D1596202

The Chartwell Press

"Pro Fides et Ratio"
thechartwellpress.com

Appreciation for *The Incarnation: Rediscovering Kenotic Christology*

"In this fascinating and well-researched study of how best to describe the Incarnation in a way that gives no less prominence to Christ's identification with the human condition than to his full divinity, Stackpole explores developments in the Anglican, Orthodox and Protestant traditions, as well as more recent Catholic writing. That ecumenical spirit is combined with a pastoral concern that ensures that he always writes in an easily accessible way that will inspire ordinary readers as well as the professional theologian."

Revd Professor David Brown, FBA, FRSE, Emeritus Professor of Theology, Aesthetics & Culture, University of St Andrews, Author of Divine Humanity: Kenosis and the Construction of a Christian Theology (Baylor University Press, 2011)

"A useful anthology of works on Anglican Kenoticism, which will be of great help in orientating readers in the debate. Clarity of argument is essential with regard to a topic as complex as kenosis. This book does theology a great service in providing such a clear exposition and critique of kenotic theology, while at the same time making clear the resources Kenoticism continues to offer for thinking through the significance of the Incarnation."

David R. Law, Professor of Christian Thought and Philosophical Theology, University of Manchester, Author of Kierkegaard's Kenotic Christology (Oxford University Press, 2013)

The Incarnation:
Rediscovering Kenotic Christology

Robert A. Stackpole, STD
Director of the John Paul II Institute of Divine Mercy
Stockbridge, MA;

Emeritus Professor of Theology
Redeemer Pacific College, Langley, British Columbia;

Founding Member:
The Fellowship of Catholics and Evangelicals
"thefce.com"

Text Copyright © 2019
Robert A. Stackpole

Published by "The Chartwell Press"
"Pro Fides et Ratio"
www.thechartwellpress.com
ISBN 978-0991-988075

Cover Photo:
Nativity Scene
St. John's Episcopal Church
Williamstown, Massachusetts
Used with Permission

"We look on the woes of the world. We hear the whole of creation, to use Paul's language, groaning and laboring in pain. We see a few good men vainly striving to help the world into life and light; and in our sense of the awful magnitude of the problem and of our inability to do much, we cry out "Where is God? How can he bear this? Why doesn't he do something?" And there is but one answer that satisfies: and that is the Incarnation and the Cross. God could not bear it. He has done something. He has done the utmost compatible with moral wisdom. He has entered into the fellowship of our suffering and misery and at infinite cost has taken the world upon His Heart that he might raise it to Himself."

Bordon P. Bowne, *Studies in Christianity*

Author's Dedication:

For Tom Hamel: Founder and President Emeritus of Redeemer Pacific College, Founder of The Chartwell Press, and Founder and Executive Director of The Fellowship of Catholics and Evangelicals; but most of all a True Friend in Christ.

Acknowledgements

I am deeply grateful to the many people who have assisted me with this project over the years. Most especially my thanks go to the Rev. Dr. David Brown, himself an expert in Kenotic theology and the history of the Kenotic movement, and to the Rev. Dr. David Law, who has similar expertise. Their feedback on drafts of several of the chapters of this manuscript was crucial to the development of my own thought, and to the fashioning of readable chapters to express it. They did their best not only to encourage me, but at times also to challenge some of my reflections, and where I have failed to heed their good counsel, the responsibility is entirely my own.

Similarly, my thanks go to Rev. Thaddeus Lancton, MIC, who provided valuable feedback for me on Part Two, Chapter Two at a time when he was burdened himself with research for his own doctoral thesis.

Finally, of course, my wife Katherine patiently endured my long hours and late nights at the computer, fashioning and editing this work; her love and companionship through everything is a grace that never fails.

A note with regard to format: I have adopted an overall style of presentation in this book which can be annoying to some readers: namely, emphasizing key words, phrases and sentences with the use of italics — and a generous use of bold type as well to highlight longer key passages and summary paragraphs. Scholars in particular tend to find this particularly bothersome (as if they did not have the ability to locate the key passages themselves!). I have adopted this mode of presentation, however, after the example of Roch Kereszty O.Cist, who used it to good effect in his classic work, *Jesus Christ: Fundamentals of Christology*, and for the sake of students of theology, seminarians and others who might find the extra guidance helpful in coming to grips with such a complex topic. For their sake, I beg pardon from the rest of the readers of this volume.

Robert Stackpole, STD

June, 2019

The Incarnation: Rediscovering Kenotic Christology

The Incarnation

Introduction:
The Anglican Heritage and the Incarnation

Even a cursory glance at the Anglican tradition reveals the central place accorded to the doctrine of the Incarnation. The great Elizabethan theologian Richard Hooker (d. 1600), for example, claimed that no greater grace could be shown to humanity than that God should unite to human nature the person of the divine Son. God in Christ thereby became the fountain of life and redemption.[1] In the early seventeenth century, the Incarnation played a leading role in the preaching of Bishop Lancelot Andrewes. Andrewes delighted in the paradox of God-made-man, and in his Nativity sermons displayed the necessity of the Incarnation to the Atonement.[2] In 1690, William Sherlock described the Incarnation as "the fundamental mystery of the Christian religion" which supremely proved the love of God.[3] In the mid-nineteenth century, Frederick Denison Maurice based his social theology on the Incarnation. Through the Incarnation, Maurice believed, God had joined the whole human race to himself, and every sphere of life was therefore made sacred to God, and meant to be incorporated into a divine society.[4] In the same century, the great preacher at St. Paul's Cathedral in London, H.P. Liddon wrote in lyrical fashion of the wonder of the Incarnation in his book *The Divinity of Our Lord and Saviour Jesus Christ* (1864):

> **Jesus is the Almighty, restraining His illimitable powers; Jesus is the incomprehensible, voluntarily submitting to bonds; Jesus is Providence, clothed in our flesh and**

---

[1] Richard Hooker, *Laws of Ecclesiastical Polity, Book V* in *The Works of Richard Hooker*, vol. II, arranged by John Keble (Oxford: Oxford University Press, 1836), p. 298 ff.

[2] See, for example, Lancelot Andrewes, *Seventeen Sermons on the Nativity* (London: Griffin, Farran, Okeden and Welsh, 1887), p. 18-31.

[3] William Sherlock, *A Vindication of the Doctrine of the Trinity* (W. Rogers, 1690), p. 238-242.

[4] See the brief discussion of the thought of Maurice in Francis Penhale, *Catholics in Crisis* (Oxford: Mowbrays, 1936), p. 124.

blood; Jesus is infinite charity, tending us with the kindly looks and tender handling of a human love; Jesus is the eternal wisdom, speaking out of the depths of infinite thought in a human language. Jesus is God making Himself, if I may dare so to speak, our tangible possession.[5]

Even John Henry Newman admitted that the Incarnation is "the central truth of the Gospel;" in fact, he saw it as central to the whole conception of Christianity he had been developing throughout his life, both as an Anglican and as a Roman Catholic.[6]

This strong incarnational focus continued in twentieth century Anglicanism. In a scholarly study of Anglican thought from the late nineteenth century to the start of the Second World War, Michael Ramsey pointed to the central place of the Incarnation in Anglican theology throughout this entire era.[7] Then in 1986, in what amounted to an official ecclesiastical response to a simmering controversy over the Incarnation among Anglican theologians, the House of Bishops of the Church of England reaffirmed their faith that "The central miracle, the heart of the Christian understanding of God, is the Incarnation itself."[8]

In fact, not only in Britain, but throughout the world, Anglican theologians often have defended the centrality of the Incarnation. William Porcher Dubose (1836-1918), for example, perhaps the most original American Episcopalian theologian, saw in Jesus "not only the supreme act of humility in God, but the supreme act of humanity in

[5] H.P. Liddon, *The Divinity of Our Lord and Saviour Jesus Christ* (London: Pickering and Inglis, 1864), p. 187.
[6] John Henry Newman, *An Essay on the Development of Christian Doctrine* (London: Pickering, third edition 1878), p. 324; cf. p. 93-94. S.W. Sykes offers a full discussion of Newman's view in *The Identity of Christianity* (London: SPCK, 1984), p. 114-116.
[7] A. Michael Ramsey, *An Era in Anglican Theology: From Gore to Temple* (London: Longmans, 1960), p. 27-29.
[8] *The Nature of Christian Belief* (London: Church House, 1986), p. 32.

God."[9] In his book *The Anglican Vision* (1997), Episcopalian James Griffis insisted that the centrality of the Incarnation is a distinctive mark of the Anglican form of Christianity:

> The doctrine of the Incarnation … came to be of particular importance in the development of Anglicanism, affecting the way we think, pray, and worship to a degree that is unique within the larger Christian community. … The Incarnation of God in Christ has become for us something more than a truth or doctrine about Jesus. It has become for us an expression of our *way of believing* — our way of believing in God and what our believing in God says about us. Belief in the Incarnation is a matter of *identity* for Anglicans and is important to the way we understand the church and the way we interpret the Bible.[10]

It is hardly surprising, therefore, that in several extensive studies of the Anglican heritage, Anglicans themselves have focused on the Incarnation as the central belief of their tradition.[11] For example, when Stephen Sykes attempted an historical definition of Anglican identity in *The Integrity of Anglicanism* (1978), he argued that the Incarnation is the central doctrine, because it is repeatedly affirmed by all parts of the Anglican liturgical tradition. In fact, he claimed, "one could argue that the incarnation is the basis of dogma in the Anglican church, provided that by 'dogma' one understood not what the church defined, but more generally that for which it publicly stood."[12] Furthermore, Sykes pointed out that Anglicans themselves often point to their emphasis on the Incarnation as a criterion by which to mark their own theology

---

[9] Cited without reference in Urban T. Holmes, *What is Anglicanism?* (Wilton, Ct: Morehouse-Barlow, 1982), p. 25. Dubose rooted his Christology in Hegelian philosophy; see the brief discussion of his thought in A. Michael Ramsey, *The Anglican Spirit* (New York: Seabury Classics, 2004), p.69.

[10] James E. Griffis, *The Anglican Vision* (Lanham, MD: Cowley Publications, 1997), p. 70 and 87.

[11] In addition to the studies discussed here, Archbishop Michael Ramsey noted the same incarnational emphasis in *The Anglican Spirit*, p.11.

[12] Stephen Sykes, *The Integrity of Anglicanism* (Oxford: Mowbrays, 1978), p. 51.

as distinct from others.[13] This clearly distinguishes it from the Lutheran tradition, for example, with its emphasis on justification by faith, or Calvinism, with its emphasis on the mysteries of predestination, election and Divine Providence. Christians from other denominations also have noticed the incarnational focus of Anglicanism: Paul Tillich even famously quipped that the Incarnation is "the Anglican heresy." In his book *What is Anglicanism?* (1982), Bishop Urban T. Holmes of the Episcopal Church in the United States attempted to unpack some of the reasons why the Incarnation has been so important to Anglican identity:

> First, the Incarnation means that God created everything that is. This is the beginning point of Christian belief for the Anglican: the doctrine of creation. The Incarnation is the ultimate act of creation, and if humanity had never sinned God would have become flesh. The material world is good. …
> Secondly, the Incarnation means that sin cannot be explained by identifying it with matter or the physical world. …
> Thirdly, the Incarnation embraces the totality of life. It is the doctrine which undergirds the Anglican commitment to sensibility, the openness to the entire experience [of life] with all its conflict and ambiguity. … If our intention in thinking is to draw together as much of an experience as possible, with items unresolved and with large, nagging questions in the middle of what we have described, then we are thinking with the left hand. … We Anglicans are not given to writing great theology. There are notable exceptions, but they are difficult to remember; but when Anglicanism is at its best its liturgy, its poetry, its music and its life can create a world of wonder in which it is very easy to fall in love with God. We are much more adept at [thinking with] the left hand than the right.[14]

---

[13] Ibid., p. 64.

[14] Holmes, *What is Anglicanism?*, p. 27, 5. On those rare occasions when Anglicans do step out and systematize their thought, the Incarnation often occupies center stage. The theology of American Anglican Kathryn Tanner, for example, centers upon the Trinity as "the overflowing superabundant source" of all good gifts, and an "incarnation centred Christology" in which God's glory as

It is not clear why the doctrine of the Incarnation would be needed to establish the first two of Holmes' three points, when it would seem that a robust understanding of the doctrine of Creation would do just as well. But he may have struck upon something significant in his third consideration. There is a hallowing of the whole of human life that happens when God assumes human nature through taking flesh and dwelling among us as Jesus of Nazareth. And it may indeed be true that the depth and ramifications of this mystery can be more fully expressed through sacred art, liturgy, poetry and song than by systematic theology and doctrinal definitions.

---

self-giving love has its "centre and meaning in God's only Son, Jesus Christ" (*Jesus, Humanity and the Trinity.* Minneapolis: Fortress Press, 2001, p. 68 and 37). In a remarkably rich ecumenical synthesis (drawing primarily upon the ancient Fathers of the East, and upon Karl Barth), Tanner weaves together a thoroughly Christocentric worldview:

> The triune God is a God who perfectly communicates the goodness of Godself among the three Persons of the Trinity in perfect self-unity. Expressing this dynamic life outward in a grace of beneficent love for what is not God, the triune God brings about a variety of different forms of connection with the non-divine, for the sake of perfecting what is united with God, in an effort to repeat the perfection of God's own triune life. ... God's work begins with creation, continues in historical fellowship with a particular people, Israel, and ends with Jesus as the one through whom, in the Spirit, all people and the whole world will show forth God's own triune goodness in unity with God. ...

> Most generally, Jesus is the one in whom God's relationship with us attains perfection. In Jesus, unity with God takes a perfect form; here humanity has become God's own. That is the fundamental meaning of incarnation .... [J]ust to the extent that we are one with Christ in faith and love; unity with Christ the gift-giver is the means of our perfection as human beings, just as the union of humanity and divinity in Christ was the means of his perfect humanity. United with Christ, we are thereby emboldened as ministers of God's beneficence to the world, aligning ourselves with, entering into communion with, those in need as God in Christ was *for us* in our need and as Christ was a man for others, especially those in need. (p. 35-36 and 9)

The Incarnation

Nevertheless, the community of faith cannot bypass theology and doctrine altogether, and beginning in the late nineteenth century, Anglican incarnational theology faced some serious obstacles. The new historical consciousness of the western world, and the new historical critique of the gospels encouraged Christians to believe that in order to share our human condition, Jesus must have had a human mind and personality that grew and developed over time (as all human personality does), a mind informed by the culture in which he was nurtured. How could Jesus really be seen as the omniscient or infallible Son of God of traditional theology and popular piety, if he actually had the consciousness and "mental furniture" of a Jew of first century Palestine?

The Kenotic movement in Christology arose, in part, to meet this difficulty. The word "kenotic" comes from the Greek *kenosis*, meaning "to empty, or to pour out," a word used by St. Paul in Philippians 2:7 to describe how the divine Son of God came to share our human condition. In the famous collection of essays entitled *Lux Mundi* (1889), Bishop Charles Gore (1853-1932) was among the first in the Anglican world to turn to this general concept (which already had been explored by German and Danish theologians earlier in the nineteenth century) to try to shed light on the mystery of the Incarnation.[15] As Archbishop of Canterbury, Michael Ramsey summarized Gore's attempt to harmonise faith in the Incarnation with the new historical approach to Jesus Christ:

> Now what did Gore mean by *kenosis*? He and his colleagues taught that in the Incarnation, there was a "self-limitation" of the divine wisdom of Jesus. While Jesus was an infallible revelation, he had a mind that was subject to the limitations of

---

[15] For the roots of Kenoticism in Martin Luther and in nineteenth century Lutheran Theology, see Claude Welch, *God and Incarnation in mid-19th century German Theology* (New York: Oxford University Press, 1965), and David R. Law, "Luther's Legacy and the Origins of Kenotic Christology" in *Bulletin of John Ryland's Library*, 93/2 (2017), p. 41-68.

his time. That is, of course, a very important matter, one reaching far beyond biblical criticism into areas of history and metaphysics. ... Charles Gore answered ... critics by saying that the human mind of Jesus was limited to the knowledge of his day. While he had the mind of God in perfectly revealing God's character and purpose, he was not there to anticipate all knowledge, all sciences, all human investigations. In fact, in such matters Jesus was not setting out to teach humanity, for he had only the knowledge of his time.[16]

Gore wrestled with this understanding of the Incarnation throughout his life, and never claimed to have settled all the metaphysical issues involved (e.g. how could God "self-limit" his unlimited divine attributes, such as His infinite knowledge and power, without ceasing to be God? How could Jesus be entirely infallible and trustworthy in some areas of knowledge, such as matters of faith and morals, but strictly bound by the limitations of his culture in all other areas of knowledge?). Nagging questions remained. Toward the end of his life, however, Gore summarized the underlying principles behind his kenotic approach to the Incarnation in his monumental work *The Reconstruction of Belief* (1926):

> [T]he measure of Christ's self-sacrifice within the limits of his mortal life cannot be said to be greater, at any rate, than that of multitudes of martyrs. But it is not within these limits that the uniqueness of Christ's self-sacrifice is found. It lies in the region of his pre-existent life. It consists in this, that **one who existed in the nature of God consented to abandon this to us inconceivable glory of life, in order to accept the conditions and limitations and sufferings of real manhood. ...**
>
> [T] he divine person in the Gospels is certainly presented to us as growing in wisdom, as being tempted, as asking questions, apparently for information, as praying, as overwhelmed with

---

[16] Ramsey, *The Anglican Spirit,* p. 72-73.

anxiety, as asking upon the Cross the great question of the perplexed and dismayed the world over, and finally, as at least in one respect, asserting His ignorance. And negatively, He never showed shows any sign of transcending the knowledge of natural things possible to His age, country, and condition.

…

The divine Son in becoming man must, we conclude, have accepted, voluntarily and deliberately, the limitations involved in really living as a man — even as a sinless and perfect man — in feeling as a man, thinking as a man, striving as a man, being anxious and tried as a man. … The incarnation is the supreme act of self-sacrificing sympathy by which one whose nature is divine was enabled to enter into human experience.[17]

Although not expressed with metaphysical precision, here was a succinct statement of the Kenotic position: in Jesus the divine Son of God, through self-limitation, has come to experience all the joys and pains, struggles and sorrows of a real human life.

Throughout the early decades of the twentieth century, a kenotic viewpoint prevailed in British theology generally (e.g. in the writings of P.T. Forsyth and H.R. Mackintosh) and in British Anglican theology in particular (especially in the work of Bishop Gore, and Bishop Frank Weston).[18] Nevertheless, difficulties with this position proved hard to eradicate. William Temple voiced the misgivings of many when he argued in *Christus Veritas* (1924) that the Kenotic Theory had an overly mythological appearance. It seemed to involve a metamorphosis, a pagan story of a god changing into a human being. Besides, Temple asked, what was happening to the rest of the universe when the second person of the Trinity, who supposedly "upholds the universe by his

---

[17] Charles Gore, *The Reconstruction of Belief* (London: John Murray, 1926), p. 510, 521-522.

[18] Thomas Langford, *In Search of Foundations: English Theology 1900-1920* (Abingdon Press, 1969), p.202-216, and Ramsey, *From Gore to Temple,* p. 30-43.

word of power" (Heb 1:3), was confined to the human limits of his earthly life in Palestine?[19]

In his book *Doctrines of the Creed* (1938), however, O.C. Quick, Regius Professor of Divinity at Oxford, offered a rejoinder. If theological statements involve analogy, he claimed, "and if we must speak of divine *actions* in the heavenly sphere, we must speak of them in the same analogical way, which means that we tell a myth about them."[20] Besides, Quick wrote, kenotic theory did not necessarily claim that the second person of the Trinity changed himself into a man, abandoning his divine powers. It could be said that he took upon himself all the conditions and limitations of a human life and human consciousness, even while retaining his creative and sustaining work throughout the universe: "Granted that the [divine] Word, without ceasing his creative and sustaining work, added something to it, what he added is precisely that experience in which his divine consciousness was limited and his divine state surrendered."[21] Quick's volume on Christian doctrine became a standard textbook in Anglican seminaries for the next two decades, and thus, despite heavy criticism, kenotic theory remained influential in the Anglican world throughout this period.

In 1958 British Methodist Vincent Taylor produced a fresh defence of kenotic theory in his work *The Person of Christ*. Meanwhile, in the Anglican Communion Archbishop Michael Ramsey and philosophical theologian Austin Farrer at least kept kenotic themes alive:

> **The divine Creator has humbled himself to take on himself the entire experience of existence as man, in all the conditions of humanity. That is what we call the Incarnation. That is the heart of Christian belief. ... God's**

---

[19] See the discussion of Temple's position in David Brown, *The Divine Trinity* (London: Duckworth, 1985), p. 234.
[20] O.C. Quick, *Doctrines of the Creed* (London: Nisbet, 1945), p. 136.
[21] Ibid., p.138.

answer to our need is to give himself utterly to us in the total self-donation of the Word-made-flesh.[22]

> [In the Incarnation we are confronted by] infinite God, living the existence of one of his creatures, through self-limitation to a particular created destiny. ... This was how God's love was shown as utterly divine — in accepting every circumstance of our manhood. He spared himself nothing. He was not a copy book man-in-general, he was a Galilean carpenter, a free-lance rabbi; and he wove up his life, as each of us must, out of materials that were to hand.[23]

In 1970, John Austin Baker published a one volume philosophical theology entitled *The Foolishness of God* that centered upon a kenotic theme. Neither Ramsey, Farrer nor Baker, however, attempted to develop a kenotic understanding of the Incarnation with the depth and intellectual rigor that Weston and Quick had done. This general failure to address the lingering intellectual difficulties involved in Kenotic Christology contributed to its decline in influence in Anglicanism in the 1960s and 1970s.

During the debate over the controversial book *The Myth of God Incarnate* (1977), however, Brian Hebblethwaite at Cambridge revived and defended the Incarnation in an explicitly kenotic fashion:

> We affirm with the tradition that, out of his great love, and in order to reconcile men to himself, God, without ceasing to be God, came among us as one of us, making himself vulnerable to suffering and evil. ... The doctrine

---

[22] A. Michael Ramsey, *Introducing the Christian Faith* (London: SCM: 1961), p. 42-43; cf. A. Michael Ramsey, *God, Christ, and the World* (London: SCM, 1969), p. 95.

[23] Austin Farrer, *Interpretation and Belief*, Charles Conti, ed., (London: SPCK, 1976), p. 130; and Austin Farrer, *A Celebration of Faith* (London: Hodder and Stoughton, 1970), p. 89, cited in Brian Hebblethwaite, *The Philosophical Theology of Austin Farrer* (Leuven: Peeters, 2007), p. 101.

of the Incarnation is more profoundly grasped when it is articulated in terms of kenosis.[24]

In the same year, Canon W.H. Vanstone produced the spiritual classic *Love's Endeavour, Love's Expense*, an analysis of authentic love, both human and divine, including a profound meditation on how all of creation springs from "The Kenosis of God." In *The Work of Love: Creation as Kenosis* (2001), Anglican scientists John Polkinghorne and Arthur Peacocke led the way in exploring how God's act of creation through an evolutionary universe might be seen as an act of divine self-limitation.

Meanwhile, among Anglican theologians, David Brown at Oxford presented a fresh exploration of the Kenotic Theory of the Incarnation in its boldest form in *The Divine Trinity* (1985). Returning to this theme many years later in *Divine Humanity* (2011), Brown offered his own original, kenotic model. In short, while no longer ascendant in Anglican Christology (or anywhere else, for that matter) kenotic theories of the Incarnation and kenotic themes have continued to influence Anglican thought right into the twenty-first century.

Anglican theologians were not the originators of the Kenotic Theory — the credit for that goes to Lutheran theologians such as Gottfried Thomasius in the nineteenth century. While the theory largely disappeared from mainstream discourse in other Christian denominations by the 1940s, it remained important to Anglicans long thereafter, and continues to be so right up until the present day. Indeed, this *persistence* of Kenotic Christology is distinctive to the Anglican Communion. Moreover, as we shall see, this Anglican heritage of Christology endured *in its own distinctive theological stream and trajectory*.

The principle argument of this book is that the Anglican tradition of Kenotic Christology not only gives us a fairly coherent understanding

---

[24] Brian Hebblethwaite, *The Incarnation* (Cambridge: Cambridge University Press, 1987), p. 47-48.

11

of the Incarnation, but it should be the *preferable* one, given its strong implications (1) for God's identification with human suffering, (2) for the doctrine of Christ's Saving Work, and (3) for the Social Gospel. Indeed, I shall endeavor to show that Kenoticism is an even stronger stance than its Anglican proponents have so far recognised. In the end, I will propose that Kenotic Christology is a hidden treasure of the Anglican tradition, and a special contribution that Anglicanism can make to the understanding of these mysteries of the Christian faith.

Even to outside observers (I am a Roman Catholic), it seems clear that some sense of direction is desperately needed in contemporary Anglican Christology. On the one hand, as we shall see, there has been a tremendous diversity of viewpoints expressed over the last century. To some extent, this may be a sign of healthy theological creativity and dialogue. On the other hand, as this study also will show, much of contemporary Anglican Christology can no longer be termed "incarnational." Not only in the famous collection of essays, *The Myth of God Incarnate*, but more generally throughout the entire post-war era, many Anglican theologians have drifted away from a clear incarnational stance. Anglican diversity now threatens Anglican theological identity at its vital center.

If Stephen Sykes, James Griffis, and Urban T. Holmes were correct, however, and the doctrine of the Incarnation is indeed central to Anglican identity, then it is particularly vital to Anglicans to articulate what they mean by the term "incarnation." This is especially true of the Church of England, and the Episcopal Church in the United States, from which "the lion's share" of Anglican theological scholarship still emanates. Anglicans need to come to some clarity and consensus as to what they mean by "the Incarnation," and why it is so central to the whole pattern of Christian belief. Only in this way can the Anglican Communion clarify and preserve its distinctive theological identity (and I will make the case in this book that, at least with regard to the mystery of the Incarnation, that heritage is well worth preserving!).

The survival of a particular denominational identity, of course, should not be seen as an end in itself. In our ecumenical age, it is merely a stage on a journey of discovery: the discernment of what each Christian tradition can contribute to the mind of Christendom as a whole. Down through the ages, each tradition, by divine grace, has pondered and developed some aspects of divine revelation more fully than any other tradition; thus, each has something to offer to enrich the others. Pope St. John Paul II suggested that this was one of the reasons why Divine Providence permitted the fracturing of the unity of the Church in the second millennium:

> Yes indeed, we can truly ask ourselves: *Why did the Holy Spirit permit all these divisions?* In general, the causes and historical development of these divisions are well known. It is legitimate, however, even to wonder if there is perhaps a *metahistorical reason as well*.
>
> There are two possible answers to this question. The more *negative* one would see in these divisions the bitter fruit of sins committed by Christians. The more positive answer is inspired by trust in the One who is capable of bringing forth good even from evil, from human weakness. Could it not be that these divisions have also been *a path continually leading the Church to discover the untold wealth contained in Christ's Gospel and in the redemption accomplished by Christ?* Perhaps all this wealth would not have come to light otherwise ....[25]

As a result, each Christian tradition has something to contribute to all the others: a gift fashioned by the Holy Spirit, the Spirit of Truth, from within its own history. Rome, it may be said, offers its experience of, and adherence to a universal pastorate, its long and in-depth reflection on the mystery of God's grace working in Mary, the Mother of God, and its rich social and sacramental teaching; Lutherans offer a consistent adherence to the principles of the primacy of grace, and justification by faith; Eastern Orthodoxy contributes its matchless traditions of liturgy and iconography; Pentecostals offer their

---

[25] John Paul II, *Crossing the Threshold of Hope* (New York: Alfred A. Knopf, 1994), p. 153.

rediscovery of the special gifts of the Spirit (healing, tongues, and prophecy); Evangelicals their devotion to the authority of the Word of God, and the importance of adult conversion to the process of salvation; and Calvinists their focus on the sovereignty of God in predestination, election and providence. Without lapsing into a facile syncretism, a full and rich Christian faith surely must include all of these elements, in some measure.

Anglicans have important insights to contribute to this mosaic as well. For one thing, **at the heart of Anglican identity lies the mystery of the Incarnation, and within this heritage, over the past 130 years, lies a particular stream of interpretation of that doctrine waiting to be rediscovered by Anglicans themselves, and by the wider Christian community. This book is but a small step toward that goal.**

This volume also takes its place as an authentic exercise of "receptive ecumenism." Traditionally, ecumenical dialogue between church bodies has proceeded along two parallel tracks: on the one hand, the quest to locate and articulate common ground, while at the same time engaging in respectful dialogue about remaining differences. "Receptive ecumenism" takes this process one step further: it involves asking in earnest what each Christian tradition might be able to learn from the historical experience and theological reflections of the others, without necessarily violating its own core beliefs. This involves listening more than speaking, and breaking down boundaries, where possible, rather than simply defining and clarifying them. In short, receptive ecumenism enables Christians to find enrichment from the treasury of gifts that God has given to other Christian traditions.[26] The reader of this book will quickly find that it is an earnest attempt to do just that: to explore how Christian theology can be enriched by the reflections on the Incarnation of the Anglican stream of Kenotic Christology.

---

[26] For an excellent example, see Gordon T. Smith, *Evangelical, Sacramental, and Pentecostal: Why the Church Should be All Three* (Downers Grove, IL: InterVarsity Press, 2017).

My intention here is not to write a history of Kenoticism. Anglican scholars such as David Brown and David Law have already undertaken the essential historical research in this regard. Rather, in this first (of two) volumes, I will locate the Anglican tradition of "Moderate Kenoticism" against the backdrop of the broad spectrum of contemporary (that is, twentieth and twenty-first century) Christian thought, both Anglican and non-Anglican. *Along the way, I will let the principal proponents of Kenotic Christology speak for themselves, quoting for the reader the most important passages from their writings. As a result, this book also serves as an anthology of key passages from authors and works of Kenotic Christology largely unknown outside of Great Britain.*

Given that since the Second World War, Anglican theology has become a virtual microcosm of the wider Christian theological debate, this survey will not be as restrictive as one might suppose. At the same time, I will seek to demonstrate the coherence, and potential fruitfulness of the Anglican Kenotic heritage, first of all, within its own frame of reference — that is, against the backdrop of the classical Anglican theological tradition, and the philosophical movements, especially Idealism and Anglo-American Analytic theism, that have prevailed in Anglican thought over the past century and a half.

In volume one of this study, therefore, my primary goals will be to re-awaken Anglicans themselves to the richness of their own incarnational heritage, and at the same time to introduce, commend, and defend this stream of Kenotic Christology to a wider, ecumenical audience.

At various points in this book, and in greater depth in a forthcoming second volume, I will place this Kenotic perspective into dialogue with the Catholic tradition of Christology (my own tradition), in order to try to answer the question: "Can the Anglican heritage of Kenoticism enrich Catholic faith in the mystery of Jesus Christ? Can it ultimately become what the Catholic tradition would call a legitimate 'development of doctrine'?"

15

The Incarnation

In his influential work *Mysterium Paschale: The Mystery of Easter*, the Roman Catholic theologian Hans Urs von Balthasar, commenting briefly on the work of Anglican Kenotic theologians Charles Gore and Frank Weston, stated respectfully: "these speculations lead nowhere: their only result is to bring to our attention in striking fashion how deep the mystery of the Kenosis lies."[27] On this matter I believe von Balthasar was profoundly mistaken. While Gore, Weston and their followers certainly have not exhausted the mystery of the Incarnation, nor answered every question, they have penetrated that mystery in important and illuminating ways. In this book, and in the volume that will follow it, I hope to show how all Christians can benefit from their efforts.

---

[27] Hans Urs von Balthasar, *Mysterium Paschale: The Mystery of Easter* (San Francisco: Ignatius Press, 1990), p. 33.

Part One
Anglican Kenoticism: Location and Coherence
Chapter One
The Meaning of "Incarnation": Exploring the Alternatives

To begin, we will survey three main schools of Anglican thought concerning the Incarnation from the past century and a half — perspectives which effectively mirror those found elsewhere in Christendom: Non-Incarnational Christology, Action Christology, and Two-Nature Christology. Along the way I will point out problems inherent in each of these schools of thought, problems which render them unsatisfactory as ways of understanding the mystery of the Word made flesh. Then, in the chapter that follows, we will begin our exploration of a fourth way: the Kenotic Theory of the Incarnation.

First of all, by "incarnation" I shall mean the identity claim that lies at the heart of the definition written by the Ecumenical Council of Chalcedon in 451 AD: the belief that in Jesus Christ one finds two "natures," divine and human, fully present in one "person." By "nature" (Greek: *physis*) the Council fathers meant the characteristic attributes of a being that define it as the kind of being it is, and by "person" (Greek: *hypostasis*) they had in mind the ontological subject or referent of all the attributes, acts and experiences of a personal kind of being. C. Stephen Layman reminds us of the slightly different way that the term "person" (hypostasis) was used by the ancient Fathers as compared with our modern use of the word "person":

> Essentially, "one person" here [at Chalcedon] means "one individual." Prosopon does not have the connotations of consciousness and self-awareness as does the modern English term. (That said, there was, of course, no doubt on the part of those who drew up the document that Jesus Christ was a conscious and self-aware being.) In context, **the force of "hypostasis" … is again to emphasize that Jesus Christ**

**was (is) one being, one "bearer of properties," not two.
...**

Now I agree that the Greek and Latin terms often translated by English "person" do not have the connotation of "conscious being." But the fact remains that the biblical materials indicate that the Father, Son, and Spirit are conscious entities that can know, have purposes, and act. Thus they apparently are persons in a sense that strongly overlaps the modern English sense of the term.[28]

---

[28] C. Stephen Layman, *Philosophical Approaches to Atonement, Incarnation, and Trinity* (New York: Palgrave Macmillan, 2016), p. 81-82, and 131-132. On Chalcedon's terminology generally, see H.E.W. Turner, *Jesus the Christ* (Oxford: Mowbrays, 1976), p. 58. On personhood and the Incarnation see Alfred J. Freddoso, "Human Nature, Potency, and the Incarnation," in *Faith and Philosophy*, 3 (1986) at https://www3.nd.edu/freddos/papers/humnat.htm. On personal identity see David Brown, *The Divine Trinity* (La Salle, IL: Open Court, 1985), p. 260-271; cf. Richard Swinburne, *The Coherence of Theism* (Oxford: Clarendon Press, 1977), p. 119-123.

Frank Weston in the second edition of his book *The One Christ* (London: Longmans, Green and Co., 1914), p. 16, summarized the importance of the meaning of "person" to discussion of the Incarnation, and applied his own special meaning to the word:

> Christology assumes in man a certain underlying reality called "I," inseparable from soul and body in existence, yet in fact distinct from and the ground of both. This "I" is the subject of all thought, perception, change and consciousness. ...
>
> The essential functions of this "I" require the soul, through which the "I" wills, thinks, and chooses; and for its true and complete life it requires the body, the material expression of which the soul is the essential form. But the "I" is not the soul, nor the body, nor the composition of the two, but the ground in which both subsist.

When Weston states that the "I" is not the soul, he is evidently distancing himself from the Cartesian notion of the human person, and when he says the "I" is not "the composition of the two" (that is, of a human soul and a human body) he seems to reject the Aristotelian, hylomorphic notion that a human person is a whole, a composite consisting of body and soul as the primary substance or

Similar to Layman, throughout this book, I assume that *a "person" is a subject or entity* (or as the Greek Fathers would have said, a "hypostasis," or as the Latin Scholastics would have said, a "suppositum") *that is the bearer of properties of a "personal" kind, in particular the inherent capacity for self-consciousness, rational thought, and voluntary agency.* Following Richard of St. Victor, we must also say that implicit in this notion of "person" is the property of "incommunicability": *persons always exist as unique and incommunicable subjects* (i.e., no one else can fully be "me"). This is a basic, general *philosophical* notion of "person" that I assume to be true for all persons — both human persons and (by analogy, at least) divine

---

subject of all its natural human attributes. According to Classical Christianity, however, only Jesus Christ is a human body- soul composite that is not in itself a human person, but which has as its ultimate subject a divine person. It is arguable, therefore, that Weston's definition of the human person or ego (in the 1914, second edition of his book, at any rate) is actually drawn from the unique metaphysical case of the Incarnation itself, and may not be transferrable to all created human persons.

Again, according to classical Latin Scholasticism, only in Jesus Christ is there a suppositum (or to use Weston's term, an ego) that is distinct from his individual human nature, that gives existence to that nature, and that serves as the ultimate subject of all his human attributes, acts, and experiences. In a Cartesian framework, of course, it is the human soul or mind that is the person or ultimate subject of all the acts and experiences of a human being, and therefore in the Incarnation it must be the case that the divine Son took upon himself the form, state, and limitations of a human soul interacting with a human body in order to become the subject or suppositum of his human nature. As we shall see later in this book, it is Richard Swinburne who utilized this Cartesian theory in depth in his Christology. A fruitful, mediating position between Aristotelian and Cartesian notions of the human person would be that *a human person* is *a human kind of soul that is meant to be embodied in a genetically human body.*

It is also important to note that "person" in Christology is not the same as "personality." Each person has a "personality," which is simply the sum of the thoughts and attitudes, dispositions and memories within the range of consciousness of any sentient being. Personality is therefore an aspect of human nature, and an indicator of personal identity, but it does not constitute personhood. **The "person" is the ultimate, unique, incommunicable subject of all the experiences, rational thoughts and voluntary actions of a personal being.**

persons — whatever else we may want to say about them. Distinguishing one human person from another can be done with the help of certain indicators: principally, a person's character and unique set of memories, though "personhood" is not constituted by these indicators, and these indicators may not always be fully adequate in identifying a person. It follows that the traditional doctrine of the Incarnation involves "the claim that the person who was and is Jesus of Nazareth is one and the same individual as God the Son, the Second Person of the Trinity — a literal statement of absolute, numerical identity."[29]

A notion of "person" fully informed by philosophical *theology*, of course, will want to add that a person is not only a subject that is the bearer of "personal properties," but also one that is essentially *relational* in nature: for example, every human person is brought into existence by God and held in existence by him at every moment as a free gift of his love, and fashioned in his "image" (i.e., the human person's personal properties are analogous, in a limited and creaturely way, to the infinitely perfect personal properties of God: his infinite power, intellect, and will). Moreover, since the human person is made in the image of a God who is a *communion* of divine persons — that is, a *perichoresis* (a mutual indwelling) in which love is eternally given, received, and returned among the persons of the Blessed Trinity — it follows that human persons can only fulfill their true nature as *imago dei* by living in loving communion with one another. Finally, a human person by definition is characterized by a longing for the transcendent (that is, for union with infinite beauty, truth, and goodness), which ultimately can be fulfilled only through union with infinitely perfect Being, the Trinitarian God himself.

In other words, to put it as simply as possible: "person" tells us "who" is being referred to, while "nature" tells us "what kind" of thing is being referenced. American Episcopal theologian James E. Griffis provided a handy summary of what the bishops assembled at Chalcedon intended to convey:

---

[29] Thomas Morris, *The Logic of God Incarnate* (Ithaca: Cornell University, 1986), p. 18.

Jesus Christ, according to Chalcedon, is one person; in him we can discern the reality of God and the reality of man; he is the presence of divine transcendence in history, the God who is with us without ceasing to be God, who in Jesus commits himself to our humanity without restriction or reservation; he is God with us for our salvation. But he is present with us in such a way that Jesus shows us what it is to be truly human. The humanity of Jesus, that which we share with him, finds its center, its reality in God …. There were many subsequent interpretations of the Chalcedonian definition, some of which, by defining the mystery of personal unity too precisely, obscure its essential witness. But the abiding contribution of Chalcedon to the doctrine of the Incarnation remains: in a truly human life God is with us for our salvation.[30]

At Chalcedon, the Church officially settled on these definitive parameters for the word "incarnation," — a word not found in the New Testament, but derived from later tradition to sum up the scriptural witness to the identity of Jesus Christ. Hence, as Anglican philosophical theologian David Brown once wrote, any theology which claims to uphold belief in the Incarnation must use the word in its conciliar sense, "otherwise, 'incarnation' will become yet another instance of the confusion endemic in theology because of the desire to retain traditional language even when the meaning is transformed almost out of recognition."[31]

One must also beware of appeals to the authority of Chalcedon that add elements not strictly or explicitly required by the core of the definition itself, for example, belief in the absolute impassibility of the divine nature, or in Christ's infallibility in all areas of knowledge. Sarah Coakley located eight important issues on which the core of the

[30] James E. Griffiss, "Jesus Christ: God with Us" in Arthur A. Vogel, *Theology in Anglicanism* (Wilton, CT: Morehouse-Barlow, 1984), p. 73.
[31] Brown, *The Divine Trinity,* p. 226.

Chalcedonian decree does not explicitly commit itself.[32] Each of these elements may have played a role in developing the phrasing of the definition at Chalcedon, and each may have developed further after Chalcedon, and treated as among the essential implications of the apostolic and conciliar faith, but they are not strictly required by the actual wording of the core of the definition itself. According to Coakley, these are: (1) in what the divine and human natures consist; (2) what hypostasis means when applied to Christ; (3) how *hypostasis* and *physis* are related to one another (how to solve the problem of the *communicatio idiomatum*); (4) how many wills Christ has; (5) Who the hypostasis in Christ is (e.g. whether it is the Divine Word); (6) what happens to the natures at Christ's death and resurrection; (7) whether the meaning of hypostasis in the Christological context is the same or different from that in the Trinitarian context; (8) whether the risen Christ is male.

---

[32] See the discussion of Coakley's perspective in Marilyn McCord Adams, *Christ and Horrors: The Coherence of Christology* (Cambridge: Cambridge University Press, 2006), p. 54. Here is the full text of the Definition of Chalcedon in a traditional Anglican translation (www.countryparson.org/creeds):

Following therefore the holy Fathers, we confess one and the same our Lord Jesus Christ, and we all teach harmoniously [that he is] the same perfect in Godhead, the same perfect in manhood, truly God and truly man, the same of a reasonable soul and body; consubstantial with the Father in Godhead, and the same consubstantial with us in manhood, like us in all things except sin; begotten before ages of the Father in Godhead, the same in the last day for us; and for our salvation [born] of Mary the virgin theotokos in manhood, one and the same Christ, Son, Lord, unique; acknowledged in two natures without confusion, without change, without division, without separation — the difference of the natures being by no means taken away because of the union, but rather the distinctive character of each nature being preserved, and [each] combining in one Person and hypostasis—not divided or separated into two Persons, but one and the same Son and only-begotten God, Word, Lord Jesus Christ; as the prophets of old and the Lord Jesus Christ himself taught us about him, and the symbol of the Fathers has handed down to us.

We do not need to unpack all eight of these elements here (and the first two and the fifth, at least, would be debatable).[33] Suffice it to say

---

[33] Briefly, regarding Coakley's eight points: Chalcedon did at least minimally define human nature as consisting of a rational soul and body, and did seem to use the word *hypostasis* to mean the ontological subject of Christ's two natures. Moreover, with regard to number 5 in Coakley's list, while it is certainly true to say that the core of the conciliar definition itself did not clearly specify whether the one person of the Incarnate is the second person of the Trinity, or whether that person, in which the divine and human natures subsist, is some form of hypostatic fusion of persons, divine and human (as found, for example, in the fourth century in the writings of St. Ephrem the Syrian), nevertheless, Chalcedon gave its full approval to the first two *Letters of Cyril*, the great Alexandrian theologian, who had stressed the fact that the divine person of the Son was the one subject of all the acts and experiences of Jesus Christ. Chalcedon also officially ratified the Council of Ephesus, which had endorsed St. Cyril's *Twelve Anathemas* — and these certainly teach the same doctrine in this regard as St. Cyril's first two letters. Moreover, Chalcedon also approved the *Tome of Leo*, in which the one person of Christ is the subject of two distinct natures, and the distinctive kinds of activity (divine and human) proper to those two natures. Since in this regard these two perspectives (i.e., that of St. Cyril and that of Pope St. Leo the Great) are not necessarily contradictory, *it can be said that the Chalcedonian definition, if read in the light of the acts of the Council as a whole, implies that there is one ultimate subject of all the acts and experiences of Jesus Christ: the divine Son, the second person of the Trinity.*

In *Ecce Homo: On the Divine Unity of Christ* (Grand Rapids: Eerdmans, 2016), Aaron Riches argues that the bishops at Chalcedon did not endorse the teachings of both Cyril and Leo merely in an attempt to fashion an ecclesiastical compromise, but because they saw no essential incompatibility between them (other than in semantics) regarding the unity of Christ:

> [Leo] was absolutely of one accord with Cyril. Cyril declared in anathema 12 of the *Twelve Chapters* that the Logos, who is the Life and the life-giving one, tasted death in the flesh in order to destroy death by death; whereas Leo in his *Tome* declares that Jesus, the impassible God, was subjected to the laws of death in order to destroy mortality by the mortality of the immortal one. The core of the apostolic proclamation of the Crucified Lord, preserved and reaffirmed in the *Credo* [at Nicea], was boldly upheld at Chalcedon in the Tome. Hence the famous acclamation of the Fathers: "Peter has uttered this through Leo. The apostles taught accordingly. Leo taught piously and truly. Cyril

for now that Chalcedon did not intend to "solve" the mystery of the Incarnation by presenting one standard theory for all to accept; rather, it set parameters to which any theory of the Incarnation must adhere if it is to represent the orthodox faith of the Church.

Non-Incarnational Christology

On this reckoning, some Anglican theologians over the past century or so have been explicitly non-incarnational. One thinks, for example, of the writings of Maurice Wiles, Geoffrey Lampe, and Don Cupitt.[34] For them, **the language of incarnation is held to be a way of telling important truths about God merely in poetic or mythical form.[35] The kernel of truth that these ancient stories and metaphors convey is that God's Spirit was at work in the life of Jesus to an exceptional degree, inspiring his teachings, and his life of loving service. But Jesus was not a divine person in human flesh.** Wiles, Lampe and Cupitt were all important contributors (in various ways) to the *Myth of God Incarnate* debate of the 1970s and 1980s.

Anglican philosophical theologian John Macquarrie, however, took issue with these theologians on this very point. For one thing, he wrote, a myth is a narrative, and the Incarnation is traditionally expressed not only in narrative fashion (e.g. "he emptied himself,

---

taught accordingly. Eternal is the memory of Cyril. Leo and Cyril taught the same. (p. 87)

Nevertheless, these teachings of Chalcedon were tragically obscured by its rehabilitation of the crypto-Nestorians Theodoret of Cyrrhus and Ibas of Edessa, and the apparent absence in the definition itself of any theopaschite formula similar to those found in the writings of St. Cyril. These were among the principal factors leading to the rejection of Chalcedon throughout major portions of Egypt.

[34] See Maurice Wiles, "Christianity Without Incarnation" in John Hick, ed. *The Myth of God Incarnate* (London: SCM, 1977), p. 1-10; Geoffrey Lampe, *Explorations in Theology: 8* (London: SCM, 1981), p. 124; Don Cupitt, *The Debate About Christ* (London: SCM, 1979), p. 73. It should be noted that Cupitt later developed a considerably more radical, non-theistic perspective on Christ.

[35] Wiles, "Christianity Without Incarnation," p. 161-165.

taking the form of a servant," Phil 2:7), but also as an ontological proposition (Jesus Christ is one person in two natures, fully human and fully divine).[36] Moreover, David Brown pointed out that scripture-based images of this ontological claim have had tremendous impact on the Christian community of faith, down through the ages:

> **Is it not God defenceless in the stable and suffering on the cross around which all the emotive and evocative power is concentrated? … It is simply because the image is so shocking when taken as the literal truth it is that it compels further reflection on what it must imply about the nature of divine love.[37]**

In short, the "myth" of God Incarnate, whether expressed in scriptural narrative or in images derived from that story, seems to have most power to move us when the ontological claim behind it is accepted as literal truth. The Incarnation means that God loved us so much that he did not think being born in Bethlehem and dying on Calvary too great a sacrifice to make in order to draw near to us and save us.

Throughout the entire *Myth of God Incarnate* controversy, Brian Hebblethwaite insisted that Non-Incarnational Christology squanders the very core of the historic Christian Faith:

> There can be no doubt that the doctrine of the Incarnation has been taken during the bulk of Christian history to constitute the very heart of Christianity. Hammered out over five centuries of passionate debate, enshrined in the classical Christian creeds, explored and articulated in the great systematic theologies, the doctrine expresses, as far as human words permit, the central belief of Christians that God himself, without ceasing to be God, has come amongst us, not just in

---

[36] John Macquarrie, "Christianity without Incarnation? Some Critical Comments" in Michael Green, ed., *The Truth of God Incarnate* (London: Hodder and Stoughton, 1977), p.140.
[37] David Brown, *Continental Philosophy and Modern Theology* (Oxford: Blackwell, 1987), p. 66.

but *as* a particular man, at a particular time and place. The human life lived, and the death died have been held quite literally to *be* the human life and death of God himself, in one of the modes of his own eternal being. …

(T)he incarnational christologian will insist that Christ must be thought of as coming to us from the side of God, the ultimate subject of his words and deeds being God himself in one of the modes of his triune being, while the non-incarnational christologian will suggest that it is enough to speak of God's unique acts by his Spirit in and through the man, Jesus of Nazareth. … The rival Christologies cannot both be true, even though both parties have *some* awareness of the religious realities whose more specific interpretation is in dispute. …

(T)here is a difference between God's making himself known through the awe-inspiring medium of "the holy" or through a prophet, and God's coming himself incognito, and winning a purely personal response. To suppose that God's acts in or presence to the man Jesus is simply a higher example of the kind of inspiration or illumination to be found elsewhere in the history of religions and is thus of supreme exemplary significance for our own "God-consciousness" is not to reinterpret the Christian tradition. It is to lose the peculiarly Christian contribution, namely that experience of God can now take a much more direct and personal form, since God himself has humbled himself and come among us as one of us.[38]

Throughout the rest of this book, I will trace the importance of the doctrine of the Incarnation for the wider pattern of Christian belief. Suffice it to say here that it seems impossible to square a Non-Incarnational Christology with the historic Christian Faith, much less with the historic Anglican expression of Christianity, with its special focus on the mystery of God made man.

---

[38] Hebblethwaite, *The Incarnation*, p. 1-2, 150, 5.

To the extent that authentically Anglican theology must be rooted in the consensus witness of the ancient Fathers of the Church, Non-Incarnational Christology leaves us with another problem. The Fathers were careful to define the parameters of the doctrine of the Incarnation at Nicea and Chalcedon, and made it a test of Christian orthodoxy. This shows that they believed the doctrine was vital to a proper understanding of the gospel story of the person and saving work of Jesus Christ. They could have left the whole matter in metaphorical and narrative form, much as they tended to do with apostolic teaching about the Atonement and the Parousia (the second coming of Christ), but they chose otherwise.

The question arises, therefore, whether for an Anglican being true to the heritage of the early Church Fathers includes adherence to what they held by consensus to be vital to the Apostolic Faith. After all, among the foundational documents of Anglican Christianity the same Convocation in 1571 that imposed subscription to *The 39 Articles of the Church of England* also gave the following instructions to Anglican preachers: "to be careful that they never teach ought in a sermon, to be religiously held and believed by the people, except what is agreeable to the doctrine of the Old and New Testaments, and *what the Catholic fathers and ancient bishops have collected out of the same doctrine.*"[39] And this commitment echoes down

---

[39] Cited in Vernon Staley, *The Catholic Religion* (Wilton, CT: Morehouse, 1983 centenary edition), p. 79. Wiles would disagree with this status accorded to the writings of the Fathers in Anglicanism: see his *Working Papers in Christian Doctrine* (London: SCM, 1976), p. 99-100, and *The Making of Christian Doctrine* (Cambridge: Cambridge University Press, 1967), p. 173. By contrast, Macquarrie tended to view the Anglican theological tradition both as a matter of adherence to their general method (scripture, tradition, and reason) as well as to their doctrinal affirmations: see his essay "The Anglican Theological Tradition" in Richard Holloway, ed., *The Anglican Tradition* (Wilton, CT: Morehouse-Barlow, 1984), p. 36 and 39. That the status of the ancient Fathers in Anglicanism remains unclear was evident from an essay by Tom Wright in *Believing in the Church* (London: SPCK, 1981), p. 112, a Report of the Church of England's Doctrinal Commission. Stephen Sykes made the case that in classical Anglicanism, the authority of Fathers, Councils, and Creeds was always held to be subordinate to Holy Scripture, and loyalty to them was upheld only in so far as they can be

through Anglican history. We find it in the same century in John Jewell in his *Apologia*: "We have returned to the Apostles and the Old Catholic fathers. We have planted no new religion, but have only preserved the old that was undoubtedly founded and used by the Apostles of Christ and other holy Fathers of the Primitive Church."[40] We find the same commitment also in the early 17th century in Lancelot Andrewes, who famously summed up the matter: "one canon … two testaments, three creeds, four general councils, five centuries and the series of the Fathers in that period … determine the boundaries of our faith."[41] We find it a few decades later in Archbishop William Laud's *A Relation of the Conference* (1639): "And I believe both Scripture and Creed in the same uncorrupted sense which the primitive Church believed them; and am sure that I do so believe them, because I cross not in my belief anything delivered by the primitive Church. And this, again, I am sure because I take the belief of the primitive Church as it is expressed and delivered by the Councils and ancient Fathers of those times."[42] We find it toward the end of the same century in John Bramhall, who spelled out the adherence of the Church of England to "the authority of the primitive fathers and the General Councils … the old faith of the whole Christian world, that is, the creed of the apostles, explicated by the Nicene, Constantinopolitan, Ephesine, and Chalcedonian fathers."[43]

Historically, therefore, the Anglican Communion has upheld the central teachings of the early Ecumenical Councils, and the statements of faith they endorsed or produced. The Bishops of the Anglican world

---

shown to be "agreeable" to Scripture. See Stephen Sykes, John Booty, and Jonathan Knight, eds. *The Study of Anglicanism* (London: SPCK/Fortress Press, 1998 revised edition), p.466. **The Anglican writers of the 16th and 17th centuries, however, generally were not in any doubt that the first four ecumenical Councils, the early Creeds, and the consensus teachings of the early Fathers of the same period could be shown to be fully in accord with Scripture. For them Scripture and early Christian Tradition formed one, seamless robe.**

[40] Cited in H.R. McAdoo, *Anglican Heritage: Theology and Spirituality* (Norwich: The Canterbury Press, 1991), p. 3.

[41] Ibid.

[42] Ibid., p. 95.

[43] Ibid., p. 105.

assembled at Lambeth in 1888, for example, specifically pointed to the vital importance for Christian unity of the Nicene Creed as "the sufficient statement of the Christian faith." That creed, of course, includes the teaching that the "only-begotten Son of God, begotten of the Father before all worlds ... begotten, not made, being of one substance with the Father, through whom all things were made ... for us men and for our salvation came down from heaven, and was incarnate by the Holy Ghost of the Virgin Mary, and was made man."[44] In accordance with the Book of Common Prayer, and for over four centuries, this creed was recited at every Anglican service of Holy Communion. In the light of this creedal and incarnational heritage, it surely strains credulity to hold that Non-Incarnational Christology should be able to find a home in the Anglican Communion as an acceptable doctrinal option.[45]

Action Christology

Another stream of Anglican thought holds that, while the mystery of the Incarnation should not be relegated to the category of mere myth or poetry, it needs to be re-interpreted and re-expressed for our time. Advances in modern thought, it is said, leave the traditional philosophical language of "person," "substance" and "natures" unconvincing to scholars, and incomprehensible to the faithful.

These concerns led to the development of what we may call "Action Christology."[46] By this we mean that *the underlying principle of Christology concerns God's revelatory action in and through Jesus Christ. The fact that Christ's action is so completely in accord with God's action means that they can be seen as united in a "personal" way.* In short, by divine action Jesus reflects the will and character of God so completely that he

---

[44] Translation taken from *The Book of Common Prayer* (Toronto: Anglican Book Centre, 1962), p. 71.

[45] See the Appendix to this volume entitled "Sed Contra" for further discussion of the normative status of the early creeds and councils of the Church.

[46] A category borrowed from Hebblethwaite, *The Incarnation*, p. 61, and 69.

is utterly transparent to the divine nature, the definitive revelation and self-expression of God in human terms.

Action Christology spread far and wide after the Second World War. Donald Baillie's book *God Was in Christ* (1948) was especially influential in launching the movement in the English-speaking world.[47] In Anglican circles it arose from suggestions made by W.R. Matthews in 1950, developed later by Hugh Montefiore, and in the Bampton lectures of David Jenkins.[48] Christ was seen as the "moving pattern" of Divine Love (Matthews), a pattern of personal life so completely in accord with the divine pattern that he may be called God manifest in the flesh. By the 1970's and 1980's, this perspective had been adopted by many of the leading theologians of the Anglican world, including John A.T. Robinson, Norman Pittenger, John Macquarrie, Keith Ward, and A.T. Hanson.

On this model of the Incarnation, the pre-existence of the Son of God is usually taken to mean the pre-existent intention and purpose in the mind of God the Father to call forth one such as Jesus in human history as the clear self-expression of the Father's truth and love.[49] Thus, the initiative in Christ's work always comes from God.[50] Jesus is the man in whom God's grace evokes

---

[47] D.M. Baillie, *God Was in Christ* (New York: Charles Scribner's Sons, 1948).

[48] W.R. Matthews, *The Problem of Christ in the Twentieth Century* (Oxford: Oxford University Press, 1950), p. 70-71; Hugh Montefiore, "Toward a Christology for Today," in A. Vidler, ed., *Soundings* (Cambridge: Cambridge University Press, 1966), and David Jenkins, *The Glory of Man* (London: SCM, 1967), p. 101-103. It could be argued, however, that incipient forms of Action Christology were already present in the pre-war era, as reflected, for example, in *Doctrine in the Church of England: The Report of the Commission on Christian Doctrine Appointed by the Archbishops of Canterbury and York in 1922* (London: SPCK, 1938), p. 75.

[49] John A.T. Robinson, *The Human Face of God* (London: SCM, 1973), p. 161, and 179. See also my discussion of the Christology of John Macquarrie later in this chapter.

[50] Ibid., p. 198.

a free, loving and total surrender, and so God comes to supreme, active self-expression in history through him.[51]

Keith Ward, for example, argued that Jesus is the "Word of God" because he expresses the character of God most fully: "He is a real man, but because of his position in world history, he becomes the place where the divine nature, the Word of God, is expressed with sharp clarity."[52] Similarly, for A.T. Hanson, Jesus is "the man who was completely open to God," and therefore "the unique instrument and manifestation of God's being."[53] In other words, the man Jesus was so completely responsive and obedient to divine grace that he supremely reflected God's character in his own.[54]

---

[51] This "dialogic" conception of the personal unity between God and Jesus is also evident in the Kenotic Christology developed by the Roman Catholic theologian Lucien J. Richard in *Christ: The Self-Emptying of God* (New York: Paulist Press, 1997), p. 90-92 and 95:

> The unity of Jesus Christ with God is primarily a personal community with the Father expressed in total dedication and obedience. ... As the one fully obedient and responsive to the will of God, Jesus is the one in whom the fullness of divinity dwells, the one to whom God is fully present ....This community is as the coming together of God's self-emptying and Jesus' acceptance. Without the divine self-communication and Jesus' receptivity there would be no incarnation. Two activities, each requiring and complementing the other, are indispensable to the full and irrevocable coming together of God and man. ... The person of Jesus is constituted by a reciprocal movement: of God to Jesus, of Jesus to God. It does not emerge from the synthesis of two static natures. We have here a unity of agency rather than of substance, of activity rather than natures, a *homo-praxis* rather than a *homoousia*, a personal, because dialogical, unity.

[52] Keith Ward, *The Living God* (London: SPCK, 1984), p. 104-106; cf. his essay "Incarnation or Inspiration—a False Dichotomy" in *Theology*, July, 1977, p. 254-255.
[53] A.T. Hanson, *Reasonable Belief* (Oxford: Oxford University Press, 1980), p. 98-99.
[54] A.T. Hanson, *Grace and Truth: a study of the Doctrine of the Incarnation* (London: SPCK, 1975), p. 46, 59, 89-90, 108.

The Incarnation

In *The Divine Trinity* (1985), David Brown offered a substantial critique of this whole approach: it is actually Nestorianism in modern dress.[55] It cannot make a truly incarnational claim, for it leaves no reason to think of one person in Christ, instead of two persons: one divine and one human. **In effect, Brown claims that Action Christology involves a limited and contingent notion of personal union:**

> **A unity of will in a common purpose, no matter how complete, would not justify us in speaking of a single person, rather than two persons. In the first place, it would remain a contingent unity (one person could will differently from the other, and so break the unity at any moment) and, secondly, there remain vast areas of personhood which still would not be united, there continuing to be no unity of common experience, despite the common purpose.[56]**

As we shall see, Brown's critique of Action Christology seems basically correct. If we look at three major re-interpretations of the Incarnation by Anglican theologians since the Second World War, we find that each one was an example of this perspective, and each fell short of a truly incarnational claim, despite a sincere effort by the authors to remain true to Chalcedon.

In *The Human Face of God* (1973), for example, Bishop John A.T. Robinson (1919-1983) claimed that the real intention behind the

---

[55] We need not wade into the ongoing debate about what Nestorius actually taught and intended; Brown's point in essence is that Action Christology is metaphysically the equivalent of the extreme wing of the ancient Antiochene Christological tradition, as in, for example, the writings of the fourth century proto-Nestorian Theodore of Mopsuestia. In *Ecce Homo*, p. 27-30, Aaron Riches outlines the thought of the Theodore in a way that shows him to be a forerunner of modern Neo-Nestorian Action Christology. For Theodore "divinity and humanity" in Christ are "discrete agents, separate ontological existences," and his teachings about a "prosopic union" in Christ is simply a way of designating "the manifestational unity of two separate ontological essences."
[56] Brown, *The Divine Trinity*, p. 230.

Chalcedonian decree was to assert not two natures so much as two "languages" with one subject, or better, two kinds of predicates of one subject.[57] We can speak in a *factual* way about Jesus as human — his birth, growth, weariness, hunger and death — but to assert his divinity is to speak of his *significance*; it is to interpret his life as the revelatory activity of God. Jesus functions for us as God's personal representative, through whom God reveals himself in a definitive and decisive way. He is a man, human in the fullest possible sense, but he functions as the instrument of the self-expressive activity of God.[58]

It is doubtful, however, that Robinson's Christology faithfully preserved the intentions of the Council fathers at Chalcedon. For when Robinson wrote of the humanity of Jesus, he spoke in factual, *ontological* terms, but when he wrote of the divinity of Jesus, he spoke of significance, that is, in *functional* terms.[59] Chalcedon makes no such distinction. The bishops at Chalcedon did not say that to assert that Christ has the divine nature means speaking in a fundamentally different way from saying that he has a human nature. Chalcedon seems to use the term "nature" (*physis*) consistently and ontologically, i.e., Christ was said to possess all the characteristic and definitive attributes of both divinity and humanity. Moreover, to claim as Robinson did that Jesus is solely a human person is actually to violate the parameters of the Chalcedonian definition. For as we have seen, while the core of the definition did not explicitly state whether the person of the Incarnate is solely divine, or a fusion of a divine person and a human person into one (a *tertium quid*), it does predicate both human and divine natures of a single subject or *hypostasis*. Chalcedon tells us that in the Incarnation, one subject, or person, Jesus Christ, has all the divine and all the human attributes.

---

[57] Robinson, *The Human Face of God*, p. 114.

[58] Ibid., p. 104.

[59] Ibid., p.182-184. Similarly, see Trevor Williams, *Form and Vitality* (Oxford: Clarendon Press, 1985), p. 271-273, 277-278, who reinterpreted the divinity of Jesus as his "unique revelatory significance," supremely manifesting the character or "form" of God.

The Incarnation

Robinson summarized his understanding of the incarnation with characteristic flourish:

> One who was totally and utterly a man — and had never been anything other than a man or more than man — so completely embodied what was from the beginning the meaning and purpose of God's self-expression ... that it could be said, and had to be said of that man, "He was God's man" or "God was in Christ," or even that he *was* "God for us." This way of putting it clearly involves no whit less of a stupendous claim.[60]

Unfortunately, Robinson's use of language was more than a little confusing. Drawing heavily upon the work of continental Christian thinkers such as Bonhoeffer and Tillich, he referred to Jesus as "God to us and for us," and often claimed that "what Jesus was and did was the direct expression and implementation of God in action."[61] Although Robinson sometimes wrote of a divine "identity claim,"[62] it is clear that for him "identity" means something less than "equation," and is a matter of verbs rather than substances or substantives.[63] Jesus is "a human figure raised up from among his brothers to be the instrument of God's decisive work and to stand in a relationship to him to which no other man is called ... he *functions* as God."[64] **This is a harmony of wills, or of activity in a common purpose between two persons, God and Jesus, and therefore a unity of work and expression. But the union between God and Christ is accomplished by God's "using, acting through a man,"[65] and while this may be of profound theological significance, it clearly falls short of the Chalcedonian claim that Christ is one person, or one subject, in two natures, fully human and fully divine. As** David Brown explained, it gives us no reason to believe that in Jesus

---

[60] Robinson, *The Human Face of God*, p. 179.
[61] Ibid., p. 114, and 180-181.
[62] Ibid., p.183 and 197.
[63] Ibid., p. 180 and 183. See footnote number one, above, for a brief discussion of the meaning of "person" and "personal identity" in Christology.
[64] Ibid., p. 184.
[65] Ibid., p. 197.

Christ we have one person, rather than two persons, divine and human, in close cooperation. As such, it is not an authentically "incarnational" Christology.

In a similar way, Norman Pittenger (1905-1997) reinterpreted the "divinity" of Jesus as "act of God":[66] "For Christian Faith, by the prevenient action of God a human life was taken and made the instrument of the gracious divine operation."[67]

The question naturally arises as to what kind of union between God and a human being this implies. In *Christology Reconsidered* (1970), Pittenger wrote:

> I should prefer to speak of the relationship or union of God and that man, rather than of godhead and manhood, thereby running the risk of attack as Antiochene if not Nestorian. … Furthermore, it is not a mechanical union in which godhead and manhood, or God and that man, are stuck together in some less than personal manner. It is to be conceived after the analogy of personal union such as we know in, say, human marriage, or the love of a lover and his beloved.[68]

Drawing upon the categories of Alfred North Whitehead's Process Philosophy, Pittenger explained that Jesus was united with God's love-in-action in a supreme way because he freely and totally responded to the alluring power of God's love, and thereby consented to become the instrument of God.[69]

Clearly, what Pittenger has in mind is a loving, intimate union of will and purpose between two persons: God as initiator, and the man Jesus in response. We do not have *one* person in two natures here. Yet

---

[66] Norman Pittenger, *Christology Reconsidered* (London: SCM, 1970), p. 2.
[67] Norman Pittenger, *The Lure of Divine Love* (New York: Pilgrim Press, 1979), p. 109.
[68] Pittenger, *Christology Reconsidered*, p. 12.
[69] Norman Pittenger, "Christology in Process Theology," in *Theology*, March, 1977, p. 191.

The Incarnation

Pittenger persisted in using the term "incarnation" to describe this unity. He called it incarnation in a "climactic" sense:

> In Jesus the energising and indwelling activity of God in human creation reaches a climactic stage. To say this presupposes that in all men and women there is some working of deity, varying in degree and intensity, while those in whom there is a greater fullness of response to the divine working become more adequately the personal instruments of God. … Much official theology seems to have gone wrong in confining the incarnating act of God to Jesus alone.[70]

Classical Christianity, however, has always preferred to speak of the varying degrees of divine presence and activity in human beings as instances of divine "inspiration," or as "the indwelling, and sanctifying work of the Holy Spirit." Although the human nature of Jesus certainly shared in the indwelling presence and activity of the Holy Spirit to an unsurpassable degree, historically Christian orthodoxy has always seen that as a mystery distinct from the mystery of the "Incarnation." The latter term refers specifically to the fact that Jesus is one person in two natures, truly human and truly divine (and some would argue that it is precisely because we know that Jesus is the divine Son Incarnate that we can know his human will was totally surrendered to the Spirit — more on that later).

In the overall framework of Pittenger's Process philosophy, God's union with Jesus was seen as an intensification of his mode of action everywhere in the world. In fact, Pittenger claims, we live in an incarnational universe:

> God's involvement identifies himself with the world to the extent of his incarnating himself in that world. … God remains unsurpassably God, yet he is active in and present in the world, working in every occasion or occurrence … surrounding and soliciting and luring and attracting each occasion towards its

---

[70] Pittenger, *The Lure of Divine Love*, p. 112 and 114. Similarly, see H.A. Williams, "Incarnation: Model and Symbol" in *Theology*, January, 1976, p. 17.

fulfilment, never over-riding its own freedom of decision, yet always seeking to invite the occasion to become truly itself.[71]

Unfortunately, Pittenger thereby left his readers in a semantic muddle. As we have seen, sometimes he used the word "incarnation" (or "climactic" incarnation) for God's luring of the human will into loving action (what might better be called "inspiration" or "the sanctifying work of the Holy Spirit"), while here he wrote of God "incarnating himself" in the world as a synonymous expression for God's creative, alluring presence throughout the entire universe (what might better be termed divine "immanence"). Neither use of the word "incarnation" is true to the understanding of the doctrine formulated at the Council of Chalcedon. Pittenger only causes needless confusion by retaining the term, while transforming its meaning almost beyond recognition. In fact, what Pittenger offered us was not a truly "incarnational" Christology at all. Rather, it was another modern Anglican reinterpretation of the Incarnation in which Jesus Christ was not held to be one person in two natures, fully human and full divine. The divine side of the incarnational identity claim was never established. Jesus was seen by Pittenger as a solely human person who freely surrendered to God's gracious will and purpose, thus becoming God's supreme earthly instrument and expression.

Perhaps the most subtle contemporary Anglican statement of Christology may be found in the writings of John Macquarrie (1919-2007), a Scotsman who taught in the USA for many years, then returned to Britain as Lady Margaret Professor of Divinity at Oxford. His magnum opus was his *Principles of Christian Theology* (second edition, 1977). The Incarnation, Macquarrie asserted, means "the bringing together of Godhood and manhood," — a conscious effort on

---

[71] Pittenger, *Christology Reconsidered,* p. 150. Similarly, in *Christ: The Self-Emptying of God*, Catholic theologian Lucien Richard states: "The incarnation is not exhausted in the one unique historical person of Jesus of Nazareth, but as Teilhard de Chardin could affirm, it is a process that strives toward the Christification of the cosmos" (p. 102).

The Incarnation

Macquarrie's part to restate Chalcedonian orthodoxy.[72] That Jesus has a divine nature, Macquarrie wrote, is clear from the scriptural confession of Christ's Lordship, giving to him our ultimate allegiance, "for if we gave such allegiance to anyone else [than God], we would be idolaters — and this, as has often been pointed out, was the basic objection to Arianism." Yet Jesus also has a human nature, for "this Word has met us and addressed us on the level of human existence."[73]

On the other hand, Macquarrie was also highly critical of Chalcedonian terminology. Today, he claimed, we cannot take "nature" to mean "a fixed stock of characteristics which constitute anything as the kind of thing it is," and then say that Christ has two "natures" in this sense in one "subsistence," in other words, in one particular being.[74] The reason for this is that man does not have a fixed nature; he is always incomplete and on his way: "In the case of man as existing and as not having a fixed essence there is no end in sight along the road he can travel."[75] At the same time, Macquarrie claimed that Christ himself is at the furthest point along the road to the fulfilment of human nature.[76] Certain potentialities of human nature must therefore be "fixed" in the sense of originally intended by creative Being, and realised and made manifest in Jesus.[77] What Macquarrie seemed to mean is that there is a boundless openness in human nature to continual growth in the likeness of God: that is, to the outpouring of one's own being in self-giving love.[78] Therefore, it is better not to speak of Christ or the saints as fulfilling a "fixed" human nature, but as progressing into a perfection not limited by any boundary.[79]

---

[72] John Macquarrie, *Principles of Christian Theology* (New York: Scribner's, second edition 1977), p. 295.
[73] Ibid., p. 296.
[74] Ibid., p. 297.
[75] Ibid., p. 298.
[76] Ibid., p. 296 and 305; cf. John Macquarrie, *The Humility of God* (Philadelphia: Westminster, 1978), p. 4.
[77] For Macquarrie's definition of God as Being, see *Principles of Christian Theology,* p. 107-122.
[78] Ibid., p. 396.
[79] Ibid., p. 499.

It is hard to see the force of Macquarrie's objection to Chalcedonian terminology here. After all, one might ask, what further possibilities for self-giving love could there be in this life beyond the crucifixion of the Incarnate Son? Was there anything he held back? How could love progress beyond the upper limit of the Cross, which was surely God's act of *total self-giving* in and through his human nature? One could apply this also to the entire life of the divine Son Incarnate: Christian belief has always seen in Jesus Christ the exemplary, "fixed," "upper limit" of human nature in its likeness to God in self-giving love.

Macquarrie also objected to the assertion that Christ had a divine nature in the "fixed" Chalcedonian sense. Instead, he sees the divine nature as "emerging" over time, in the sense that God as expressive Being only achieves his highest earthly self-expression through the whole life story of Christ Jesus.[80]

The question then arises as to how these two "emerging" natures are brought together in one person. Macquarrie claimed that "the incarnation is to be understood not as an instantaneous happening, but as a process of coming together."[81] For as Jesus increasingly matures as a person, he manifests more and more of the possibilities of humanity, and therefore of the intended self-expression of creative Being through humanity. This process is completed on the Cross, where full "convergence" of the two natures takes place. On the Cross, Being manifests itself through an act of perfect human love.[82] Macquarrie showed himself indebted here to the work of the Catholic theologian Karl Rahner. Rahner taught that "God takes on a human nature of his own" in an "unsurpassable" way when the nature which surrenders itself to the divine mystery belongs so little to itself that it becomes the nature of God himself. "The Incarnation of God is therefore the unique, the *supreme* case of the total actualisation of

---

[80] Ibid., p. 299.
[81] Ibid., p. 300.
[82] Ibid., p. 303, but cf. p. 396.

human reality, which consists in the fact that man *is* in so far as he gives up himself."[83]

For Macquarrie, Christ's humanity is the key to his divinity. Jesus is the clear image and expression of holy Being for us precisely because he manifests true manhood, the pinnacle of God's work in the universe as creative Being.[84] Thus, Christology must begin "from below." The first thing Jesus brings to light is true humanity: "He makes unhidden what human beings have it in them to become."[85] He fulfils the highest potentials of human personality. But we can say more, for human beings can be the most complete manifestation of creative, self-giving Being lying behind the universe.[86] Leaning heavily upon the philosophy of Heidegger, Macquarrie argues that Being is present and manifest through all created beings, but most especially in the highest personal being, Jesus Christ. Jesus is therefore to a supreme degree the self-disclosure of creative Being: through him God has revealed with supreme clarity who he is and what he has always been striving for everywhere in the universe as self-expressive, reconciling Being. Jesus Christ is therefore truly called "the paradigmatic revelation of God," "the symbol of Being," and "the focus where the mystery of Being is disclosed."[87]

Macquarrie added three important points of clarification here.

First of all, he was careful to point out that it is the entire "constellation" of the personal qualities of Jesus which makes him the true man, and not just one or two of his characteristics (e.g. his self-giving love, his devotion to his Father, or his freedom).[88]

---

[83] Gerald A. McCool, ed., *A Rahner Reader* (London: Darton, Longman and Todd, 1975), p. 146.
[84] Macquarrie, *The Humility of God*, p. 31.
[85] Ibid., p. 30.
[86] Macquarrie, *Principles of Christian Theology*, p. 225-226.
[87] Ibid., p. 270-271.
[88] Ibid., p. 305.

Second, Macquarrie reassured his readers that by calling Jesus "the symbol of Being," he did not mean that Jesus is merely a mental image, or a figure from a timeless myth. It is essential that Jesus be seen as an historical individual, otherwise we could never be sure that his way of life, his true manhood as the Gospels portray it, is actually a possibility in this world: "The way of life which lies at the heart of the Christian proclamation is not something utopian or belonging to a wish-world, but something that has been realised in human history, under the conditions of being-in-the-world."[89]In fact, the Jesus of history is the basis for our belief that Jesus is truly our "best clue to the mystery of the Father," the Being at the heart of this real universe in which we live.[90] Macquarrie thereby showed that it is essential for Christology to be based on a solid historical core. We have to know, as best we can, if the Jesus reached by historical research provides any basis for the significance accorded to him as the revelation of true manhood and true Godhood. Drawing primarily upon the New Testament scholar Bultmann, he concluded that a certain historical core in the Gospels is practically unassailable: in the face of what Jesus of Nazareth held to be the imminent arrival of the world's end, he gave himself away in love to God and to others, even unto death.[91]

Third, Macquarrie made it abundantly clear that Jesus is not to be seen as the ideal Pelagian man, as if his exemplary and revelatory life was simply a matter of human moral effort: "From first to last, this is the work of Being."[92] Jesus only reached the heights of personal being because God expressed himself through him. The human Jesus does not earn his place as the self-disclosure and focus of Being. The initiative lies always with God's Word, his self-expressive Being. Thus, according to Macquarrie, the symbol of the pre-existence of the Word is vital to Christianity. It tells us that the same self-expressive Being who is active in all creation is the one present and manifest in Jesus: "Christ has been present in creation from the beginning as its aim,"

---

[89] Ibid., p. 278.
[90] John Macquarrie, *Christian Hope* (Oxford: Mowbrays, 1981), p. 68.
[91] Macquarrie, *Principles of Christian Theology*, p. 277.
[92] Ibid., p. 310.

for "even before history began to run its course, Christ and his saving work were present in the mind and intention of the Father."[93] Christology "from above," in this sense, definitely has its place.

Clearly, what Macquarrie offered was another, more sophisticated version of Action Christology. Being is said to be present and manifest in a supreme way through Jesus Christ because Christ's self-giving love, the outpouring of his own being, is the best "symbol," "clue," "focus," "paradigm," and "expression" of the self-giving love that characterises the Creator.

Unfortunately, this understanding of the person of Christ — or rather, of God's self-expressive activity through Christ — is not as incarnational as Macquarrie believed. For example, while he asserted "the closeness, even the identity of Christ with God," it is not clear how he justified or made coherent such a claim.[94] To begin with, he told us that self-expressive Being is present and manifest in every being. His presence and manifestation in Christ seems only a matter of degree. Many people respond to Being's gracious presence and activity, and thereby manifest in their lives God's presence and character as holy Being. Perhaps Jesus was the one who most fully and lovingly responded to his presence, and manifested him to the highest degree. But surely this alone does not mean that Jesus was one in identity with a divine person, the Divine Word. To establish such an identity, it is not enough to point to the whole "constellation" of a man's highest personal qualities, and show that he is the supreme expression and reflection of the character of God in human history. For personal identity is not indicated or established by a high degree of similarity in *personal character* alone. Many philosophers at least would want to add *having the same experiences* as an essential indicator as well.

---

[93] Macquarrie, *Christian Hope*, p. 61.
[94] Macquarrie, *The Humility of God*, p. 64; Macquarrie, *Principles of Christian Theology*, p. 296 and 321.

Was Macquarrie able to sustain this other aspect of a divine identity claim for Jesus Christ? At one point, he tells us that God's attribute of omniscience means that God "occupies every perspective at once."[95] It seems that in some way God shares completely in the experience of every creature in the world. This may not be intelligible (can anyone else, even God, occupy my perspective and experience my experiences precisely as I experience them? Does God feel my depression or wanton lust when I do? Does God feel the guilt of my guilty conscience, or share my disordered desire to go on sinning?). But even if this is intelligible, how can we assert an "identity of Christ with God" in any way closer than in his sharing in the experiences of the rest of us? Macquarrie could reply that Jesus can be seen as one in identity with God because they have both a common character and common experiences (i.e., his character perfectly reflects God's, and his experiences are experienced by God as God's own), whereas other human beings do not fully reflect the loving character of God. However, even this would not rescue Macquarrie's position, for presumably, when the followers of Jesus are fully sanctified in heaven, they too will fully reflect God's character of self-giving love. Will we then become one in identity with God along with Christ? Are we each to lose our own distinct personal identity in the end, like drops falling into the ocean of the divine Being?

Suffice it to say that Macquarrie did not make a clear divine identity claim for Christ. In fact, there seems to be considerable avoidance of the question altogether in his writings. On the one hand, he was quite explicit about his concern for ontology: "I agree with Tillich that the honest theologian cannot avoid facing and exploring the metaphysical or ontological implications of his utterances about God, Christ, man, and the world."[96] On the other hand, such avoidance seems precisely what happens in his essay on this very subject, "The Concept of the Christ Event" (1981).[97] Macquarrie asked: which is more central to

---

[95] Macquarrie, *Principles of Christian Theology*, p.206.
[96] John Macquarrie, "The Concept of the Christ Event" in A.E. Harvey, ed., *God Incarnate: Story and Belief* (London: SPCK, 1981), p. 32.
[97] Ibid.

Christology, the Christ-event or Jesus the individual? He points out that whenever we refer to a person, we have to refer to him/her in a descriptive context. For example, "Jesus" is the one who lived at a certain time and place, with certain relations, in a certain culture, whose life had certain historical effects. All this describes the personal "event." Nevertheless, Macquarrie did not seem to distinguish the personal identity of the individual from the wider contextual "penumbra" by which we locate him/her in human history.[98] In other words, that wider penumbra or event does not help us much with questions such as "Is Jesus a solely human person?" or "Is he a reincarnation of the Buddha?" or "Is he the second person of the Trinity Incarnate?" In fact, there was considerable avoidance of ontological-identity questions altogether in this important essay. For example, Macquarrie tells us that when we think about Jesus as the Christ-event, rather than trying to isolate him as a single, historical individual, we can better understand the doctrine of the Incarnation. We should think of the Incarnation as God expressing himself in the world in a "new and fuller way" through all that led up to and prepared for the life of Jesus, as well as the entire "new humanity" that results from him.[99] Doubtless, all that is true as far as it goes, but it does not fully answer the underlying ontological-identity question: "Who is Jesus?" And it confuses the doctrine of the Incarnation, an identity claim, with the historical preparation for, and the historical effects of, God's incarnate life.

To sum up what we have said so far: the doctrine of the Incarnation is an ontological-identity claim. Jesus of Nazareth is said to be one person in two natures, fully human and fully divine; in other words, he is one subject, who possesses all of the characteristic and definitive attributes of divinity and humanity. Non-Incarnational Christology simply rejects this claim, and seeks to salvage kernels of spiritual truth from the discarded husk of the traditional doctrine. Action Christology has also fallen short of this claim, despite an evidently sincere desire on

---

[98] Ibid., p. 70.
[99] Ibid., p. 78.

the part of its proponents to remain true to the intentions of Chalcedon, and to retain the word "incarnation."

As we have also seen, since the Second World War Anglican Christology has been like a microcosm (albeit an imperfect one) of many of the streams of theology flowing outside of the Anglican world. Anglicans in this period drew heavily on the thought of philosophers such as Tillich, Whitehead, and Heidegger, and on theologians such as Bonhoeffer, Bultmann, and Rahner. **Unfortunately there has been a general reluctance by Anglican theologians in this era to mine the treasures of their own Anglican tradition on the mystery of the Incarnation. Moreover, in so far as authentically "Anglican" theology is committed to the ancient Nicene and Chalcedonian faith, and to its own incarnational heritage, both Non-Incarnational Christology and Action Christology must be deemed unsatisfactory.**[100]

Two-Nature Christology

One place that contemporary Anglican theologians might have looked for guidance regarding the mystery of the Incarnation would have been to reach back to the classical model of Two-Nature Christology (TNC). **This theory states that the two natures of Jesus Christ, divine and human, are present and operative simultaneously in the one person, while each nature remains distinct.** *In other words, when God becomes incarnate as Jesus of Nazareth, no*

---

[100] According to the Doctrine Commission report of the Church of England *Believing in the Church* (London: SPCK, 1981), the Creeds themselves were compiled with explicit reference to the higher authority of Scripture, and are held by the Anglican tradition to be under Scripture (see p. 28-30 and 112). A significant modification of the generally received sense of the Nicene Creed and the Chalcedonian definition, therefore, would have to be justified at the bar of Scripture, and not merely in the light of new trends in philosophy (such as Process or Existentialist philosophies). Among contemporary Anglican proponents of Action Christology, only John A.T. Robinson attempted to do this in his writings, especially in his *Redating the New Testament* (1976), *The Priority of John* (1987), and in his chief Christological statement *The Human Face of God* (1973).

divine attributes are abandoned, limited, altered or affected in any way by the union. **In addition to his eternal divine nature, the divine Son simply added a human nature and a human life to the unchangeable reality of who he is.**

For example, an Anglican disciple of St. Thomas Aquinas, Eric Mascall (1905-1993), viewed the human nature of Christ not as a fetter, limiting and constraining the divine Son, but as an instrument of the one who remains, even while incarnate, the universal, unchangeable Divine Word.[101] The absolute impassibility of the divine nature (that is, God's transcendent invulnerability to suffering), so Mascall believed, is not in any way compromised by the Incarnation.[102]

This, of course, leads to the obvious question: how can God be utterly impassible, changeless, and timeless in his divine nature, and yet also be the subject of a human life, with all of its experiences of time, change, and suffering? Mascall explained: "By providing the eternal Word with a complete and concrete human nature which is subject to suffering, it makes it possible for the eternal Word, who is absolutely impassible in his Godhead, to be really and literally passible in his manhood."[103] Hence, Mascall wrote of the paradox that God must remain immutable in becoming man so that it is truly God who is mutable and passible as man.[104]

The classical Two-Nature Theory of the Incarnation, however, remains controversial. For example, David Brown argued that if the divine nature remains entirely impassible, completely unaffected in that nature by his incarnate life, we would not be able to distinguish between God the Son's relationship to the human nature of Jesus and his relationship to any other instance of human nature.[105] Of course, a

---

[101] Eric Mascall, *Christ, the Christian, and the Church* (Longmans and Green, 1946), p. 49

[102] Eric Mascall, *Whatever Happened to the Human Mind?* (London: SPCK, 1980), p. 95.

[103] Ibid., p. 34.

[104] Ibid., p. 72.

[105] Brown, *The Divine Trinity*, p. 264-265.

proponent of classical TNC could reply that only in the case of Jesus is a divine person the ultimate subject of all the acts and experiences of a human life. He is uniquely the one operator of two natures. Yet, such a reply would hardly seem adequate. For in everyday life, we normally speak of someone as the "subject" of human experiences (and "subject to" human experiences) because certain events have actually affected their individual human nature, in mind, body, spirit, and/or emotions. What analogy could we possibly find for the claim that a person can be completely unaffected by his own human life and death? Again, *a defender of classical TNC could argue that God is not, in fact, "unaffected" by his own human life and death as Jesus of Nazareth; he is simply affected solely in his human nature, but not in his divine nature.* Becoming incarnate in this way in another nature is something that only God can do, but it is not logically or theologically impossible.

Nevertheless, even if this is merely a paradoxical, rather than a logically self-contradictory theory of the Incarnation, *classical TNC leaves us wondering whether God was really involved in his incarnate life and death in any significant or comprehensible way.* O.C. Quick, for example, put the objection like this:

> For a theologian who holds deity to be strictly impassible and not subject to any limitation, it seems to follow that Jesus Christ suffered and was subject to limitation only as man, and that as God he remained unaffected by any of the human experiences which involve suffering or limitation. ... To me the suggestion that God, *but not deity*, became incarnate is unintelligible.[106]

Similarly, Frank Weston remained unconvinced of a strictly classical TNC in which Christ was seen as being "so nearly dual in personality that the divine person, as it were, watches Himself as man suffering."[107] In other words, *the divine person of the Son of God, in his divine nature, seems to be left as the mere operator*

---

[106] Quick, *Doctrines of the Creed*, p. 125 and 133.
[107] Weston, *The One Christ*, p. 210.

and spectator of his own human life and death. In today's world, by way of analogy, think of the relationship between a video game player and his/her on-screen character. He operates the on-screen character, and it is, in a sense, his own character in that (virtual) world — but he does not experience the struggles and sufferings of his on-screen character in his own proper nature, even if in some sense he does have metaphysical ownership of them.[108]

---

[108] Some of the ancient Fathers seem to have spoken in similar terms. For example, Eusebius calls the humanity of Christ an "instrument which he had before him," and compares it to the relation between a musician and his lyre, who is not himself affected by the blows which strike the strings. On Eusebius see Charles Gore, *Dissertations on Subjects Connected with the Incarnation* (London: John Murray, second edition, 1907), p. 101-102. Giles Emery, O.P., points out that St. Athanasius, St. Cyril of Alexandria, and St. John Damascene all wrote of the humanity of Christ as an "instrument" of his divinity; Gilles Emery, O.P., *The Trinity: an Introduction to the Catholic Doctrine of the Triune God* (Washington, DC: The Catholic University of America Press, 2011), p. 180. For the later Fathers of the Church, one of the preferred analogies for the Incarnation was the fact that a created human person is the subject of both his soul and his body at the same time; see St. Cyril of Alexandria, *ad Nest.* 2:6,10: "If anyone kills and ordinary human being, he is not to be accused of two crimes, even if a man is to be considered as composed of soul and body, and the experiences of these two components are by nature different. We should think of Christ in the same manner: he is not twofold, he is one single Lord and Son, the Word of God the Father, in the flesh. ... Something like this can of course be observed in our experience: for a single man is really a composite being, made up of unlike elements, namely soul and body" (cited in Henry Bettenson's anthology, *The Later Christian Fathers.* Oxford: Oxford University Press, 1970, p. 253-254). But this analogy breaks down for classical TNC because in the human person the soul and body affect each other profoundly; the human soul, for example, is not impassible with relation to the sufferings of the body. Another analogy for the Incarnation used by proponents of classical TNC was the analogy of a man who puts on a garment. Saint Athanasius, for example, wrote: "[J]ust as Aaron put on his robe, so the Word took earthly flesh, having Mary for the Mother of his body .... As Aaron remained the same and did not change by assuming the high priest's dress ... so the Lord did not become another by taking the flesh, but remained the same and was clothed in it" (*Contra Arianos* ii, 7, 8, cited in Henry Bettenson's anthology, *The Early Christian Fathers.* Oxford: Oxford University Press, 1956, p. 281). In what sense, then, was the Divine Word really the subject of the sufferings and tribulations of the outer garment, so to speak, of his humanity? If

As we shall see in our next chapter, Kenoticists of all kinds share this same objection to classical TNC. American philosopher C. Stephen Evans, for example, has asked:

> If there is no change in God, what could it mean to say that God himself *takes on* human nature? A real incarnation must not be merely an addition to God; it must make some difference to God and in God.[109]

---

we tear in half someone's coat while he is wearing it, we do not say that we have torn that person in half!

[109] C. Stephen Evans, "Kenotic Christology and the Nature of God" in C. Stephen Evans, ed., *Exploring Kenotic Christology* (Vancouver, BC: Regent College Press, 2006), p. 197. Similarly, the Russian Orthodox Kenotic theologian Sergius Bulgakov in *The Lamb of God* (Grand Rapids: Eerdmans, 2008 edition, Boris Jakim, trans.) sharply criticized classical notions of the Incarnation in which "Although the human flesh is received into the hypostatic union for the sake of its redemption, in itself it remains, as it were, outside the life of the God-man. It remains an instrument (St. John of Damascus), a veil, or a kind of annex or accident in the theophany" (p. 256). He even goes so far as to say that all this is a violation of the teachings of Chalcedon:

> Thus, while acknowledging that the Word had accepted the suffering of the flesh, St. John of Damascus denies that these sufferings had any relation to the divine nature, which is "impassible." However, can one separate the hypostasis from the nature in this manner (as John in effect does) and consider that which is proper to the hypostasis (the suffering of the flesh) to be totally alien to the divine nature? Does this not contradict both the letter and the meaning of the Chalcedonian definition, according to which the natures are united *without separation ...?* (p. 258-259).

Perhaps Bulgakov "overshot the mark" here. From the Patristic discussion leading up to and surrounding Chalcedonian definition, the early Fathers such as St. Leo the Great and St. Cyril of Alexandria seemed to be comfortable with the notion that the hypostasis of the divine Son could be the subject of the simultaneous and harmonious operation of two natures, without compromising the impassibility of the divine nature. Nevertheless, Bulgakov, like Weston, Quick and Evans, has raised important questions here about the intelligibility of the classical Two-Nature Theory of the Incarnation.

Anglican theologian Marilyn McCord Adams addressed this issue in her defence of TNC in her book *Christ and Horrors: The Coherence of Christology* (2006): "[T]he Word made flesh is not a mere aggregate of Divinity and humanity; the individual nature is *assumed* by the Divine Word. But what is the metaphysical difference between mere aggregation and inherence?"[110] To answer this crucial question, Adams drew upon the work of the medieval Franciscan theologian and philosopher John Duns Scotus. The relationship between the human nature assumed and the divine Son of God, Scotus taught, is best understood as akin to the ontological dependence of an accident upon its subject.[111] An accident has no act of existence of its own, nor does it necessarily actualize any unrealized potential in its subject: an accident is merely a mode or modification of an existing substance in quality, quantity, or relationship to other substances. Accidents would include modes of, or modifications in color, position in space, height and weight, and so on, that are not essential to a substance, and do not necessarily make an essential change in the kinds of substances they modify — or even effect any real change in those substances at all. For example, consider the accidental change that occurs to me when, after standing on my left side, you move to stand on my right. Your relation to me in space is an accidental modification of my substance (in its relation to other things) that does not necessarily affect me at all (I may be asleep and completely unaware of this change in your location). *The Incarnation, therefore, would be similar to this: an accidental modification and addition to the divine Son that does not alter or affect his divine nature in any way.*

In a highly abstruse section of her book, Adams wrote: "[T]he ontological dependence of the human nature on the Divine Word would suffice for the truth of 'The Divine Word is human' and be enough to license the further creedal predications: 'born of the Virgin Mary, suffered under Pontius Pilate, was crucified, dead, buried, but rose on the third day.'"[112] David Brown, however, in *Divine Humanity*

---

[110] Adams, *Christ and Horrors*, p. 125.
[111] Ibid., p. 125-128.
[112] Ibid., p. 128.

(2011) questioned whether Adams had really succeeded here in illuminating the mystery of the Incarnation:

> So [for Adams] the only anchor maintaining the appropriateness of ascribing to God the full horror of what Christ endured is metaphysical: the sheer claim that he has been made the subject of such horrors. Yet what does that mean? We are simply not told, beyond the rather unhelpful analogy of the possibility of adding a bovine nature to Socrates. … Even if the proposed metaphysics is logically coherent, bolting human nature onto the divine hardly in itself gives its experiences supreme significance for the divine being: a mere pinprick in its total life … .[113]

Then, anticipating the ground we will cover in the next few chapters of this book, Brown adds:

> Certainly, Adams' accusation that the English Kenoticists were vague about their metaphysics is fair, but they were at least clear what they wanted, that the pain [of Christ] should be taken into the divine nature, something achieved by definition on their account, since (by whatever means) divine nature was now placed on the same level as human nature itself.[114]

Of course, any claim that God the Son has suffered and been affected *in his divine nature* through his incarnate life and death raises huge metaphysical issues (for example: how can the God who is — so classical Christian tradition holds — infinitely perfect Being experience "suffering" in his divine nature without this involving a diminution of his Being in some sense, and thereby cease to be God?). Some of these issues I will attempt to tackle in the upcoming chapters of this book, and some in the next volume in this series. Much about Kenoticism stands or falls on the outcome of this debate. Suffice it to say here that

---

[113] David Brown, *Divine Humanity* (Waco, TX: Baylor University Press, 2011), p. 207.
[114] Ibid.

The Incarnation

Anglican Kenoticists, among others, have asked penetrating questions about the intelligibility and incarnational significance of classical TNC that still need to be faced, even if they have challenges of their own to overcome.

Nor is this debate about the suffering of God confined to discussion of kenotic theories of the Incarnation. It is surely one of the most hotly debated topics in theology over the past century. In his essay "Does God Suffer?" (and his book in 2000 of the same title), Roman Catholic theologian Thomas Weinandy, OFM Cap, spoke for many in his ecclesial tradition when he wrote that "the great Judeo Christian mystery which finds its ultimate expression in the Incarnation" is the mystery that "He who is completely other than the created order can be present to and active within the created order without losing His *complete otherness* in doing so."[115] But what can it mean to say that the One who has assumed and definitively expressed himself through all the limitations and conditions of a real human life is "*completely* other?" The Incarnation is only possible, intelligible, and of saving significance because it manifests an analogy of being between the divine nature, and human nature in its perfected state (an analogy already implied in Gen 1:26-28, where we are told that God made man "in his own image," echoed as well, perhaps, in Heb 2:5-18). That is surely why God's incarnation as a human being is intelligible in a way that God becoming incarnate as a stone or a vegetable is not. When Jesus said to his disciples "He who has seen me has seen the Father" (Jn 14:9), surely he meant more than just that the disciples had now seen the Father's "complete otherness"! It is the incarnational analogy — the fact that the infinite love of a personal God can be revealed definitively and analogically through the human nature of Jesus Christ — that places the Incarnation at the heart of the "Good News." Human nature is shown to have the capacity to be a vehicle and revelation of the divine.

---

[115] Thomas Weinandy, OFM Cap, "Does God Suffer?" in *First Things*, November, 2001, p. 7 (emphasis mine).

It follows that if one insists that the divine nature really is unalterably impassible, then there must be some analogy drawn from human life as *imago Dei* that can help us at least *begin* to understand what it might mean to say that the Son of God, in his divine nature, remaining immune to all suffering, entered into our human condition and shared in our suffering in some intelligible and significant way. It is the failure to illuminate this mystery any further than by appeals to the incomprehensible "otherness" of God, or to contentious philosophical gymnastics,[116] that has kept this debate simmering.

In an attempt to avoid some of the difficulties inherent in classical TNC, Catholic philosopher Brian Leftow and Reformed philosopher Oliver Crisp have developed **a "compositional" theory of the Incarnation. Jesus Christ is said to be a whole composed of three parts: the person of the divine Son, a human soul, and a human body**. Crisp defines his position this way:

> According to compositional Christologists, in the incarnation the Second Person of the Trinity assumes a human nature, understood to be a concrete particular. The concrete human nature and divine nature of God the Son together compose Christ. That is, God Incarnate is a whole composed of the proper parts of God the Son and (the parts of) his human

---

[116] Significantly, at the end of her exceptionally complex discussion of Duns Scotus, Adams admitted and explained in detail why the author of a recent, major scholarly work on the Incarnation in medieval thought, Richard Cross, would disagree with her assessment of the coherence and adequacy of Duns Scotus' understanding of the Incarnation. See Adams, *Christ and Horrors*, p. 127, and Richard Cross, *The Metaphysics of the Incarnation* (Oxford: Oxford University Press, 2002). Can the mystery of the Incarnation really depend for its intelligibility upon debate over such hair-splitting philosophical distinctions among a tiny elite of philosophical theologians? It seems more likely that the principle known as "Occam's razor," is being violated here: Adams may have opted for an unnecessarily abstruse understanding of the Incarnation, when simpler and more intelligible explanations are close at hand. In fact, in her clear exposition of Richard Swinburne's "Two-Minds" theory of the Incarnation, she came very close to endorsing one (see *Christ and Horrors*, p. 114-123)!

nature. According to compositional Christologists, this human nature comprises a human body and a human soul. ... We might say that the human nature of Christ is the instrument of God the Son, in which he is "embedded" post-incarnation. ... [B]rian Leftow ... speaks of Christ's human nature as being like a diver's dry suit. The suit is intimately connected with the body of the diver, enabling it's wearer to maneuver and act in an alien environment without getting wet.[117]

Philosopher C. Stephen Layman has pointed out several problems inherent in the compositional model:

Christian theology affirms that the eternal Son became a human being. But did that happen, given the compositional account? The Son became part of a whole that included Christ's body and Christ's mind. Does this make the Son a human being? It is not clear that it does.[118] ...

Layman also contends that if, on this model of the Incarnation, the person of the divine Son unites himself with, and becomes the personal subject of a human nature (that is, a body-soul composite) understood as a concrete-particular, then we have evidently lapsed into Nestorianism: for a concrete, human, body-soul composite is the very definition of a fully human person. In other words, on this model, the divine person of the Son has united himself with a human person:

[O]n a compositional account, an ordinary human being is a composite of a human body and a human mind (or soul). And

---

[117] Oliver Crisp, *The Word Enfleshed : Exploring the Person and Work of Christ* (Grand Rapids: Baker Academic, 2016), p. 97 and 99-100. But this seems a woefully inadequate analogy for the Incarnation: for the rest of humanity is not privileged to be able to move and maneuver through the "alien environment" of this fallen world with a similar "dry suit" that preserves us from getting "wet" with the sufferings and sorrows of this mortal life. For further discussion of this point see Part Two, Chapter One, below.
[118] Layman, *Philosophical Approaches to Atonement, Incarnation, and Trinity*, p. 88.

an ordinary human being is also a person, that is, a conscious entity that can know, have purposes, and act. But ... the eternal Son is also a person in this sense. So ... the compositional account seems to imply that two persons are involved in the incarnation. And that is Nestorianism.[119]

According to Classical Christian orthodoxy, on the other hand, the divine person of the Son was (and is) the uncreated act of Being in which the human body and soul of Jesus subsist (apart

---

[119] Ibid. Crisp has attempted to respond to the charge of Nestorianism. He writes:

> One could claim that the logic of the three-part compositional model is that there are not two persons in Christ, because his human nature is subsumed into a larger whole. Or, his human nature fails to be a person distinct from God the Son in virtue of its being part of a larger composite that includes God the Son. Another way to block the nature-person inference is to argue that no proper part of a person constitutes a person (*The Word Enfleshed*, p. 110)

But we have to ask in response: what is it exactly that is being "*subsumed* into a larger whole" here, and becoming "*part of* a larger composite," and that is being referred to here as "not a proper *part* of a human person"? On the compositional model, each of these phrases evidently refers to a human body-soul composite as a concrete particular: and what else could that be but a human person? So God the Son united himself with a concrete human person in the Incarnation — which is Nestorianism, pure and simple. Crisp also writes:

> [A]t no time does the human nature of Christ exist apart from God the Son, the divine person who assumes [subsumes?] it at the first moment of its existence. So the human nature is never in a position to form a fundamental substance or supposit distinct from God the Son .... (p. 111)

This is actually the very line of defence that Nestorius used long ago, but it doesn't extricate Compositional Christology from the problem. For if there never was a moment when the human nature of Christ existed on its own as a concrete particular, then the divine Son did not assume or subsume human nature as a concrete particular into a greater whole in the Incarnation. The Compositional Model must be false. But if he did assume human nature as a concrete particular, then the divine person of the Son united himself with a human person in the Incarnation — which again is the Nestorian heresy.

from which that human body and soul composite has no existence; in other words, Jesus' very existence is an extension of God the Son's own existence). And through that human nature divine Sonship is expressed in human terms. The person of the Son is therefore not a "part" of Jesus, but the ultimate subject of the entire earthly reality of Jesus Christ — all his human attributes, acts and experiences — whereas fully human persons commonly are *created* subsistences (i.e., created individual instances of human nature) composed of a human soul united to a human body. In other words, the Incarnation is not God and a man joined together, but God dwelling among us *as* a man.[120]

---

[120] The Byzantine Emperor Justinian insisted on this in his treatise *Confessio rectae fidei* (PG 86a. 997b and 1011b) issued just prior to the Fifth Ecumenical Council (Constantinople II):

> Hypostatic union means that God the Word, that is one hypostasis from the three hypostases of the divinity, was not united to a previously existent man, but in the womb of the Holy Virgin fashioned for himself from her in his own hypostasis flesh ensouled by a rational and intelligent soul, which is human nature. … Neither is the human nature of Christ ever spoken of on its own, nor did it possess its own hypostasis or person, but it received the beginning of its existence in the hypostasis of the Word.

Saint Thomas Aquinas endorsed a similar, "subsistence theory" of the Incarnation. According to Thomas Weinandy, this theory designates "a twofold oneness in Christ. … [C]hrist is one ontological reality/supposit, and the one ontological reality/supposit that Christ is is *the one person/hypostasis of the Son existing as man*" ("Aquinas: God *Is* Man and the Marvel of the Incarnation" in Thomas Weinandy, *Jesus: Essays in Christology*. Ave Maria, FL: Sapientia Press, 2014, p. 129; italics mine). In fact, Aquinas seems directly to distance his subsistence theory of the Incarnation from the kind of Two-Nature theories proposed by Adams and Leftow when he writes in *De Unione Verbi Incarnati*, 2 : "[T]he human nature in Christ does not subsist separately through itself but exists in another, i.e. in the hypostasis of the Word (indeed not as an accident in a subject, nor properly as a part in a whole, but through an ineffable assumption) …" (Ibid., p. 136).

Anglican theologian David Brown offered his own, modified version of TNC in his book *The Divine Trinity*. **There could be a "flow" of experience between the two natures of Christ, Brown suggested, analogous to the flow between the conscious and subconscious of a single human mind. This unifying flow would enable us to speak of Christ as one person in two natures.**[121] While God the Son receives experiential input from his intimate union with a particular human nature, he nevertheless "retains such a total perspective on pain and its ultimate meaning and purpose that it legitimises the use of the term 'impassible.'"[122] Presumably, God in his divine nature sees clearly the probable outcome of his incarnate pains and struggles, the place they hold within his overall saving purposes for humanity, and is constantly aware of his own ability to absorb suffering without being destroyed or overwhelmed by it. The Son of God in his divine nature thereby views the sufferings of his human body and the troubles of his human mind from an omniscient perspective on events, and in that sense remains relatively impassible.[123] Moreover, God in Christ freely chose to subject himself to these experiences of human suffering; he was not subjected to them involuntarily.[124]

Brown's version of TNC, however, has several liabilities of its own.

First, much as with Leftow's compositional theory, we have to ask: is this really an "incarnational" Christology? The answer to this question depends in part upon the status accorded to the Fifth Ecumenical Council (Constantinople II) in 553 AD. The Anglican heritage generally has given preference only to the first four councils. The Fifth Ecumenical Council, however, made it crystal clear that the one person of the Incarnate simply *is* the uncreated person of the divine Son, and not a joining together, fusion or collaboration of two persons, a created human person and an uncreated divine person (just as Chalcedon had

---

[121] Brown, *The Divine Trinity*, p. 261-263 and 265. W.R. Matthews had suggested a similar view in Matthews, *The Problem of Christ in the 20th Century*, p. 80.
[122] Ibid., p. 253.
[123] Ibid., p. 264-265.
[124] Brown, *Divine Humanity*, p. 203.

said that the Incarnation does not involve a confusion of the two natures). ***Thus, according to mainstream Christian orthodoxy, the one subject or person of Christ pre-existed as the second person of the Trinity, and then assumed all the limitations and defining attributes of human nature, so that it can be truly said that there is one ultimate subject of all the human attributes, acts, and experiences of Christ, the eternal and pre-existent Son of God, born of Mary, who suffered and died on the Cross.*** This position was held to be rooted in Scripture (commonly cited, for example, was I Corinthian 2:8: "None of the rulers of this age understood this; for if they had, they would not have crucified the Lord of glory."). It was preserved in the east through the writings of St. John of Damascus, and in the west by St. Thomas Aquinas.[125] More recently, it was reaffirmed by the *Catechism of the Catholic Church*, directly quoting the Fifth Council twice in entry 468:

> After the Council of Chalcedon, some made of Christ's human nature a kind of personal subject. Against them, the fifth ecumenical council at Constantinople in 553 confessed that "there is but one *hypostasis* [or person], which is our Lord Jesus Christ, one of the Trinity." Thus, everything in Christ's human nature is to be attributed to his divine person as its proper subject, not only his miracles but also his sufferings and even his death: "He who was crucified in the flesh, our Lord Jesus Christ, is true God, Lord of glory, and *one of the Holy Trinity*."

One could argue that the principal achievement of Constantinople II was simply to ensure that the Chalcedonian definition would be read in the light of the teachings of Ephesus, the Third Ecumenical Council, that defined that Mary, the Mother of Jesus, also rightly could be called the "Theotokos" (literally, the God-bearer). In other words, already at Ephesus (under the guidance of St. Cyril of Alexandria, and officially endorsing his incarnational theology in the form of his *Twelve*

---

[125] On St. John Damascene see Gerald Bray, *Creeds, Councils, and Christ* (Leicester: InterVarsity Press, 1984), p. 168-169; on St. Thomas Aquinas see Riches, *Ecce Homo*, p. 155-176.

Anathemas), it was implicit that there was no independent, created person with whom the divine Son was joined or fused in some way to become a *tertium quid*, a composite divine-human person, much less a cooperative alliance of two persons. For Ephesus, the one whom Mary bore in her womb is clearly a single, uncreated, divine person: the second person of the Trinity in human form. Ephesus was the precursor of Constantinople II in this regard.[126] Thus, even in a traditional Anglican framework that privileges only the main teachings of the first four councils, incarnational models such as Brown's TNC may not be a live option.

Second, Richard Swinburne questioned Brown's understanding of "personal identity" at work in this version of TNC. According to Swinburne, Brown seems to understand personal identity here as constituted by a causally connected stream of memories and character traits, so that personal identity over time is a matter of "more or less." This does not seem to do justice to the metaphysical ultimacy of what it means to be an individual "person," Swinburne insisted.[127]

Third, Brown states that God the Son shared in Christ's human condition of suffering and struggle to some extent, but only as seen from the vantage point of a divine, omniscient perspective on events. **Even through his unifying "flow" of experience with Jesus of Nazareth, therefore, God has not really experienced suffering as we experience it, in the form of bodily and emotional helplessness, and a limited understanding of its meaning and purpose. Thus, this model of the Incarnation does not establish that the divine Son has fully identified with human sufferings**

---

[126] See for example, the anathemas of St. Cyril endorsed by the Council of Ephesus, including anathema 7: "If anyone says that as man Jesus was activated by the Word of God and was clothed with the glory of the Only-begotten, as a being separate from him, let him be anathema."

[127] See my footnote number one, above, and Richard Swinburne, in *Oriel Review*, 1986, p. 41f, as discussed in Brian Hebblethwaite, *Philosophical Theology and Christian Doctrine* (Oxford: Blackwell, 2005), p. 64.

and the human condition. Brown himself was aware of this shortcoming.[128]

Finally, Brown's position can be criticised with the perceptive comment, offered in another context, by Anglican theologian Maurice Wiles: "If it is logically conceivable for God to be actually identified with a human person, without in any way taking away from the full and genuine humanity of that person, it follows that God does not, in fact, draw near to us individual men and women, or share our suffering as directly as apparently he could."[129] **In other words, Brown's TNC leaves us wondering: if God the Son drew so near to Jesus of Nazareth that, from the moment of his conception onward, he shared in some way in the human experiences of Jesus (through a unifying "flow" of experience between them), and sanctified his human will, then why does God not draw this near to *every* person he created? The answer of the Classical Christian tradition, of course, is that in the Incarnation God the Son did**

---

[128] Brown, *The Divine Trinity*, p. 271. Sergius Bulgakov seemed to run into a similar difficulty in his understanding of the limited participation of Christ's divine nature in the sufferings of his human nature:

> [T]he human nature puts its imprint on the life of the divine nature, in a manner unfathomable for us. To be sure, it is not possible to say that the divine nature in Christ could suffer together with the flesh, as flesh. But the soul too, after all, even the human soul, while suffering with the flesh, suffers not in a fleshly manner but in spiritual manner. ... Even though the flesh is, of course, foreign to it, the Divinity of the Lord Jesus Christ spiritually co-suffers in relation to the fleshly passion of the hypostatic Word, for the nature cannot fail to suffer if its hypostasis suffers. (*The Lamb of God,* p. 259)

The trouble with this solution is that both Brown and Bulgakov imply that there are aspects of human suffering in which the divine nature cannot fully share. It would seem to follow that God cannot become fully incarnate: he cannot truly share our lot.
[129] Maurice Wiles, "A Survey of Issues in the Myth Debate" in Michael Goulder, ed., *Incarnation and Myth* (London: SCM, 1979), p. 7-8.

not draw near to one of us; rather, he came among us *as* one of us, in order to draw nearer to us all.

Chapter Two

Understanding The Kenotic Theory of the Incarnation

Before we explore the strong implications of the Anglican heritage of Kenoticism for the wider pattern of Christian belief, we need to be sure that we can locate this stream of kenotic theory, and articulate it in a coherent fashion. For if the theory does not make any logical,[130] philosophical, or theological sense, it is no use developing it further. Nonsense, after all, is nonsense.

By the concept of "kenosis" I shall mean *self-giving love for others expressed through an act (or acts) of self-limitation, even, if need be, to the point of total self-sacrifice.*[131] This definition of

---

[130] Throughout this book, I assume that basic standards of logic (such as the law of non-contradiction) properly apply to talk about God — his nature, character, purposes, and actions in the world — just as they do in any other field of inquiry. Contra the Protestant Neo-Orthodox and Emerging Church movements, logic should not be a dirty word to theologians, and is not an attempt to squeeze God into human categories of thought. Rather, logic is essential to meaningful verbal communication and human discourse; it was built into the structure of the universe itself by God the Creator so that his creation would be intelligible (at least to some extent) to human minds; and it reflects the eternal nature of God, who is always himself and not otherwise (cf. Ex 3:14). Use of logic also does not preclude the recognition of paradoxical mysteries in heaven and earth, for a paradox is not actually a logically self-contradictory statement: it is a statement that seems self-contradictory at first, but when examined more closely can be shown not to be so.

[131] Although I have not followed David Law's more detailed classification of the various types of kenotic theory, I have found most useful his approach that *kenosis* should be understood as "limitation," a general, umbrella concept which is worked out in different ways by different incarnational theorists:

> In my view, the most helpful way of understanding kenosis is to interpret it as meaning 'limitation'. This allows us to include theologians in our discussion who do not hold that Christ 'abandoned' his divine attributes, but hold that Christ's divine nature was placed under real restrictions which limited his exercise of his divine attributes during his earthly existence. Kenosis theories can then be organized according to the degree of limitation they ascribe to Christ. This allows us to see 'emptying', 'abandonment', 'self-divesting', 'renunciation', 'concealment',

"kenosis" fits at least with the general intention behind St. Paul's use of the word in Philippians 2:5-8, where he described the love of Christ for us in taking upon himself human limitations and sufferings:

> Have this mind among yourselves, which is yours in Christ Jesus, who, though he was in the form of God did not count equality with God a thing to be grasped [NB: the Jerusalem Bible here has: "did not cling to equality with God," which may be a more accurate translation], but emptied himself [*kenosis*], taking the form of a servant, being born in the likeness of men; and being found in human form he humbled himself, and became obedient unto death, even death on a cross. (RSVCE)[132]

'reduction', and 'humiliation' as different ways in which the limitation imposed on the Logos by the assumption of human nature may have come about. Interpreting kenosis as limitation, rather than the more narrow definition of Christ's 'emptying' himself of something, also has the advantage that it accommodates the other biblical passages which have been drawn into the discussion of kenosis, notably those touching on Christ's development, human experiences and emotions, and lack of knowledge. (David Law, *Kierkegaard's Kenotic Christology*. Oxford: Oxford University Press 2013, p. 23)

[132] That this passage can be interpreted as an expression of St. Paul's belief in the Incarnation has been ably defended in recent years by Larry Hurtado in *Lord Jesus Christ: Devotion to Jesus in Earliest Christianity* (Grand Rapids: Eerdmans, 2003), p. 118-126, and Gordon Fee, "The New Testament and Kenosis Christology" in Evans, ed., *Exploring Kenotic* Christology, p. 30-35. See especially their response to the work of New Testament scholar J.D.G. Dunn, the principal proponent of a non-incarnational reading of this passage. Stephen T. Davis argues that the phrase "emptied himself" fits well with a kenotic Christology, without strictly requiring that interpretation:

> He 'emptied himself, taking the form of a servant,' the text says. Some who oppose the kenotic interpretation insist that since the text does not precisely say what he emptied himself of (which is true), it follows that he did not empty himself *of* anything. But that is not a very impressive argument. Both in English and in Greek, some verbs, when used, immediately cry out for a direct or indirect object. If I say, 'I repeat,' you can sensibly wonder what I am about to repeat. If I say 'I

This passage finds an echo in another place in St. Paul's writings, when he says to the Corinthians: "For you know the grace of our Lord Jesus Christ, that though he was rich, yet for your sake he became poor, so that by his poverty you might become rich" (II Cor 8:9). The Kenotic Theory, however, does not strictly depend upon the exegesis of Philippians 2 or II Corinthians 8; it is a broadly based incarnational model. **According to Anglican theologian O.C. Quick,** *the central principle of the Kenotic Theory of the Incarnation is that "the eternal Son or Word, in his incarnation by a voluntary act limited himself to a historical human consciousness and human faculties of knowledge and action."*[133] **Through this act of self-limitation, the divine Son may be said to have experienced all the joys and sorrows, struggle and pain of a real human life as Jesus of Nazareth.**

As we shall see, some Kenotic theorists believe that the act of self-limitation by the divine Son in the Incarnation involved *an actual reduction, renunciation, or even "abandonment" of divine attributes in order to conform to all the conditions and limitations of human life.* Others hold that the act of self-limitation involved was really just *a self-restraint by the divine Son of the exercise of some of his divine prerogatives within a certain sphere — those divine prerogatives incompatible with sharing our lot and living an authentically human life.* Either way, **the Kenotic Theory necessarily involves a modification of traditional notions of absolute divine changelessness (or "immutability"),** for *in all kenotic theories the divine Son in some way reduces the scope or operation of his*

---

listen,' you can sensibly wonder what I am listening to …. Now any vessel that is 'emptied,' whether that vessel be a bottle, a room, a human life, or even a divine life, must be emptied 'of' something. So what the hymn [in Phil 2:5-11] implies or presupposes that Christ Jesus emptied himself 'of' is still an open question. (Davis, "Is Kenosis Orthodox?" in Evans, ed., *Exploring Kenotic Christology*, p. 131-132).

The trouble is that the phrase "he emptied himself" also could be a metaphor that means simply "he gave of himself without reserve, holding nothing back;" the issue can only finally be settled by the context of the passage as a whole, and not by the phrase taken in isolation.

[133] Quick, *Doctrines of the Creed*, p. 132.

divine attributes in order to dwell among us in human form. Moreover, the traditional notion of absolute divine immunity to suffering ("impassibility") must also be revised, for according to the Kenotic Theory, the incarnate life truly affects the divine nature — the divine mind or consciousness, so to speak. As a result of his sojourn on earth, it is said, the divine Son has added to his store of experience an experience of all the conditions and limitations of an authentically human life.[134]

Kenotic theologians tend to express their wonder at the mystery of the Incarnation by celebrating the paradox of divine self-limitation that it entails. P.T. Forsyth, for example, once wrote: "We face in Christ a Godhead self-reduced but real, whose infinite power took effect in self-humiliation, whose strength was made perfect in weakness, who consented not to know with an ignorance divinely wise, and who emptied himself in virtue of his divine fullness."[135]

Kenotic theorists also claim to be faithful to the gospel message of the Incarnation proclaimed in Phil 2:5-8, II Cor 8:9, and throughout the New Testament. For example, in their volume *Exploring Kenotic Christology* (2006) a collection of (mostly non-Anglican) Protestant

---

[134] Throughout most of this book I shall assume (for the sake of argument) that God does not dwell in a realm of timeless eternity, with all time present before his gaze at once. Anglican theology over the past century has been nearly unanimous in rejecting the notion of God's timeless eternity, and so, to abide by an Anglican frame of reference in this volume, and to evaluate Kenoticism first from within the general context of Anglo-American Analytic Theism (as well as to keep the present discussion within manageable proportions!), I will postpone for now consideration of this important issue. In the final, Conclusion section of this book, however, and in volume two of this series, we shall have to widen our discussion when we explore whether the Anglican stream of Kenoticism can enrich the Catholic Faith, given Catholicism's very different philosophical and magisterial frame of reference. Moreover, by speaking of the divine memory or store of experience, I do not mean to imply that God has a retrieval system, for all of his memories of the past surely must be readily available to the divine consciousness.

[135] P.T. Forsyth, *The Person and Place of Jesus Christ* (Grand Rapids: Eerdmans, third edition 1909), p. 294.

scholars from the United States vaunted the biblical roots of their theory:

> [A]n orthodox biblical Christology almost certainly must embrace some form of a 'kenotic' understanding of the Incarnation, that the One who was truly God, also in his incarnation lived a truly human life, a life in which he *grew* both in stature and in wisdom and in understanding (Luke 2:52), learned obedience through what he suffered (Heb 5:8), and who as Son of the Father did not know the day or hour (Mark 13:32). ...[136]

> [T]he assurance in Hebrews that Jesus was tempted suggests another aspect of his self-emptying: 'For we do not have a high priest who is unable to sympathize with us in our weaknesses, but we have one who has been tempted in every way just as we are — yet he did not sin' (Heb. 4:15). Even Jesus' prayer to the Father that he be glorified with the glory he had in the presence of the Father before the world existed (John 17:5) suggests that the Incarnation involved the giving up of some aspect of divine glory. ...[137]

> Kenoticists are in no way uncomfortable with the supernatural dimension that Jesus exhibits ... but they explain this dimension by pointing to another fundamental characteristic of the biblical portrait: Jesus lived his life in complete dependence upon, and in complete union with the Father and the Spirit. **When Jesus performs a miracle, on a kenotic view of the Incarnation, he does not suddenly draw upon a hidden 'power-pack' of divine properties that he has been holding in reserve all along, to be pulled out on special occasions. Rather, he draws upon the power of the Father through a life lived in the Spirit. We believe that it is crucially important to notice, in the context of a discussion of kenosis, an obvious but overlooked fact,**

---

[136] Fee, "The New Testament and Kenosis Christology," p. 43.
[137] Ronald J. Feenstra, "A Kenotic Christology of the Divine Attributes" in Evans, ed., *Exploring Kenotic Christology*, p. 151.

namely, that Jesus lived his life in complete and
continuous dependence on the Holy Spirit, and that he
lived a life of perfect submission to the Father.[138]

Not all Kenoticists would fully agree with this last statement about the
miracles of Christ. Some might wish to say that in the Son of God's
incarnate life, while his power to perform miracles would not violate
the boundaries of his human nature as Jesus of Nazareth — and
therefore all must be done by the power of the Holy Spirit (Mt 12:28;
Lk 4:18; Acts 10:38) — nevertheless, the *manner* in which those
miraculous acts were accomplished must reflect in some way the
uniqueness of his person. For unlike any other saint or holy figure,
Jesus was a *divine* person, the divine Son in human flesh. Thus, as
incarnate he did indeed perform miracles only by the power of the
Spirit, but usually not by prayer and supplication; rather, he did them,
according to his Father's will, by touch or word of command. This is
what made the disciples exclaim "Who then is this, that even the wind
and the sea *obey* him?" (MK 4:41). Led by the Holy Spirit, he spoke
with divine authority, and with the power of the same Spirit healed the
sick, raised the dead, and calmed the waves of the sea.

**In fact, the divine Son Incarnate, dwelling among us under all
the conditions and limitations of human life, was necessarily so
completely open and surrendered to the Holy Spirit that even his
flesh was healing and life-giving (Mk 5:27-29), and his human
mind contained all truth that pertained in any way to his mission
(Mt 11: 27, Jn 1:14, Col 2:3). In short, Kenotic theologians usually
claim that, given the human limitations that the Son of God
assumed in the Incarnation, Jesus of Nazareth accessed divine,
supernatural, prophetic knowledge, and the divine,
determinative power to perform miracles — all that he needed
for the accomplishment of his mission — only through the Holy**

---

[138] Stephen T. Davis and C. Stephen Evans, "Conclusion: The Promise of Kenosis"
in Evans, ed., *Exploring Kenotic Christology*, p. 319-320. Russian Orthodox
theologian Sergius Bulgakov was another Kenoticist who strongly emphasized
the dependence of the human nature of the divine Son upon the Holy Spirit in
every aspect of Christ's mission; see *The Lamb of God*, p. 307-308.

Spirit. **We will return to these issues for more in-depth discussion later in this book.**

In order to grasp more clearly the Kenotic perspective on the Incarnation, let us look at the writings of two very different theologians, representing two distinct ecclesial traditions.

Kenotic Themes in the Writings of Austin Farrer

Among Anglican Kenoticists of the twentieth century, few expressed the mystery of the Incarnation with greater evocative power than Austin Farrer (1904-1968), for many years the Warden of Keble College, Oxford. Farrer never wrote a book or treatise on the subject, but scattered throughout his works of philosophical theology, as well as in his homilies, one finds many moving and memorable expressions of this doctrine.

To begin with, he defined the Incarnation as "infinite God, living the existence of one of his creatures, through self-limitation to a particular created destiny."[139] Farrer explained:

> **This was how God's love was shown as utterly divine — in accepting every circumstance of our manhood. He spared himself nothing. He was not a copy book man-in-general, he was a Galilean carpenter, a free-lance rabbi; and he wove up his life, as each of us must, out of materials that were to hand.**[140]

> [T]he ancient and medieval conception of Christ's person was not poisoned by philosophy: it was starved by a lack of historical sense. Those ages saw him too much in the colourless abstraction of man-in-general, or in the borrowed clothes of a contemporary with themselves. We see him as a Galilean villager of the first century. The tools of his thinking came from the local stock; only he made a divinely perfect use of them. The Jewish ideas he inherited, broken and reshaped

---

[139] Austin Farrer, *Interpretation and Belief*, p. 167.
[140] Austin Farrer, *A Celebration of Faith*, p. 89.

in the course of his life, served him for mental coinage, in the traffic of his unique sonship to his Father, and his assertion of God's kingdom over mankind. He had what he needed, to *be* the Son of God; as for defining the divine sonship, that was a task for other hands, using other tools; the Apostles began a theology of his person, and the Fathers continued it.[141]

Doubtless there are metaphysical ambiguities here. For example, how can God the Son limit himself to live under all the conditions of "a particular created destiny" without ceasing to be divine? Does he give up for a time his eternal cooperation with the Father and the Spirit in the providential care of the universe in order to limit himself to "accept every circumstance of manhood?" And how did Jesus of Nazareth — who allegedly had to "weave up" the contents of his mental and moral life solely from "the materials that were at hand" in Galilee in the first century — "make divinely perfect use of them" without violating the boundaries of an authentically human existence? Farrer does not attempt to answer these difficult questions.

One important contribution that Farrer made to British and Anglican reflections on the Incarnation, however, was to remind his readers that when we are speaking of this mystery, it is not entirely accurate to describe Jesus Christ as "God Incarnate." To be more precise, He is the *divine Son* Incarnate:

> It is not just Godhead that becomes incarnate, it is Godhead in the special form or person of Sonship. Divine Son becomes incarnate: and since Divine Son draws his whole person and being from the divine fatherhood anyhow quite apart from his incarnation, when he becomes incarnate he does not cease to do so. ...[142]

> He is the Son of God, and his sonship is simple and unalloyed derivation ... The Son of God is the Word of the Father, and

[141] Austin Farrer, *Saving Belief* (London: Hodder and Stoughton, 1964), p. 80.
[142] Farrer, *Interpretation and Belief,* p. 131.

more alive than any utterance because he comes new every moment from out of the heart of God. ...[143]

We cannot understand Jesus simply as the God-who-was-man. We have left out an essential factor, the sonship. Jesus is not simply God manifest as man, he is the divine Son coming into manhood. What was expressed in human terms here below was not bare deity; it was divine sonship. God cannot live an identically godlike life in eternity and in a human story. But the divine Son can make an identical response to his Father, whether in the love of the blessed Trinity, or in the fulfilment of an earthly ministry. All the conditions of action are different on the two levels; the filial response is one. Above, the response is cooperation in sovereignty and an interchange of eternal joys. Then the Son gives back to the Father all that the Father is. Below, in the incarnate life, the appropriate response is obedience to inspiration, a waiting for direction, an acceptance of suffering, a rectitude of choice, a resistance to temptation, a willingness to die. For such things are the stuff of our existence and it was in this very stuff that Christ worked out the theme of heavenly sonship, proving himself on earth the very thing he was in heaven; that is, a perfect act of filial love.[144]

Thus, Farrer reminds us that the divine Sonship on display throughout the human life of Jesus of Nazareth reflects the eternal relationship of derivation and love between the Son and the Father. The doctrines of the Incarnation and the Trinity, therefore, are inextricably linked — and this is certainly true of kenotic approaches to the mystery of the Incarnation, as we shall see later in this book.

The Kenotic Christology of Hugh Ross Mackintosh

---

[143] Austin Farrer, *Lord I Believe. Suggestions for Turning the Creed into Prayer* (London: The Faith Press, 1955), p. 39.
[144] Ibid., p. 101-102.

Hailing from the Scottish "Free Church" tradition, Hugh Ross Mackintosh (1870-1936) at New College in Edinburgh wrote one of the classics of the twentieth century Kenotic movement: a massive tome entitled *The Doctrine of the Person of Jesus Christ* (second edition, 1913). Mackintosh made a valiant attempt in this book to work out the metaphysical difficulties with the Kenotic Theory of the Incarnation, drawing upon most of the work in this area that had preceded him. Moreover, his book was so well received (at least in Scotland) that it remained a standard text on the subject for many years.

Although the work of Mackintosh antedated that of Farrer by several decades, excerpts from his great book can fill out for us the basics that we need to know about the general Kenotic perspective, including areas that Farrer did not explore. We shall quote the testimony of Mackintosh at length here, not to plunge the reader at this point into his metaphysical speculations (more will be said on those later), but to let Mackintosh "paint the picture" for us, in broad brushstrokes, of a general kenotic approach to this mystery. Arguably, in that respect no one has ever done it better:

> The Incarnation of the divine Son involved a real self-limitation of His Divine mode of existence. ... Somehow — to describe the method exactly may of course be beyond us — somehow God in Christ has brought His greatness down to the narrow measures of our life, becoming poor for our sake.[145]

> The Kenotic theologians, one and all, proceed upon orthodox assumptions as to the Trinity and the two natures present in the one person of our Lord. Their object is to show how the Second Person of the Trinity could so enter human life as that there resulted the genuinely human experience which is described by the evangelists. To this problem they are unanimous in replying — of course with individual variations — that the eternal Logos by a wonderful suspension or

---

[145] H.R. Mackintosh, *The Doctrine of the Person of Jesus Christ* (Edinburgh: T. and T. Clark, second edition, 1913), p. 265 and 466.

restriction of His Divine activities reduced Himself within the limits and conditions of manhood.[146]

He did not remain all that He was in the pre-existent glory, but stooped down, by a real surrender and self-impoverishment, and took a lower place. In the light of that renunciation we gain a new glimpse of the lengths to which Divine love will go for man's redemption. This I believe to be the profoundest motive operating in the Kenotic theories — this sense of a sacrifice on the part of the pre-existent one; and it is a conception notoriously absent from the Christological arguments of not a few that have criticised these theories with great severity.[147]

Hearts have thrilled to this message that Christ came from such a height to such a depth! He took our human frailty to be His own. So dear were human souls to God, that he travelled far and stooped low that He might thus touch and raise the needy. Now this is an unheard of truth, casting an amazing light on God, and revolutionising the world's faint notions of what it means for Him to be Father; but traditional Christology, on the whole, has found it too much to believe. Its persistent obscuration of Jesus' real manhood proves that after all it shrank from the thought of a true "kinsman Redeemer" — one of ourselves in flesh and spirit. Christ's point of departure was Godhead, no doubt, yet in His descent He stopped half-way. The quasi-manhood He wore is so filled with Divine powers as to cease to belong to the human order.[148]

Notice in these passages a three-fold insistence. First, the Incarnation means that the divine Son must have limited himself, restricting or restraining his infinite divine attributes in some way in order to dwell among us within the confines of an

---

[146] Ibid., p. 266. As we shall see, Mackintosh's statement here that the Kenotic theorists "one and all" proceed on orthodox assumptions with regard to the Trinity and the Incarnation is hardly accurate with regard to the "pure" Kenoticism of theorists like Gess and Godet.

[147] Ibid., p 267-268

[148] Ibid., p. 467.

authentically finite human life; second, this act of self-diminution is the supreme expression of his sacrificial love for us; and third, the divine Son must have come "all the way down" into the depths of the human condition, with all of its real limitations and sufferings. Mackintosh's book abounds in wonderfully evocative and lyrical expressions of this threefold mystery:

> We are faced by a Divine self-reduction which entailed obedience, temptation and death. So that religion has a vast stake in the *kenosis* as a fact, whatever the difficulties as to its method may be. No human life of God is possible without a prior self-adjustment of deity. The Son must empty Himself in order that from within mankind He may declare the Father's name, offer the great sacrifice, triumph over death; and the reality with which, to reach this end, He laid aside the form and privilege of deity is the measure of that love which has throbbed in the Divine Heart from all eternity.[149]

> It would seem that the self-imposition of limits by Divine love must be conceived of as a great supra-temporal act by which, in the almightiness of grace, the Son chose to pass into human life. An infinitely pregnant act, for in truth it involved all the conflict, renunciation, and achievement of the life to which it was the prelude. But it is not possible to conceive this act as having been continuously repeated throughout the earthly life. We cannot think of the Incarnate One as confining Himself from moment to moment, by explicit volition, within the frontiers of manhood. That would simply lead back to the old untenable conception of a *krypsis* by which the Divine Self in Christ veils His loftier attributes, now less now more, and is actuated in each case by didactic motives. To return thus to a theoretic duality of mental life in our Lord against which all modern Christology has been a protest, is surely to sin against light.[150] The acceptance of human relationships — to nature,

---

[149] Ibid., p. 470
[150] Mackintosh seems to forget for a moment that some Kenotic theorists (e.g. Martensen and Weston) would argue not for a divine-human duality of mental

to man, to God — belongs to the eternal, transcendent sphere, as a definitively settled act, it is not something consciously and continually renewed in time. What *is* continuous with the decisive act of self-reduction is the moral quality of life on earth, the permanent self-consecration of Jesus' will. But the self-limitation, transcendently achieved as a single, final deed, inaugurates a permanent condition or state of life, amid circumstances of change and suffering once for all accepted.[151]

The position defended here is that only so — only by contracting His Divine fullness within earthly limits — could the redeeming God draw nigh to man. Further, the life of Jesus exhibits to us precisely that rendering of true deity in human terms, that absolute perfectness of life "in short measures," which answers to the Kenotic principle as rightly understood. We read the Gospels, and we find that in Jesus there was faith and hope and love in perfect fullness; that he lived in unbroken intimacy with his Father; that He manifested God to men as absolute holiness, love, and freedom; that He acted a Divine part in the experience of the sinful, forgiving their iniquities and imparting a new and blessed life. In Him there is realised on earth the human life of God, and it is a life whose chiefest glory consists in a voluntary descent from depth to depth of our experience. It is the personal presence of God in One who is neither omniscient nor ubiquitous nor almighty — as God absolute must be — but is perfect Love and Holiness and Freedom in terms of perfect humanity.[152]

---

life in the human nature or human soul of Jesus, but for a duality of mental life in the divine nature of the Son as a result of the Incarnation.

[151] Ibid., p. 482. Again, Mackintosh did not speak for all Kenotic theologians here. Some (such as Charles Gore and Frank Weston) would have seen the incarnate state as something continuously willed by the divine Son by an act of the *Logos asarkos*, that is, by the unlimited Divine Word, and not by the human mind and will of Jesus.

[152] Ibid., p. 486. The distinction that Mackintosh draws here between "God absolute" (fully exercising omniscience, omnipotence, and omnipresence), and his incarnate state, having "contracted His Divine fullness within earthly [human] limits" sounds very much like the Christology of nineteenth century German

The Christology of Mackintosh, like that of all Kenoticists, is motivated in part by the desire to remain true to the real human limitations exhibited by Jesus in the synoptic Gospels:

> Jesus bodily and mental life obeys the rules of natural human development. Luke sums up the scanty recollections of His childhood in the statement that "Jesus continued to advance in wisdom and stature, and in favour with God and man" (2:52); and the words enunciate a principle that covers the entire life. It is impossible to conceive a point at which the evangelists would have held that He had nothing more to learn of His Father's will. In the physical sphere He is authentically man. When the temptation was past, He hungered; on the cross He thirsted and longed to drink; He slept from weariness in the boat upon the lake. His career closed in pain and death and burial. And His soul-life is equally normal. There were hours when He rejoiced in spirit; the unbelief of His countrymen moved His astonishment; He marvelled at the centurion's faith; glimpses of His heart broke out in His compassion for the unsheperded multitude or for the widow of Nain, in the brief anger with which He drove the money-changers from the Temple, in the desire for the companionship of the Twelve, in His tears over Jerusalem. Every wholesome emotion touched Him, finding fit outlet in word or act. Most significant of all, His piety is human. The Baptism and Temptation were scenes of prayer; He was found by disciples praying in secret; it was with prayer on His lips that he healed the man deaf and dumb, that He fed the multitude, that in the garden He wrestled through the agony, and at the end gave up His spirit. No shadow of estrangement fell on His communion; yet the unquenched longing with which He resorted to the Father betokens a deep, consuming sense of need. ...

---

theologian Gottfried Thomasius. As we shall see later, Mackintosh offers a revised version of the Thomasian theory.

Nowhere does Jesus's trust in God appear more wonderful than in the presence of the catastrophe which, in outward semblance, was to sweep down His person and His cause to common ruin. If He triumphed in prospect of a death for sin, it was through a confident reliance upon His Father. And from this flowed His *peace*. The untroubled calm of soul we mark in Him ... [F]requently in the course of His public ministry there is a visible and profound contrast between the tumult and uproar around Him and the interior calm of a heart at rest in God. This inward rest He strove to impart to others (Mt 11:28 ...). Finally, He was actuated by an infinite *love*, which may be said to have formed the very substance of His nature. It was primarily love to God, in whom were the wellsprings of His life, but it overflowed in a comprehensive love toward man.[153]

He appears on the page of history as a Jew of the first century, with the Jewish mind and temperament. To interpret his message we need not travel out beyond the Hebrew frontier; nothing is here from the wisdom of Buddha or Plato, nothing even from the fusion of Hellenism and Hebraism in the crucible of Alexandria. He was nurtured in Galilee, where He must have encountered some impressions of the larger world, but little in His teaching recalls Greco-Roman civilization. ...

The realm of scientific knowledge is one in which he became like unto His brethren. Incontestably He exhibits at different times a wholly abnormal penetration, a perception of men's thoughts which far outstrips the insights even of prophets. But we cannot speak of His omniscience except as we desert the sources. "Of that day or that hour," He said plainly, "knoweth no one, not even the angels in heaven, nor yet the Son, but the Father" (Mk 13:32) — a declaration of ignorance which, it is suggestive to note, is not insisted on after the resurrection

---

[153] Ibid., p. 10-12. It is strange that in painting the picture for us here of Christ's fully human life (including his piety, with its uninterrupted communion with God and the "untroubled calm" of his inner peace) Mackintosh neglects to mention the agony of Christ in the Garden of Gethsemane, and the cry of dereliction on the Cross.

(Acts 1:7). Along with this goes the fact that He makes inquiries and manifests surprise; but that in doing so He was acting a part is credible only to the incurable docetic mind. …

Not only is it related that Jesus asked questions to elicit information — regarding the site of Lazarus' tomb, for example, or the number of loaves, or the name of the demented Gadarene — but at one point there is a clear acknowledgement of ignorance: "Of that day or that hour," He said, respecting the Parousia, "knoweth no man, not even the angels in heaven, neither the Son, but the Father." If He could thus be ignorant of a detail connected in some measure with His redemptive work, the conclusion is unavoidable that in secular affairs, His knowledge was but the knowledge of His time. …[154]

To ignore the human conditions of His historic life, therefore, is to miss the contrast of earthly humiliation and ascended majesty. It is also to miss the redeeming sacrifice of God; for these circumstances of self-abnegating limitation form the last and highest expression of the love wherewith the Father bowed down to bless us in the Son.[155]

Mackintosh not only sought to make his theory of the Incarnation harmonize with the real humanity of Christ on display in the synoptic Gospels; he also believed that a kenotic understanding of the Incarnation was the best fit with the teachings of St. Paul and St. John:

Finally, there is the Phil. 2:5-7, a passage "marked by epic fullness and dignity," the amplest and most deliberate of all St. Paul's declarations on the theme. Lightfoot has thus paraphrased vv 6 and 7: "though existing before the worlds in the eternal Godhead, yet He did not cling with avidity to the

---

[154]Ibid., p. 10-13, and 97. Mackintosh seems to posit here a *limited* knowledge in the human soul of Christ concerning things of redemptive significance, at least prior to the resurrection, and a *limited and fallible* knowledge of secular and scientific matters, akin to the viewpoints on these subjects of the people of his ancient culture.

[155] Ibid., p. 14.

prerogatives of His Divine majesty, did not ambitiously display His equality with God; but divested himself of the glories of heaven, and took upon Him the nature of a servant, assuming the likeness of men." Christ, that is, came into our world from a previous state of Divine existence; in that estate He possessed self-conscious independent life, with a will that ruled itself; a will that might have been exerted in other modes, but actually was exerted in this mode of self-abnegation. It is asserted — and on this assertion hinges the thrilling moral appeal of the passage — that before He came as man Christ's life was Divine in quality; not merely *like* God but participant in His essential attributes (*morphe*). The crucial fact is that the apostle, even though refraining from speculation as to the relationship to God of the Eternal Son, does not scruple to describe Him as subsisting in, and then giving up, "a being so in the form of God that to be equal with Him is a thing of nature." He took a life of manhood through the abdication of infinite glory. And the *motif* of the passage — metaphysical only so far as it is ethical — lies in the subduing thought that when it was open to Christ so to employ the powers of His inherent Divine dignity as to insist on being worshipped as God, He chose to reach this supreme position of Lordship acknowledged universally, by the path of lowliness, obedience, and death. Thus His descent reveals the vastness of His love, and justifies His later exaltation.[156]

While Mackintosh finds a kenotic understanding of the Incarnation explicit in St. Paul's Letter to the Philippians, it is perhaps more surprising that he finds the Kenotic perspective embedded especially inthe Gospel According to St. John. To begin with, he says, the central theme of this Gospel is the descent of the Divine Word into human flesh and mortality, in order to give his life for us on the Cross:

> By the phrase of deep simplicity, "the Word became flesh," it appears to be taught that He passed into a new form of

---

[156] Ibid., p. 66-67.

existence, a form essentially qualified by human mortality and dependence. ...

Yet when it is read, as it ought to be, with constant reference to the Gospel it has introduced, no one can miss the clear indication of the *motive* which is conceived of as underlying the advent of Jesus Christ. It is the Divine desire to impart life to a perishing and darkened world. No doubt it is characteristic of St. John, in contrast to the Pauline view, to regard the earthly life of Jesus less as a humiliation than as a revelation of divine glory, the beams of which shine forth clearly in His wondrous works. Nevertheless, he is wholly at one with St. Paul in the conviction that the redeeming work of Christ centres in the sacrifice of the cross (1:29). Jesus speaks of His death as the hour of His being glorified (12:23-24, 13:31) and declares that He came into the world to die (12:27)[157]

Mackintosh also claims — contrary to popular belief (and much scholarly opinion as well) — that St. John does not compromise or obscure the full humanity of Christ:

To say that the Logos-Jesus [in St. John's Gospel] is incapable of human weakness, and that the writer has obliterated all traces of struggle in His life, is totally misleading in view of the cry for deliverance from the passion in 12:27; and in chapter 5, where Jesus is represented as the Judge, it is noticeable that His fulfilment of the office is made wholly dependent on his obedience to the Father. "I can of Myself do nothing; as I hear, I judge" (5:20). The real fact is that manifestations of the humanity of Jesus are recorded with greater vividness in the Fourth Gospel than in any of the first three. He is shown to us wearied at Jacob's well, weeping beside the grave of Lazarus, grateful for the companionship of the Twelve, anticipating the cross with alternate shrinking and desire, athirst on Calvary, and bearing even after the resurrection, the marks of the spear and the nails. ... He is subject, moreover, to the limits of earthly experience; for although more than once very

---

[157] Ibid., p. 119-120.

remarkable knowledge is attributed to Him, yet definite details, such as His inquiry regarding the place of Lazarus' tomb, make it impossible to say that He is depicted as omniscient.[158]

The Christ of the Fourth Gospel, then, is truly man, one with us in all points, except sin. The secret of His uniqueness lies in an unparalleled relation to the Father. Men can be children of God only by new birth; Jesus is the Son of God by eternal nature.[159]

Finally, having carefully constructed his case for a kenotic understanding of the person of Jesus Christ, Mackintosh tells us that *the move from classical Two-Nature Christology to the newer Kenotic Theory is not a revolution in Christian thought, but an organic development and deepening of the Church's faith*:

The fact that each reasoned view of Christ should call for criticism and modification at the hands of later ages, so far from being an embarrassment, is a profound testimony to the magnitude of the theme. Christological theory is in truth like a great cathedral. "It is ever beautiful for worship, great for service, sublime as a retreat from the tumult of the world, and it is forever unfinished." The Christ whom any mind or group of minds can reproduce is not the infinite Redeemer of the world.

Further, it will scarcely be denied that the task of interpreting Christ afresh is a vital part of our religious service. He is to be loved with the heart, but also with the mind. It is all but impossible for a thoughtful man to adore Jesus Christ, finding in Him blessedness and eternal life, and not be conscious of a powerful desire to reach coherent views of His person. What

---

[158] Ibid., p. 99-100.

[159] Ibid., p. 102. Mackintosh may be contradicting himself here, because he admits in his discussion of the witness of St. John's Gospel that Jesus exhibits there extraordinary supernatural knowledge. Thus, in John Christ's humanity is not only unlike ours in its unique mode of dependence on the Father, but also in the results of that dependence on his human mind: an extraordinary participation in divine knowledge in his human soul, by the Holy Spirit.

we already know of Him has led us to faith and worship; may not (he will ask) a deepened knowledge, if it be attainable, add yet profounder significance to our confession of His name?[160] ...

The coinage of far-off ages may doubtless be defaced and soiled; the inscriptions set upon it may be in part undecipherable. Yet the ore from which the ancient currency was struck is still in our possession; and the task of modern Christology, as we believe, is to stamp the mintage freshly, sending it forth for the service of a new generation.[161]

With the help of Austin Farrer and H.R. Mackintosh, we have surveyed the terrain of the Kenotic project. Yet, as we have seen, many difficult questions remain to be answered. **Are kenotic theories of the Incarnation really just an exercise in futility, that ultimately "lead nowhere," as von Balthasar (and many others) have claimed, or has Kenoticism in general, and the Anglican heritage of Kenoticism in particular, opened up new and profound dimensions of the mystery of the person and work of Jesus Christ?**

To answer that question, throughout the rest of Part One of this book we shall look at the two main two schools of kenotic theory: "Radical" and "Pure" Kenoticism, on the one hand, and "Moderate," "Two-Minds" or "Two Spheres" Kenoticism on the other. The first will be termed "Radical" simply because of its degree of departure from historically mainstream Christian understandings of the nature of God and the metaphysics of the Incarnation. The second will be termed "Moderate" because (arguably) it remains closer to those traditional parameters. Moreover, I will endeavor to show that the "Radical" approach has no significant Anglican pedigree, and in any case, suffers from severe philosophical and theological difficulties (although, as we shall also see, as amended by P.T. Forsyth, H.R. Mackintosh, and Vincent Taylor, Radical Kenoticism can withstand some of the objections commonly brought against it). **Moderate Kenoticism, on**

---

[160] Ibid., p. 300.
[161] Ibid., p. 305.

the other hand, has been nurtured in Anglican soil and restated in several forms. Here, I will suggest, is a coherent and illuminating approach to the mystery of the Incarnation that has profound implications for the wider pattern of Christian belief. Indeed, that will be the central argument of this book.[162]

---

[162] The label "Radical" here is not intended in a pejorative sense: the gospel, after all, is a radical claim about Divine Love (Jn 3:16), and "moderation," however characteristically Anglican such a temperament may be, is not necessarily the best way to approach the wonder of the Incarnation. But in this case, as we shall see, "Moderate Kenoticism" can include the fundamental advantages of the Radical perspective, while avoiding the most severe problems that the latter entails.

Chapter Three
Radical and Pure Kenoticism

This stream of kenotic theory represents an attempt to remain true to the spirit, if not always to every letter of Chalcedonian orthodoxy regarding the Incarnation. **In general, the Radical Kenotic Model (hereafter, Radical KM) states that Jesus Christ is one person in two natures, human and divine, but in Radical KM the two natures are held to be fully operative and manifest *successively* rather than *simultaneously*. In other words, *the pre-existent Divine Word completely "abandons," or "renders latent" — and therefore fully or partially inaccessible and inoperative for a time — some or all of his divine attributes in order to live solely within the confines of human nature, as a fully human being.***

Radical Kenoticism first came into prominence in Germany in the mid-nineteenth century in the writings of Gottfried Thomasius (1802-1875), and in a somewhat different form in the work of Wolfgang Friedrich Gess (1819-1891) and in France, Frederic Louis Godet (1812-1890). Among Anglican theologians, however, Radical KM has had few defenders. Austin Farrer came close at times. He believed that the divine Son limited himself to conform to a particular human destiny — even to the point of being ignorant of his divine identity — yet he knew "how" to be the loving and obedient Son of the Father at every moment of his life: he thereby lived out for us an earthly parable and expression of his everlasting love for the Father in the Blessed Trinity.[163]

Gess and Pure Kenoticism

In *The Divine Trinity* (1985) David Brown offered a hypothetical defence of Radical KM in its boldest form (which we shall call "Pure KM"), as found in the work of Gess. Brown reasoned that if Kenoticism could be shown to be coherent even in this most extreme

---

[163] Farrer, *Interpretation and Belief*, p. 130, and 135-137; cf. Hebblethwaite, *The Incarnation*, p. 116-119.

form, then kenotic models of the Incarnation in general should not be dismissed without careful consideration (as they all too often have been over the past half-century). **On the Pure Kenotic Model, the divine Son is said to have completely abandoned all the attributes of his divine nature in order to sojourn on earth as a human being. In other words, divine attributes such as omniscience, omnipotence and omnipresence are left behind in such a way that they cannot be ascribed to him during his incarnate life in any way (they are not even held to be latent or in cold storage in some fashion). In fact, the divine Son chose to lay aside *all* of his divine attributes and literally changed himself into a human being.** Brown explains:

> All one need say is that divine attributes apply exclusively before the Incarnation, human attributes exclusively to the period of the Incarnation, and divine attributes again exclusively to the post-Incarnation period, and both divine and human predicates to the one continuing person who is the subject of all these experiences when no temporal segment is indicated.[164]

Brown's version of Pure KM, however, like that of Gess, raises many difficult questions.

First, can a person change his/her nature from one kind to another, and still remain the same person? In other words, can a personal being abandon one set of attributes (e.g. the essential angelic attributes) in favor of another — and even if they can, would they be able to retain their personal identity in the process? Brown defines "person" as a subject whose identity is indicated and constituted by a certain character and set of memories.[165] If we define "person" in this way, then it would seem logically coherent to say that a person (e.g. a divine person) could change his nature (e.g. for a human nature) and still remain the same person, provided that the new nature adopted can preserve the key features of character and memory which might give

---

[164] Brown, *The Divine Trinity*, p. 257.
[165] I defined "person" somewhat differently in the first chapter of this book.

us grounds for claiming that personal identity has been preserved. Presumably, all things are possible for God in his absolute freedom, including this kind of transformation or metamorphosis.

The defense "God can do anything," however, is hardly convincing if we cannot state in a logically coherent and intelligible manner what he is alleged to have done. After all, according to Pure KM, in the infancy of Christ there would be vast personal discontinuities with the pre-existent Son: lost memories of his pre-existent, divine life, and a divine character as yet undisplayed.[166] Even in his adult life major discontinuities surely would remain. Then how can we assert that Jesus of Nazareth was one and the same person as the pre-existent divine Son?

David Brown suggested that the divine character and memories could be latent.[167] He notes that there are some people who suffer from amnesia, and later recover fully; they remember both stages of past life. Similarly, the divine Son, while incarnate may have retained his divine memories in a hidden way, in "cold-storage," so that he was no longer conscious of them. Then, at the resurrection or ascension he might conceivably recover the memory of both stages of his past life. Moreover, it could be said that divine moral character was gradually manifest in Jesus' earthly life as he matured, and this may be taken as an indication that there had been a latent divine character in the infant.

It is not immediately clear how there could be a latent ethical character in a child. Brown argues that it might be latent "in much the same way as a human character is unexpressed in the gap that is presumed to exist between death and the appearance of resurrected bodies."[168] But this parallel does not seem a very apt one: that "gap" occurs only after a person has already had a full life of character development, building habits of the will (virtues and vices) through freely chosen acts of the will. On the other hand, Classical Christian orthodoxy has always claimed that *every* child born into this world possesses what we may call

---

[166] Brown, *The Divine Trinity*, p. 269.
[167] Ibid., p. 269-270.
[168] Ibid., p. 270.

a "latent" moral character: the inherited condition known as "original sin," including disordered desires (concupiscence), a clouded mind and a weakened will, all of which results in a strong inclination to sin. Thus, from a Christian theological standpoint there would not seem to be anything either extraordinary or super-human about a latent moral character in the human soul of the infant Jesus, a character that gradually manifested itself more and more throughout his life (although in his case it was never in a disordered state, but always enriched with grace and virtue).

Pure KM might be said, therefore, to preserve a coherent understanding of the abiding personal identity of the Son of God. He was fully divine, then fully human, then fully divine again. But Brown can only do so by importing into Pure KM the idea that the divine Son temporarily rendered "latent" in some way his divine character and memories (i.e., Divine Goodness and Omniscience). If the divine Son has preserved at least these divine attributes during his incarnate life, even if only in latent form, then it can hardly be said that divine attributes apply to the Son "exclusively" during his pre-incarnate and post-incarnate life, and human attributes "exclusively" during his sojourn among us. As we shall see, Brown's adjustment of Pure KM here moves the theory onto ground laid out by P.T. Forsyth, H.R. Mackintosh, and Vincent Taylor — that is, out of Pure KM altogether.

In any case, the cost of adopting Pure KM is very high. For one thing, we end up with a radically "voluntarist" understanding of the divine nature. Evidently, a divine person can choose to be whatever he wants to be: he can even enter a state in which he is completely unable to access or exercise his divine attributes. Indeed (if we stick with the Pure KM of Gess unaltered), he is cut off from them in such a way that they can no longer be ascribed to him at all. What attributes, therefore, are essential to what it means to be divine? What would define a divine person that can incarnate himself in this way (without committing suicide!), other than God's sovereign Will to be whatever he chooses to be? As we shall see, Gottfried Thomasius attempted to address these very issues in his version of Radical KM.

Also, with such a radically voluntarist understanding of the divine nature, what would be left of natural theology or Christian philosophical apologetics? As Richard Swinburne has pointed out, almost every philosophical argument for the existence of God claims to show the rational certainty, or at least the rational probability, of the existence of a being who is essentially all-powerful and all-knowing?[169] We shall return to this issue later.

Pure KM leads to other difficulties as well. The question arises: how could the divine Son ever regain divine attributes such as omniscience, omnipotence, and omnipresence, having completely shed them for his sojourn on earth? If these attributes did not remain latent within him in some way, they would have to be restored to him by another. Can the eternal Father fashion the person of Jesus of Nazareth into a deity? Can the Father bestow divine attributes upon a solely human subject who has no trace of these powers latent within him at all? This lands us in one version of the ancient heresy of "adoptionism": that a solely human being, Jesus of Nazareth, was ultimately raised to divine status (i.e., his life ended in apotheosis rather than ascension). Needless to say, this is hard to conceive, if by "raised to divine status" one means changing from a finite to an infinite being. Alternatively, and more plausibly, one could argue that after dwelling among us as Jesus of Nazareth, the person who was (formerly) the divine Son never fully regained his divine status and omni-attributes. The sacrifice of his divine status in becoming human was as a permanent one. But this would turn the Holy Trinity from that point onward into a Binity, violating (among other things) the entire liturgical heritage of Christianity in its worship of a Trinitarian God. Moreover, it runs up against the indications of Scripture that the Son of God "*upholds* the universe" and that in him "all things *hold together*" (Col 1:17; Heb 1:3; notice the use of the present tense). He can hardly do these things if he is no longer omniscient, omnipotent, and omnipresent.

Even if the Son of God can in some way regain his divine attributes at the close of his sojourn on earth (and Gess and Brown assume that he

---

[169] Richard Swinburne, *The Christian God* (Oxford: Clarendon Press, 1994), p. 232.

does), does he have to shed his human nature to do so? Presumably he would, since he had to shed his divine nature to become fully human.

Some theologians and philosophers have argued that nothing would be lost to Christian belief if we hold that the divine Son gave up his human nature at the Ascension. They often cite St. Paul's teaching in I Corinthians 15 that the glorified Jesus has a "spiritual" not a physical body (I Cor 15: 44-50). For example, C. Stephen Layman writes: "[I]t is open to Kenotic theorists to suggest that Christ's resurrection body did involve *some* limitations, but his embodiment in a resurrection body was temporary, and *in his subsequent glorified state he is unembodied and unlimited in knowledge and in power.*"[170]

This view is based, however, on an unlikely interpretation of St. Paul's teaching. In I Corinthians 15, verses 12-22 he specifically points to Christ's resurrected and glorified body as the sign and promise of our own everlasting destiny if we remain united to him in faith. In other words, we are to have everlasting, resurrected, glorified, and in that sense "spiritual" bodies like his. Moreover, in verses 35-41 he speaks of a continuity between the earthly human body that is sown in the ground at death and the "celestial body" that springs from it. It was evidently essential to the good news that St. Paul preached that the fullness of our humanity will be attained when Christ will "change our lowly body to be like his glorious body, by the power which enables him to subject all things to himself" (Phil 3:20-21). The implication is that Jesus Christ remains fully human even in heaven, and offers us a share in that fully human destiny, which is not a purely divine and bodiless existence, but a glorious fullness of human nature, body and soul, in an everlasting and glorified state. That is certainly the way the consensus of the early Fathers of the Church interpreted St. Paul's teaching on Christ's resurrection.

Besides, without the good news of the everlasting, glorified human body of Jesus, what happens to the doctrine of the presence of Christ in the Eucharist? In the Eucharist the bread and wine actually become

---

[170] Layman, *Philosophical Approaches to Atonement, Incarnation and Trinity*, p. 110; italics mine.

the body and blood, soul and divinity of the glorified Jesus (according to the Catholic view: transubstantiation), or the bread and wine are substantially united with the heavenly body and blood of Christ (Lutheran consubstantiation) or the bread and wine at least convey to the believer a spiritual union with the heavenly Christ, including his ascended and glorified humanity (the classical Calvinist view). In short, Christians historically have been nearly unanimous that Holy Communion unites them in some intimate way with the full humanity as well as the divinity of their Savior. If the divine Son loses his human nature once and for all at the Ascension, however, "Holy Communion," so defined, becomes impossible.

All this leads us to yet another problem: Pure KM obviously requires a radically "social" model of the Trinity if it is to be coherent.[171] Only a view of the Trinity that sharply distinguishes between the three divine persons as three independent, primary substances will do. For the Father and the Spirit must sustain creation with divine power, at least temporarily, while the divine Son relinquishes all his divine attributes, as well as his universal, creative role, in exchange for a human life, death, and resurrection. Hence, Pure KM implies that the divine Son can give up his participation in the divine nature, as well as his office of "holding together" the universe, at least temporarily, and let the other persons of the Trinity "pick up the slack."[172]

It is far from clear how such a conception of the Trinity avoids the charge of tritheism, since there is no mutual indwelling[173] of the three persons essential to the divine nature. One (or more) person(s) of the Trinity can simply choose to go on temporary, or even permanent furlough from the divine reality. Again, the Trinity can become (temporarily or permanently) a Binity! Even if we say that the three always choose to cooperate in divine purposes and share eternal joys,

---

[171] Brown, *The Divine Trinity*, p. 234.

[172] This was clearly the teaching of Gess; see Mackintosh, *The Doctrine of the Person of Jesus Christ,* p. 268.

[173] Also known as the "coinherence" of the divine persons of the Trinity, it means that they share essentially one divine nature and one act of being. This doctrine was defined by the 15th century ecumenical Council of Florence, but it had a long Patristic and Scholastic lineage before that.

if that is *all* that constitutes their abiding unity, then it is merely a relationship of love, sharing and cooperation among three gods, not three subjects or three personal relations within one God. We are on Mount Olympus here, rather than abiding in the mystery of God as Blessed Trinity.

On closer examination, the Trinitarian confusion gets even worse. For Pure KM also entails that the Holy Spirit does not eternally originate from the Father and the Son, since the Son has abandoned the divine nature (temporarily or permanently) and exchanged it for a human nature. It follows that at least during his incarnate life, the Son would have no capacity to generate the person of the Spirit with the Father. The western doctrine of the *filioque*, therefore, would be a casualty of Pure KM. Moreover, at the Incarnation the Father would lose his characteristic Trinitarian identity as one who eternally generates an eternal Son, and the Son would lose his Trinitarian identity as one who eternally proceeds from the Father (since the Son would have given up his divine Sonship by becoming incarnate, and for the entire period of the Incarnation). It would follow, therefore, that the revealed names of the persons of the Trinity (Father, Son and Holy Spirit) do not refer to anything eternal, essential or truly distinctive about them. Thus, the Christian understanding of the Trinity would be completely undermined.

The "Pure" version of Radical KM also has hurdles to clear with regard to the fundamental sources of divine revelation, which certainly seem to imply that the Son of God was human and divine simultaneously rather than successively. For example, it would take exceptional ingenuity to square Pure KM with the New Testament witness that "God was in Christ reconciling the world to himself" (2 Cor 5:19) and "in him the whole fullness of deity dwells bodily" (Col 2:9) and "I and the Father are one" (Jn 10:30).

Finally, the Pure KM of Gess does not abide within the parameters of the Chalcedonian definition. His theory may be said to preserve the integrity of the two natures, divine and human, in one person successively rather than simultaneously. But the Council fathers evidently meant to reject any notion of the conversion of God the Son into a man (e.g. they wrote of "the distinctive character of each nature being preserved, *and [each] combining in one Person and hypostasis"*). But Pure KM, with its complete abandonment of divine attributes by the Son, would seem to imply just such a conversion.[174]

Thomasius and Radical Kenoticism

Rather than try to find a way through the minefield of difficulties inherent in Pure KM, most defenders of Radical KM have embraced it in a somewhat different form, turning to the work of Gottfried Thomasius for guidance. **In the mid-nineteenth century, Thomasius wrote the first in-depth presentation of Kenoticism. He tried to solve the metaphysical conundrums in the notion by making a distinction between the "immanent" and "relative" attributes of God. The "immanent" divine attributes, he said, are those essential to God's being; they are eternally operative in the life of the Blessed Trinity (such as his self-existence, the power of his absolute freedom, his truth and his love) while the "relative" attributes are those which pertain to his relationship to the world which he made (omnipotence, omniscience, and omnipresence), and thus can only be ascribed to him contingently, not essentially (i.e., they are contingent upon God's will to create a universe and sustain it in being). Anglican historian of the Kenotic movement David Law summarized Thomasius' theory as follows:**

> Kenosis thus consists in the Son's divesting himself of his relative attributes of omnipotence, omnipresence and omniscience. It is because he divests himself of these attributes that he is able to live a genuinely human life. But Christ does

---

[174] The sixth century Athanasian Creed is more explicit about this than Chalcedonian definition. Speaking of Christ it says: "Who, although He be God and Man, yet He is not two, but is One Christ; One, however, not by conversion of Godhead into flesh, but by taking of Manhood into God." Historically affirmed by Anglicans, part of this Creed still can be found as an "Authorized Affirmation of Faith" in the recent (2000) *Common Worship* liturgy of the Church of England (p. 145).

not divest himself of the immanent attributes of absolute power [i.e., His boundless capacity for self-determination; his absolute freedom to determine what he will be], truth, holiness, and love. On the contrary, one of the purposes of the incarnation is to reveal these to humankind and thereby disclose God's essential nature. Christ still remains fully divine because he has not renounced any of the attributes essential to divinity (absolute power, truth, holiness, and love) but only those which pertain to God's relation to the world (omnipotence, omniscience, and omnipresence). Since God is not dependent upon the world, the attributes by means of which he relates to the world can be divested without undermining Christ's divinity. Christ remains — as the Chalcedonian Definition affirms and which Thomasius believed he was defending — truly divine and truly human.[175]

The result of this understanding of the Incarnation is that Jesus Christ can be seen as fully human: **the Son's retention only of the essential attributes of divinity during his incarnate life means that he possessed no divine omni-attributes that might over-step the boundaries and limitations of a truly human life.** Law again describes this for us:

The divesting of omnipotence means that Christ did not exercise his cosmic powers during his incarnate life, nor indeed was he in possession of them. Christ 'was not an omnipotent being.' Omniscience too is divested on Christ's assuming human nature. The insights of the incarnate Christ are not instances of omniscience, but of prophetic perception. Christ had no knowledge of the universe as a totality, but had only sufficient divine knowledge to carry out his redeeming purpose. Consequently, 'The mediator was not an omniscient

[175] David R. Law, "Case Studies in Lutheran and Anglican Kenoticism: The Christologies of Gottfried Thomasius and Frank Weston" (unpublished English version provided by the author), p. 11; originally published in a French version, "Le kénotisme luthérien et anglican: les christologies de Gottfried Thomasius et Frank Weston", Études Théologiques et Religieuses, vol. 89, no. 3 (2014), 313-340.

human being.' Finally, the Son divests himself of his divine omnipresence, for if he did not, he could not exist as a human being, for human beings are not omnipresent but limited in time and space.[176]

One of the advantages of the Thomasian form of Radical KM is that it enables us to envisage how Jesus could share in the journey of every human being by growing and developing in knowledge and wisdom throughout his life. Law tells us:

> The incarnate Son [according to Thomasius] has no consciousness or knowledge outside the human consciousness that he has assumed on becoming a human being. Nor does the Son exercise any functions outside of those possible by means of a human consciousness. ... Thomasius argues that the divine consciousness is expressed and develops wholly within the confines of the human consciousness. It is wholly within the human consciousness that the divine essence and glory of the Logos is expressed. ... The limitation of divinity to what can be expressed through the medium of a human consciousness allows Thomasius to deal with the New Testament witness to Christ's *development*. ...

> Like all human consciousnesses, Christ's human consciousness undergoes development. Every human consciousness is characterized by 'potency,' i.e., the potential latent within every human being which needs cultivation if it is to come to fulfilment. ... Thomasius is prepared to concede that Christ underwent a temporary period of unconsciousness as an unborn child and at his death. This application of the concept of potency to Christ allows Thomasius to solve the problem of how Christ could undergo human development during his earthly existence. Christ's potency, as it were, is his divinity. It is the 'memory' of the glory which he possessed as the pre-existent Logos. He was not born with a full awareness of his divinity, however, but developed an increasingly divine self-

---

[176] Ibid.

consciousness during his earthly existence and to the point where he became aware of his relationship with the Father and his role as redeemer of the world.[177]

As in Brown's version of Pure KM, notice the appeal here in Thomasius to the idea that the divine Son must have rendered at least some aspects of his divinity "latent," or in "potency," in his human nature, for this model of the Incarnation to work. In other words, Thomasius brought into his idea of the life of the Incarnate (with all divine omni-attributes abandoned) a latent sense in Jesus of his own identity and mission that arose from within and was gradually manifested in his life over time. Thomasius would claim that knowledge of this kind of "truth" is one of the "essential" attributes of the divine nature, and that the divine Son retained this kind of knowledge in his incarnate state. Nevertheless, it was still a measure of divine and supernatural knowledge, not natural knowledge, which was made available here to the human mind of Jesus.

Positing this kind and degree of latent divine knowledge, however does not seem sufficient to render the Thomasian theory coherent. For David Law also documents the withering critique that Thomasian metaphysics suffered in the nineteenth century. In 1887, for example, **Adolf von Stahlin argued that the distinction between immanent and relative divine attributes was a fatal weakness in the theory. The relative attributes must in some way be contained in the immanent attributes.[178] In other words, in so far as God can create and sustain a world by using omni-attributes if he so chooses, the capacity to exercise those attributes must be in some way essential to his being, and cannot be *completely* abandoned by a divine person.** Anglican Bishop Frank Weston summed up the objections of many when he wrote:

> In short, God's attributes are in one sense aspects of God Himself. And God cannot abandon aspects of Himself. He

---

[177] Ibid., p. 13-14.
[178] Ibid., p. 26.

may so order things that any particular aspect is lost sight of and hidden, but that is self-limitation, not self-abandonment.[179]

Moreover, given the "voluntarist" understanding of the divine nature in Thomasius, one wonders why God's absolute power of self-determination essentially requires him to be loving rather than wicked. How does Thomasius' claim that God is *essentially* "love" fit with the claim that he is *essentially* free to be whatever he chooses to be?[180] Here there appears to be an inherent contradiction in Thomasian metaphysics. If God is essentially Unconditioned Will, then why cannot God choose to be a wicked God instead of a loving one? Is this merely an arbitrary choice on his part — and couldn't he simply change his mind and be an evil God tomorrow, if he willed to be so? Classical Christianity, by contrast, saw Divine Love and Divine Will as expressions of the one divine substance or essence: the one, infinite, eternal act of Perfect Being in which God is himself, and in which he always wills what he knows to be good. Divine Love and Divine Will, therefore, are essentially (not "voluntarily," contingently, or by external constraint) united in God's nature.

Furthermore, the problems we have seen with Pure KM recur here in Thomasius with regard to Swinburne's concern about the survival of Christian natural theology and rational apologetics (again, more on this later).

With regard to the doctrine of the Trinity, Thomasian Radical KM might be able to avoid the lapse into tritheism that Pure KM entails,

---

[179] Weston, *The One Christ,* p. 136.

[180] Thomas R. Thompson claims that for Thomasius "the divine essence as self-determining will plays a supreme role in his kenoticism." Thomas R. Thompson, "Nineteenth Century Kenotic Christology" in Evans, ed., *Exploring Kenotic Christology*, p. 84. Law reports that for Thomasius "'Absolute self-determination' or 'will' is a divine characteristic because God alone determines or wills what he is." See Law, "Case Studies in Lutheran and Anglican Kenoticism" (English version), p. 6. NB: For this reason, *Thomasian Kenoticism does not have any difficulty in holding that the divine Son could recover his omni-attributes after his resurrection/ascension: the Son had never lost his essential divine attribute of absolute self-determination, so he was presumably free to will at any time the resumption of his role in the governance of the universe.*

The Incarnation

since Thomasius sees the divine, absolute power of self-determination that grounds the life of the Trinity as retained by the Son during his incarnate life. The Trinitarian life remains uninterrupted: the Father wills the Son to be, and the Son wills himself to be willed by the Father, and together they will the Holy Spirit to be. Still, the other two persons of the Trinity must "cover" for the cosmic role of the divine Son, at least during his sojourn on earth when he is not able to exercise his "relative" divine attributes toward all of creation.[181] It is not clear what warrant such an idea might have in Scripture or mainstream Christian Tradition. As Frank Weston put it: "The general tendency of the New Testament is towards the doctrine of the permanence of the universal life and cosmic functions of the eternal Word [Col 1:17; Heb 1:3; see also Jn 1:18 and 5:19]. ... and all down the ages the Church has received and maintained that the Word never for a moment ceased from His activity in upholding creation."[182]

In addition, Thomasian Radical KM has hurdles to jump with regarding the recovery by the divine Son of all of his divine omni-attributes after his sojourn on earth. How can he do so in a way that does not violate the boundaries of his risen and glorified humanity? Contemporary Thomasians seem to want to hold (along with the New Testament, as in Philippians 3:20-21, and the classical Christian Tradition) that the divine Son remains in a perpetually incarnate state even in heavenly glory. But to fit with a Thomasian understanding of "incarnation," they claim that this somehow involves the assumption of a heavenly human body and soul by the Son at the resurrection/ascension that (unlike his earthly body and soul) can be the vehicle of the possession and exercise of all the divine omni-attributes.[183] This may not be coherent (surely, a risen and glorified human body and soul still must be *finite and human*, rather than infinite and divine, and therefore must have at least *some* human limitations, even if not exactly the same as earthly human limitations). But even if the claim is coherent, in this respect Thomasian theory seems to give

---

[181] This is precisely what some contemporary Thomasians posit: See C. Stephen Evans, "Kenotic Christology and the Nature of God," p. 213-214.
[182] Weston, *The One Christ*, p. 128-129.
[183] Evans, "Kenotic Christology and the Nature of God," p. 201-202.

us a picture of the risen and ascended Christ akin to the "Monophysite" heresy, with his divine nature ultimately swallowing up much that is definably human about him.

The understanding of Divine Omnipotence operative in the Thomasian theory is also problematic, since it presupposes that Divine Omnipotence must be "abandoned" in some way by the Son in order to make way for his love to achieve his saving purposes for humanity. In short, in Thomasian theory there seems to be dissonance between an "essential" divine attribute ("love") and a "relative" divine attribute ("omnipotence"). We shall return to this important point later.

Finally, it is arguable that despite his sincere attempt to remain true to Chalcedon, Thomasius failed to abide by the phrase in the Chalcedonian definition of the Incarnation which says that the two natures are united in Christ "without change." Thomasius would argue that the "essential," or "immanent" divine attributes remain unchanged and fully operative during the incarnate life of the Son; but if Stahlin was correct, and the sharp distinction that Thomasius made between the essential or immanent, and the relative attributes of God is incoherent and cannot be sustained, then the "abandonment" of those relative or omni-attributes by the Son (in the sense that they cannot be attributed to him in any way during his life as incarnate) would constitute just the kind of essential "change" in the divine nature that the bishops at Chalcedon were worried about.

Contemporary followers of Thomasius seek to overcome at least Stahlin's critique by positing a capacity for divine self-limitation with regard to the exercise of the omni-attributes. In the book *Exploring Kenotic Christology* (2006), for example, Protestant scholars from the United States Stephen T. Davis and C. Stephen Evans sought to resurrect Thomasian theory in this fashion:

> [I]n the Incarnation, Jesus Christ 'emptied himself' by temporarily giving up those divine properties that are inconsistent with being truly human, while retaining sufficient divine properties to remain truly divine; and he did not assume those common human properties that are inconsistent with

being truly divine, but assumed sufficient human properties to be truly human. ... A coherent kenotic theory accordingly will hold that what is essential to God is not, for example, omniscience, but the rather the more complex property of being omniscient-unless-freely-and-temporarily-choosing-to-be-otherwise. The same point will then be made with other divine properties such as omnipotence, omnipresence, and so on.[184]

The suggestion of the kenotic Christologist is that, in becoming human, God decided to divest himself at least temporarily of some of the divine properties, such as omnipotence, omniscience, and omnipresence. A decision to become a human being is, for example, a decision to be located in a particular time and place, and this seems incompatible with omnipresence. Naturally, this view implies that such properties as omnipotence, omniscience, and omnipresence are not essential to be divine, since on an orthodox view Christ retains his divinity and thus divine nature during his earthly career. Contrary to what we might otherwise have thought, the kenoticist says that this provides us with good reason to think that what is essential to being divine is not the possession of such properties as omnipotence and omniscience, but rather such properties as 'being-omnipotent-unless-freely-choosing-to-limit-one's-power.'[185]

It is not entirely clear what Davis and Evans are proposing here. On the one hand they state that in the Incarnation the Son of God "gave up" or "divested himself" of some of his divine properties, the ones that are "not essential to be divine" in order to assume a fully human life that exemplifies Divine Love. This sounds very much like Thomasius — and would therefore be subject to Stahlin's

---

[184] Stephen T. Davis, "Is Kenosis Orthodox?' in Evans, ed., *Exploring Kenotic Christology*, p. 117-118.
[185] Evans, "Kenotic Christology and the Nature of God," p. 197-198.

aforementioned critique.[186] On the other hand, they write of God as possessing a capacity "temporarily" to "limit" his omni-attributes: and as Weston had pointed out, self-limitation in the form of the "self-restraint" of the "exercise" of divine attributes is not the same thing as abandoning them altogether, for the latter involves the claim that those attributes can no longer be ascribed to the divine Son during his incarnate life in any way at all.

Radical Kenoticism Revised: Forsyth, Mackintosh and Taylor

In the 20th century several British theologians offered revised versions of Thomasian Radical KM that attempted to iron out some of the difficulties involved. Scotsmen from the Congregationalist and Free Church traditions, such as P.T. Forsyth (1848-1921) and H.R. Mackintosh, as well as English Methodist New Testament scholar Vincent Taylor (1887-1968) presented an arguably less radical version of Kenoticism than either Gess or Thomasius.[187] Taylor, for example, suggested that the divine Son, through an act of self-limitation, merely relegated some of his divine attributes to a state of "potency," rendering them "latent" in his human nature in order to live under the conditions of human existence. The Son chose to renounce only his conscious awareness, control, and exercise of these attributes, including his omniscience, omnipotence and omnipresence.[188] **In other words, in order to live and die as one of us, Taylor suggested,** *the divine Son somehow limited his conscious awareness of, and thereby his ability to exercise, the omni-attributes of his own divine nature.* **In this way he rendered these**

---

[186] Evans: "What is retained will chiefly be the self-giving love that is regarded as lying at the heart of divinity and which is exhibited precisely in God's willingness to empty himself for the sake of his creatures." Cited in Edwin Chr. Van Driel, "The Logic of Assumption," in Evans, ed., *Exploring Kenotic Christology*, p. 266.

[187] Writing in 1958, long after Forsyth and Mackintosh had finished their work, Taylor refers to them as offering "the best form" of the Kenotic Theory. See Vincent Taylor, *The Person of Christ* (London: Macmillan, 1958), p. 267 and 299.

[188] Ibid., p. 286-304. Similarly, see P.T. Forsyth, *The Person and Place of Jesus Christ*, p. 307-311. On Forsyth, see also the discussion of his perspective in Brown, *Divine Humanity*, p. 108-114.

attributes latent, without completely abandoning them. The powers remained hidden, untapped, inaccessible and inoperative during his sojourn on earth. Taylor explained:

> The Christology which seems most in accord with the teaching of the New Testament is the doctrine that, in becoming man, the Son of God willed to renounce the exercise of divine prerogatives and powers, so that in the course of his earthly existence, He might live within the necessary limitations which belong to human finitude. Divine attributes of omniscience, omnipotence, and omnipresence were laid aside, not in the sense that they were abandoned or destroyed, but in such a manner that they became potential or latent because no longer in exercise. … No just reason has been given why, within the limitations necessary to the Incarnation, the attributes of omniscience, omnipotence and omnipresence should not have remained latent, or potential, existent, but no longer at the centre of the Son's consciousness and in conscious exercise. … As in all Christological questions our difficulty is that there is really no adequate illustration available; but with this necessary limitation, there are many cases in human life in which powers are latent, either by an act of will, or because their presence is not known.[189]

The validity of Taylor's proposal here depends on the coherence of the notion that a divine person can render latent in his human nature — and therefore at least temporarily inaccessible and inoperative — his divine omni-attributes. Let us look at each of these attributes in turn.

a) The question of how God the Son could self-limit his *omnipresence*, rendering it latent and inoperative, has been discussed by the American Protestant philosopher Thomas Morris. In short, his view is that if it is coherent to say that the divine Son can limit his own omniscience, then it must be coherent to say he can limit his omnipresence, since omnipresence by definition should mean "the property of

---

[189] Taylor, *The Person of Christ,* p. 277-278 and 293.

being everywhere in virtue of knowledge of and power over any spatially located object."[190]

b) The question of how God the Son can self-limit, by rendering latent and inoperative, his own *omnipotence* has also been discussed by Morris. He tells us that, once again, it all depends upon God's ability to put limitations on his own omniscience:

> [I]f the Son then lacked at least omniscience, one piece of knowledge he may be said to have lacked is the knowledge of his being omnipotent. And anyone who has restricted his knowledge of the range of his own power may be argued thereby to have restricted the exercise of his power, since, presumably, no one usually draws on resources he does not believe he has.[191]

Obviously, Taylor's theory would be cleaner and simpler if it could be said that the divine Son, while incarnate as Jesus of Nazareth, was unaware of his own divine identity and powers. But it does not strictly necessitate that view. It may be that, although Jesus was conscious of being the divine Son under the limitations and conditions of human life, he was at the same time aware that those conditions, originally and voluntarily self-imposed, now rendered him unable to access his omni-attributes, so that he had to live instead in complete dependence upon his heavenly Father and the Holy Spirit (the issue of Christ's awareness of his divine identity will be explored in the next chapter of this book).

In any case, Morris is surely right: human beings cannot fully use or develop talents or gifts of which they are completely unaware, or at least ones that by some act in the past they have rendered inoperative and beyond their

---

[190] Morris, *The Logic of God Incarnate*, p. 91.
[191] Ibid., p. 92.

present power to access. In a similar way, it could be said that the Word as incarnate cannot exercise powers that he does not even know he possesses, or at least, knows that he cannot access through the human nature he freely chose to assume. Thus, according to this version of Radical KM, God the Son renders latent certain of his powers, such as his universal sway over physical events, in order to sojourn on earth as a human being.

The definition of "Divine Omnipotence," however, must be carefully stated here if Taylor's theory is to avoid a serious distortion of the Christian understanding of God. For if we define divine power simply as an all-determinative and generally coercive force, then Radical Kenoticism in any form leaves us with the impression that the Word of God is like an absolute monarch who, through the self-limitation involved in the Incarnation, completely changed his providential *modus operandi* for a while in order to win us over. This would make Jesus of Nazareth the supreme anomaly, rather than the supreme instance and manifestation of the loving power of God in the world. Through Jesus, God would be living and acting "out of character," so to speak. Moreover, we could also end up envisioning a "strife of attributes" in the divine nature, with Divine Omnipotence seen as an obstacle to (and something that needs to be completely set aside for) the achievement of his saving purposes on earth — a problem we saw with the theory of Thomasius.

Later in this book we shall take an in-depth look at proposals for understanding the divine nature as essentially kenotic, expressed in God's relationship with all of humanity, with all of creation — and even within the inner life of the eternal Trinity. Suffice it to say here that prior to the Second World War, most Anglican theologians were reticent to drive a wedge between God's love and his almighty power. The two were seen as inseparable, and their unity vital to the gospel. Michael Ramsey, for example, asked of all Gessian and Thomasian versions of Kenoticism: "Is not the unity of Love and Omnipotence of the very essence of Christian theism?"[192] Frank Weston insisted:

> [I]n our experience the child ascribes omnipotence to the mother in the measure that he loves her. He sees no antithesis; perfect love requires omnipotence, that it may never fail the beloved. So thinks the child.
>
> Surely God's omnipotence is His eternal love, manifested and directed to the fulfilment of the desires of His fatherly Heart; as His omnipresence is His eternal love seeking to unite Himself with all His children; and His omniscience is His love embracing each one of them, holding them to His Heart, knowing them and becoming known of them.
>
> The love of God did not come into action first at the Incarnation: it came under men's observation.[193]

This tension between Divine Love and Divine Omnipotence, however, is a problem for Taylor's Radical KM — and indeed, for all versions of Kenoticism. If kenotic theories of the Incarnation, by definition, involve some measure of self-limitation by the divine Son of his omni-attributes in order to share in all the conditions and limitations of a real human life, then how can we avoid seeing Divine Omnipotence as something that needs to be set aside, to some extent at least, lest it pose an obstacle to the saving work of Divine Love?

Weston had already hinted at a possible solution of this dilemma when he wrote of Divine Omnipotence as God's love "directed to the fulfilment of the desires of His fatherly Heart." **With greater clarity and precision, O.C. Quick explored**

---

[192] A. Michael Ramsey, *An Era in Anglican Theology: From Gore to Temple* (Eugene, OR: Wipf and Stock, 1960), p. 33.
[193] Weston, *The One Christ*, p. 135.

this mystery in *Doctrines of the Creed* (1938). "Power," he wrote, "is the ability to achieve purpose":

> Almightiness or omnipotence is then the attribute of one who can make all things serve his will or achieve his purpose in all things. What he does is necessarily determined or, if you will, limited by what he purposes or wills to do. ... **[T]he strongest power in the world is that of agape [love] itself, which does not work by force to achieve its highest purposes or win its greatest victories. The cross is the power and wisdom of God [I Cor 1:24-25]. ... For this power converts even suffering itself into something active and creative, and makes the very forces of evil, even through the apparent completeness of their triumph over it, nevertheless subserve its own purpose of good.**[194]

It follows that *God never exercises his power apart from his wise purposes of love.* Thus, Kenoticism, properly conceived, cannot be said to make of Jesus an anomaly. The same God, out of the power of his selfless love, bestows existence on all creatures, guides them toward his benevolent purposes for them, and became incarnate in human history to bring us salvation. Whether as Creator and Sustainer, as Providential Lord, or as Incarnate Redeemer, everything he does is an expression of the power of his steadfast love to achieve his purposes for his creatures. God consistently seeks the good of all things with his loving power no matter which mode of action (universal, cosmic, and largely determinative; or self-limited-in-manhood) he chooses to adopt to achieve those good purposes.

To refine Radical Kenoticism, therefore, one should not say (with Gess or Thomasius) that the divine Son

---

[194] Quick, *Doctrines of the Creed*, p. 62, 65, 66. Cf. Keith Ward, *Holding Fast to God* (London: SPCK, 1982), p. 35-38.

completely "abandoned" or "divested himself" of his omnipotence in the Incarnation, nor even (with Taylor) that he rendered his power *fully* latent, *completely* inaccessible and inoperative for a time. Rather, *through his incarnate life his omnipotence — that is, his infinite, unsurpassable, and indefatigable ability to achieve his loving purposes in all things — was utilized and expressed, but in a new way.* The divine Son simply rendered latent and inoperative *one form* in which Divine Love exercises power — namely, his universal sway over physical events — in order to exercise and express his loving omnipotence in a new and unique way through his human limitations and sufferings as Jesus Christ. Among the ancient church Fathers, St. Gregory of Nyssa expressed this paradox when he wrote:

> The fact that the all-powerful nature was capable of stooping down to the lowliness of the human condition is a greater proof of power than are the miracles, imposing and supernatural though these be … The humiliation of God shows the super-abundance of his power, which is in no way fettered in the midst of conditions contrary to its nature. … The greatness is glimpsed in the lowliness and its exaltation is not thereby reduced.[195]

This divine, self-sacrificial love has an alluring, attractive radiance that is able (without coercion) to convert even the hardest of human hearts — in that sense it is the greatest of all forms of divine power. As the Reformed theologian Karl Barth repeatedly pointed out, God is sovereign Lord even in his servant form. His omnipotence is activated and expressed through Jesus Christ because God's power is "the power of the ordering of his love," the power which orders the very

---

[195] St. Gregory of Nyssa, *The Great* Catechism, chapter XXIV, quoted in von Balthasar, *Mysterium Paschale*, p. 34.

community of love in the Blessed Trinity.[196] The Anglican *Book of Common Prayer* captures something of this truth in its Collect for the Eleventh Sunday after Trinity, which begins, "O God, who declarest thy almighty power most chiefly by showing mercy and pity."[197]

If this account of Divine Omnipotence is plausible, then we would need to make a further amendment to Taylor's version of Radical KM to make it cohere with the historically mainstream Christian faith. H.R. Mackintosh pointed the way in his classic exposition of Kenotic Christology, *The Doctrine of the Person of Jesus Christ* (1914). **According to Mackintosh, God the Son has not rendered *fully* latent and inoperative his omni-attributes in the Incarnation, but "transposed" the exercise of them for a time so that they operated, and were manifest, only in and through the conditions and limitations of the human nature that he assumed. In other words, the divine Son expressed and utilized those omni-attributes in a unique way, through a limited vessel, in order to achieve his loving purposes for humanity.[198]** Mackintosh writes:

> [T]hough not parted with, attributes may be *transposed*. They may come to function in *new ways*, to assume *new forms of activity*, readjusted to the new condition of the Subject. It is possible to conceive the Son, who has entered at love's behest on the region of growth and progress, as now possessing *all* the qualities of Godhead in the form of concentrated potency rather

[196] Karl Barth, *Dogmatics in Outline* (London: SCM: 1949), p. 49; cf. Donald Dawe, *The Form of a Servant: an historical analysis of the Kenotic motif* (Philadelphia: Westminster, 1963), p. 172-173.

[197] *The Book of Common Prayer* (Canada, 1962), p.234.

[198] Arguably, his version of Radical Kenoticism in this respect is quite similar to the position put forward by the Reformed theologian J. H. A. Ebrard (1818-1888): see Thomas R. Thompson, "Nineteenth Century Kenotic Christology," p. 86. But it has its roots especially in the work of P.T. Forsyth in 1909 in *The Person and Place of Jesus Christ*, p. 307-311.

than of full actuality, *dunamei* rather than *energeia*. For example, in its eternal form the absolute intelligence of God acts as an intuitive and synchronous knowledge of all things; when the Eternal passes into time, however, knowledge for Him must take on a discursive and progressive nature. Similarly, a man who has tested his own abilities may know that all mathematics is potentially in his grasp, although in point of fact he has mastered no more than is needful for his calling. So Christ, who in virtue of his relation to the Father had Divine knowledge within reach, took only what was essential to His vocation. Though on many subjects He shared the ignorance as well as the knowledge of his contemporaries, yet he had at command all higher truth which can be assimilated by perfect human faculty. In his unique knowledge of God He knows that relatively to which all else is but subordinate detail. This is the kind of *spiritual* omniscience that seems to be claimed for him in the Gospels.

The same principle may be applied to omnipotence, provided that we bear well in mind that there is no such thing, even in God, as omnipotence which is not morally conditioned. … [I]n the historic Jesus there is a derived power over the souls of men, as over nature, which may be viewed as a modified form of the power of Godhead. It is not omnipotence *simpliciter*, but it is such power within human limits as we feel to be akin to almightiness, and prophetic of the hour when the Risen Lord should say: "All power is given to me in heaven and earth." Omnipresence is more baffling; and yet perhaps only at first sight. … [W]hat faith asserts is not that He is everywhere present in an infinitely extended universe, with a physical ubiquity like that of ether, but that He is absolutely superior to, and independent of, the limitations of space and distance. … Now this transcendence of spacial limitations, combined with these positive relationships, is present or implicit in Christ's redemptive mission — in his triumphant capacity, that is, to accomplish in Palestine a universally and eternally valid work unhampered by the bounds of "here" and "there." As part of history, His work has a date and place, yet its power far transcends them. So the eternal form of divine existence and the time-form are here vitally related to each other. The exchange of one for the other is no negation of God's specific being; it is the supreme energetic act of perfect Love. Love is the link which binds the pre-temporal Word to the living and dying Jesus.[199]

All of this may be "true as far as it goes," but problems still remain. Mackintosh claims that on his theory there is "no *negation* of God's specific being,"— but there is definitely a radical *self-diminution* of the divine attributes of the Son involved. After all, to "transpose" a reality from a richer to a more limited medium must involve the assumption of narrower boundaries and limitations. For example, a Beethoven symphony, transposed for piano, is analogous to the full orchestral score, but clearly not its exact equivalent. The same notes on the piano keyboard that in one passage of the score must reflect a melody originally given to the string section, must represent in another place the notes originally played by the flutes and oboes. In other words, one single instrument, with all its limitations, must try to express, as well as can be expressed, the richness of the whole orchestra. Thus the "spiritual omniscience" that Mackintosh finds in the Incarnate Lord is not the same thing as boundless Divine

---

[199] Mackintosh, *The Doctrine of the Person of Jesus Christ*, p. 477-479. Notice that Mackintosh assumes here that God abides in a realm of timeless eternity, with "synchronous" knowledge of all things. This perspective was soon to fall into disrepute in much of twentieth and twenty-first century Christian thought (see the final, "Conclusion" chapter of this book for further discussion).

Omniscience; it is Divine Omniscience self-limited and transposed. And the same is true of the other omni-attributes Mackintosh discusses.

In short, if the Forsyth-Mackintosh-Taylor version of Radical KM is to be taken seriously, we must still ask if there is a coherent way to understand how these divine omni-attributes can be self-limited and transposed, rendered latent in Christ's human nature, and therefore at least partially inaccessible and inoperative.

c) According to Thomas Morris, much depends upon whether or not it is coherent to say that the divine Son can radically "contract" (i.e., "transpose," that is, render latent, and at least partially inaccessible and inoperative) his Divine Omniscience within the boundaries of his human mind as Jesus Christ. For if he can, then, as we have seen (letters a and b above), it will be coherent to say that he can transpose and render latent his attributes of omnipresence and omnipotence as well.

Here, for the sake of argument, and in order to abide by the parameters of this study, I will assume (as most 20th and 21st century Anglican theologians have) that God's omniscience does not mean that he has all times and events present before his gaze at once; I will assume that he can and does know all the facts about the past, all the facts about the present, and all future possibilities and probabilities, but not the future voluntary actions of beings with free-will.[200] (We will explore further this perspective on Divine Omniscience in Part Two of this book).

What, then, can it mean to say that the divine Son has self-limited his own omniscience (so defined), "transposing" it so that it abides within the limits of an authentic human life, rendering it "latent" in his human nature, and therefore at least partially inaccessible and inoperative?

---

[200] See, for example, Richard Swinburne, *The Coherence of Theism*, p. 175-176.

Vincent Taylor wrote: "There are many cases in human life in which powers are latent, either by an act of will, or because their presence is not known."[201]

We can imagine, for example, a concert pianist who gives up her career for a time in order to raise her children, and only years later begins to recover her old musical knowledge and skill, stored in her memory. She knows all the while that she has the hidden ability to play the piano at a certain level, and sometimes plays songs that she remembers for her children, but her knowledge and skills have been rendered latent and inoperative in such a way that she is unable to access them in full measure for a time — and this sacrifice is undertaken and sustained out of love for her family. In short, her talents have temporarily been self-limited and "transposed" in order to conform to all the limitations and conditions of loving motherhood.

Also, we can call to mind the history of a Catholic religious order in the Middle Ages and Early-Modern period, the Order of our Lady of Ransom founded by St. Peter Nolasco in the 13th century, whose members sometimes exchanged places with Christian slaves in North Africa in order to set them free, especially those slaves who were losing their faith by their imprisonment among the Muslims. Here is another act of sacrificial self-limitation — the setting aside of a natural right, rendering latent and inoperative the capacity to exercise human liberty — in order to reach out in love to others. The self-limitation of power involved, the acceptance of a state with new limitations and conditions, and the motive of love behind it all in order to achieve God's highest purpose — the salvation of souls — all this echoes what Christ has done for humanity through the Incarnation.

---

[201] Taylor, *The Person of Christ,* p. 293.

Thus, it seems that human beings can self-limit and transpose their attributes of knowledge and power, rendering them latent and largely inaccessible for a time. This establishes at least a *prima facie* case that, by analogy, God can do something similar. In other words, it is not utterly inconceivable that in the Incarnation the divine Son can render latent in his human nature, and thereby partially inaccessible and inoperative, his capacity to exercise omniscience and omnipotence.[202] The basic structure of the Forsyth-Mackintosh-Taylor version of Radical KM, therefore, would seem to be intelligible and coherent — provided, of course, that one can accept the radical view of the divine nature which this theory presupposes.

Radical Kenoticism and Voluntarism

Here is a critical issue for any version of Radical KM, an issue that we mentioned in passing before. According to Catholic philosopher and theologian Thomas Joseph White, OP, in Radical Kenoticism, at least:

> The continuity between the heights of divine identity and his human lowliness is guaranteed by a kenosis originating from the divine freedom and love that constitute the divine essence. … In his love, God is free to be both supreme and lowly, both impassible and suffering, both eternal and temporal, and so on. The wedding between these two seeming contraries is guaranteed by God's freedom to diversify his attributes. The free self-emptying of God incarnate in Christ takes place because of love, and reveals that love to man in human

---

[202] Forsyth offered a number of analogies, of varying degrees of value; see the summary and discussion of them in Brown, *Divine Humanity*, p. 112-113.

historical terms, particularly in and through the Paschal mystery. …[203]

In other words, we are confronted in Radical Kenoticism with various forms of a "voluntarist" understanding of the divine nature, arrived at not so much by prior philosophical speculation as by the alleged implications of what God has revealed about himself through the life and death of Jesus Christ.[204] God has revealed that he is free to be whatever he wills to be, and to limit himself in any way he chooses in order to reach out in love to his creatures. In other words, as P.T. Forsyth put it: "If the infinite God was so constituted that he could not live also as finite man then he was not infinite."[205] According to voluntarism, God freely determines the kind of God he wills to be; or as Karl Barth wrote: "God's being is … his willed decision."[206]

One major problem with voluntarism (as we have seen before in our discussion of Thomasius) is that it is hard to grasp how a God who is truly and absolutely "free" in this sense is at the same time essentially and reliably loving (as Thomasius, Mackintosh, and other proponents of Radical KM have claimed). Protestant voluntarist-theologian Paul Fiddes admitted as much in his reflections on creation as an expression of Divine Love. He wrote:

---

[203] Thomas Joseph White, OP, *The Incarnate Lord: A Thomistic Study in Christology* (Washington, DC: Catholic University of America Press, 2015), p. 343-344.

[204] An exception here might be Austin Farrer, who gradually adopted a voluntarist understanding of God, in his last book defining God as "Unconditioned Will … a determinator who is nothing but what he determines to be — a free Spirit." Austin Farrer, *Faith and Speculation* (Edinburgh, T. and T. Clark, 1967), p. 118, and 142.

[205] Forsyth, *The Person and Place of Jesus Christ*, p. 315.

[206] Karl Barth, *Church* Dogmatics, II/I, G. Bromiley and T.F. Torrance, translators (Edinburgh: T. and T. Clark, 1936-77), p. 271-272; cited in Paul S. Fiddes, "Creation out of Love," in John Polkinghorne, ed., *The Work of Love: Creation as Kenosis* (Grand Rapids: Eerdmans, 2001), p. 181.

> There are admittedly some logical strains in this [voluntarist] solution that God is entirely what God wills to be. Most evidently, it does not seem to square with the common-sense view that there must already be a nature in existence with the powers of knowledge and intention in order to make choices.[207]

Indeed, if God's essential nature consists above all in his unlimited power of making choices, including the power to "diversify" all his other attributes (as White put it), then what God chooses will not necessarily be in accord with attributes such as wisdom or love (attributes which, on this reckoning, do not essentially belong to him). Thus, God's choices to be truthful, and to act in loving ways would always be merely *arbitrary* choices on his part, not a real reflection of who he essentially is. **According to the classical conception of God, by contrast, God always chooses what he knows to be true and good, because he is essentially not only free, but also all-knowing and all-loving: He always lives out all of these compossible divine attributes at once, and he would not want to do otherwise, for he cannot be other than true to himself.**

Fiddes tries to avoid the voluntarist quagmire here by appealing to God's covenant faithfulness:

> If God's will is not to be arbitrary, then God's faithfulness [in love] must be unchanging. This may seem to require a nature possessing the quality of absolute fidelity, which exists as the *basis* for God's making of choices. However, it is possible to think of this 'covenant faithfulness' (*hesed* in Old Testament faith) from the perspective of God's will .... God promises to be faithful to what God chooses to be, and we take a risk of faith on the consistent character of God's will which is manifested in the promise.[208]

---

[207] Fiddes, "Creation out of Love," p. 182.
[208] Ibid., p. 183.

It is far from clear how this appeal to divine promises avoids the voluntarist trap of an arbitrary God. For God's promises would be just as arbitrary as anything else he chooses to do. If God is essentially Absolute Freedom, Unconditioned Will, then there is nothing about God's covenant love and making of promises to us that necessarily expresses the kind of God he essentially is. He just happens for the time being (and arbitrarily, as far as we know) to choose to be loving and truthful toward us, but that choice is not based on any essential attributes in him of wisdom and love — for love and truth do not necessarily condition his will, if his will is essentially unconditioned. He is entirely free to choose to be a different kind of God tomorrow. Since divine promises are just as arbitrary as any other choice the voluntarist God might make, our only way to relate to him would be to cling to those promises with utterly blind faith.

To be sure, a voluntarist God is free to make promises and could will to keep them — but the main point here is that even if he did so, this would not tell us anything about the essential nature of God. All we could know is that on this particular occasion, or in his dealings with the people of Israel, or in his relationship with humanity generally, he seems (from all we can tell from our past experience of him) to keep his promises. Yet even this is not guaranteed, because he could will to make us *believe* he will always keep his promises to us, only to break them later in the sovereign freedom of his Unconditioned Will. For, again, **with voluntarism there is nothing essential about his nature that necessarily moves him always to will the true and the good. If his essential nature is Unconditioned Will, then that Will is not necessarily conditioned by Divine Knowledge or Divine Goodness.**

All of this is a far cry from the biblical and Classical Christian conception of God, whose essential nature and character (and not just his acts of will) can be known from his works of creation and salvation (Is 6:1-4; Ps 103: 6-8; Ps 139; Rom 1:19-21; I Jn 1:5, 4:8).[209] Moreover,

---

[209] The Scripture text traditionally used to justify an essentialist rather than a voluntarist approach to the divine nature was Ex 3:14, where God discloses his

Christians have always believed that the divine nature essentially includes infinite Goodness and Wisdom, and not just infinite Will and Power. Even if one could devise a coherent metaphysics in which the divine essence is reducible to infinitely *loving* Will, it would still hardly measure up to the guidance of Scripture and mainstream Christian Tradition concerning the nature of God. For Christianity always ascribed *infinite Divine Knowledge* to God's nature as well (e.g. Job 38-39; Ps 139; Dan 2:20; Rom 11:33-36; Heb 4:13; I Jn 3:19-20).

One could still defend the Forsyth-Mackintosh-Taylor version of Radical KM as the one that has the fewest problems. For example, it tries to avoid Stahlin's critique of Thomasius' absolute distinction between immanent and relative divine attributes — although it retains some of the other problems common to all forms of Radical KM (e.g. the problem of the full recovery by the divine Son of the exercise of all his divine attributes at the Ascension in a way that does not overwhelm the reality of his risen and glorified human nature).[210] **This**

---

name as "I am who I am" (RSV) or "I am that I am" (KJV). Saint Thomas Aquinas took this to be a divine self-disclosure that God is Being itself ("I am he who is"), essentially infinite in all perfection, but contemporary biblical scholarship insists that the Hebrew text here does not necessarily carry that meaning. For it could also mean "I am what I am," or "I will be what I will be" (which sounds closer to the voluntarist notion that God chooses whatever he wants to be). Often overlooked in this discussion, however, is the way the New Testament conveys this same divine self-disclosure in the words of Christ, and translates it into Greek as *ego eimi* ("Before Abraham was, *I am*" Jn 8:58; cf. Mk 6:50; Jn 6:20), the same words found in the Greek Septuagint translation of Exodus 3:14 (*ego eimi ho on* :"*I am* He who is"). Given that the Greek text of Ex 3:14 carries the connotation that God is "the Being One," so these New Testament passages might be taken as an implicit extension and endorsement of that aspect of the divine self-disclosure in Exodus.

[210] This difficulty is on full display in P.T. Forsyth's *The Person and Place of Jesus Christ*, where he starts out with a model of the Incarnation which will be closely followed a few years later by H.R. Mackintosh:

> Here [in the Incarnation] we have not so much the renunciation of attributes, nor their conscious possession and concealment, as the retraction of their mode of being from actual to potential. The stress falls on the mode of existence of these qualities, and not on their

expression of Radical KM merely requires a softer version of the distinction than Thomasius had posited between the "immanent" and "relative" divine attributes. The immanent ones would be those essential divine attributes that must *always* be fully operative and manifest by a divine person, whereas the relative, or omni-attributes would be those essential attributes *capable of divine self-limitation,* including the capacity to transpose them into a state of "latency": an inability fully to access and operate them when abiding solely under the confines of another nature. In that sense, even these relative attributes could never be abandoned altogether. At least in intention, therefore, the defender of this form of Radical Kenoticism may want to uphold an understanding of God with a fairly traditional set of essential divine attributes — and avoid fully lapsing into voluntarism.

---

presence or absence. ...The attributes of God, like omniscience, are not destroyed when they are reduced to potentiality. They are only concentrated. The self-reduction, or self-retraction, of God, might be a better phrase than the self-emptying. (p. 308)

But then Forsyth speculates that the *kenosis* of the divine Son became a *plerosis* through his death and resurrection, when the Son of God finally regained his full consciousness of, and exercise of his omnipotence and omniscience without shedding his human nature. In the end, this seems to leave us with an Apollinarian or Monophysite Christ in heavenly glory:

The divine omniscience, morally retracted and potential in Christ [on earth], developed by his exercise in a life-series of moral crises and victories; till culminating in the cross and its consummate victory, it emerged into actual consciousness and use in the Glorified, to whom all things were delivered of the Father, all power given in heaven and on earth — when he was determined by the resurrection so as to be the Son of God with power. What he achieved was not the realisation of an old ideal but the reintegration of an old state. ... In finding the sheep that were lost he gradually finds the self, the mode of self, the consciousness he had renounced. Even for himself the losing of his life was the regaining of it. The diminuendo of the Kenosis went on parallel with the crescendo of a vaster Plerosis. He died to live. And his post-resurrection power is other than that of his earthly life. The form of a servant gives place again to the form of God. (p. 311)

A major problem with any version of Radical KM, however, is that in order to defend it *one has to put aside almost the entire Christian heritage of natural theology and its contribution to our understanding of the divine nature.* Thomas Morris, for example, feared that [Radical] Kenoticism requires "a real departure from what most theists, Christian as well as non-Christian, have wanted to say about the nature of God."[211] For example, the divine consciousness of a divine person would no longer be seen as necessarily immune to temporary states of extreme and extensive ignorance concerning his own divine identity and essence, and concerning the world that he made (even if he can be said to retain that knowledge in some kind of latent, or potential way in the human nature that he assumed, knowledge which he was temporarily unable fully to access, especially during his infancy). Moreover, a divine person would no longer be seen as immune to states in which he was no longer capable of accessing or utilizing some forms of his divine power. Morris fears that all this violates fundamental Christian religious intuitions about the divine nature. He writes:

> [P]art of what it means to be God is to have the properties of goodness, omnipotence, and omniscience, and to have them essentially. That is to say, it is a conceptual requirement of deity that any individual who is God is God in every possible world in which he exists, and at any and every time at which he might exist. There is no ascending to, or abdicating this throne. ...

> Well, then, on the [Radical] kenotic view, what *are* the necessary truths about divinity? What is it to be God? The kenotic suggestion, perhaps, is something like this: In order to be literally divine, it is necessary for an individual to have in all possible worlds the property of *being omnipotent unless freely and temporarily choosing to be otherwise*, the property of *being omniscient*

---

[211] Morris, *The Logic of God Incarnate*, p. 100.

unless freely and temporarily choosing to be otherwise, and likewise for omnipresence.[212]

But if God the Son can freely choose to be otherwise than omnipotent and omniscient, in the sense of *retaining little or no access to these attributes*, then these attributes could not really belong to him "essentially," only "contingently," upon his choice. In other words, a divine person could choose whether or not to be able to access his own divine attributes at any given time — and that would be voluntarism, pure and simple.

Going further in this vein, Richard Swinburne pointed out:

> The difficulty with [the Radical Kenotic] theory is that all the arguments to the existence of God are arguments of a simple source of all … to whom omnipotence and omniscience belong essentially; and any being who was divine would have to have the same essential properties as such a creator — otherwise he would be less than the creator source of all, and there would be no Incarnation of God.[213]

Counter-arguments, however, are available to defenders of the Forsyth-Mackintosh-Taylor version of Radical KM.

First of all, again, proponents of this form of Radical KM might accept that the divine "relative" or omni-attributes of God must be just as essential to the divine nature as his "immanent "attributes — at no point can a divine person shed them altogether — but the Incarnation reveals that these relative attributes are capable of self-limitation and transposition within the boundaries of human nature (in a way that renders them latent and at least partially inaccessible and inoperative for a time). **Arguably, since the divine Son never *completely* loses or abandons any divine attributes, there is no essential change in**

---

[212] Thomas V. Morris, *Our Idea of God* (Downer's Grove, IL: InterVarsity Press, 1991), p. 108 and 167.
[213] Swinburne, *The Christian God*, p. 232.

the divine nature involved in the Incarnation, and he still can be
said, in some sense and at all times, to be an essentially
omnipotent, omniscient, and omnipresent divine person (just as,
in our analogy, the mother who has temporarily rendered latent
and largely inoperative her concert-pianist skills can still
legitimately be called, in some sense, a "pianist"). For the same
reason, this version of Radical KM might be said (to that extent, at
least) to adhere to the parameters set at Chalcedon, for the divine Son
does not *completely* abandon or divest himself of any divine attributes in
the Incarnation.

Second, C. Stephen Layman has argued that a kenotic incarnation (in
what we would call a Thomasian form), would still leave Jesus as a
being fully worthy of worship, for his essential divine attributes (such
as his uncreated self-existence, and his sacrificial love) were retained
and fully operative during his incarnate state:

> Perhaps the crucial issue is this: Is a being having the attributes
> [Radical] Kenotic theorists assign to divinity *worthy of worship,*
> worthy of total devotion? Should a human refuse to worship a
> Being on the grounds that it temporarily gave up some
> knowledge and power for the sake of redeeming humankind?
> Once the latter question is posed, the answer seems obvious:
> No. … If the Son remains worthy of worship throughout the
> narrative of his redemptive work, then he remains divine. And
> I submit that he does plausibly remain worthy of worship in all
> phases of his redemptive work.[214]

Doubtless Layman's point would be strengthened further if coupled
with a theory of the Incarnation like that of Mackintosh, in which the
divine Son did not so much completely "give up" infinite knowledge
and power in the Incarnation as temporarily "transpose" these
attributes into his human nature into a latent, and only partially
accessible form.

---

[214] Layman, *Philosophical Approaches to Atonement, Incarnation and Trinity*, p.
102 and 108.

We need to draw a distinction, however, between what makes a person worthy of our admiration, loyalty and love, and what might make them actually worthy of "worship." The apostles loved, admired and followed Jesus as a great prophet, a compassionate healer, and even as the long-awaited Messiah, but arguably they did not begin to worship him as "My Lord and my God" (Jn 20:28) until after he was vindicated by divine power at the resurrection.[215] This stems from the fact that in a biblical sense to worship someone as fully divine is to acknowledge them as the Lord of all, the transcendent source of all creation and Lord of history (Is 6:1-4; Ps 95 and 96; Dan 2:21; Rom 1:18-25; Rev 4:11). A self-existent and sacrificially loving being who was *not* at the same time all-wise and all powerful (Dan 2:20), the transcendent Creator and Lord of all, simply would not have the same status as the Lord God of Israel, and should not be worshipped.[216] In fact, the Bible insists that God is by definition the maximally greatest being we can conceive — indeed, beyond what we can conceive: "Great is the Lord, and greatly to be praised, and his greatness is unsearchable [i.e., unfathomable]" (Ps 145:3; cf. Ps 89:6, and Heb 6:13-14). **Thus, unless we have grounds to believe that the divine person who was (and is) Jesus *always* fully possessed (that is, always had full access to) the infinitely great omni-attributes (omniscience, omnipotence, and omnipresence), and that in some way that divine person continually reigned as Lord over all creation and**

---

[215] They were evidently tempted to do so even earlier by remarkable displays of his power over nature, such as the calming of the storm at sea: "Who then is this, that even wind and sea obey him?" (Mk 4:41)

[216] Both Protestant New Testament scholar Richard Bauckham and Jewish theologian Pinchas Lapide have argued that early Jewish monotheism, and the monotheism of Second Temple Judaism inherited by St. Paul and St. John, contrasted the worship of Yahweh with polytheism not primarily as a numerical reality (there is one God not many) but as a functional and qualitative reality (there is only one Creator and Ruler of all); only Yahweh is the Creator and Ruler of everything that is not him, and only Yahweh is all-holy, and so worthy of worship. See the discussion of Bauckham and Lapide's work in Thomas McCall, *Which Trinity? Whose Monotheism?: Philosophical and Systematic Theologians on the Metaphysics of Trinitarian Theology* (Grand Rapids: Eerdmans, 2010), p. 59-61.

history, even simultaneously with his self-limited incarnate state as Jesus Christ (which presumably lasts forever), it would seem to be a violation of the biblical revelation to hold him as worthy of worship "in every phase of his redemptive work." And if the divine Son is not worthy of worship while he abides solely in his incarnate state, then only in a much attenuated sense can we say we encounter "God" in Christ.[217]

Third, a defender of the Forsyth-Mackintosh-Taylor version of Radical KM might argue that the belief that God is essentially omniscient and omnipotent is derived more from the heritage of ancient Greek philosophy than from the biblical revelation of God.[218] Over the centuries theologians all too often have allowed their understanding of God to be strictly governed by prior metaphysical ideas. We have not allowed Christian theology to be sufficiently criticised and corrected in the light of the Incarnation and the Cross. In Germany, Lutheran theologians Jurgen Moltmann and Eberhard Jungel argued extensively along these lines.[219] In Anglican circles, Donald Mackinnon echoed similar concerns.[220] They insisted that man has preconceptions of the form which God's self-revelation should take, and these preconceptions often inhibit him from recognising that self-revelation when it does take place. In other words, as Mackinnon asked, *what if our God should disclose himself to us as the Trinitarian, crucified God — in violation of our expectation of one who is the*

---

[217] This was the element of truth in the otherwise extreme attacks on Kenotic Christology made by the American Episcopalian priest Francis J. Hall in *The Kenotic Theory* (London: Longmans, Green and Co., 1898); see especially p. 96, where he insists that the Kenotic theory inevitably undermines the full divinity of Jesus Christ.

[218] See Quick, *Doctrines of the Creed,* p. 135 –although he does not make the argument to support Radical KM.

[219] See the summary and discussion of the perspectives of Moltmann and Jungel in Alister McGrath, *The Making of Modern German Christology* (Oxford: Blackwell, 1986), p. 192-193 and 202.

[220] Donald Mackinnon, *The Problem of Metaphysics* (Cambridge: Cambridge University Press, 1974), p. 114-121.

maximally perfect being that we can preconceive: simple, immutable, and impassible?[221] Jungel once wrote:

> [T]he mode of speaking of the Christian tradition insists that *we must be told* what we are to think of the word 'God.' It is thus presupposed that only the God who speaks himself can finally tell us what we are to understand by the word 'God.'[222]

The contributors to the volume *Exploring Kenotic Christology* (2006) put forward a similar perspective. Ronald Feenstra claims to follow the insights of the early Christian writer Tertullian when he says:

> We should not decide in advance what God can or cannot do … but we should look at what God has done. Then, in the light of what God has done, we know that even *this* is possible for God, although it may seem impossible to us.[223]

A Christian philosopher, however, may rightly ask how we can possibly conclude that "God" has done something or told us something, if we have no prior knowledge of what "God" is like and what the word "God" means? At least a rudimentary knowledge of the divine nature is required to be able to discern that such a being has "done" something in history from which we might be able to learn more about him. For this reason, C. Stephen Evans in the same volume stated more cautiously than Feenstra the same underlying point:

> I do not, of course, want to claim that one could develop an account of the nature of God entirely by beginning with the Incarnational narrative, however interpreted; if we did not have some prior understanding of what the term 'God' means

---

[221] Donald Mackinnon, *Themes in Theology: The Threefold Chord* (Edinburgh: T and T Clark, 1987), p. 159-160 and 234-235.

[222] Eberhard Jungel, *God as the Mystery of the World* (Edinburgh: T and T Clark, 1983), p. 13.

[223] Feenstra, "A Kenotic Christology of the Divine Attributes," in Evans, ed., *Exploring Kenotic Christology,* p. 160.

we could attach no meaning to the claim that Jesus was God. The fact that we must have such a prior understanding of God to formulate an account of the Incarnation does not, however, mean that our concept of God cannot be significantly reshaped in the light of that doctrine.[224]

But Evans is struggling here too. After all, where would such a "prior understanding" of the nature of God come from other than from the Old Testament (i.e., from divine revelation in human history prior to the Incarnation, where God is always held to be Almighty and All-knowing, e.g. Ps 136: 4-5 and Dan 2:20) and from natural theology (i.e., from philosophical reason reflecting on God, manifest in his creation as essentially omnipotent and omniscient; cf. Rom 1:18-21)? The idea that a divine person could choose to become incarnate by restraining some forms of the exercise of these divine omni-attributes at a particular time and place (while continuing to have full access to them, and to exercise them in a broader way elsewhere) would certainly amount to a significant "reshaping" of the traditional biblical and philosophical understanding of the divine nature. We will encounter that new perspective in our discussion of the Moderate Kenotic Model in the next chapter, as well as in the concluding chapter of this book. *But the idea found in Radical KM that a divine person could render himself unable fully to access his own essential omni-attributes seems closer to an outright contradiction of that Christian, theistic heritage.* And again: the Incarnation and the Cross may reveal unexpected depths of the divine nature, but those changes in our understanding of the divine must not be so radical that they contradict the "prior understanding" of "God" that enables us to posit an incarnation of God in the first place.

Feenstra writes:

> [I]t would be odd if the Incarnation of God contributed to our knowledge that God is triune, but contributed nothing to our understanding of the divine attributes. If Jesus Christ is the most direct revelation of God, as Christians believe he is, then surely our understanding of what God is like seems likely to

---

[224] Evans, "Kenotic Christology and the Nature of God," p. 194.

need revision in the light of what is revealed through his presence and teaching. So we need to be willing to revise our concept of God in the light of the Incarnation. …

God's revelation in the Incarnation has led Christians to the belief that God is triune, so too the revelation of God in the Incarnation, as attested by Scripture, leads to the belief that God has unsurpassable knowledge that can, during the Son's humiliation for the purpose of redemption, take a form that involves non-omniscience. Following the method for understanding the divine attributes used by kenotic Christology offers a fruitful method for deepening our understanding of the divine nature.[225]

In one respect, at least, Feenstra must be right: what God clearly has revealed through Jesus Christ must be allowed to "trump" what we *think* we already know about God from Old Testament theology and from natural theology. So, for example, through the Incarnation of the Son we come to know the richness of Divine Love as an eternal Trinitarian communion of divine persons, although this truth abides in some tension with Old Testament monotheism, and the philosophical notion of the simplicity of the divine nature.

Still, it is not clear that the Incarnation involves quite as drastic a revision of our understanding of the divine attributes as Feenstra and many Radical Kenoticists seem to think. Certainly, the proponents of Moderate KM, as we shall see, would take issue with their claim. It is one thing to say that *God can express his omni-attributes in more than one way* (e.g. God's loving omnipotence expressed in his universal sway over natural history, and expressed also in saving the world through his self-imposed human limitations, weakness and sufferings as Jesus Christ; or God's omnipresence expressed in his providential knowledge and power over the entire cosmos, and also through his unique form of presence and loving power in Bethlehem and on Calvary, with its universal, saving effects). But it is another thing to say that *God can only*

---

[225] Feenstra, "A Kenotic Christology of the Divine Attributes," p. 162 and 164.

utilize and express the fullness of his omni-attributes in these ways successively rather than simultaneously, so that in order to become incarnate God the Son can and must abandon, or render latent and at least partially inoperative — *and inaccessible even to himself!* — some forms of his own power and knowledge. *This inevitably leaves us with the voluntarist notion that a divine person can freely choose to cease to fully possess his own, allegedly "essential" omni-attributes (that is, that he can render himself unable fully to access and utilize them) in order to become incarnate.* God viewed in this way would seem to be the voluntarist God of Unconditioned Will, the equivalent of the mythological "shape-changer." Or to put it less crudely, and in more Scholastic, philosophical terminology: God cannot be the Pure Act of infinitely perfect Being if he puts aspects of his divine nature into a state of "concentrated potency" (Mackintosh's phrase) in the Incarnation. To do so makes him less than fully divine. Or, to put it in terms of Analytic Theism: it is just not clear how a divine person can be said *essentially* to possess the capacity to exercise the attributes of omniscience, omnipotence and omnipresence, *if he can render himself unable to access and utilize these attributes.* **Self-restraint of the full exercise of the divine omni-attributes at a particular time and place is one thing (as in the Moderate Kenotic Model); a divine person who can actually cripple his own capacity fully to access and exercise his omni-attributes for a time, however — much less divest himself some or all of his divine attributes altogether! — is something very different.**

Thus, even if a defender of Radical KM sincerely wants to avoid philosophical voluntarism, still, with any form of Radical KM he inevitably ends up swimming in voluntarist waters. And these waters ultimately leave us spiritually drowning, able to know God only as the arbitrary author of a series of gracious acts, rather than the One who has revealed himself, through his creation and his work of redemption, to be essentially infinite in wisdom, love, and power, the infinite source of all good from which gracious acts will always spring.

Besides, while theologians should welcome the chance to supplement and deepen from divine revelation what we can

know of God from natural theology, still, as Swinburne pointed out, preference should be given to models of the Incarnation that do not involve an actual *contradiction* of most of the heritage of Christian natural theology. That heritage is vital to discerning the fact of an incarnation of God in the first place, and vital also (among other things) to the whole evangelistic enterprise of Christian apologetics.

An Excursus on the Value of Natural Theology

In fact, it is divine revelation itself, conveyed through Scripture, which mandates the integrity of natural theology.

The classic biblical text on this matter is Romans 1:18-21, where St. Paul explains why the Gentiles are without excuse for their alienation from God, even though they did not have the benefit of the Jewish Law and the Prophets:

> For the wrath of God is revealed from heaven against all ungodliness and wickedness of men who by their wickedness suppress the truth. For what can be known about God is plain to them because God has shown it to them. Ever since the creation of the world his invisible nature, namely his eternal power and deity, has been clearly perceived in the things that have been made. So they are without excuse; for although they knew God they did not honor him as God or give thanks to him, but they became futile in their thinking, and their senseless minds were darkened.

Reformed theologian C.G. Berkouwer argued in his book *General Revelation* (1955) that St. Paul emphasizes the *rejection* by the pagans of God's general revelation through creation.[226] They "exchange" their knowledge of God for the false gods of idolatry. Thus, according to Berkouwer, St. Paul gives no encouragement here to the formation of

---

[226] C.G. Berkouwer, *General Revelation* (Grand Rapids: Eerdmans, 1955), p. 137-192.

a purely "natural" theology, from the use of reason alone. But to "exchange" that natural knowledge of God, and to be at fault for doing so, the pagans first had to possess it. Just as their conscience sometimes "excused" the pagans when they obeyed the natural moral law, of which they had at least a rudimentary understanding (Rom 2:15), so it must be possible for a pagan philosopher or poet to obtain glimpses of the truth about God: to "clearly perceive" Him reflected in nature (Rom 1:18-21) and to "feel after him and find him" in the depths of the human heart (Acts 17:27-28). It may be a rare achievement for any of them not to cast away this rudimentary knowledge of God, but it has to be possible for pagans at least to obtain it — arguably, Plato, Aristotle, Cicero, and some of the Stoics and Neo-Platonists would be good examples — and how much more likely, therefore, that Christian philosophers, using reason, and analyzing the same data of nature and of conscience, can find pathways to the reality of God. The interpretation of this passage by Reformed theologian R.C. Sproul, therefore, makes much more sense:

> God directs his wrath to mankind because of their repression of natural revelation. God may be known because he has "shown" what may be known about himself. This showing or revealing is "manifest" or clear. Since Creation itself, God's invisible attributes, though invisible, are "clearly seen" — that is, they are seen by or through the things that God made. This is almost universally understood to mean that God clearly reveals himself in and through nature, that there is a general or natural revelation.

> Does this manifest revelation "get through" to us and yield any knowledge of God? Paul does not leave us in any doubt. He says this divine revelation is "seen" and "understood." To see and understand something is to have some kind of knowledge about it. ...

> People reject the natural knowledge of God. This rejection, however, does not annihilate either the revelation or the knowledge itself. The sin of mankind is in refusing to

acknowledge the knowledge they have. They act against the truth that God reveals and they clearly receive.[227]

The *Catechism of the Catholic Church* (1994), in accord with Catholic Tradition, teaches that the existence of God the Creator "can be known with certainty from the created world by the natural light of human reason. ... Man has this capacity because he is created 'in the image of God'" (*CCC*, 36). In a section of the *Catechism* entitled "Ways of Coming to Know God," we are told:

> Created in God's image and called to know and love him, the person who seeks God discovers certain ways of coming to know him. These are called proofs for the existence of God, not in the sense of proofs in the natural sciences, but rather in the sense of "converging and convincing arguments" which allow us to attain certainty about the truth. (*CCC*, 31)

We should notice here (1) that our human capacity to seek and find God by reason, reflecting on his creation, is said to be rooted in the biblical truth that human beings are created in the "image" of a rational Creator (cf. Gen 1:26; Jn 1:1), and (2) that the *Catechism* does not necessarily promise that we can have deductive proofs of the existence of God, and "certainty" in that sense; it may be that our rational certainty will be based instead on solely inductive or abductive arguments: evidences that converge toward a strongly probable case for the existence of the Creator. This would give us "moral certainty" rather than deductive certainty, similar to the way converging lines of evidence in a court of law can give us a form of rational certainty, commonly described as a verdict "true beyond a reasonable doubt."

Whether or not these "converging and convincing arguments" can be deductive proofs (such as the famous five ways to the existence of God

---

[227] R.C. Sproul, *What is Reformed Theology?* (Grand Rapids: Baker, 1997), p. 15-16. Sproul is using the New King James Version translation of the passage, another "close" translation of the Greek text, in that respect much like the RSV that I used to quote this passage.

in the *Summa Theologiae* of St. Thomas Aquinas) remains a matter for debate among Christian philosophers. What should be beyond doubt, according to the *Catechism*, is that rational "certainty" regarding the existence of God is in fact obtainable. The *Catechism* points to two legitimate points of departure for such arguments (*CCC*, 31-33): from "the physical world" (that is, from movement, becoming, contingency, and the world's order and beauty), and from within "the human person" (that is, from human openness to truth and beauty, our sense of moral goodness, our freedom and the voice of conscience within, and from our longings for the infinite and for happiness).

These rational pathways to the reality of God are not only encouraged by the Catholic magisterium, they are also indicated in Holy Scripture. Since the Bible was written and compiled primarily for believers, it assumes rather than tries to demonstrate the existence and nature of God. Nevertheless, the Scriptures offer plenty of indications as to how rational argumentation for the reality of God fruitfully can proceed. For example, the pathway from the beauty and order of nature to the reality of the Creator is suggested in Psalm 19:1: "The heavens declare the glory of God, and the firmament proclaims his handiwork." Similarly, in Acts 14:15-17, St. Paul argues that nature attests to the work of "a living God who made the heaven and the earth, and the sea and all that is in them." In particular, he points to the fact that "In past generations [God] allowed all the nations to walk in their own ways; yet he did not leave himself without witness, for he did good and gave you from heaven rains and fruitful seasons, satisfying your hearts with food and gladness" (v. 16-17). A pathway to the reality of God from within the human soul is suggested in Romans 2:14-15, where St. Paul writes of the natural moral law that is "written on the hearts" of the Gentiles by God, in their "conscience." This implies that the natural moral law in the hearts of all people is evidence of the work of a supernatural moral Lawgiver. Furthermore, in Athens St. Paul appeals to the nearness of God to every human heart (Acts 17:27-28), which gives us hope that people everywhere "might feel after him and find him… for 'in him we live and move and have our being,' as even some of your [pagan] poets have said, 'for we are indeed his offspring.'" The implication here is that God gives to all people an experience of his presence, and a corresponding longing and desire for him as a pathway at least to a rudimentary knowledge of himself. In his Encyclical Letter *Fides et Ratio* (1998), Pope St. John Paul II discussed these same Scripture passages:

> In Athens, we read, Saint Paul entered into discussion with "certain Epicurean and Stoic philosophers" (17:18); and exegetical analysis of his speech at the Areopagus has revealed frequent allusions to popular beliefs deriving for the most part from Stoicism. This is by no means accidental. If pagans were to understand them, the first Christians could not refer only to "Moses and the prophets" when they spoke. They had to point as well to natural knowledge of God and to the voice of conscience in every human being (cf. Rom. 1:19-21; 2:14-15; Acts 14:16-17). Since in pagan religion this natural knowledge had lapsed into idolatry (cf. Rom. 1:21-32), the Apostle judged it wiser in his speech to make the link with the thinking of the philosophers, who had always set in opposition to the myths and mystery cults notions more respectful of divine transcendence. (no. 36)

In Romans 1:18-21, St. Paul evidently refers to a simple, cosmological argument for the existence of God that lies within the capability of all people, but that most people suppress. That this was his intended meaning becomes clear when we compare Romans 1:18-21 with the deutero-canonical passage that he was alluding to here, that is, Wisdom 13:1-9:

> For all men who were ignorant of God were foolish by nature; and they were unable from the good things that are seen to know him who exists, nor did they recognize the craftsman while paying heed to his works; but they supposed that either fire or wind or swift air, or the circle of the stars, or turbulent water, or the luminaries of heaven were the gods that rule the world. If through delight in the beauty of these things men assumed them to be gods, let them know how much better than these is their Lord, for the author of beauty created them.

And if men were amazed at their power and working, let them perceive from them how much more powerful is he who formed them. *For from the greatness and beauty of created things comes a corresponding perception of their Creator.* Yet these men are little to be blamed, for perhaps they go astray while seeking God and desiring to find him. For as they live among his works they keep searching, and they trust in what they see, because the things that are seen are beautiful. Yet again, not even they are to be excused; for if they had the power to know so much that they could investigate the world, how did they fail to find sooner the Lord of these things?

Here the author of the book of Wisdom claims that as pagan peoples inferred the existence of the gods behind the beauty and power of the forces of nature, so they should have been able to infer that there is One even more beautiful and powerful who created and formed all things, their "craftsman" and their "Lord." Saint Paul's language and train of thought in Romans 1:19-21 seems in part to be an echo of this passage from the book of Wisdom, a deutero-canonical book with which his audience in Rome would have been familiar, because the book usually formed part of the Greek Septuagint version of the Old Testament that was in common use among the early Christian churches outside of Palestine. Of course, neither Wisdom nor Romans refer to arduous causal proofs for the existence of God as the basis for this natural knowledge of him, but to the simplest insight of the "man on the street" that there must be a First Cause, a Supreme Power behind all natural powers, that explains how everything came to be as it is. The universe just does not explain its own order (that is, its design and beauty), its capacity to change (or undergo "motion"), or even its own existence. Surely, there must be a Creator and Craftsman as the ultimate explanation for everything. For the man on the street, this is simply the Principle of Sufficient Reason that he uses in everyday life, applied to "the whole show."

In short, natural theology provides us with that basic, "prior understanding" of the nature of God that Evans admitted is essential to discerning that "God" has become incarnate in

history as Jesus Christ in the first place. It also provides Christian apologetics with a rational *preambula fidei* which helps to draw unbelievers to accept the existence of God, and thereby serves as a springboard to faith in God and his Son.

Anglican Evangelical theologian J.I. Packer claimed that natural theology can add nothing of substance to dogmatic theology:

> We do not need natural theology for information. Everything that natural theology, operating upon general revelation, can discern about the Creator and his ways is republished for us in those very Scriptures that refer to the general revelation of these things (see Ps. 19; Acts 14:17; 17:27-28; Rom. 1:18-32; 2:9-16). And Scripture, which we rightly receive on the ground that it is God's own word of testimony and law, is a better source of knowledge about God than natural theology can ever be.[228]

Roman Catholic theologians would object, however, that while natural theology may not give us brand new, entirely extra-Scriptural, supplementary information about God, it is surely necessary for the clearest interpretation of divine revelation that we can attain. It helps unfold the truths implicit in Scripture itself. For example, the Scriptures tell us that God is "eternal" (Is 46:9-10; Heb 9:14; II Pet 3:8), but do not fully or clearly explain for us what that eternity means. Does God dwell merely on a different linear time-scale than his human creatures, or does He have all linear time present before His gaze, and present before His infinite knowledge and power? Bold would be the exegete who would claim to be able to settle that question *sola scriptura*! Again, the Bible says that God is in some sense "changeless" (Ps 102: 25-27; Jas 1:17). But what can this mean? And if we can speak analogically about God, because there is some kind of "analogy of being" between God and His creatures (Ps 19:1; Rom 1:18-21), and especially between God and His human creatures (Gen 1:26), is it also true that we can make some univocal statements about Him? These

---

[228] J.I. Packer, *Knowing God* (Downers Grove, IL: InterVarsity Press, 1995), p. 46.

are difficult, yet far from unimportant matters, and Holy Scripture does not seem to be sufficiently perspicuous, all by itself, to answer such questions for us. **It would seem that dogmatic theology can use the aid of the long tradition of Christian metaphysics, or "natural (rational) theology," even regarding some of the most basic biblical truths about the nature of God.**

Pope St. John Paul II endorsed this use of philosophical reason in the work of dogmatic theology in *Fides et Ratio*:

> For its part, dogmatic theology must be able to articulate the universal meaning of the mystery of the One and Triune God and of the economy of salvation, both as a narrative and, above all, in the form of argument. It must do so, in other words, through concepts formulated in a critical and universally communicable way. Without philosophy's contribution, it would in fact be impossible to discuss theological issues such as, for example, the use of language to speak about God, the personal relations within the Trinity, God's creative activity in the world, the relationship between God and man, or Christ's identity as true God and true man. This is no less true of the different themes of moral theology, which employ concepts such as the moral law, conscience, freedom, personal responsibility and guilt, which are in part defined by philosophical ethics (no. 66).

Conclusion

Why this digression on the value of natural theology? To begin with, it is important to recognize the full cost of adopting any Radical version of KM. As we have seen, one might be able to state a version of Radical KM that seems intelligible and coherent in itself, and fits to some extent with an orthodox (Chalcedonian) understanding of Jesus Christ — Forsyth, Mackintosh and Taylor seem to have come closest to doing so — *but how would one fully accomplish this task without embracing a "voluntarist" understanding of the divine nature that overthrows the whole enterprise of Christian natural theology, and that undermines the biblical self-*

revelation of God as essentially all-knowing, and infinite in love? That is a heavy cost indeed, as I have endeavored to show. After all, even this (most defensible) version of Radical KM posits that a divine person can render himself unable fully to access or utilize allegedly "essential" attributes of his own divine nature — which surely requires Christian theology radically to reconfigure its understanding of the nature of God (and in a way that fits with no version of Christian natural theology known to this author).

This is certainly one reason why Anglican theologians historically have been reluctant to embrace any version of Radical KM. As we saw in the Introduction, Anglicanism traditionally holds a high view of the goodness and dignity of the created world, and of God as manifested throughout his creation, a divine manifestation amenable at least to partial understanding by human reason. That is why Anglican theologians often have attempted to fashion a synthesis between what they saw as the best of human philosophy based on rational reflection on the world, and the revealed truths of the faith. Whether they drew primarily upon the philosophy of Plato (e.g. Maurice and Westcott), or Aquinas (Hooker and Mascall) or Heidegger (Macquarrie) or Tillich (Robinson) or Whitehead (Thornton and Pittenger) or some form of philosophical Idealism (Dubose, Gore and Temple), or some form of Analytic Theism (Hebblethwaite, Swinburne and Brown), Anglicans traditionally have looked to various forms of natural theology as an aid – albeit an imperfect one, and subject to continual revision — in the comprehension of God through his creation, and the penetration of the mysteries of divine revelation. Thus, broadly defined, at least, "natural theology" usually has found a place within the Anglican theological tradition.[229] For Anglicans, the Word made manifest in

---

[229] This does not mean that Anglicans have always accepted the traditional Roman Catholic understanding of "natural theology." John Macquarrie, for example, argued for a "new style" of natural theology, one that would be "descriptive" of the human condition in the world and its openness to God, rather seeking to demonstrate the existence and nature of God in a "deductive" fashion. Nevertheless, even this new approach, according to Macquarrie, would preserve the essential features of any Christian "natural theology." It would "provide a bridge between our everyday thinking and experience and the

human flesh is always the same Logos through whom the whole world was made, manifest throughout creation (Jn 1:1-14).[230] Any theory of the Incarnation that seems to rupture the integrity of either of those two ways that God manifests himself to us, or the harmony between them, is thereby rendered suspect.

In addition, as we have seen, the Anglican theological tradition historically has sought to remain true to the faith of the ancient and relatively undivided Church of the early Fathers, the first four Ecumenical Councils (including the Chalcedonian definition of the Incarnation) and the Apostles and Nicene Creeds. **Of course, all versions of Kenoticism require at least some revision of the Patristic consensus that the divine nature is absolutely immutable and impassible. A God so-conceived would be incapable of the kind of self-limitation and exposure to human suffering that a kenotic theory of the Incarnation requires. Radical KM in any form, however, represents an even more extreme, "voluntarist" departure from what the ancient Church would have recognized as the nature of God and the manner of the Incarnation.** This too has rendered Radical KM somewhat suspect as a way forward for Anglican Christology.

By way of summary and review, we can say that *any* version of Radical KM involves at least four intractable problems:

---

matters about which the theologian talks: it will relate religious discourse to all other areas of discourse ... and investigate the universal conditions that make any religion or theology possible," including "rational reflection as a way of testing or even confirming what has been given in revelatory experience." Macquarrie, *Principles of Christian Theology,* p. 57-58.

[230] On this characteristic feature of a major stream of Anglican theology going back to Hooker, see Archbishop Michael Ramsey, *The Anglican Spirit,* p. 11: "For what God does in revelation brings to a climax what God does in nature; what God does in nature is a necessary key to the understanding of what God does in revelation." As Charles Gore put it: "If the Word or Son reveals God through the Incarnation, He has previously revealed Him in the body of nature through its beauty, order, and power" (Charles Gore, *The Incarnation of the Son of God.* London: John Murray, 1891), p. 41.

The Incarnation

(1) Radical KM tells us that the divine Son assumed an incarnate state in which he was not able — at the same time, and apart from the human nature he assumed — to be the Lord of all creation and cosmic history. The unique ability to do such things would seem to be essential to the biblical view of God. Thus, on biblical principles, the divine Son was not worthy of worship while he existed *solely* in such a radically self-limited state. **In other words, from a biblical perspective at least, the divine person who became Jesus Christ arguably was *no longer fully divine* while living solely in his limited, "incarnate" form.** The biblical doctrine of the Incarnation, however, is that Jesus was "Emmanuel, God with us" (Mt 1: 23; Jn 20:28), the fully divine Son dwelling among us in a fully human way.

(2) Radical KM usually asserts the resumption by the risen and ascended Lord of full access to, and the full exercise of his divine omni-attributes (omnipotence, omniscience, and omnipresence) — the very attributes which enable him to act as Lord of creation and cosmic history — but the theory cannot explain how those divine attributes do not overwhelm the reality and limitations of his glorified human nature. **Thus, the risen and ascended Jesus ends up as the Monophysite Christ, *no longer fully human.***

(3) **Radical KM implies that a divine person can render himself (temporarily, at least) *unable fully to access or utilize some of his essential divine attributes* (such as the capacity to exercise omnipotence, and omniscience). This necessarily involves the adoption of a "voluntarist" view of the divine nature:** that God can render latent and temporarily inaccessible to himself — or even divest himself completely — of some of the properties that traditionally and essentially define him as "God." It is unclear how the divine omni-attributes can be held to be "essential" to the divine nature, rather than just "contingent" on such a theory. **As a**

result, Radical KM overthrows almost the entire enterprise of Christian natural theology and rational apologetics, integral both to dogmatic theology and to the Church's evangelistic witness.

(4) **Radical KM depends on a theistic voluntarism that undermines our biblical and philosophical assurance that the divine nature is essentially all-knowing, and all-loving.** God defined essentially as Unconditioned Will can only be the arbitrary agent of a series of gracious acts toward humanity, from which no deeper conclusions about his divine nature legitimately can be drawn. Some proponents of Radical KM (e.g. Thomasius and Mackintosh) insisted that God is essentially both Absolute, Unconditioned Will *and* Infinite Love. Besides the danger of contradiction between these two divine attributes, so conceived, however, positing that God is essentially infinitely loving Will, but not also essentially infinite in Knowledge, hardly fits with the biblical and mainstream Christian understanding of the divine nature.

Finally, it is important to note that most of the critique of Kenoticism over the last century and a half has been focused on its radical forms. In fact, some of the Anglican theologians who offered sharp critiques of Radical Kenoticism (e.g. Weston, Temple, and Swinburne) were themselves proponents of a moderate version of Kenoticism without giving it a "kenotic" label. The point is that the main stream of the Anglican tradition of Kenoticism has not run through these more "radical" configurations. If we are seeking to locate that valuable heritage, we will need to look elsewhere.

Chapter Four

Moderate, Two-Minds, or Two-Spheres Kenoticism: the Anglican Stream

The Moderate Kenotic Model of the Incarnation (hereafter: "Moderate KM") offers an alternative to the Radical versions of Kenoticism that we have explored so far. Much like Two-Nature Christology, Moderate KM states that in Jesus Christ we have one divine person, the Son of God, in two natures, divine and human, with both sets of attributes present and fully operative *simultaneously*. **According to Moderate KM, however,** *without ceasing his universal role as the Logos who oversees, upholds and guides all of creation, the divine Son enters into history in a unique way in the Incarnation: by an act of the self-limitation and self-restraint of the exercise of his omni-attributes, he conforms himself to an additional, fully human mode of consciousness and will. In his divine nature, therefore, he is able to add to his store of experience an experience of all the conditions and limitations, joys and sorrows of an authentically human life as Jesus of Nazareth.* **Moreover, within the sphere of his incarnate state the divine Son acts solely through human limitations, expressing and revealing himself in fully human terms.**

In some respects, therefore, Moderate KM is very close to traditional Two-Nature Christology, since in Moderate KM the Incarnation involves the assumption of an *additional* sphere or state, rather than (as in Radical KM) the reduction of the divine nature of the Son, without remainder, to the confines of a human state. But as O.C. Quick pointed out, that addition necessarily involves an experience of human limitations, and therefore an element of change in the divine nature itself: "Granted that the Word, without ceasing his creative and sustaining work, added something to it, what he added is precisely that experience in which his divine consciousness was limited and his divine state surrendered."[231]

Frank Weston suggested that this understanding of the Incarnation fits well with the New Testament. Regarding the classic kenotic Scripture passage, Philippians 2:5-8, Weston remarked:

> Saint Paul, in the passage in question, is presenting our Lord to us as an exemplar of the race in humility. Of what exactly, then, did He empty Himself in order to be a true example of humility? The Apostle contrasts equality with God and a state of servitude; freedom and limitation. There is no evident hint that our Lord laid aside the omnipotence and omniscience of God in order to become man. The Apostle's point seems to be that the eternal Son deliberately chose to empty Himself of all the characteristics that mark the state of equality with God, and to make his own the characteristics that mark the state of human slavery. The Incarnation meant for him not only taking our manhood, but assuming the characteristics of slavery.
>
> Now slavery is a purely negative state. It is the state of a man who is by right possessed of all human qualities, but by the accident of his state is prevented from the exercise of them, either in part or altogether. He is at the mercy of his master, whose will may change from day to day, and who may at any moment free his slave from his limitations. Were he to do so, the slave would be found to possess all the proper attributes of manhood. Thus slavery is based as a state, not on the absence of rights and powers, but on the absence of the actual liberty to exercise them. Limitation, therefore, and not abandonment, is the keynote of slavery.
>
> For St. Paul, the divine love of the eternal Son is the motive that has constrained Him to enslave Himself in order that men may come to give Him love for love. Under this law of loving

---

[231] Quick, *Doctrines of the Creed*, p. 138.

self-limitation the Son lives, possessing all His rights as God, but hindered from the exercise of them. The limits of the self-emptying are fixed. A slave cannot part with the essential attributes of manhood: he is merely hindered from the exercise of them. **And on this analogy Christ may not be said to have been self-emptied of any essential attributes of God or Godhead: He merely limited himself in, or restrained Himself from, the free use of the divine powers that are his.**[232]

Stated in this way, the Radical Kenotic theory of Forsyth-Mackintosh-Taylor would seem to fit with this biblical passage almost as well as Moderate KM. As we have already seen, however, *Weston was convinced that any theory of the Incarnation in which the divine Son relinquishes the universal operation of his omni-attributes, ceasing for a time to exercise his cosmic role, does not measure up to Scripture or Tradition*:

> The general tendency of the New Testament is towards the doctrine of the permanence of the universal life and cosmic functions of the eternal Word. The Pauline doctrine of the Son is that He is the expression of God, the divine self-manifestation, from whom all things come, in whom all things are, and to whom all things move. Without Him the universe would not be [I Cor 8:6; Col 1:15-20]. To this the Epistle to the Hebrews also witnesses [1:1-3]. And all down the ages the Church has received and maintained that the Word never for a moment ceased from his activity in upholding the creation.[233]

Church historians do not have to look far to find evidence for Weston's claim here about what the Church has believed "all down the ages." For example, St. Irenaeus of Lyons in the second century wrote that the Son of God "was made man, while all the same existing in the world and invisibly sustaining all creation."[234] The great Patristic

[232] Weston, *The One Christ*, p. 131-132.
[233] Ibid., p. 128-129.
[234] St. Irenaeus, *Adv. Haer. V.18.3.*

theologian of the Incarnation, St. Athanasius (d.373), had this to say on the matter:

> He was not, as might be imagined, circumscribed in the body, nor, while present in the body, was he absent elsewhere; nor, while he moved in the body, was the universe left void of his working and providence; but, thing most marvelous, Word as he was, so far from being contained by anything, he rather contained all things himself; and just as while present in the whole of creation, he is at once distinct in being from the universe, and present in all things by his own power... thus, even while present in a human body and himself quickening it, he was, without inconsistency, quickening the universe as well.[235]

Weston's knew very well, however, that the particular theory of the Incarnation that he advocated could not be found in its fullness anywhere in the Christian tradition before the nineteenth century (although there may be the beginnings of such a perspective in the writings of St. Irenaeus of Lyons, Origen, St. Gregory of Nyssa and Bl. Theodoret).[236] **None of the ancient Fathers or medieval saints clearly held or stated that in the Incarnation the Son undergoes change in his divine nature, self-limiting and restraining the exercise of his divine omni-attributes at a particular time and place in order to become incarnate (without ceasing his universal, cosmic role), and thereby assuming human experiences of change and suffering into himself. Moderate KM, therefore, necessarily involves at least some modification of traditional notions of divine immutability and impassibility.**

---

[235] Athanasius, *On the Incarnation of the Word* I.17.1 in Edward R. Hardy, *Christology of the Later Fathers,* Library of Christian Classics (Philadelphia: Westminster Press, 1954), p. 70-71. Pope St. Damasus was even more direct in his *Tome* (382 AD) when he wrote: "Anyone who says that the Son, while incarnate on earth, was not in heaven with the Father, is a heretic." (section 13)

[236] Gore, *Dissertations*, p. 99-100, 108-112, 118-119, 131-132, and 140.

Weston himself was inconsistent on the point. On the one hand, he stated that any change in the divine nature is impossible:

> While, then, we strongly maintain that the Son of God suffered only in respect to His human nature, we must not minimize the fact that he who suffered is actually the Son of God Himself. We must not think of the Incarnate as if He is two selves: the one divine, standing aloof from the Passion; the other human, or divine-human, the subject of the sufferings and death. The Self of the Incarnate is one and only one. He who was mocked, scourged and crucified, was not conscious of another self that could not in any way be mocked or scourged or crucified.[237]

However, if the divine nature of the Son, including the divine range of consciousness and experience, is not affected in any way by his incarnate life and sufferings, it is hard to see how Weston can avoid the critique of Two-Nature Christology we met earlier (and that Weston himself endorsed): that it makes the Son in his divine nature a mere spectator of his own human life and death (recall our analogy for TNC in Chapter One: the relationship between a video-game player and his on-screen character). Weston seemed to be aware of this problem:

> The Incarnate really felt all the sufferings Himself, in His divine self: and the medium of His suffering was the manhood in which He had willed to live a life of limited self-consciousness.[238]

> [W]e are far too ignorant of the nature of God to be able to measure the effect upon Him of the assumption of manhood ....[239]

---

[237] Weston, *The One Christ*, p. 208.
[238] Ibid., p. 210.
[239] Ibid., p. 163.

For it is necessary to bear in mind that although the state of the Incarnation is merely the sum of new relationships, yet it was only entered at the cost of very real self-sacrifice, and continuance in it involves very real humiliation. God cannot be related to sinners through manhood without something of that which in us would be a sense of humiliation.[240]

One might ask: where does this "sense of humiliation" reside, if not in the divine nature of God the Son, "the divine self" who "really felt" those human sufferings as his own, and who bore the "cost" of that self-sacrifice? And that means we must ascribe the experience of change and suffering, in some respect at least, to the divine nature itself.[241]

---

[240] Ibid., p. 165.

[241] Weston struggled to fit his theory of the Incarnation with the traditional doctrine of the ancient Fathers of the Church that the divine nature is completely immutable and impassible:

> [W]hen God becomes man God's knowledge of Himself is a knowledge of Himself as man, as it were an added knowledge, external to His eternal self-knowledge. Each added relationship of God to His creation is both the occasion and the condition of a new form of self-knowledge or self-consciousness.

> If it be answered that in saying this we postulate a change in the content of the divine knowledge, the answer is that since God is eternal, and all that is is the expression of His eternal mind and Will, there was in fact no real change. There was only an expression in terms of created life of what was hidden in the Divine mind. (*The One Christ*, p. 178-179).

It could be argued, therefore, that what was hidden from all eternity in the divine nature was precisely the capacity to self-limit the exercise of his divine attributes at a certain location in time and space, and thereby to experience and share the sufferings of his creatures. We shall return to this dilemma later in the concluding chapter of this book.

Early Proponents of Moderate KM: Martensen and Gore

Moderate KM actually originated with the Danish Lutheran Bishop Hans Lassen Martensen (1808-1884). **In his work *Christian Dogmatics* in 1849, Martensen claimed that there is a "double-life" in Christ: not within the human nature of Jesus, but within the divine Logos. In his divine nature the Logos continually pervaded and sustained the world while simultaneously, from his servant form as Jesus of Nazareth, "God felt the limitations of his human nature as his own limitations."**[242] Martensen explained:

> He lives a double life in his world-creating and his world completing activity. As the pure *Logos of Deity* he works through the kingdom of nature by his all pervading presence, and creates the presuppositions and conditions of the revelation of his all-completing love. As the *Christ* he works through the kingdom of grace, of redemption, and perfection, and points back to his pre-existence.[243]

Martensen's Christology was heavily based on Hegelian philosophy, and his formulation of a "double-life," "two-centers" or "two-spheres" version of Kenoticism lacked sufficient clarity. Weston provided the best summary of Martensen's position in *The One Christ*:

> The main points on which [Martensen] insists are these. The Logos lives a double life: He continues in His full life of glory and divine activity as the Word of the Father, and within the sphere of the Incarnation He also lives a life of limitation and poverty, marked by the renunciation of all true exercise of the physical attributes of Godhead. ... Thus, in the Christ we see not the naked God, but the fullness of deity framed within the ring of humanity, and the physical [omni] attributes of

---

[242] H. Martensen, *Christian Dogmatics* (Edinburgh: T and T Clark, 1880), p. 264-270.
[243] H. Martensen, *Christian Dogmatics*, 1871 edition, cited in Brown, *Divine Humanity*, p. 61.

Godhead are in some sense perfected and vitalized by their expression in terms of humanity. …

In all this we see an advance in the idea of Kenosis: the eternal Son remains master of His powers, however, He may restrain them; and the emptying of them is not the putting of them away, but the pouring of them into a personal manhood, in the measure in which they could be assimilated. …

The implication that divine attributes of the physical order are perfected by their expression in manhood may be accounted for by [Martensen's] plea that the Logos has eternal relations with creation; relations which at first existed in essence only, but later were manifest in visible form. Thus the Incarnation of the Word is really the crown of His self-expression as the eternal Word. The completeness of the divine Being required, as it were, the manifestation of the divine world-activities in terms of creation.[244]

In this idea that God needs to complete and perfect his divine nature through his activity in time as Creator, and through the crown of his creative work in the Incarnation, we can see Martensen's Hegelianism on full display. That God somehow needs to accomplish all this in order to perfect himself, however, seems far removed from the biblical revelation of the Sovereignty of God ("… as though he needed anything," Acts 17: 25). Besides, the historic Christian tradition is that God's love for creation is an expression of selfless generosity precisely because he does *not* need to love us; he creates, redeems, and sanctifies to meet the needs of his creatures to be and to be blessed, not to meet his own needs. Precisely because God is infinitely perfect Being, all his acts *ad extra* can be seen as acts of *agape*: pure, selfless, self-giving love.

The main problem with Martensen's theory of the Incarnation, however, was that he did not make it clear how the "double-life" of the Son, operating from two psychological centers or spheres

---

[244] Weston, *The One Christ*, p. 121-123.

of consciousness at once, can be construed as belonging to one person, rather than two persons. We shall return to this important issue later.

In the late 19th and early 20th centuries, some Anglican theologians struggled to state Moderate KM in a more coherent fashion. In his reflections on the Incarnation, Bishop Charles Gore, for example, sounded at times like Thomasius, claiming that in the Incarnation the divine Son "abandoned" his own divine prerogatives in order to dwell among us as a fully human being.[245] But at other times Gore wrote instead merely of the abandonment of the "exercise" of certain divine attributes.[246] In fact, in his *Dissertations on Subjects Connected with the Incarnation,* he stated his preference for the theory of Martensen, with the Son operating during the Incarnation from two spheres or ranges of consciousness, one limited and kenotic, the other unlimited and non-kenotic.[247]

Gore's perspective was driven by a strong desire to remain faithful to the apostolic testimony to the authentic humanity and limited human consciousness of Jesus, manifested in the synoptic Gospels:

> [T]he self-sacrifice of the Incarnation appears to have lain, in great measure, *so far as human words can express it*, in His refraining from the divine mode of consciousness within the sphere of His human life, that He might really enter into human experience.[248]

> There are constantly attributed to our Lord human experiences which seem inconsistent with practical omniscience. Thus, He

[245] For example, See Gore, *Dissertations*, p. 206.
[246] Ibid., p. 90.
[247] Ibid., p. 93 and 192-193; cf. the juxtaposition of language of the divine Son "abandoning what he possessed" with that of "ceasing to exercise certain natural prerogatives of the divine existence" in Gore, *The Incarnation of the Son of God*, p. 158. See also David Brown's discussion of Gore's evolving kenotic viewpoint in *Divine Humanity*, p. 138-142.
[248] Gore, *Dissertations*, p. 97.

expresses surprise at the conduct of His parents, and the unbelief of men, and the barrenness of the fig tree, and the slowness of His disciples' faith. He expresses surprise on many occasions, and therefore we must believe he really felt it; and on other occasions He asks for information and receives it, as when He came down from the Mount of Transfiguration and was presented with the child which the disciples had failed to cure, He asked the father, like any physician, 'How long time is it since this hath come unto him?' and when He is on His way to heal Lazarus, He asks 'Where have ye laid him?' It is of course a common form of human speech for men to ask questions in order to draw out the feelings of others or to reproach them, without any implication of ignorance on their own part. Thus, some of our Lord's questions are not asked for the sake of information — and this is apparently true of all those asked after the resurrection — but there are a number on the other hand of which this is not at all a natural explanation. They represent a natural need for information.[249]

It was only because the future was not clear that he could pray: 'O my Father, if it be possible, let this cup pass away from me.'...

Though our Lord knew so well, and told so plainly, the moral conditions of the great judgement to come, and discerned so clearly its particular application in the destruction of Jerusalem, yet he expressly declared, as St. Matthew as well as St. Mark assure us, that of the day and the hour of His second coming no one knew except the Father, 'not even the angels of heaven, neither the Son'; and we cannot hold this declaration apart from the other indications that are given to us of limited human consciousness. It may fairly be contrasted with the phrase used to the apostles after the resurrection, 'It is not *for*

---

[249] Ibid., p. 82.

you to know times or seasons, which the Father hath set within his own authority.'[250]

Our Lord exhibits insight and foresight of prophetic quality. … But He never enlarges our stock of natural knowledge, physical or historical, out of the divine omniscience.

The recognition of these phenomena of our Lord's life leads us to the conclusion that up to the time of His death He lived and taught, He thought and was inspired and was tempted, as true and proper man, under the limitations of consciousness which alone makes possible a really human experience.[251]

For Gore, the most difficult aspect of Martensen's two spheres theory was trying to conceive how the divine Son, self-limited to an authentic human consciousness in his humanity, could at the same time sustain the whole of creation. Gore speculated that the best analogy for this two-minds state of the divine Son while incarnate is the act of human sympathy. The divine Son retained his attributes of omniscience and omnipotence in the sphere of his cosmic role, even as he entered fully and sympathetically into the experience of the human condition as Jesus of Nazareth:

To sympathise is to put oneself in another's place. Redemptive sympathy is the act of the greater and better putting himself at the point of view of the lower and the worse. He must not abandon his own higher standing-ground if he is to benefit the object of his compassion; but remaining essentially what he was he must also find himself in the place of the lower; he must come to look at things as he looks at them; he must learn things over again from his point of view. … It is the grown one learning to speak as a child; it is the Divine putting himself at the point of view of the human. …

---

[250] Ibid., p. 83-84.
[251] Ibid., p. 87.

All real sympathy of the unconditioned for the conditioned demands, as far as we can see, real self-limitation.[252]

David Brown offered a critique of Gore's comparison of the Incarnation with the human act of sympathy: "[T]he problem with the suggested analogy is that in sympathy we merely *imagine* ourselves different from what we are; we do not become something different. There is also the further difficulty that it is far from clear that the notion of sympathy makes sense when extended to something of which one has had no experience at all."[253] Perhaps Gore could defend himself against the first charge, at least, by saying that in acts of sympathy, while we do not change our metaphysical status from one kind of being into another, we do significantly modify our own being, taking on new perspectives and feelings we did not have before.

A good summary of Gore's overall perspective can be found in Weston:

> Dr. Gore, Bishop of Oxford … appears to follow the line that leads to the conception of the Logos as remaining in supreme control over His divine powers, regarding Him as abandoning their use entirely within the limited sphere of the Incarnation: those divine powers, that is, which may be supposed to be incompatible with the proper development of His manhood. Thus with the extreme Kenotists [sic] he can practically differentiate the moral [or immanent] attributes from the physical [or relative]; but with Martensen he refuses to postulate a cessation of the Logos from His cosmic functions; and he marks off a state within which he argues for a relative abandonment by the Logos of His physical attributes. …
>
> Briefly stated, the Bishop's theory is this. The eternal Son, in His cosmic position as Logos continued in the full possession and exercise of His divine prerogatives and powers. But within

---

[252] Ibid. p. 218-220.
[253] Brown, *The Divine Trinity*, p. 247; italics mine.

a certain sphere, for a fixed period, for a definite purpose, He willed to abandon some of those prerogatives and powers, and to live entirely and personally, under conditions of manhood identical with our own, except as to sin. Of this abandonment the purpose is our redemption and the motive His infinite love.

Thus we are to think of Him as being actually ignorant, and, in matters unconnected with His mission, accepting and holding the views of His contemporaries. But in all that concerns His work of redemption, He is to be acknowledged and obeyed as an infallible Teacher, the true divine light of the world.[254]

Gore's position failed to convince most theologians at the time, and its shortcomings remain apparent today.

First of all, what can it mean to say that the second person of the Trinity "abandoned" his omni-attributes in the Incarnation if on another level he was still accessing and utilizing them to uphold and guide the universe? As Weston pointed out, the word "abandonment" is just not accurate here, because if the Son merely holds those attributes to some degree in abeyance in the sphere of His incarnate life, while exercising them in other ways elsewhere, that is really an act of *self-restraint*, a limitation of the *exercise* of divine attributes by the Logos *asarkos* (that is, by the eternal, unlimited Logos) in relation to a certain place and time, not the "abandonment" or loss of those attributes.[255]

Second, Weston worried about how we can understand the self-consciousness of Jesus. On Gore's theory, Weston claimed, "It seems possible to argue that the Word as self-abandoned has a different self-consciousness from the eternal Word as unlimited ...."[256] As we shall see later, Weston's own version of Moderate KM has to face a similar difficulty.

---

[254] Weston, *The One Christ* (1914), p. 124-125.

[255] Ibid., p. 127.

[256] Ibid., p. 126.

In the end, Gore's approach often seems to be an unsuccessful attempt to stick together aspects of the theories of Martensen and Thomasius. Moreover, as we have seen, his analogy for the Incarnation with the act of human sympathy has significant limitations. As a result, while his reflections on the mystery of the Incarnation were not fully convincing in themselves, they did spawn several generations of Anglican theologians who saw the value of Moderate Kenoticism in general, and attempted to improve upon the theory.

As we have seen, many theologians in the first decades of the twentieth century embraced Kenoticism because they thought it might give them a way to harmonize advances in the understanding of the historical contextualization of human consciousness, and the historical criticism of the Gospels, with an orthodox understanding of Jesus Christ as a divine person incarnate. Historical criticism tended to say that like any human being, Jesus must have grown and developed in knowledge and wisdom as a youth (Lk 2:40), must have been as limited, or even fallible with regard to scientific and historical knowledge as people of his time and culture — for example, regarding the authorship of the Torah and Psalter (Mk 10:3, 12:36) — and even ignorant at times of some matters pertaining to his unfolding mission (e.g. in his infancy, and as an adult ignorant of the date and time of the end of the world, Mk 13:32). Later, Anglican Kenoticists such as Farrer, Hebblethwaite, and Brown would even question whether the pre-Paschal Christ could be fully human if he was explicitly aware of his own divine identity.

In any case, Moderate KM offered a way to explain all this: the earthly range of consciousness of Jesus of Nazareth was held to be fully human, subject to cultural and historical limitations and influences, and human ways of gaining and holding knowledge. From the Holy Spirit Christ may have received a measure of supernatural revelation — for example, infused prophetic knowledge, in-depth knowledge of his Father and the Kingdom, and the capacity to read the hearts of those to whom he came to minister — but only such knowledge as was needed for the fulfilment of his mission, and only obtained in such a way, and

to such an extent, that the boundaries of what fully human minds can receive and hold were never violated.

Frank Weston and Moderate Kenoticism

During this period, no one explored the mystery of the Incarnation in a kenotic fashion with greater depth and penetration than the Anglican Bishop of Zanzibar Frank Weston (1871-1924) in his classic work, *The One Christ* (in two editions: 1907 and 1914). **For Weston, Jesus Christ is "God the Son self-limited in manhood." The Incarnation is an initial, continuous and everlasting act of self-limitation by the second person of the Trinity *asarkos*, in which he restrains the exercise of some of his divine attributes at a particular time and place in order to live without interruption under all the conditions of human life:**

> In time and through eternity the Christ is God the Son self-limited in manhood. ... [T]he self-limitation is continuous from the moment of the conception onwards ... at every moment He willed to live in the conditions of manhood, and ... in His acceptance of the law that governs this life lies the value of the Incarnation as an act of divine-self-sacrifice.[257]

> To sum up then, the Logos, in His state of Divine Glory, possesses a true consciousness of Himself as God the Son, omnipotent and omniscient. In virtue of His omniscient wisdom, by His omnipotent power, He ever imposes upon Himself a law of self-restraint, so framed that, in the Incarnate state, His exercise of His own proper powers is at every moment to be adapted to the measure of the capacity of His ever-growing manhood. He knows Himself not as God the Son exercising full divine power through a free and unlimited Divine Nature, but as God the Son limited and conditioned in manhood; and unable to act or speak or think outside the limits imposed upon Him by His manhood. So living and so

---

[257] Ibid., p. 138-139.

conforming to the law of self-restraint, He is the centre of the new relationships with His Father and His creatures that make up the life of the Incarnation ….[258]

The Incarnate is God the Son conditioned in and by manhood. His divine powers are always in His possession; but the conscious exercise of them is controlled by the law of restraint which He imposed upon himself at the moment of the Incarnation. Within the sphere of relationships that are His as Incarnate this law is valid and binding forever. It is the self-sacrifice of the eternal Son for our sakes. And by this law the Incarnate has no possible *media* of self-knowledge or the exercise of His divine powers that He cannot find in the manhood that He has assumed. These means are not of fixed content, for as the manhood grows and moves onward to its glory its power of mediating the divine must necessarily increase. *But for ever the manhood is the measure of the self-consciousness and the self-manifestation of the divine Son as Incarnate.*[259]

The great prayer of our Lord written down for us by St. John will afford a very real test of our theory. … The Incarnate speaks of Himself as "Jesus Christ whom thou hast sent" [Jn 17:3]. … His state can only be described under a human name, Jesus; and the essential character of it is self-surrender. He was sent to it. That is, He knows Himself as divine Son under limitations, in conditions of manhood. … These are not words of the eternal Son, unlimited and free. Nor are they words of the Son after He has abandoned all His divine attributes. But they do exactly suggest the Incarnate conditioned in manhood, holding communion with the Father through His manhood, and desiring to raise that manhood and His people in it and through it to the state of divine glory.[260]

---

[258] Ibid., p. 179-180.
[259] Ibid., p. 219-220; italics mine.
[260] Ibid., p. 280-281.

Weston often prefers to speak of the one "ego" of the divine Son Incarnate rather than a divine "person." But this does not mean that he completely "psychologized" the notion of "person."[261] *For Weston, the "ego" is not merely a psychological phenomenon (such as an act of self-consciousness); rather, it is an underlying ontological subject whose identity is indicated (but not constituted) by an act of self-consciousness with that subject as its referent. In other words, an act of self-consciousness points to the ego in which it subsists, and of which it is an expression:*

> [T]he human subject or Ego is defined as "the individual substance of rational nature." That is, the human Person is an immaterial being, in whom are constituted soul and body as to be his very own nature, in which he will be a responsible centre of relationships with all that is not constituted in him as its ground of being. …
>
> In any case, Christology assumes in man a certain underlying reality called "I," inseparable from soul and body in existence, yet in fact distinct from and the ground of both. This "I" is the subject of all thought, perception, change and consciousness. …
> The essential functions of this "I" require the soul, through which the "I" wills, thinks, and chooses; and for its true and complete life it requires the body, the material expression of which the soul is the essential form. But the "I" is not the soul, nor the body, nor the composition of the two, but the ground in which both subsist.[262]

---

[261] In a chapter in her book *Christ and Horrors*, entitled "Psychologizing the Person," Adams misinterpreted Weston's thought in this regard by relying on the first edition of *The One Christ* (1907), rather than on the second edition (1914). See especially the passage she quoted from Weston, 1907, p. 130, on p. 91 of *Christ and Horrors*, which was significantly revised by Weston in the 1914 version of his book, p. 142.

[262] Ibid., p. 15-16. See Chapter One, footnote one, for a critique of Weston's generic notion of "person."

For Weston, therefore, the unfathomable mystery of the Incarnation is that this subsisting "ground" or "person" or "ego" of the divine Son becomes the subject of two sets of relationships simultaneously:

> In the act of assuming manhood the divine Son *added to Himself* new powers of a level infinitely beneath His own, new modes of self-expression, inadequate to His Deity, and new relationships with his creatures; together with certain necessary limitations proper to our human nature.[263]

> How can the Logos as self-limited be the subject of the passion, the agony, the desolation and death upon the cross, and yet at the same moment be the living and life-giving son of God? No one has answered this question, no one can answer it. ... The Holy Spirit has not given us a revelation concerning the conception of a single person as the centre of two sets of relationships at the same moment: He has, however, revealed to us the actual relationships themselves.[264]

> It will be suggested that the state of the Son of God at any one moment is merely the sum of His relationships. As His glorious heavenly state is in fact His eternal relations with the Father and the Holy Spirit together with His relation to the world that His wisdom has created; so His state of incarnation is the sum of certain new relations which He has willed to form, in respect to the incarnate activities, with his creatures, and with the Father and the Spirit in so far as His peculiar indwelling of the redeemed and His office of Mediator render necessary an addition to His essential relations. ... That the Person who sat wearied on the well of Samaria is personally and identically the Eternal Son of God, who upholds all things by the word of His power, must ever be maintained. Our problem is to determine how the two sets of relations can exist

---

[263] Frank Weston, *The One Christ* (London: Longmans, Green and Co., 1907 edition), p. 12.
[264] Weston, *The One Christ* (1914 edition), p. 181 and 187.

side by side without essential separation and yet without encroachment.[265]

In the first place, then, the Person who became incarnate is purely divine. In His eternal essence He is of one substance with the Father, God of God, possessed of all divine powers, prerogatives, and attributes. His incarnation in no way interferes with his true life in the eternal Godhead, or hinders Him from His divine activities in the universe. He remains true Word of God, "upholding all things by His word of power" [Heb 1:3]. Nor on the other hand does His Incarnation involve him in the absolute abandonment of any one of the attributes of His divinity. Whatever of self-limitation is required, He always remains in possession of His powers, recognizing a law of restraint where restraint is necessary. His continuous respect for this law of self-restraint constitutes His act of self-sacrifice and obedience.[266]

[W]e must adore the eternal Logos in His glory and majesty, and watch Him begin to form new, limited relations with men, the first of which leads him to add to Himself babyhood, as the centre of a new sphere of limited and conditional activity.[267]
...

Never for a moment may we say that the Babe Jesus, as Babe, ruled the universe from His mother's knee. The Person who is Mary's Babe is at the same moment Ruler of the Universe through His divine relations therewith. But through His assumed, human relations He can only enter upon His full lordship as He advances in glory, beyond the grave (I Cor 15: 25-28; Eph 1:21-22). Thus we may not say that the eternal Son was to the same extent self-limited when man as when He was an infant. For in considering the self-emptying of the eternal

---

[265] Ibid., p. 22.
[266] Ibid., p. 149-150.
[267] Ibid., p. 178 and 162.

Son we have not to discuss how much of His power He retained, but how far at any stage of His life the manhood that he had assumed was able to mediate His power.

It follows that for Weston, the divine Son in his incarnation restrained the universal exercise of his divine attributes in order to assume a second, additional, fully human state. This human state included a state of self-consciousness which is "of different content" from his heavenly state of self-consciousness as the eternal, unlimited Logos (in both states, however, the ultimate referent of his acts of self-consciousness is the same: the ego or person of the divine Son):

> The Incarnate is the Son of God existing only under conditions of manhood. In what sense, then, was He conscious of himself?

> We may arrive at an answer by a process of elimination. First He did not know Himself as God the Son possessed of and exercising unlimited power. His state of eternal glory was, at were, a memory to Him (Jn 17:5): but His human mind was, and is, so inferior to the Divine Nature that it could not mediate an act of self-knowledge as Eternal God in the glorious liberty of divine power; otherwise manhood would indeed be equal with Godhead.

> Secondly, He did not know Himself as merely a man; for His self is divine. He was conscious of divinity (Jn 5:17, 8:58, 10:30, 14:23, etc). And thirdly, He did not know Himself as divine-human in composite consciousness; for He had not associated any human person with Himself.

> It remains therefore to say that He was conscious of Himself as God-in-manhood. He knew Himself as God just in so far as a perfect, sinless, God assumed soul could mediate the divine-self-consciousness.[268]

---

[268] Ibid., p. 167-168.

[T]here is a permanent ego of the manhood whose self-consciousness is of different content from that of the divine Son in His freedom and glory ….

[W]hen God became man God's knowledge of Himself is a knowledge of Himself as man, as it were, an added knowledge, external to His essential self-knowledge. Each added relationship of God to His creation is both the occasion and condition of a new form of self-knowledge or self-consciousness.[269]

The new-born babe, wrapped in swaddling clothes, has no more consciousness of self than may be possible to an infant soul, sinless, flawless, unburdened, and constituted in the person of God the Son. Nay more, the Incarnate as unborn babe has no consciousness that is not proper to the soul of babyhood, again sinless, flawless, unburdened, and constituted in the person of the Son of God. We must not let this thought stagger us. For in the first place, it behoved God to condescend to the lowest form of human life in order to redeem it.[270]

In fact, I do not know that it would be dangerous to the dogma of the incarnation to allow a practical absence of self-consciousness in the Incarnate during these first months of His life on earth …. No theory of the incarnation has any satisfactory explanation of these nine months of mysterious life …. [T]he law of self-restraint, self-imposed before the act of Incarnation, required of Him that he should taste of the unconsciousness or practical unconsciousness of the unborn child. But on the other hand we are to recall St. Luke's record of the small measure of consciousness found in the unborn Baptist, and to be prepared to allow to the full for some small

---

[269] Ibid., p. 128 and 178.
[270] Ibid., p. 176.

measure of consciousness in the Incarnate which could be mediated by His soul, as yet unborn ....."[271]

As the time of the Passion grows nearer we become more and more aware of the conditions of the Savior's self-knowledge.

He is pictured as anticipating His glory (Jn 17:1,5), as moving calmly forward to his glorification with and by the Father (Jn 13:1); but always His language and His actions are tempered by a recognition of limitation (Jn 16:7. Cf. 14:28, 7:39). He cannot escape from the sense of trouble that possesses His soul (Jn 12:27; Mt 26:38); He cannot avoid the prayer of agony in the garden (Mt 26: 39-46; Lk 22: 40-46) nor the feeling of desolation on the Cross (Mt 27:46). Son of God He is, and Son of God He knows Himself to be: but it is Son of God in manhood. He does not know Himself apart from manhood. It is He Himself who is troubled; He Himself who is in bitterness of soul; He himself who prays in agony and cries aloud in desolation; it is He Himself who cannot come to the Father except in and through His manhood.[272]

For Weston (as for Mackintosh) the divine Son in his incarnate state is able to manifest all of the divine attributes, but only to the extent that they can be expressed (or, as Mackintosh would say, "transposed") within the limits of his ever growing and developing human nature.[273] It is important to remember — and

---

[271] Weston, *The One Christ* (1907 edition), p. 181-182.

[272] Weston, *The One Christ* (1914 edition), p. 207.

[273] This notion seems to have a precursor in St. Gregory of Nyssa. According to Sarah Coakley, Gregory taught that the relationship of the divine and human natures of Christ is "like a glass being filled from an (incomprehensibly larger, indeed qualitatively and incomprehensibly different) container, till everything divine has been taken in *that can be.* Not — says Gregory — that the characteristics of divinity and humanity are *compatible*; but nor are they meant to be: one (the divine) is infusing the other (the human) until it is fully restored to its proper perfection in the resurrection." Sarah Coakley, "Does Kenosis Rest on a Mistake?" in Evans, ed., *Exploring Kenotic Christology*, p.259.

Weston repeatedly emphasizes this point — that we do not know *in advance* **precisely what those human limits are, because it is only in Christ that we see for the first time the full potential of human nature to be the vehicle and expression of the divine:**

> We cannot at all set a limit to the capacity of manhood for union with God, nor do we know at what point the human soul ceases to be able to advance in the comprehension of God. Limits there must be; but they may be wider than we think. … It seems therefore natural for us to find in the Gospel the record of the limitations under which the Incarnate lived and worked. … [W]e can see that the Incarnate Son must at every moment live under a law of self-restraint as to all His divine powers, in some measure. The measure of the self-restraint is the capacity of perfect manhood to receive, assimilate, and manifest divine power. … It would appear that the measure of His self-restraint was not one and the same at every period of His [human] development. It varied as the capacity of His manhood varied. As His human soul grew and developed, so did its capacity widen, and the degree of His self-restraint was always determined by the state of His human soul; it was never arbitrary. For the act of self-sacrifice lies in His determination to possess Himself and His powers within the conditions of manhood, and to allow the needs and the capacity of His manhood to determine at every moment the limits of His freedom. Thus, the Incarnate state is one of progress at every moment; beginning with the life of the unborn child and looking for its consummation to the day when He shall mediate to His mystical body the beatific vision of the Godhead.[274]

> [L]et us remember that we cannot measure the consciousness of the unborn or the infant. Of John the Baptist we know that he leapt in his mother's womb at the approach of Mary immediately after her conception of Christ; a fact that may

---

[274] Ibid., p. 152-154.

perhaps imply some kind of consciousness which, even if we ascribe it to some special action of the Spirit or to some extraordinary endowment of holiness, points to the possibility of extraordinary capacity in the soul of Jesus. But in the last resort we must be content to leave the matter unexplained, knowing that we are moving in the region of mystery.[275]

As a child the Incarnate was wise, but His wisdom was limited by the conditions of perfect, sinless, God-assumed childhood (Lk 2:40, 4:22). How wide these limits were St. Luke has been at pains to shew us. He tells us that the boy Jesus was at every moment being filled with wisdom, his human faculties exhibiting, that is, an understanding and power that was the highest possible to a boy (Lk 2:40).

As an instance he records the astonishment of the learned teachers and their followers in the Temple at the understanding and answers of the boy at the age of twelve. Our Lord seems to have exhibited an insight into the divine law that was beyond the power of an ordinary child. The cause of this extraordinary understanding, which no one suspected to be more than human, and which was, in fact, truly and perfectly characteristic of this perfect, God-assumed boyhood, the Evangelist traces to the underlying self-consciousness of the Incarnate (Lk 2:41-47).[276]

His ascension is, therefore, the enlargement of His human capacities to a degree that we cannot measure, and it carries with it a corresponding increase of the content of His consciousness and of the exercise of His powers.[277]

---

[275] Ibid., p. 177.
[276] Ibid., p. 201. By "underlying self-consciousness" here Weston seems to mean the fact that in the Temple the boy Jesus referred to God as "my Father."
[277] Ibid., p. 320.

The Incarnation

Based on these selections from Weston's *The One Christ*, we can see several things.

(1) Weston's theory of the self-restraint of the divine Son in assuming the limitations and conditions of human nature is similar in many respects to the Radical KM of Mackintosh, but with two major differences. First, for Weston the divine Son's self-restraint of his omni-attributes is a *continual* act of self-limitation by the divine *Logos asarkos* (that is, by the Divine Word from outside of the sphere of the Incarnation) at every moment of his human life, whereas for Mackintosh this act of self-restraint is a *once and for all* act of the *Logos asarkos* at the first moment of his human existence, when he contracts and transposes his divine attributes into his incarnate state in the womb of Mary. Second, for Weston, the divine Son self-limits (or transposes) the exercise of his divine attributes into the vehicle of his human nature *without losing access to, or ceasing the exercise of his divine omni-attributes throughout the universe as the Logos asarkos.*[278] This move seems to preserve Weston from having

---

[278] To be precise, Mackintosh claimed that we do not know whether the divine Son ceased his cosmic role during his incarnate sojourn on earth, because, Mackintosh said, the scriptural passages relating to this question are "insufficient" to answer it. But Mackintosh clearly leaned toward the view that the Son must have relinquished that role, and he developed his theory of the Incarnation without worrying about how to make coherent any idea that the Son of God operated in two "states," or from two centers or ranges of consciousness simultaneously. See Mackintosh, *The Doctrine of the Person of Jesus Christ*, p. 483-485. Vincent Taylor was similarly reticent to make a firm commitment on this important issue:

> It has been conjectured that, in consequence of the Incarnation, the cosmic functions of the Son are taken over by the Father and the Holy Spirit; but this suggestion is crude and mischievous …. To say that the cosmic activities of the Son are not suspended although not present to His consciousness, is an alternative speculation which may be entertained, but cannot be established by human reason. In what way the divine consciousness of the Son functions while He is incarnate, is not revealed to us, but it would be idle to suppose that the Godhead is

to adopt a "voluntarist" understanding of the *kenosis* in which God the Son actually can choose not to be fully divine, temporarily abandoning some or all of his divine attributes in order to become incarnate (Thomasius, Gess), or in which God the Son can choose to render himself unable fully to access and exercise his own divine omni-attributes, abiding *solely* in that limited, incarnate state (Forsyth-Mackintosh-Taylor). We have already seen some of the major difficulties associated with the voluntarist-Radical KM option, and Weston's Moderate KM evidently can avoid them.

(2) Moreover, by rejecting all notions that the divine Son must completely abandon, or render latent and fully inoperative his divine omni-attributes to assume his incarnate state, Weston, somewhat like Mackintosh, opens the door to a new idea: that in the act of incarnation, *God utilizes and expresses his omni-attributes in an additional and unique way through his human life and death.* This "transposition" of the divine attributes by the divine Son *asarkos*, in and through his human nature, can be seen as the completion of the expression of these divine attributes in the created order, rather than as a mere setting aside or diminution of those attributes. Thus, paradoxically, the infinite "power" of God to achieve his highest purposes is supremely operative and uniquely expressed through the weakness and sufferings of the human nature of the Son, and in some measure the infinite Wisdom of God is communicated to,

---

impoverished by the supreme act of love by which the Son of God is sent into the world. (*The Person of Christ*, p.298)

Taylor's speculation here, however, is surely untenable. How could God the Son, possessing nothing more than an amnesiac human consciousness during his sojourn on earth (i.e., unaware of his divine identity and omni-attributes, or at least aware of his inability to fully access those powers), nevertheless, at the same time providentially guide and sustain the entire cosmos without consciously knowing what he was doing throughout the universe? This is one reason why Moderate KM posits *two* ranges of consciousness in the divine nature of the Son, operative simultaneously in the mystery of the Incarnation, through one of which he continues providentially to govern all of creation.

stored in, and expressed through the human mind of the Son. We will return to this latter issue in Part Two, Chapter Two of this book.

Further difficult issues, however, arise in this regard, namely: what is the relationship between the self-limited state of the divine Son and the work of the Holy Spirit? The Church has always taught that the Incarnation of the Son happened "by the power of the Holy Spirit" (Nicene Creed; cf. Lk 1:35). We have already met this issue before, in Part One, Chapter Two (above), with regard to the measure of supernatural, prophetic knowledge and supernatural, determinative power that Jesus needed for the accomplishment of his mission. There I suggested that *in his self-limited and authentically human state, the divine Son ensarkos could only access the divine, determinative power to perform miracles, and supernatural, prophetic knowledge from the same source that any human being can access such power and knowledge: through perfect surrender to, and cooperation with the Holy Spirit.* The Kenotic Theory allows that Jesus accessed these particular forms of divine power and knowledge in a *limited* way — and exercised them in a *filial* way in obedience to his Father (Jn 4:34). But in and through his human nature, he could only do so at the prompting of the Holy Spirit, and only by relying on the Holy Spirit's power and knowledge.

(3) Finally, Weston never actually considered himself a Kenoticist, and from these passages it should be clear why he hesitated to do so. In his version of Moderate KM he treads on very dangerous ground by speaking of the unknown limits of divine "knowledge" and "power" of which human nature can be the vehicle and expression, limits discovered only through the Gospel record of the life of Christ. It is not that Weston is wrong on this point: the question is how far he is willing to go with it. Since Weston takes the Gospel According to St. John as reportage of the actual words and deeds of the Savior in Palestine (a contentious point in historical criticism of the New Testament) his view of the extent of the supernatural

knowledge and power mediated and exhibited by the historical Jesus Christ is very expansive indeed. As a result, while Weston's theory is certainly kenotic, (for he posits an incarnation of God in Christ by means of the self-limitation, in the form of self-restraint, of divine attributes by the Son), the question will arise in volume two of this study whether he inadvertently lapsed into Docetism or the Monophysite heresy in this respect: compromising the reality of the human nature of Jesus, his real human sufferings and struggles — which is precisely what Gore, Mackintosh and the other Kenoticists were trying to avoid.[279]

After Weston, a number of Anglican theologians in the twentieth century expressed versions of Moderate KM in their own work, including O.C. Quick, H.E.W. Turner, Norman Anderson, John Austin Baker, Brian Hebblethwaite, Richard Swinburne and (into the twenty-first century) David Brown.[280] Central to any version of the Moderate Kenotic Model, as we have seen, is that the divine Son continued to exercise, and remain conscious of, his cosmic functions as the universal, omniscient and creative Word, even as he experienced human limitations of consciousness, knowledge and power as Jesus of Nazareth.

---

[279] Perhaps these difficulties could have been avoided if Weston had seen more clearly that the divine identity of the Son entails that in his human nature as Jesus, he would completely and totally surrender himself to the Holy Spirit at every stage of his human life. Again, it was solely by the power of the Spirit that Jesus performed miracles and attained the measure of supernatural, prophetic knowledge needed for his mission. Weston actually comes close to embracing this perspective in *The One Christ*, p. 266-275.

[280] Quick, *Doctrines of the Creed*, p. 132-139; H.E.W. Turner, *Jesus the Christ*, p. 73-85; Norman Anderson, *The Mystery of the Incarnation* (London: Ecclesia, 1978), p. 145-155; John Austin Baker, *The Foolishness of God* (London: Darton, Longman, and Todd, 1970), p. 206-207 and 319-320; Hebblethwaite, *The Incarnation*, p.1-2, 30-31, 45-46, 57, 65-68. I am indebted to Turner for his distinction between Radical and Moderate Kenoticism.

Does Two "Minds" Equal Two "Persons"?

In his book *The Divine Trinity*, David Brown put simply and directly the strongest objection against this whole approach to the mystery of the Incarnation: "The split personality it postulates in the divine nature of the Son is so intense as to make it incomprehensible why we should continue to speak of only one person being involved in the two contrasted types of activity."[281] In short, Moderate KM seems to assign to the divine Son two distinct "personalities" or "ranges of consciousness" simultaneously: one omniscient and unlimited, governing the whole universe, and the other fully human, limited, culturally formed and influenced — and, perhaps, in some respects even fallible. **How can we render coherent and intelligible the claim that these two vastly different minds or ranges of consciousness are included in the divine nature and belong to the same divine person?**

Brian Hebblethwaite was well aware of this critique. It is "paradoxical," he wrote "to suppose that a human life lived out within the framework of first-century Jewish consciousness could actually *be* the incarnate life of God himself in one of the modes of his infinite and eternal being."[282] Hebblethwaite does not intend to remove the element of paradox, but he reminds us that a paradox is not necessarily a logical contradiction. Thus, he has little patience with the suggestion made by Don Cupitt, and others, that the idea of one person in two natures is as illogical as the idea of a square circle:

> What after all is the basis for comparing talk of one who is both God and man with talk of a square circle? Certainly, a square circle is a contradiction in terms. The terms 'square' and 'circle' are precisely defined terms, and their logical compatibility is obvious from the definitions. But 'God' and 'man' are far from being such tightly defined concepts. It is difficult enough to suppose that we have a full and adequate

---

[281] Brown, *The Divine Trinity*, p. 233.
[282] Hebblethwaite, *The Incarnation*, p. 45.

grasp of what it is to be a human being. We certainly have no such grasp of the divine nature. *Who are we to say that the essence of God is such as to rule out the possibility of his making himself present in the created world as a human being, while in no way ceasing to be God as he ever is?* ... Certainly the eternal God and a historical man are beings of a different ontological status. But the claim of the Christian tradition has been that the ontology of God is such as to permit the infinite source of all created being to come among us as a man. Again, who are we to say that the ontological status of God is such as to render this logically impossible?[283]

Nevertheless, if we cannot completely comprehend the divine essence, western Christianity claims that we can know *something* of God's essence by way of analogy. It is hard to understand how God the Son can limit the exercise of his omniscience and omnipotence at a particular time and place, experiencing all the limitations of a particular human mind and body, and yet all the while remain the omniscient sustainer of the universe. Does this not leave us in Moderate KM with two distinct minds, two separate ranges of consciousness in the divine nature of the Son during his incarnate life — and therefore two persons? If we possess at least some analogical understanding of the divine mind (i.e., God is said to be "omni-scient" and to possess "infinite knowledge"), then we ought to be able to come up with some analogy for the Incarnation, an analogy which can ease the tension involved in claiming that a single person both knows all truth and transcends all suffering in some way in his divine nature, and yet at the same time is limited (and perhaps fallible) in knowledge, and can share fully in creaturely suffering through his human experience as Jesus of Nazareth. It was the failure of many theologians to find adequate analogies that rendered the intelligibility of Moderate KM suspect.

Weston, for example, likened the dual state of the Son in the Incarnation to the story of St. Francis De Sales acting as the confessor to his own parents. As a priest in the confessional, St. Francis had to

---

[283] Ibid., p. 3; italics mine.

limit his knowledge and affective relationship with his parents as a son in order to relate to them for a time solely in and through his priesthood. Weston wrote:

> It is an analogy only, and clearly is very inadequate, but it does touch our problem at two points: it affords an analogy with the co-existence of two sets of relationships in the one subject, the Logos; and an analogy with the limitation necessary to the second relationship.

> And … it gives us a faint hint of the possibility of locating the power of self-limitation in the subject of the wider relationship. It was as son that Francis willed to act as priest to his parents; it was as son that he put aside all such knowledge of them as his priesthood might not mediate.[284]

It is not clear, however, that Weston's second point makes sense. After all, St. Francis must have agreed to hear his parents' confessions primarily out of a sense of duty as a priest, because they needed a confessor, rather than solely out of love for them as their son. Moreover, as Weston himself seemed to realize,[285] all the analogies he offered for his theory of the Incarnation (e.g. a general's son who wills to fight as a soldier on the front lines; a king's son who wills to share the state of his subjects as a workman), while they show us the capacity of persons for *kenosis* — that is, for loving acts of self-limitation — they do not show us how it is intelligible to say that a person can love in a kenotic way while *simultaneously* exercising broader knowledge and powers in a non-kenotic way.

Hebblethwaite at least kept the issue clear in this discussion by repeatedly insisting that in Moderate KM we are positing two levels or ranges of consciousness, two mental spheres of subjective experience, not in the human mind of Jesus, but in the mind of the divine Son while incarnate:

[284] Weston, *The One Christ*, p. 167.
[285] Ibid., p. 183-184.

[I]n fact, the tradition has carefully distinguished what can be said of the human subject, Jesus, from what can be said of the divine subject, God the Son, whose human expression and vehicle, in his incarnate life, the human subject Jesus is. ... For this reason, incarnational Christology attributes two consciousnesses not to Jesus, but to God incarnate. ... [M]uch depends on what one sees as the primary subject of Christological statements. ... The primary subject of all Christological statements is God. It is God *qua* God, who cannot die, and it is God incarnate, i.e., God *qua* man, who suffers and dies for our salvation. Nor is there any question of sundering the natures here, when it is made clear that *we are not talking of two separate individuals, but of the divine substance, which is such as to include within its own subjectivity the human subject, Jesus, as the expression and vehicle of God's incarnate life.*[286]

Still, we are left with our dilemma: what can it mean to say that such radically different ranges of consciousness, knowledge and subjective experience, one infinite and the other finite, belong to, and are fully operated by the same divine person simultaneously? Are we just up against an impenetrable mystery and paradox here? *The danger is that without any good analogies to help us, the "Incarnation," the heart of the Christian faith, is almost completely incomprehensible to us; we hardly know what we mean by the term, except as a matter of logic* (i.e., all we really know is that the claim that one divine person can possess and operate two sets of properties simultaneously, divine and human, is not necessarily self-contradictory).

A proper analogy for the Moderate Kenotic Model of the Incarnation might be found, however, in the way that the vast pool of subconscious images and thoughts exists within human beings on a different level from our more limited, conscious selves, without leading us to deny our own unity of person. The

---

[286] Hebblethwaite, *The Incarnation*, p. 31; italics mine.

analogy would work as follows: the human subconscious would correspond to the omniscient knowledge and infinite range of consciousness of the divine Son, while the human conscious life would be comparable to the limited, human range of consciousness (i.e., both the human conscious and subconscious life) that the divine Son assumed in the Incarnation.[287]

This analogy might go some way toward easing our problem, for we can easily see how we can know or believe many things on a sub-conscious level without being explicitly or consciously of aware of them. For example, I may be terribly upset by how I was treated on a certain occasion by my best friend, but so afraid of admitting this to myself that I will not let myself be consciously aware of that dismay. Or I might have had an experience in my infancy of a loving mother that is stored mostly in my subconscious memory, which I can never fully access on a conscious level, but that subconscious memory may affect how I feel about and relate to women and mothers on a conscious level for the rest of my life. In fact, if the famous depth-psychologist Carl Jung is correct, then each of us has a subconscious store of mythical archetypes and stories that are common to humanity.[288] My individual share in these, however, may never come to light until with the help of a Jungian therapist I begin consciously to analyze my dreams. Such knowledge remains mostly hidden, deep within me. And yet, all the while, the fact that we possess such different levels and ranges of consciousness within our own human nature does not lead us to doubt that we are one person. **In fact, there seems to be what has been called an "asymmetric accessing relationship" between the human subconscious and the human conscious mind: the subconscious mind seems to store in the subconscious memory just about everything that a person experiences on a**

---

[287] On this analogy, see David Brown, *Divine Humanity*, p. 181-182. It is important to bear in mind here that we are merely drawing an analogy; we are not following William Sanday in trying to locate the divine presence in Jesus solely in his subconscious. On this see Brown, *Divine Humanity*, p. 158.
[288] Christopher Bryant, *Jung and the Christian Way* (London: Darton, Longman and Todd, 1983), p. 30 and 38.

conscious level, while the conscious mind has only limited access to what is stored in the subconscious.

Similarly, the divine Son may have, on one level, an infinite range of consciousness and knowledge that does not, or cannot fully rise to the level of his limited, human range of consciousness as Jesus of Nazareth (a range which, again, must include both human subconscious and human conscious levels). Thus, it is conceivable that at one "level," or in the depths of his divine nature, the divine Word retains his omniscience — and therefore can exercise his cosmic, creative, role — even while, at the same time, on another level, he can experience a fully human life, with all of its limitations and conditions.

At least two further questions arise with regard to appropriate analogies for the Moderate Kenotic Model of the Incarnation.

1) What can it mean to say that the divine Son has *added* to his own infinite level or range of consciousness a brand new level or range, and therefore new types of experience, without ceasing from the old? Perhaps an analogy can be drawn with those who attain by divine grace a state of mystical union with God. The result is a whole new level of awareness, including supernatural, infused knowledge of many of the mysteries of the faith, and experiences of wordless, imageless adoration of Divine Love. At first, this new level to which the soul has been raised by the Holy Spirit is so radically different from anything experienced before that the poor human soul is swept away in ecstasies, "transports," and "flights of the spirit." But after long experience with the gift of mystical union, the soul learns to live and operate on two levels at once, carrying on with daily duties on a conscious level even while, at another supra-conscious level (so to speak), the soul remains totally absorbed in contemplating the infinite light and love of God.[289] In fact,

---

[289] On the whole phenomenon of mystical union, see Thomas Dubay, *The Fire Within* (San Francisco: Ignatius Press, 1989), p. 97-107.

it is the teaching of some of the Catholic saints that even while abiding in this state of mystical union with God, the human soul at the same time can experience the most terrible bodily and emotional suffering.[290]

The analogy with the Incarnation, however, is not a very close one, for the person who is raised to a state of mystical union with God receives an additional, *expanded* range of consciousness, and level of awareness. In the Incarnation, on the other hand, Moderate KM posits that the divine Son assumes an additional, *more limited* range of consciousness. But the analogy at least enables us to see how even a human person can attain an additional mental range or level that can operate simultaneously with his original range of consciousness. If human beings can do this, under certain conditions, it is hardly unintelligible or inconceivable that the divine Son could do something similar.

2) Granted that at least two levels of consciousness, containing different ranges of knowledge and experience, can and do exist in human beings (the conscious and subconscious levels — and also in rare cases an added, supra-conscious level of knowledge and experience in the form of mystical union with God) — still, in human souls these different levels affect each other constantly. There is a constant flow between them. For example, human conscious experience is often stored in the subconscious memory, and subconscious thoughts and emotions sometimes rise to the level of daylight consciousness. Also, in mystical union, supernatural knowledge of the mysteries of the faith experienced on the supra-conscious level can be infused into the conscious or subconscious mind in the form of concepts and images. The question arises, therefore, whether in the mind of the divine Son, while incarnate, the two

---

[290] For example, see St. Francis De Sales, *Treatise on the Love of God* (Westminster, MD: Newman Press, 1944), sections 9.3 and 9.12, p. 371-372 and 395-397.

levels or ranges of his consciousness, divine and human, interact at all. For if they do not, the divine Son would be operating with a completely "split-personality" in his divine nature, with two "minds," "levels," or "ranges" of consciousness, and little or no connection between them at all. How then could we claim that this analogy really helps us understand what it means to say that these two "minds" or "ranges of consciousness" belong to a single divine person?

Contemporary Contributions to Moderate KM: Thomas Morris, Brian Hebblethwaite and Richard Swinburne

One of the most lucid defenders of what we have called Moderate KM, or the Two-Minds Theory, was the Protestant philosopher Thomas Morris. In his book, *The Logic of God Incarnate* (1986), and in his essay summarizing his theory, "The Metaphysics of God Incarnate" (2009), Morris tried to explain more clearly the relationship between the divine and human minds of Jesus Christ:

> **[O]n the two-minds view, the Incarnation involved not just a duality of abstract natures, but a duality of consciousness or mentality which was thus introduced into the life of God the Son. *The two-minds of Christ should be thought of as standing in something like an asymmetric accessing relation: the human mind was contained in, but did not itself contain the divine mind, or, to portray it from the other side, the divine mind contained, but was not contained by the human mind.* Everything present to the human mind of Christ was thereby present to the divine mind as well, but not vice versa. … Jesus had all the mental, intellectual, emotional and volitional resources we all have, lacking none. And it was these, not his divine resources, that he typically drew on for the personal history enacted on this earth. But this living of a human life through human resources was, on the two-minds view, going on at the same time as he, in**

his properly divine form of existence, was continuing to exercise his omnipotence, with the wisdom of his omniscience, in his omnipresent activities throughout creation.[291]

It follows that the mind of the divine Son experienced all the joys and sorrows of a human life, in and through his limited, human range of consciousness as Jesus of Nazareth, while simultaneously these experiences were translated onto the level of the divine Son's omniscient perspective on all events. We need not deny that he is still a single "person." In fact, we can illustrate this from actual cases of multiple personality. Morris explains:

> **In some cases of multiple personality, there exists one personality with apparently full and direct knowledge of the experiences had, information gathered, and actions initiated by one or more other personalities, a sort of knowledge which is not had by any other personality concerning it. In other words, there seem to exist asymmetric accessing relations in such cases.**[292]

In other words, one personality knows and remembers the experiences of another. The second personality, however, does not have such access to the first, and may see it as another individual altogether. **Hence, we can claim an analogy here with the divine mind of the Son in the Incarnation: the mind of the divine Son is like a central, accessing personality; the human personality of Jesus is its offshoot and self-expression, and the original divine mind has full access to the experiences of that secondary personality.**[293]

---

[291] Thomas V. Morris, "The Metaphysics of God Incarnate," in Michael Rea, ed., *Oxford Readings in Philosophical Theology 1: Trinity, Incarnation, and Atonement* (Oxford: Oxford University Press, 2009), p. 220; italics mine.

[292] Morris, *The Logic of God Incarnate,* p.106. Cf. William Confer and Billie Ables, *Multiple Personality* (New York: Human Sciences Press, 1983), p. 17.

[293] Please see Chapter One, note 1, for the definition of "personality" assumed throughout this book, which is not the same as "person."

We need to bear in mind that in Moderate KM, two levels or ranges of consciousness, or two minds, one infinite and the other finite in scope, are attributed not to the human mind of Jesus, but only to the divine mind of the Son while incarnate. Jesus of Nazareth did not have a split-personality; he had a fully healthy and integrated human mind. Again, Morris explains:

> The divine mind of God the Son contained, but was not contained by, his earthly mind or range of consciousness. That is to say, there was what can be called an asymmetric accessing relation between the two minds.[294]

It is important to remember that Morris was only drawing analogies here; he was not stating that the Incarnation is *exactly* like a state of human multiple personality. For one thing, multiple human personalities exist on the ontological level of finite, created being, whereas the divine mind is an aspect of infinite, uncreated being,

---

[294] Ibid., p. 103. It seems to me that Morris wounds his own position with the following argument, neatly summarized by Thomas Senor in "Drawing on Many Traditions: an ecumenical kenotic christology" in Anna Marmadoro and Jonathan Hill, eds., *The Metaphysics of the Incarnation* (Oxford: Oxford University Press, 2011):

> [T]he asymmetric accessing relation that the earthly mind of Jesus has to the mind of God the Son is also had by each of us with the mind of God the Son. The Son has complete access to our mental life and we have whatever access to his he allows us to have. So wherein is the uniqueness of Christ? Morris's answer is that unlike us, the causal and cognitive powers of the earthly mind are none other than the causal and cognitive powers of God the Son. But the rest of us have independent cognitive and causal powers. Our mental powers are brought about by God but they are numerically distinct; the powers of Jesus just are the powers of God the Son.

As the reader will discover, in Part One, chapter five I find myself in agreement with Morris that the cognitive and causal powers of Jesus are identical with those of God the Son, but as will be made clear in Part Two, Chapter One of this book, I am not in agreement with Morris that God has an asymmetric accessing relationship with the subjective experience of every human being.

and the additional, finite, human limitations that he assumed would be a subset of his divine nature and experience. Morris' argument was simply that if we find it inconceivable that a divine person can be the subject of two such very different minds, levels and ranges of consciousness at once, divine and human, we can find analogies for this in human mental phenomena. These include the relationship between the subconscious and conscious life of a single human mind, and a particular kind of split personality belonging to a single person, analogies that can render the two-minds view of the Incarnation more intelligible.

Still, one might object that the comparison of the state of the divine mind in the Incarnation with a human type of split-personality is demeaning to God. As Morris pointed out, however, this objection hardly fits the case. A split-personality is said to be unhealthy for a human being because it is generally an involuntary state that blocks the goals valuable to the person involved. But this would not apply to the analogous state of divided personality assumed by the divine Son in the Incarnation. The self-extension of the divine mind into an additional, human range of consciousness and will was entirely voluntary, and conducive to his loving, saving purposes for humanity.[295]

If the multiple-personality analogy is felt to be unhelpful, Morris found other analogies for the Two-Minds theory:

> [T]here are numerous earthly phenomena with which we are familiar that provide very helpful partial analogies to the two-minds view of Christ. There seem to be cases of dreams in which the dreamer both plays a role within the environs of the dream story, operating with a consciousness formed from within the dream, and at the same time retains an over-arching consciousness that the drama of the dream is just that — only a dream. Another sort of analogy is provided by thought experiments dealing with artificial intelligence, in which two

---

[295] Ibid., (Morris), p. 107.

physical systems are each such as to be credited with mentality
and yet stand in such an asymmetric accessing relation that one
can be considered a sub-system of the other, with its own
distinctive origin and functions, but belonging to the unity of
the larger system of mentality.[296]

Perhaps what renders all such analogies for the Incarnation suspect is
that they seem so much less inspiring than the kind of analogies we
found for the Forsyth-Mackintosh-Taylor version of Radical KM: for
example, the woman who places her musical knowledge and skills in
abeyance for a time in order to look after her children, or the members
of the Order of Our Lady of Ransom in the Middle Ages, who
exchanged places with slaves to set them free. These analogies seem to
show us divine kenotic love in action in a much more moving and
"preachable" way than analogies drawn from the human conscious-
subconscious life, or from cases of multiple personality, or dreaming,
or artificial intelligence systems. However, the analogies for Radical
KM can still be used for Moderate KM, and for preaching the gospel
of the Incarnation, as long as we are aware of the point at which they
break down: they do not show us a single person with two different
minds, levels and ranges of consciousness fully operative *simultaneously*.
Since the act of an infinite person becoming incarnate and living on a
finite level without ceasing fully to carry out his universal, cosmic role
is something only God can do, it is of the nature of the case that the
closest analogies for the Incarnation available to us lie at the very
boundaries of what we can experience or comprehend. After all,
philosophical theology is not designed to give us sermon illustrations,
but to provide us with coherent and intelligible perspectives on God
and his action in the world.

Morris's view was favorably received by Anglican advocates of
Moderate KM such as Brian Hebblethwaite":[297]

---

[296] Morris, "The Metaphysics of God Incarnate," p. 221.
[297] Morris himself actually contrasted his Two-Minds view with the Kenotic
Theory, but by the latter he clearly had Radical Kenoticism in mind, and as
Stephen T. Davis put it, Morris himself was "an unwitting kenoticist": "What the

177

The Incarnation

What does it mean to say that with Jesus Christ we have to do not simply with a supremely great teacher, prophet, and exemplar, but with God made man? It means that for Christian understanding, the whole life and work of Jesus Christ were lived out from a centre in God. God, in person, is believed to have come to share our human lot, thereby showing us, in action and passion, the depths and extent of his love for humankind, and enabling men and women to be drawn, for ever, into the all-embracing life and love of the divine.

Clearly, such an incarnation must have involved self-limitation, self-emptying, *kenosis*, on the part of God. ... For Incarnation to be real, the human vehicle of the divine life had to be a genuine human being — in fact ... a Jew nurtured in the faith of Israel. This self-emptying must have entailed limitation in knowledge and power, compatible with Jesus being a first-century Palestinian Jew. ... But such a Kenotic Christology is pressed too far if it is held to involve the abandonment of the divine attributes of omnipotence and omniscience by God the Son. The divine subject of the incarnate life must have remained aware of what he was doing in taking our nature upon him and living a human life on Earth.

This means that we have to distinguish between two subjectivities where God incarnate is concerned. *Qua* God, he retained the divine attributes and powers. *Qua* man he was limited to a first-century Jewish viewpoint. Such a "two-consciousnesses" view of the incarnation has been argued for, in detail, by T.V. Morris. According to Morris's analysis, the divine mind of God the Son has to be thought of as containing the human mind of Jesus without being constrained by it. But the logic of God incarnate requires much more than this.

---

two-minds theory entails that the Logos 'gave up' or 'emptied itself of' in the incarnation was invulnerability to human pains and sufferings." Stephen T. Davis, "Is Kenosis Orthodox?" p. 122.

Morris insists, quite rightly, that God the Son has to be thought of as the ultimate subject of Jesus' thought and action, even if Jesus, *qua* man, was aware of no more than a profound love of, and communion with, God and a unique vocational insight. In other words, the human subject has to be distinguished from the divine subject, even when the former was the incarnate form of the latter.

To develop this view further: the incarnate one, *qua* man, was not omnipotent. But it was the omnipotence of God that included the power to channel his divine personality through the humanity of Jesus, and it was the Divine Omnipotence that manifested itself humanly in Jesus' healing powers and in what he made of his Jewish inheritance. Presumably, too, it was his being God incarnate that ensured his sinlessness. Similarly, Jesus himself was not omniscient; but the omniscience of God the Son included knowing what it was like to be one of us. And it was the divine omniscience that manifested itself humanly in Jesus' knowing both the secrets of the human heart and the reconciling power of God's love.[298]

In the years before he became an Eastern Orthodox Christian, Anglican philosophical theologian Richard Swinburne also explored and defended the Two-Minds Theory.[299] Trying to encapsulate his perspective in a short space, as we must do here, is exceptionally difficult because of his distinctive philosophical system. According to Marilyn McCord Adams, Swinburne actually captured most of what Frank Weston had been trying to say in his own version of Moderate KM. Here we shall quote at length Adams' summary of Swinburne's

---

[298] Brian Hebblethwaite, *In Defence of Christianity* (Oxford: Oxford University Press, 2005), p. 118-120. Note here the somewhat different way that Hebblethwaite understands the role of the omnipotence and omniscience of God in the Incarnation compared to what I argued in Chapters Two and Three, and earlier in this present chapter.
[299] Swinburne's reflections on the Incarnation were developed in *The Christian God*, published in 1994, the year before his conversion to Eastern Orthodoxy.

Christology, as probably the best and clearest introduction to his thought:

> **For God to become human, a divine individual soul [NB: Swinburne prefers to call the divine persons "souls", since they are immaterial persons] would have to take a human body from our gene pool and permit Itself to become causally interactive with that body in the way human souls normally are.** The Divine individual soul would not thereby lose the cognitive contents, the thoughts and preferences that it has by virtue of Its essential Divine attributes. Since it is *essentially* Divine, and since omniscience, omnipotence, and perfect goodness are essential to Divinity, that would be metaphysically impossible. Rather, **the Divine individual soul would allow itself to acquire a further range of contents — sensations, feelings, beliefs, and desires — by virtue of Its connection with a human body. As on Weston's theory, Incarnation would mean not [radical] kenosis, but an *extension* of Its normal mode of operation. Besides the Divine Way of thinking and acting, the Divine individual would have a human way of thinking and acting.**[300]

What Swinburne proposes here is that a divine person, the divine Son, limited himself to act as fully human soul in relation to the human body that he assumed in the womb of the Blessed Virgin Mary. Swinburne therefore supplements the theory of Morris by showing how God the Son became incarnate in the first place, whereas Morris had focused simply on analyzing the incarnate state of the Son. Moreover, *pace* Adams and Swinburne himself, this is indeed a "kenotic" theory of the Incarnation, for it posits an act of self-limitation of the divine nature by the Son in order to become incarnate (that is; in order to dwell under all the limitations and conditions of a human soul), and it results in new kinds of experience and suffering being taken into the divine nature through its union with human flesh. **The fact that the divine**

---

[300] Adams, *Christ and Horrors,* p. 119.

Son at the same time carries out his omniscient and omnipotent cosmic role does not mean that his act of becoming incarnate is not a kenotic one. The joys, sorrows and sufferings of Jesus Christ really modify the divine nature, in the sense of giving God the Son new kinds of experience.

Adams writes:

> Metaphysically, what Swinburne offers is one [divine] soul substance with two ranges of consciousness: a divided mind. … Swinburne reckons that soteriological motives for the Incarnation would furnish God with good, non-neurotic reasons for dividing his mind. The partition would be created and enforced by a conscious decision informed by the comprehensive Divine consciousness, which would have access to everything. But there would be a vast gap between the range of consciousness out of which the Divine Word operates as God, and that out of which he functions as human …. The human range would have to house ignorance, growth, temptation, experiencing infirmities, learning obedience through suffering. The human range would have limited access to the comprehensive contents of the Divine mind.
>
> **Moreover, Swinburne envisages the Divine Word acting out of Its comprehensive consciousness to exercise some editorial control over the contents of its narrower consciousness. … Swinburne reckons that Christ's human belief-set should include enough to guarantee reliable knowledge of his human duties and the doctrinal content his earthly ministry was supposed to convey.**[301]

The question obviously arises how Swinburne's theory of the Incarnation fits with the basic pattern of Christian (and classical Anglican) orthodoxy. First, is this just a modern version of the ancient heresy of Apollinarius, who taught that in the Incarnation the

---

[301] Ibid., p. 120.

omniscient mind of the Son replaced the human mind? Was Jesus a divine-human hybrid, so to speak? Thomas Weinandy, for example, complains that in the (Moderate) Kenotic Christology of Gore and Weston, "The consciousness, etc., of Christ is not really human, but merely the divine consciousness, etc., brought down to a human level."[302] **Swinburne persuasively argued, however, that what the ancient Fathers objected to in the Apollinarian heresy was the way it deprived Jesus of a fully human soul with a fully human psychological life. On Swinburne's theory, the soul of Jesus was** *fully* **human, with authentic human limitations, without being** *merely* **human; the soul of Jesus was the divine Son of God assuming all the limitations and conditions of a human soul united with a human body.**[303]

Swinburne (and Morris) also might be charged with violating the parameters of the Chalcedonian Definition, which stated that in the Incarnation the divine and human natures were present in Jesus Christ "without confusion." But Swinburne and Morris presumably could respond, again, that the intention of the bishops at Chalcedon was to insure that Jesus had an authentically human body and soul, and all the essential human attributes. Jesus was not some kind of blending of the divine and human natures, a *tertium quid* possessing neither a fully human nor a fully divine nature. Of course, the only way the Council fathers could conceive of this at the time was in terms of classical Two-Nature Christology (see Chapter One, above). On Swinburne's and Morris's theory, however, "housing the human range of consciousness in numerically the same soul as the divine consciousness does not swallow up or fail to preserve the properties of human nature."[304] **The human range of consciousness of the divine Son is definably human, with authentic human limitations, even though it is included within the divine range of consciousness as the vehicle and expression of the divine life. Moreover, the divine Son does**

[302] Thomas Weinandy, OFM Cap., *Does God Change?* (Still River, MA: St. Bede Publications, 1985), p. 117.
[303] Swinburne, *The Christian God*, p. 197-198.
[304] Adams, *Christ and Horrors*, p. 123.

not cease to possess and exercise his omniscience, omnipotence and omnipresence throughout the cosmos, even while he assumes human limitations in the sphere of his incarnate life. So, on this model both the human and divine natures are preserved.

Answers to Objections Raised by Bayne and Layman

Perhaps the most in-depth critique of the coherence of Moderate KM, in the form developed by Morris and Swinburne, was offered by philosopher Tim Bayne from Macquarrie University in Australia. Based on his own background in the philosophical and scientific study of the unity of human consciousness, **Bayne wrestled with the alleged "Achilles heel" of Moderate KM: how can two such dramatically different spheres or ranges of consciousness belong to, be experienced by and be fully operated by the same personal subject simultaneously? Bayne expressed three main concerns:**

    1. The Privacy Objection

Simply put: how can two such vastly different ranges of consciousness literally share *the same* experiences? Doesn't this violate the essential privacy (i.e., the ownership or privileged access) of what it means to have an "experience"? As Bayne also wrote: "particular experiences can only be had by a single consciousness."[305]

Bayne terms the theory of Morris and Swinburne "inclusionism": the theory that Christ had two minds, a human and a divine mind, with the human contained within the divine. On this version of Moderate KM the mind of the divine Son in his divine nature experienced a limited, human range of consciousness, with all the joys and sorrows, suffering and pain that his human life as Jesus Christ entailed, and also, simultaneously translated those experiences onto the level of his properly divine and omniscient perspective on events. In other words,

---

[305] Tim Bayne, "The Inclusion Model of the Incarnation: Problems and Prospects," *Religious Studies* 37, p. 12.

in both ways his human experiences as Jesus of Nazareth were included and preserved as a subset of his overall divine store of experience.

To better understand this, we need to ask the question: who or what is the "person" (Greek *hypostasis*, Latin *suppositum*) that experiences human limitations — including ignorance and suffering — as Jesus of Nazareth?[306] If Jesus was merely a human being, and nothing more, then perhaps his "person" was simply the whole body-soul composite that people referred to as "Jesus of Nazareth" in the first century AD (that would fit with an Aristotelian notion of "person"). Or by his "person" we could mean just his human mind or soul (as a Cartesian philosopher might say).

The doctrine of the Incarnation, according to Moderate KM, however, claims that unique among all the human beings that have ever lived, in Jesus *it is the second person of the Holy Trinity, in his divine nature, that is the ultimate subject of a fully human mode of existence. The human acts and experiences of Jesus are included as a subset and expression of the divine mode of existence of the Son of God.*

Granted that two human personalities or ranges of consciousness, standing "side by side" (so to speak) in two distinct human persons, from two distinct bodily perspectives, cannot have exactly the same experiences in every respect; but why does that necessarily imply that two ranges of consciousness in which one is a subset of another in the same person cannot have identical experiences? As Morris pointed out, we have an analogy for this in cases of multiple personality where there exists in one human person an asymmetric accessing relationship between a central, accessing mind, and one or more additional minds. We have a similar analogy in the possession by each one of us of a subconscious and conscious mind, with something very like an asymmetric, accessing relationship between the two. Moreover, as Hebblethwaite insisted in this context, we have no comprehensive understanding of

---

[306] See Chapter One for a discussion of the meaning of "person" in Christology.

the divine nature that would enable us to say that God is incapable of doing this:

> [W]e are not talking of two separate individuals, but of the divine substance, which is such as to include within its own subjectivity the human subject, Jesus, as the expression and vehicle of God's incarnate life .... Certainly the eternal God and a historical man are beings of a different ontological status. But the claim of the Christian tradition has been that the ontology of God is such as to permit the infinite source of all created beings to come among us as a man. Again, who are we to say that the ontological status of God is such as to render this logically impossible?[307]

To be sure, in the Incarnation we are dealing with something unique that only God can do: include and preserve within his infinite divine mind — by self-restraint of his divine attributes at a particular time and place — the experiences and thoughts, joys and sorrows of a limited human soul and body. But it is not clear that the privacy or privileged access of Jesus to the unique experiences of his human body and soul have thereby been violated, since the "he" to whom those human experiences belonged was the divine person who assumed that form to begin with. In other words, there was no experience of Jesus that "he" (the divine Son) cannot share, because Jesus has no experiences at all that could be separate from the ontological reality of who he is: the divine Son Incarnate. The point of the Incarnation is that Jesus is not a created human person (conceived either in Aristotelian or Cartesian fashion) to whom God the Son has drawn near in some way (logically violating the private ownership of the human experiences of Jesus in the process!); rather, he is God the Son, a divine person, dwelling among us *as* one of us, having limited himself to conform to all the conditions and limitations of human nature.

---

[307] Hebblethwaite, *The Incarnation*, p. 3, and 31.

2.   The Self-Consciousness or "I –Thought" Problem

Bayne writes:

> One would assume that Christ's 'I' thoughts had the same referent irrespective of the consciousness in which they were tokened. ... Surely it was possible for Christ to think of himself (as himself) in either of his consciousnesses, and if he wasn't able to do this by means of I-thoughts, how was he able to do it? ...

> Giving a uniform account of all of Christ's 'I' thoughts seems to prevent us allowing Christ's human consciousness and self-consciousness a truly human character. The problem isn't just that of seeing how 'I' thoughts tokened within two minds can have the same referent ... rather, the problem is seeing how all of Christ's 'I' thoughts can have the same referent given the vastly different nature of his two minds.[308]

This is the problem of the self-consciousness of the Son of God with which Weston struggled, and never fully resolved. The Son must have the same divine person or ego underlying his two distinct sets of relations and vastly different ranges of consciousness, divine and human. **But what does the divine Son Incarnate mean in his human mind when he says "I"? — and is it the same thing that the unlimited *Logos asarkos* understands by "I"? If not, how can Jesus and the Logos be one and the same person? Can two minds or ranges of consciousness, one infinite and the other finite, see themselves as the same "I," the same person? Even if it is not impossible, is it even intelligible?**

The best that Weston could do was to posit that simultaneously the divine Son knows himself as God the Son unlimited, exercising fully all his omni-attributes in his cosmic role, and continually committing himself to all the limitations of his incarnate state, while in addition, at the same time he knows and experiences himself as God-the-Son self-

---

[308] Bayne, "The Inclusion Model of the Incarnation," p. 20-21.

limited in manhood, perceiving himself from within all the conditions of human life.[309] In each state, the self-conscious "I" always refers to his divine person, the second person of the Trinity, although not always to that person in the same set of relations or under the same conditions.

The mystery of self-consciousness of the divine Son in his two natures is not liable to be fully comprehensible to us, given the utter ontological uniqueness of the Incarnation. Again, there seems to be an analogy available to us in cases of asymmetric accessing relationship between multiple human personalities. In such cases, as we have seen, a central accessing personality is aware of its own mental states, and remembers as its own all the thoughts and experiences of a secondary personality as well.

With regard to the Incarnation we are in the realm of mystery for sure, but it is not clear that Moderate KM leaves us in the realm of blatant self-contradiction here. Moderate KM can ease this tension if it is coupled with the belief that in his human soul, Jesus, at first subconsciously, was aware of his unique, filial relationship with his heavenly Father, and ultimately became fully conscious of his own divine identity as an adult.[310] Otherwise, the radical split between these two simultaneous acts of self-consciousness of the divine Son, divine and human, would mean that there is almost no unity of self-consciousness at all in the divine mind of the Son while incarnate. The most we could say would be that in his human mind, Jesus remained aware of having a unique and supremely intimate relationship with the Father, but he never attained an understanding what made it unique — and all this makes it, if not impossible, then at least improbable that these two acts

---

[309] Bulgakov offered a similar perspective in *The Lamb of God*, p. 229 and 284.

[310] **Roch Kereszty, O.Cist., draws a distinction between Christ's human "awareness" of being the divine Son Incarnate, an awareness which he must have had from the very beginning of his human life, and his conscious, reflective "self-knowledge" of his identity in his human consciousness.** See Kereszty, *Jesus Christ: Fundamentals of Christology* (Staten Island, NY: Alba House, third edition, 2002), p. 366-367.

of self-consciousness, divine and human, belong to the same person at the same time.

Some of the later Anglican Kenoticists have been reluctant to ascribe to Jesus explicit knowledge of his divine identity at any stage of his earthly life. Hebblethwaite, for example, endorses the view of Austin Farrer when he writes:

> Jesus did not know that he was God the Son. An omniscient being cannot be very man. But he knows how to be the Son of God in the several situations of his gradually unfolding destiny.[311]

It is not clear, however, why "omniscience" would be required for Jesus of Nazareth to come to conscious and explicit knowledge that he was the divine Son Incarnate. All that would be needed would be for him as a youth to experience a supremely intimate relationship with his heavenly Father (see Lk 2:49), which at some point (probably at his baptism: see Lk 3:22) became an explicit knowledge of his divine identity through a gift of infused insight from the Holy Spirit. Given that all prophetic knowledge of God's nature, character and purposes comes from the Holy Spirit (II Peter 1:21), this kind of prophetic insight cannot be said to require the presence of "omniscience" in a human mind.

David Brown suggests, however, that human self-knowledge of a divine identity would pose a threat to that person's mental equilibrium:

> [I]t is hard to see what sense could be made of a truly human consciousness being aware of itself as divine. Would a conviction of omnipotence, for instance, however derived, not lead a human being to have doubts about his or her own sanity?[312]

---

[311] Hebblethwaite, *The Incarnation*, p. 121; cf. p. 68.
[312] Brown, *Divine Humanity*, p. 183.

More likely, for Jesus an infused knowledge from the Holy Spirit of his own divine identity (probably at his baptism) finally would have made sense for him of his experience since childhood of his supreme and unique intimacy with the Father. His divine Sonship also would have been corroborated by knowledge of the miracle — no doubt communicated to him by Mary and Joseph at some point — of his conception without human fatherhood. Furthermore, the explicit, infused knowledge in his human soul of his divine identity would include the fact that he was the divine Son *under the conditions of manhood*, and thus unable fully to access his omnipotence and omniscience through his human consciousness, in the sphere of his incarnate state. It is hard to see, therefore, how this kind of self-knowledge necessarily would lead him to question his own sanity — although it did lead him to go immediately into the wilderness to wrestle with his identity and his mission.

In fact, one could plausibly argue that the proverbial "shoe is on the other foot": if Jesus really was the divine Son dwelling among us under all the limitations and conditions of human life, then it would be a *lack of knowledge* of his own metaphysical identity that would give us grounds for questioning his sanity. Presumably, if one cannot clearly and accurately answer the question "Are you a divine person?" by the time you are an adult, then you do not have anything remotely close to a healthy sense of personal identity (and a belief in one's own divine identity would only be a clear sign of insanity if that belief was not true).

Moreover, a lack of explicit knowledge by Jesus of his own divine identity would mean that he was not fully aware of the mission he was given by the Father. *For Jesus would have been ignorant of the central tenet of the very gospel that he came to reveal: that "God so loved the world that he gave his only-begotten Son ...." (Jn 3:16). It would mean that in saving the world, in his human range of consciousness Jesus really did not understand what he was accomplishing for humanity, and how he was able to accomplish it.* In so far as that saving work was based on the fact that he was the Divine Word made flesh, if he was unaware of his

**own divine identity he would not have known in his human mind
what he was doing.**

In part, Hebblethwaite, Brown, et al seem to be driven to posit
ignorance in Jesus of his own divine identity by an alleged consensus
of Scripture scholarship on this point — and even more by what it
would mean for Jesus truly to share our lot in his total kenotic
identification with the human condition. But as far back as 1909, P.T.
Forsyth strongly contested this view in *The Person and Place of Jesus*
Christ:

> He knew himself to be among men for certain universal
> purposes, to be final king, judge, and redeemer. Could it have
> escaped him that these were functions which in Israel's ideal
> were reserved for God alone? He calls himself king in God's
> kingdom. He is the bridegroom of the true Israel, whose
> husband, in all the Old Testament, was God alone. He is to sit
> on the throne of glory, where no Jew could place any but God.
> The angels he sends forth are *his* angels. The blessed of the
> father are *his* elect. … He knows himself to be final judge, and
> there is no appeal, and no revision of his sentence. …
>
> Christ's sense of finality we must recognise, which is his faith,
> however implicit, in his own Godhead. We must acknowledge
> his sense of his own finality in the last moral issue of the world,
> the supreme human issue, the issue between God and man, life
> and death. He knew he was decisive in that issue. And who
> could be final or decisive there but God? The final revelation
> could only be God revealing Himself, in the sense of
> bestowing Himself, and Himself coming to men to restore
> communion. … A message could never be the final revelation,
> nor could a messenger. … **[W]e possess God in a Christ
> who does, and knows he does, things reserved always for
> God to do. … Was the Great Saviour so dull as not to
> realise that?** As he felt his own mission alone among all men
> to save, how did he feel as he read in his Bible words like these:
> "I am God, and besides me there is no Saviour"? How would

that have struck him as he knew himself to be not merely the herald of salvation but the Saviour, when he not only forgave particular cases but knew he was there to ransom the world by an offering for sin?[313]

We shall return to this important issue later in this book. Suffice it to say here that the pendulum in biblical scholarship has swung back a bit on these matters in recent years. As I wrote in an essay for the *Canadian Journal of the Fellowship of Catholic Scholars:*

> Arguably, from the earliest days of the Jesus movement on record, a follower of Jesus was someone who confessed at least implicitly that Jesus is the divine Lord (I Cor 12:3, cf. I Cor 8:6), someone who worshipped and prayed to him as such (Acts 7:59; I Cor 16:22; Phil 2:6-11; Rev 22:20), and someone who was "baptised into Christ" (Gal 3:27) — all concepts that shatter the boundaries of pre-70 AD Palestinian Judaism ....

> The real "historical Jesus," one suspects, cannot be easily confined either to Greco-Roman or to Palestinian-Jewish categories of thought. There is plenty of data in the Gospel accounts that suggests that Jesus of Nazareth made extraordinary claims that fit no one's clear expectations at that time, and no one's pre-conceptions: for example, he claimed the absolute trust, loyalty and devotion of others in a way proper to God alone [Mt 8:22, 11:28-30; Lk 14:26]; he claimed to be the only true and authoritative interpreter of the Torah [Mt 5:17-48, 19:3-12], and the unsurpassable and unique revealer of God the Father as the only one who truly knows him (even according to "Q": Mt 11:27, Lk 10:22); he claimed to be greater than the Temple [Mt 12:6] and Lord of the Sabbath [Mk 2:28]; he sometimes spoke of himself in biblical images and metaphors that properly belonged to God alone (such as the "Bridegroom" and the "Good Shepherd" [Mk 2:19-20; Mt 26:31; Lk 15:3-7]); he exhibited a unique intimacy

---

[313] Forsyth, *The Person and Place of Christ*, p. 90 and 92-93; my emphasis.

with God, calling him "Abba," Father [Mk 14:36], and "My Father in Heaven" [Mt 11:27, 16:17; Lk 2:49], but never "Our Father" in a way that included himself [Lk 11:2]; he exhibited extraordinary supernatural power, not only in healing the sick, but also in calming a storm at sea and multiplying loaves and fishes to feed multitudes — miracles most often accomplished not by means of prayer and supplication (as the prophets had done), but by his own personal authority and command; he claimed to be the physician of sinners [Mt 9:12], the Son of Man sent from heaven with authority on earth to forgive sins [Mk 2:1-12], to give his life as a ransom for sinners [Mk 10:45 14:22-25], and ultimately to be the final judge of the world [Mt 25: 31-46]. In all this we have left on one side consideration of the sayings of Jesus in St. John's Gospel, and focused largely on the multiple attestation of Jesus' self-revelation in the synoptic Gospels. The central *explicit* message of Jesus in the synoptic Gospels was indeed the proclamation of the dawning of God's Kingdom ... but one could also argue that the *implicit* message that permeates his words and deeds was that the Kingdom of God is breaking into the world precisely because God Himself has come to dwell among us, sharing our lot in a truly human way, in the person of His Son [Mt 22:41-46; Mk 12:6, 13:32; Lk 10:22][314] ....

---

[314] In his ground-breaking work, *Did Jesus Know He was God?* (Chicago: Franciscan Herald Press, 1984), Francois Dreyfus, OP, of the Ecole Biblique in Jerusalem reminds us that Christ's knowledge of his own divinity in his human soul must have been a purely reflexive and relational knowledge of his divine Sonship — just as it is the life of the eternal Trinity:

[I]n his psychological and existential dimension ... we can say that it is radically impossible for Jesus himself to glance upon himself. Since he is a divine person who is only the relationship of love to the Father, he is himself, Jesus of Nazareth, related the Father by all fibres of his being, totally and integrally. And certainly Jesus himself is aware of himself; he had an awareness of himself infinitely greater and better than we. But it is an awareness which is uniquely and totally filial. He is aware of himself in and through the Father, without any backward glance upon himself. It is in his look of love toward the Father that Jesus himself is

In the end, we are left with the same reactions to the real, historical Jesus that his own contemporaries had, and with the same questions that cry out for an answer: "Where did this man get this wisdom and his mighty works?" (Mk 13:54) and "Why does this man speak thus? ... Who can forgive sins but God alone?" (Mk 2:7), and "Who then is this, that even the wind and the sea obey him?" (Mk 4:41).[315]

For all of these reasons, a radical split with regard to the self-consciousness of the divine Son — with the Son in his human range of consciousness as Jesus of Nazareth unaware of his own divine identity, both subconsciously as a child and consciously as an adult — does not seem to be historically necessary, or psychologically or theologically plausible, nor is it the best fit with Moderate KM.

3. The Divine Infallibility Problem

Given that in Moderate KM, the divine mind of the Son contains, or includes within itself, the human mind of the Incarnate, Jesus of Nazareth, the question arises whether the divine mind of the Son held any false beliefs in his human range of consciousness

aware of himself, totally, since he only exists by the Father, in the Father, for the Father. Jesus knows that he is God: this formula, however correct it is, is nevertheless inadequate. It would be better to say: In his look of love toward the Father Jesus sees that the Father has given everything to him [as his only Son], everything that he is, everything that he possesses, and that this total gift is completely reciprocal: "All I have is yours and all you have is mine" (Jn 17:10). (p. 107)

[315] Robert Stackpole, "Promise and Perils in contemporary 'Jesus Research,'" in *Journal of the Canadian Chapter of the Fellowship of Catholic Scholars,* Winter-Spring, 2012, p. 107-108. I have added some minor edits and scripture references to the original article here, but with no attempt to include all the synoptic parallels. A somewhat similar perspective can be found in New Testament scholar N.T. Wright's book *Simply Jesus* (New York: Harper One, 2011), p. 79-80, 132-133, 135,142-143, 169, 171, and 176.

that contradict what he knows to be true in his properly divine, unlimited range of consciousness. Bayne explains the problem for us (and Morris' attempted solution of it):

> [T]he model does not seem to be consistent with the claim that God is infallible. The argument is straightforward: (1) Jesus had false beliefs. (2) All of Christ's beliefs are properly attributable to God [that is, to his divine mind, in the human range of consciousness included within it]. Therefore, (3) God had false beliefs. … [Morris replied]: "From the earthly mind of Jesus containing the belief that the sun moves around the earth, it thus would not follow that this is something believed by God the Son in his properly divine mind. The divine mind would have perfect access to the contents of the human mind and thus would know this belief to be contained in the human mind. It just would not thereby have this belief as one of its own beliefs." (Morris, 1986, 159f.)

Clearly, something is wrong with the response here; for Morris has already told us that the divine mind "contains" the human mind of Jesus Christ as its own. If a false belief of Jesus is not contained within and attributable to the divine mind, then whose belief is it? Bayne comments:

> This response [by Morris] is untenable. The inclusion model claims that God the Son, a single person, acquired human form and a human consciousness. It follows from this that the *entire* contents of the human consciousness can be ascribed to God the Son. … [W]hat is the ontological basis for the claim that only some of Christ's conscious states belong to Christ? Orthodoxy doesn't claim that Jesus was God the Son only on certain occasions or in certain respects. Nor does it claim that God is infallible only in the divine mind. Its claim is simply that God does not have any false beliefs.[316]

---

[316] Bayne, "The Inclusion Model of the Incarnation," p. 21-24.

Unfortunately, Bayne rejected a possible solution to this dilemma right from the outset. **Given that Jesus was fully human, Bayne wrote, a Jew of first-century Palestine whose human consciousness (like that of all human beings) grew and developed in a fallible cultural context, "one would expect a thoroughly human consciousness to contain false beliefs."**[317] **But this is to presuppose that error (and not just limitation of knowledge and growth in knowledge) is a natural and essential condition of the human mind. On the contrary, it could be the case that Jesus Christ had a fully human mind with a *limited* range of knowledge, but that he never had *false* beliefs that contradicted those in his properly divine, omniscient range of consciousness.** This in fact was Weston's position:

> [A]ttempts must be made to re-assert the inerrancy of the divine Redeemer without in any way minimizing the reality of His manhood. ... He could not through His divine nature see a thing as black, which in His Incarnate state He knows as white. ... For nothing will ever make it legitimate to say that a matter was related to the Son as Incarnate as being a truth which at the same moment was related to the Son as unlimited logos as being untrue. The unity of the person of the Word is the pledge of the infallible truth of every word He spoke. The mind of Jesus was only Jewish in so far as the Jewish mind of His age reflected the truth. Every word that He uttered is for ever true. Human the mind was and is to this day: human truly and completely; but whatever its limitations, whatever the measure of its ignorance, whatever the medium of its self-expression, it was infallibly true.[318]

Nevertheless, the question for Moderate KM would remain: how could Jesus be preserved from accepting the errors of his culture that he was taught as a boy, and still be considered a fully human youth, with a fully human mental life?

---

[317] Ibid., p. 22.
[318] Weston, *The One Christ*, p. 7 and 226.

C. Stephen Layman expressed a similar difficulty with Moderate KM (which he calls the "Divided-Mind" view of the Incarnation):

> If we say that Jesus did not hold such beliefs [that is, false beliefs taught to him as a child] then we apparently deny that Jesus had a child's natural, deep trust in authority figures. The only viable alternative would be to claim that the child Jesus had such trust but was somehow prevented (by his divine consciousness?) from exercising it in every case in which an authority figure asserted a falsehood. Either way, we sharply qualify the sense in which Jesus took on a human mind.[319]

Still, one wonders: couldn't the child Jesus have been led by the Holy Spirit to trust adults up to a point, but prevented from accepting any falsehoods that they might teach him simply by enabling him to withhold his judgment on such matters? At every stage of his maturation process, he would then remain infallible, but limited and subject to growth in consciously apprehended knowledge. That does not seem to violate the parameters of authentic humanity any more than forms of genius possessed by children make them a different species from their peers.[320] Consider, for example, the child Mozart, who must have had a child's natural trust in authority figures too, up to a point, yet even from an early age his musical "ear" could spot errors in composition and harmony by his tutors to an astonishing degree. The child Jesus, it may be said, was a genius in faith and morals in the only way one can be a genius in such aspects of mental life, that is, by a supernatural rather than a natural gift: the gift of the Holy Spirit.[321]

---

[319] Layman, *Philosophical Approaches to Atonement, Incarnation, and Trinity*, p. 94.

[320] A similar analogy is discussed in Dreyfus, *Did Jesus Know He Was God?*, p. 116.

[321] Of course, this analogy — intended to establish the plausibility that Jesus was infallible in matters of faith and morals in his human soul, without violating the boundaries of what is truly human — still does not fully solve the problem that Bayne raised with "inclusion" (i.e., Moderate Kenotic) models of the Incarnation. To avoid the problem of false beliefs being attributed to God we would need to

We will discuss the infallibility of Christ's human mind in greater depth in Part Two, Chapter Two of this book. **Suffice it to say here that the obvious escape from Bayne's "divine infallibility" problem for Moderate KM would be to posit not *omniscience* in the human mind of Christ (as if he knows all things), but *infallibility* (i.e., what he believes to be true, he knows truly).**

Layman added another concern with Moderate KM when he proposed that this model makes it hard to understand in what sense the divine Son may be said to have taken on a human body:

[N]ote that several of the grounds for claiming that a person has a body involve clear limitations:

a. Limits on how much of the physical world one can control through basic actions
b. Limits on *how* one knows (e.g., so much of human knowledge depends on sense experience and the proper functioning of the brain)
c. A limited point of view on the world
d. Limits on mental functioning when the body (especially the brain) is not functioning properly.

But since the Divided-Mind view insists that Jesus Christ was at all times omnipotent and omniscient, it cannot allow that he had any of these limitations. Thus, it seems that the Divided-mind view either implicitly denies that the Son took on a human body or it claims that he had a body only in a very attenuated sense. At the very least we can say that a theory of

---

say that the divine Son, dwelling among us as Jesus of Nazareth, was infallible in his human mind with regard to *every* kind of knowledge. I shall leave further discussion of this latter possibility — and how it might fit with Christ's authentic humanity — to Part Two, Chapter Two of this book. **For now, I simply ask the reader to consider that infallibility can be ascribed to the human mind of Jesus *at least* on matters of faith and morals, without implying that his human mind was omniscient, for infallibility is certainly in accord with a limited and ever growing store of knowledge in his human soul (Mk 13:32; Lk 2:40).**

the incarnation that provides for a stronger sense of embodiment would have at least one important merit that is lacking in the Divided-Mind view.[322]

Layman's concern here, however, trades upon a certain ambiguity in his treatment of the Two-Minds Theory of the Incarnation. Several times in his book Layman says that the Incarnation means that Jesus Christ is "identical" with the divine Son of God. But at best that is shorthand for the doctrine of the Incarnation, which holds that **Jesus Christ is identical with the divine Son *as incarnate*, that is, *the divine Son in the human state that he assumed*. In other words, "Jesus Christ" and "the divine Son" are not precise synonyms (for example, it would be awkward to say that "*Jesus* created the world"); rather, Jesus Christ is identical with, and the name for the divine Son *in his incarnate form, the Logos ensarkos*. Technically, when we refer to "Jesus Christ," therefore, we are speaking of the divine Son in his human form as Jesus of Nazareth, not the *Logos asarkos* in his states which are not limited by, nor included in that form.** Thus, we can say in the Nicene Creed we believe in "one Lord Jesus Christ, the only begotten Son of God, begotten of his Father before all worlds," but we do not mean by this that the human form that the divine Son assumed was "begotten by His Father before all worlds." Rather, we mean that numerically the same *divine person* who was eternally begotten of the Father came among us as one of us in time and history as Jesus Christ.[323]

It follows that it would be misleading to say that "Jesus Christ" was at all times omnipotent and omniscient. Rather, to be more precise, Moderate KM claims that the divine Son retained the exercise of his omniscience and omnipotence throughout the

---

[322] Ibid., p. 98.

[323] Norman Anderson makes a similar point in *The Mystery of the Incarnation*: "There is no reason that I can see ... why we should equate the divine Logos or Son so *completely* with Jesus, or Jesus with the Second Person of the Trinity, as to suggest that *Jesus as Jesus* was pre-existent, or that the Logos was altogether confined to ... Jesus during his earthly life" (p. 102).

universe even while restraining the exercise of these omni-attributes at a certain time and place in order to dwell among us in a fully human way as Jesus Christ. In that human state, he could be said to have had all of the bodily limitations listed by Layman.

Bayne ends his own discussion of Moderate KM (or "inclusionism") with these remarks:

> Perhaps none of the objections presented against standard inclusionism amount to outright refutation of the model — given the deep obscurity of the concepts involved it is difficult to see how one might *prove* that the model is false — but they do, I think, pose serious challenges for the model.[324]

It would seem that Bayne has exaggerated the problems here, in two respects.

First, any model of the Incarnation is going to have difficulties, precisely because of the ontological uniqueness of the Incarnation. The best we can do is draw analogies that help to make the model intelligible, and try to avoid blatant contradictions within the model itself, as well as contradictions of the wider pattern of Christian belief.

Second, the best theory of the Incarnation is not one that has no challenges at all, but one with the fewest and least critical challenges. In this respect Moderate KM in the Anglican tradition, originating with the Lutheran Martensen, but developed further by Anglicans Gore, Weston, Quick, Hebblethwaite and Swinburne (with a bit of help from the Protestant philosopher Thomas Morris), can offer a fairly coherent and intelligible model of the mystery of the Incarnation. Moreover, the nature of the difficulties it presents pale in comparison with the problems we had to face with Radical KM. As we have seen, even the version of Radical KM with the fewest serious problems (the Forsyth-Mackintosh-Taylor approach), leaves us having to radically re-

---

[324] Bayne, "The Inclusion model of the Incarnation," p. 26.

configure the classical Christian understanding of the nature of God as infinitely perfect Being — or at least, as essentially omniscient, omnipotent and omnipresent — for in the mainstream Christian tradition a truly divine person cannot be said to lack full access to any of his divine attributes, or render himself unable to utilize them. Furthermore, in classical, mainstream Christianity, God is *essentially* all-knowing and infinitely loving, and not just by arbitrary edict of his (allegedly) Unconditioned Will, as Radical KM seems to imply. In short, some form of "voluntarist" understanding of the nature of God seems inevitable with Radical KM, with all its attendant problems.

The Anglican stream of Moderate Kenoticism, on the other hand, avoids these problems, and yet retains most of the advantages of the general kenotic approach. On this model, the divine Son exercises all of his cosmic functions and attributes as the omniscient, omnipotent, and omnipresent Word, even as he takes on the form of a human consciousness and will, with human limitations, conditions and choices. As Jesus of Nazareth, he truly shares our lot, with all its cares and struggles. This fully human experience is taken into the very divine nature itself, included and preserved in the divine store of divine experience. The Son of God freely willed to make this loving self-sacrifice, becoming incarnate among us out of love for us. As St. Paul put it: "You know the grace of our Lord Jesus Christ, that though he was rich, yet for your sake he became poor, so that by his poverty you might become rich" (2 Cor 8:9).

David Brown and the Method-Acting Analogy

We also need to consider a unique case of Anglican Moderate KM. In his book *Divine Humanity: Kenosis and the Construction of a Christian Theology* (2011), David Brown offered a fresh analogy and theory of the Incarnation that fits with some of the basic features of the Moderate Kenotic Model. Brown has done a tremendous service to the wider Church by keeping alive in-depth consideration of kenotic theories of the Incarnation, tracing the complicated history of Kenoticism, and rebutting the all too often facile and misinformed critique it has suffered. The Kenotic Theory he presents in *Divine Humanity*, however, presents the reader with some significant challenges of its own.

Brown proposes that there is a flow of experience between the two natures of Jesus Christ, but this time (unlike his version of TNC that we considered in Chapter One) he posits that God the Son has *totally* identified with a historical instance of human nature, analogous to the way that an actor using the Stanislavsky method imaginatively identifies as much as possible with the dramatic character he assumes. Brown sees the Incarnation as a *complete* projection of one self into another self, in a way that is only possible for God. He calls it "the deliberate merging of the projected divine consciousness with a particular human history .... The divine 'nature' becomes the subject of the specific humanity derived from Mary, which also sets it within a specific social and cultural context."[325] This means that during his kenotic identification with the human life of Jesus, God fully shares the perspectives and experiences of Jesus "from the inside," so to speak, from a fully human perspective, and learns what it is like to be human. At the same time, that human experience flows back into his properly divine mind, and there is experienced on the divine level from an omniscient perspective on events. Thus, the consciousness of the divine Son during his incarnate life would include two levels or ranges simultaneously: his kenotic, fully human experience, and that experience also translated onto the non-kenotic, properly divine, omniscient level. Meanwhile, of course, the effect on the human nature of this total projection of the divine self is that Jesus draws "into his life from the divine the pattern of how divine [Trinitarian] life might be lived under purely human conditions."[326]

Discussion of David Brown's theory among scholars is only just beginning. This is a version of Moderate KM that sees the divine Son fusing in a mysterious way with the historical reality of a

[325] Brown, *Divine Humanity*, p. 252-253.
[326] Ibid., p. 256-257.

created instance of human nature, Jesus of Nazareth. But for that very reason, the theory appears to suffer from some of the same problems we saw with his version of TNC (see the end of Chapter One, above). For example, **is this really an "incarnational" Christology, one that fits within the parameters of what was taught by the Third, Fourth and Fifth of the Ecumenical Councils of the Church regarding the mystery of the Incarnation? In other words, is Jesus Christ a *created* person or an *uncreated divine* person (as we have seen, the latter is what the Third and Fourth Councils implied, and the Fifth Council explicitly attested)?** Arguably, he cannot be both without lapsing into some form of Nestorianism. Moreover, what understanding of "person" is at work here? Can two persons, one created and the other uncreated, actually come together to become a single "person"?[327] If

---

[327] In Brown's defence, it should be said that his theory has a precursor in the fusion language in the *Hymns on the Nativity* composed by St. Ephrem the Syrian in the fourth century, who, for example, likened the Incarnation to the blending of pigments in a painting. Moreover, Brown can make a claim that Jesus and the divine Son become one and the same person in the incarnation *if* having the same character and the same set of memories are always fully sufficient indicators of personal identity. The point remains a contentious one, however, in contemporary philosophy. In *God in a Single Vision*: *Integrating Philosophy and Theology* (London: Routledge, 2016), Brown explains that in his theory of the Incarnation, he posits "a real merging into a single consciousness, even if its contents are derived from two quite distinct sources and so technically remain 'two'" (p. 99). But in what sense are they "distinct" sources that "remain two" in the Incarnation? Again, if they are two distinct *persons* (one divine and one human) whose natures have co-mingled in the way Brown describes, and if it is the *persons* that "remain two," it would seem we have violated the teachings of the Council of Chalcedon here (which clearly spoke of one person in the Incarnation as the subject of the two natures) and we have lapsed into a form of Nestorianism. On the other hand, if they are two distinct *natures* from two distinct persons that have commingled to produce a *single* person, we are left asking: is that person created or uncreated? For only if Christ is an *uncreated, divine* person dwelling among us under all the conditions of humanity would Brown's theory match the implicit teachings of the Third and Fourth Ecumenical Councils, and the explicit teachings of the Fifth. On these conciliar teachings see our discussion of Brown's Two-Nature model of the Incarnation in Chapter One, above.

not, again, Brown's theory leaves us with two persons in the Incarnation rather than one.

In an address delivered at a theological conference in Augsburg, Germany in June, 2018, Brown responded to these concerns by explaining that on his model, "the coincidence [in Jesus] of the two movements (divine to human and human to divine) can appropriately be seen as divinely constituted in a single person," and added in a footnote: "That is, [can be seen as] a common ontological basis that grounds their relational movements"[328] In both classical Two-Nature Christology and Kenotic Christology, however the "hypostatic union" of human and divine in Jesus was not usually seen as the movement of a divine person into some kind of merger or fusion with a created, human person — not even by the gracious initiative of that divine person. Rather, a different kind of unifying "two movements," a synergistic union, was held to be the result of the prior act of the divine Son in taking flesh, and dwelling among us under all the conditions of humanity, body and soul: the divine Son Incarnate opened his human soul completely to the mind and will of the Father, by the Holy Spirit. In other words, there is a kind of divine-human "synergy" that is the *result* of the Incarnation, not the *definition* of it.

Finally, Brown has compared the divine act of incarnation with the projection of self into the reality of another human life involved in "method-acting." But in human method-acting, the capacity to do this is largely driven by the human capacity for empathy and sympathy. As we shall see in Part Two of this book, it is not clear how a person can closely empathise and sympathise with the life-situation of another, if he has never undergone experiences that are at least generically similar. Tim Bayne wrote:

---

[328] To date unpublished; quoted with permission of Dr. Brown. The address will be published in 2019 as part of a collection of essays in English and German, Thomas Marschel and Thomas Schartl, eds., *Trinitat als Revision des klassichen Theismus?* (Munster: Aschendorff, 2019).

It is very plausible to suppose that one can only know what it's like to have an experience of a certain type by having had a similar sort of experience. If that is right, then God needed to have had human experiences in order to know what it is like to be human. God couldn't know what it is like to suffer and be abandoned without himself suffering and feeling abandoned.[329]

Brown himself insisted on this point in his earlier book, *The Divine Trinity.*[330] **But it would seem that in his version of Moderate KM in *Divine Humanity,* he has put the proverbial "cart before the horse": he posits that the divine Son can fully and completely empathise and sympathise with all the experiences of a human being, Jesus of Nazareth, *without ever having experienced human life before, from a fully human perspective.***

David Brown's theory stands somewhat apart from the mainstream of Anglican Moderate Kenoticism. Nevertheless, his proposal at least shows that in-depth work to develop a kenotic understanding of the Incarnation is still alive in the Anglican world, and hopefully will continue to move forward in the generations to come.

---

[329] Bayne, "The Inclusion Model of the Incarnation," p. 4.

[330] Brown, *The Divine Trinity,* p. 247. In *God in a Single Vision*, Brown argues that in his version of Moderate KM, "What occurs is ... significantly different from empathy. The latter is a matter of trying to enter into another's experience while fully aware that it is not one's own" (p. 99). But this is also what happens in method acting; however much the actor tries to deeply empathize with the character he is playing, imagining himself "in the shoes" of that character, he remains at some level well aware that he has not completely exchanged one identity for another. Thus, the only way we can apply the method-acting analogy to the Incarnation would be to see the Incarnation as an instance of *perfect empathy*, in which the divine Son was able completely to empathize with the human experiences of Jesus of Nazareth, and in that sense totally identify with them (without, of course, losing the sense of his own, eternal divine identity) — and the question remains how he can perform such a feat of perfect empathy for a particular human being without ever having experienced the human condition himself before.

Chapter Five
Critique of All Forms of the Kenotic Theory

As we saw at the very outset of this book, many theologians and philosophers over the past century and a half have extensively criticized the Kenotic Theory of the Incarnation. The Roman Catholic theologian von Balthasar claimed that it "leads nowhere." Even in the Anglican world, there have been no shortage of severe critics. John A.T. Robinson, for example, dismissed the whole kenotic enterprise as "a fruitless expenditure of theological ingenuity."[331] In this book, I have endeavored to "let the other side be heard," so to speak, and to show that some forms of the Kenotic Theory, especially the Moderate KM pursued by several Anglican thinkers in the 20th century, can survive most of the charges brought against it.

So far, however, we have focused our attention on the critique levelled at specific types of the Kenotic Theory. We need to close by looking at the charges levelled at the theory in general, no matter what form is under discussion.

The German Lutheran theologian Paul Althaus, for example, rejected Kenoticism on the grounds that it implies that God was not fully present and manifest in the humanity of Christ; God could only reveal himself by limiting or abandoning his divine nature. Althaus emphasised "the *whole* glory and power of God in the uncurtailed, unchanged humanity of Jesus," a mystery open only to the eyes of faith.[332] There is certainly some truth in this charge, at least in so far as it is levelled against "radical" forms of Kenoticism. As we have seen, Radical KM implies that in the Incarnation the divine Son, while dwelling solely in a limited and incarnate state, is not able fully to access his divine, omni-attributes, and no longer able to act as Lord of creation and history. It follows that he is not fully divine or worthy of

---

[331] Robinson, *The Human Face of God*, p. 207-208.
[332] Paul Althaus, "Kenosis," in K. Galling, ed., *Die Religion in Geschichte und Geganwart*, vol. III (Tubingen, 1959), p. 1243-1246. Similarly, See Colin Gunton, *Yesterday and Today* (London: Darton, Longman and Todd, 1983), p. 172.

worship when he dwells among us as Jesus of Nazareth. But this kind of criticism hardly seems fair when levelled against *all* forms of Kenoticism. Moderate KM, for example, would not be open to this charge. In any case, the Bible teaches that finite and sinful man cannot see the *whole* glory of God manifest in this life (Ex 33:18; cf. Jn 1:14 with I Cor 13:12), not even through Christ. Saint John implies that the Logos *left* the fullness of his divine glory to become incarnate, and returns to it only after his resurrection, though to some extent he manifested that divine glory on earth as well (Jn 1:14; 17:5, 24). Even God's incarnate self-revelation, therefore, must involve a measure of *veiling* (as Althaus himself admitted).

Besides, as we have seen, Kenoticism in some of its forms can hold (along with all authentically "incarnational" Christianity) that the wisdom and power of God's merciful love was uniquely operative, and most fully revealed (insofar as it can be revealed to us) in the wondrous act by which he chose to share our human condition to save us from sin and death: "In this the love of God was made manifest among us, that God sent his only-begotten Son into the world, so that we might live through him" (I Jn 4:9).

The Reformed theologian Emil Brunner, for example, once wrote that the Cross of the Incarnate manifests Divine Love not in spite of, but because of the weakness and frailty of the Son's humanity: "It is precisely the supreme point of the ... Kenosis which is the supreme height of the self-manifestation of God."[333] In other words, the Cross shows the depths of God's love for us: the extent of the self-sacrifice that God was willing to undergo for our salvation. Indeed, if our previous discussion of the omnipotence of God is acceptable, then *the Son-in-kenosis manifests not only the depths of Divine Love, but also, paradoxically, the supreme power of that love at work in human history.* As Frank Weston put it: "If we are driven to speak of limitations and conditions imposed upon the Word by His own will, we think not of a diminution

---

[333] Emil Brunner, *The Christian Doctrine of Creation and Redemption: Dogmatics volume II* (London: Lutterworth, 1952), p. 361.

of power so much as the manifestation of a powerful Love."[334] In this way, at least, the "glory" of the Lord was truly manifested in and through his kenotic incarnation.

Althaus further contended that rational speculation into the manner of the Incarnation significantly reduces the element of faith involved for the believer. But again, this criticism seems to "overshoot the mark." We need not be afraid of a measure rational exploration in Christology, for we are exhorted by Christ himself to love God with all our "mind," as well as all our heart, soul and strength (Mk 12:30). Moreover rational scrutiny in Christology merely seeks to establish the coherence and intelligibility of what we mean when we speak of "the Incarnation," so that we speak as clearly as we can of this mystery, and sing the praises of God "with understanding" (Ps 47:7; I Cor 14:15). Rational analysis also tries to insure that our understanding of the Incarnation fits with — even illuminates and strengthens, if possible — the wider pattern of Christian belief. To believe that the divine Son has *actually* taken flesh in human history, however, and to commit one's whole life to Jesus Christ as Lord and Savior, still involves a tremendous act of faith.

Furthermore, no responsible proponent of a kenotic theory of the Incarnation is going to claim that their model gives us a *comprehensive* understanding of the Incarnation. Where the saving acts of God are concerned, we are dealing with holy mysteries. To paraphrase Karl Rahner: a holy mystery is not something we know nothing about (hence doctrines, creeds, and theories!), but something about which there always remains more to be said. There are depths upon depths of the mystery of God in Christ that we can never fully fathom with our finite minds: "now we see in a mirror dimly" (I Cor 13:12). **With regard to the mystery of the Incarnation, Charles Gore stated: "It must have involved an act of self-limitation *greater than we can fathom*, for the eternal to begin to think and act and speak under the conditions of humanity."[335] The best of our doctrines and theories, therefore, may be "true as far as they go," but they can**

---

[334] Weston, *The One Christ*, p. 228.
[335] Gore, *The Incarnation of the Son of God*, p. 161, italics mine.

never entirely capture the wonders of Divine Love. As the poet Tennyson wrote: "Our little systems have their day, they have their day and cease to be, they are but broken lights of thee, and thou O God, art more than they."[336]

Kenoticism and Classical Chalcedonian Doctrine

Some critiques of Kenoticism arise from sharp questions being asked about modern theology as a whole. For example, in her book *Jesus, Humanity and the Trinity* (2001), Anglican theologian Kathryn Tanner argued that Christian orthodoxy begins to be compromised when we look upon God and humanity as two contestants trying to occupy the same space, so that God has to recede from the world or limit himself in order to make room for his creation. Classical Christianity did not see any such competition between the Creator and his creatures. Rather, God in his goodness was held to bring about the whole plane of creaturely being and activity from beyond, from the transcendent plane of uncreated being, and God was said to be everywhere present to creatures, not crowding them out but *enabling* them to be. **Similarly, Tanner argued, in Christology we do not need to try to blend or squeeze together two natures, divine and human, on the same plane or level of reality. Rather, in the Incarnation there is a unique intersection of opposites, in which an incomprehensibly greater divine person, who creates and sustains the universe, is at the same time "hypostatically" united with human nature.**[337]

Tanner's is indeed a trenchant critique of much of modern theology. A clear example of the problem she is addressing can be found in an essay by Jurgen Moltmann entitled "God's Kenosis in the Creation and Consummation of the World."[338] According to Moltmann, God must

---

[336] Alfred Lord Tennyson, "In Memoriam A.H.H.," stanza five.

[337] Tanner, *Jesus, Humanity, and the Trinity*, p. 1-33.

[338] Jurgen Moltmann, "God's Kenosis in the creation and Consummation of the World" in Polkinghorne, ed., *The Work of Love*, p. 145. Similarly, see the Roman Catholic theologian Lucien Richard's exposition of creation as *kenosis* in *Christ: The Self-Emptying of God*, p. 138-139: "Seen from God's side, creation may be

get himself out-of-the-way as much as possible to provide living space for his creatures:

> God's determination to be Creator is linked with the consideration for his creation that allows it space and time and its own movement, so that it is not crushed by the divine reality or absorbed by it. By differentiating himself as Creator from a created world, God creates a reality that is not divine, but is not Nothing either, and preserves it by distancing himself from it. How can a finite world co-exist with the Infinite God? Does it set a limit to the limitless God, or does God limit himself? If this limit or frontier between infinity and finitude is already 'fore-given' to God, then God is not infinite. If God is in his very essence infinite, then any such limit or frontier exists only through his self-limitation. That makes it possible for a finite world to co-exist with God …. Before God went out of himself in order to create a non-divine world, he withdrew himself into himself in order to make room for the world and to concede it a space.[339]

Moltmann simply does not consider the possibility that infinite, uncreated being might be of an entirely different order than finite created being, and therefore that God's infinity would pose no threat to the reality of finite existence. To draw an analogy: it is not the case that the more a room is filled with musical sound, the less it can be filled with color: sound and color just do not compete for living space,

---

considered as a sort of yielding, a making room for an 'other.' In order to create a world 'outside,' God must have made room for finitude in Godself. The 'nothingness' in the creation *ex nihilo* comes to be because God withdraws God's overwhelming presence and restricts God's power. … Creation emerges as empty space, as God-forsaken space, as space set free for creation's own creativity." One wonders what possible foundation this kind of radically kenotic notion might have in Genesis 1 and 2, or with the teachings of the saints and Fathers of the Church on the doctrine of creation. Richard certainly does not bother to tell us where this can be found, even implicitly, in the fonts of divine revelation for a Catholic theologian: namely Scripture and Sacred Tradition.

[339] Ibid., p. 145-146.

as very different orders of being. Of course, lurking behind Moltmann's perspective here is Hegel's idea of the "true infinite": the idea that an infinite being must include everything that exists in its own being or it would not be infinite. Moltmann escapes from Hegel's extreme panentheism only by positing a necessary divine self-limitation of God's own infinite nature in order to enable all his creatures to be.[340]

Tanner's critique of this understanding of God's act of creation is surely right on target. **Unfortunately, she seems at times to confuse the issue of God's universal presence and work as Creator with the very different issue of his special form of presence and work in the world in the Incarnation. In the latter, we are dealing with the loving and self-sacrificial act of God in which somehow, without ceasing to be fully divine, God truly meets us and addresses us *on our level,* on the fully human plane of reality, by coming among us as one of us, taking upon himself our human condition and limitations. In other words, the Incarnation is precisely the act in which God has come to inhabit our "space," — as St. John put it, the Word became flesh and "tabernacled" (literally in Greek, "pitched his tent") among us (Jn 1:14). This inevitably raises questions about how an infinite, uncreated being can do this, without ceasing to be the God he ever is.**

---

[340] There are strong philosophical reasons for believing Hegel's notion of the "true infinite" to be false. Arguably, he has confused infinity as a quantitative or spatial concept with infinite being. After all, if by infinite being we mean a being who possesses infinite "transcendentals" (truth, beauty, and goodness), then it is clear that infinite being can create finite being without those creatures competing for a share of those transcendentals with him, and without requiring him to limit his own possession of them in order for his creatures to receive a share. Imagine, for example, a university lecturer with infinite knowledge of physics. The fact that he bestows some of that knowledge of truth on his students through his lectures does not mean that he thereby loses some of that truth in the process, or that he has to limit his own knowledge of truth in order to "make room" for their reception of knowledge; rather, infinite truth, as an aspect of infinite being, can be shared without loss and received without diminishing its source. The same would hold for the transcendentals "'beauty" and "goodness."

Simply to retreat back into classical Two-Nature Christology, and speak of an incomprehensible hypostatic addition to God's normal _modus vivendi_ as Creator is not very illuminating (see our discussion of classical TNC in Chapter One of this book).

Tanner challenges Kenotic Christology, claiming that it holds that divine and human attributes would be incompatible in the same personal subject — in competition which each other, so to speak — whereas, in reality, divinity and humanity operate on radically different orders of being. As a result, "[T]he characteristics that distinguish God need not be covered over and held in abeyance ... for God to be brought near to us, indeed to become one with us. Immanence and transcendence, closeness and difference, are simply not at odds in God's relations with us."[341] But this is to miss something important about the Incarnation: it is not primarily just a new and special way that God relates _to_ us or becomes one _with_ us; it is not even a special way God draws _uniquely close to one of us_ (that is, to Jesus of Nazareth). Rather, it is where God _actually becomes one of us._ At times Tanner clearly accepts this, expressing Christ's metaphysically unique status in terms of classical conciliar orthodoxy: "Jesus has a human existence, but only in virtue of having his existence in God. Jesus does not just get his existence _from_ God, as we do; he exists in God; his very existence is God's existence."[342] This underlying insight about the Incarnation, however, she couples with a classical Two-Nature theory of the Incarnation. **As we have seen, the main problem that many Moderate Kenoticists have with classical TNC is _not_ that it is necessarily _self-contradictory_ — as if divine and human properties _logically_ cannot be attributed to the same divine person simultaneously. The main problem with TNC (as we saw**

---

[341] Tanner, _Jesus, Humanity and the Trinity,_ p. 13.

[342] Ibid., p. 25. This leads to a difficulty, however, because if God is essentially immaterial (Jn 4:24; II Cor 3:17), then in the Incarnation his human body cannot be an extension of his divine existence in quite the same way that his human soul can be. As we have seen in Chapter Four (above), Richard Swinburne's version of Moderate KM avoids this problem by positing that in the Incarnation the divine Son assumes all the limitations of a human soul in a Cartesian mode of unity with a human body.

in Chapter One) is that talk of God "taking on" or "assuming" human nature in a TNC way is a problem of *intelligibility*. In particular, the theory provides us with no assurance that in a significant way God the Son has really "borne our griefs and carried our sorrows." To put it in a nutshell: in classical TNC the divine Son, in his divine nature at least, was a mere spectator of, and entirely immune to his own earthly sufferings. The divine Son thereby "suffers impassibly" — the rest of us are not so lucky.

Critics have also questioned whether any form of Kenoticism can be said to abide within the parameters of the Chalcedonian Definition of the mystery of the Incarnation. **Catholic theologian Thomas Weinandy, OFM, Cap., has been the most persistent critic. For example, he states directly: "If the Son of God suffered as God, it would mean, contrary to the Council of Chalcedon, that there was a confusion and mixing and so a changing of natures."**[343] In particular, the Council condemned those who "foolishly imagine that there is *one nature* of the flesh and of the Godhead," and "monstrously suppose that by reason of the confusion [of natures] the divine nature of the Only begotten is passible."[344] The Council's warning here, however, was not part of the definition itself (and in the Catholic theological tradition, at least, reasons given in support of a conciliar or papal definition, and disciplinary or pastoral applications of that teaching, are not held to be fully under the guidance of the charism of "infallibility" of the Church's authentic magisterium — only the core definition itself). Moreover, this warning was directed specifically at the Monophysite (one nature) heretics who mixed and confused the two natures, so that Jesus Christ was either less than fully divine, or less than fully human, or both. It is not clear, however, that Kenoticism in all of its forms implies this kind of "confusion" of the two natures. The Pure KM of Gess would be open to criticism for precisely the opposite reason: as a theory of the Incarnation that implies the radical

---

[343] Thomas Weinandy, OFM, Cap., *Jesus: Essays in Christology* (Ave Maria, FL: Sapientia Press, 2014), p. 309.
[344] See discussion of this point in J.K. Mozley, *The Impassibility of God: A Survey of Christian Thought* (Cambridge: Cambridge University Press, 1926), p. 94-95.

sundering of the two natures, so that the doctrine of *one* person in two natures *simultaneously* is abandoned. Moreover, **if the divine nature is such that the Son of God can limit himself to include and preserve within his own divine store of experience an experience of all the conditions and limitations of human life, as most kenotic theories hold, it does not necessarily follow from this that the divine nature has thereby undergone an *essential* change that renders him less than fully divine. In Moderate KM, at least, nothing essentially divine is violated or lost in the Incarnation.** As we shall see in Part Two and in the concluding chapter of this book, some philosophical theologians (including some from the Anglican tradition such as Hebblethwaite, Swinburne and Brown) have argued that *the sense in which God is properly "immutable" does not necessarily force us to say that he is also utterly "impassible" in his divine nature.* The warnings issued by the Council fathers at Chalcedon, on the other hand, were predicated on a philosophical understanding of the divine nature as absolutely immutable and impassible. If that understanding of divine impassibility can be shown to be unnecessary (and perhaps even unhelpful) to the whole pattern of the orthodox Christian faith, then the way is clear for rethinking kenotic theories of the Incarnation. Again, more on this later.

Weinandy insists, however, that the changes in the divine nature posited by Kenotic theories of the Incarnation, "whether it be Gore's 'real self-emptying' and 'abandonment' of certain divine prerogatives, or Weston's 'self-restraint'" are "not only impossible since God is immutable," but "even impossible to conceive."[345] He writes:

> How can an omnipotent being give up or restrain his omnipotence? How does an omniscient being give up or restrain his omniscience? How can a being who is said to be God, because he is omnipotent and omniscient give up or restrain these attributes, and yet remain God? Even on a human level that is ontologically impossible. How can a man

---

> remain a man if he gives up his rationality? Rationality is an essential element of what it means to be a man.[346]

Weinandy confuses the issue here, however, by treating the "giving up" (or "abandonment") of divine attributes in the Incarnation (as in Radical KM) as the equivalent of the "self-restraint" of the exercise of divine attributes (as in Moderate KM) — but the two positions are simply not the same. To begin with, even on a human level, a person can certainly restrain the full exercise of his attributes of rationality or power without losing those attributes altogether and ceasing to be fully human — we do so every time we choose to go to bed at night and fall asleep. Indeed, we can restrain the exercise of our rationality and power without even ceasing to exercise those attributes in another way, on another level. For example, a woman might be driving to work in the morning, figuring out what she is going to say to her boss to explain why she is late, and focusing her conscious attention on this problem, while at the same time her mind — operating under the temporarily chosen restraints of lack of conscious attention to the task of driving the car — successfully multi-tasks by driving on "auto-pilot," so to speak. Or a policeman may physically overpower and handcuff one criminal while at the same time he uses "soft-power" by trying to convince another to give himself up voluntarily.

In the case of God, it is not hard to see how he could restrain the exercise of his omnipotence in his relationship to particular creatures at various times and places in world history without ceasing to be the omnipotent God he ever is: for example, he does this every time he permits human voluntary agency to affect the course of events. The form of power God *could* wield over the human will and the course of events is self-restrained whenever he permits human beings to exercise their free-will; meanwhile, God is using his determinative power to guide the wider course of the non-human and non-angelic universe. It is a bit harder to conceive of how God can self-restrain his omniscience in the Incarnation, but as we have seen, Moderate

---

[346] Ibid., p. 115.

KM advocates such as Richard Swinburne speculate that God the Son became incarnate by choosing to relate to a particular human body in time and space (that is, to an ovum in the womb of Mary, fashioned by the Holy Spirit into a biologically male human body), in precisely the way that a human soul normally interacts with a human body. He thereby formed for himself a sphere of activity in which he knows and wills in a fully human way, in union with that body, under self-imposed human conditions and limitations — without ceasing to guide the whole course of the universe with unlimited knowledge and power, apart from the sphere of his humanity, as the Divine Word. Doubtless this would still violate Weinandy's understanding of God's absolute divine immutability (more on this in the "Conclusion" chapter of this book). But it is not the same position as the abandonment or "giving up" of divine attributes by the divine Son altogether, or rendering of them inaccessible even to himself — notions that we met in the more radical kenotic theories.

Weinandy also complains that Kenotic Christology "defines personhood as psychological self-consciousness," which distorts the meaning of "person" used in the classical, conciliar tradition of Christianity: "How can one person, who is defined by his self-consciousness, have two self-consciousnesses [divine and human], two intellects, two wills, without destroying the person? It is impossible. A person can have only one self-consciousness, etc., since that is how he is so defined."[347] To be sure, Kenotic theorists sometimes wrote in confusing ways in this regard: Weston, for example, seemed at times to adopt this perspective in the original, 1907 edition of his landmark book, *The One Christ*. But he tried to correct that mistake in the 1914 edition, as we have seen. Moreover, there is nothing about Moderate KM, at least, that requires such a fully psychologized notion of "person" (see our definition of "person" in Chapter One). In the end, Moderate Kenoticists are more concerned that in the Incarnation there must be some kind of psychological unity between the two

---

[347] Ibid., p. 120.

"states" and ranges of consciousness of the divine Son, human and divine; otherwise, it would be harder to conceive of him as a single person. As we have seen in Chapter Four, it was Thomas Morris who explored in depth the possibility of an asymmetric accessing relationship between the divine and human minds of Christ. Unfortunately, Weinandy fails to notice or critique this option at all.

Another serious charge against the orthodox Christian credentials of the Kenotic Theory is that it leaves us with only one will in Jesus Christ rather than two wills, divine and human. Allegedly, this violates the teachings of the Sixth Ecumenical Council in 680 AD. After all, in Kenoticism the human will of Jesus Christ is seen as the divine will itself, self-limited in manhood. Kenotic theory, therefore, seems to say that Jesus had just *one* will, one power of volition, although one which legitimately can be defined as fully divine and fully human. The question arises whether this theory is really the ancient Monothelite heresy in modern dress, since it fails to preserve the reality of both a fully divine and a fully human will acting in harmony, so to speak, in the Incarnation.

Thomas Morris helps us to understand just what is meant by the doctrine of one person in two natures:

> The Christian claim is that in order to be fully human, it is not necessary to be merely human. ... Consider now an alligator. It has all the essential properties of being a physical object. It is *fully* physical. But there is a sense in which we can say it is not *merely* physical. It has properties of animation as well. It is an organic being ... according to orthodox Christology, Jesus was fully human without being merely human.[348]

In a similar way, **both the mind and will of Jesus Christ can be said to be *fully* human, without being *merely* human.** We have already discussed in depth the issue of this kind of double-mind of the divine

---

Son in Kenoticism in Chapter Four; now we must look more closely at the issue of his double-will.

First, in kenotic theory the will of Jesus is authentically "free." Minimally, free-will means the capacity of the conscious self to direct itself, the ability to exercise voluntary agency in making rational choices, without being subject to any all-determining set of external coercions and/or internal, non-rational compulsions. Presumably, at least in this minimal sense both God and human beings possess "free-will."[349] If the will of Jesus Christ is actually the will of the divine Son

---

[349] By human free-will in a "minimal" sense I mean the notion of free-will put forward by Duns Scotus: the ability of human persons to bring about effects as an uncaused-cause, such that neither God, nor the coercive force of other human beings, nor internal neurological processes, nor any other event is causally responsible for these actions (although God might be said to be a concurrent cause of human free actions, in so far as he sustains all things in existence, including each human will, at every moment). This is the view known as "originalism," because it holds that human actions, to the extent that they are free actions, originate with the person as their cause. By ascribing this minimal form of freedom both to God and to human beings (and to Jesus), I am not intending to deny that human beings can also possess what many have called "freedom for excellence": i.e. freedom understood as the capacity to act virtuously for true human happiness. Indeed, I do not believe that these two notions of freedom are incompatible. In order to be truly responsible for our actions and to be able freely to choose the good, we must possess freedom of origination, but that kind of freedom is undermined in fallen humanity: to a considerable extent we are trapped and enslaved by the false values of the world and our disordered passions (concupiscence), and thereby remain relatively powerless against demonic temptation until this triple-stranglehold (the world, the flesh, and the Devil) is broken with the help of divine grace, and by the gift of the light of the truth of who we are, and who we were created to be. Nevertheless, divine grace and divine truth only *restores* our freedom of origination, and *enables* it to choose the good; it does not *compel* us to do so (which would utterly cancel out our freedom of origination, and with it our responsibility for our own actions). Divine grace is precisely what assists and enables us freely (that is, with restored freedom of origination) to pursue and attain freedom of excellence. The more we freely choose the good with the help of grace, the more we attain habits of virtue which incline us to choose the good with constancy.

operating under all the conditions of human life, it is still an instance of authentically free-will, being under no set of all-determining, non-rational causes.

Second, in kenotic theory the will of Jesus is fully human because it operates under human limitations: in other words, it operates within the context of a particular human consciousness, in a particular life-situation, in which the human range of

---

That Jesus in his human nature also possessed this "freedom for excellence" is clear from John 1:14, which tells us he was right from the start "full of grace and truth." His human freedom of origination did not need to be restored, because it was already fully assisted by grace from the beginning of his earthly life, and already informed by the light of truth, so that from infancy he was as empowered with the seeds of virtue as an infant soul possibly could be, and no obstacles arose within him to the growth and strengthening of those virtues throughout his life.

God has "freedom for excellence" only in an analogous sense of the phrase, of course, for he possesses all goodness and all truth by nature, and infinitely so, and not by the supernatural gift or assistance of another. Rather, he eternally and freely lives his divine life (with freedom of origination) according to his infinite goodness and truth (that is, with infinite excellence) without obstacle or hindrance. In an analogous way, when human persons attain the heavenly kingdom, they too will freely live without obstacle or hindrance in accord with the truth and goodness they perceive in the Beatific Vision, and therefore without the possibility of sin. Thus, the ultimate goal of human freedom of origination is to choose irrevocably to commit itself to truth and goodness, to give itself away and surrender itself in love, thereby attaining everlasting and heavenly freedom for excellence. This also shows that the lack of any possibility for committing sin which characterized the divine-as-human will of Jesus during his sojourn on earth, does not necessarily contradict the authenticity of his human nature. It simply entails that he was as "full of grace and truth" from the Holy Spirit as his developing human nature could be at every stage of his life journey. Precisely because he was a divine person incarnate, he was as completely surrendered to the Holy Spirit at every moment, and therefore as completely dedicated to truth and goodness as his human nature possibly could be at every step of his human development. We will explore this matter in greater depth in volume two of this series. On the compatibility and interplay of these two kinds of human freedom, see Joseph Laporte, "What Does It Mean to Have Free Will?" at https://www. Bigquestionsonline.com/2017 /10/11/what-does-mean-have-free-will/.

consciousness is aware of solely human powers and options at his own disposal. Put another way: the human soul of Jesus cannot will to use to the full his divine powers of omniscience and omnipotence because he is either not explicitly conscious that he is a divine person who has such powers, or at least, he knows he is unable fully to access or utilize them from within the human, incarnate state which he originally and voluntarily assumed.

Finally, in Kenoticism we can say that the will of Jesus is fully human because like us, he could be tempted to sin (Mt 4:1; Mk 1:13). By "temptation" here I shall mean the capacity to be assailed by disordered passions — irrational bodily or emotional desires — which cause psychological conflict and difficulty in moral decision-making. It may seem implausible at first that a divine person incarnate, for whom choosing to sin is essentially an impossibility (since, presumably a divine person would never, and in that sense at least *cannot* sin, even through the exercise of his human will) could still be said to be able to experience temptation. But we can follow Thomas Morris here in his claim that temptation is a psychological event which does not depend upon any metaphysical possibility of sinning. For example, I can be tempted to lie to my best friend, even if, unknown to me, my friend had died an hour earlier. The fact of my temptation is not altered by the impossibility of actually committing such a sin. Moreover, in theological terms, although Jesus could not be tempted by disordered passions arising from within himself (since he never inherited any disordered passions due to original sin, or formed any within himself due to actual sin), the New Testament tells us that he was subject to extraordinary Satanic assaults designed to sway him from his mission. These demonic assaults must have caused him tremendous internal, psychological conflict; for example, he sweated drops of blood in the Garden of Gethsemane in anguish at the depths of suffering he would have to undergo to accomplish our redemption (Lk 22:44). Furthermore, kenotic theorists have often pointed out that a person's inherent goodness often *increases* rather than decreases the intensity of their experience of temptation. As H.R. Mackintosh put it, "the resistance of temptation may be torture to a good man, whereas a bad man yields easily."[350]

For all these reasons, it is hard to see how the Kenotic Theory (other than in its Pure form) clearly undermines the Chalcedonian claim that Jesus Christ simultaneously had a definably human as well as a fully divine will. In Radical KM, the will of Jesus can be defined as fully human, without being merely human. The divine Son's power of volition pre-existed in the Trinity as the will of the second person of the Trinity, and then was included in the Son's descent into all the conditions and limitations of human life: the state in which many of his divine attributes were transposed into a fully human form of operation and expression (being rendered latent and to some extent inoperative, especially during his infancy). In the context of those human constraints, despite experiencing temptation in his human soul as a youth and as an adult, all the actions of Jesus were necessarily good, because they proceeded from the volitional power of the divine Son in his perfect love for the Father and for us, operating under human conditions.

A similar defense can be mounted for Moderate KM. On this version of kenotic theory, the will of the divine Son exercises all his cosmic functions, and by means of that will he helps to sustain and guide the universe from an omniscient perspective. At the same time he acts freely within the confines of his limited human life and consciousness as Jesus of Nazareth, in which he is subject to the experience of temptation.

In short, in at least some versions of Radical KM, and certainly in Moderate KM, the will of Jesus of Nazareth simply *is* the volitional power of the divine Son himself, operating under all the conditions of a truly human mode of life.[351] The Sixth

---

[350] Mackintosh, *The Doctrine of the Person of Jesus Christ*, p. 403.

[351] In this discussion I have focused on the "will" as "the power of volition," in other words, as the capacity for voluntary agency. Arguably, the same conclusions hold if we consider the will in a broader sense as including the faculty

Ecumenical Council tells us: "For as his flesh is called and is the flesh of God the Word, so also the natural will of his flesh is called and is God the Word's own will."[352] This seems to be very close to what the Kenotic theologians were trying to say. As Vincent Taylor put it, for Radical Kenoticism:

> The human will is the divine will restrained by conditions which are accepted fully and completely ... one will, the will of the Eternal Son, manifesting itself under different conditions.[353]

Taylor's way of phrasing the mystery, however, does not capture **the nuance available to Moderate KM: that the divine will of the Son, operating kenotically under human conditions and limitations (*ensarkos*), was at the same time perfectly in accord with, and fully expressive of the unlimited divine will (*asarkos*) that the Son eternally shares with his heavenly Father in the divine nature, operative throughout the entire universe.[354] Thus, with Moderate KM we can say that in one sense the divine Son, while incarnate on earth, had two wills fully operative simultaneously: his divine will in its authentically human, self-limited state, acting in accord with his divine will in its properly divine, unlimited state, and therefore also totally surrendered to the will of his Father:** "Father, if thou art willing, take this cup from me; nevertheless, not my will but thine done" (Lk 22:42; cf. Jn 5:30 and 6:38). In other words,

---

of desire. Saint Thomas Aquinas gave the classic exposition of this perspective in his discussion of the various aspects of the "will" in the human nature of Jesus Christ on display in the Garden of Gethsemane. Christ naturally shrank from the prospect of torture and death that is so contrary to the natural goods of human life, but his "rational will" remained in surrender to the "divine will," which enabled his "natural and sensual will" to submit as well; see Aaron Riches in *Ecce Homo*, p. 179-181.

[352] Cited in Hardy, ed., *The Christology of the Later Fathers*, p. 383.
[353] Taylor, *The Person of Christ*, p. 295-297.
[354] This would seem to be the perspective of Bulgakov as well; see Paul Gavrilyuk, "The kenotic theology of Sergius Bulgakov" in *Scottish Journal of Theology*, vol. 58, Issue 3, August, 2005, p. 263.

the divine will of the Son, operating under all the conditions of human life, was completely and freely surrendered to the divine will of the Father — an earthly expression and manifestation, we might say, of the eternal derivation of the Son (and all that he is) from the Father in the life of the Blessed Trinity.

In any case, the Anglican theological tradition has traditionally held that the Fifth, Sixth, and Seventh Ecumenical Councils should not be accorded the same authority as the first four, allegedly "undisputed" councils, and that the concept of an order or "hierarchy" of truths usefully can be applied to conciliar decisions.[355] The Sixth Council remained true to the Chalcedonian faith that Jesus Christ is one person in two natures, possessing all the essential attributes of both divinity and humanity simultaneously. Thus, the work of our salvation "was willed by a divine person through a human will."[356] Moderate KM at least would seem to be able to sustain a similar claim, albeit in the framework of the Kenotic notion of the divine Son's self-restraint of the universal exercise of his divine omni-attributes in the sphere of the Incarnation, even while he retained the full use of those attributes throughout the cosmos. This understanding of *kenosis* was a notion that the ancient Fathers, in their nearly unanimous belief (derived from Hellenistic philosophy) in the absolute immutability and impassibility of the divine nature, could not even begin to consider as a live option. Given a contemporary and alternative philosophical framework that can fit with the wider pattern of Christian belief, however, a kenotic notion of the Incarnation may turn out to be a live option for the legitimate development of the doctrine of the Incarnation in the Church today. And as we shall see in the concluding chapter of this book, it may not be as far removed from the intentions of the Fathers as some critics fear.

---

[355] See, for example, the Anglican-Orthodox Joint Doctrinal Commission, *Anglican-Orthodox Dialogue: the Dublin Agreed Statement, 1984* (London: SPCK, 1985), p. 52-53.

[356] International Theological Commission (Roman Catholic), "Select Questions on Christology," section 7, at www.vatican.va/roman_curia/congregations/cfaith/cti_documents/rc_cti_1979_cristologia_en.html.

Kenoticism and Orthodox Parameters for the Doctrine of the Trinity

Finally, we must look at the Trinitarian objections brought against Kenoticism. All forms of the Kenotic Theory have been criticised for forcing us to adopt an extreme and exclusively "social" model for the Trinity: in other words, the model that the closest and least-inadequate analogies for the mystery of the Divine Trinity must be drawn from our experience of loving communion among human persons.

For Brian Hebblethwaite, the Social Analogy for the Trinity is rooted in the very reasons why Christians believe in the Holy Trinity in the first place. First, Hebblethwaite claims, there is the argument from Divine Love. Saint John clearly teaches in 1 John 4:8 that "love" is an essential attribute of God. If God is perfect love, then that must include the perfection of loving personal relationship: love given, received, and returned. If God is a solitary person, then to enjoy this perfection of love he would have to create a world to love, and creatures that could love him back — but that would make God dependent upon his creation for the fulfillment of his nature, and therefore not, in himself, perfect love. **Thus, for God to possess the perfection of love within his own eternal being, there would have to be the perfection of loving personal relationship within his essence.** Hebblethwaite writes:

> If God depends on his creation for the perfection of personal relation, then it seems that God is being thought of as dependent on his creation for being personal at all. And if the personality of God depends on creatures, what sort of God is it that we are really thinking of? ... The argument should run: God *is* Love and therefore in himself relational, the perfection of love given and love received.[357]

---

[357] Hebblethwaite, *The Incarnation*, p. 134-135. Notice that Hebblethwaite's argument here does not depend on perfect love among the divine persons consisting solely of *self-giving, agape* love. It can fit also with the idea of Richard

Hebblethwaite then points to God's historical revelation of himself through Jesus Christ, and the Christian experience of the Holy Spirit, to bring us from belief in *loving personal relationship* within God to belief in a *trinity* of divine persons[358]:

> The starting point of the argument is that the Incarnation and particularly the relation between the incarnate one and his heavenly Father reveal and portray to us in terms we can readily understand the eternal relation of love given and love received within the deity. … God is sufficiently rich and complex in his own being to be able, without ceasing to be God, to make himself personally present in human history as a man, and to relate himself to himself in the manner in which we read of Jesus' prayers to the Father. Precisely that relation was the revealed form of the eternal personal relation subsisting within the Godhead. …

---

of St. Victor that God's perfect, divine love must include both *dilectio* and *condilectio* (see note 367 below).

[358] When philosophers demonstrate the existence of "God," what they are actually doing is demonstrating the existence of a self-existent, transcendent, eternal, personal being who is the source of all created existence, and who has the essential attributes of omniscience, omnipotence, and perfect goodness — indeed, some theistic philosophers would add: One who is Being itself, Being in its fullness, infinitely perfect Being. It is only closer analysis of the nature of this divine, personal Being that compels one to say that he must somehow include loving, personal relationship within his own nature or essence in order to be perfectly good. In the light of Christ we then come to realize that this "God," this "source without source" of creation as a whole whom we have been contemplating philosophically, is actually God the Father, the eternal "source without source" of the fullness of the divine reality as well. **It is not surprising, then, that the New Testament often refers to God the Father simply as "God" (e.g. I Cor 8:6; II Cor 13:14; Phil 2:9-11). This is not because he is more fully divine than the other two persons of the Trinity, as if he had more of the essential divine attributes, but only because he comes eternally (non-chronologically) first as the source and origin of the other two divine persons, and because he is first known of the three by human beings, both in natural theology and in salvation history.**

Consider what Paul writes about the Spirit in Romans 8. In the cry 'Abba! Father!', he says, 'the Spirit of God joins with our spirit in testifying that we are God's children' and 'We do not know how we ought to pray, but through our inarticulate groans, the Spirit himself is pleading for us, and God, who searches our inmost being, knows what the Spirit means, because he pleads for God's people in God's own way.' I am not trying to prove anything just by quoting scripture. All I am suggesting is that the experience reflected in the kind of language used in Romans 8 seems to consist in a sense of being caught up, when our prayer falters, into God's own interior dialogue. Is there not here, after all, another indication of relation in God? The way in which our prayers are caught up into God's own self-address reveals the reality of further internal relation in the deity.

The social analogy is an *analogy*. It invites us to consider the possibility that the 'infinite richness and complexity' of the one God embraces the fullness of love given and love received within the infinite being of the source of all things. ... God *is* love, not just that he loves us, but that love — and that means love being given and received — is of the essence of his inner being.[359]

The Social Analogy for the Trinity also can claim support from the contemplative wisdom of the Gospel According to St. John. It was John among the apostles who contemplated the Trinitarian life of God in greatest depth; especially in chapters 13-17, it seems clear that the mystery of the Trinity for John is a mystery of persons-in-relation. Thomas McCall sums up for us the evidence from the climax of John's gospel in chapter 17:

---

[359] Ibid., p. 15-16, 17, 20, 132. Hebblethwaite's Trinitarian reading of Romans 8 is echoed by NT scholar Tom Wright in his book *The Day the Revolution Began* (London: SPCK, 2016), p.292-293; the "groaning" and "sighs" of the Holy Spirit mentioned by St. Paul are an expression of a kind of "conversation" and "dialogue" going on between the Father and the Spirit, in which our prayers are taken up.

> [I]n John 17 we find that the Father gives authority (17:2), work (17:40), words (17:8) his name (17:11), and glory to the Son (17:22), and that the Father loves the Son (17:23,24,26). The Son prays *to* the Father (17:1), gives eternal life to those whom the Father has given him (17:2), and brings glory to the Father (17:4). It seems reasonable, then, to conclude that in John 17 there is some sort of "social analogy" being employed, that we see the Father and the Son portrayed as distinct agents, that we see their love for one another, and that indeed they are presented as distinct centers of will and consciousness.[360]

There are also plenty of indications in the writings of the Fathers of the Church that they looked upon each divine person as analogous to a distinct, conscious agent. Tertullian certainly implies that the divine persons are three centers of consciousness and will in his disputes with the Modalists (See *Against Praxeas*, 7 and 11). Michael Barnes and Cornelius Plantinga, Jr., have argued that especially in his discussion of the Holy Spirit, St. Gregory of Nyssa implicitly writes of the Son and the Spirit as distinct actors, knowers, willers, and lovers — in other words, as centers of consciousness and will, although Gregory did not use that phrase or define *hypostasis* in that way explicitly.[361]

Still, the question remains: how far do we have to press a social analogy and a social understanding of the Trinity in order to fit with a kenotic approach to the Incarnation? In some cases of kenotic theory, as we have seen, the distinction and division between the divine persons cuts so deeply that it inevitably leads us into "tritheism": that is, to the idea that the Holy Trinity involves three independently existing and separable divine beings. The Pure KM of Gess, at least, seems wide open to this charge. But Thomasius tried to avoid this pitfall with his insistence that no essential attributes of the divine nature are abandoned in the Incarnation, and that the divine attribute in which

---

[360] McCall, *Which Trinity? Whose Monotheism?*, p. 71.
[361] See discussion of their perspectives in McCall, *Which Trinity? Whose Monotheism?*, p. 239.

he believed the Trinity is grounded — the power of absolute Divine Will — remains operative even in the incarnate state of the Son. The Radical KM of Forsyth, Mackintosh and Taylor might try to take shelter under much the same defense as Thomasius on this point. In short, versions of Radical KM united with a voluntarist understanding of the divine nature can be found that at least attempt to fend off the charge of tritheism (if voluntarism can be swallowed at the same time!).

These versions of Radical KM also force their adherents to speculate that the other two persons of the Trinity must have "covered" for the cosmic assistance of the Son during the Incarnation. The divine role of sustaining the whole universe in existence, and guiding it providentially according to divine purposes would need to be maintained by the Father and the Spirit alone, at least during the Son's sojourn on earth — perhaps also during his ongoing, glorified, incarnate state in heaven after the Resurrection and Ascension. As previously discussed, what is lost here in Radical KM is the full doctrine of the "coinherence" of the persons of the Trinity: if not in their unbroken sharing (in some sense) of the divine nature, at least in their joint participation in all divine acts *ad extra*. As this doctrine was not formally defined by the Church until the 15th century Council of Florence, Anglican theologians have not usually considered themselves strictly bound to it. But it has a long Patristic and Scholastic pedigree,[362] and in some form at least, it seems essential as a hedge against tritheism. It seems clear that if the divine persons do *not* share and cooperate in all of God's acts in the world (in this case, if the divine Son does not share in the governance of the universe while in his incarnate state) then the three are not one God after all, but three separate and separable gods.

---

[362] For Patristic and Scholastic references see Ludwig Ott, *Fundamentals of Catholicism* (Charlotte, NC: TAN Books, fourth edition, 1960), p. 71-72. In the theology of the Fathers of the East, the Greek term "perichoresis" (meaning "encircling," or "encompassing") was often used to express the mystery of the mutual interpenetration of the divine persons.

Moderate KM, at least, does not compromise the doctrine of divine coinherence to quite the extent that Radical KM does, for on the Moderate KM model the divine Son continues to share with the Father and the Spirit the task of upholding and guiding the whole universe, even as he assumes human limitations as Jesus of Nazareth. Still, a stronger doctrine of coinherence can lead Kenoticism into an equal and opposite danger: the ancient heresy of "Patri-passianism." This is the doctrine that all three divine persons experienced the suffering and death of Jesus Christ. After all, if (as all kenotic theory holds) the divine nature of the Son, and not just the divine person of the Son, is what assumed the limitations of human nature and human experience in the Incarnation, including the suffering and death of Jesus on the Cross, then how is this experience of crucifixion not fully shared by all three divine persons — since all three supposedly share the one divine nature or "essence" (i.e., the same set of divine attributes in act)? **In the end, if we want to hold on to a kenotic theory of the Incarnation, do we have to embrace a social doctrine of the Trinity that crosses the line into tritheism in order to avoid Patri-passianism?**

We need to carefully discern, therefore, the contours of an orthodox understanding of the Trinity that can fit well with the Moderate Kenotic Model of the Incarnation. To do so, we shall start with two basic presuppositions.

First, any attempt to unfold the doctrine of the Trinity today can only be a tentative one. This is so not only because of the unfathomable depths of the divine mystery itself, but also because this doctrine is presently under review in the Catholic-Orthodox ecumenical dialogue process by some of the best minds in Christendom. That ecumenical dialogue has only just begun the process of seeking to re-receive, re-express, and more fully integrate the riches of both eastern and western traditions on this, most central doctrine of the faith — and this surely leaves individual efforts undertaken apart from that dialogue process (such as my own in this book) as tentative and exploratory at best.[363]

Second, let us recall the generic philosophical definition of "person" with which we started in Part One, Chapter One of this book. A person was said to be a subject or bearer of properties of a "personal" kind: namely, the capacity for self-consciousness, rational thought, and voluntary agency. We also said that from the perspective of philosophical theology, human "persons" only fulfill their nature as *imago dei* in relationships of loving communion with others and with God, for God is himself essentially a loving, Trinitarian communion of "persons." Of course, divine "persons" are only analogous to human persons; for divine persons possess personal properties in an *infinite* way: they are characterized by an infinite mode of self-consciousness, infinite knowledge, infinite freedom, and infinite love.

a) *Three distinct, fully divine centers of consciousness and will*

Given that starting point, it is hard to see how any model of the mystery of the Trinity can completely side-step the idea that divine consciousness or mind is instantiated somewhat differently by each of the divine persons. For example, the Father must surely possess a unique and incommunicable awareness of himself as the "Father" who eternally begets his Son, who in turn must possess a unique and incommunicable awareness of being the eternal "Son" begotten by his Father, and who, together in their mutual love, eternally generate the Holy Spirit, who must possess a unique and incommunicable consciousness of himself as the Spirit who proceeds from both. These three distinct acts of reflexive self-consciousness by the three divine persons do not *constitute* them as distinct persons (that is, their

---

[363] The most in-depth statement produced to date is "The Greek and Latin Traditions Regarding the Procession of the Holy Spirit" (1995) by The Pontifical Council for Promoting Christian Unity. It should be noted that there is no indication at all in this document that the Roman Catholic Church expects the Orthodox Christians of the East ultimately to embrace the full Latin doctrine that the divine persons should be defined as "subsistent relations."

hypostatic distinction; to say so would be completely to "psychologize" the persons of the Trinity), but these acts of self-consciousness are *grounded in* and *manifest* the underlying distinctions of origin among them (the Father as origin without origin; the Son as originated by the Father and in some sense co-originator of the Spirit; and the Spirit as originated by the Father and the Son, but not an originator). In other words, each divine person possesses and lives out the divine nature, the full actualization of all the divine attributes, but each in his own unique way — paternal, filial and pneumatic respectively — based on the unique relations of origin proper to each one.[364] So, the Father always manifests the characteristic of divine Fatherhood (as source without source, pure provision and gratuity, Jn 16:15, 17:24) in all that he is and does; the Son always manifests the characteristic of divine Sonship (pure derivation, perfect reflection, and perfect missional obedience Jn 1:1,14, 14:9; Col 1:15; Heb 1:3; Jn 5:19, Jn 17:4-5), and the Holy Spirit the characteristic of divine Spirithood (pure receptivity and pure gift, Lk 1:35, 38; Jn 14:15-16, 20:22; Acts 2:3; Rom 5:5; I Cor 12:4-7). The unique act of self-consciousness proper to each divine person is just another manifestation of these characteristics (unless we are going to hold that the Father is *not* uniquely conscious of himself as Father, the Son *not* uniquely conscious of himself as Son, etc., in violation of the implications of the New Testament witness; see for example Mt 26:39, Jn 6:38, and Rom 8:15-16, 26).[365]

---

[364] We might find an analogy in the way both men and women equally possess fully human natures, but in the distinctive manner proper to them as male and female. The difference, of course, is that men and women possess the same nature merely generically, but the divine persons not only possess the same divine nature generically, but also, as we shall see, they are united in a unique way both "socially and organically" in one Tripersonal act of being.

[365] By "act of self-consciousness" I mean an awareness of oneself as a distinct personal subject: that is, as an "I' or "ego," with ownership of one's rational thoughts and voluntary actions, and unique, privileged access to the experience of being that particular personal subject. Unlike the case with groups of human beings, in the Trinity each divine person necessarily thinks and acts in complete harmony with the other two: they hold all the same factual knowledge, purposes and decisions in common. Each divine person, therefore, would be aware that

To put it another way: each of the persons of the Trinity, as fully "divine" persons, actualizes and exercises all of the divine attributes, such as the greatest possible goodness, knowledge, and power. But each person does so from his own unique "perspective" within the life of the Trinity, which means they each can have their own experiences (some of which — such as their own act of self-consciousness — cannot be fully shared with the other persons of the Trinity) and their own distinctive acts in the world (thus, only the divine Son became incarnate, and only he directly and fully experienced what it is like to have human limitations, and to suffer and die from within a fully human consciousness), all with the support and cooperation of the other two divine persons.

All this is not to posit that the divine persons are three primary substances, three separate, independent beings, distinct centers of consciousness and will in *that* sense (which surely would be tritheism).[366] Rather, *they are three personal subjects united in a unique act of being as One God.*

---

his factual knowledge, purposes and choices were his own, and also that they were in perfect accord the other two persons. However, it does not seem to be the case that the awareness of being one particular divine person rather than another can similarly be held in common, or the unique privileged access to the experience of being that divine person within the life of the Trinitarian communion as a whole. Only the Father knows himself to be the Father and fully experiences what it is to be the Father in the life of the Trinity; only the Son knows himself to be the Son, and fully experiences what it is to be incarnate, etc. Thus, the factual knowledge of each of the three persons is infinite, and fully shared, as well as their common purposes and choices, but experiential knowledge, it would seem, cannot be held in common in the same way, or to the same degree.

[366] The phrase "centers of consciousness" for divine persons, used by some 20th century theologians, does not necessarily imply tritheism. It all depends on what is meant by the phrase. A "center of consciousness" could simply mean a subject that has the property of the inherent capacity for consciousness of a "personal" kind (i.e. a kind that involves the capacity for self-consciousness, rational thought, voluntary agency, and loving relationships). See the discussion of this in Taylor, *The Person of Christ*, p. 20-21.

b) *United "organically" (by eternal generation) and "socially" (by loving cooperation) in one Tripersonal act of being*

In fact, the divine revelation to which Scripture and Tradition bear witness implies that there can be no such thing as an independent, or solitary divine person. The Father cannot be fully divine, or be "Father" at all, without eternally generating his Son (that's why his very name is "Father;" Fatherhood is not just something he decides to do: it is who he eternally and essentially is — it is his own unique and incommunicable way of possessing and expressing the divine nature). Following St. Thomas Aquinas, we might say that the Father necessarily generates his Son by an act of self-knowledge (*per modum intellectus*), who is therefore called in Scripture his Word or Image (Jn 1:1; Col 1:15; Heb 1:3). And the Son is the divine person who exists and possesses the divine nature only through being eternally begotten by the Father. Moreover, the love between them would not be complete unless it eternally generated (*per modum amoris*) a third divine person, the Holy Spirit (Rom 5:5).[367] **In short, no fully "divine" person can exist, and therefore the divine nature itself**

---

[367] By the language chosen here—"the love between them would not be complete unless …" I am deliberately alluding to the Social Trinitarian thought of Richard of St. Victor (d. 1173). Richard argued that it takes three divine persons for the eternal perfection of love to exist in the life of the Divine Trinity. It takes two persons, the Father and the Son, to express and enjoy between them the perfection of *dilectio* (selfless, self-giving love), but love between two persons has not reached its perfection unless the two also express and enjoy a second kind of love, *condilectio*, which occurs when two persons perfectly love a common object. Richard's argument should not be taken as a rational proof for the doctrine of the Trinity, but it does show that at least these two kinds of love are needed for the perfection of charity, and therefore it is fitting that God should be at least a trinity of persons united by such bonds of love. It is only by divine revelation that we know for sure that there are actually three persons in God, and that no more than that are needed for the perfection of love in the divine nature. We see a created analogy of this in the human family, of course, where the marital commitment of self-giving love between a man and a woman naturally seeks to express and complete itself in the procreation and nurture of their children. See the essay by Paul Burgess, "Three are the Perfection of Charity: the *De Trinitate* of Richard of St. Victor" at www.paulburgess .org/richard.html.

cannot exist, save in this tri-personal manner, with the three persons in relationships of eternal ontological dependence upon each other, and only together fully manifesting the divine "personal" perfections in each one of infinite knowledge and love.[368]

Given that the three persons of the Trinity eternally and perfectly know and love one another, it stands to reason that they would always necessarily and fully cooperate in carrying out divine purposes in the world through the shared exercise of the divine attributes of omniscience, omnipotence, and omnipresence. Indeed, unless they did so, theoretically they could thwart or hinder each other's exercise of those attributes. This is one reason why David Brown argued in his book *The Divine Trinity* that the divine attributes are most appropriately applied to the Godhead as a whole: the Trinity-in-Unity fulfills those attributes in a more rich and perfect way than each person would considered separately.[369] In one sense, at least, this must be true. As previously discussed, **each of the divine persons possesses, experiences, and expresses the divine nature in his own distinctive way (paternal, filial, or pneumatic) — and**

---

[368] It follows that we must distance ourselves here from the position of the Orthodox theologian John Zizioulas, who argues that "person" is logically and ontologically prior to the concept of "nature," "essence" or " substance" in God, in particular, that the undefinable "person" of the Father in his absolute freedom is the source of the entire divine reality (including his own). This seems unintelligible; it also attributes a radical "voluntarism" to the nature of the Father which gives him an altogether different nature from the Son and the Spirit. A real "person" is by definition a subject or primary substance possessing a particular kind of nature or essence or secondary substance — namely a nature consisting of personal properties (See Part One, Chapter One). "Person" and "nature," "essence" and "substance" (both primary and secondary) are therefore inseparable realities. In God, his divine "nature" or "essence" is ontologically and logically inseparable from its uniquely and necessarily Tri-personal subject: i.e., the divine nature can only exist in this Tri-personal way (which is a truth that Zizioulas also strongly wants to affirm, but it does not cohere with the radical freedom that he attributes to the Father). On Zizioulas see Keith Ward, *Christ and the Cosmos: A Reformulation of Trinitarian Doctrine* (New York: Cambridge University Press, 2015), p. 151-165.
[369] Brown, *The Divine Trinity,* p. 300-301.

this implies that only **God the Trinity, the Tri-personal communion of divine persons as a whole, eternally united by relationships of generation and cooperation among the three, includes all the ways of being "divine" in one act of being.**

With regard to the traditional divine property of *aseity* (independent existence, self-existence) things get a bit more difficult. Much depends on what we mean by the word. If aseity means "having no source of being beyond of oneself," then of the three divine persons only the Father has this divine property, for he alone is the eternal "source without source" of the other two persons of the Trinity. On the other hand, if by aseity we simply mean "to be uncreated," then all three persons possess this divine property.

c)   The mystery of the eternal relations of origin among the divine persons

The doctrine of the Trinity involves the claim that it is possible to be an uncreated person, and yet to receive one's being from another. The Son and the Spirit receive their existence from the Father not by being created *ex nihilo* (they are not dependent beings in *that* sense), but through the mystery of eternal divine "generation" or "origination," "begetting" and "procession." *Their existence is an uncreated, derived form of divine existence, ultimately emanating, so to speak, from the divine life of the Father.*

By divine relations of "origination," "generation," "begetting" and "proceeding," we have in mind the simple distinction between "begetting" and "making" that C.S. Lewis explained so well in *Mere Christianity*: *"When you beget, you beget [generate, or originate] something of the same kind as yourself.* A man begets human babies, a beaver begets little beavers and a bird begets eggs which turn into little birds. *But when you make, you, you make something of a different kind than yourself.* A bird makes a nest, a beaver builds a dam, a man makes a wireless set ...."[370] *Of*

---

[370] Lewis, *Mere Christianity* (New York: Harper Collins, 2001 edition), p. 157; italics mine.

course, these terms "begetting and "making" can only be applied to God by analogy. For the divine Father *eternally* (ever and always) "begets" or "generates," and in that sense enables the Son to be — as Lewis puts it: '[W]e must think of the Son always, so to speak, streaming forth from the Father, like light from a lamp or heat from a fire, or thoughts from a mind. He is the self-expression of the Father — what the Father has to say. And there never was a time when He was not saying it."[371] Moreover, only God the Trinity can "make" a world *ex nihilo* (out of nothing). No creature can "make" things in that way. **The closest earthly analogy for divine "begetting" probably would be the biological phenomenon of cell division, especially in the "mitotic" phase of an animal cell cycle, in which the mother cell divides into two daughter cells genetically identical to each other. The daughter cells are in all important respects equal in nature to the original mother cell.** Of course, the analogy breaks down in so far as each mitotic cell division is a limited, temporal event, not an eternal process.

    d)   *Essentially inseparable persons — each divine person is only fully divine by sharing in the eternal, Tripersonal communion of origination and cooperation*

Again, the mystery of the Trinity includes the fact that each of the persons of the Trinity is only fully divine because he shares in the life of the Trinitarian communion as a whole. Brian Leftow clearly states this option (without actually endorsing it) when he writes: "[E]ach Person's deity is tied to the others, for each helps the others qualify as divine: the Persons are 'one God' in that they are divine due to the way they are one." And again: "[T]here are two ways to be divine — by being a case of deity, and by being a Trinity of such cases"[372] —

---

[371] Ibid., p. 173-174.

[372] See Brian Leftow, "Anti Social Trinitarianism" in Stephen T. Davis, Daniel Kendall, SJ, and Gerald O'Collins, SJ, *The Trinity: an Interdisciplinary Symposium on the Trinity* (Oxford: Oxford University Press, 1999), p. 212 and 221. Leftow claims that all talk of "different ways of being divine" implicitly leads to the Arian heresy, with its distinctions between greater and lesser degrees of deity among the persons of the Trinity (p. 208 and 211). But this claim clearly involves a *non-*

and as we have seen, it is simply impossible for any personal subject to be "a case of deity" apart from sharing in the Trinitarian communion of persons. **So "God" is a Trinity of personal subjects, each one possessing all the essential divine attributes, with the divine persons united in a unique way, essentially inseparable both by eternal generation and by wise and loving cooperation.** For example, only in so far as the divine persons participate in the Trinitarian communion as a whole can it be said that each one is truly *omnipotent* (in the sense of being able to exercise unlimited power). Each divine person considered separately would be limited by having to cooperate with the others: in other words, if God is a Trinity of fully divine persons, then the exercise of infinite power must be a shared exercise of power.[373] Furthermore, it is only by participating in the Trinitarian communion as a whole that each person is truly *omniscient*, since each divine person has experiential knowledge which the others lack, and without at least some partial way of sharing that kind of knowledge with the others, it would be totally unavailable to them.[374]

---

sequitur. It is entirely coherent to hold that each divine person instantiates the divine nature somewhat differently, and at the same time hold that the three are co-equal and co-eternal in possessing all the essential divine attributes. Moreover, the similarities with Arianism here are superficial. The Arians held that the Son and the Spirit are created beings, created lesser gods, and in that sense at least autonomous and independent persons, while the Social Trinitarian model we are proposing here entails no such polytheistic beliefs.

[373] To the objection that a subject cannot be truly omnipotent if his plans or actions can be thwarted by another, Richard Swinburne replies that each of the divine persons qualifies as omnipotent in the sense that each has the power to do anything that it is logically possible to do, and each cannot fail at anything he tries to do. It is simply not possible that any divine person would *actually* choose to thwart the plans and actions of the others (although each theoretically has the power to do so); given that they each possess the attributes of infinite knowledge and love through their relations of origin, they will always in fact cooperate in the exercise of omnipotence. See Richard Swinburne, *The Christian God* (New York: Oxford University Press, 1994), p. 129 and 175.

[374] To the objection that a divine person cannot be truly omniscient unless he has the full and complete knowledge (both factual *and* experiential) possessed by the other divine persons, we can reply that to be omniscient is to possess all knowledge that it is possible to possess, and it is not logically possible for divine

Finally, it is only through participation in the Trinitarian communion as a whole that each person is fully *good*, since "goodness" presumably means the capacity to fulfill one's nature, as we have seen, the divine nature must exist in the form of a Trinity of divine persons in order to fulfill the divine nature of each one — and therefore of all together in the Trinitarian God — as perfect in Love. At the same time, all cooperation and sharing by the divine persons in their acts and experiences *ad extra* is accomplished and experienced by each divine person in his own unique way, according to his unique manner of instantiating the divine nature, reflecting his own unique, eternal mode of origin.

e) *The Trinitarian ramifications of the Incarnation*

What happens in the Incarnation, according to Moderate Kenoticism, is that the divine Son adds to his consciousness of himself as eternal Son (eternally begotten by the Father, through whom and for whom all things are made, and who continually upholds the universe by his word of power) an experience of what it is to be the divine Son dwelling under all the conditions and limitations of human life as Jesus of Nazareth. Thus, as Weston explained, in the Incarnation the divine Son must be eternally conscious of himself, and relate to the other eternal persons of the Trinity and all of creation, as the unlimited Logos, and at the same time he must be conscious of himself as divine Son operating under all the limitations of his humanity, from the perspective of a limited human consciousness. It is the same divine person at the center of these two "sets of relations," limited and unlimited, and as the subject of these two states of self-consciousness at once.

Only the Son as divine Sonship Incarnate, therefore, enacts and experiences his human life, agony and passion personally and directly, and in his own unique, filial way of possessing and expressing the divine nature. That is why, for example, Jesus speaks of himself as

---

persons fully to possess all experiential knowledge in common, See footnote 365 above.

"sent" from the Father into the world to do his Father's will: it is a temporal, human expression of his eternal derivation from the Father in the life of the eternal Trinity (he eternally "comes from" the Father, and all that he is and does, therefore, in eternity and in time, comes from the Father). But the other divine persons might be said to share in the Son's life, agony and passion in their own distinctive ways too — in a paternal and pneumatic way respectively. In some manner the Father and the Spirit share in the Son's experience of suffering and death as Jesus of Nazareth, through what some theologians have called a mysterious act of "compassion" with the Son in his passion. This might be seen reflected in the New Testament language of the Father "giving up" his Son, which implies an experience of loss: "He who did not spare his own Son, but gave him up for us all …" (Rom 8:32).[375] The book of Hebrews speaks cryptically of the sacrifice of the Son being made "by the eternal Spirit" (9:14; cf. Eph 4:30: "And do not grieve the Holy Spirit of God…."). We are on the edge of deepest mystery here, and must continue this discussion of the suffering and compassion of God, both in the next chapter, and in the concluding chapter of this book. Suffice it to say for now: **Moderate Kenoticism implies a social doctrine of the Trinity, but it is not necessary for Moderate KM to go so far as to embrace tritheism in order to avoid the patri-passianist heresy.**

---

[375] According to Bulgakov, for example, the Father "co-suffers" in the sending and sacrifice of his Son; see *The Lamb of God*, p. 260. Pope St. John Paul II vaguely alluded to this as well in his encyclical letter *Dominum et Vivificantem* (1986), section 39. 3-4:

> The concept of God as necessarily the most perfect being excludes from God any pain derived from deficiencies or wounds; but in the depths of God there is a Father's love that, faced with man's sin, in the language of the Bible reacts so deeply as to say: "I am sorry that I have made him." But more often the Sacred Book speaks to us of a Father who feels compassion for man, as though sharing his pain. In the end, this inscrutable and indescribably fatherly "pain" will bring about above all the wonderful economy of redemptive love in Jesus Christ … in whose humanity the "suffering" of God is concretized.

f)   Why this social-organic model is not tritheism

To summarize: If the persons of the Trinity are in eternal and necessary relationships of ontological dependence upon each other; if they can only fully possess and actualize divine perfections such as self-knowledge, love, aseity, omnipotence, omniscience, and goodness through their relations of origin and cooperation with each other; and if the distinctive way that each divine person possesses and actualizes the divine nature is grounded in, and expressive of the unique, eternal relations of origin of each one, then, arguably, we have preserved a fair measure of Trinitarian "coinherence," and we have moved some distance from tritheistic social models of the Trinity.

Indeed, we have opted instead for what might be called a ***social-organic*** model; for the unity of the Church, the Body of Christ — which is itself a mystery of both social and organic unity in the Holy Spirit — may offer us the closest possible analogy for the perfect unity of the Blessed Trinity. Our Lord himself indicated this when he prayed that all his followers might be one, "even as thou Father, art in me, and I in thee, that they all may be one in us ... that they may be one even as we are one, I in them and thou in me, that they may become perfectly one ... (Jn 17: 21-23). The model for ecclesiastical unity is therefore the Trinitarian communion as a whole: the wondrous mystery of perfect, unifying interdependence and coinherence in the life of the Blessed Trinity.

C. Stephen Layman offers a persuasive explanation of the divine unity possible in a social-organic doctrine of the Trinity in his book *Philosophical Approaches to Atonement, Incarnation and Trinity*:

> [T]he extraordinary unity of the divine persons enables us to see that the charge of polytheism is misplaced. The persons of the Trinity are so very unlike three Greek or Roman gods. (1) *The persons of the Trinity are bound together by necessity. They form a metaphysical unit.* It is the nature of the Father to necessarily [and eternally] generate the Son and the Spirit. (Or from a more

Western point of view, it is the nature of the Father to necessarily generate the Son and the nature of the Father and the Son jointly to generate the Spirit.) The Trinity is a unique entity in this respect. (2) *By virtue of the bonds of perfect love, the Trinity is a self-maintaining event ... analogous to a living thing.* Thus, if a living thing is a primary substance, the Trinity is plausibly one also. It is not simply a group of divine persons who have gotten together to plan and rule. (3) *The persons of the Trinity do not act independently. They have different roles, but each fully supports the other and none acts simply on its own.* Each acts with the assistance and support of the others. There is perfect cooperation in all things and what one divine person wills, the others also will. Given the extraordinary ways in which the divine persons are unified, I submit that *the claim that the [Social Theory of the] Trinity is tritheism just doesn't fit — it simply doesn't ring true.*[376]

g) The quaternity objection

Some may object that a social-organic model of the Trinity makes each divine person a mere "part" of the Trinity, and therefore less than fully divine in himself — and therefore also subordinate to a *fourth* divine person, the Trinity as whole, who alone is fully and completely divine. But there are several ways to reply to this objection.[377]

First, it is not strictly true that a social-organic model holds that each divine person is a mere "part" of the Trinity. **"Part-whole" language for the Trinity is merely analogical — and imperfectly so, for the divine persons are not initially separate or in any way separable parts or pieces of God that are ontologically prior to God, and**

---

[376] Layman, *Philosophical Approaches to Atonement, Incarnation and Trinity*, p. 166-167; italics mine. Richard Swinburne sums up the matter well when he writes: **"The claim that 'there is only one God' is to be read as the claim that the source of being of all other things has to it this kind of indivisible unity."** See *The Christian God*, p. 181.

[377] See also the discussion of the "simplicity" of God in the "Conclusion" chapter of this book.

that merely come together (or are brought together somehow) as a collection or compound to make up the one God. Divine persons can only exist in the eternal, Trinitarian communion of origination and cooperation which the Social-Organic Model describes, and none of them can exist as divine persons apart from the others.[378]

Second, if it is permissible to draw an analogy between the mystery of the infinite divine essence and the mathematical concept of "infinity": an infinite series of numbers can include within itself other infinite series that are equal in magnitude to itself, and equal to each other. Take, for example, the infinite, endless series of whole numbers. Included in that infinite series are several others: for example, the infinite series of even numbers, and the infinite series of odd numbers. Yet these two series are equal to each other in magnitude (both are endless), and equal also to the infinite, endless series of whole numbers. In other words, the subsets, so to speak, are of no lesser magnitude than the whole. One-third of infinity is still infinity, and three infinities add up to infinity. In a somewhat similar way, each case of deity (Father, Son, and Holy Spirit) is infinite in itself, and the Trinity as a whole is equally infinite. There is no subordination here. And yet, just as only the Trinity as a whole includes all three ways of being "divine," even so, only the set of all whole numbers includes all even numbers and all odd numbers.[379]

Third, the one God, the Trinitarian communion as a whole, does not possess all the properties necessary to be defined as a "person" (for example, the Trinity as a whole does not possess its own *single* center of self-consciousness, rational thought and voluntary agency). Rather, **God is Tri-personal: a communion of *three* distinct centers of**

---

[378] At least one of the early Fathers and Doctors of the Church, St. Hilary of Poitiers (310-368) seemed to lean toward something like a part-whole analogy or social-organic model for the Trinity: "Each divine person is in the Unity, yet no person is the one God" (*On the Trinity* 7.2, cf. 7:13, 32).

[379] Of course, this analogy breaks down (as all analogies do at some point) because the paradoxes or internal contradictions in the notion of mathematical infinity lead some philosophers to conclude that an infinite series of objects or events cannot exist in the real world.

divine consciousness and will — united and interdependent in a unique way through their eternal relations of origin, and in mutual love and cooperation — because God is *three* persons sharing one act of being, thereby fulfilling the divine nature of each one; he is not *one* person.

Finally, this objection also fails to take into account an important dimension of the Trinitarian mystery that we have discussed already: **on a social-organic model each divine person shares in the full actualization of divine attributes such as aseity, omnipotence, omniscience and goodness only in so far as he organically (by origination) and socially (by cooperation) participates in the life of the Trinity as a whole.** Theoretically to extract a divine person from that Trinitarian communion and to examine his attributes as a *separate and solitary* divine person is to remove from the equation precisely what makes him fully divine. For example, the Son is always fully divine *in the context of the life of the Trinity as a whole.* All the divine attributes can be fully attributed to him through his relationships of origin and cooperation with the other divine persons. Thus, Divine Omnipotence can be fully attributed to the Son through his cooperation with the Father and the Spirit, as together they share the exercise of omnipotence; and perfect Divine Love can be attributed to him through his relationships of giving, receiving, and returning love with the other divine persons. The same holds true for the Father and the Spirit. Not only in their necessary and eternal relations of origin, but also in their sharing and cooperation in the full actualization and exercise of all the divine attributes, they are interdependent — in some respects analogous to the interdependence of functioning organs within a living body. Only because they live and act in Trinitarian communion, as organs of the living, interdependent whole as one God do they share fully in the attributes fulfilled by all three together. Divine life is what the whole, Tri-personal communion of God has: in other words, each person within that communion is only fully divine by means of his eternal relationships with the others, and only by participating together with them in the life of the whole.

h) The helpful confluence and inevitable limitations of Trinitarian analogies

We are not trying to solve a metaphysical puzzle here so much as exploring a divine mystery, a mystery for which we have only more or less inadequate analogies at our disposal. Thus, even the organic aspect of the analogy necessarily breaks down at some point. Each "organ" within the "body" would have to be generically identical in nature to sustain the comparison with the three fully and equally divine persons of the Trinity. (In the earthly, biological realm, no living creature composed of three generically identical organs — say, three hearts or three lungs — is known to this author!) Also, each of the three organs would have to be the distinct subject of a capacity for self-consciousness, rational thought, voluntary agency, and self-giving love. If human conjoined triplets can exist and flourish in the real world, then we might have the beginnings of a close earthly and natural analogy for the Divine Trinity: an analogy consisting of three equal persons sharing organically in one life, one communion of being.[380] Given that our knowledge of the infinite divine reality (in most respects) is merely analogical, however, any such finite analogy for the infinite will break down at some point. That is why an *organic analogy* for the Trinity (living organs of an interdependent, living whole) must be supplemented by a *social analogy* (the loving union of sharing and cooperation among three equal, personal subjects: three centres of consciousness and will). Moreover, as we have seen, divine revelation in Holy Scripture and (at least western) Tradition also suggests that the three co-equal divine persons can be held to originate from eternal "spiritual" acts, such as the act of self-knowledge (again, the first divine person eternally generates his Word or Image as a distinct divine

---

[380] To be sure, images of the Trinity as a man with three heads were condemned by St. Thomas Aquinas (ST IV.8.4.11), St. Antoninus of Florence (d. 1459), and finally by Pope Urban VIII in 1628. They pointed out that a three-headed human being would be a "monstrosity of nature," and therefore not a fit representation of the divine in sacred art. On this see David Brown, "The Trinity in Art" in Davis, Kendall, and O'Collins, eds., *The Trinity*, p. 334-335. However, I am not proposing the use of such an image for prayer and devotion, or as an aid to worship. I am simply pointing to it as an aid to establishing the intelligibility of a social doctrine of the Trinity by means of a close (but necessarily imperfect) analogy.

person in his own right, *per modum intellectus*) and the act of love (*per modum amoris*, that is, a third divine person is the fruit of the fullness of love, between the first and second persons of the Trinity); thus, even the *unitary, psychological analogy for the Trinity* of Augustine and Aquinas can play a role here, at least with regard to the relations of origin of the three. **Perhaps Charles Gore summed up this mystery best in his Bampton Lectures (1891):**

> **Thus, the Christian, taught of Christ, lifts up his mind in reverent awe, and yet in confidence, to catch some glimpse of the eternal Being. ... He beholds by faith God, self-contained, self-complete, as the Father moves for ever forth in the begetting of the Son, and the Father and the Son in the procession of the Spirit. There lies an eternal fellowship, in which the Father finds in the Son His adequate word or utterance, the satisfying expression of His being, and object of His thought, will, and love; in which the Son eternally receives and communicates the fullness of the divine life; in which the Spirit, the life of the Father and the Son, is the product and joy of both, and the bond of communion one with the other. ...**
>
> **[Only the Trinity] can explain how God can be eternally alive and yet in complete independence of the world which He created, because God's unique eternal being is no solitary and monotonous existence; it includes in itself the fullness of fellowship, the society of Father and Son and Spirit.**[381]

i)   The paradox of the Trinity

I am aware that the Social-Organic Model of the Trinity that I have outlined in this chapter still falls short of the venerable Catholic Tradition that the persons of the Trinity are "subsistent relations" — and not, as I have argued here, three eternally and ontologically

---

[381] Gore, *The Incarnation of the Son of God* , p. 135-136 and 137.

interdependent centers of self-consciousness, rational thought, and voluntary agency, united in loving communion. I trust that the understanding of the Trinity that I have presented, however, preserves at least the main intention behind the Subsistent Relations Doctrine, as defined, or at least clearly implied, at the ecumenical councils of Lateran IV and Lyons in the thirteenth century.[382] That intention I take to be that **the mystery of the Holy Trinity is a *paradox*: everything that distinguishes the three divine persons comes from and**

---

[382] In an address in Augsburg, Germany in June of 2018, David Brown offered the helpful suggestion that the Fourth Lateran Council (and Lyons and Florence after it) evidently did not intend to insist solely or strictly on a subsistent relations model of the Trinity; otherwise it would have condemned the Social Trinitarian thought of Richard of St. Victor (d. 1173), even as it condemned the Trinitarian speculations of Joachim of Fiore and Amalric. Richard had modified the definition of "person" passed down from Boethius by adding the characteristic of "incommunicability": persons exist as unique and incommunicable subjects. A person for Richard is "the incommunicable existence of an intelligent nature" (*De Trinitate*, 4.22.24). The Council condemned Joachim of Fiore's tri-theism, which allegedly amounted to the claim that the divine persons did not share a common essence. By contrast, in a social-organic model, each divine person shares the same, generic nature (in that each one possesses all the divine attributes) and each one necessarily implies the existence of the other two, since it is impossible for the Father to exist as divine Father without His Son and without their Spirit, etc. — in other words, if one is speaking of "the Father" one is automatically and implicitly speaking of the co-existent and co-equal "Son" and their co-equal "Spirit" as well.

Some Catholic ecumenists have argued (e.g. Bertrand De Margerie, SJ) that authentically ecumenical councils of the Church manifest varying degrees of "ecumenicity" due to the measure of the presence and participation of the bishops of the whole, worldwide Body of Christ. If so, then those councils manifesting lesser degrees of ecumenicity (such as Lateran IV and Lyons) are prime candidates for the re-reception and re-formulation of the their teachings through ecumenical dialogue with Eastern Orthodox Christians in a way that councils such as Nicea, Chalcedon, Florence, and Vatican II are not, councils which manifested maximum ecumenicity. See De Margerie, SJ, "L'analogie dans l'oecumenicite des Conciles. Notion clef pour l'avenir de l'oecumenisme" in *Revue Thomiste* LXXXIV. 3 (1984), p. 425-426. I put the case that there is nothing in the Social-Organic Model of the Trinity proposed in this book that violates the in-depth teachings on the Trinity of the Ecumenical Council of Florence. For further discussion, see Appendix B of this book.

reflects the unique relations of origin of each one, while everything that unites them as one God flows from the fact that each one not only possesses in the abstract the same attributes (that is, the divine nature as a kind-essence or secondary substance), they also participate inseparably with one another in the eternal actualization of those divine attributes (the divine being as a primary substance), through the mystery of the divine Tri-personal communion.[383]

In the Anglican world, Richard Swinburne attempted to develop a social doctrine of the Trinity in a way that harmonizes with the Two-Minds theory of the Incarnation. As we have seen, he preferred to speak of the divine persons as "souls," since each one is an immaterial and personal subject. Swinburne, therefore, sees the Trinity as constituted by three divine souls, which he identifies as three concrete, individual essences (that is, three distinct persons, each of whom instantiates the essential kind we call "divinity"), but the three are both eternally bound together and individuated from one another by their unique and everlasting relations of origin (the Father everlastingly causes the Son to be, and the Father and Son everlastingly cause the Holy Spirit to be). On the basis of the Divine Goodness and Divine Omniscience possessed by each one, the three necessarily and fully cooperate in the loving purposes common to all. In addition, Swinburne argues that it is not essential to the "divine" kind of nature to be completely immutable and impassible. Thus, it is possible for divine persons, in pursuit of their loving and common purposes, to think different thoughts, perform different actions, and have different experiences — including the experience by the divine Son of an incarnate life and death as Jesus of Nazareth (with "incarnation," as we have seen, understood in accord with Moderate KM).[384]

---

[383] By which I mean the mystery of the eternal generation of, and loving and wise cooperation among the divine persons.

[384] On Swinburne's Trinitarian thought, see the summary in Adams, *Christ and Horrors*, p. 114-118. The idea that the second and third persons of the Trinity are "caused" to be, however, is ambiguous, and could leave us with three independent divine entities, that is, with tritheism. In *Was Jesus God?* (Oxford: Oxford University Press, 2008), Swinburne quoted St. Augustine's argument that

Cardinal Kasper's Catholic Explorations of Kenoticism and the Social Trinity

In the Catholic world, Cardinal Walter Kasper has also made explorations in forming a social doctrine of the Trinity. These fit with his preference for a more kenotic understanding of the Incarnation than the Scholastic tradition in Catholicism usually has been willing to accept.

---

if the Father "wished to beget" the Son (that is, wished to cause the Son to exist), but was unable to do so, then he would have been weak, and if he was able to do it but did not wish to, he would have lacked generosity (p.29). But this implies that there is a fully divine person (the Father) who can exist apart from and logically prior to the begetting of his Son (which is impossible if his Son is his Word, the fruit of his necessary and eternal act of self-knowledge). It also makes the eternal begetting of the Son a voluntary act of will on the part of the Father, which hardly seems to fit with the ontological necessity of the divine processions and the essential Trinitarian reality of God. The fact that God is a Trinity of persons might then be a merely *contingent* feature of the divine reality. God the Father certainly loves the Word or Son whom he begets, but he does not generate the Son by "choice," but by ontological necessity (*per modum intellectus*, as the Latin Scholastic theologians would have said).

Swinburne also claims that when the Nicene Creed described the eternal Son as "not made," the theologians of that era had in mind merely "not made out of pre-existing stuff, and the Creed is thus denying that the Son was made out of anything pre-existing" (p. 36). But the council Fathers surely had more in mind than that, for they were responding to the Arian heretics who held that the Son was created *ex nihilo*, prior to the rest of creation. In short, it was not an option for the ancient, orthodox Fathers to hold that the eternal Son was merely a contingent reality, caused to exist out of nothing by a creative act of free choice of the Father. Rather, the notion of divine "begetting" was seen as analogous to the necessary "emanations" of the deity in Neo-Platonism, which is one reason why several of the early Fathers drew upon Neo-Platonic philosophy to unfold the mystery of the Trinity, and why they often used impersonal images for the divine processions to balance the personal metaphors: for example, the Son is like light ever shining from a lamp, or waters ever streaming forth from their source.

First, Kasper sees a strong social dimension to the Trinity at work in the medieval, Thomistic doctrine of the divine persons as "subsistent relations":

> The statement that the distinctions in God are in the form of relations is of fundamental importance because it represents a break-away from a one-sidedly substantialist type of thought. The final word belongs not to the static substance, the divine self-containment, but to being-from-another and being-for-another. ... In God substance and relation are identical; God is relation and exists only in the intra-divine relations; he is wholly love that surrenders and bestows itself. This relational reality of God, which is identical with his being or substance, presupposes real, mutually distinct relational realities. ... [W]e are saying that the numerically one divine nature or substance is 'possessed' by three subjects or that it exists in three relatively distinct modes of subsistence.[385]

> This understanding of God as communion-unity has far-reaching implications for our understanding of reality. ... God's unity is the fullness and even overflowing of selfless giving and bestowing, of loving self-outpouring; it is a unity that does not exclude but includes; it is a living, loving being with and for one another.[386]

One major problem with this Thomistic doctrine, however, is that we have no experience of anything even remotely analogous to "persons" existing *solely* as "relations" (as opposed, for example, to persons who are naturally "in relation" to one

---

[385] Walter Kasper, *The God of Jesus Christ* (New York: Crossroad, 1984), p. 280.
[386] Ibid., p. 307.

another, such as a mother and her unborn child).[387] At best, therefore, the doctrine of the divine "persons" as "subsistent relations" is about as minimally intelligible as a theological statement possibly can be. Some contemporary theologians even claim that to call such subsistent relations "persons" is simply an equivocation: "[O]n no reasonable understanding of *person* can a person be equated with a relation. Relations do not cause things, know truths or love people in the way the Bible says God does."[388] Even St. Augustine, the originator of the Subsistent Relations Doctrine, recognised this problem: "When the question is asked 'What three?' human language labours altogether under great poverty of speech. The answer, however, is given three 'persons,' not that it might be completely spoken, but that it might not be left wholly unspoken."[389]

Contemporary proponents of the "subsistent relations" doctrine such as Cardinal Kasper claim that it shows us that the essence of God includes internal relations of "self-giving love." In this way they attempt to lay claim to the moral and religious value of Social Trinitarianism. The problem, again, is that it is nearly impossible to conceive how a mere "relation" is equivalent to a "self" that can personally give itself to other "selves" out of love. A "self" or person surely implies a distinct subject of consciousness and will. Of course, the defender of the Subsistent Relations Doctrine might claim, as St. Thomas Aquinas did (see ST Ia.28.3), that each of three subsistent relations in God (traditionally called Fatherhood, Sonship, and passive Spiration) is "in reality the same thing as" the one divine nature in act (Aquinas), the divine essence as existence itself, "the one supreme reality" (Fourth Lateran Council, 1215) — and since that essence includes divine attributes analogous to human personal properties (e.g. infinite knowledge and infinite love), then each subsistent relation in

---

[387] For further discussion of this point, see Appendix A of this book on Keith Ward's recent work on the Trinity, *Christ and the Cosmos: A Reformulation of Trinitarian Doctrine*.

[388] J.P. Moreland and William Lane Craig, "The Trinity" in Rea, ed., *Oxford Readings in Philosophical* Theology, vol. 1, p. 34.

[389] St. Augustine, *De Trinitate* 5.10.

God rightfully can be called (by remote analogy) a "person." However, this move raises severe difficulties of logical coherence. After all, if Father is numerically identical to the one supreme reality whole and entire, and the Son is numerically identical to the one supreme reality whole and entire, and the Holy Spirit is numerically identical to the one supreme reality whole and entire, then it is very hard not to draw the logical conclusion that all three are, numerically and generically, the same thing as each other: they are just three names for exactly the same reality, the one supreme reality whole and entire. **There would be no *real* distinction of persons at all in God — and certainly not as "selves" (distinct centers of consciousness and will) that can give themselves to each other in love.**[390]

In the Orthodox tradition of the East, the divine persons are not held to be reducible to relations. That would be a meager understanding of "person." Rather, according to St. Gregory Palamas (1296-1359) the unique relations of each one do not *constitute* the persons, they *characterize* the persons. Relations, while they designate and characterize each person as a distinct person, do not exhaust the mystery of divine personhood.[391]

---

[390] As philosopher Thomas McCall writes, based on ""Leibniz's Law of the "Indiscernability of Identicals": "If the divine persons are all identical with the divine essence, then ... the divine persons will be identical with one another. Such a doctrine seems hopeless for trinitarian theology" (McCall, "Trinity Doctrine, Plain and Simple" in Oliver Crisp and Fred Sanders, eds., *Advancing Trinitarian Theology: Explorations in Constructive Dogmatics*. Grand Rapids: Zondervan, 2014, p. 58). Apart from appeal to some form of the highly controversial philosophical notion of "relative identity," there does not seem to be any way forward for the Thomistic position here. And that seems a very thin thread on which to hang the central doctrine of the Christian Faith. On these difficult issues see Brown, *The Divine Trinity*, p. 289-291.

[391] See Timothy Ware, *The Orthodox Church: An Introduction to Eastern Christianity* (Milton Keynes: Penguin, third edition, 2015), p. 208-209. Again, there does not seem to be any indication from the contemporary Catholic-Orthodox dialogue process that the Catholic side insists that the East must ultimately embrace the full-blown, Thomistic Subsistent Relations Doctrine. Such an insistence might very well doom the process right from the start.

Social-organic models of the Trinity also contain elements of paradox and mystery. They are based on the self-revelation of the Tripersonal God to which the New Testament bears witness, and as we have seen, on revealed analogies drawn from the most closely bonded human social relationships (such as the Church and the family, in John 17), as well as on forms of organic unity found in God's general revelation in nature. Thus, the uncreated Trinity tends to illuminate all of created reality as the pattern of authentic unity-as-communion. Anglican theologian Leonard Hodgson expressed this beautifully in his book *The Doctrine of the Trinity* (1943):

> The Christian doctrine of God thus contains an assertion about the nature of unity. It asserts that all actual unities of our earthly experience, from the unity of the hydrogen atom to the unity of a work of art, of the human self or of a human society, are imperfect instances of what unity truly is. We may find in them analogies to that true unity, and learn from them something of what perfect unity must be. But perfect unity itself is to be found only in God, and it is through the revelation of God in Christ that we find the unity of God to be of such a kind as to cast light upon all our lesser unities. Thus the Christian revelation brings with it a contribution to human thought on the subject of unity, a contribution which theologians and philosophers have not always rightly appreciated either as a matter of historical fact or as a source of enlightenment. ...

> [T]he essence of the doctrine of the Trinity is the doctrine that true unity is what I have called "internally constitutive unity," that is to say, a unity which by the intensity of its unifying power unifies distinct elements in the whole. A unity can be deficient as unity, it can fail to exhibit perfection of unity, in either or both of two ways: either by failing to maintain its elements in their distinctness, or by failing in its power to unify them, or both. ...

Thus, the doctrine of the Trinity is directly relevant to all our endeavors to promote the peace and unity of mankind. For the unity of different types of churchmanship within the Church, for the unity of different groups and classes within a nation, for the unity of different nations within a commonwealth of mankind, we need to look to the pattern of unity which has been shown us in the mount. We need to pray that the Church, by contemplating the unity of the Divine Trinity, may find its own true unity, and thus be able to lead the groups, classes, races and nations of mankind into that peace and unity which is God's will for them. ...

Because for us the unity of God, which is the archetype and pattern of all true unity, is a life in which the Divine Love eternally unites and yet keeps distinct the Persons of the Trinity, therefore we, when we are taken up to share in that life, may hope each to be united with God, and with his fellows in God, in a life of love which shall preserve eternally our personal distinctness. Through countless ages, by means of our bodily life in space and time, God our Creator has been fashioning us into uniquely individualised personalities. This creation is no transient illusion, or mere appearance, as certain monistic and pantheistic theologies would have us think. ... [H]e Himself is such that that creative purpose can be fulfilled, as He takes those created souls to be one while remaining many in the unity of the Blessed Trinity.[392]

Writing at almost exactly the same time as Hodgson, **Christian apologist C.S. Lewis (also an Anglican), summed up this mystery in words that have been cherished by Christians of all denominations ever since:**

And that, by the way, is perhaps the most important difference between Christianity and all other religions:

---

[392] Leonard Hodgson, *The Doctrine of the Trinity* (London: Nisbet and Co., 1943), p. 96, 183, 187, 189:

that in Christianity God is not a static thing — not even a person — but a dynamic, pulsating activity, a life, almost a kind of drama. Almost, if you will not think me irreverent, a kind of dance. …

The whole dance, or drama, or pattern of this three-Personal life is to be played out in each one of us: or (putting it the other way round) each one of us has got to enter that pattern, take his place in that dance. There is no other way to the happiness for which we were made.[393]

Throughout his whole discussion of the Trinity, we can see Kasper groping to find ways to keep in balance the two traditional Catholic poles of understanding the essence of God: as "Being" and as "Love."[394] He leans pretty heavily, however, toward the latter approach. In his understanding of the intra-Trinitarian relations, for example, Kasper seems to shy away from the Latin tradition that the second and third persons originate from the Father's essential, spiritual acts of perfect self-knowledge and perfect love. Kasper bases his model instead solely on what is necessary for perfect love to exist in God:

Perfect and complete communion within the one being of God … includes distinctions in the way this one being is possessed. In the Father, love exists as pure source that pours itself out; in the Son it exists as a pure passing-on, as pure mediation; in the Spirit it exists as the joy of pure receiving. These three modes in which the one being of God, the one love, subsists, are in some sense necessary because love cannot be otherwise conceived; to that extent the Trinitarian confession has an intrinsic plausibility to the believer. …[395]

---

[393] C.S. Lewis, *Mere Christianity*, p. 175-176.

[394] See St. Bonaventure, "The Soul's Journey into God," chapters 5 and 6, in *Bonaventure* (New York: Paulist Press, 1978), p. 94-109, and Pope Paul VI, *The Credo of the People of God* (1968) at http://w2.vatican.va/content/paul-vi/en/motu_proprio/documents/hf_p-vi_motu-proprio_19680630_credo.html .

[395] Kasper, *The God of Jesus Christ*, p. 308-309.

Each of the three modes in which the one love of God subsists is conceivable only in relation to the other two. The Father as pure self-giving cannot exist without the Son who receives. But since the Son does not receive something but everything, he exists only in and through the giving and receiving. On the other hand, he would not have truly received the self-giving of the Father were he to keep it for himself and not give it back. He exists therefore insofar as he receives himself wholly from the Father and gives himself wholly back to the Father, or, as it is put in the farewell prayer of Jesus, glorifies the Father in his turn. As an existence that is wholly owed to another, the Son is therefore pure gratitude, eternal eucharist, pure obedient response to the word and will of the Father. But this reciprocal love also presses beyond itself; it is pure giving only if it empties itself of, and gives away, even this two-in-oness and, in pure gratuitousness, incorporates a third in whom love exists as pure receiving, a third who therefore exists only insofar as he receives his being from the mutual love between Father and Son. The three persons of the Trinity are thus pure relationality; they are relations in which the one nature of God exists in three distinct and non-interchangeable ways. They are subsistent relations.[396] ...

There are certainly ambiguities in Kasper's thought here. For example, he poetically describes the characteristic properties of the divine persons who eternally give or receive existence from each other (e.g. "pure self-giving," "pure gratitude, eternal eucharist") — but logically it does not necessarily follow (and it is nearly unintelligible!) that these divine persons are nothing more than "relations." They could be described more properly as "personal subjects, distinct centers of consciousness and will, essentially united in relationships of ontological interdependence and loving cooperation with each other"— as in a social-organic model of the Trinity. Moreover, given the way he defines the relations of origin of the second and third divine

---

[396] Ibid., p. 309.

persons, it would seem that the Father is not eternally and directly involved in the procession of the Spirit. According to Kasper, the Spirit proceeds from the Father as the pure source of love, *through* the Son as the one who eternally mediates and passes on that love to the Holy Spirit, who is the pure divine receiver of love. And yet Kasper also states that the Spirit "receives his being from the mutual love between the Father and the Son."

Cardinal Kasper also wants to maintain a balance between eastern and western approaches to the Trinity — but here again, his nearly exclusive focus on the divine essence as Divine Love dominates his discussion:

> [A]fter the fashion of the Eastern doctrine of the Trinity, we must start with the Father as the origin and source of the Trinity and show that the Father possesses the one divine substance in such a way that he gives it to the Son and to the Spirit. ... This new approach, which we owe to the Eastern Church, need not lead to an abandonment of the achievements of Augustinian Trinitarian theology. For if we start with the Father as the origin and source of the Trinity we are led to conceive of the one divine nature as love. Then it becomes possible, more than in Eastern theology, to understand the Trinity entirely in terms of its innermost root, as is done, for example, by Richard of St. Victor; that is, as the mystery of perfect love that communicates and empties itself and, to that extent, as the grammar and summary of the entire Christian mystery of salvation.[397]

Kasper even goes so far as to say that "the meaning of being is the selflessness of love" – as if love is the *only* category in which the divine essence can be discussed and understood.[398] How this can be squared with the Catholic Tradition that the God of love is also in some sense

---

[397] Ibid., p. 314.
[398] Ibid., p. 310.

simple and immutable in essence, the eternal and pure act of infinite power and knowledge, is not readily apparent.

Kasper also briefly discusses perhaps the most difficult issue for social models of the Trinity: *the Trinitarian consciousness of God:*

> From the standpoint of the traditional doctrine of the Trinity it is clear that the unity of being in God entails unity of consciousness. It is impossible to accept three consciousnesses in God. ... [A]ccording to the traditional terminology, we must say that the one divine consciousness subsists in a triple mode. This means a triple *principium* or subject of the one consciousness must be accepted, and at the same time, that the three subjects cannot be simply unconscious, but are conscious of themselves by means of the one consciousness (*principium quo*). ... We have no choice, then, but to say that in the Trinity we are dealing with three subjects who are reciprocally conscious of each other by reason of one and the same consciousness which the three subjects 'possess,' each in his own proper way.[399]

The understanding of the divine mind here is starkly paradoxical: somehow one divine consciousness can be possessed in a unique and distinctive way by each of the persons of the Trinity — and yet remains one divine act of consciousness, in the one divine nature of the Trinity as a whole.

Whether or not all this is coherent is difficult to say. We are certainly in a realm of deep mystery here. David Brown has pointed to one way in which this mystery might begin to be understood: the phenomenon found in some (especially primitive and medieval) societies in which there is a social, group consciousness, a common vision and accepted wisdom which antedates individual reflection, is accepted as given by all (although some individuals in the society are better able to articulate and justify it than others), and which provides the foundation for

---

[399] Ibid., p. 288-289.

community life and the pursuit of common goals (although each individual in the group is also aware of himself or herself as a distinct individual, sharing in that common social vision). This feature of pre-modern societies might be taken as an analogy for the shared consciousness of the persons of the Holy Trinity.[400]

There may be an opening here in Brown to what we proposed earlier: that each of the three persons of the Trinity possesses, experiences, and expresses the divine-kind of nature in his own distinct manner — characterized by divine Fatherhood, Sonship, and Spirithood respectively — while sharing in the knowledge, purposes and decisions common to all three. Brown has given us an analogical way of understanding how (to use my own terminology) *there can* be *something analogous to a common Tri-personal consciousness in God.*

To be sure, the Trinity as a whole is not a single center or subject of divine self-consciousness or consciousness. In other words, there is not a single personal subject who experiences himself as, and knows himself to be the Divine Trinity — because the Trinity is not *a person*, but a Trinity-in-Unity: *a communion of three persons;* in a mysterious way, God's self-consciousness is threefold rather than singular.[401] Nor is the Trinity a single personal subject that originates thoughts or intentions — because the Trinity is not comparable to *a single personal subject*, but more like *a social-organic union of three personal subjects* who *jointly* originate *common* thoughts and intentions. Nevertheless, in the wondrous Tri-personal life of God there must be something analogous to a single, *common* divine consciousness made up of the knowledge, purposes, and choices that the three divine persons eternally originate in their life

---

[400] Brown, *God in a Single Vision*, p. 116-122.

[401] **In other words, in God there must be an eternal Father who knows and experiences himself as the Father-of-the-Trinity; there must also be an eternal Son who knows and experiences himself as the Son-of-the-Trinity; and there must be a Holy Spirit who knows and experiences himself as the Spirit-of-the-Trinity; these three together are the self-consciousness of God. But there is no single personal subject who can say "I am the Trinity."**

together, and eternally hold in common.[402] In trying to comprehend the unique, supernatural and infinite Trinity, we are left reaching for analogies to helps us at least begin to plumb the depths of this mystery: the divine reality as analogous, for example, to three torches eternally lit from each other, and radiating together one common and infinite Light.

When Cardinal Kasper writes about the Incarnation, he seems to leap out of the Catholic philosophical tradition of God as infinitely perfect Being, and into a position that sounds very similar to that of Radical KM (perhaps closest to the Mackintosh version of Kenoticism). It is God's freedom in love, Kasper says, that enables him to take the experience of human weakness and suffering into himself in order to overcome it on our behalf. Kasper claims, therefore, that a "solution" to the paradox of the Incarnation of an immutable and impassible God might be found in "the innermost being of God himself, in his freedom in love. ... Because God is the omnipotence of love he can as it were indulge in the weakness of love; he can enter into suffering and death without perishing therein. ... Thus God on the cross shows himself as the one who is free in love and as freedom in love."[403] This sounds awfully close to an appeal to a "voluntarist" understanding of the divine nature in order to make the divine *kenosis* of the Incarnation possible. In other words, it sounds as if Kasper is saying that God can do anything he wants to do in the freedom of his love, even if that means abandoning or contradicting his other divine attributes. Indeed, for Kasper it is precisely this absolute freedom of God's love that is all-powerful. Kasper writes:

> Because of his sovereign love, God got himself involved, so to speak, in the incarnation and lowered himself to the status of a slave. He was not overpowered by suffering. As a God who is immortal and in himself incapable of suffering, he voluntarily surrendered himself to suffering and death. ...

---

[402] In fact, as previously mentioned, *all* of the knowledge, purposes and choices of the three divine persons are held in common, without remainder, other than some forms of "experiential" knowledge. See footnote 365, above.
[403] Kasper, *The God of Jesus Christ*, p. 191-195.

In Jesus' death, God has not relinquished omnipotence, but rather has enacted all in a powerful way. With Kierkegaard, one can say: an element of omnipotence, indeed the omnipotence of love, entails allowing oneself to be affected by suffering without being under its control. ....

In his mercy, God allows himself, in sovereign freedom, to be affected by pain and suffering. In his mercy, God is shown to be masterfully free. His mercy is not induced by human need or woe. God graciously chooses to be affected and moved by the pain and suffering of humankind. Thus, many theologians today in the Catholic, Orthodox, and Protestant traditions speak of the possibility of God suffering vicariously with us.[404]

Throughout his work, Kasper has sought to find ways to reconcile what he sees as the biblical understanding of God in his sovereign freedom and love with the philosophical understanding of God as Perfect Being — both approaches which he takes to be valid and necessary to help us comprehend the mystery of God. If he has often left us with puzzling paradoxes, it only stands to reason: this is somewhat new territory for the Catholic tradition to tread. Whether or not Kasper's paradoxes in the end will be shown to be mere self-contradictions remains to be seen. My contention in this book is that these bold Catholic explorations in a social doctrine of the Trinity, and a kenotic approach to the Incarnation, could be greatly enriched by work already done in the Anglican tradition, and especially in the Anglican stream of Moderate Kenoticism. At the very least, this might provide a way for Catholic Kenoticism, as we find it in theologians such as Kasper and (as we shall see) von Balthasar, to avoid lapsing into voluntarism or tritheism.[405]

---

[404] Walter Kasper, *Mercy: The Essence of the Gospel and the Key to the Christian Life* (New York: Paulist Press, 2014), p. 119.
[405] Catholic theologian Roch Kereszty, O.Cist., also draws very close to a kenotic understanding of the Incarnation in *Jesus Christ: Fundamentals of Christology*, p. 373-374:

Chapter Six
Contemporary "Super-Kenosis" Theories

As we draw Part One of this study to a close, we need to consider the work of two theologians from outside the Anglican Communion who made significant contributions to Kenotic Christology in the twentieth century: the Roman Catholic theologian Hans Urs von Balthasar (1905-1988), and the Russian Orthodox theologian Sergius Bulgakov (1871-1944). As we shall see, their perspectives cannot be fitted neatly into the categories of "Radical" and "Moderate" kenotic theories of the Incarnation that we have used so far. Moreover, **they take Kenoticism to a whole new level, positing not just that God's actions in the world are often kenotic in form, but that** *the eternal life of the Trinity itself is characterized by kenotic relationships among the three divine persons: what von Balthasar and Bulgakov term "super" and "supra" kenotic relationships.*

As we have already seen, Kenotic Christology did not originate from within the Anglican orbit: the first to make explorations in this regard were nineteenth century Lutheran and Reformed theologians on the European continent, such as Thomasius, Gess, and Martensen. Before the First World War, Protestant theologians from Great Britain, both Anglicans and others, sought to adopt, and in a few cases further develop this same stream of Christology (with H.R. Mackintosh and Anglican Bishop Frank Weston as the most in-depth contributors to the discussion). Meanwhile, the theory continued to percolate in British Anglicanism through important contributions from O.C.

[I]n the process of the incarnation, [the Word] empties himself of his divine "status," renounces — it seems — the direct use of his divine consciousness and knowledge, and becomes aware of himself as a human being and as such learns gradually about God, himself, people, and the world. ...

We might say that he "translates" his divine Sonship into the language of human words, attitudes, actions, and relationships, as he constantly listens to his Father and says and does nothing other than what he hears from his Father.

Quick, Brian Hebblethwaite, Richard Swinburne, and David Brown. Due to their stature as two of the preeminent systematic theologians of the era, however, it was von Balthasar and Bulgakov who had by far the greatest influence, and no discussion of this topic would be complete without an exploration of the insights that might be gleaned from their work.

Von Balthasar and the Kenotic Life of the Trinity

We will survey the Trinitarian thought of Hans Urs von Balthasar first, although he died nearly a half-century after Bulgakov. But the latter has some broader insights that will be taken up later in this study.

Von Balthasar's work is also notoriously difficult to translate from the German, much less to comprehend, so we will lean primarily on the clear explanations of his position provided by his interpreters, rather than on major selections from his own writings. For example, here is how Gilles Emery, OP, summed up von Balthasar's perspective on the Holy Trinity — so crucial to his theological project as a whole:

> **[Von Balthasar] understands the eternal generation of the Son by the Father (the "Immanent Trinity") as an "initial 'kenosis' within the Godhead that underpins all subsequent kenosis":** "The Father strips himself, without remainder, of his Godhead and hands it over to the Son." Inherent in the Father who begets the Son from all eternity is an "absolute renunciation" (*ein absoluter Verzicht*) to be God for himself alone; the Father by love "lets go of his divinity" (*ein Losslassen des Gottsteins*). The eternal act of the Son's generation by the Father is grasped as "the positing of an absolute, infinite distance" (*die Setzung eines absoluten unendlichen Abstands*) within the Godhead itself, a "distance" that contains all the other distances that are possible within the world ("including the distance of sin"). Proceeding from the Father and the Son as "their subsistent We," the Holy Spirit maintains "the infinite difference" (*die unendliche Differenz*) between the Father and the Son, and he bridges this difference, since he is the Spirit of

both. **The kenosis of God in the covenant and on the cross, then, is based upon this "initial kenosis" (*Urkenosis, Urkenose*).** The thought of Balthasar rests upon a knife-edge. On the one hand, he rejects all fashionable talk of "the pain of God" (Moltmann). Yet on the other hand, by recourse to negative theology and to a complex theory of language concerning God, Balthasar posits an event (*ein Geschelen*) that happens within God. It is worthwhile to note the form this kenotic language takes: the eternal generation of the Son is explained in terms of a "separation of God from himself" (*Trennung Gottes von sich selbst, Trennung von Vater und Sohn*). For it is only from within this trinitarian separation, for Balthasar, that other separations can take place: in creation, the history of salvation, and even those that are most alienating and painful. The "emptying" (*Entleerung*) of the Father's heart is the original trinitarian "drama" which constitutes the condition of possibility for the drama that unfolds between God and the World.[406]

Another commentator who has wrestled with the Trinitarian thought of von Balthasar, Aristotle Papanikolauo, clarifies for us that for von Balthasar the concept of "person" itself has an inescapably kenotic dimension:

> The Trinity is, according to Balthasar, an event of kenotic love. … [T]he Father "*is* this movement of self-giving that holds nothing back." This movement is one of kenotic "self-destitution which constitutes the person of the Father, and at the same time, those of the Son and the Spirit. …"

The Father freely gives all that the Father is to the Son, who, in receiving the self-gift of the Father, freely returns all that is

---

[406]Gilles Emery, OP, "The Immutability of the God of Love" in in James F. Keating and Thomas Joseph White, O.P., editors, *Divine Impassibility and the Mystery of Human Suffering* (Grand Rapids: Eerdmans, 2009) , p. 49-50; my emphasis in bold type.

offered back to the Father in an eternal act of thanksgiving. The Spirit exists as the "holy intimacy between Father and Son," whose own self-giving constitutes the unity between the mutual self-giving of the Father and the Son.

The divine persons are constituted in and through movements of kenotic self-giving and receiving. ... *Kenosis* in this sense refers to the *ecstatic* movement of the one toward the other, the self-destitution in favor of the other. This self-destitution, however, is at one and the same time within the triune life a making-space for the reception of the "other."... In the kenotic movement of self-giving and reception the divine persons are constituted as unique and irreducible, as "Other." This otherness of the divine persons implies a "distance," *diastasis* or "*hiatus*" between them. This *diastasis* is implied in the trinitarian difference between the persons. In this sense, the Trinity is, as Ward puts it, "a community constituted by differences which desire the other."[407]

It follows, of course, that in the "Theo-drama" of God's love-relationship with the world, the eternal kenotic love among the persons of the Trinity manifests itself in the kenotic descent, and the whole kenotic life and death of the Son of God. Von Balthasar writes in *Mysterium Paschale*:

We shall never know how to express the abyss-like depths of the Father's self-giving, the Father who, in an eternal 'super–Kenosis,' makes himself 'destitute' of all that he is and can be so as to bring forth a consubstantial divinity, the Son. Everything that can be thought, or imagined where God is concerned is, in advance, included and transcended in this self-destitution which constitutes the person of the Father, and at the same time, those of the Son and the Spirit. God as the 'gulf'

---

[407] Aristotle Papanikolauo, "Person, *Kenosis* and Abuse: Hans Urs Von Balthasar and Feminist Theologies in Conversation" in *Modern Theology* 19:1, January, 2003, p. 47.

(Eckhart: *Un –Grund*) of absolute Love contains in advance, eternally, all the modalities of compassion, and even of 'separation' motivated by love and founded on the infinite distance between the hypostases — modalities which may manifest themselves in the course of a history of salvation among sinful humankind.

God, then, has no need to 'change' when he makes a reality of the wonders of his charity, wonders which include the Incarnation and more particularly, the Passion of Christ, and, before him, the dramatic history of God with Israel, and no doubt, with humanity as a whole. All the contingent 'abasements' of God in the economy of salvation are forever included and outstripped in the eternal event of Love. And so, what, in the temporal economy, appears as the (most real) suffering of the Cross is only the manifestation of the (Trinitarian) Eucharist of the Son: he will forever be the slain Lamb, on the throne of the Father's glory, and his Eucharist — the Body shared out, the Blood poured forth — will never be abolished, since the Eucharist it is which must gather all creation into his body. What the Father has given he will never take back.[408]

It would be hard to imagine a more thoroughgoing theological Kenoticism than this, since the eternal life of the Trinity itself, as well as all his dispositions and acts *ad extra* toward his creatures, are said to be marked by an eternal, kenotic pattern. And yet, as tempting as it might be for those inclined to Kenotic Christology to leap on-board and embrace this wider kenotic context, there are several things that should give us cause for concern here.

First, what can von Balthasar possibly mean by an "infinite distance" between the Father and the Son that is somehow overcome by the Holy Spirit as the intimate bond of love between them? After all (as

---

[408] Von Balthasar, *Mysterium Paschale*, "Preface to the Second Edition," p. viii - ix.

we saw in Part One, Chapter Five of this book), the Son and the Spirit, in the very act of their eternal generation from the Father, share with him in the eternal Being of God: they all share the infinite divine nature in-act, through the mystery of divine coinherence. **Unless we are implicitly thinking of the Trinity as three distinct primary substances — which of course, would be tritheism, pure and simple — not only is there no "infinite distance" between the divine persons, there is the closest imaginable (indeed unimaginable!) unity among them. To begin with, therefore, I would suggest that the idea that God the Father in begetting his eternal Son posits an infinite distance between himself and his Son, which then needs to be overcome somehow through the Holy Spirit, is metaphysically unintelligible.**

Second, the idea that the eternal love among persons of the Trinity — the Father, Son, and Holy Spirit — is essentially kenotic in form also appears to be confused. The eternal generation of the Son from the Father, and of the Spirit from the Father and the Son, has no eternal obstacles to overcome, no "distance" or barriers to cross, and therefore involves no death-to-self nor denial-of-self by each divine person, and no conceivable act of "self-destitution," "absolute renunciation" or "stripping of self" (as if there was something within the person of the Father that would need to be stripped away, renounced or restrained to enable the Trinitarian relations of origin, and the Trinitarian mutual love to happen!); **rather, *the eternal generation of the divine persons involves an infinite, unhindered expression and fulfilment of each one.* In other words, in the act by which the Father eternally begets his Son, he gives of himself completely and expresses himself completely *without loss*, for his resources for self-expression are infinite. And there is also no act of "self-emptying" as "self-limitation" of the divine persons toward one another in order to "make space" for each other. On the contrary, in their love for each other they eternally generate and enable each other to be without loss to themselves; indeed, through these very relations of origin they eternally fulfill the divine nature of each person. So the Father does not kenotically renounce or limit himself to allow the Son to be; rather, he** perfectly expresses and fulfills himself, eternally constitutes himself as "Father" precisely in begetting his fully divine Son, without whose existence he would not be Father, nor able to know and love himself without doing so in and through his eternal Word.

It follows that there is no pre-Trinitarian, primordial first person of the Trinity who needs to "renounce" being God for himself alone: the Father does not exist as Father, or possess the fullness of the divine nature, without begetting his Son (again: he could neither know nor love himself alone, in solitude, without his Divine Word. He constitutes himself as the fully divine Father, therefore, in his very eternal act of begetting his Son). And the Son does not limit or renounce anything in receiving and returning all that he is to the Father: he actually constitutes himself as Son in that reception and return of love to the Father, and only eternally knows and loves himself as Son in the loving gaze of his Father, without whom he would not exist as a divine person at all. **In short, *where love requires no self-limitation or self-sacrifice, there is no kenosis.***

What von Balthasar has done is confuse the eternal, Trinitarian love with the kind of love needed among created persons, where there really is a true ontological "distance" between persons as distinct primary substances. In human relationships, not only must that "distance" be overcome, by the Holy Spirit, but also the self-centered, fallen human nature of each one of us. Thus, among human beings authentic love often needs to take a kenotic form; we are challenged to overcome this "distance," as well as all of the obstacles born of sin, through acts of self-restraint and self-sacrifice: by the Holy Spirit dying to our old, fallen self for the good of others.

Von Balthasar has also confused love as "ecstatic or complete self-giving" with "kenotic" love. Granted that the highest love involves total self-giving, still, not all authentic, self-giving love among human beings is always kenotic in form, involving true self-limitation or self-sacrifice (see our discussion of this point coming up in Part Two, Chapter One). There would seem to be no reason to assume, therefore, that the perfect and eternal love among the persons of the Blessed Trinity must always be kenotic in form.[409]

Scott Hahn seems to get the balance right in his reflections on the mystery of the Trinity in *First Comes Love: Finding Your Family in the Church and in the Trinity* (2002):

> [G]od is love, and the essence of love is self-giving. The Father pours out the fullness of Himself; He holds nothing of His divinity back. He eternally fathers the Son. The Father is above all else, a life-giving lover, and the Son is His perfect image. So what else is the Son but a life-giving lover? And the Son dynamically images the Father from all eternity, pouring out the life He's received from the Father; He gives that life back to the Father as the perfect expression of thanks and love. That life and that love, which the Son receives from the Father and returns to the Father, is the Holy Spirit.
>
> We imitate God by giving ourselves in love. Love demands that we give ourselves totally, holding nothing back. In eternity, the complete gift of self is the Trinity's life. In time, the image of that love is a *sacrificial* love, *life-giving* love. We must die to ourselves for the sake of another.[410]

Finally, what von Balthasar has shown (at best) is that it was *fitting* that God (whose eternal Trinitarian life is said to be marked by pure, kenotic self-giving among the three divine persons), should lovingly

---

[409] Lucien Richard seems to repeat von Balthasar's misunderstanding when Richard writes of an "eternal passibility" within God that flows from the total self-giving love among the three divine persons, who all the while must "remain other" to each other; see *Christ: The Self-Emptying of God*, p. 106.

[410] Scott Hahn, First Comes Love: *Finding Your Family in the Church and the Trinity* (New York: Image Books, 2002), p. 73-74. In accord with the Trinitarian theology of Richard of St. Victor, it might be better to define the Holy Spirit as the fruit of the love between the Father and the Son, rather than as synonymous with the life and love between them, for the latter notion easily could be confused with the idea that the Holy Spirit is merely a divine attribute, rather than a full divine person in his own right.

enter by *kenosis* into our human condition. The fact is that God reached out to us in love in a way that, in this fallen and broken world, necessarily involved self-limitation, and ultimately self-sacrifice. But von Balthasar has not shown how an essentially omnipotent, omniscient, omnipresent divine Son, whose intra-Trinitarian life is also marked by eternal joy and beatitude, can actually do all that — kenotically assume our human condition and limitations, and for our sake bear our griefs and sorrows — without ceasing to be fully divine. For the eternal love among the persons of the Trinity (even if conceived in some kenotic fashion) is not the only essential divine attribute with which we have to reckon: not according to Scripture, Tradition, or the Christian heritage of natural theology, at any rate. After all, what happens to God the Son's omniscience, omnipotence, and omnipresence in the Incarnation? Von Balthasar never clearly tells us. In other words, he has not shed greater light on the central kenotic conundrum; to some extent he has merely side-stepped it.

Bulgakov and the Divine Kenosis in Creation and the Incarnation

The ideal of the kenotic, humiliated Christ — obedient, humble, poor, sacrificing himself for others in non-violent love — has a long tradition in Russian Orthodox religious culture. We find it in some of the lives of the early Russian saints who were often seen as "holy fools" for Christ, such as St. Theodosius (d. 1074) and (in the 18th century) St. Tikhon of Zadonsk.[411] We find it also in many of the great works of

---

[411] In his Preface to the anthology *A Treasury of Russian Spirituality* (Buchervertriebsanstalt: 1988), p. 9-10, George Fedotov holds that the kenotic way of following Jesus Christ is a defining characteristic of Russian spirituality:

> The most remarkable phenomenon of early Russian spirituality is the immediate impact of the Gospels upon the minds of the first Russian saints. Thus the rediscovery of the Christ of the Gospels, of the Christ in His human nature behind the Byzantine Pantokrator (the "omnipotent" or the "Divine Monarch"), which was a great feat of the twelfth century in the West, was anticipated by almost a century in the spiritual life of Russia. Doubtless the use of the Slavonic language in the Bible, and the celebration of the Liturgy contributed to the originality of the Russian

nineteenth century Russian literature (both those written by believers and by non-believers): for example, in the character Lukeria, the "Living Relic" in Turgenev's *A Sportsman's Sketches*; in Tolstoy's short story *Feodor Kuzmich*, a tale about a hermit believed to have been Tsar Alexander I, who kenotically abdicated his throne in order to live as one of the faithful poor; we find it in some of Tolstoy's peasant characters too such as Nikita in *Master and Man*; and above all in Dostoevsky's Prince Myshkin in *The Idiot*. The nineteenth century Slavophiles believed that this ideal of kenotic self-abasement as an expression of faith and love was preserved in the Russian heartland in the culture of the peasants, and that this ideal was the special gift that Russian Christianity could contribute to the healing of the world. It was summed up in a poem by Tyutchev that one author calls "the heart of Slavophilism":

> Those poor villages,
> That featureless nature....
> Land of patient fortitude,
> Land of the Russian folk.
>
> The proud glance of the stranger
> Will not notice or understand
> The radiance which transpires
> Thy naked poverty.
>
> Laden with the burden of the cross,
> All through thee, my native land,
> In the form of a servant, the King of heav'n
> Went about, bestowing his blessing.[412]

religious genius, but whatever its cause, kenoticism, in the sense of charitable humility as well as of non-resistance, or voluntary suffering, remains forever the most precious and typical, even though not always the dominant motif of Russian Christianity.

[412] Nadejda Gorodetzky, *The Humiliated Christ in Modern Russian Thought* (London: SPCK, 1938), p. 7.

This image of the divine Son who humbled himself to dwell among us, even entering into the depths of human affliction with us, and who showed us the way of pure, sacrificial love in the midst of poverty and suffering, was taken up into the writings of two great Russian theologians of the early twentieth century: M.M. Tareev (1866-1934) and Sergius Bulgakov (1871- 1944). In Bulgakov in particular we also find complex speculations on the role of the Divine Wisdom (*Sophia*) in the creation of the world and the preparation for the Incarnation. This aspect of his thought actually resulted in his Orthodox brethren bringing charges of heresy against him in the 1930s. Nevertheless, we can extract from Bulgakov's writings many rich Christological insights, and some that connect with the Anglican tradition of Kenotic Christology that we have found in Gore, Weston, Quick, Swinburne, Hebblethwaite, and Brown.

With regard to the mystery of the Trinity, we find strands of Kenoticism that later influenced von Balthasar. Paul Gavrilyuk explains:

> For Bulgakov, the manifestation of God's love for the world reflects the eternal relationship between the persons of the Trinity. … The Father pours himself out, empties himself in begetting the Son. The Father gives himself entirely to the Son. The Father comes out of himself, finds fulfilment in, and identifies himself with the being of the Son. The Father empties himself into the Son without in any way being limited by him because the Son shares in the same infinite and unfathomable divine nature.
>
> The Son on his part empties himself by submitting to be begotten from the Father and by being obedient to the Father. The love of the Father is 'ecstatic, fiery, conceiving, active'…. The love of the Son, in contrast, is 'sacrificial, self-denying humility of the Lamb of God, "destined before the foundation of the world" (I Pet 1:20)' (*AB*, 122). **To capture the depth of this mutual sacrifice Bulgakov speaks of the 'supratemporal suffering' (*predvechnoe stradanie*) within the Trinity, of the Father's death to his divine self in**

begetting the Son, and of the Sonship as 'supratemporal kenosis' of the divine being (*AB*, 122). He qualifies these rather bold statements by saying that this suffering is not a result of external limitation, for nothing can limit the absolute being from outside, but rather is an expression of the reality of sacrificial love.[413]

Of course, we could simply repeat here much the same critique that we made of the Trinitarian speculations of von Balthasar. **In addition, one has to wonder: why is there this pressing need in both theologians to push a kenotic form of love right back into the inner life of the Trinity itself? While such a move may add to the "fittingness" of subsequent divine acts of *kenosis* in creation and incarnation, it solves none of the metaphysical conundrums of kenotic models of the Incarnation (such as the ones with which we wrestled in Part One of this book) and it simply adds another tier of problems of its own. After all, what real sense can be made of a "supratemporal suffering" in the eternal Trinitarian life of God? And in any case, why is such an idea needed in order to say that the eternal self-giving love among the persons of the Trinity must take a specifically kenotic form when God reaches out to**

---

[413] Paul L. Gavrilyuk, "The kenotic theology of Sergius Bulgakov," p. 255-256; my emphasis in bold type. Bulgakov argues that the Word "seems to become wordless (in Himself) when he makes himself the Word of the Father," and "becomes poor and sacrificially silent in the bosom of His Father" (Gorodetzky, *The Humiliated Christ in Modern Russian Thought*, p. 162). But surely, the Son does not kenotically "make himself" wordless, poor and silent in his eternal relationship with his Father, because his hypostatic particularity as the Word is given to him in the very act in which he is begotten by the Father, and he knows himself as the co-equal divine Word in knowing the Father. Bulgakov also denies that there is any tragedy or unresolved suffering in the eternal, immanent Trinity, because it is triumphantly overcome by the Holy Spirit as the joy, blessedness, "bond" and "bridge" of love, a love that overcomes the "transtemporal suffering" of the eternal relationship between the Father and the Son (Gavrilyuk, "The kenotic theology of Sergius Bulgakov," p. 256). But (as I argued above, contra von Balthasar) if there is no real "distance" between the Father and the Son, then there is no "transtemporal suffering" in the life of the immanent Trinity, or eternal divine "wound" of any kind, for the Holy Spirit to bridge and heal.

his creatures in the work of creation and incarnation? In other words, what possible incoherence could be involved in saying that *ad intra* the perfect, eternal, self-giving love of the Trinity is without suffering or self-limitation of any kind, while that same perfect love expressed *ad extra*, toward his creatures in linear time, making space for their free-will, and entering into their broken and fallen condition in order to save them, must involve kenotic self-limitation and self-sacrifice? An intra-Trinitarian *kenosis* is simply not needed in order for God's perfect love legitimately to take kenotic form in his relationship with his creatures.

For Bulgakov, *the eternal life of the immanent Trinity is the life of God in himself and for himself.* **But in creation and incarnation he comes out of himself, so to speak, and lives no longer for himself alone. He gives up being for himself alone for the sake of creatures, and especially for the sake of his human creatures in the Incarnation. This necessarily exposes him to suffering. In other words, God eternally abandons his absolute immunity to all temporal suffering by choosing to create and become incarnate. Thus, the *immanent* Trinity accepts to become temporal and passible in the *economic* life of the Trinity.**

Gilles Emery, OP, summarizes this aspect of Bulgakov's thought as follows:

> The first economic action of kenosis occurs in the creation, which is conceived as an overflowing of the life of God by a voluntary self-diminution, a metaphysical kenosis with respect to the divinity itself. "The kenosis in creation of God who is Holy Trinity signifies his self-diminution with respect to his absoluteness. The absolute God, correlated with nothing but himself, becomes correlative with something outside himself." The kenosis consists in the passage from the immobility of the Absolute toward the becoming of the relative; he who is only absolute and not relative becomes relative by the creation. "The absolute God, who exists in himself, self-contained in his

absoluteness, self-sufficing in his majesty, abandons this state and establishes in dependence upon his own absolute being a relative creaturely being." The consequence … is that we can no longer think of "God" without the world, because the notion of "God" is a relative one.[414]

We need to be clear that for Bulgakov, this "change" in God is something he freely willed to undergo by creating a world. God's plenitude is immutable in his immanent being (by and for himself), but he can freely choose to limit or diminish that plenitude of divine life for the sake of his creatures, thereby to some extent refusing his own beatitude. **In other words, God has the freedom to choose *how* he wishes to live out the divine fullness of his being in his loving relationship with the world, even if this involves for him self-limitation and temporal suffering. (As we shall see, this perspective will be of crucial importance in our discussion in the concluding chapter of this book).** Bulgakov describes the paradox this way in his Christological masterpiece, *The Lamb of God* (1933):

> For God, self-limitation or, in general, distinction in the mode of the living out of the divine fullness is determined only by God Himself; it is the realization of His aseity and freedom. To attribute immobility and unchangeableness to God in the living out of the [divine] nature would be to diminish His absoluteness and His aseity. It would be to assert that a law of necessity exists for God Himself, or that His Divinity exerts a power over Himself that is greater than He Himself (this is the

---

414 Emery, "The Impassibility of the God of Love," p. 45. Perhaps we can still think of God as immutable and impassible, and without the world, if we think of the divine nature of the immanent Trinity as a theoretical "remainder concept": i.e., what God would be in himself if he had not timelessly chosen to create a world or become incarnate in it. This would define for us the fullness of what God is in and for himself, and the infinite resources from which he acts *ad extra*. Also, there could be senses in which God remains unchangeable and impassible — even a-temporal — despite his experiences of change and suffering in relation to his creatures. We will explore these issues further in the next chapter, and in the concluding chapter of this book.

impersonalistic conception of the Absolute, which is totally inadequate to the idea of a Personal God). *Nothing can limit God's freedom in His proper life; and there is no principle that would necessarily define God's life in the fullness that is exclusively possible for it.*[415]

In his study of the kenotic theme in the theology of Bulgakov, Paul Gavrilyuk identified three distinct aspects of the divine *kenosis* involved in God's relationship with his creation.

1) **God freely accepts the constraints of time and space in his actions in the world.**[416] **In other words, having created time and space, he limits himself to relate to the world in accord with those boundaries.** Although God is beyond the temporal unfolding of creation, nevertheless, he freely enters the world of temporality and becoming, and limits his manifestations by the conditions of time and space.

It is not clear, however, what Bulgakov means by God making himself "relative" to time and space and having to "limit himself" by acting within those boundaries. One would think that for a God to whom all time is present at once (at least according to the Classical and Scholastic conception of the divine nature), there would be no problem at all about acting within linear time without accepting or being bound by the

---

[415] Sergius Bulgakov, *The Lamb of God* (Grand Rapids: Eerdmans, Boris Jakim, trans., 2008), p. 122; italics mine. Here Bulgakov seems to tread perilously close to the kind of theistic voluntarism we criticized in Part One of this book. Nevertheless, this need not be voluntarism if, in the act of making himself subject to change and suffering in relation to his creatures (that is, in the economic life of the Trinity), it can be said that somehow, at the same time God transcends all change and suffering (in the immanent life of the Trinity) — which, as we shall see, is precisely what Bulgakov wants to say. This would mean that in making himself subject to change and suffering he has added new kinds of experience to his divine nature without loss of the essential plenitude of his divine nature. Again, see the "Conclusion" chapter at the end of this book for further discussion.

[416] Gavrilyuk, "The kenotic theology of Sergius Bulgakov," p. 258.

limitations of time and space. All of God's acts toward his time-bound creatures would be just so many aspects of the one, timeless, eternal act in which he is all that he is, and does all that he does.

2) **God limits his power, allowing creatures to exist with authentic free-will.**[417] Gavrilyuk states that according to Bulgakov

> God freely chooses to limit his omnipotence by giving human beings a degree of independence from himself. Bulgakov boldly states that human freedom remains 'unbreakable and impenetrable for God' . ... [D]ivine grace works only by persuasion, not by external compulsion. Using the image of Rev 3:20, Bulgakov states that God knocks at the door of human freedom, but never breaks it. Divine grace cooperates with human will, never violating it.[418]

As we will see in Part Two, Chapter One of this book, this is an understanding of creation-as-*kenosis* common to many in the Anglican stream of Kenoticism.[419] It is also characteristic of those writing from the perspective of Process philosophical theology. Bulgakov differs from Process theology here, however, in two respects: first, while divine "persuasion" is God's characteristic mode of action in his relationship with human beings, for Bulgakov he is not *confined* to that mode in his relationship with the cosmos as a whole; and second, God's use of loving persuasion with humanity is an act of voluntary

---

[417] Ibid., p. 257.

[418] Ibid., p. 258.

[419] I argued in Part One, Chapter Three, however, that in Kenotic Christology God the Son "limits" his omnipotence" in the Incarnation only in the sense that he restrains *one form* of his divine power (his determinative power) in favor of *another form* (the alluring power of his kenotic, self-sacrificial love as Jesus of Nazareth). In each form he is exercising divine power as his infinite, unsurpassable, inexhaustible "ability to achieve purpose" (O.C. Quick).

self-limitation on his part, according to Bulgakov; *it is not an expression of an inherent limitation in the divine nature itself.*

3) **According to Bulgakov, God even gives up his foreknowledge in order to preserve human freedom.**[420] **In order to enable genuinely human free choice, he limits his own knowledge of the future.** Gavrilyuk explains: "To put it briefly, God chooses not to know future contingents in order not to determine the future and take away human freedom ...."[421]

Of course, as far back as the sixth century, the Christian philosopher Boethius contested the idea that divine foreknowledge (in the form of a-temporal knowledge) is incompatible with genuine human freedom.[422] It remains a contentious point in the philosophy of religion to this day. Thus, it is not clear that Bulgakov really needed to ascribe this particular form of kenotic self-diminution to God in order to make a coherent claim that human beings have been given the capacity for authentic voluntary agency.

Despite his in-depth discussion of how God abandoned his immutability and his impassibility, and even self-limited aspects of his omniscience and omnipotence in his work of creation, Bulgakov still insisted that in his eternal being God all the while remains omniscient, knowing himself and all things in one supratemporal act.[423] In fact, he claims that the eternal, immanent Trinity remains *unchanged* amid all of his kenotic acts *ad extra*. Bulgakov writes:

> There is no place for change, becoming, or process in the eternity of the unisubstantial Trinity. This eternity transcends not only the world with its becoming, but also God Himself

---

[420] Ibid., p. 257.

[421] Ibid., p. 259

[422] See Boethius, *The Consolation of Philosophy*, (Oxford: Oxford University Press, P.G. Walsh, trans., 1999), Book Five, p. 97-114.

[423] Gavrilyuk, "The kenotic theology of Sergius Bulgakov," p. 258-259.

insofar as He defines Himself *in relation to the world* as the Creator and Providence.[424]

Thus, Bulgakov, tries to maintain a distinction between the eternal, immutable, and impassible life of the immanent Trinity, and the kenotic life of the economic Trinity voluntarily immersed in time, change, and even suffering. Precisely how God simultaneously can be both completely immutable and impassible in himself, and mutable and passible in his relationship with his creatures, Bulgakov never really succeeds in explaining with any clarity. As we shall see in the next chapter of this book, Anglican Kenotic theologians and others in the twentieth century would try to unpack this mystery, speculating (for example) that there are aspects the divine nature — such as his possession of the omni-attributes, and his steadfast disposition of love — that endure throughout all of God's acts and experiences in time in his relationship with his world. But writing in the early 1930s, Bulgakov did not have the benefit of these speculations from the realm of Anglo-American Analytic theism. He leaves us therefore, with a sharply di-polar understanding of God, and we shall have to explore later whether that is an aid or a detriment to working out a proper Kenotic Christology.

Bulgakov's theological project is equally challenging when he unfolds for us the mystery of the Incarnation. In *The Lamb of God*, for example, he makes clear his embrace of Kenotic Christology, which he even calls "the most important current of Christological thought since the ecumenical councils."[425] His own model of the Incarnation is boldly and unapologetically kenotic:

---

[424] Bulgakov, *The Lamb of God*, p. 222. Changeless indeed, and yet, paradoxically, according to Bulgakov, that changeless state of the eternal and immanent Trinity includes the "supratemporal suffering" of the Father and the Son in their eternal relationship with each other. It is not easy to see how this apparent contradiction in Bulgakov's thought can be overcome, unless it be understood as a changeless, eternal Trinitarian act of suffering.

[425] Ibid., p. 220.

We must be guided here not by the idea of "taking on" humanity by Divinity or the "inhabitation" of Divinity in human flesh, but by the idea of the descent of Divinity down to man, the self-diminution of Divinity, His humiliation or kenosis. ... The kenotic principle must be understood with an acuteness and clarity that did not by any means characterize the classical epoch of Christological disputes (if we ignore certain scattered statements of St. Cyril or St. Hilary).[426]

The kenosis consists precisely in the fact that the Son diminished Himself in His Divinity and became the *subject*, the hypostasis, of the *Divine-Human* life, experiencing hypostatically all that His humanity experienced. His proper Divinity was therefore so diminished for itself, was so hidden in its own depths or potentiality, that it was no longer an obstacle for death, and did not exclude its possibility. Unfathomably, His proper Divinity experienced death, without itself dying of course, but without resisting it.[427]

In fact ... the God-Man, having a divine personality and nature, *willed not to be God* during His earthly ministry; instead, He accepted humiliation and kenotically concealed His Divinity in *becoming*, having His Divinity, but not actualizing it. *How* could it in fact have been actualized? God and the world are so incommensurable that this relation cannot even be conceived except on the basis of divine kenosis.[428]

Some of Bulgakov's statements here seem to echo the Radical Kenoticism of Gess (e.g. the divine Son "willed not to be God" in the Incarnation) or of Thomasius and Mackintosh (i.e., the reduction of divine attributes by the Son from a state of actualization to one of "potentiality" in order to become incarnate). At other times, however,

---

[426] Ibid., p. 219; my emphasis in bold type.
[427] Ibid., p. 312.
[428] Ibid., p. 236-237

he sounds more like Martensen or Weston, for example: "In becoming man, God does not stop being God; even after descending from heaven, He remains in heaven."[429]   We can only explain this by recognizing that, on the one hand, Bulgakov retains a sharp distinction between the state of the divine nature in the eternal life of the Trinity, and the kenotic state of the divine nature in the outreach of the Trinity to the world (as discussed above); he writes: "The 'immanent Trinity' does not know the kenosis of the Word, which exists only in the 'economic Trinity.'"[430] In addition, Bulgakov insists (as all proponents of the Moderate Kenotic Model do) that even while incarnate, the Divine Word retains his creative and sustaining role throughout the universe:

> [T]he kenosis does not affect the participation of the Logos in creation (as is powerfully shown in the prologue to the Gospel of John, where the doctrine of the Word by whom all things were made, is juxtaposed with the testimony about the incarnation of the Son). The Word created the world, and the words of the Word are the foundation of the world's multiplicity and "allness." The pre-eternal Word, uttered at the creation of the world, remains in it as the indestructible foundation of its reality. Here we encounter in their full power the most audacious Christological paradoxes: sleeping on the stern, the Lord contains the universe in His Word; hanging on the cross and tormented by the suffering unto death, the Lord is the Creator and initiator of life, who contains all created things in His Word; born in the manger and reposing in the grave, the Lord is the Sovereign ruler of all creation; and so on. For this word about the world, resounding in the world, is His very personality, begotten of the Father and overshadowed by the Holy Spirit. The world is not shaken in this verbal foundation by the personal kenosis of the Word ....

---

[429] Ibid., p. 220.
[430] Ibid., p. 227.

A final problem arises: that of the participation of the Logos in His state of kenosis in the providential government of the world. The solution to the problem must show that this participation is not abolished or diminished by the descent of the Logos from heaven.[431]

Perhaps, then, Bulgakov's incarnational thought is closest to that of Charles Gore, with its unique (and not entirely successful) juxtaposition of the kenotic models offered by Thomasius and Martensen. Thus, Bulgakov can speak of the divine Son "diminishing" his own divinity, in the sense of reducing his divine attributes to a hidden state of mere "potency" in order to dwell among us as one of us, but at the same time he can say that the divine Son, even during his sojourn on earth, retains his cosmic role as the universal Word upholding and guiding all of creation.

How can the Divine Word be the subject of both states simultaneously? Bulgakov offers his own solution to this (the main hurdle for Moderate KM) with a unique set of distinctions. Paul Gavrilyuk explains:

> A crucial question for Bulgakov, as well as for the fifth-century patristic and nineteenth-century kenotic thought, was what precisely did God empty himself of [in the incarnation]? Bulgakov answers that Christ did not empty himself of his divine nature, for he remained truly God …. Instead, the Son of God surrendered the 'form of God,' which Bulgakov interpreted as divine life and glory: 'God voluntarily gave up his divine glory, divested himself of it, became naked, emptied himself, became poor, and accepted a form of a slave.' God freely limits the fullness of his life and renounces its joy and blessedness. He enters into human life and makes it his own …. This key distinction between the divine nature, which remains intact in order to safeguard Christ's divinity in the

---

[431] Ibid.

Incarnation, and the abandoned glory, was a common motif in the kenotic theories of the Protestant theologians from the time of Thomasius. ...

[Bulgakov] criticizes Thomasius' distinctions between the immanent and relative attributes of [of God] as artificial and affirms that the kenosis must affect all the divine attributes. In its place, Bulgakov introduces a quasi-Hegelian distinction between God-in-himself and God-for-himself. Bulgakov proposes that God's existence 'in himself' corresponds to the divine nature and remains unchangeable in the incarnation. In turn, God's existence 'for himself' embraces God's relationship with his creatures and corresponds to his life and glory: Christ remains God-in himself, but ceases to be God-for-himself.[432]

Unfortunately, Bulgakov's kenotic, incarnational model here appears to be neither coherent nor intelligible. The incoherence lies in his self-contradictory statements that "the divine nature of the Logos ... remains unchanged and undiminished in Christ,"[433] while at the same time he insists that the *kenosis* must affect all the divine attributes, and that his "proper Divinity" is "diminished" in the Incarnation. Are the divine attributes and his "proper Divinity" not aspects of Christ's "divine nature"? If the former are affected and "diminished" in the Incarnation, how can the latter remain unchanged in every way? Moreover, unintelligible, if not also incoherent, is the distinction he makes between the "glory" or "form" of God and the divine attributes themselves. Bulgakov writes:

The "form" is precisely the glory, which the Son has as God but which He removes from Himself in His humiliation, although He will later once again put on this garment of glory (see Jn 17:5). The glory, in turn, is Sophia in the capacity of the divine nature manifested, and revealed in itself. The glory is the

---

[432] Gavrilyuk, "The kenotic theology of Sergius Bulgakov," p. 260-261.
[433] Bulgakov, *The Lamb of God*, p. 224.

love of the hypostatic God for His Divinity. It is the bliss and joy that proceed from this love. And it is precisely this joy that the Son deprives himself of, empties Himself of: "[Instead of] the joy that was set before Him, [He] endured the cross" (Heb 12:2 …).[434]

What precisely is Bulgakov saying here? If he is defining the "form" or "glory" that the divine Son "diminished" or "deprives himself of" in the Incarnation as the joy and bliss of God's own love for himself, then how can Bulgakov distinguish that "glory" from the attributes of the divine nature: are not intra-Trinitarian joy, love, and beatitude attributes of God?[435] Wouldn't the Incarnation then involve an abandonment or limitation at least of these divine attributes in the Incarnation? On the other hand, if Bulgakov is defining the divine "glory" that the Son of God sheds in the Incarnation as "the divine nature manifested and revealed" *ad extra*, then we do not have a true kenotic self-limitation in the Incarnation at all — at least not one that would enable the divine Son to experience all the conditions and limitations of human life and suffering. It would be a mere veiling or hiding of his divine perfections, a *krypsis* rather than a true *kenosis*. Gavrilyuk, therefore, joins most commentators in their conclusion that "Bulgakov's attempt to replace Thomasius's distinction between the immanent and relative attributes [of God] with the quasi-Hegelian categories was overall unsuccessful."[436]

---

[434] Ibid.

[435] As we saw in Part One, Chapters Three and Four, Mackintosh and Weston argued that none of the divine attributes of the Son were fully abandoned in his incarnation, but all were in some way "transposed" into a limited human form. Moreover, Weston would insist that the divine Son retains all his divine attributes in-act in his state as sustainer and providential guide of the universe even while he simultaneously restrains and self-limits the exercise of those attributes, at a particular time and place in human history, in order to dwell among us in a fully human state.

[436] Gavrilyuk, "The kenotic theology of Sergius Bulgakov," p. 261. I have refrained from summarizing here what Gavrilyuk describes as the "further complication" that Bulgakov "introduces into this already complex discussion when he speaks of Christological kenosis as God's surrender of the divine Sophia and God's

These problems then have a ripple effect on Bulgakov's approach to the passion and death of Christ. On the one hand, as we have seen, Bulgakov claims that the kenosis of the Son involves only the economic Trinity, and not the unchangeable nature and being of God in the eternal, immanent Trinity. On the other hand, he insists that the divine nature of Christ does not remain impassible when he is on the Cross. As Gilles Emery, OP, puts it:

> For, following Bulgakov, the divine nature cannot fail to suffer if its hypostasis is subject to suffering. This is why the cross of Christ also engages the other divine persons in a kenotic participation. The mystery of Golgotha takes place in heaven in the heart of the Father — this heart which is the Holy Spirit. It is the "sacrifice of the Father" who offers his only Son in the Holy Spirit.[437]

As we discussed in Part One, Chapter Five of this book, a mysterious "compassion" with the passion of the Son by the Father and the Spirit does seem to be indicated in the New Testament. But Bulgakov takes this notion to patri-passianist extremes. As Emery explains:

> On the subject of the "sacrificial kenosis of the Father," Bulgakov makes some extremely strong statements that seem to suggest a "mutual exile" of the divine persons and, in a certain sense, a crucifixion of the Trinity. Bulgakov explains that the Father deprives himself of the Son: the Father at the

---

descent into the realm of creaturely Sophia" (p. 261, fn 37). Given that Bulgakov had defined the divine Sophia or Wisdom as "the equivalent of the divine nature, the richness of possibilities in God from which creation derives," it is far from clear how the divine Son can surrender the divine Sophia without ceasing to be divine. The "creaturely Sophia" into which the Son allegedly descends is, after all, the limited, created reflection of the infinite divine Sophia (Troy A. Stefano, "Christology after Schleiermacher" in Francesca Aran Murphy, ed., *The Oxford Handbook of Christology* (Oxford: Oxford University Press, 2015), p. 370.

[437] Emery, "The Immutability of the God of Love," p. 47.

cross is without the Son (the Father no longer has a Son), and the Son is without the Father (the Son no longer lives in union with the Father). The crucifixion of the Son sent by the Father becomes, then, their common crucifixion. It is the *crucifixion of the Trinity*. In the human crucifixion of the Son and the divine co-crucifixion of the Father, the very Love of the Father and the Son, the Holy Spirit, is co-crucified.[438]

Indeed, Bulgakov says that the sufferings of the Father and the Holy Spirit when the Son is on the Cross are distinct from, but no less intense than the sufferings of the Son. Being forsaken by the Father, the Son experiences spiritually the equivalent of all the sufferings of hell. Thus, the Son suffers as condemned by the Father for all the sins of the world, but the Fathers also suffers in judging and forsaking His Son, and the Holy Spirit experiences the suffering of God's sacrificial love for the world.[439]

This survey of the contributions to the Kenotic project of Bulgakov and von Balthasar, therefore, leaves us with something of an anti-climax. Rich and thought provoking as their kenotic explorations certainly are, it is not clear that they offer us a better way forward for Kenotic Christology than the (primarily Anglican) stream of Moderate Kenoticism. Indeed, the expansive notions of the Trinity-in-*kenosis*, and creation-as-*kenosis* offered by Bulgakov and von Balthasar would seem to add more problems to Kenotic Christology than they actually solve.

---

[438] Ibid.

[439] Gavrilyuk, "The kenotic theology of Sergius Bulgakov," p. 264. It would be better to say (in accord with Part Two, Chapter Two, below) that the Father does not actually judge or forsake his Son, but merely *permits* his Son's human nature to experience on the Cross the subjective feeling of divine judgment on sin, and the loss of any sense of the divine presence, through the crucifixion inflicted on him by the Romans and the Jews, so that his Son might assume the eternal penalty for sin as the sin-bearing substitute for all.

And yet, as we shall see at the end of Part Two of this book, aspects of Bulgakov's di-polar (immanent-economic) understanding of the divine nature may help us to comprehend one of one of the most difficult theological mysteries of all.

Conclusion of Part One

In conclusion, let us briefly review the ground we have covered in this part of the book. I have attempted to show:

1) Ever since Charles Gore at the end of the nineteenth century, there has been a recognizably Anglican approach to the Kenotic Theory of the Incarnation. Anglicans have rarely taken seriously the more radical kenotic models, given the minefield of theological and philosophical problems that these radical theories entail. Instead, they have focused on developing or defending what we have called Moderate, Two-Minds or Two-Spheres kenotic theories. This approach can be found especially in the writings of Anglican writers such as Gore, Weston, Quick, Hebblethwaite, Swinburne (before his move to Eastern Orthodoxy), and Brown, with some help from the Protestant philosopher Thomas Morris. These writers have developed their perspective in critical dialogue — even within the Anglican world itself — with other, very different approaches to the mystery of Christ: Non-Incarnational Christology, Action Christology, and Two-Nature Christology.

2) Nevertheless, Anglican Kenoticism is not of mere historical or antiquarian interest. I have endeavored to show that some forms of the Kenotic Theory — and especially the Moderate stream of Kenoticism found within the Anglican heritage — can withstand much of the critique levelled against them, and at least in terms of its intelligibility and coherence, Moderate Kenoticism should be treated as a live option for the

development of an orthodox Christian understanding of the mystery of the Incarnation.

In all this, we have yet to explore in-depth what Brian Hebblethwaite considered the most powerful reasons for adopting an incarnational and kenotic doctrine of Christ: namely, "the moral and religious value" of the doctrine.[440] What makes the Incarnation so central to the Christian faith is not only the beauty and power of the doctrine itself, but the light that it shines on every other aspect of God's revelation of his love, and his saving purposes for us. In Part Two of this study, therefore, we will explore the implications of a kenotic understanding of the Incarnation (especially in the form of Moderate KM) for the wider pattern of Christian belief: that is, for God's identification with human suffering, for the doctrine of the Saving Work of Jesus Christ, and for the social implications of the gospel. In each case, I hope to show that a kenotic understanding of the Incarnation can shed new rays of light on the mainstream Christian tradition.

---

[440] Hebblethwaite, *The Incarnation*, p.27-44.

Part Two
Anglican Kenoticism and its Implications

Chapter One
Kenoticism and God's Identification with Human Suffering

In the first part of this book, we saw that the Anglican stream of Kenoticism provides us with a model of the Incarnation that avoids many of the difficulties inherent in rival viewpoints. I also argued that one of the distinctive strengths of Kenotic theories in general is their ability to show that God has fully identified with human joys and sorrows, experiencing them from a limited, human perspective as Jesus of Nazareth.

All of this assumes, however, that an incarnation of God is necessary to enable God to identify and sympathise with the human condition. Is that true? After all, one could argue that a personal, loving, and omniscient God would always and everywhere empathise and sympathise with the sufferings and struggles of his creatures. Why would he need to become incarnate to do so?

The central concern of this chapter, therefore, is to explore whether belief in an incarnation of God, especially in a kenotic form, is necessary to enable us to say that God can closely empathise and sympathise with human suffering in his world. As a matter of fact, Anglican theology over the past century, and modern theology in general, are filled with in-depth discussion of this issue. As in Part One of this book, we shall draw primarily upon Anglican sources in the pages that follow, as we continue to explore the extent to which the incarnational and kenotic heritage of Anglican Christianity has contributed to discussion of these mysteries of the faith. At the same time we need to acknowledge that Anglican theology since the Second World War actually has been a microcosm of the wider discussion of these matters in the Christian world.

Throughout this chapter, I will use the phrase "identification with human suffering" to mean the experience of human affliction from a limited, human perspective on events. By "empathy" I shall mean the act of imagining oneself in the place and situation of another person. By "sympathy" or "compassion" I shall mean the affective accompaniment of empathy: that is, feelings of grief, sorrow, or pity over the afflictions of others.

Although it is not the focus of this chapter, we should note at the outset that in identifying with our human condition, the divine Son has not just borne the burden of our griefs and sorrows. He has shared with us all the characteristic joys and blessings of human life as well: wholesome food, refreshing sleep, intimate family bonds, close personal friendships, creative work in the carpenter shop, wonder at the beauties of nature, community celebrations of marriage and other social and religious festivals, replete with wine and music, dance and song. His life full of labors and sufferings was punctuated by these refreshments along the way, and in sharing our lot the Son of God has hallowed and blessed them all.

O.C. Quick and the Passibility of God

To begin, we can clarify our question with the help of some philosophical categories provided for us by the Anglican theologian O.C. Quick in *Doctrines of the Creed* (1938). Quick suggested that God's passibility means that he can be subject to suffering or passion; he can be moved, and effects can be produced upon or within him. According to Quick, we can speak of the passibility of God in three ways: "external," "internal," and "sensational."[441]

1. External Passibility

This form of passibility refers primarily to the capacity of the divine will to be acted upon by something outside itself, the capacity to be opposed or moved by some other free agent. Quick's definition of "external passibility" was not entirely clear, but he emphasized that:

---

[441] Quick, *Doctrines of the Creed,* p. 122, 184-187.

[I]n creating free agents other than himself, God voluntarily limited himself, so as to allow them really to act of their own motion, and even to rebel against his will if they would. In this way, therefore, God makes himself externally passible by creating.[442]

In other words, God limits himself in creation because he refuses to override the freedom he has given to some of his creatures. In this sense at least, his act of creation involves a voluntary *kenosis*. Charles Gore expressed it this way in *The Reconstruction of Belief* (1926):

Without fear of discord, then, with legitimate science, we must hold to the conviction that God has created beings with the responsibility of freedom — that within the scope of His universal presence and energy He has so far limited Himself as to leave room for their free activity, with all its disordering effects upon His creation, when it is misused; and in each act of our moral choice, however largely determined by conditions over which we have no control, such as circumstances, heredity, and the character generated by our whole past, we must recognize that the determination is not complete — there remains a spontaneous element in each choice which constitutes, according as it is exercised, our moral worth or our sin, our moral liberty or our moral servitude.[443]

Of course, in the strictest sense God is never subject to the action of any other being, because he freely willed to create free agents, holds them in existence at every moment, and presumably could remove them from existence at any time if he willed to do so. External passibility simply points to the fact that God permits his will to be opposed and his purposes in the world to be blocked, to some extent at least, by the misuse of creaturely freedom, both human and angelic. In effect, he allows his free creatures the dignity of choosing their own character and destiny.

---

[442] Ibid., p. 184-185.
[443] Gore, *The Reconstruction of Belief,* p. 143.

Some theologians and scientists (not least some from the Anglican tradition), have expanded upon this point. They have posited that there must be a self-limitation of Divine Omnipotence not only in God's respect for the free-will of some of his creatures (angels and human beings), but also in his choice to utilize evolutionary processes to unfold all the potentialities of life on our planet. Arthur Peacocke, for example, has made the case that God by *kenosis* relinquished a degree of control over natural history when he fashioned an evolutionary biosphere in which randomness and chance would be significant drivers of biological diversity and evolutionary advance:

> Biological evolution impels us to take more seriously and more concretely than hitherto the notion of the immanence of God-as-Creator — that God is the Immanent Creator creating in and through the processes of the natural order …. The traditional notion of God *sustaining* the world in its general order and structure now has to be replaced by one with a dynamic and creative dimension — a model of God giving continuous existence to a process that has an inbuilt creativity, built into it by God, and manifest in a 'time' itself given existence by God. As Frederick Temple said in his Bampton lectures of 1885, "God did not make the things, we may say, but he made them make themselves."…

> There is a creative interplay of 'chance' and 'law' apparent in the evolution of living matter by natural selection. … For biological evolution depends on a process in which changes occur in the genetic-information carrying material (DNA) that are purely physiochemical and random with respect to the biological form and needs of the organisms possessing the DNA …. What we call 'chance' is involved both at the level of the mutational event in the DNA itself; and in the intersecting of two causally unrelated chains of events — namely, the changes in the DNA and the consequences of such changes for survival in its biological niche ….

Instead of being daunted by the role of chance in genetic mutations as being the manifestation of irrationality in the universe, it would be more consistent with the observations to assert that the full gamut of the potentialities of living matter could be explored only through the agency of the rapid and frequent randomization which is possible at the molecular level of DNA.[444]

If all this is true, then it would certainly imply that God's creation of the entire biosphere involves a continual *kenosis*: in other words, he permits the biosphere, through the influence of randomness or chance, to fashion its own path and destiny (although the laws God creates and sustains, and with which chance interacts, will insure that it is an evolutionary path). The Anglican scientist John Polkinghorne echoes his colleague's perspective here, and goes beyond it by saying that a

---

[444] Arthur Peacocke, "The Cost of New Life" in Polkinghorne, ed., *The Work of Love*, p. 23, and 25-26. There are a multitude of difficulties with this perspective, however, on philosophical, theological and even scientific levels. For example, it is not clear that it is philosophically coherent to say that God can make creatures make themselves: see Michael Chabarek, OP, "Could God have used Evolution?" in Paul D. Brown and Robert Stackpole, eds., *More than Myth? Seeking the Full Truth about Genesis, Creation and Evolution* (Chilliwack, BC: The Chartwell Press, 2014), p. 228-245. Nor do we have any reason to believe that God could *only* unfold the potentials for biodiversity in the universe through a process in which randomness or chance play a significant part. There are other scenarios for God's interaction with creation in natural history that fit with the progressive appearance of ever higher and more complex life-forms on the earth over millions of years, but that do not require such a radical act of creation-as-kenosis. See Robert Stackpole, "Fact and Fiction in Genesis 1" in Brown and Stackpole, eds., *More Than Myth*, p.87-134, and in the same volume, the Introduction, and the essays by astrophysicist Hugh Ross and Greg Moore on the "Progressive Creation" and "Day-Age" perspectives. On the scientific level, major questions still remain to be answered about almost every aspect of the Neo-Darwinian evolutionary mechanism that Peacocke takes for granted here. In the same volume, *More Than* Myth, see the essay by Casey Luskin of the Discovery Institute, "The Top Ten Scientific Problems with Biological and Chemical Evolution." In short, it is not just biblical fundamentalists and Young-Earth Creationists who have trouble seeing the necessity of the Neo-Darwinian story of life on planet earth upon which Peacocke so heavily depends.

theology of "Creation as Kenosis" adds a vital dimension to Christian theodicy:

> There is an unavoidable cost attached to a world allowed to make itself. Creatures will behave in accordance with their natures: lions will kill their prey; earthquakes will happen; volcanoes will erupt and rivers will flood. I have called this insight "the free process defense" in relation to physical evil, in analogy with the familiar free-will defense in relation to moral evil. These defenses do not by any means solve all the problems of theodicy, but they temper them somewhat by removing a suspicion of divine incompetence or indifference. From this point of view, the classic confrontation between the claims of divine love and the claims of divine power is resolved by maintaining God's total benevolence but qualifying, in a kenotic way, the operation of God's power.[445]

2. Internal Passibility

Internal Passibility refers to conflicts and disharmony within a conscious being or personality. Human beings, for example, frequently

---

[445] John Polkinghorne, "Kenotic Creation and Divine Action" in Polkinghorne, ed., *The Work of Love*, p. 95-96. It is very hard to see the force behind Polkinghorne's argument here. The obvious response to such a radical, creation-wide *kenosis* on God's part is to ask why he insisted on creating a "free process" involving such massive wastage, and pervasive animal and human suffering. Human free-will is necessary to make such things as love and reason and human creativity possible, and the misuse of human (and angelic) free-will doubtless causes suffering. But what is there about biodiversity that can *only* arise from a "free process" based largely on genetic mutations and survival-of-the-fittest? In short, Polkinghorne's worldview seems to be long on *kenosis* but short on love. Nor is it clear why God inspired the creation narratives of Genesis 1 and 2 to be written (even if they are to be interpreted more figuratively than literally) when they contain little that coheres with "Creation as Kenosis," and much that seems to contradict it. Again, see my essay in *More Than Myth?* — cited in the previous footnote. For a Roman Catholic perspective similar to that of Polkinghorne, see Archbishop Josef Zycinski's *God and Evolution: Fundamental Questions of Christian Evolutionism* (Washington, D.C.: Catholic University of America Press, 2006), p. 161-164, 181-194 and 250. Zycinski leans especially on Rahner, von Balthasar, and Alfred North Whitehead.

experience mental anguish and struggle in their decision making. They agonise over what to do. Human emotions such as anger or sadness can influence and even overwhelm the rational mind, and move one to act contrary to right reason. Such irrational feelings Quick calls "passions." But God is without passions, so defined; in other words, his wisdom and his holy will cannot be touched or swayed by irrational feelings.[446] Quick does not mean by this that all feelings are irrational, for sometimes our affections can move us to live in harmony with right reason. And, Quick does not deny that God has affections in accord with right reason. What he means is that "The divine will and reason are not passive to changing emotions, as are the will and reason of man."[447] In other words, in himself God is never tempted or swayed by irrational feelings. He has no bodily or emotional passions that might control him, or cause him internal conflict. In this sense, he is impassible in mind and will, immovable in his wise disposition of love. God's nature is simple and impassible in that everything he does and is accords with his wise and steadfast love; as Quick puts it: "we conceive God's changelessness to consist simply in the absolute steadfastness of his perfect will of love."[448]

Of course, God may be possible with regard to the ways he actually *exercises* his love toward his creatures (but this would more accurately be described as a form of *external* passibility). In other words, given his kenotic respect for human free-will, our petitions and intercessions in prayer move him to come to our aid in the sense that they give our consent and *permit* him to love us in ways that he otherwise would not do — but our prayers do not *persuade* God to help us. For *internally*, he is already disposed to love us in every way that he can, and every way that we will allow. As Christ says in Revelation 3:20: "Behold, I stand at the door and knock; if any one hears my voice and opens the door, I will come in to him and eat with him, and he with me." Thus, God may be said to be internally impassible in that his wise disposition of love is unchangeable.

---

[446] Quick, *Doctrines of the Creed*, p. 185.
[447] Ibid.
[448] Ibid., p. 135.

This understanding of divine immutability found an echo in the writings of the Anglican theologian Brian Hebblethwaite. In his collection of essays entitled *The Incarnation* (1987), Hebblethwaite explained:

> There seem to be two elements in the idea of divine immutability … that Christian theists must retain. In the first place, they will want to insist on the unchangeable nature of God's character as manifested in his acts — his steadfastness both in purpose and in action, his reliability and his trustworthiness. And in the second place they will want to insist on the fact that what God has done he has done. If he has provided a unique and normative revelation of himself in Jesus Christ, then that is what he has done. That fact stands fast, however we may change and develop in our comprehension of God's self-revealing act.

> So God remains the same yesterday, today and forever in his character and purpose. And what he has done by acts of self-revealing love, he has done, and there is no changing those facts — if facts they are. It seems then that something is left of the notion of immutable divine reality and truth. God may exist in process and becoming and acting. There may indeed be a divine history — but this history constitutes itself an immutable reality, in the sense that what God has done he has done, and the reality of God's unchanging character and trustworthiness, as manifested in the divine history, remains immutable as well.[449]

Even from within the stream of Analytic philosophical theism, however, it would be possible to admit much more than this regarding divine immutability. For example, it is arguable that according to both Scripture and philosophy, the essential attributes of the divine nature are not lost over time: God is always by nature self-existent, everlasting, all-powerful, all-knowing, and infinitely good. Whatever

---

[449] Hebblethwaite, *The Incarnation*, p. 99.

the divine history may be, arguably this essential nature of God remains intact. As we saw in Part One of this book, this form of philosophical theism is a challenge to some of the more radical kenotic theories of the Incarnation.

Some philosophers in the Analytic tradition, however, such as H.P. Owen and Peter Geach, have gone even further. They have argued that although he is omniscient, God does not know all future *actualities* (because the future depends in part upon the decisions of free creatures which, arguably, cannot be foreseen), but God does know all future *possibilities*. In other words, God does not know everything that *will* be, but he does know everything that *may* be. Thus, he always knows how he will respond to every possible situation that may arise, so that his loving purposes for his world can be fulfilled. In this sense, God's will is internally impassible not only as a general, steadfast purpose and benevolent disposition; even with regard to particular people and events his decisions cannot be altered, for he has already decided from the beginning how he can most lovingly respond to every possible situation that may arise, and every possible prayer. Our prayers and actions might still move him with respect to which of these divine decisions actually will be implemented in his world (again, another form of external passibility), but God has perfectly loving and immovable "contingency plans," so to speak.[450] In this sense, also, he may be said to be internally impassible and immutable.

3. Sensational Passibility

By this phrase Quick meant "liability to those feelings of pleasure and pain, and more especially those of pain, which are caused within a conscious being by the action of some other being upon it."[451] This includes divine affections such as God's sympathy and compassion for the sufferings of his children, his sorrow over their sins, and his joy over their acts of virtue. Quick believed that God made himself

---

[450] See the discussion of the views of Owen and Geach in Richard Creel, *Divine Impassibility* (Cambridge: Cambridge University Press, 1986), p. 17.
[451] Quick, *Doctrines of the Creed*, p. 185.

passible and vulnerable to these affections by choosing to create beings who can sin and suffer, and thereby cause him to experience the appropriate emotions in response, in accord with his love for them. In short, *God's omniscient care for the condition of his creatures makes him sympathetically responsive to their plight.*

It is easy to see why the kind of perspective Quick offered on divine sensational passibility — coupled with developments in the idea of external passibility (discussed above) — has led many theologians to embrace a wider kenotic perspective. Not only is there a divine *kenosis* in the Incarnation, it is said, but the Incarnation reflects other kinds of divine *kenosis* pervasive in his work as Creator. A great variety of viewpoints have been expressed on the doctrine of creation as *kenosis*, and as we have seen, some of these perspectives make connections with the scientific theory of the evolution of the entire biosphere. But for those not willing to go quite that far, Anglican theologian Keith Ward, summed up the thoughts of many when he wrote:

> [N]ot just the incarnation, but the creation of conscious and rational beings itself is a kenotic act on God's part. For it will involve a giving up of pure divine bliss, and accepting many experiences of pain and suffering. It will involve a giving up of complete control, and accepting the freedom of created beings to make their own decisions, however misdirected. It will involve the giving up of complete knowledge, and accepting that much about the future must be unknown until it is determined by the actions of creatures. These are real limitations, and this may be thought of as a sort of kenosis, a giving up of some great goods, in order that free creatures may exist in independence, community, and creativity.[452]

Are Ward and Quick correct about divine "sensational passibility"? Our first task in this chapter is to ask (with special reference to the framework of the Anglican theological and philosophical tradition) whether, or to what extent, God can be said to experience "sensational

---

[452] Keith Ward, "Cosmos and Kenosis," in Polkinghorne, ed., *The Work of* Love, p. 157-158.

passibility" in relation to his creatures, apart from or prior to the Incarnation. In other words, we need to know if God as Creator, Sustainer, and Providential Guide of his universe identifies, empathises, and sympathises with human afflictions.

Panentheism and God's Compassion for Human Suffering

The "sensational passibility" of God as Creator, Sustainer, and Providential Guide of history is a common theme of twentieth and twenty-first century theology. A lucid example can be found in the writings of British Protestant theologian John Hick:

> It is a highly preachable thought that in the incarnation God became our fellow sufferer. But do we not want to say that in his total awareness and sympathy with his creatures, God has *always* participated in every pain and joy, every hope and fear, every feeling and volition, every success and failure of all his human children? Do we not want to say that all the consequences of all his creatures, all their experiences, have always been open to the divine omniscience? … [T]he doctrine of unceasing divine sympathy and suffering removes this particular need for incarnation, since God is already fully involved in all his creatures' joys and sorrows. A God who knows his creatures through and through and who participates from the beginning in their joys, feels their sorrows, and grieves at their sins, does not have to become incarnate to do this.[453]

We need to know, however, in what way God's "participation" in every human joy and sorrow is being understood here. Does God actually experience the hurts and feelings of limited creatures as if they were his own? Or does he just sympathise with us from his own omniscient perspective on events?

---

[453] John Hick, "Evil and Incarnation" in Michael Goulder, ed. *Incarnation and Myth* (London: SCM: 1979), p. 81.

Some form of pantheism or panentheism may be required to make Hick's view of the sympathy of God intelligible here. *By "panentheism" I mean the theory that the universe is a part, aspect, or strictly necessary expression of God, so that without the universe he would not be God.* For example, panentheists may hold that creation is like a body that God fashions for himself for the completion of his own being; or that the material world necessarily emanates or overflows from God's transcendent being (Plotinus), or that God comes to self-consciousness through his involvement in human history (Hegel), or that he grows in value in some way alongside his world as a result of his inter-actions with it (Whitehead). *Perhaps belief in a general panentheistic presence of God throughout the universe is necessary if we are to hold that God sympathetically participates in all human afflictions, so that their suffering necessarily has an effect on him as well.*

Anglican theologian John Macquarrie argued along these lines in his book *Principles of Christian Theology* (1977). Macquarrie defined God as holy Being. God is not a being, nor a property of beings, nor an inclusive totality of all beings. Rather, Being is the act or condition of existence, the act or energy by which beings exist.[454]

Being is that which lets all things be, or enables them to be, and thereby brings them into being. Moreover, Being contains all the potentialities which it can actualise in the world: "Since letting-be is prior to particular instances of being, though other than these, we are justified in claiming that Being is more beingful than any particular being it lets be."[455] While Macquarrie referred to Being as the power of "letting-be," and therefore as the transcendent Creator, Being is also immanent in the whole creation: "there 'is' no Being apart from beings, and Being 'is' present-and-manifest in every being."[456] In other words, God is by definition he-who-necessarily-creates, and is thereby manifest in all his creative work. This is certainly not pantheism, but it can be termed a form of panentheism, in that God is said to depend upon his work of creation for the realisation of his nature as self-expressive Being.[457] In

---

[454] Macquarrie, *Principles of Christian Theology*, p. 107-122, especially p. 120.
[455] Ibid., p. 113.
[456] Ibid., p. 120.
[457] Ibid., p. 120 and 200.

fact, "God cannot be conceived apart from the world, for it is of his very essence (letting-be) to create."[458]

Macquarrie believed that all the creative action of holy Being must be costly to him:

> He puts himself into the creation. He commits himself to it and takes responsibility for it, though at the same time he commits a share of responsibility to the creatures. And in all this there is inevitably not just a limitation of power, but also God making himself vulnerable, for there cannot be this love and sharing and conferring of freedom without the possibility of suffering on the part of him who loves and shares and confers.[459]

> It must be at real cost to himself that God creates, reconciles, and consummates. Such at any rate would seem to be implied in any understanding of God that looks to the cross of Christ for the centre of revelation.[460]

> The Kenosis which was of such interest to the traditional Kenoticists, the Kenosis implied in incarnation, is seen to be only one moment, though indeed the climactic one, in a whole history of Kenosis. For instance, creation too is Kenosis ....[461]

Macquarrie's panentheism is clearly in evidence here. This is what he called an "organic" model of the God-world relationship "in which God as Creator is affected by the world as well as affecting it, for his very act of creation entails risk and vulnerability to his own fulfilment as well as to that of his creatures."[462]

Macquarrie's viewpoint, however, can be challenged in several respects.

---

[458] Ibid., p. 121. See the further discussion of this issue in the "Conclusion" chapter of this book.

[459] Macquarrie, *The Humility of God*, p. 4.

[460] Macquarrie, *Principles of Christian Theology*, p. 256.

[461] John Macquarrie, "Kenoticism Reconsidered" in *Theology*, March, 1974, p. 124.

[462] Macquarrie, *Principles of Christian Theology*, p. 121.

First of all, it is not clear how God suffers with us, in other words, how human sins and afflictions are costly to him as well. Macquarrie seems to mean that whenever God's self-expression in creation is thwarted, when his loving purposes for creatures are at least partially blocked (as in Quick's "external passibility"), then Being fails to fully realise his own self-expressive nature, and thereby suffers loss (as in Quick's "sensational passibility").[463] But surely this would mean that God (who, in Macquarrie's view, *must* create a world in order to be God) strictly depends upon a proper response from his creatures if he is to find his own blessedness and fulfilment. His act of creation must at the same time be a striving for fulfilment. A lack of response to God's love, therefore, would cripple the divine self-realisation, understood as self-expression through creation.

What Macquarrie has done here is abandon the classical, Scholastic distinction between God's intrinsic and extrinsic "glory": the former, his intrinsic perfection of Being; the latter, the reflection of those divine perfections in his creation. If Macquarrie was right to make this move, then we had better refer to God as "Striving-after-Being" or "Hopefully-Emerging-into-Expression-Being" rather than simply as "Being." Also, we would have to recognize that by defining God in this way, we have removed from him the capacity for purely selfless and generous love (*agape*) toward his creatures. His love for us would always, necessarily, involve a striving for his own elusive fulfilment. And we would also have to ask whether a God who *necessarily* depends upon a positive response from his creatures for his fulfilment as self-expressive Being is really the God of the Bible (Acts 17:25; cf. Ps 145:3 and Is 6:1-5).

Second, even if we accept that God our Creator feels in some way for the sufferings of his creatures, this would still leave us with the question of whether God has ever shared the human condition from a limited perspective similar to our own. For God's perspective on suffering would be one of omniscience. But human beings do not have the advantage of such a total perspective on the meaning and purpose of their sufferings, on God's resources for dealing with suffering, or

---

[463] Ibid., p. 199-201.

on the temporal boundaries of suffering, and its possible or probable results. Marilyn McCord Adams summed up the matter in her book *Christ and Horrors* (2006):

> God's feeling *in the Divine nature* all the pains that creatures feel will not constitute adequate solidarity with human horror-participants. Divine consciousness is of immeasurable scope. God's clear and comprehensive awareness of the Good that God is would radically recontextualize any creaturely pain and suffering that God might feel: what swamps a human consciousness would be a miniscule fragment of what occupies Divine attention. Moreover, what is distinctive about horrors is that they stump the meaning-making resources of the horror-participant. This is not possible where the Divine mind is concerned — a fact on which human salvation ultimately depends! To show solidarity with horror-participants, God must experience evils within the limits of a finite human consciousness, with a mind that can be "blown" and at least *prima facie* unable to cope with horrors.[464]

Adams then pointed to the Incarnation of the divine Son in an individual human nature as precisely meeting this need, enabling him truly to share our lot as the crucified God: the God who lives and dies as one of us (Jn 1:14). As Jesus Christ, God himself could journey through the depths of human affliction with us.

Macquarrie could not make this move, however, because he believed that God's omniscience means that he already occupies every creaturely perspective at once (a view we questioned in Part One of this book, in our discussion of his theory of the Incarnation). It would follow that God cannot attain any closer participation in human sufferings than he already and ever has. Indeed, Macquarrie nowhere states that the human life and death of the Divine Word adds any new kind of knowledge or experience to the divine nature.

Third, it is not clear why the doctrine of the Cross requires us to believe that God suffers in his role as Creator and Sustainer of the universe.

---

[464] Adams, *Christ and Horrors*, p. 197-198.

Macquarrie said that he was compelled to believe in the universal vulnerability of God to suffering by the Christian tradition that God is the God of suffering love, as revealed on the Cross. Only if God's continuous creative action is "costly" to him can he truly be called loving and worthy of worship.[465] "A God of love is inevitably vulnerable," he wrote, "for there is no love that does not suffer."[466]

This raises the question of whether all true love involves suffering. **Let us define the highest form of human love (agape) as a selfless (i.e., self-forgetful) seeking of the good of others, even, if need be, at the expense of one's own temporal good. It follows that true love is willing to be vulnerable, take risks, and make sacrifices for others if and when the need arises. But the highest love is not sacrificial or suffering by definition.** Otherwise, why would Scripture say that in the highest unity of love in heaven, there shall be no more pain or sorrow, and all tears shall be wiped away (Rev 21:4)? A true lover is willing to suffer pain and loss for his beloved, *if need be*. For this reason, a willingness to suffer may reveal the depth of one's commitment to the beloved. But love can be strong and true in days of good fortune when circumstances do not require us to suffer. Suffering is never a good or end in itself. Moreover, even in human experience we know of authentic acts of love for others that require little, if any suffering: for example, playing with one's children, sharing conjugal love with one's spouse, and singing the praises of God at worship ("Be filled with the Spirit, addressing one another in psalms and hymns and spiritual songs, singing and making melody to the Lord with all your heart, always and for everything giving thanks in the name of our Lord Jesus Christ to God the Father." Eph 5:19-21). Macquarrie is surely mistaken, therefore, when he claims that "there is no love that does not suffer."

God as Creator might then be seen as truly loving (though without suffering) in that he selflessly confers blessings on his creatures by bringing them into being, and enabling them to share, in a creaturely and limited way, in his infinite perfections.

---

[465] Macquarrie, *Principles of Christian Theology*, p. 256.
[466] Macquarrie, *The Humility of God*, p. 69.

God's vulnerability to suffering might then be more the result of his incarnation, than of his general work of creating, sustaining and providentially guiding his world. His incarnate life could then be seen as his act of identification with our vulnerable human condition, even unto death on a cross, which he freely and lovingly undertook for our sake and at our need. Indeed, in the two main Kenotic Models of the Incarnation that we explored in Part One of this book (Radical and Moderate), the depth of human suffering was said to have been taken into the everlasting divine "memory," or store of experience of God the Son through his passion and death as Jesus of Nazareth. Through this experience, God came to empathise and sympathise with the afflictions of humanity in the closest possible way.

A helpful clue here might be the words of St. Paul in II Corinthians 8:9" "You know the grace of our Lord Jesus Christ, that though he was rich, yet for your sake he became poor, so that by his poverty you might become rich." Paul does not say "God was from everlasting poor and sympathetically vulnerable to all the sufferings of his creatures, and so he enacted an earthly sign and symbol of that poverty on the Cross." In the Scriptures the descent from divine riches to human poverty and servanthood refers more to God's incarnation in Jesus Christ than to his general activity as Creator and Providential Lord of the cosmos and of human history (Phil 2:6-11).

Finally, Macquarrie offered a pastoral reason for believing in a universal pathos in the creative work of the Divine Spirit. He saw God as "from the very beginning ... in the creation and among men, sharing their suffering and striving for their liberation."[467] Macquarrie believed that this truth keeps Christian spirituality from becoming a tranquil contemplation of an impassible divine realm. True spirituality means "letting ourselves be invaded by the striving and passion of the Spirit of Christ for his people."[468] In this way our spiritual life becomes ethical rather than escapist.

---

[467] Ibid., p. 63.
[468] Ibid.

The Incarnation

If a kenotic Incarnation lies at the center of Christian spirituality, however, it is surely in no danger of otherworldly escapism. For if the Divine Word has become "Emmanuel," God with us, living in person a human life with all its sorrows and joys, then this human experience remains part of his everlasting memory: the reference point and touchstone of his closest sympathy and compassion for us. Thus, God is not utterly tranquil and detached from human experience; through the Incarnation he has chosen to be involved in the deepest way with his children and their destiny. The ethical aspect of our contemplative life, therefore, can be preserved even without the idea of a God who suffers as Creator, Sustainer, and Providential Guide of the world. For the Christian can truly say: God loved us so much that for our sake he came to share our human condition, living and dying as one of us: "In this the love of God was made manifest among us, that God sent his only-begotten Son into the world, so that we might live through him. ... Beloved, if God so loved us, we also ought to love one another" (I Jn 4:9-11).

In short, Macquarrie's panentheistic theology has not given us adequate grounds for believing that apart from the Incarnation and its effects, God has ever fully identified with the human condition, or that he can closely empathise and sympathise with human afflictions.

Much the same critique can be made of the panentheistic Process theology of Norman Pittenger. Pittenger tells us that God is nothing other than pure, unbounded love.[469] As a result, we cannot think of God as impassible, or unmoved by the sins and sufferings of his children:

> With his creatures he both suffers and rejoices — and (as I believe we must also say) he is 'enriched' in his own divine experience by what happens to and in his world.
>
> To say this last, however, is not to suggest that God becomes 'more divine' in consequence of his relationships. It is to say that although God is always supreme and worshipful,

---

[469] Norman Pittenger, *The Christian Church as Social Process* (Philadelphia: Westminster Press, 1971), p. 188.

> unsurpassable by anything which is not himself, his own 'existence' as love-in-action may be given more opportunities of loving and more ways of acting in love, as the free decisions of the creatures provide him with new material on which he can work.[470]

This seems clear enough. God does not *become* loving through relating to his creatures, but he does find more concrete ways to *enact* and *express* his love. Moreover, his Divine Omniscience must include some kind of awareness of the sins and sufferings of his children.

Difficulties start to arise, however, when Pittenger starts to speak of God as "the ultimate recipient of cosmic occurrence"[471] who in some way needs human love for his own fulfilment. Pittenger warned us not to think that "divine love is entirely selfless, without any need for response, and without any desire to receive," for the Bible speaks of "the yearning love of God, urgently seeking a response, finding value in the beloved, desiring the returning love of the other, and essentially concerned to establish a relationship between the two."[472] **But God's desire to elicit a response of love from us does not necessarily spring from a need *in him* to receive our love and worship. His desire to receive our love and worship may spring instead from a selfless desire to draw out of his children our own potential for good, and for the enjoyment of his presence. In other words, God does not necessarily desire our love out of his own need, as if something were lacking to his own fulfilment or beatitude. Rather, he desires that we love him for *our* own good.**

Even if we can claim, based on a panentheistic Process theology, that in some remote way God as Creator feels for our pains and sorrows and grieves over our sins, again, this does not yet enable us to say that God has ever identified with the human condition, or that he can closely empathise and sympathise with us now. For apart from or prior to the Incarnation, he has never known what it is like to suffer from a

---

[470] Ibid., p. 51-52.
[471] Pittenger, "Christology in Process Theology," p. 188.
[472] Pittenger, *Christology Reconsidered*, p. 130.

finite, human perspective as we do. The American Process theologian Daniel Day Williams stressed that in Process theology, we can only speak of God's participation in suffering by way of analogy:

> Suffering is what it is for us in part because we do not see its full consequences. In our doctrine of God, even God's knowledge does not encompass all the specific aspects of future free decisions. But God's being includes his knowledge of all possible outcomes. He knows the boundaries of all tragedy, just as he knows the infinite resources for dealing with every evil. Suffering is thus transformed in God without being eliminated. God participates in the world's suffering, but without all the limitations that beset finite sufferers.[473]

A third Anglican attempt to work out a theology of universal divine pathos (i.e., a theology of divine participation in human suffering that is not metaphysically dependent upon the Incarnation) was put forward by W.H. Vanstone in his influential book *Love's Endeavour, Love's Expense* (1977). **Based on a phenomenological analysis of "love" among human beings, Vanstone defined authentic love as inherently "limitless, as precarious, and as vulnerable."**[474] Authentic love is *limitless* in that it implies a "totality of giving — that which we call the giving of self or self-giving. The self is the totality of

---

[473] Daniel Day Williams, *The Spirit and the Forms of Love* (New York: Harper and Row, 1968), p. 127-128. It is important to note that despite its acceptance of universal divine pathos, Process theology is not really a stream of Kenoticism. It does not involve divine *self-limitation*, but severe metaphysical restrictions on Divine Omnipotence itself which leave God *unable* to act in his world in any other way than through "persuasion," that is, by presenting his creatures with the attractive ideals he hopes to fashion in creation. In addition to the scriptural problems involved here for the Christian (i.e., how is this kind of God really the God of the Bible?), John Polkinghorne's critique of Process theology cuts right to the heart of the matter: "It is a noble concept, but it is open to question whether deity has not been so evacuated of power that hope in God as the ground of ultimate fulfilment has been subverted …. The matter can be put in the bluntest terms by asking whether Whitehead's God could be the One who raised Jesus from the dead." Polkinghorne, "Kenotic Creation and Divine Action," p. 92.
[474] W.H. Vanstone, *Love's Endeavour, Love's Expense* (London: Darton, Longman and Todd, second edition 2015), p. 53.

what a man has or is: and it is no less than this that is offered or made available in love."[475] Authentic love is also *precarious*, for it does not coerce or control its object; it does not compel a response of love. Thus, it may "fail to 'arrive'— through misjudgment, through misunderstanding or through rejection. Love may be frustrated: its most earnest aspirations may come to nothing...."[476] Furthermore, authentic love is *vulnerable*:

> The power over itself which love gives to its object ... is power to make angry or to make glad; to cause grief or joy; to frustrate or fulfill; to determine tragedy or triumph. It is the 'power of meaning'— the power of having meaning to, or value for, the one who loves. It is the power of affecting the one who loves. It creates a new vulnerability in the one who loves.[477]

Vanstone then argued that God's love as Creator, if it is truly authentic, must be expressed in a similar way toward his creation.

God's love must be "limitless" in that the self-gift of his own being can only be expressed as an infinite gift, through the creation of an infinite object of his love, an infinite universe.[478] Moreover, this infinite self-gift must not be "easy" for him; he must "spend himself" in it. Vanstone therefore critiqued the biblical language that "By the Word of the Lord were the heavens made, and all the hosts of them by the breath of His mouth" (Ps 33:6), because there is no sacrificial "giving of self" implied here.[479]

The activity of God in creation must be "precarious" because he must relinquish absolute control over its outcome:

> It must proceed by no assured programme. Its progress, like every progress of love, must be an angular progress — in which each step is a precarious step into the unknown, in which each triumph contains a new and potential tragedy, and

---

[475] Ibid., p.45.
[476] Ibid., p. 46.
[477] Ibid., p. 52.
[478] Ibid., p. 59.
[479] Ibid., p. 60-61.

each tragedy may be redeemed into a wider triumph; in which, for the making of that which is truly an 'other,' control is jeopardized, lost, and through activity yet more intense and vision yet more sublime, regained; in which the divine creativity ever extends and enlarges itself, and in which its endeavour is ever poised on the brink of failure. *If creation is the work of love, then its shape cannot be predetermined by the Creator, nor its triumph foreknown:* it is the realisation of vision, but of vision which is discovered only through its realisation: and faith in its triumph is neither more nor less than faith in the Creator Himself — faith that he will not cease from his handiwork nor abandon the object of His love. *The creation is 'safe' not because it moves by programme towards a predetermined goal but because the same loving creativity is ever exercised upon it.*[480]

Finally, the love of the Creator for his world must be "vulnerable." But in this respect Vanstone drew back from ascribing to God susceptibility to literal "hurt," "sadness," or being "made glad" by his creatures, fearing that such language might be too anthropomorphic, and say more than we really know about the mystery of God.[481] What we do know, Vanstone claimed, is that Divine Love cannot be diminished or destroyed by that which it loves, nor can it be changed into something other than love. It is inexhaustible and indefatigable. But according to Vanstone it surrenders to the beloved the power to determine its issue: whether completion or frustration. Thus, at this point in his book, Vanstone drew back from ascribing "sensational passibility" to the divine nature (to use Quick's terminology), and collapsed the idea of divine "vulnerability" into the previous category of its "precarious" nature (a form of "external passibility"):

> The vulnerability of God means that the issue of His love as triumph or tragedy depends upon His creation. There is given to the creation the power to determine the love of God as either triumphant or tragic. This power may be called 'power

---

of response': upon the response of the creation the love of God depends for its triumph or its tragedy.[482]

Vanstone then summed up his vision of the kenotic love of the Creator for his world:

> **If God is love, and the universe is His creation, then for the being of the universe God is totally expended in precarious endeavour, of which the issue, as triumph or as tragedy, has passed from His hands. For that issue, as triumphant or as tragic, God waits upon the response of His creation. He waits as the artist or the lover waits, having given all.[483] …**

> Drained is love in making full;

> Bound in setting others free;

> Poor in making many rich;

> Weak in giving power to be.[484]

It is not easy to unpack the metaphysics implied in Vanstone's discussion of Divine Love here. To his credit, he admitted in several places in this book that he was dealing with mysteries too deep to be easily defined and comprehended. Nevertheless, several responses could be made to his threefold understanding of the universal, kenotic love of the Creator.

1. Vanstone's argument that the created universe must be infinite in order to be the proper self-expression and object of the infinite self-giving of God falls afoul, first of all, of modern science. Contemporary physics since Einstein has argued that the space-time-matter continuum is certainly not boundless. Besides, as Vanstone himself admitted elsewhere in his book, God does not need to create an infinite object in order to have an infinite recipient of his love, because within the life of the

---

[482] Ibid., p. 67.

[483] Ibid., p. 74.

[484] Ibid., p. 119.

eternal Trinity there already exist three infinite persons who give and receive love without limit:

> Christian theology asserts that this 'need' is met within the being of God himself, and requires, for its satisfaction, no response from the creation. In the dynamic relationship within the being of the Trinity, love is already present, already active, already completed and already triumphant: for the love of the Father meets with the perfect response of the Son. Each, one might say, endlessly enriches the Other: and this rich and dynamic inter-relationship is the being and life of the Spirit. Therefore nothing beyond the being of God is necessary to the fullness or fulfilment of God. God is not like man — who must look beyond himself to another who, by responding, will satisfy his need to love. Within the mystery of the divine being there is present both the power to love and the triumphant issue of love in the response of the Beloved.[485]

Still, Vanstone could argue that the love of God expressed *ad extra* must be analogous to the infinite Trinitarian relationships of *complete self-giving, with nothing held back*, and therefore the biblical language of God creating the universe by a series of almighty verbal commands is inadequate, even as a metaphor.

This objection only stands, however, if we are compelled to see all authentic acts of Divine Love toward creation as equal in degree and intensity. More traditional Christian theology would have seen God's act of bestowing existence on all things, enabling creatures to share in a limited way in his divine perfections, as a pure act of selfless generosity, undertaken solely for the good of creatures themselves. This is why St. Irenaeus of Lyons in the 2nd century famously taught that "the

---

[485] Ibid., p. 68.

glory of God is man fully alive."[486]Returning to our working definition of "love": if authentic *agape*-love always consists in "the selfless seeking of the good of others," then how can God's powerful act of bestowing existence on creatures, and holding them in existence at every moment, not be called an act of authentic love? The Incarnation may involve an even deeper and more complete act of self-giving love for his creation. But again, our working definition of authentic love spoke of "seeking the good of others, even, *if need be*, at the cost of one's own temporal good." If there is *no need* for a great act of divine self-sacrifice in creating and sustaining the world, how can the lack of such a sacrifice render his creative love less than authentic?

2. From a biblical standpoint it would seem that Vanstone's language about the "precarious" nature of God's creation-project is over-blown. The "safety" of creation in the providential hands of the Creator is surely not reducible to the fact that God will never give up in his attempts to reach out to the world with his "creative love." It must also consist in the fact that God knows his own infinite resources for bringing "un-thought of goods out of permitted evils," and knows that these resources will bring about the final triumph of his purposes for creation.[487] Only so can we make sense of the promises and reassurances given to us in biblical apocalyptic prophecy, especially in the eschatological discourses of Jesus, and in the book of Revelation. God may not be able to insure that particular individuals will participate in his final victory over evil — that depends upon their own free response to his love — but he surely knows he has the loving power to bring his creation in general to a joyful consummation. In this way, he might be likened to a perfect chess player. He gives his creatures the right to freely choose the moves they want to make within the framework of the game, and he knows that

---

[486] St. Irenaeus, *Adv. haereses.* 4,34,7: PG 7/1,037.
[487] A phrase used by Austin Farrer in *Saving Belief*, p. 57.

some of the pieces on the board will be lost in the struggle. But he also knows he has the unsurpassable wisdom and love to win the game in the end, and so he can assure us (through scriptural promise and prophecy) of the fact of that triumph, and of at least the general nature of the final outcome.

Does this mean that God's Love as Providential Lord of history is less than fully authentic because it involves a degree of "control" of the final issue? Vanstone had argued that authentic love never uses force or control to avoid tragedy and compel a positive response. But this is surely open to qualification. *The biblical narrative shows God using what we shall call "determinative power" to achieve some of his purposes in salvation history* (e.g. the creation of the world *ex nihilo*; the fresh start for humanity through Noah and the Flood; the overcoming of Pharaoh and his armies at the Red Sea; Jesus casting out demons and calming the storm at sea; the resurrection of Christ from the dead; the defeat of God's unrepentant enemies at the Final Judgment, and the triumphant resurrection of all the faithful). Of course, divine acts of control or determinative power are never used to achieve God's *highest* purposes of love (such as the salvation of sinners through the Cross), and they are never used to *compel* a return of his love, for an authentic response of love must always be freely given. But divine acts of determinative power can be acts that initiate a new stage of creation or of history, or effective acts of "damage control," so to speak, for the common good, in a world rife with sin and rebellion — and to that extent, they are surely acts of authentic love. For *it is not true that authentic love is never coercive: it certainly can be, if the need arises, for the sake of the good of others.* For example, consider the parent who compels her child to go to school, the lifeguard who rescues (by taking total control of) a helpless swimmer who is drowning, the judge who compels a man to pay his taxes, and the policeman who compels a violent criminal, afflicting the innocent and helpless, to "cease and desist" — these are hardly violations of authentic love. As O.C. Quick wrote, God cannot use this kind of love to achieve his greatest victories and achieve his highest purposes.[488] But it is not clear why Vanstone insisted that all expressions of authentic love, human and divine, must be exactly the same as the sacrificial love of the Incarnate Son on the Cross.[489]

All of this means, of course, *that it is not essential to Kenoticism to hold that authentic acts of Divine Love are always and only kenotic in form* (that is, that they always involve self-limitation, or self-sacrifice). Love is only kenotic *if need be*. Again, God's act of creating the universe *ex nihilo* at the beginning of time involved a unique form of power, which is not easily interpreted as kenotic; nor does biblical teaching about the final consummation of the world, and the creation of a new heavens and a new earth seem kenotic in form. As David Brown has written:

> Some aspects of the divine promise do depend on unqualified power. Most conspicuously, there is nothing inherent in human beings that can guarantee life after death: our faith in Christ's promise that we will one day be with him is thus a matter not just of grace but also of divine power to defeat death. Likewise, the attempt to follow Christ in this world should not always take the kenotic path. Sometimes power is the right instrument to use.[490]

---

[488] Quick, *Doctrines of the Creed,* p. 62.

[489] Graham Tomlin argued for the same perspective as Vanstone on this point in *The Power of the Cross: The Theology of Christ in Paul, Luther, and Pascal* (Carlisle: Paternoster Press: 1999), p. 278-279: "[T]he cross represents the characteristic pattern of God's action in the world ... a paradigm of the way in which God always works."

[490] Brown, *Divine Humanity,* p. 264.

To be sure, the *highest* form of Divine Love, by which God achieves his supreme purposes for us — the love that makes the most difference to humanity — does indeed seem to take kenotic form. As discussed earlier in this chapter, this is true both in one aspect of his work of Creation (where God limits himself to permit the exercise of voluntary agency by both angels and human beings) and in the Incarnation (when he assumes human limitations and dies for us on the Cross). Nevertheless, the expressions of God's infinite love in creation and in history are various and manifold — as various as the needs of his creatures that he seeks to meet.

3. At one point in his book, Vanstone offered a remarkable speculation regarding the "vulnerability" of Divine Love: that God relinquished his affective invulnerability when he created human beings to be members of his own "family" (so to speak):

> Trinitarian theology asserts that God's love for His creatures is not the love that is born of 'emptiness.' It is not analogous to the love with which a woman, deprived of children, may love a dog or a doll. It is the love which overflows from fullness. Its analogue is the love of a family who, united in mutual love, *take an orphan into their home.* They do so not out of need but in the pure spontaneity of their own triumphant love. Nevertheless, in the weeks that follow, the family, once complete in itself, comes to need the new-comer. Without him the circle is now incomplete: his absence now causes anxiety: his waywardness brings concern: his goodness and happiness are necessary to those who have come to love him: upon his response depends the triumph or the tragedy of the family's love. In spontaneous love, the family has surrendered its own fulfilment and placed it, precariously, in the orphan's hands. *Love has surrendered its triumphant self-sufficiency and*

created its own need. This is the supreme illustration of love's self-giving or self-emptying — that it should surrender its fullness and create in itself the emptiness of need. Of such a nature is the Kenosis of God — the self-emptying of him Who is already in every way fulfilled.[491]

Vanstone clearly meant the reader to understand that this affective "Kenosis of God" (the title of his chapter) happens through God's work of creation. It comes out most clearly in the last stanza of his poem on the last page of his book:

Thou art God; no monarch Thou
Throned in easy state to reign;
Thou art God, whose arms of love
Aching, spent, the world sustain.[492]

Here Vanstone clearly echoes the thought of Sergius Bulgakov. As we have seen, Bulgakov taught that from all eternity God chose to surrender his absolute invulnerability to suffering in his loving relationship with his creatures. Even if Vanstone also intended to introduce here Quick's notion of divine "sensational passibility," however, this whole speculation raises as many questions as it answers. One would have to ask: what would be the point of the Trinitarian "family" taking on such a remote form of sympathy for the plight of human beings simply by creating them? — What good would that do for us? How would that be an act of "love" (that is, of "selflessly seeking the good of others") that would make any real difference to us, given that it would be a sympathetic bond with our plight that does not proceed from God ever having shared in human afflictions from a fully human perspective? How then could he empathise and sympathise with our plight in a way that truly comforts and consoles us?

---

[491] Vanstone, *Love's Endeavour, Love's Expense*, p.69; italics mine.
[492] Ibid., p. 120.

Suppose, however, that the great divine act of self-emptying, of "surrendering its fullness" and abandoning its invulnerability, occurs through the Incarnation rather than through God's general presence and work throughout the universe as Creator. *Suppose the Incarnation is the principal act in which God surrenders his own immunity to tragedy and loss, for our sake and at our need.* Then the plight of humanity would affectively "matter" to him in the most profound way because he had taken the world and its sorrows on his heart through his own human life and death as Jesus Christ. From this we would know for sure that "he has borne our griefs and carried our sorrows" (Is 53:4). If so, then his incarnation really would make a difference to us in a way that might console and comfort us in our sorrows. For it would give us, in all our afflictions, *the human companionship of God.*

After all this, the central question of this chapter remains unanswered: apart from or prior to the Incarnation, do we have any reason to believe that God – though loving us truly as our Creator, Sustainer, and Providential Guide — has ever identified with the human condition, experiencing human afflictions from a limited human perspective on events? *Do we have any grounds, therefore, for believing that merely in his universal awareness and creative work he can closely empathise and sympathise with the human condition, in such a way that can make a significant difference to us in our time of need?* Anglican panentheists such as Macquarrie and Pittenger, and spiritual writers such as Vanstone, do not seem to have provided us with any clear reasons to believe that he can.

Biblical Perspectives on God's Compassion for Human Suffering

Another alternative would be to argue for the universal sympathy of God from a biblical perspective. After all, the compassion of God for his people does seem to be a recurrent theme in the Old Testament (e.g. Is 63:9: "In all their afflictions he was afflicted.").[493] Perhaps we do not need to speak like panentheists — as if God is the World-Soul, or as if creation is an emanation or necessary self-expression of him — in order to believe that God has compassion for human afflictions. Anglican theologians Geoffrey Lampe and Maurice Wiles, for example, were convinced that the Old Testament gives evidence of the suffering of God as Creator and Providential Sustainer of the world. They noted that Hosea's broken heart over Gomer's unfaithfulness is portrayed in the Bible as a parallel to God's sorrow over the apostasy of his beloved bride, Israel.[494] Lampe and Wiles offered no detailed exegesis of Hosea, however, and it must be said that it is God's faithfulness in love for his wayward people that stands at the heart of this prophetic book, and not divine sorrow from rejected love. The most we can say is that Hosea 11:8 offers us a hint of divine pathos. But it may be wiser to interpret this passage in the light of the Old Testament tradition as a whole, in which God's universal care for human suffering and sin seems more a factual awareness of the human predicament, coupled with an earnest, active commitment to save his people, rather than a close sympathetic participation in their plight. The latter is sometimes expressed, but the former is always emphasized.[495]

In *The Foolishness of God* (1970), John Austin Baker placed great importance on the idea that God suffers in affective sympathy with the plight of his creatures, apart from and prior to the Incarnation. Without the possibility of human pain, he argued, human beings could

[493] This was also one of the main points of the classic work by Old Testament scholar Abraham Heschel, *The Prophets* (New York, 1962); see especially Chapter 18: "Religion of Sympathy," p. 307-313.

[494] Geoffrey Lampe, *God as Spirit* (Oxford: Clarendon Press, 1977), p. 21; Maurice Wiles, *The Remaking of Christian Doctrine* (London: SCM, 1974), p. 71.

[495] See Ps 103:13-14, Ex 3:7-8. For an interpretation of Hosea similar to that of Lampe and Wiles, see Gerhard Von Rad, *Old Testament Theology,* vol. II (Edinburgh: Oliver and Boyd, 1965), p. 63. For a more in-depth and nuanced view, interpreting v.8 with v.9, see James Luther Mays, *Hosea* (London: SCM, 1969), p. 156-157; cf. George A Buttrick, ed. *The Interpreters Dictionary of the Bible,* vol. 2 (New York: Abingdon Press, 1965), p. 652-653.

never attain virtues such as concern, courage, and sacrificial love. If we regard these as among the highest values for which we exist, then we are permitted to see this pain-ridden creation as the work of a loving God. For God permits pain and affliction in his world for the sake of our possible attainment of these heroic values.[496]

If the universe has been created with the purpose of attaining these values, Baker argued, then God himself must be committed to them.[497] And this means that God himself, as Creator, must have loved in a sacrificial way, and opened himself to suffering. First of all, by granting all things the right to exist and to be themselves, his act of creation itself is "an act of love, a sacrifice, a self-denying."[498] Moreover, by granting the freedom to his creatures to accept or reject his love, he has "bared himself to suffering." Baker asked:

> Is it not the price of love, of having real values, that is, ones which we genuinely care about, that it makes us vulnerable? So, too, by creating, God makes himself vulnerable. For the very values which he most cherishes, and for which he intends his creation to be the setting, all depend on freedom; and in the process of learning to share these values, to achieve this freedom, his creatures misunderstand and misuse his work, with terrible consequences not only to each other, but precisely because he loves, to himself as well.[499]

Baker may sometimes be faulted for portraying God's love in an overly anthropomorphic fashion, as if God is emotionally wounded by unrequited love. Nevertheless, despite his occasional rhetorical flourishes in this regard, and much like Vanstone, he actually made a slightly more modest claim than Macquarrie did. Neither Baker nor Vanstone claimed that all love must be suffering-love; their argument,

---

[496] Baker, *The Foolishness of God*, p. 63-64, and 68.

[497] Ibid., p. 132-133.

[498] Ibid., p. 133. Baker seems to have in mind here an idea similar to what Quick would call divine "external passibility."

[499] Ibid. Here Baker seems to ascribe to God Quick's notion of "sensational passibility."

to be precise, was that *all authentic love, including Divine Love, is vulnerable to rejection, and sympathetically concerned for the beloved.* Thus, true love by definition makes the lover a *potential* sufferer: *God must always and everywhere be vulnerable to the betrayal of his values, and sympathetic to the plight of his creatures.* As Baker put it: "If God suffers, then he has suffered whenever his personal relationships with his free beings enslaved by moral evil has made him suffer, whenever the pains of his children have struck home to his compassion."[500]

As we have seen, God's universal sympathy does seem to be implied in certain passages of Scripture. Moreover, what Quick and Baker (and also, perhaps, Vanstone) claimed as true for God, universal divine "sensational passibility," also seems to fit with all human love as we know it and experience it. Loving human beings are generally compassionate toward human suffering, and grieve over human misery and wrongdoing, especially of their loved ones. On the other hand, it is worth pondering precisely why this is true for human beings. It seems that we need to be "moved" with empathy and compassion in order to seek the good of others. It could be argued, however, that this is precisely what makes human love different from Divine Love: presumably, God does not need to be "moved" in order to move out of himself to love his creatures; rather, he is always, eternally moving in selfless, self-giving love among the persons of the Trinity, and always moving toward his creatures to help meet their needs and overcome their miseries.

In any case, neither Baker nor Vanstone consider that God's omniscient perspective on events would radically temper and ease God's vulnerability. Hence, even if we must believe that a loving God would have something analogous to sympathetic affection for us — that Scripture indicates this, and, perhaps, that authentic love is inconceivable to human beings without such feelings — this still would not amount to God ever actually experiencing the human condition from a limited, finite perspective on events, like ours. And if he has not identified in

---

[500] Ibid., p. 308.

this way with our condition, it is hard to see how he could empathise or sympathise with our plight very closely.

A Case for Divine Impassibility?

At the opposite end of the theological spectrum from the Anglican writers we have so far considered in this chapter, a number of theologians from various ecclesial traditions have sprung to the defense of the classical doctrine of divine impassibility.

In his essay "The Involvement of God" (1985), for example, the British Roman Catholic theologian Herbert McCabe made a case for the utter impassibility of God in his relationship with his creation. He sought to defend

> the classical doctrine of God derived from Augustine and Aquinas: that it is not in the nature of God to be involved in the suffering of the world as spectator, sympathiser, or victim, but it is in God's nature nonetheless to be involved with his creatures more intimately than any creature could be involved with any other. Secondly … that the Christology of Chalcedon does make sense of the notion that God suffers and indeed was tortured to death ….[501]

Unlike the Anglican authors we have surveyed so far, McCabe sought to hold on to a classical notion of the divine nature as absolutely impassible. He tells us that it is not in the nature of God to suffer in any way.[502] But if God has no natural capacity or potential for suffering, what is the meaning of saying that he is "involved" with his creatures more "intimately" than any creature could be, or that he was "tortured to death" on a cross? McCabe explained that God is the first cause of every act of being in the world, and thus "there case be no actual being

---

[501] Herbert McCabe, "The Involvement of God" in *New Blackfriars*, November, 1985, p. 464.
[502] Ibid., p. 470.

which does not have the creator at its center, holding it in being."[503] True as this may be, it hardly implies that God is "involved" in human suffering in any "intimate" (i.e., experiential, affective or sympathetic) way. He is not necessarily intimately involved: he is simply the first cause of the existence of the sufferer. McCabe then claimed that although God does not have feelings of sympathy or compassion in any literal sense, still he identifies with human suffering in a "spiritual way"— a way which McCabe never defined.[504] In short, it is not clear that McCabe brought us any nearer to understanding how an utterly impassible God can identify with the human condition, or empathise and sympathise with human suffering. An essentially impassible God can hardly be "intimately involved" with his creatures, if these words are meant to include an affective or sympathetic dimension, as they normally do in the English language.

In another notable defence of divine impassibility, the Protestant philosopher Richard Creel presented a rebuttal of seven arguments commonly used to establish God's passibility in feeling (Quick's "sensational passibility").[505] Two of these arguments directly relate to our concern here: whether or not God can be said to closely sympathise with human afflictions, apart from or prior to any incarnation.

1. Omniscience requires "sensational passibility"?

As Creel explained, some make the argument that "in his omniscience, [God] must know more than *that* we suffer, he *must know our suffering itself*, and it is impossible to know someone's suffering without suffering sympathetically with them."[506]

---

[503] Ibid., p. 469.
[504] Ibid., p. 471. With similar lack of clarity, Roch Kereszty, O. Cist., wrote of God the Father's "personal vulnerability" to the sins and sufferings of his creatures, a vulnerability "commensurate with God's infinite love," but in a way that "excludes ontological vulnerability." Kereszty, *Jesus Christ: Fundamentals of Christology*, p. 412-413.
[505] Creel, *Divine Impassibility*, p.113-116.
[506] Ibid., p. 114.

Creel strongly rejected, however, any idea that God identifies with each of us by sheer intuitive participation:

> I do not believe it follows that one who knows someone else's feeling must therefore share that feeling with them. If it were so, the implications for theology would be disastrous. God would have to be thought of as suffering, feeling stupid, feeling horny, taking pleasure in vicious acts, and so forth, because we humans do. Rather than accept such implications, it would seem preferable to argue that God does not know any of our feelings directly because it is in principle impossible for any being to know directly the subjectivity of another. ... To go a bit further, to know the feeling of another is to know that, if you were that individual, that is how you would feel — but it is not necessarily to feel that way yourself. Hence, it is conceivable that God can know our pain and pleasure, our joy and grief, our distress, relief, etc., without thereby having these experiences as his own.[507]

While this seems to be an effective response to philosophical theologians such as John Macquarrie and Keith Ward who taught that God in his omniscience must share every human perspective at once, it does not really address the position of those like Quick, Vanstone, and Baker, who argued that a God who loves and cares for the plight of his creatures, in beholding their sufferings and sorrows, would be sympathetically moved by them.

Going beyond all of these writers, however, we are forced to say again: even if God does feel for us in some way, pitying our afflictions and sorrowing over our sins, it can only be from his omniscient perspective on all events, including his full knowledge of the limits of suffering, his own ability to heal suffering and bring good out of permitted evils, and his full knowledge of the meaning, purpose and general outcome of

[507] Ibid., p. 129, and 130.

suffering in his overall plan for history. In short, God in his blessed and heavenly life may have something analogous to empathy and compassion for us. But, apart from or prior to the Incarnation, he has not really identified with the human condition. He has never experienced anything like the depths of human suffering, with all the mental and emotional trauma this entails. Thus, he has never truly "borne our griefs, and carried our sorrows" (Is 53:4). And if not, then it is not clear how he can be said to empathise and sympathise with our afflictions very deeply — at least not in a way that enables us to look to him and find (in Whitehead's phrase) "the fellow sufferer who understands."[508]

2. Morality requires "sensational passibility"?

Creel reports the claim of some philosophers and theologians that to some extent our Creator is responsible for the suffering of his creatures because he made us, and holds us in existence at every moment, knowing full well the certainty that sin, pain and sorrows of all kinds will afflict us. Given this situation, it is said, morality requires that the God who made us not remain aloof and detached. He must take a share in our suffering, sympathising with us in our condition, and struggling alongside us against evil.

For his part, Creel rejected this argument. Insofar as God's act of creation is truly a loving act, giving us a form of existence in which even the risk and actuality of human miseries are instrumental to higher goods, then, according to Creel God is under no obligation to share our plight.[509] Indeed, we argued earlier in this chapter that even apart from any possible sympathetic bond with his creatures, the Creator's free gift to them of existence is an authentically loving act.

---

[508] Alfred North Whitehead, *Process and Reality* (New York: The Macmillan Company, 1929), p. 532.
[509] Ibid., p. 147.

On the other hand, *we normally think it wrong for a person to require behavior and difficult experiences of another that he would not undergo himself, in companionship with the other, if he could.* We admire the military commander (like General Omar Bradley in World War II) who goes into the trenches with his soldiers. *Surely it is not wrong to have the same desire and expectation of God — especially since we may need such divine companionship to help us make it through our worst afflictions* (after all, there was a reason why Catholic hospitals traditionally had a crucifix on the wall in each room). In fact, God the Son offers us a form of divine companionship which he himself did not have access to in the midst of his own human sufferings, when he "trod the winepress alone" on the Way of the Cross (Is 63:3): namely, the companionship in all his afflictions of a divine person incarnate. *Moreover, it seems especially incumbent upon God to offer us this closely empathetic and sympathetic companionship, since human suffering in his world is not always directly conducive to the highest goods of each individual sufferer.* For example, free-will is certainly good for human beings to have, because without it we could not love (the highest good of all). But if a Gestapo agent uses his free-will to torture me unmercifully, then his use of his free-will is not liable to be directly conducive to *my* highest goods, unless I am extraordinarily advanced in sanctity and grace (and, as Catholics would say, willing and able to "offer up" my terrible sufferings in union with Christ for the salvation of others).[510] Doubtless, the Lord opens the gates of heaven as compensation to all relatively innocent and faithful souls who have to suffer in such excruciating ways ("I consider that the sufferings of this present time are not worth comparing with the glory that is to be revealed to us," Rom 8:18), but in this life the passage of most people through such horrific experiences is often little more than a desperate struggle against despair.

---

[510] This is not to say that it is *impossible* for persons less advanced in sanctity to attain their highest goods through the experiences of victimization and torture — only that it is an extraordinarily difficult path to tread. Presumably, God would not permit it to happen at all if it was not at least *possible* for the victim, with the help of divine grace, to grow to the heights of sanctity in this way. See also note 540, below.

Thus, it would seem to be morally fitting that our Creator would identify in some way with the worst sufferings of his creatures. And this identification would need to be more than just a remote sympathy with our plight. *The most fitting thing for God to do would be to enter into solidarity with us, to "join us in the trenches," so to speak, by sharing in the human condition of suffering and struggle from a finite perspective similar to our own.* Clearly, the Incarnation might be seen as just such an act of divine solidarity. As Brian Hebblethwaite put it:

> If the suffering and Cross of Jesus can be seen as God's own suffering and Cross in the world, then we have a much more morally powerful and credible conception of God .... The revelatory and moral force of the belief that God wins our love by coming as a servant and by "loving his own to the end" is very great. In particular, it is the manner in which our God is believed to have taken upon himself the burden of the world's evil that renders him morally credible. For Christian belief, God takes responsibility for the suffering and evil entailed in creation by making himself vulnerable to it and by himself experiencing its pain and dereliction.[511]

Presumably, by "taking responsibility" for the sufferings and evils in his creation, Hebblethwaite did not mean taking "the blame" for these things. He simply meant that God created us knowing full well the many kinds of sorrows and sufferings that would befall humanity, primarily due to the misuse of angelic and human free-will — and in this light, *he does not ask us to walk through any depth of moral challenge or mortal affliction that he was not willing to walk through himself as Jesus of Nazareth.* Richard Swinburne came to much the same conclusion:

> [I]t seems to me highly plausible to suppose that, given the amount of pain and suffering which God allows humans to endure (for a good purpose), it would be obligatory on God to share a human life and suffering. This would be achieved by a

---

[511] Hebblethwaite, *The Incarnation*, p. 64.

divine person becoming incarnate as a human (that is, becoming a human being) and living a life of much suffering ending with the great crisis which all humans have to face: the crisis of death.[512]

Keith Ward has objected that an incarnation would not fulfil this moral requirement:

> We must conceive any good God as suffering with all his creation. But then it is not a unique incarnation which makes this suffering possible; that would limit the amount of God's suffering to a finite time.[513]

From the perspective of a kenotic theory of the Incarnation, however, the sufferings of the divine Son, through his incarnate life and death, would not be limited to a finite time, because they would be present to his unfading memory as the risen and ascended Son, and included in the store of experience in his divine nature — and thereby forever provide a touchstone for the closest possible empathy and compassion for all human suffering.

In fact, this empathetic understanding of the human condition also would be *retroactive*. In other words, assuming that God does not dwell in a realm of timeless eternity (an assumption we have made throughout this book), then prior to the Incarnation, God the Son would have in his perfect Divine Omniscience full knowledge of all the trials and tribulations of those who had suffered throughout human history in the run-up to his incarnate life and death. As a result of his sojourn on earth as Jesus of Nazareth, however, he would attain a closer empathy and deeper compassion for these sufferers of ancient times. Thus, added to his Divine Omniscience would be a new kind of knowledge. To his perfect factual knowledge of human affairs would be added experiential knowledge of the human condition, as a

---

[512] Swinburne, *Was Jesus God?*, p. 40.
[513] Ward, "Incarnation or Inspiration — A False Dichotomy," p. 253.

touchstone for his affective compassion for all people, of all times: past, present, and future.

An important defence of the classical tradition of divine impassibility also has been offered by the Catholic theologian Thomas Weinandy, OFM Cap. Weinandy insists that the whole theology of pathos in the divine nature merely "imprisons" God in the same state of misery as suffering humanity, and thereby effectively undermines the gospel. In his essay "Does God Suffer?" (2001), for example, he writes:

> If God, having lost His singular transcendence, is now infected by evil and suffering, then He too is immanently enmeshed in an evil cosmic process from which He, like all else, cannot escape.

> God may now suffer in union with all who suffer — and those who espouse a suffering God boast this to be of singular value — but in so suffering, humankind, and even God Himself, are deprived of any hope of ever being freed from evil and so the suffering it causes. There is no hope of divine justice ever setting things right, nor is there any hope of love and goodness vanquishing evil. The transcendent One, All-Holy God of the Bible who, as Creator, is present to all creation, and who, as Savior, acts immanently within creation, vanishes. …

> [T]he truth that God does not suffer is at the heart of the gospel, making it truly good news. This is especially in contrast to the bad news, which has become something like a "new orthodoxy," that God is in as much trouble as we are.[514]

We will examine the more philosophical arguments that Weinandy presents for divine impassibility in our final chapter, where I will begin to explore the question of how Kenoticism might be reconciled with the Catholic magisterial and philosophical traditions. With regard to the *theological* objections to divine passibility that Weinandy offers here,

---

[514] Weinandy, "Does God Suffer?" p. 13 and 18.

however, we can acknowledge the importance of the arguments he presents. For if human suffering is somehow taken into the divine nature itself through the Incarnation of the Son (as all Kenotic Theories of the Incarnation hold), and if, as a result, the divine nature now has a close, affective compassion for the struggles and sufferings of all people, of every time and place, then surely there must be a sense in which these experiences of suffering never pass away for God, since divine memories would not fade. Perhaps this is something of what the book of Revelation is driving at when the author speaks of "the Lamb slain from the foundation of the world" (Rev 13:8, KJV); in other words, he freely chose from the beginning of time to abandon his absolute immunity to human suffering by taking flesh and dwelling among us. The same author says of Christ the Lamb, "I saw a Lamb standing as though it had been slain" (Rev 5:6), in other words, still bearing the wounds of his passion (Jn 20:27), wounds which do not pass away. This should move us to wonder at a love so deep that God would, in a certain sense, accept to bear the Cross for us for all eternity.

Weinandy's arguments against divine passibility, however, seem to be *non sequiturs* in several respects. Even on the notion of divine passibility that we are defending here, it is certainly not the case that "God is in as much trouble as we are," helplessly imprisoned in the cosmic web of suffering and death. First, he is never merely the helpless subject of suffering and sorrow; in becoming incarnate as Jesus of Nazareth he has only taken upon himself what he willed, and always in the service of his infinitely wise plan of salvation for his creatures. Moreover, his infinite divine nature cannot be overwhelmed by his finite experience of human suffering and universal sympathy, for he has infinite resources to absorb and transcend it. He knows its limits; he knows the extent to which he can bring the highest goods out of such permitted evils; and he is risen to new and glorious life in his human nature as well, which is also part of his everlasting store of experience. Third, if God in some sense takes on an everlasting burden of compassion in his divine nature, it does not necessarily follow that all hope is lost of "goodness vanquishing evil." Presumably, he has taken on this burden

through the Incarnation precisely because he knows that in so doing he can thoroughly vanquish evil *in us*, by bringing to salvation all those who will receive and return his love. He can overcome evil and suffering in us by bearing it in his own heart, in some sense, forever. Again, this should move us to wonder and love, not to despair.

We will return to these issues in the final, "Conclusion" section of this book. For now, we need to acknowledge that Weinandy is rightly concerned about exaggerated forms of Kenoticism that do not carefully explain in what sense the divine nature transcends the experiences of suffering that God has voluntarily undertaken for our sake. In his book *Looking Through the Cross* (2014), Anglican (now Bishop) Graham Tomlin explained the importance of this theological intuition:

> [W]hen we say that God suffers, we must be careful to check what we are saying. God knows what it is to suffer in the human nature of the incarnate Son, which since the incarnation has been taken up into God. Yet suffering is simply not strong enough to overcome the eternal God. …
>
> What this means is that while we can have utter confidence that God knows what it is to suffer in his Son Jesus, at the same time we can also have utter confidence that suffering is too weak to storm the strongholds of God. Suffering cannot pierce the very essence of God. It does not make it into the new heavens and the new earth. This is the final victory over suffering: God is eternal. And suffering is not. …
>
> The Christian insight into suffering tells us that in an ultimate sense, even when we feel alone and in despair over our suffering, that both of these things are true. We are not alone in our suffering, because God, in the person of his Son Jesus, has tasted physical pain, despair, betrayal, and death, that he knows intimately what it is to suffer and stands close to us in it. At the same time, suffering is transitory. There is a form of

existence that is beyond all suffering: the heart and essence of God, and it is into that heart that we are beckoned in our journey in and with Christ. That is where the journey of faith ends: beyond the possibility of suffering in the heart of God.[515]

Tomlin is careful to explain in his book that the traditional way all this has been understood is that God identifies with our suffering solely in his human nature as Jesus Christ, but not in his divine nature, which forever remains beyond all pain and sorrow. As we have seen in Part One, however, there is a significant cost to that move — a heavy cost to the intelligibility of the mystery of the Incarnation, which is the very heart of the gospel. With a classical Two-Nature Christology, how can we really use the kind of language that Tomlin does (in the passages quoted above) that "what it is to suffer" has been "taken up into God" through the passion of his Son, and that as a result God "knows intimately what it is to suffer and stands close to us in it"? This kind of language is surely very hard to reconcile with a theory of the Incarnation that says that in his divine nature, throughout his incarnate life, passion, and death, the divine Son was essentially an impassible spectator of his own earthly sufferings.

In the concluding chapter of this book, therefore, we shall explore another option. Suppose we draw the line between God's experience of human suffering and his transcendence of all suffering — that transcendent place where he longs to bring each one of us with the risen Christ at our journey's end — not between his human and divine natures, but (rather less clearly, but more appropriately) *within the mystery of the divine nature itself.* For this is the mystery of all mysteries that any human mind can ever attempt to comprehend: the mystery of the essence of God. Suppose the location of God's transcendence of all pain and sorrow lies in *the unfathomable depths of his divine nature*, in which God has infinite resources for absorbing the suffering he freely assumed as Jesus of Nazareth, and from

---

[515] Graham Tomlin, *Looking Through the Cross* (London: Bloomsbury, 2013), p. 114-116.

which he has an infinite capacity to bring good out of permitted evils.

The Compassion of God as a Result of the Incarnation

Considered apart from or prior to the Incarnation, we have so far found no reason to believe that God has ever identified with human afflictions, in other words, that he has ever known what it is like to suffer from a limited bodily and mental perspective like ours. Moreover, it is not clear how God can closely empathise and sympathise with the human condition now, if he has never truly shared our lot. By way of contrast with the classical doctrine of absolute divine impassibility, we have sketched some reasons to believe that a divine solidarity with us in all our joys, pains, and sorrows is indicated in Scripture, morally fitting, and an important part of the gospel. But we have not found any grounds for belief in that solidarity — or that God can have anything more than a remote affective sympathy for our plight — unless he has taken flesh among us as Jesus Christ.

Now we shall develop further the argument that the Incarnation deepens God's empathy and compassion for us. *For if the Word of God has become incarnate as Jesus of Nazareth, then he has indeed fully identified with the human condition. He has shared our lot. He has come to experience human sorrow and affliction from a fully human, limited perspective on events, and thereby enabled himself to empathise and sympathise in the closest way with all human beings.*

Arguably, this is one aspect of the message of the Book of Hebrews in the New Testament. The biblical author tells us that "for a little while" the divine Son was "made lower than the angels," which even included his "tasting death for every one" (Heb 2:9). In order to become a "merciful" high priest for humanity (2:17), a Savior who could truly "sympathise with our weaknesses" (4:15), it was necessary for him to "partake of the same nature" as those he came to rescue from the power of death and the devil (2:14), and to be "in every respect ... tempted as we are, yet without sinning" (4:15). It is precisely this kinship with us in our struggles and sorrows that enables us to turn to him with "confidence … that we may receive mercy and find grace to help in time of need" (4:16). As H.R. Mackintosh wrote in *The Doctrine of the Person of Jesus Christ* (1913):

> It is one of the most treasured convictions of the Christian mind that in the Divine sympathy for the children of men there is now a depth and intimacy to which that earthly career [of Jesus] contributed, that the Son who came forth from the Father has taken out of time an eternal gain. So the grace which flows to us has been enriched by all things which Jesus underwent.[516]

All this is not to say that prior to the Incarnation God did not care about human pain and human sin. David Brown explains that believing that God *cares* about human suffering is quite different from saying that he *identifies* with our suffering:

> There is a major difference between the claim that God knows that someone suffers and cares and the claim that God knows that someone suffers and he himself once suffered likewise. The difference lies in the fact that in the latter case, suffering is part of the memory of God (and divine memories presumably do not fade!), and if that is so, then self-identification means exactly what it says, that God has direct experiential knowledge of the situation, and not just an abstract factual knowledge.[517]

Along with O.C. Quick, therefore, let us say that by taking human flesh, "God enters upon a further passibility than that which was involved in the first creation."[518] He experiences human "internal

---

[516] Mackintosh, *The Doctrine of the Person of Jesus Christ*, p. 371.

[517] Brown, *The Divine Trinity*, p. 11.

[518] Quick, *Doctrines of the Creed*, p. 187. Cf. Hebblethwaite, *The Incarnation,* p. 71 and Leonard Hodgson, "The Incarnation," in A.E.J. Rawlinson, ed., *Essays on the Trinity and the Incarnation* (London: Longmans, 1928), p. 396.

passibility," in other words, human mental anguish, conflict and interior struggle, for he becomes the subject of human emotional experience and temptation. Secondly, he experiences human "sensational passibility," including bodily pain, emotional sorrow and grief, all from the perspective of a limited human consciousness. In short, the divine Son Incarnate identifies with human afflictions, and this experience becomes the reference point of a closer empathy and compassion for the afflictions of us all.

Against this, Herbert McCabe claimed that God does not need to share in our lot before he can closely sympathise with our condition:

> Sharing in actual pain is neither necessary nor sufficient for compassion, whose essential components are awareness, feelings of pity and concern. I can have all three without suffering myself from the pain or tragedy that afflicts my companion. And conversely I may be smitten with exactly the same kind of pain without experiencing any compassion at all.[519]

But David Brown has persuasively argued that at least some actual experience of the human condition from a human perspective is required to enable us to use such words as "sympathy" and "compassion" in a meaningful way:

> [I]t is far from clear that the notion of sympathy makes sense when extended to something of which one has had no experience at all. For how can one 'feel with' someone if one has never felt anything comparable? This being so, there is doubt about whether the notion of sympathy can be properly applied to a being (i.e. God) who by definition experiences no emotions or physical sensations.[520]

---

[519] McCabe, "The Involvement of God," p. 469.
[520] Brown, *The Divine Trinity*, p. 247. "Who by definition feels no emotions ..." could be taken to mean "no human emotions in the literal sense," for presumably Brown would admit that God might be able to experience something

Similarly, Anglican philosophical theologian Basil Mitchell claimed that the Incarnation makes intelligible God's real identification with the human condition, and therefore his close sympathy with us. Mitchell calls this the "logic of condolence":

> If we are to know that God has shared our lot, we need to know that he has been subject to the limitations of human nature which are the necessary conditions of pain being for him what it is for us. If this is true, there is a logic of condolence to which the traditional doctrine [of the Incarnation], if it is intelligible, conforms.[521]

Anglican theologian Keith Ward has been a vocal opponent of this idea that an incarnation of God is necessary to enable his deepest compassion for our plight. He wrote:

> It may well be thought … that no being is truly omniscient if it lacks knowledge of what it feels like to experience suffering or happiness. If I know that the proposition 'You are in pain' is true, but I do not know what it feels like for you to be in pain, then there is something that I do not know — and that something, you may well think, is the most important thing of all. If that is so, then any omniscient being must know what it feels like for creatures to feel as they do. That may be called affective knowledge, a much more involving and intense thing than propositional knowledge.[522]

This is precisely the same point that we encountered earlier in our discussion of the work of Richard Creel — that "Omniscience requires emotional passibility" — and is subject to the same response. The idea

---

remotely analogous to human sympathetic sorrow, in the context of his omniscient perspective on events, and/or that his eternal beatitude would consist of something at least remotely analogous to human joy.

[521] Basil Mitchell, "A Summing-up of the Colloquy: Myth of God Debate" in Goulder, ed. *Incarnation and Myth*, p. 240.

[522] Ward, "Cosmos and Kenosis," p.156-157.

that God in his omniscience must be able to share all my feelings is fraught with difficulty. Suppose I am suffering from uncontrollable, homicidal anger at my spouse: does God share that feeling with me? Suppose I am suffering from clinical depression due to disordered brain chemistry: does this mean that God falls into clinical depression too? Moreover, how can one have an experiential knowledge of all human pain and sorrow, if that is not based on sharing in human experience, from a human, limited perspective on events? In his heavenly state, God may indeed be able to experience some kind of kind of feeling for the plight of all his creatures that is remotely analogous to human sympathy, and he certainly experiences something analogous to human happiness in his own eternal beatitude as well, but again, none of this is the same as having fully "human" feelings, apart the real experience of sharing our human nature — and it is simply not clear how God can closely empathise and sympathise with our human condition apart from having had an experience of what it is like to be human from within all the limitations of human life. *Divine Omniscience presumably means that God knows all that can be known, all that is logically possible to know: but "experiential awareness" that is not based on ever having had similar experiences would seem to be a contradiction in terms, and therefore not possible even for Divine Omniscience.* David Brown drives the point home the point with lucidity:

> While it is true that omniscience guarantees that God will know all it is possible to know, this still precludes the type of experiential knowledge that only comes from the inside of an experience, as it were …. To my mind the advantage of a kenotic account [of the incarnation] is not that it allows God to wallow in suffering, but that his experience of the world would remain radically different from ours unless he has somehow entered into the human condition. In virtue of having done so, he can then come alongside the sufferer, and offer grace from the inside, as it were, showing how the situation might, potentially at least, be transformed, or at the very least endured.[523]

---

[523] Brown, *Divine Humanity*, p. 254 and 208-209.

Maurice Wiles, by contrast, argued vigorously throughout the entire *Myth of God Incarnate* debate of the 1970's and 1980's that God's incarnation in Christ would not actually enable him to identify with all human suffering. In other words, to say that God suffers in and through Christ's life and passion would not establish that he has experienced *every kind* of human trauma, e.g. as a victim of disease, accident, or old age.[524] The claim that God identifies with and sympathises with human sufferings like ours, therefore, does not necessarily follow from the assertion of an incarnation. Instead, Wiles wanted to see the sufferings of Jesus as a "sacramental representation" of God's universal identification with the sufferings of each individual, and "this self-identification must be of a different order."[525]

Of course, this raises the obvious question: what "different order"? The Incarnation, especially as understood in kenotic theory, would at least give us *some* grounds for believing that God can, in a close way, empathetically understand our afflictions, and sympathise with us with reference to his own, personal experience of human life and death as Jesus of Nazareth.

Wiles had asked, however, whether the crucifixion of the Incarnate Son would enable him to identify with or sympathise with *all* forms of human suffering:

> On the face of it, it does. But it is possible that we are being misled here by the abstract nature of the concept of 'suffering." Suffering is not some single entity in which different people share. There is my suffering and your suffering — and they are of many kinds. If the eternal drank of the chalice of sufferings in the passion, in how direct a sense is that the same chalice as the one drunk by the mother of a brain-damaged child or the chance victim of a psychopathic assault?[526]

---

[524] Wiles, *The Remaking of Christian Doctrine*, p. 72.
[525] Ibid.
[526] Ibid.

In claiming that the Incarnate Son has "borne our griefs and carried our sorrows," however, the Kenotic theologian is not being misled by an abstraction. He or she simply posits that the word "suffering" refers to a set of real human experiences which are so similar in significant respects that they can be named by the same word. The point is that God has entered his created structures and truly suffered — indeed, he has experienced dark, cruel, and bitter physical, emotional and mental suffering. This experience was of the same *class* of experience which people go through regardless of the particular *ways* in which they come to suffer.

Jesus Christ and Total Human Affliction

Christians traditionally have believed that the Word-made-flesh, Jesus Christ, entered into the very *depths* of human suffering on the Cross. In his passion, he underwent the three-fold abandonment that characterises *total human affliction*: excruciating pain in the loss of his physical life, abandonment by his friends and rejection by his society, and seeming abandonment by God himself. He even lost the sense of the presence of his heavenly Father at the very moment he most needed him. At least in part, this spiritual aspect of his suffering was the result of the physical aspect: in the midst of the most horrible forms of death, bodily pain and misery can become so extreme that it totally rivets and enslaves the conscious attentive faculties, shutting off those faculties from the subconscious and the depths of the spirit. All spiritual consolation is thereby blocked, and God seems far away when his felt-presence is most desired.

In fact, in one sense Christ's afflictions were even greater than ours could ever be, because his agony was that of a pure and righteous soul — conscious as neither Job nor the author of the Psalms could be of the seeming inexplicable silence of God in the face of injustice and death. Hence, as he was dying he cried out "My God, My God, why have you forsaken me?" (Mk 15:34). As Simone Weil once pointed out:

There is not real affliction unless the event which has seized and uprooted a life attacks it, directly or indirectly, in all of its parts, social, psychological and physical …. Affliction constrained Christ to implore that he might be spared; to seek consolation from man; to believe that he was forsaken by the Father.[527]

The point here is that any particular instance of human suffering is but a foretaste, an inkling, of the experience of total human affliction — *and Jesus walked through total affliction.*[528] *Thus, whatever our sorrows or sufferings may be, we can be assured that the divine Son, Jesus Christ, can understand our condition with the deepest compassion.* If Jesus was and is the divine Son Incarnate, then he gives us a divine companionship in all our suffering. There is no dark corner of the world that he has not filled with his presence; there is no depth of the human condition that he has not taken on his Heart. As Lutheran theologian Jurgen Moltmann once put it, on the Cross, Christ

delivers himself up in order to be ours and to be with us, right into the desolation of God-forsakenness itself. Even in this

---

[527] Simone Weil, *Waiting on God* (London: Fount edition, 1977), p. 63-64.

[528] Here I am speaking of Jesus Christ experiencing total human affliction to an unsurpassable degree in an *intensive* rather than an *extensive* sense. To be sure, some human beings have been subject to torture for many months or even years, and not just for three hours as Christ was on the Cross. But it would be hard to imagine any human being suffering with the same *intensity* as Christ did for more than three hours: the human body and spirit can only take so much of that level of affliction. Christ's intensive suffering was extraordinary, first, in its unusually extreme prelude (he was mocked, spat upon, beaten, scourged, and crowned with thorns *before* being tortured to death on the Cross), and secondly, due to the multi-dimensional intensity of his emotional and spiritual agony and passion, as discussed here in this chapter, and in the chapter that follows. Similarly, John Milbank writes of the Divine Logos as "able to let [his] human nature plumb the full depths and implications of suffering," and as experiencing "the maximal possible victimage." See *Being Reconciled: Ontology and Pardon* (London: Routledge, 2004), p. 61.

hell, thou are there. That is the divine truth of Jesus' cry of desolation.[529]

This brings us to a further question. If the divine Son Incarnate, Jesus of Nazareth, has journeyed with us through the experience of total human affliction, even to the depths of the feeling of God-forsakenness itself, then has he also experienced the suffering of human guilt, the alienation from God due to sin? After all, any incarnational understanding of the person of Christ assumes that he is a divine person, and therefore incapable of sin.

Some theologians have speculated that the incarnate Son may have experienced guilt, not in the sense of being *objectively* guilty of any intentional transgression, but in the sense of participating in the human feeling of *subjective* guilt, in other words, feeling *as if* he was somehow guilty of sin, when in fact he was not. Jesus was born as a Jew, raised in a culture that saw all human beings as sinners in need of repentance (e.g. Is 53:6). If he was by *kenosis* incarnate in that culture, he may have initially (say, in his youth) felt this to be true in his own case as well — if only in the sense that he may have felt that he shared in some way in the corporate guilt of God's wayward people, Israel. Perhaps that was why he sought out the baptism of John, "a baptism of repentance for the forgiveness of sins" (Mk 1:4). In fact, on one occasion in his ministry Jesus seemed to disclaim untarnished moral goodness, saying "Why do you call me good? No one is good but God alone" (Mk 10:18). All this has led some theologians to speculate that Jesus may have shared in the human experience of subjective guilt. David Brown writes:

> [A]ssuming the usual first-century Jewish reasons for baptism, is it not possible to read Jesus' original decision at its face value? He presents himself because of his own subjective solidarity with his people. By that I do not mean what Matthew probably meant [in his Gospel], that he acts representatively

---

[529] Jurgen Moltmann, *Experiences of God* (Philadelphia: Fortress Press, 1980), p. 16.

on their behalf. Rather, it constitutes a real part of the way in which in a kenotic incarnation Jesus' own life-story becomes wholly bound up with the attitudes and assumptions of his own people, for it would presumably have been very hard for Jews at the time not to feel corporate guilt at their people's failures to live up to divine expectations of them. It would thus have become part of Jesus' general identification with our fallen condition. Incarnation with an unfallen humanity would mean rejecting as part of Jesus' story all those social settings and limitations that make us precisely the sort of people we are, including our sense of participation in the guilt of others.[530]

Brown goes even farther down this road when he claims that Jesus actually showed that he shared the cultural prejudices of his people against Gentiles, for Jesus was hesitant to come to the aid of the Syro-Phoenecian woman, and spoke derisively of the Gentiles as "dogs." For Brown, this story shows us that he shared in our struggles to overcome socially-contracted prejudice, and it marks "a decisive point of change in Jesus' attitude to Gentiles."[531] But it hardly seems necessary to interpret the Gospel text in this way. That Jesus was not in the throes of anti-Gentile prejudice when he spoke to the Syro-Phoenician woman is implied in St. Matthew's order of events, because the story of the healing of the servant of the Roman centurion, who (Jesus said) had more faith than anyone else in Israel, and Christ's teaching that "many from the east and the west" would join the sons of Abraham in the Kingdom of God appears *seven chapters ahead* of the healing of the pagan woman's daughter (cf. Mt 8:5-13 and 15:21-28). Also, the Syro-Phoenician woman was from a religious culture in which occult attempts to manipulate the gods were rife, and this woman in particular was literally grovelling at his feet like a dog, and "buttering up" Jesus with grandiose titles. The "sting" of what Jesus said to her is mitigated by the fact that the word "dogs" in Greek here is in the diminutive form: "little dogs" or "puppies," implying affection as well as critique. His remarks may have been intended to teach her

---

[530] Brown, *Divine Humanity*, p. 215.
[531] Ibid., p. 216.

that grovelling and fawning like a little dog was not the way the people of Israel, as children in God's family, had been taught to approach and relate to the merciful God and his Messiah.

To be sure, Brown was not necessarily ascribing to Jesus any objective guilt here, that is, any willful act of sin, but his description of the attitude and actions of Jesus — what Jesus did and what he had to overcome in himself — amounts at least to what is classically referred to as a state of "involuntary imperfection." Even if the story of the Syro-Phoenician woman is not an example of venial sin in Christ, Brown could still fairly argue that such involuntary, imperfect moral attitudes are an inescapable aspect of the human condition, because society always saddles each new generation with gender, ethnic, class, political and religious prejudices to which individuals are expected to conform. Even the most sincere and devout Christians, growing steadily in sanctity, will have to struggle with the help of the Holy Spirit to undo these cultural distortions of the truth. If Jesus was fully human, therefore, he would presumably have to go through the same process. *Thus, beyond sharing temporarily — perhaps up until his baptism — in Israel's sense of corporate guilt, Jesus also may have shared temporarily in the deep-seated prejudices of his people, and may have had to struggle to overcome these prejudices over time, even during his public ministry, with the help of the Holy Spirit.*

On the other hand, while it certainly would have been difficult for Jesus to transcend the prejudices of his people among whom his human personality was raised and nurtured, part of the mystery of the Incarnation is that *here in human nature was a life so utterly suffused and guided by the Holy Spirit that Jesus can even say: "He who has seen me, has seen the Father" (Jn 14:9)*. It is precisely because an instantiation of human nature has been enabled to transcend all prejudice and sin by the Spirit that Jesus is for us the true icon of God the Father. And the metaphysical fact of the Incarnation entails that in all of the attitudes, words and deeds of the Son of God, the Spirit's presence and operation was unfettered. This is no violation of the limits of authentic human nature because participation in social prejudice is not a "natural" part of the human condition: it is a corruption ultimately rooted in original sin and human alienation from the Holy Spirit — in which Jesus also did not share. **Whatever prejudices his culture may have tried to foist upon him in his youth, therefore, the Holy Spirit would have enabled Jesus to struggle successfully at least to reserve judgment, and not take these prejudices to heart, until he received further light on such issues from broader life-experience along his human journey, with the help of the Holy Spirit.**

There is a paradox here that needs to be preserved: in a properly kenotic understanding of the Incarnation, Jesus certainly must have passed through all the natural stages of human cognitive and moral development, as these have been uncovered by developmental psychologists such as Piaget and Kohlberg. **Given that he was the divine Son Incarnate, however, his humanity must have been as "full of grace and truth" from the Holy Spirit as it could be at every stage of his human journey (Jn 1:14, cf. Lk 2:52), as an ever growing receptacle of the Spirit (after all, the Son can never be separated from the Holy Spirit, either in the life of the eternal Trinity, or in his incarnate state on earth). It follows that even in the midst of this broken and sinful world, he must have passed through all of the natural stages of human development in a "sinless," Spirit-led way. At the same time, this developmental progress could not be attained without struggle against the downward pull of this fallen world: against occasional, distorted teachings from his elders; against poor examples and social pressures from his peers; and against internal, demonic temptation.** For example, we can imagine that when Jesus decided at the age of 12 to stay behind from the caravan of pilgrims returning home to Galilee, in order to confer in-depth with the teachers and scribes in the Great Temple at Jerusalem, this was an act of "adolescent rebellion," but in the natural and good sense of that phrase: he was choosing for the first time to prioritize his own mission in life, and to make decisions in the light of that mission without total reliance on the permission and understanding of his parents. Moreover, he did so under the guidance of the Holy Spirit, without succumbing to the bad examples of his peers, who (no doubt) lived out their adolescence in a far less positive way. His parents also needed to begin to appreciate the new stage in human growth and maturation that Jesus had attained, and how it was bound up with his mission as Son of the one whom he called "my Father" (Lk 2:49-50). Doubtless they did come to understand all this in time, after pondering and praying deeply over this mystery (Lk 2:52).

That as an adult Jesus saw himself as in any sense a sinner in God's eyes can be criticised on several grounds. First of all, the Gospels indicate that his baptism by John was an experience of affirmation of his divine identity, and of his unique loving intimacy with his heavenly Father ("You are my beloved Son, with you I am well pleased." Mk 1:11; Lk 3:22). It was also an experience of vocational calling and empowerment — but there is no indication at all that it included an assurance of divine forgiveness. Secondly, his alleged disclaimer of moral goodness in Mark 10:18 might be interpreted not as a confession of moral unworthiness, but as a way of saying to his questioner: Think about what you are saying — about who you imply that I am — when you call me "good!"[532] Third, if Jesus did see himself as a sinner saved by grace, it is odd that we have absolutely no record of any testimony of his own to that effect. For example, he never tells his disciples the inspiring story of how his heavenly Father raised him from the mire of his sins — or even from participation in Israel's sins — by forgiveness and sanctifying grace, nor does he present himself as an example of what God can do for sinners. On the contrary, one finds in the recorded words of Jesus not a trace of any consciousness of personal sin or guilt, despite the importance he attached to repentance among his followers (e.g. Mk 1:15; Lk 11:4, 18:9-14). As John A.T. Robinson observed, the consciousness of sin "is so universal a mark of saintliness, from Paul onwards … that the omission cannot but strike us."[533]

---

[532] See Brant Pitre, *The Case for Jesus* (New York: Image Books, 2016), p. 151-152.
[533] Robinson, *The Human Face of God*, p. 97. That Jesus never committed actual sin was the clear teaching of the apostolic Church (e.g. Jn 8:46; Heb 4:15; I Pt 1:19). If Jesus had taught them otherwise, this unanimous position is hard to explain. In addition, of course, ascribing actual sin to Christ would violate the doctrine of the Incarnation itself, in which Jesus is held to be a divine person living under all the limitations and conditions of human life. Presumably, a divine

We should also bear in mind that any ascription to Jesus of a false sense of guilt in his human consciousness — that is, that at any stage of his life he sincerely believed he was guilty of sin, when in fact he was not — would violate the infallibility of the divine Son in his incarnate state, an infallibility of which bishops Gore and Weston were convinced, and which is a logically necessary pre-requisite for adopting the Moderate Kenotic Model of the Incarnation (see the discussion of this point in Part One, Chapter Four, above). We will revisit the whole issue of Christ's "infallibility" in the next chapter of this book. Suffice it to say here that if Moderate KM is true, then Jesus Christ, fully surrendered to the Holy Spirit, the Spirit of Truth (Jn 16:13), could not have accepted (even temporarily) false notions of his own guilt, nor false ascriptions of natural inferiority or sub-human status to Gentiles, women, slaves, or any other group of people that his Hebraic culture might have tried to teach him to denigrate. *It is precisely his untarnished moral goodness and his infallible grasp of truth, by the Holy Spirit, at each step of his human growth and development, that enables us to see in him the true image of God the Father, the God of infinite truth and infinite love.*

A better way to understand Christ's identification with our subjective experience of guilt is to return to the point made by Simone Weil. As we have seen, she held that the experience of total human affliction involves a human life being attacked and uprooted in every aspect of its being: physical, social, and psychological. In the same essay, she went on to describe another aspect of such afflictions:

---

person would never do evil things. In other words, metaphysically, how could a divine person, infinite in love, commit sin as a human being? How could God the Son, dwelling among us as one of us, betray the love of God? Finally, as we shall see in the next chapter of this book, there are historical and religiously powerful theories of the saving work of Jesus Christ that depend for their coherence on the doctrine of his entire sinlessness. According to John the Baptist, for example, Jesus is the one who can "take away the sin of the world" because he is the spotless "Lamb of God" (Jn 1:29).

Affliction hardens and discourages us because, like a red-hot iron, it stamps the soul to its very depths with the scorn, the disgust, and even the self-hatred and sense of guilt and defilement which crime logically should produce, but actually does not ... "Christ ... being made a curse for us." It was not only the body of Christ hanging on the wood which was accursed, it was his soul also. *In the same way, every innocent being in his affliction feels himself accursed.*[534]

Weil roots this sense of being cast off by God in the realisation that one suffers from some blind mechanism of God's universe. Those innocently struck down by accident or disease suffer in this way. So do those trapped in the often blind, confused course of human events (wars, revolutions, etc.). Martyrs who willingly die for their cause often do not experience such total affliction. But Christ did:

He died like a common criminal, confused with thieves, only a little more ridiculous. For affliction is ridiculous.[535]

Total affliction makes one feel as worthless as a crushed worm. It completely cuts one off from all that had previously sustained one's human dignity; the affirmation of friends and community, the dignity of bodily health, and almost all sense of worth as a creature in God's hands. For it is God's universe that causes the affliction. In the same way, *Jesus experienced in his human soul the feeling of utter abandonment by God on the Cross, and could only cry out to him in the darkness.* In addition, as previously discussed, his sense of separation from God was in on sense even greater than ours could ever be, because it happened to one who knew that he had been completely faithful to his heavenly Father. The injustice of his total affliction, and the total silence, and

---

[534] Weil, *Waiting on God*, p. 80-81; italics mine.

[535] Ibid., p. 84. The absurd nature of the suffering of Christ included his being paraded in front of the people of Jerusalem as a mock king — scourged, robed, and crowned with thorns — and crucified under the taunting sign "The King of the Jews," misunderstood and rejected by almost everyone.

seeming total absence of God in the face of it, must have been all the more unfathomable for being completely undeserved. *Thus, Jesus' feeling of being utterly forsaken and cut off from God was analogous to our experience of extreme guilt: an experience of worthlessness, divine judgment, and alienation from God as the direct result of our mortal sins.*

David Brown has suggested another aspect of the depth of total affliction suffered by Jesus Christ on the Cross. In a way similar to Marilyn McCord Adams, who had written of the way participation in "horrors" can overwhelm the "meaning-making resources" of its victims, Brown points to the "essential arbitrariness" and at least initial "meaninglessness" of such intense human suffering:

> God's involvement with suffering in Christ is an involvement with that most frightening aspect of suffering, its essential arbitrariness. *There is no providential reason* why one of us will die in his forties of cancer, while another will enjoy a ripe old age; no reason why a Mother Teresa of Calcutta lives universally honoured by almost all, while a fellow believer languishes in a Soviet psychiatric hospital, forgotten even by his fellow Christians. It is this which makes Christ's cry of dereliction from the cross the cry of all sufferers — Why me? Why has God abandoned me to this fate? Of course, the cry had been heard before, most poignantly of all, perhaps in Psalm 88 with its unrelieved gloom. But here in Jesus we have God himself endorsing that cry, the tragic element in his creation that each new sufferer must discover for himself, *that there is no reason why it has befallen him rather than another.* Many a hospital chaplain has commented on the need for patients to let their anger loose against God. In the incarnation we have God taking part in the tragic element of his creation by railing against himself. …

> Now dying, he finds himself abandoned by all and so enters that most painful experience of them all, the assigning to one's life by others of a label one cannot accept — to the Jewish authorities, a blasphemer, to the Romans, a common criminal, and, worst of all, to his own disciples a failure. …

So it is a God who has entered into the most awful pain of all, the pain of meaninglessness, who offers us his aid in giving our pain a meaning. It is surely here that special providence enters the picture. It is no part of the divine plan that any specific individual suffer pain. But because pain is a tragic consequence of the values that creation embodies, God has chosen to enter into our pain at its most acute and now is always available to help creatively transform whatever befalls us as one who knew pain at its worst and potentially most destructive.[536]

In order properly to understand what Brown is proposing here, we need to appreciate the philosophical presuppositions behind it. Brown clearly and helpfully spelled these out for his readers:

If God has given free will to human beings, this must have introduced a *radical indeterminacy* to the world, which even God cannot fully control. So, if one accepts the free will defence there is just no avoiding the admission that there is an incurably tragic dimension to the creation, both in the sense that not everyone *may* be redeemed, since that is ultimately in our hands, not God's, and in the sense that not every event in our lives now can be used for the good, since the opportunity for that to be so has passed, and here again God has no power to alter the nature of time.[537]

---

[536] Brown, *God in a Single Vision*, p. 36-37; italics mine. Perhaps "Why me?" is an exaggeration here: after all, Jesus *voluntarily* exposed himself to suffering and death by going up to Jerusalem, taking his message of the dawning of God's Kingdom right into the heart of the nation, and publicly challenging the integrity of the Temple establishment by driving off the money-changers from Temple courtyard. He suffered neither "arbitrarily" nor unexpectedly. On the other hand, he might have asked "why me?" in another sense, as if saying to the Father: "I freely accepted to drink the cup of suffering for the sake of the kingdom — then why have you abandoned me in the midst of that suffering?"

[537] Ibid., p. 34, italics mine. "The free will defence": in other words, that God gave his creatures free will in order to make possible their attainment of such values as love, compassion, creativity, and wisdom, but that free will also can be misused, and thereby cause disorder and innocent suffering in the world.

Brown makes it sound as if God is able to guide his creation in general by his providence, but that the destinies of individuals — including their liability to experience extreme suffering at the hands of others, or from the vicissitudes of the natural world — are largely arbitrary and beyond God's control. This does not seem to fit, however, with the teaching of Jesus that God's providential care for each individual in this life is so personal and intimate that we need not be anxious for any of our true needs:

> Are not two sparrows sold for a penny? And not one of them will fall to the ground without your Father's will. But even the hairs on your head are all numbered. Fear not, therefore; you are of more value than many sparrows. (Mt 10:29-31; cf. Lk 12:22-34)

Perhaps there is a way to soften Brown's position here on the "radical indeterminacy" of the course of individual human lives, and the "arbitrary" nature of many of our sufferings, without losing the important, underlying point he is making.

First of all, we could bring in the traditional distinction between God's *absolute* and *permissive* will. God may not have chosen to inflict extreme misery on any particular individual as part of his original and eternal plan to achieve the values of his creation; but he does at least *permit* those terrible evils to befall particular individuals; he sees these evils and does nothing to stop them from happening to particular people, and so he must have a good reason for that kenotic restraint in each case (after all, on some occasions, apparently, he intervenes by miracles to stop or reverse grievous ills that afflict people).

Second, we can draw a distinction between the misery experienced by us when we run up against the limits of our ability to *see and understand* the meaning and purpose of our suffering, and Brown's assertion that sometimes there really is *no reason in divine providence* why we have been permitted to suffer. In the Old Testament, after all, Job's biggest complaint was that he could not see or understand the justice or purpose of his suffering, and God's response was to point to his own infinite power and wisdom as largely incomprehensible to finite human minds. Not to be able fully to understand why he lets us suffer grievously in particular cases is a terribly hard cross for us to bear, but it does not necessarily imply that God has no good reason, in accord with his loving providence, for permitting us to do so.

Finally, Brown pointed to the best solution of this human predicament by writing that God has made himself "available to help creatively transform whatever befalls us."[538] In other words, to put it in traditional terminology: it is the will of God that we cooperate with him to bring good out of permitted evils. In the worst circumstances, perhaps we may only be able to do so through prayer, or through suffering patiently without giving in to despair — but there must always be a way provided.[539] *Surely, a loving God would not allow any individual to suffer total human affliction unless it was at least possible, with the help of his grace, to bring good out of that permitted evil for that individual — indeed, a greater good than had he not permitted it to happen — and this must be so even if we do not yet fully understand what that greater good could be, or see it come to full fruition in our lifetime.* This certainly does not mean that we will all in fact *succeed* in cooperating with God to bring good out of such terrible evils, nor does it mean that it will ever be *easy*; moreover, other human beings, by their gross misuse of their free will, can make the path to finding meaning and purpose in our sufferings *maximally difficult*. But God's permissive will takes all that into account as well (I Cor 10:13).[540]

---

[538] Ibid., p. 37.

[539] In grave circumstances, Catholic Christians often turn to their tradition (based in part upon Col 1:24) of "offering up" their sufferings, in union with the merits of the Passion of Jesus Christ, in order to obtain graces for the Church, and for souls on earth and in Purgatory. See *Catechism*, entries 1508 and 1521, and Pope St. John Paul II's Apostolic Letter *Salvifici Dolores* ("Redemptive Suffering," 1984).

[540] To return to the case previously discussed of an ordinary Christian suffering torture: it must be at least *possible* for such a person to be radically transformed within through this experience — with the help of divine grace identifying with the crucified Christ, and offering up those sufferings in love for others — and thus to become a great saint. Unless this highest human good was at least a

As Brown has pointed out, one of the key ways that God has come to our aid was to reassure us that the discovery of meaning and purpose can happen even in the most horrific instances of permitted evil (such as the murder by public torture of the only entirely innocent and righteous human being who ever lived). For God himself entered into that depth of human suffering as Jesus of Nazareth, dying in total affliction on the Cross, yet without ceasing to love those around him, to pray for his persecutors, to surrender to God's will in the midst of utter darkness — and finally rising to new life and ultimate triumph on Easter morning.[541]

The inescapable conclusion of this whole discussion of human suffering is that we can only assert God's identification with the human condition, and therefore his close sympathy for human suffering of every kind, if we believe that God has become incarnate in a real human life, and rejoiced and sorrowed, struggled and died in total affliction as one of us. It is through this event that God has come to experience human afflictions from the perspective of a fully human consciousness, and thereby gained a touchstone for deepest compassion with the sorrows and griefs of all his children.

---

possible outcome of those sufferings (even if not their *probable* outcome) — perhaps the most terrible sufferings a human being can experience — it is hard to see why a loving God would permit them. Similarly, in the case of an unbeliever lost in mortal sin who undergoes such torture, it must be at least *possible* for this experience of dreadful suffering to lead him to at least rudimentary repentance and conversion, and the avoidance of eternal loss — the highest possible good for him at this stage of his journey. Otherwise, again, it is hard to see why a loving God would permit these sufferings to befall him.
[541] Brown, *God in a Single Vision*, p. 150.

God's Identification with Human Suffering and Theories of the Incarnation

It seems clear from everything we said in Part One of this book that if an incarnation is necessary for a strong assertion of divine identification with, and compassion for the human condition, then only a kenotic theory can make this doctrine intelligible and coherent.

Non-Incarnational Christianity, as we have seen it expressed (for example) by Hick, Lampe and Wiles, may want to hold fast to belief in the universal sympathy of the Creator for the sufferings of his creatures. But we have argued that at best, such divine feelings can only be predicated of God in some way remotely analogous to the human act of sympathy. This is because, apart from an incarnation, God could experience human suffering and struggle only from an infinite, omniscient perspective on events, which would vastly temper and ease that experience. Suffering would never have been for him what it can be for us: total affliction in mind, body, and spirit. And no one has ever made it clear how God can be said to closely empathise and sympathise with our condition if he has never shared our lot, experiencing human life and afflictions himself, from the finite perspective of a fully human consciousness.

Those who have approached this subject from the standpoint of what we have called "Action Christology," or with a "panentheist" theological perspective, such as Macquarrie, Pittenger, and Ward, have much the same difficulty as the Non-Incarnationalists in this respect. The phenomenology of "love" by W.H. Vanstone, and the philosophical theology centered on love by John Austin Baker also did not give us any reason to doubt the metaphysical necessity of the Incarnation to the depths of divine compassion.

In addition, Two-Nature Christology seems unable to make an intelligible claim that God has ever fully identified with human suffering.

The Incarnation

As we saw in Part One, David Brown's Two-Nature Theory (found in his book *The Divine Trinity*) entails that God identified with the human condition of suffering and struggle to some extent, but only as translated onto the level of a divine, omniscient perspective on all events. Even in Christ, therefore, God has not included and preserved in his eternal, divine store of experience an experience of real human suffering, from a limited perspective on events like ours, with all the mental and emotional trauma that this entails.

More classical versions of Two-Nature Christology, as we found them expressed in the writings of Anglicans Eric Mascall (following Aquinas) and Marilyn McCord Adams (following Duns Scotus), and in similar perspectives offered by Roman Catholic philosophical theologians such as Herbert McCabe, and Thomas Weinandy — and even the "compositional theory" of Brian Leftow and Oliver Crisp — all leave us with an abstract puzzle precisely where we need clarity and assurance. In each of these versions of TNC, the *person* of the divine Son is said to suffer in a fully human way, while the essentially impassible *divine nature* remains unmoved, unchanged, and unaffected. *But how can an utterly impassible God experience as his own, in a significant and intelligible sense, the life and passion of Jesus?* If his divine nature is not involved in the sufferings of his human nature, we are left with a view of the Incarnation in which God the Son, in his eternal and immutable divine mind or divine range of consciousness, was a mere spectator of the human life and death of Jesus that he operated and directed on earth.

It is certainly a blessing that centuries of popular Christian devotion to Jesus Christ have been oblivious to this theological problem, and despite the handicap of an insufficient theory of the Incarnation, have been inflamed by the Holy Spirit with the love of the Crucified God. But since the rise of Kenotic Christology in the nineteenth century, there has been a persistent attempt to match that fire of love with a theory of the Incarnation that can fully support and sustain it.

In his contribution to the collection of scholarly essays titled *Divine Impassibility and the Mystery of Human Suffering* (2009), Protestant theologian Bruce Marshall tried to reassure his readers that the logic of Two-Nature Christology is easy to understand. On closer inspection, however, his assurances fail to convince. Marshall writes:

> Impassibility and exposure to suffering — passibility — are opposites, which naturally prompts the thought that they cannot be predicated of the same subject or person. But since we do not predicate them of the incarnate Word in the same respect, the appearance of contradiction is easily disposed of …. "The Impassible God suffers and dies" is no more puzzling than "corruptible man is incorruptible"— corruptible with respect to his flesh, incorruptible with respect to his soul, as all of us are. The logic of the matter can be illustrated, in fact, by the most metaphysically prosaic cases. "That man is curly" (in virtue of his hair, not in virtue of what makes him a human being), we say without logical strain, or "The Ethiopian is white" (with respect to his teeth, but black with respect to his skin). The rule is that opposites can be predicated of the very same thing, and yield true statements, as long as we can make a distinction between that in virtue of which, or the respect in which (*id secundum quod*) each is predicated. This works for the metaphysical case of the curly man, and for the metaphysically unparalleled case of the incarnate God.[542]

Coming up with a theory of the Incarnation that passes the test of logic, however, is not the same thing as finding a *theologically* satisfactory incarnational model. Logical coherence is necessary, but not fully sufficient for the task. The example of "The man is curly" that Marshall gives, for instance, is based on the distinction between what is essential to a substance, and what is accidental. Do we really want to say that the incarnate life and death of the Son of God had a mere accidental relationship to his divinity? — indeed, that it was the kind of accident that made no real difference to, and had no impact on the

---

[542] Bruce D. Marshall, "The Dereliction of Christ and the Impassibility of God," in Keating and White, editors, *Divine Impassibility and the Mystery of Human Suffering*, p. 279-280.

divine substance at all? (See our discussion of the Scotist view of Marilyn McCord Adams in Part One, Chapter One of this book). How does that illumine for us what it means to say that the Word became flesh and truly shared our lot? Furthermore, the other two examples that Marshall gives — "Corruptible man [in the flesh] is incorruptible [in his immortal soul]" and "The Ethiopian is white (with respect to his teeth), but black (with respect to his skin)"— are both adequate analogies of a "compositional" theory of the Incarnation, such as that proposed by Leftow and Crisp. According to this theory, Jesus Christ suffers only in part of what he is, not in the whole of what he is. But do we really want to say that the divine person of the Son is only one part of a greater whole called "God Incarnate"? As previously discussed in Part One, Chapter One, above, Leftow likens the Incarnation to a diver who puts on wet suit so he can jump in the water and swim without getting wet. And Crisp writes: "God the Son acts in his human nature rather like one might use a tool to perform a certain task."[543] Crisp then tells us that when Jesus wept over the death of his friend Lazarus, "The divine person who possesses this human nature is the one that moves his human nature to weep"[544] With all due respect, this sounds more like the description of a puppet show than the story of the God who entered into the very depths of our human condition out of love for us. Finally, with Aquinas and the Classical tradition, do we really want to say that in his divine nature the Son of God merely watches himself suffering as man, without sharing in that suffering? None of these theories seem to move us closer to understanding with sufficient clarity the mystery of God's identification with the plight of humanity.

My contention is that only Kenoticism can help us here. For both of our main Kenotic Models show that God has fully identified with the human condition through Jesus Christ, experiencing it from the perspective of a fully human consciousness. The divine Son of God became incarnate as Jesus of Nazareth: either by rendering latent — that is, partially inaccessible and inoperative

---

[543] Crisp, *The Word Enfleshed*, p. 113.
[544] Ibid., p. 116.

for a time — his divine omni-attributes in order to live within all the limitations of human life (the Radical KM of Forsyth, Mackintosh and Taylor); or better, the divine Son became incarnate by restraining the exercise of his omni-attributes at a particular time and place in history, extending his own divine mode of being (even while continuing to uphold and guide the whole creation as the universal Logos) into an additional, human mode of consciousness and will — multiplying his own personality, as it were, to take the form of a limited, human range of consciousness and action as Jesus of Nazareth, to which his infinite, divine consciousness has an asymmetric accessing relationship — in order to experience all the conditions of a fully human life (with individual variations, the Moderate KM of Martensen, Gore, Weston, Quick, Hebblethwaite, Morris, Swinburne and Brown). Only with a kenotic model of the Incarnation, it would seem, are we permitted to say that God the Son has truly come to share our lot from the perspective of a fully human consciousness, and thereby gained a touchstone for closest empathy and sympathy with the joys, struggles, pains and sorrows of every human being.

Roman Catholic theologian Lucien J. Richard found in Kenoticism a unique capacity to address the needs of suffering humanity:

> The strength of kenotic Christology is both intellectual and symbolic; its imagery of the self-emptying of God revealed in the person of Jesus is one that resonates with the deepest elements of our human nature. This Christology addresses the issue of human suffering in stark and challenging terms, and it provides Christianity today with a fundamental understanding of the transformative power of love ....[545]

Protestant theologian C. Stephen Evans summarized the case for Kenoticism in similar terms in *Exploring Kenotic Christology* (2006):

---

[545] Richard, *Christ: The Self-Emptying of God*, p. 8.

An incarnation that includes suffering to the point of painful death is powerful testimony to the goodness of God .... I believe that a kenotic understanding of the Incarnation significantly deepens the ground of this faith, for on the kenotic view God has in Christ completely identified with the human condition. He has made himself vulnerable to all the common ills of humanity, and has no hidden powers to be called forth in a pinch.[546] In facing the frustrations and even terrors of human existence, Christ must depend entirely on the Father and the comfort of the Spirit. An assurance of love toward us as sufferers is far more powerful if it comes from one who has shown a willingness to share fully in our sufferings.[547]

Indeed, the kenotic Christian can truly say that God the Son does not ask us to walk through any depth of human struggle, misery or grief that he was not willing to walk through himself.

Furthermore, if God has indeed entered into the fellowship of our sufferings through his incarnate life and death, then (as we have already seen) this "touchstone" experience is also *retroactive*: God now has the closest possible compassion for the sufferings of every human being who has ever lived, even those who lived before his incarnate sojourn on earth, through his unfading memory of their lives and his greatly augmented capacity for empathy and sympathy.

---

[546] It is important to remember that for Jesus of Nazareth to be authentically "vulnerable" to the "common ills of humanity," — social, physical, psychological, and spiritual — does not necessarily mean that he succumbed to the pressures of those miseries. In particular, I argue throughout this book that, although he experienced sufferings from these human ills, *he did not succumb by embracing either sin or error at any stage of his human journey*. By the Holy Spirit, he successfully struggled against these shortcomings of fallen humanity in fulfilment of his mission to be the Savior and Light of the World.

[547] Evans, "Kenotic Christology and the Nature of God" in Evans, ed. *Exploring Kenotic Christology*, p. 203.

In short, it is not because authentic love in every form always involves suffering that we must say that God sympathetically suffers with his creatures. Rather, it is because he has freely chosen to assume all the conditions and limitations of human life as Jesus of Nazareth, for our sake and at our need; he has thereby taken upon his heart the ultimate depths of compassion for our plight — a depth of compassion for us which abides forever.

Chapter Two
Kenoticism and the Saving Work of Jesus Christ

God has limited himself to share our lot through his incarnate life and death as Jesus of Nazareth. Through this act, he has made himself vulnerable to the suffering and evil to which his creatures are subject, assuming into his divine nature the depths of human pain and affliction. Such has been the claim of Kenotic theorists — not least from the Anglican Communion — since the latter half of the 19ᵗʰ century.

At the same time, Christians have always been driven to say much more about the Incarnation, for we live in a world full of human arrogance and injustice, cruelty and oppression, greed and lust, godlessness and indifference. The fact that God the Son, the second person of the Trinity, has walked alongside us in our struggles and our sufferings, and therefore can closely empathise and sympathise with us, is simply not "good news" enough. The gospel message is more than just an assertion of divine compassion for us. For God has also undertaken dramatic, costly and decisive acts to come to our rescue and save us from the guilt and power of sin.

Our central concern in this chapter, therefore, will be with the doctrine of the Saving Work of Jesus Christ, also known as the doctrine of *Redemption* or *Atonement* (meaning all that makes us "at-one" again with God). More specifically, *this is the doctrine that God acts in Christ, and especially in the death of Christ, to save the world from sin* ("… and you shall call his name Jesus, for he will save his people from their sins," Mt 1:21; "Christ Jesus came into the world to save sinners," 1 Tim 1:15).[548] In his book *The Doctrine of the Atonement* (1951), Leonard Hodgson summed up the biblical understanding of atonement like this: "The Atonement is (i) an act of God, (ii) restoring fellowship, (iii) by

---

[548] This chapter will focus exclusively on the impact on humanity of Christ's saving work, but this is not to deny that his work of redemption also has implications for the liberation and transformation of the entire created order; see, for example, Rom 8: 18-25, and the next chapter of this book.

forgiveness of sins, (iv) through the death of Christ …. 'On these aspects of the Atonement there is general agreement among the various writers of the New Testament.'"[549]

Throughout this chapter, by acts of "sin" I shall mean human acts of betrayal of God's love, who brought us into being and trusted us with the stewardship of his creation: the care of ourselves, each other, and all living creatures (Gen 1:26-28, 2:15). A prime example of sin in the biblical story, of course, is Judas Iscariot, the friend and apostle of Jesus, who in the end betrayed him. This is not because Judas was necessarily the worst of all sinners, but because he is archetypical of what all of us do, in ways great or small.

By divine "forgiveness" I shall mean the pardoning of the *objective guilt* for sin (i.e., the erasing of our moral debt to God for our sins), always coupled with, and expressed by a renewal of the gift of the Holy Spirit and his sanctifying grace in our hearts, to enable us to overcome the *power* of sin in our lives (i.e., the inner disorder and corruption that inclines us to sin in the first place). In other words, God never forgives us merely by erasing our demerits in a heavenly accounts book somewhere, but by giving *himself* to us, uniting us to himself in the Holy Spirit, which is the gift that he merited for us by his passion and death on Calvary — symbolized by the blood and water that flowed from his pierced heart on the Cross (Jn 19:34).

The reticence of contemporary Anglican theologians to write in-depth about the mystery of the Atonement, however, is widely recognised. For example, in his classic study of Anglican theology *From Gore to Temple* (covering the period roughly from 1889-1939), Michael Ramsey pointed to several abiding features of Anglican thought: the continuing influence of Platonism and humanism, and a special emphasis on the doctrine of the Incarnation, sometimes at the expense of proper concern for other key Christian doctrines.[550] Anglican theologians in

---

[549] Leonard Hodgson, *The Doctrine of the Atonement* (New York: Charles Scribner's Sons, 1951), p. 15.
[550] Ramsey, *From Gore to Temple*, p. 27-28, 164.

this period such as William Temple and Lionel Spencer Thornton sought to fashion a broad rational synthesis of philosophy and theology. They developed an evolutionary view of the cosmos with the Incarnation as its crown and revelatory key, and shied away from equal concern for the doctrine of Redemption. Of course, given the historical realities of the day, a general confidence in the rational powers and progressive goodness of humanity is not surprising. Throughout most of this period, Britain remained a world super-power with a worldwide empire. Though shaken and wounded by the First World War, she had not suffered as much as other European powers such as France, Germany, and Russia. Also, much of the Anglican Communion's theological work was still being written in the cloisters of Oxford and Cambridge, at that time largely populated by the children of the upper classes.

The sufferings of Britain during the Second World War, however, proved a further shock. Archbishop Temple began to write of a new theological task: the need for a theology of redemption rather than merely of explanation, a theology that takes with deadly seriousness the "self-sufficiency and arrogance" of the world.[551] Soon thereafter, Britain's initial burst of post-war political idealism turned sour in the face of industrial conflict and the explosion of the first Soviet A-bomb.[552] Yet Anglican theologians still did not respond to Temple's concerns. As if the fundamental Christian doctrines were clear and assured, in the 1950s they concentrated instead upon matters of liturgy, ministry, and biblical interpretation.[553] This prolonged failure to think deeply about doctrinal fundamentals may have contributed to an over-reaction in the following decades: the radical questioning of basic Christian doctrines by so many leading Anglican theologians throughout the world in the 1960s-1980s.[554]

---

[551] Ibid., p. 161.
[552] Paul A. Welsby, *A History of the Church of England: 1945-1980* (Oxford: Oxford University Press, 1984), p. 24-25.
[553] Ibid., p. 56-68.
[554] Ibid., p.110, and 235-238.

In fact, it could be argued that Anglican scholars still have not taken up Temple's challenge. The doctrine of the Atonement all too often has been neglected. Looking at the period from World War II to the present, we can find only five truly in-depth treatments of the subject by Anglican theologians: Leonard Hodgson's *The Doctrine of the Atonement* (1951), F.W. Dillistone's *The Christian Understanding of Atonement* (1968), John Stott's *The Cross of Christ* (1986), Fleming Rutledge's *The Crucifixion* (2015), and Tom Wright's *The Day the Revolution Began* (2016).

The history of post-war Anglican theology might have been rather different if the strong implications of Kenoticism for the saving work of Jesus Christ had been more fully appreciated and developed. The founders of the Anglican stream of Kenoticism, Charles Gore and Frank Weston, had certainly laid the groundwork, for as Michael Ramsey pointed out, "the Kenotic theology of Gore and his disciples was emphatically a theology of redemption."[555] Nevertheless, that mantle has fallen, and much work needs to be done.

In this chapter we shall survey and critique four general approaches to the doctrine of Redemption (Exemplarist, Sacrificial, Penal, and Classical), categories often used by systematic and historical theologians to describe the many dimensions of Christ's saving work. Our focus will remain primarily on Anglican contributions to this discussion, but as usual, we shall see that post-war Anglican thought largely reflects the mind of the wider Christian community on this subject. Moreover, our approach will be more analytical than historical. **Each theory of Atonement we examine will build upon insights gained from the previous ones, until we are able to complete a mosaic (although such a mosaic could never really be complete!) of the *multi-dimensional mystery* of all that Jesus has done to save us.**[556] Finally, I will

---

[555] Ramsey, *From Gore to Temple*, p. 27.

[556] This is similar to the method of approach taken by the Doctrine Commission of the Church of England in its 1995 report *The Mystery of Salvation* (Church House Publishing, 1995), p. 92-93, 97, and 101:

endeavor to show that Kenoticism, especially in the form developed within the Anglican tradition, can shed further light on this great mystery.

As an initial guideline, we shall keep before our eyes the marvellously synthetic approach to the doctrine of Redemption of Anglican bishop and Kenotic theologian Charles Gore:

> There are, in fact, three relations in which our Lord stands to us in the New Testament. There is Christ in front of us, who sets before us the standard of the new life — in whom we see the true meaning of manhood. That is to kindle our desire. There is Christ for us — our propitiation or atonement — winning for us, at the price of His blood-shedding, freedom from all the guilt and bondage of the past, the assurance of free forgiveness and a fresh start. Then there is Christ in us — our new life by the Spirit, molding us inwardly into His likeness, and

---

It is important for Christian doctrine to be able to trace the fact and work of atonement to Jesus himself, but elaborate theories of the atonement are secondary, necessarily diverse, and all to some extent inadequate to the reality of their subject and to the profundity of its meaning. ...

Christian tradition taken as a whole seems intuitively to recognize this fact of the diversity of images for the atonement in the New Testament and has not tried to impose one particular theory. ...

Eventually, doctrines of the atonement emerge, which are attempts to devise as coherent answers as possible to the questions raised by [the biblical] narrative; and these doctrines have been many, and varied in the history of Christian thought. To try to reduce this variety to a single agreed statement of the doctrine of the atonement would be untrue both to the New Testament and to our Anglican heritage. Far better, and more consistent with our rich Christian tradition, is to provide a series of angles of vision, or reference points, to sketch the great mystery of the atonement. These are complementary insights and are not in competition with each other; they are facets of the central jewel of the Christian faith, that in the cross and resurrection of Jesus God has won our salvation.

conforming us to His character. And the three are one. Each is unintelligible without the others. The redeeming work of Christ lies in all together.[557]

Exemplarist Theories of Atonement

The first set of theories we will examine will be called "Exemplarist," because they tell us that **Christ's saving work consists in the fact that through his teachings and his lived example, and especially by his death on the Cross, he has demonstrated and revealed the love of God for us, as well as the proper love of humanity for God. In other words, he "exemplifies" the truth about humanity and divinity.** God intended this revelatory and didactic work to bring about a change in human hearts that might reconcile sinners to himself (I Jn 4:7-12; Rom 5:8; II Cor 5:18-20). For example, *the life and death of Jesus, perfect in love, is said to be the supreme example and attractive ideal of human devotion to God, an ideal which we must always aspire to imitate.*[558] Yet Exemplarist theologians typically wish to say more, for the good example of Jesus from the past is usually not held to be enough to save us from the guilt and power of sin. The depths of the human predicament was expressed by St. Paul when he wrote:

> For I do not do what I want, but I do the very thing I hate …. For I delight in the law of God in my inmost self, but I see in my members another law at war with the law of my mind and making me captive to the law of sin which dwells in my members. Wretched man that I am! Who will deliver me from this body of death? (Rom 7:15-24)

Exemplarist theologians claim, therefore, that the life and death of Jesus is also the supreme declaration of the merciful love of God for us, intended to awaken in us a response of love, with the help of the Holy Spirit. *Above all, it is through the passion and death of Jesus that God*

---

[557] Gore, *The Reconstruction of Belief*, p. 595-596.

[558] Evangelical theologian Norman Anderson, for example, included this as an aspect of Christ's saving work in *Jesus Christ: The Witness of History* (InterVarsity Press, 1985), p. 79.

convincingly demonstrates his suffering, patient, and forgiving love for sinful and struggling humanity.

In post-war Anglican thought, Exemplarism has been very popular — as it has been throughout the Christian world.[559] F.W. Dillistone, for example, listed it as one of the two basic forms in which atonement has been conceived down through the ages. According to Dillistone, there is an eternal idea, true for God and the whole cosmos which must be revealed and affirmed: "through-death-to-life," or better, "reconciliation through sacrifice." The self-offering of the Son of God is the full expression of this idea as true for both God and humanity.[560] Hence, Exemplarism fits very well with the Platonic and relatively optimistic strains of Anglican thought. Allegedly, all that is needed to save us is a clear and convincing demonstration of the truth of this idea, and of Divine Love for humanity as an expression of this idea.

Exemplarism comes in two distinct forms: incarnational and non-incarnational.

1) Non-Incarnational Exemplarism

This model may be found, for example, in the writings of Maurice Wiles and Geoffrey Lampe. In general, they held that **by his grace God led a solely human Jesus to attain supreme intimacy with himself, and supreme love and faithfulness even unto death. Jesus was so surrendered to the divine will and purpose for human life that he became for us a true reflection of God, a living parable of God's character and loving outreach to the world.** Anglican theologian Trevor Williams summed it up in these words:

> [T]he mystery of Jesus is still the reality and constancy in his experience … of a personal relationship with God. Within this

---

[559] Among contemporary Roman Catholic theologians, Gerald O'Collins, SJ, has been a leading proponent of Incarnational Exemplarism. See his book *Jesus our Redeemer: A Christian Approach to Salvation* (Oxford: Oxford University Press, 2007).

[560] F.W. Dillistone, *The Christian Understanding of Atonement* (London: SCM, 1968), p. 410-412.

relationship of love, one might say that Jesus' own life conformed to or took on the character of God's life without violence to his humanity. Hence, under the conditions of human existence he gave visible expression to the eternal character of God, and at the same time to God's creative, life-giving power, which overflowed in the love Jesus showed.[561]

In a non-incarnational theology such as this, Wiles contended, we can still believe that Jesus is the true or ideal man, and we can still see Jesus as our Savior: "It would still be possible to see Jesus not only as one who embodies a full response of man to God, but also, as one who expresses and embodies the way of God towards men. ... It is supremely through Jesus that the self-giving love of God is most fully expressed."[562]

While all of this may be true as far as it goes, we are still left with the crucial question of how God supremely demonstrated his love for us on the Cross through a solely human Jesus. In *The Remaking of Christian Doctrine* (1974), Wiles offered two ways of conceiving this. First, "the death of Christ exemplifies the love of God." Second, "the Passion of Christ has been remarkably effective as an historical phenomenon in the transformation of human lives."[563] Allegedly, neither of these points requires or justifies any divine identity claim we may want to make for Jesus Christ.

Wiles wanted to continue to see the Cross as the supreme exhibition of God's love for humanity, even in a non-incarnational framework. However, it makes little sense to speak of the death of Jesus as a demonstration of Divine Love unless something has been done for our benefit on Calvary, some loving act accomplished for us there. Surely, *love cannot be fully expressed except in action for the benefit of another.* Yet Wiles never clearly explained what a solely human Jesus actually accomplished for us on the Cross that can save us from the guilt and power of sin. Moreover, if the Cross is truly an act of God's love for

---

[561] Williams, *Form and Vitality*, p. 202.
[562] Wiles, "Christianity Without Incarnation," p. 8.
[563] Wiles, *The Remaking of Christian Doctrine*, p. 79-80.

humanity, and not just an act of one man's love for God, then it must be God himself who both performs and experiences it. For surely, *love cannot be fully enacted and expressed by proxy*. God must do more than simply call someone else, on his behalf, to do his saving work, and he must do more than just sympathise with the sufferings of his ambassador from a distance. In response to Wiles, therefore, we must repeat Brian Hebblethwaite's question: "How one may ask, does someone else's death reveal *God's* love?"[564] In short, ***if Jesus on the Cross is not God in person, performing a salvific act of love for us by suffering and dying for us, then on what grounds can we assert that the Cross "exemplifies the love of God" in a significant way?***

If we follow Wiles' non-incarnational path, the most we could say about the doctrine of the Atonement would be something like this: (1) that God can help people to love, even in the face of death, just as he inspired Jesus to do, and this shows us that to some extent God cares about us; and (2) since God led Jesus to suffer patiently at the hands of sinners, this shows us the Father's patient and forgiving love for humanity. Now all this is certainly true and helpful, as far as it goes, but it surely does not have the kind of life-changing, transformative power needed from a gospel of redemption.

Geoffrey Lampe offered a clearer and fuller statement of Non-Incarnational Exemplarism in his book *God as Spirit* (1977). Lampe claimed that Jesus' character was fully shaped and sanctified by the Spirit into the earthly image of God.[565] By meditating on the life of Jesus in Scripture, therefore, we can see reflected in him God's own character, as well as God's creative purposes for us. Through the attractive power of the life and death of Jesus, people are called to share "his trusting and hoping response to God's providential care, his moral demand, and his call to service."[566] We are thereby invited to

---

[564] Hebblethwaite, *The Incarnation,* p. 33.
[565] Lampe, *God as Spirit*, p. 19.
[566] Ibid., p. 13.

attain true "sonship" — to love and trust the Father as Jesus did — and enabled to do so by God as Spirit dwelling within us.[567]

Lampe did not say that we are saved by Christ's moral and religious example alone. Rather, Christ's attractive example of inspired sonship calls us to receive the same Spirit of God within our own hearts, who alone can transform us into his true disciples.[568] Anglo-Catholic theologian Eric Mascall, therefore, overstated the case when he complained that Lampe had "ignored without comment the historic witness of Christendom that, in order to be reconciled to God, man needs something more from Jesus than the example of someone whose life was so perfect that he himself needed no reconciliation at all."[569] Lampe never denied the need for the inner, re-creative action of the Spirit in every human soul. In fact, that is the center of his whole understanding of God as Spirit. The moral and religious example of Jesus is but the supreme occasion and opportunity of the call of God. Through the inspired example of Jesus, God attracts us to Christ's moral and religious ideals and beckons us to follow. To do so we must open our hearts to the strengthening, sanctifying power of his indwelling Spirit.

The Cross also plays a part in this understanding of the Atonement. Lampe rejected traditional ideas of Christ ransoming us from slavery to Satan, or sacrificing himself vicariously for our sins. Instead, "the death of Christ may still be seen to have a central and focal place ... as the climax, culmination, and fulfilment of his entire life of faith and obedience, and as the point where the essential character of 'sonship' toward God is most fully disclosed."[570] But salvation is not something that was accomplished once and for all in a past event.[571] It is a process of being transformed by the Spirit, of growing into the likeness of Christ in self-giving love, daily dying to self and being raised in the Spirit to a new life centered in God.

---

[567] Ibid., p. 29.

[568] Ibid., p. 24.

[569] Mascall, *Whatever Happened to the Human Mind*, p. 105.

[570] Lampe, *Explorations in Theology: 8*, p. 21.

[571] Ibid., p. 21.

Lampe's dual emphasis on the attractive power of Jesus' human example of faith and love, and on the work of the Holy Spirit within us, enabling us to become Christ's true disciples, surely should be taken to heart. It neatly supplements what we found was true and helpful in Maurice Wiles' approach to Christ's saving work. Nevertheless, as Lampe has a non-incarnational model of atonement, it suffers from similar defects. Let us grant that Jesus, led by the Spirit, gave us a supremely attractive example of human faithfulness to the Father, culminating in his martyrdom, and let us also grant that the Divine Spirit is active in our hearts to help us follow Christ's Way. But is this all that God has done to save us? Is this really enough to save us from the burden of *guilt* we carry for our past sins, and the *power* of our ongoing proclivity to sin? Furthermore, let us grant that when a solely human and innocent Jesus was put to death on the Cross, God showed his patient, forbearing love for us all by not giving up on humanity right there and then. But is this really the great act and demonstration of God's love for us that can move us to deeply love and trust him in return? How does this accomplish anything more than to republish what was already well known to the ancient Jews, and recorded in the Old Testament (see for example Psalm 103: "Bless the Lord, O my soul, and all that is within me, bless his holy name! … [W]ho forgives all your iniquity, who heals all your diseases ….")? Where is the gospel-extra here? ***In the Christology of Lampe and Wiles, the Cross in particular seems to accomplish very little for us, and the full cost of it, in bodily pain and mental agony, is borne by Jesus of Nazareth, and not by God.***[572] This hardly amounts to a very convincing demonstration of God's own love for us. H.R. Mackintosh put it this way:

> Love in essence is desire and will to suffer for the sake of the beloved: to enter his condition, to take his load, to renounce every privilege. Not to send a sympathetic message simply, or appear by deputy, but to come in person, obstacles and

---

[572] Geoffrey Lampe, "The Holy Spirit and the Person of Christ" in S.W. Sykes and J.P. Clayton, editors, *Christ, Faith and History* (Cambridge: Cambridge University Press, 1972), p. 124.

counter-reasons notwithstanding. Otherwise, love is not known as love ....

It is not that God cannot be known as Love apart from His incarnation in Christ. To say so would be false. But it is not false to say that apart from the gift of Christ out of an eternal being, God's love would not be displayed so amazingly, in a form and magnitude which inspire awe and overwhelm the soul.[573]

2) Incarnational Exemplarism

Advocates of this model attempt to include insights from the non-incarnational form, but seek to articulate more clearly the way in which the life and death of Jesus Christ shows us God's love for human beings. The key to the model lies in the Incarnation. As John Austin Baker wrote:

> **It is inconceivable to me that love could ever say: 'I must save these children of mine, and that will mean the most terrible suffering. I will find someone else to do the job.' Love does not send others to suffer in its place. Love comes itself.**[574]

In short, *authentic love cannot be fully expressed by proxy, through an ambassador.* True love can only be expressed in person, and if need be in personal sacrifice for the sake of the beloved. God became incarnate as Jesus Christ to exemplify and demonstrate this authentic love for all of humanity.

The principle features of Incarnational Exemplarism were first expounded by Peter Abelard in the Middle Ages. They can be found

---

[573] Mackintosh, *The Doctrine of the Person of Jesus Christ,* p. 425, and 460. Mackintosh's words harken back to the lyrics of the hymn by Isaac Watts, "When I Survey the Wondrous Cross," which exclaim at the end: "Love so amazing, so divine, demands my life, my soul, my all." It is very hard to see how Non-Incarnational Exemplarism can inspire such faith and devotion.
[574] Baker, *The Foolishness of God,* p. 407

also in brief, summarizing statements by two post- World War II Anglican theologians. First, Austin Farrer:

> What, then, did God do for his people's redemption? He came among them, bringing his kingdom, and he let events take their human course. He set the divine life in human neighbourhood. Men discovered it in struggling with it, and were captured by it in crucifying it. What could be simpler? And what more divine?[575]

Some years later, Brian Hebblethwaite unpacked this perspective in greater detail, summing it up in these words:

> By his own identification with human suffering and evil, with the effects of betrayal, cruelty and judicial murder, God in Christ at once shows us the truth about ourselves, reveals the nature and the cost of divine forgiveness and draws us into union with the triune God.[576]

> It is God's own act of self-involvement through incarnation to the point of crucifixion that, as it were, transmits God's forgiveness and God's love, and enables the divine Spirit, the Spirit of both God the Father and Christ crucified, to penetrate human hearts and human society and begin the work of sanctification.[577]

A yet more detailed presentation of an Incarnational Exemplarist approach to the doctrine of Christ's saving work can be found in an essay by philosophical theologian J.R. Lucas., entitled "Atonement and Redemption" (1976).[578] According to Lucas, Jesus gave us the supreme

---

[575] Farrer, *Saving Belief*, p. 99.

[576] Hebblethwaite, *Philosophical Theology and Christian Doctrine*, p. 92. In this passage Hebblethwaite is summarizing with approval the soteriological perspective of Anglican theologian Donald Mackinnon.

[577] Ibid., p. 103. Here Hebblethwaite is unpacking the meaning of the quote on Christ's saving work by Farrer from *Saving Belief*.

[578] J. R. Lucas, *Freedom and Grace* (London: SPCK, 1976).

example of human life lived on the basis of sincere love for God and humanity, even in the face of death.[579] Today we can easily identify with Jesus. We find his teaching and example especially attractive because he was a real human being like us, sharing our condition; he is not just an abstract ideal or a character from mythology.[580] Furthermore, the resurrection of Jesus gives us a double-assurance: that God's love for us is stronger than the grave, and that Jesus is still with us in some way (Mt 28:20).[581] We can open our hearts to him and share with him our sorrows and our joys, our hopes and fears, knowing that as a human being himself, he can truly understand us.[582]

Lucas pointed out, however, that fulfilling human relationships, even with Jesus, "do not constitute a complete resolution of Adam's predicament."[583] They cannot fully assuage the alienation of free moral agents, the solitariness of the individual ego which, Lucas believed, lies at the origin of human self-centeredness.[584] In other words, accepting Jesus as our supremely inspired human example, and relating to him personally as our risen Lord, is still inadequate to save us from the disorder of sin. *The attractive example of Jesus from the past, the presence of the risen Christ beside us today, and the hope of eternal life with him in heaven — all this is good news, but it is still not enough.*

The Christian Faith, therefore, takes us further. Jesus is held to be not only a sincere prophet and martyr, risen from the dead. He was and is divine. All that he has done for us is God's own work, in person: "His death is therefore not only proof of his humanity and sincerity, but of

---

[579] Ibid., p. 50.

[580] Ibid., p. 52.

[581] Ibid., p. 51.

[582] Ibid., p. 52.

[583] Ibid., p. 54.

[584] Ibid., p. 42-49. Lucas calls this the human "logical inadequacy," and "the inevitable isolation of the human ego" (p. 54-55). Thus, he claims that human beings are "naturally bad" (p. 46), which hardly fits Christian faith in God as the loving Creator who made all things "very good" (Gen 1:31). Nevertheless, ego-centrism (with its origin in the fall of the human race, resulting in the universal, wounded condition of original sin) is indeed the plague of humanity, and as Lucas shows, only Divine Love can rescue us from it.

God's love … [God] cares to the extent of making the greatest sacrifice he possibly could."[585] Thus, in Incarnational Exemplarism God comes to us in the flesh, and not by proxy, through a mere human ambassador. In this way the life and death of Jesus is the supreme elucidation of God's self-sacrificial love for us, and we are drawn to love him because he so loved us (I Jn 4:9-11).

Lucas needed to spell out more clearly, however, just what the divine self-sacrifice on the Cross actually accomplished for us. A demonstration of sacrificial love must be in the form of a costly act, performed for our benefit. As we said earlier, love cannot be fully expressed except in action for the benefit of another. But how do we benefit from the death of Jesus? How was the Cross instrumental and decisive in helping remove both the objective guilt (i.e., the moral debt) of our past sins, and our present proclivity to sin that has such power over us? Lucas claimed that the best hope for humanity is to come to know that we are loved by God in such a sacrificial way that it can break down the barriers of our ego-centrism, and lead us to acknowledge a center of worth and devotion beyond ourselves (and beyond our own social group: our race, class, and nation).[586]

Let us grant that God the Son made a tremendous act of self-sacrifice by entering into our human condition, showing us the way to live in the Holy Spirit, and accepting a martyr's death at the hands of sinful men. Let us grant that he also offers us his ongoing companionship and guidance as the risen Lord, and the hope for everlasting life with him at our journey's end. *The question remains: how has the death of Jesus on the Cross in particular benefited us in a salvific way? In what way is it God's decisive act to liberate us from the guilt and power of sin, and therefore the supreme revelation of his love, as the Christian Faith has always claimed: "God shows his love for us in that while we were yet sinners Christ died for us" (Rom 5:8)?*

---

[585] Ibid., p. 55-56.
[586] Ibid.

In their debate with non-incarnational theologians, Anglican writers have made it clear that an incarnational approach can add several things to Exemplarist theory.

1) **First of all, the Incarnation establishes the definitiveness, or "finality" of God's self-revelation through the words and deeds of Jesus Christ.**

Most of those operating with a kenotic understanding of the Incarnation (including many from the Anglican tradition: e.g. Gore, Weston, Quick, Farrer, Hebblethwaite, Swinburne, and Brown) have been willing to admit that the human mind of Jesus must have been formed and nurtured by the first century Jewish culture in which he was raised — a social conditioning process that is similar for all authentic human beings. Nevertheless, the same writers have insisted that **the divine Son must have chosen the precise moment in history, "the fullness of time" (Gal 4:4), when he could accept all the conditions and limitations of human life, and mediate through them to all subsequent history, with the help of the Holy Spirit, the clearest, most complete and most trustworthy divine revelation possible in human terms**.

Charles Gore and Frank Weston defended Christ's entire trustworthiness (or "infallibility") as a vehicle and source of God's definitive self-revelation; Gore put it this way:

> [N]othing is more essential to a full faith in Christ than this recognition of his essential finality …. This means that He is not only the greatest prophet and the most conspicuous saint and the noblest leader of humanity who has ever lived; for if that were all, obviously we could "look for another" as great as He, possibly greater than He. … There may be another Christ, even conceivably a higher and more enlightened one. There is no real ground for asserting the finality of the Christ, unless he be personally God in manhood. … For there

can be no disclosure of God even conceivable which should be completer or fuller (at least under the conditions of this world) than is given us in Him who is the Word made flesh.[587]

It is surely beyond question that our Lord is represented in the Gospels as an infallible no less than a sinless teacher. He challenges criticism. He speaks in a tone of authority only justifiable to one who taught with absolute certainty 'the word of God.' 'Heaven and earth,' He said, 'shall pass away, but my words shall never pass away.' But infallibility is not omniscience.[588]

Gore's last point — that "infallibility" is not the same as "omniscience" — is a claim we discussed and endorsed earlier (in Part One, Chapter Four of this book). Gore and Weston were emphatic that it would be impossible to believe that Jesus Christ was the divine Son Incarnate, and at the same time believe that he taught error in any respect. A divine person incarnate would be entirely trustworthy, and in that sense "infallible" as a vehicle of divine revelation. But this is not the same as claiming him to be omniscient.

This point received clear expression in one of the nineteenth century Anglican classics on the Incarnation: H.P. Liddon's *The Divinity of our Lord and Saviour Jesus Christ* (1864):

[P]lainly enough, a limitation of knowledge is one thing, and fallibility is another. Paul says that "we know in part," and that "we see through a glass darkly." Yet Paul is so certain of the truth of that which he teaches as to exclaim, "If we or an angel from Heaven preach any other Gospel to you than that which we have preached unto you, let him be accursed." Paul clearly

---

[587] Gore, *The Reconstruction of Belief*, p. 510-511.
[588] Gore, *Dissertations*, p. 80.

believed in his own infallibility as a teacher of religious truth, and the Church of Christ has ever since regarded his Epistles as part of an infallible literature. But it is equally clear that Paul believed his knowledge of religious truth to be limited. Infallibility does not imply omniscience any more than limited knowledge implies error. … When we say that a teacher is infallible we do not mean that his knowledge is encyclopaedic, but merely that, when he does teach, he is incapable of propounding as truth that which in point of fact is not true[589]

Christ's conscious grasp of the truth about the nature, character and purposes of God, about his relationship with his heavenly Father, and about his mission to bring about the dawning of the Kingdom of God on earth must have grown and developed over time. Like all human beings, his human mental powers grew and expanded as he matured from infancy to adulthood; no doubt he also learned and pondered the Scriptures throughout his many years in Nazareth, and experienced in prayer more and more, in his human range of consciousness, the intimate love of his heavenly Father. An "infallible" grasp of religious truth, therefore, does not necessarily imply at any stage of life a "perfect," "complete," or "comprehensive" understanding of truth; what Jesus knew as a youth was subject to deeper penetration and clarification over time through years of deeper prayer, meditation and life experience. The gift of infallibility from the Holy Spirit simply means that in his conscious human journey into divine truth, the truth that he came to earth to live and to reveal, Jesus never wandered off into the darkness of error, or led others into error.

For Gore and Weston, Christ's finality and infallibility as a channel of divine truth also does not preclude the need for the

---

[589] Liddon, *The Divinity of Our Lord and Saviour Jesus Christ*, p. 198.

The Incarnation

Church to grow in its comprehension of what God has revealed to humanity through Him. Gore put it best in *The Reconstruction of Belief*:

> [C]hrist and the doctrine of Christ is so rich and manifold that it will take all races and all ages and all sorts of individual characters to realize all that it involves. ... [A]s Jew and Greek and Roman and Frenchman and Englishman and German have contributed, so will Indian and Chinese and Japanese. It will take all mankind to understand Him in who dwells all the fullness of God bodily.[590]

Some kenotic theologians have been willing to entertain broader notions of fallibility in the human mind and teachings of Jesus — for example, they claim that despite the fact that he was God Incarnate, and filled with the Holy Spirit, the human mind of Jesus was partially and at least temporarily *corrupted* by his ancient culture, even on aspects of his understanding of God, humanity, and moral principles. As we saw in the previous chapter of this book, David Brown argued that in Jesus' kenotic struggle by the Holy Spirit to overcome the limitations and blindness of aspects of the culture in which he was nurtured, by the start of his public ministry he may not have fully succeeded in transcending those distorted perspectives, even on matters of religious and moral significance (for example, on the role of women in the Church, given that Jesus only chose men to be apostles; on the naming of God, whom Jesus taught us to address as Father but never as Mother; and on the dignity of the Gentiles, whom Jesus referred to as "dogs" in Mark 7:27; on this passage see Part Two, Chapter One of this book). A complete transcendence of the blind-spots of one's own culture (allegedly) is impossible for human beings to attain; but, some theologians claim, Jesus did manifest at least the "trajectory" of that process of

---

[590] Gore, *The Reconstruction of Belief*, p. 614-615.

transcendence, a trajectory toward greater dignity and equality for all people, and therefore the endpoint of this trajectory is what is truly authoritative in his teachings and example, not the particular perspective which his human mind had attained in the context of first century Palestine.[591]

Of course, the attempt to discern in the teachings and example of Jesus what truly "transcends" the cultural blind spots to which he was allegedly and partially bound is fraught with subjectivist peril, for usually the truths that we believe transcend his own time and culture are those that happen to agree with our own. We end up sifting the teachings of Jesus for trajectories that confirm what we already believe on other grounds. Either Jesus Christ really is "the Light of the world" (Jn 8:12), or we are the ones with the greater fullness of light, a light that he only dimly and partially perceived from his vantage point in the distant past. It is one thing to draw out the full implications of Christ's teaching in the legitimate process of the development of doctrine (see, for example, *Catechism of*

---

[591]   David Brown seems to lean toward such a view in *Divine Humanity*, p. 143, 154, 209-219. However, he does not mention the issue of addressing God in prayer and worship as both Father and Mother in the context of that discussion. In *God in a Single Vision*, p. 65, he also suggests that Jesus probably believed that the world would end within a single generation (e.g. Mk 9:1 and 13:24ff), and did not foresee any mission to the Gentiles (e.g. Gal 2:11ff). But these are highly contentious issues in New Testament studies. For example, Evangelical scholar John Wenham in *Christ and the Bible* (Guildford, Surrey: Eagle, 1993), p. 71-79, offers two ways of reading the eschatological discourses in the Gospels that do not involve Jesus making any claim of an imminent end of the world; see also Catholic scholar David B. Currie in *What Jesus Really Said about the End of the World* (San Diego: Catholic Answers Press, 2012) on the hidden, chiastic structure of the eschatological discourse in Matthew; and see the extraordinary entry titled "End of the World?" in *The Ignatius Catholic Study Bible* (San Francisco: Ignatius Press, 2010), p. 50, which argues that Jesus' entire discourse in Mk 13 and Mt 24-25 is an extension of his cryptic comment in Mt 24:2 and Mk 13:2 predicting the destruction of the Temple in Jerusalem. On this reckoning Jesus was not referring directly to the end of the world at all in the so-called eschatological discourses in the gospels (surely a highly unlikely interpretation, given the way the early Church Fathers often read portions of these texts).

The Incarnation

the Catholic Church, entry 94); it is another to take Christ's teaching to "endpoints" that we desire them to reach, rather than ones that are necessarily implicit in his teachings and example.

In response to similar viewpoints expressed in his own day, C.S. Lewis once wrote:

> [I]f we once accept the doctrine of the Incarnation, we must surely be very cautious in suggesting that any circumstance in the culture of first-century Palestine was a hampering or distorting influence upon his teaching. Do we suppose that the scene of God's earthly life was selected at random? — that some other scene would have served better?[592]

Brian Hebblethwaite made much the same point in his book *In Defence of Christianity* (2005):

> The genuine humanity of the incarnate Lord did not only have to be particular, limited, and historically and culturally conditioned, as all humanity is. It had to be *thus* limited in the specifically Jewish way in which Jesus's humanity was limited. For only a Jew, with a Jew's inheritance, a Jew's faith and understanding and a Jew's hope, could be God incarnate. That faith alone could sustain the very image of God's being. It was, so Christians believe, for that purpose that God, in his providence, fashioned the Jewish way of being human and the Jewish way of being religious.[593]

To be sure, this consideration alone does not guarantee that Jesus of Nazareth was infallible in every respect. Unlike

---

[592] C.S. Lewis, *The World's Last Night and Other Essays* (New York: Harcourt, Brace and World, 1960), p. 56-57.
[593] Hebblethwaite, *In Defence of Christianity*, p. 94

Weston, most contemporary kenotic theologians have been willing to grant that as a Jew of first century Palestine, Jesus must have shared not only in some of the limitations, but even in some of the illusions of scientific and historical knowledge common to people of his time and culture, and that these errors are sometimes manifest in his teaching. Thus, it is said, Jesus probably believed along with his contemporaries that Moses wrote the entire Torah (Mk 10:3) and David the entire Psalter (Mt 22:41-46), and perhaps also that many physical and mental illnesses were caused by demonic infestation (e.g. Mt 17:14-21).[594] These theologians usually argue, however, that

---

[594] Gore argued in *The Reconstruction of Belief*, p. 482-489, that in the debate in the Gospels over the meaning of Psalm 110 (Mt 22:41-46; Mk 12:35-37; Lk 20:41-44), Jesus was just accommodating himself to the common opinion of his day that all of the Psalms were written by King David. Gore claims that Christ may not have known who actually wrote this Psalm, and that in any case he was not positively teaching Davidic authorship because that is not the point he was trying to make. Rather, Jesus was saying to the scribes, in effect: "Given that you teach that David wrote this Psalm, and that the Messiah is to be a son of David, how can you explain the fact that David here calls the Messiah his 'Lord'?" A similar argument is often made regarding Christ's ascription of Mosaic authorship to the Torah: a mere accommodation to his listener's about Mosaic authorship in order to make a deeper point about moral theology (Mk 10:3). Gore also concedes that "there must have been in our Lord's mind a world of 'ordinary' knowledge which he shared with his contemporaries ... which was part of the furniture and limitation of His real humanity; but this he did not teach" (p. 878). In short, for Gore it was the teachings of Christ — and not the entire contents of his human mind — that was always delivered with "infallible certitude." Of course, it could very well be that the Torah was substantially authored by Moses, even though later Hebrew writers (also under divine inspiration) edited his original work; and it could be that David was the original author of most of the Psalms, or at least of the substance of Psalm 110. Moreover, demonic possession is sometimes manifested in sickness, seizures, and self-inflicted injuries (see Mt 8:16; Mk 1:26, 5:2-5), and so it is not clear that Jesus mistook a case of epilepsy for demonic possession in Matthew 17. Harder to explain is the charge that Jesus was mistaken about the time of the reign of the High Priest Abiathar (Mk 2:25-26) and the lineage of the prophet Zechariah (Mt 23:35). For an in-depth rebuttal of ascription of historical error to Jesus in both cases, see John Wenham, *Christ and the Bible*, p. 81-87; on possible Davidic authorship of Psalm 110, see Wenham, p. 80. On the case of Abiathar, see also Trent Horn, *Hard Sayings: A Catholic*

such errors will be found to affect only peripheral matters, not the center of his teaching and what he came to reveal: especially the nature, character, and saving purposes of God, and the ethics of the Kingdom.

Again, most kenotic incarnational theologians seem to agree that the divine Son must have chosen to sojourn among us at just the right time, so that under the conditions of a human life and consciousness, he might be able to discern and articulate in his human mind, and effectively communicate to all subsequent generations, the saving truths about God and humanity. Moreover, most seem to hold that the Incarnation necessarily implies the total surrender of his human mind and will to the Holy Spirit, the Spirit of Truth (Jn 16:13). This means that Jesus would have been entirely free from the blindness of willful prejudice and intellectual arrogance that affects all other human perspectives. Besides, if the socio-cultural conditioning process of the human soul of Jesus Christ actually led him into errors or half-truths on matters of religious and ethical significance, then Jesus himself did not seem to have had the humility to admit his own fallibility in this respect. For he assumes, and frequently alludes to the fact, that his teachings are entirely trustworthy: e.g., "Truly I say to you" (Mt 5:18, 5:26, 6:2, 6:5, 6:16); "You have heard it was said, but I say to you" (Mt 5:21-22, 5:27-28, 5:31-32, 5:33-34, 5:38-39, 5:43-44); "No one knows the Father except the Son, and any one to whom the Son chooses to reveal him (Mt 11:27; Lk 10:22); and again: "Heaven and earth will pass away, but my words will not pass away" (Mt 24:35; Lk 21:33).

These considerations, along with those we touched upon earlier in this book, should be enough to establish that the human mind of Jesus was preserved from error, and therefore he was an entirely trustworthy teacher (and in that sense

Approach to Answering Biblical Difficulties (El Cajon, CA: Catholic Answers Press, 2016), p. 127-128.

"infallible") *at least* on any matter of significance to his revelatory mission (such as matters of faith and morals).[595] Brian Hebblethwaite summed up the heart of the matter when he wrote:

> [W]e believe that this mysterious and ineffable God, out of pure love for mankind, has made himself known to us in the most direct and comprehensible way possible, by coming amongst us as one of us, and sharing our life, its heights and depths, its joys and sorrows. ...

> [I]t is the personal presence of God this side of the divide between infinite and finite that is supremely revelatory of who God is. By this act, God overcomes the vagueness and dread that limit the experience which elsewhere and otherwise men can and do enjoy. If Jesus is God *in person*, then our knowledge of God has an intelligible, personal, human focus. In Jesus' character and acts we see the character and acts of God himself in terms we can readily understand. At the same time God does not overwhelm us in his self-

---

[595] It is also important to point out that in Catholic ecclesiology, the infallibility of the teaching authority of the Church is analogous to, but not the exact equivalent of the infallibility of Christ as teacher and revealer, as discussed above. Christ's teachings are not only supernaturally guided, and free from all error, but also implicitly comprehensive in scope: along with his deeds, the seed of all later, legitimate developments of Christian doctrine. That is why St. Jude can speak of his revelatory teachings and deeds, as delivered to the apostles, as comprising "the faith once and for all delivered to the saints" (Jude 3). The Church's charism of infallibility is merely derivative and interpretive in form: in other words, her task and charism is faithfully to guard and proclaim the revealed truth as it is in Christ, penetrate it ever more deeply, express it ever more clearly, and unfold its implications more completely for the needs of every generation, with the help of the Holy Spirit, so that Christ's promise can be fulfilled: "you will know the truth, and the truth will make you free." (Jn 8:32; cf. 16:13, and I Tim 3:15).

revelation. Instead he invites and wins our personal response.[596]

Here we also need to remember what we established in Part One, Chapter Four of this book: that the logical coherence of the Moderate Kenotic Model of the Incarnation is incompatible with Jesus ever holding false beliefs. *A Jesus who was infallible only in some areas of knowledge, such as faith and morals does not fit with Moderate KM.* Weston was therefore the only consistent moderate Kenoticist on this point.[597]

In fact, it is possible to develop a perspective on this aspect of the mystery of the Incarnation that fits well with Moderate KM, and with Weston's concerns. In his human soul Jesus certainly was not omniscient because a human mind is a limited, finite receptacle of truth. As a fully human being, there were some things he could not and did not know (e.g. Christ's confession of ignorance about the exact day and hour of the end of the world in Mk 13:32). Thus, in his human mind, Jesus did not know all *possible* things, which would involve an infinite range of knowledge (see Mt 26:39: "Father, if it be possible, let this chalice pass from me"; in his human soul Jesus did not know if it was still possible for him to be spared what he saw up to that point as God's will regarding the Cross). Nevertheless, from the Holy Spirit Jesus possessed a relatively universal knowledge of *actual* things: a supernatural, infused knowledge of all that he needed to know to be the Incarnate Son and Savior of the world (Jn 1:14 and Col 2:2-3; cf. Jn 16:30). To put it more precisely: *Jesus must have known all actual things that pertained in any way to his mission, to his teaching, and to the course of his life.* Thus, he may not have needed to know molecular physics or trigonometry, because these subjects did not come up during his life at all, and did not form any part of his mission, or of what he came to reveal. But Jesus did need

---

[596] Hebblethwaite, *The Incarnation*, p. 22-23.
[597] Weston, *The One Christ*, p. 7 and 226.

to know God as his Father, the Kingdom he was empowered by the Spirit to proclaim and inaugurate, the secrets of human hearts he came to save, and the nature, character and purposes of God he had come to reveal.[598]

Until the 20th century it was not clear how a human being could possess such extensive, supernatural knowledge, and still undergo an authentic human journey of learning and growth, and real human development in the understanding of himself, of human relationships, and of the wider world. Modern depth psychology, however, enables us to locate Christ's relatively universal knowledge in the vast ocean of his *subconscious*, where it would have been stored and acted, first of all, as *a regulator of everything Jesus would have been taught in his youth*. Whenever he was taught a falsehood by his elders and teachers on any subject, this would have resulted in a dissonance between his conscious and subconscious mind, an intuitive sense that something was wrong with what was being proposed to him, which would have led him, with the help of the Holy Spirit, at least to reserve judgment and refuse to embrace the false proposition. At every stage of his growth in human knowledge on a conscious level, therefore, he would have been preserved from believing falsehoods. Also, this store of subconscious, relatively universal knowledge would have acted as *the reservoir of the supernatural truths that Christ was sent to reveal to humanity as part of his mission*. By the Holy Spirit, these truths would have risen to his daylight consciousness at just the right moments of his life and ministry (e.g. see Jn 7:6-40). This was not an inner ocean of truth that Jesus could just dip into at any time by a conscious act of will (after all, human beings cannot access the contents of their subconscious mind anytime they wish). Rather, it is something to which the divine Son would have had access in his incarnate state only by the prompting and guidance of the Holy Spirit, especially during prayer, and in meditation on the Scriptures. In this way, it would be similar to the gift of divinely

---

[598] See *Catechism of the Catholic Church*, entries 492-493.

infused knowledge that is bestowed on authentic prophets of the Lord. Christ's relatively universal knowledge in his human subconscious, therefore, could be seen as a supremely extensive form of the charism of prophecy from the Holy Spirit. Presumably, a human mind can receive a measure of such divinely infused, supernatural knowledge without necessarily violating the boundaries of what it means to be authentically human.   Finally, this internal reservoir of relatively universal truth would have enabled him to exercise *a universal, redemptive love in and through his sacred humanity*, providing him *with a subconscious vision of every single human being for whom he was giving his life on the Cross*. As St. Paul implies, Jesus did not just die for humanity in general, but for each and every human being, past, present, and future: "the Son of God, who loved me, and gave himself for me" (Gal 2:20; cf. *Catechism of the Catholic Church*, entry 478: "Jesus knew and loved us each and all during his life, his agony, and his Passion, and gave himself up for each one of us …."). By the Holy Spirit Jesus possessed in his subconscious an infused, prophetic knowledge of all that he needed to know to be the Incarnate Son and Savior of the world. But this in no way interfered with his journey of growth in knowledge and wisdom on a conscious level throughout his life, from his infancy to his death and resurrection (Lk 2:52), and an ever clearer, conscious apprehension of his identity and mission (Lk 2:50, 3:22).[599]

---

[599] Whether or not Jesus also possessed the beatific vision and beatific knowledge during his sojourn on earth, as St. Thomas Aquinas taught, limitations of space require us to leave all discussion of that ongoing debate among Catholic theologians to the second volume in this series. Suffice it to say here that it may be possible to argue that Jesus did possess the beatific vision, without seeing it as an additional source of supernatural knowledge, and without violating the limitations and conditions of an authentic human journey. The best keys to this mystery seem to be found in the writings of 20th century Catholic theologians Karl Adam, and Bertrand De Margerie, SJ.

2) **Second, the Incarnational Exemplarist approach shows us that God's love for us is truly self-sacrificial.**

God the Son himself lived out for us this revelatory and exemplary human life and martyrdom. As Jesus Christ he has lived in human flesh the ethics of the Kingdom — the Way of faith and love even in the face of oppression and death — and thereby sealed it in the human memory and imagination forever. He has shown us the Way in person. In fact, even if we say that it was not strictly necessary for God to show us the Way himself — that he could have inspired a solely human figure to do it — it was at least fitting that he do so. It was fitting because his purpose was not only to communicate to us the Way of faithful love, but also to give us a *powerful motive* to follow him: by convincingly demonstrating his love for us. In other words, *if God is truly a loving Creator, and if he wished clearly to express that love in a way that might move us to return his love, then he could do so by taking flesh and showing us the Way he intended us to live with the help of the Holy Spirit, even at great cost to himself. This would convincingly demonstrate his love for us, and might thereby move us to open our hearts to his Holy Spirit, and to love and trust him in return*: "that those who live might live no longer for themselves, but for him who for their sakes died and was raised" (II Cor 5:15). Besides, as John Austin Baker wrote (quoted above): Divine Love would never call upon someone else to undertake the costly and decisive work needed for our salvation; he would never say "I will find someone else to do the job." Divine Love comes himself. Perhaps Keith Ward summarised this whole approach best when he wrote that by the depths of his self-sacrifice for us, God has acted to turn our hearts away from cynicism and callousness. As Jesus Christ

he shares our condition of suffering and estrangement. He shows us the way to escape — by self-sacrifice. And if we allow him to, he makes possible our escape by beginning to transform our lives from within.[600]

3) **Third, we should remember that God Incarnate accomplished all this for us while we were yet sinners. In this way, God's love was shown to be truly merciful.**

Christ came into his own world unmerited and unexpected, and at the culmination of his exemplary human life, he suffered patiently at the hands of sinful humanity. This convincingly demonstrated the extent of his offer of reconciliation, and the depth of his patient, forgiving love. As St. Paul put it" "In Christ God was reconciling the world to himself" (II Cor 5:19). And once again, it was more fitting for him to show us this himself, than merely inspire someone else to do it. An offer of forbearance and reconciliation is more convincingly made in person, not by proxy — especially if that offer is a costly one to make. As F.W. Dillistone wrote:

> God does not hold past enmity against the offender, nor does He allow present hostility to repel his advances. He makes the gracious offer of reconciliation even to the point of accepting death at the hands of those who will not heed His advances. His wounds, His sacrificial death, now speaks the word of reconciliation more eloquently than even His life of love.[601]

In the Catholic world also, Incarnational Exemplarism has been very popular over the past half-century. Here we will offer just one example, since it is one with the added merit of being so beautifully expressed. In his book *God's Mercy Revealed: Healing for a Broken World* (2005),

---

[600] Ward, *The Living God*, p. 117.
[601] Dillistone, *The Christian Understanding of Atonement*, p. 277; cf. Quick, *Doctrines of the Creed*, p. 84.

Monsignor Peter Magee, a former member of the Diplomatic Service of the Holy See, unfolded for his readers the mystery of the Cross as the supreme revelation of God's merciful love. These excerpts from Magee's work make a fitting conclusion to the case for the Incarnational Exemplarist approach to the doctrine of Redemption:

> [W]hy was Jesus crucified? The short and truest answer is, to save us from sin and death. But why would he do that? And why did he have to be crucified for that to happen? ...
>
> Since God had created us free, he wanted to find a way of rescuing us from sin and death that would still respect our freedom and yet manifest his immense desire to bring us back, to redeem us, to save us for himself ....
>
> The Son of God became incarnate, one of us, so that we might believe in his enduring love. The Incarnation is so incredibly bold and daring that those of other religions, and even many Christians — perhaps some who read this — cannot believe it ....
>
> Jesus did not manifest his divinity all at once, precisely because he wanted to respect our freedom and not overwhelm us. Rather, he appeals to our minds with the proclamation of his truth, the Gospel, the Good News, the annunciation of God's salvation near at hand for those who will freely believe. He also appeals to our hearts and even to our bodies by performing signs and miracles to excite our faith, to draw us to himself. He appeals to the deep sense of loss and confusion within us by showing mercy, by forgiving sins.
>
> Yet he knows, as we all do, that the stubbornness of pride will keep some from believing in him. Indeed, he aroused the furious anger and rejection of hardened sinners. He knew in his life on earth that rejection would lead to slander, derision, jealousy and even violence and death. Still, he had to be faithful to the will of the Father and to his own will. He had to prove

to us that no matter what we would do, he would remain faithful. He would offer the possibility of redemption to whoever would willingly receive it.

It is at this point that the Cross comes into view. Christ did not want the Cross for the sake of the Cross; he wanted *whatever it would cost* to win over our hearts to faith …. Jesus knew that the Cross would be his fate, and he transformed it into the very instrument of our salvation. For in being crucified, in surrendering himself freely to death out of loving fidelity to the Father and to us, he fulfilled all the prophecies of the Old Testament and brought Judaism to consummation in the sacrifice of the Cross. He became the innocent Lamb who was slain and whose blood saves us from the angel of death and damnation …. His death opened up for us the passage, the corridor, from the hell of sin to the heaven of grace and love ….

We must never let ourselves forget the Cross, for on it hangs the hope of every sinner, however miserable; the comfort of every sick person, however pained; the joy of every holy heart, however tried …. *The Cross speaks of persevering patience, unconditional forgiveness, limitless compassion* …. The Cross can break the hardest of hearts …. The Cross helps us to remember the price of our salvation, and to stir up our hearts in love for Jesus, whose very personal memento it is.[602]

Clearly, an incarnational version of Exemplarism adds additional and vital insights to the non-incarnational form, and helps us develop a much more powerful understanding of Christ's saving work. Nevertheless, **at least two major questions remain unanswered for any Incarnational Exemplarist doctrine of Redemption.**

First, *are there any conditions that Divine Love must fulfill so that God's offer of forgiveness for our sins — his offer of full*

---

[602] Peter Magee, *God's Mercy Revealed: Healing for a Broken World* (Cincinnati, OH: Servant Books, 2005), p. 43-47 and 42; italics mine.

pardon and transforming grace — can be made on a just basis? Or can a loving God simply forget about our past sins, and "let bygones be bygones," so to speak, for the sake of his work of reconciliation? In other words, is it not the clear witness of Scripture and of the mainstream Christian tradition down through the ages that it was precisely on the Cross that Jesus our Savior accomplished what was needed to deal with the guilt and power of our sins once and for all?

Anglican theologians such as Leonard Hodgson, Austin Farrer, John Austin Baker, Brian Hebblethwaite, Kathryn Tanner and John Milbank taught that God is free to cancel the debt of objective guilt for our sins unconditionally, without requiring any kind of compensation. Baker wrote that God's "forgiveness" simply means his suffering acceptance of the circumstances created by evil as a base from which to work for new goods. In this way the Cross becomes the manifestation of God's unconditional, and boundlessly patient love.[603] Milbank wrote that "real, positive Christological forgiveness is … not reactive, since it is only the sustained giving of the original gift, despite its refusal."[604] Hodgson pointed to the way that Christ "absorbed" the evil of his murderers by his forgiving and compassionate love on Calvary, and thereby "cut short" the power of evil to spread any further.[605] Anglican theologian (and former Archbishop of Canterbury) Rowan Williams put forward a similar perspective in *God With Us* (2017):

---

[603] Baker, *The Foolishness of God*, p. 306-307; similarly, see Hodgson, *The Doctrine of the Atonement*, p. 61-62, and Brown, *God in a Single Vision*, p. 150. Kathryn Tanner is emphatic on this point: "The cross simply does not save us from our debts to God by paying them. If anything, the cross saves us from the consequences of a debt economy in conflict with God's own economy of grace by cancelling it" (*Jesus, Humanity, and the Trinity*, p. 88), which presumably means that God's forgiveness is universal and boundless, since we have no real moral debts to God at all, at least none that he does not cancel unconditionally.
[604] Milbank, *Being Reconciled*, p. 68; see his discussion of Aquinas on this point, p. 64-67.
[605] Ibid. (Hodgson), p. 78-79.

How then does the execution of Jesus show the love of God? How does it become that sort of sign? We have a hint in Luke 23.34 and in the first letter of Peter 2.23. In Luke, as Jesus is crucified he says, 'Father forgive.' And in Peter's letter we are reminded that when Jesus is abused he doesn't retaliate: 'When they hurled their insults at him, he did not retaliate.' Here is a divine love that cannot be defeated by violence: we do our worst, and we still fail to put God off. We reject, exclude, and murder the one who bears the love of God in his words and work, and that love continues to do exactly what it always did.

...

And that's the good news: the good news of our powerlessness to change God's mind. Which is just as well, because God's mind is focused upon us for mercy and for life. God will always survive our sin, our failure. God is never exhausted by what we do. God is always there, capable of remaking the relationships we break again and again. That's the sign of the cross, the sign of freedom.[606]

All of this rings true as far as it goes: the Cross is indeed the supreme instance and sign of God's patient, forbearing, unconditional love, a love that forever absorbs the power of evil, and thereby limits its spread, inspiring others to do the same. Nevertheless, for most of the history of Christendom, this would not have passed muster as a sufficient statement of what Jesus Christ accomplished on the Cross for us, and how the Cross supremely reveals God's love.

The basic Incarnational Exemplarist perspective on the Cross was summed up by Brian Hebblethwaite, who insisted that "God's forgiving love does not *depend* upon the death of Christ, but rather is *manifested* and *enacted* in it."[607] But this way of expressing Christ's saving work on the Cross hardly seems adequate, since there is no theologian (at least none known to this author) who would say that God could

---

[606] Rowan Williams, *God With Us: The meaning of the cross and resurrection. Then and now* (London: SPCK: 2017), p. 8-9.
[607] Hebblethwaite, *The Incarnation*, p.37; italics mine.

not love us until he first died for us on the Cross. What many *have* said is that the Cross must be a manifestation of *all* of God's perfections if it is to be the pinnacle of his self-revelation (Jn 17:1), and one of those perfections is surely divine "holiness" or "justice." So our question remains unanswered: *in the very act of manifesting and enacting his love for us on the Cross, did God also, at the same time, to be true to himself, need to enact and manifest his holiness and righteous judgment upon our sin?* For example, to use traditional theological language: did God in Christ need to "pay the penalty due to us for our sins" in order to set us free from our moral debt, or did he need to make "satisfaction" or compensation for our objective guilt by his passion and death in order to express his love for sinners on a just basis? Did he also need to "merit" all the graces we need for our sanctification, so that those graces could be poured out upon repentant sinners on a just basis? If he needed to do some/all of these things in order to save us in accord with his own nature as both just and merciful, then it certainly would be a clear and powerful demonstration of his love if he accomplished all this for us primarily on the Cross. And this would certainly justify the Christian tradition of seeing in the Cross God's decisive saving act, and the supreme and definitive revelation of his love for humanity.

A second unanswered question for Incarnational Exemplarism concerns the *scope* of God's saving work through Jesus Christ. If the principal thing that he accomplished for us through his life, death, and resurrection was to *show us* something — e.g., to *demonstrate* the depths of God's forgiving and patient love — then it would seem that his saving work only makes a difference to those who know about it. It is very limited in scope, and does not in any way change the state of affairs between God and humanity as a whole. Anglican theologian Vernon White spelled out this complex predicament in his book *Atonement and Incarnation* (1991):

> '[K]knowledge' must not supplant 'effective action' as the defining characteristic of Christ's work .... Revelation conceived primarily as saving knowledge must either insist on the uniqueness of the Christ event and limit the possibility of salvation to those who know it, or else it is forced to deny that

uniqueness in order to widen the scope of potential salvation. But revelation conceived primarily as saving action is saved the embarrassment of such a dilemma ....

[S]alvation (including its reconciling effects) is constituted primarily by divine action, not by human knowledge of that action. The point is that an action may have an effect where the identity of the agent is unknown or unrecognized (as an unconscious man may be saved from the sea by a stranger he never knew). The anonymous reconciling work of Christ may be effective far beyond the bounds of Christendom. Indeed, some of the positive reconciling values of other religions may *be* Christ, the *logos spermatikos*, under another name.[608]

White is not saying here that it makes no difference at all whether people come to know the gospel of the Incarnation and the Cross. He is merely pointing out that in some versions of traditional Christianity, at least some of the effects of Christ's saving work in his life and death on the Cross were considered to be real and potentially decisive even for those who, through no fault of their own, remain in a state of "invincible ignorance" of the gospel, people who in this life never had a fair chance to become believers (e.g. because they lived before the coming of Christ, or outside the reach of Christian missions). By contrast, if Jesus Christ's saving work consists only in a *demonstration* of his love, intended to move human hearts, then it can only move the hearts of those who come to hear of it and believe it. Anyone in invincible ignorance of the gospel who comes to salvation in other ways, therefore, would have to do so *entirely apart from Christ's saving work in the Incarnation and on the Cross* — which would seem to be a direct contradiction of the New Testament: "For in him all the fullness of God was pleased to dwell, and *through him, to reconcile to himself all things*, whether on earth or in heaven, *making peace by the blood of his cross*" (Col 1:20; cf. Col 2: 13-14; Rom 3:23-24).

---

[608] Vernon White, *Incarnation and Atonement* (Cambridge: Cambridge University Press, 1991), p. 23-24 and 20.

Is there a way to conceive of Christ's saving work through the Incarnation and the Cross as decisive for human salvation *especially*, but *not exclusively*, for those who hear and receive the gospel? To find such a perspective, we will have to move beyond Exemplarist theories of Atonement.

Sacrificial Theories of Atonement

Sacrificial theories state that Jesus has made the one perfect offering of loving obedience to the Father in his life and death. On the basis of that sacrificial self-offering, the risen and ascended Lord now stands as our advocate in heaven. In union with his perfect offering and heavenly intercession, our souls can be cleansed of sin's defilement: we can be sanctified by his life within us, and also (in some versions of the Sacrificial Theory), freed from our moral debt to God.

Sacrificial theories usually harken back to the Temple worship of ancient Israel. Unfortunately, the sacrificial system of the ancient Israelites is very difficult for post-Enlightenment minds to comprehend. Rowan Williams offered a helpful summary of what biblical scholarship can tell us about it:

> We can begin to see just how much is going on in the language of sacrifice [in the Old Testament], and how very hard it is to push it into a tidy system .... [I]n the middle of it all is one great governing idea: a sacrifice is something given over to God, most dramatically when it is a life given over with the shedding of blood. That gift of life or blood somehow casts a veil over the sin or sickness or disorder of an individual or of a whole people. It removes the consequences of sin; it offers the possibility of a relationship unclouded by guilt with God; it is a gift that stands between God and the failures and disorders of the world. The gift is given — and it's a costly gift because it's about life and blood — so that peace and communication may be re-established between heaven and

earth. And this was always symbolized by the fact that a sacrificial animal would be cooked and cut up and shared in a meal, which expressed not only fellowship with one another, but restored fellowship with God.

It's a gift that in the language of the Old Testament turns away the anger and displeasure of God. In the jargon of theology it 'propitiates' God, it makes things all right with him again, but it also brings him back into active relationship with the world. At the highest point, sacrifice establishes — or re-establishes, confirms — the *covenant*, God's alliance with God's people. The gift is given, and in response God not only covers over sin, but promises actively to be there for his people.[609]

1) Pure Sacrificial Theories

According to O.C. Quick, one central intention of Israel's sacrificial system was that "the blood or offered life of a sinless victim should cleanse the offerors, or things used in worship, from the defilement of sin."[610] In other words, each sin was seen as a disease or taint which stains the soul, weakens the will, and impairs our power to see what is right, and to do it.[611] In Christian and New Testament terms, the "defilement" of sin consists in these deleterious effects on our souls, from the obstruction or loss of the life-giving Holy Spirit. This "stain" of sin makes us unable to commune properly with God. Our unrepentant hearts are hardened, we have "hearts of stone," as the Old Testament says, that are closed to the Holy Spirit. Innocent blood alone, when offered to God (so the ancient Jews believed), carried with it the almost magical power to cleanse sinners of their defilement.

Animal sacrifices, however, were eventually seen to be imperfect. For animals were sacrificed against their will, and did not share in human nature and human temptations. Echoing the theology of the Book of

---

[609] Williams, *God With Us*, p. 24-25.
[610] Quick, *Doctrines of the Creed*, p. 232.
[611] Ibid., p. 218-220.

Hebrews, Quick explained: "only the life which has conquered temptation *in man's own nature* can therefore apply to that nature a fully sanctifying power."[612]

Jesus Christ came into the world as both priest and victim of the perfect sacrifice: he sacrificed *himself* for us. According to Eric Mascall, Christ made the perfect human self-offering of obedient love to the heavenly Father, in his life and his death, an offering we could no longer make.[613] Today, by identifying ourselves with Christ's perfect self-offering, especially through Baptism and the Eucharist, we can be mystically united with him and his heavenly intercession for us (Heb 5:6, 6:20, 7:25; I Jn 2:1), and receive the renewal of the life of his Holy Spirit in our hearts (I Cor 12:12-13). Incorporated into Christ in this way, our lives can be cleansed of sin's destructive power.[614] O.C. Quick summed up this theory of Atonement (what we shall call the "Pure" Sacrificial Theory) in these words:

> **The atoning sacrifice of Christ has in itself made a real and objective difference, beyond the mere revealing Of God's constant love. ... [O]n the cross the sinless manhood was offered so that, having passed into the heavenly world, its sanctifying and life-giving power might be available to sinful man.**[615]

Here we already have an answer to one of the two "unanswered questions" left over from our survey of Incarnational Exemplarist

---

[612] Ibid., p. 234.

[613] Eric Mascall, *Corpus Christi* (London: Longmans, 1965), p. 95.

[614] Ibid., p. 102-104. The notion of incorporation into Christ in these ways as the primary means of sharing in the benefits of his incarnation, death, and resurrection, was a prominent theme in the writings of St. Thomas Aquinas. On this see Rik Van Nieuwenhove's essay "'Bearing the Marks of Christ's Passion': Aquinas' Soteriology" in Rik Van Nieuwenhove and Joseph Wawrykow, eds., *The Theology of Thomas Aquinas* (Notre Dame, In: University of Notre Dame Press 2010), p. 287-296. Similarly, see Kereszty, *Jesus Christ: Fundamentals of Christology*, p. 344-346.

[615] Quick, *Doctrines of the Creed*, p. 235 and 236-237.

theories of Atonement. On this version of the Sacrificial Theory, the saving work of Jesus Christ makes an *objective difference* to God's relationship with all of humanity even before people are able to hear and receive the gospel message. The saving agent of sanctification, Jesus Christ, passes through death and into the eternal realm, making the power of his faithful and obedient love in principle available to all.[616] Salvation through the Cross and Resurrection of Christ is therefore *especially*, but *not exclusively* available to those who become believers.

It was Vernon White who sought to develop in greater depth this version of the Sacrificial Theory. White drew heavily upon the Book of Hebrews chapter 5 (especially Heb 5:8-9) and Patristic theories of "recapitulation" dating back to St. Irenaeus of Lyons in the second century. In these, the governing idea was that Jesus Christ had to "pass through" every aspect of the human journey, and every stage of the story of his people Israel, in order to offer sanctifying grace to sinful humanity. White put it this way:

> God 'equips himself' in Christ with an experience he then offers universally through the Spirit of Christ .... Thus, God in Christ takes into his own experience that which qualifies him to reconcile, redeem, and sanctify in his relationship with all people everywhere .... [I]t is something like the mountain guide who first crosses a difficult terrain himself, in order to equip himself to take across all who follow him. It is a journey we could not make apart from him, yet we must make. It is, of course, the journey of dying to self and living wholly to God — through temptation, suffering, and death itself .... God in Jesus consistently and perfectly did the very thing which must happen to all of us: he died to self and lived to God. He does this as an individual human being under the normal conditions

---

[616] J.K. Mozley shows that this understanding of the "deifying" power of the risen and glorified Christ was also central to the soteriology of St. Athanasius in the fourth century; see J.K. Mozley, *The Doctrine of the Atonement* (London: Duckworth, 1915), p.105-106.

of a finite, fallen world, 'learning' faith as a fragile mortal. Having done this as an individual (entailing historical particularity), his spirit (transcending spatial and temporal particularity, having access to all time and space) can relate that achievement to every other individual.[617]

God overcomes evil and achieves reconciliation, first, by experiencing the consequences of [evil], both in terms of his own temptation to live for self, and in terms of the assault of other people's selfishness on him. But then, by his perfect response through such human experience, by dying to himself and living wholly for God and others, he fashions a unique relationship out of it; he is made perfect through suffering, and rises with the capacity to make others perfect through theirs.[618]

Clearly, the Pure Sacrificial Theory, as developed by Anglican theologians such as Quick, Mascall and White, adds an important element to our understanding of the Atonement.[619] It supplements the insights of the Exemplarist theories we have already explored. For this sacrificial theory tells us that the saving work of Jesus involves more than just acts done *in the past* for our benefit. As a result of his human life, death, and resurrection, perfect in love, *Jesus Christ, the divine Son Incarnate, has become a present and available power for human sanctification.* The same quality of self-giving love and faithfulness to the Father that Jesus lived on earth, he now makes available to us, through his risen and ascended life, especially (but not exclusively) by the outpouring of his Holy Spirit in the word, sacraments and fellowship of his Church, through which we are incorporated into Christ. In short, the Pure Sacrificial Theory makes an important connection between the doctrine of Redemption, and the resurrection and ascension of

---

[617] White, *Incarnation and Atonement*, p. 49-50, 53, 54-55. By his "spirit" here, White presumably meant his risen, glorified and ascended humanity.
[618] Ibid., p. 104.
[619] Similar perspectives can be found in Vincent Taylor, *The Atonement in the New Testament* (London: Epworth, 1940), p. 177-178, and 212, and H.A. Hodges, *The Pattern of the Atonement* (London: SCM, 1955), p. 28-30.

Christ[620] — a connection also made by St. Paul ("[Jesus] was put to death for our trespasses and raised for our justification"; Rom 4:25), as well as by the author of the book of Hebrews ("Although he was a Son, he learned obedience through what he suffered; and being made perfect he became the source of eternal salvation to all who obey him"; Heb 5:8). In short, our salvation is not only something done for us in the past to which we must respond today. Our very response is something accomplished in and through us by the sanctifying power of the indwelling Savior, that is, by "Christ within you, the hope of glory" (Col 1:27).

One difficulty with the Pure Sacrificial Theory is that it seems to make the Cross of Jesus merely the culmination of his whole life of self-giving love; it is not clear that anything distinctive or decisive happened on the Cross itself for our salvation —other than the fact that it transported our Savior into the realm of eternal life. For Kathryn Tanner, this is actually an advantage. "Incarnation," she claims, should be "the primary mechanism of atonement":

> Following Thomas Torrance, one can say: "Union with God in and through Jesus Christ who is one and the same being with God belongs to the inner heart of the atonement." … An incarnational model of atonement insists upon the relationship between the cross and the rest of Jesus' life, since the mechanism of salvation on the cross is at work throughout the whole of Jesus' life. And the effects of this salvific mechanism — its point — are, indeed, much clearer away from the cross than on it — for example, in Jesus' healing ministry to the sick and the outcast, the advent of the new community of God, and Jesus' resurrected life.[621]

Here the Cross is said to be an expression of the depths of God's incarnate, self-giving love, a love already on display throughout the

---

[620] Quick, *The Gospel of the New World* (London: Nisbet, 1944), p. 93-94.
[621] Kathryn Tanner, *Christ the Key* (Cambridge: Cambridge University Press, 2010), p. 252 and 262.

earlier chapters of Jesus' life. The Cross also enables the divine life that was in Jesus to pass into the eternal realm, and become a universally available gift through his risen and ascended presence in the world.

All of this may indeed be "true as far as it goes." But Tanner's admission that salvation through Christ is seen less clearly on the Cross than away from it is already a clue that something has gone amiss here. For one thing, this violates one of the most basic Christian intuitions: the intuition that traditionally made the Cross the central symbol of Christianity. Moreover, the *decisiveness* of the Cross for Christ's work of salvation lay at the very heart of the gospel message preached by St. Paul (Rom 5: 6-10; Col 1:20-21; Eph 2:16).

In addition, one of the "unanswered questions" from our discussion of the Incarnational Exemplarist Theory remains to be addressed: *are there any conditions of justice or holiness that God needs to fulfill to be true to himself, and to offer his forgiveness to us on a just basis, or can he just forget our past sins and "let bygones be bygones"?* Again, *by divine "forgiveness" we mean his act of pardoning our objective guilt (i.e., erasing our moral debt to him for our sins), coupled with his act of pouring into our hearts his sanctifying, transformative grace to enable us to overcome the crippling power of the inner disorder and corruption that strongly inclines us to sin.*

On the face of it, Scripture seems to be of two-minds about this. For example, Psalm 51 tells us that "the sacrifice acceptable to God is a broken spirit; a broken and contrite heart" (Ps 51:17). It would seem that an awakening of a spirit of penitence within us is all that is needed to enable us to receive divine forgiveness, and for God to offer that forgiveness to us in accord with his justice. On the other hand, the same Psalm later tells us that God will then "delight in right sacrifices, in burnt offerings and whole burnt offerings" (Ps 51:19) as if something in addition to our repentance, or as an expression or completion of our repentance, is also appropriate.

To answer this question, we will need to go beyond what we have called "Pure" sacrificial theories of Christ's saving work, and gain insights from other perspectives.

2) Sacrificial-Satisfaction Theories of Atonement: St. Anselm

According to Sacrificial-Satisfaction theories of Atonement, Jesus Christ's whole-life offering to the Father of obedient love, from cradle to grave, or at least his death on the Cross, "compensates" or "satisfies" Divine Justice for the moral debt of our sins. It takes away our objective guilt for sin, so that God can now pardon our sins and make his Holy Spirit and his sanctifying grace available to us on a just basis.

The Bible repeatedly tells us that "justice," "holiness" and "righteousness" are essential characteristics of God. Isaiah's favorite term for the Lord, in fact, was "the Holy One of Israel," and he does not mince words on this aspect of the divine nature: "The Lord of hosts is exalted in justice, and the Holy God shows himself holy in righteousness" (Is 5:16). Of course, it would be easy to show that by these terms the Old Testament did not mean only "retributive justice," for God's "justice" is what sets his world to rights in *every* respect, and not just by holding accountable unrepentant evildoers. For example, his justice also impels him to seek fairness and relief for the poor: "Happy is he whose help is the God of Jacob, whose hope is in the Lord his God … who executes justice for the oppressed; who gives food to the hungry" (Ps 146: 5-7).

In her magnum opus, *The Crucifixion: Understanding the Death of Jesus Christ* (2015), American Episcopalian Fleming Rutledge insisted that Jesus Christ's saving work must include the upholding of God's righteousness, so that justice is done and manifest to all. The Cross cannot be just a demonstration of the Lord's endless patience and forbearance with sinners:

> [T]here are some things that cannot go unpunished. This is not an abstract philosophical proposition. If there is to be a moral order, justice must be done and must be seen to be done. In the cross of Christ, justice is indeed seen to be done, but it is

such a strange justice that interpretation has frequently tied itself into knots trying to explain how it works. We can begin by saying this much: *contrary to the teaching of some over the years, in the crucifixion God has not declared a general amnesty.* The Christian emphasis on forgiveness and redemption has to be given its proper context, for God is not in favor of impunity. No one except a criminal is going to be satisfied with a general amnesty. *Even without reference to God's justice, our own human sense of justice demands that reparations be made, that sentences be served, that restitution be offered when there is a great offense ....*

Many of the attempts made over the years to explain the cross have arisen out of the intuition that on the cross we see some sort of justice being done .... "For Christ also dies for sins once for all, the righteous for the unrighteous, that he might bring us to God" (I Pet 3:18).[622]

Rutledge points out that Patristic and medieval Scholastic theologians were of a common mind that the human predicament of sin involves both "guilt requiring remission" and "captivity requiring deliverance."[623] Sin is what she calls "a responsible guilt for which atonement must be made," as well as "an alien power that must be driven from the field."[624] The very same message, she says, is imbedded in the New Testament: "Many interpreters have chosen to emphasize either one or the other of these, but *both* categories were of utmost importance to the apostles and Evangelists, and therefore are to us."[625] In fact, these are essentially the same two categories that in this book we have called (following the Evangelical tradition in this respect) the "objective guilt" and the "power" of sin.

---

[622] Fleming Rutledge, *The Crucifixion: Understanding the Death of Jesus Christ* (Grand Rapids: Eerdmans, 2015), p. 148; italics mine.
[623] Ibid., p. 161.
[624] Ibid., p. 181.
[625] Ibid., p. 182.

The Incarnation

The classic exponent of the Sacrificial-Satisfaction Theory of Atonement was the medieval theologian St. Anselm. In his work *Cur Deus Homo* ("Why the God-Man?"), he argued that our sins place us in moral debt to God, and this debt can only be discharged in two ways: by the wrongdoer making "satisfaction" to the offended party, or by the "punishment" of the malefactor — either way, God's offended "honor" must be compensated. But only one who is both God and man could make a compensatory satisfaction for sin on our behalf: "If it be necessary, therefore ... that [salvation] cannot be effected unless the aforesaid satisfaction be made, which none but God can make and none but man ought to make, it is necessary for the God-man to make it"(2.6).[626]

Anselm stated that a life of obedience could be required of the divine Son Incarnate, since obedience is a human duty to God, but by remaining obedient *even unto death*, Christ offers something to God which is not due, because death is the proper penalty for sin, and Jesus was innocent of all sin. Thus, by accepting death he offers to God a sufficient compensation for all human sin — indeed, his loving obedience unto death on the Cross, as the loving obedience of a divine person, was of such value to God the Father that it *more* than makes up for the debt of our sins. By his self-offering on the Cross, therefore, Christ merited a reward from the Father, which he claims now on our behalf in the form of pardons and graces poured out in abundance on those who repent and believe. *In short, the basic principles of Anselm's theory are (a) that sin is a debt to the divine honor, and (b) that atonement is made by Christ's death in the form of a satisfaction or compensation that more than covers that debt, meriting for humanity all the graces we need for salvation.*

Anselm's theory often has been criticized on the grounds that it makes sense only in a medieval context, for it seems to be based on the principle of feudal respect and "honor" owed to a sovereign. Rutledge takes pains to point out, however, that by the upholding of divine "honor," Anselm was not just referring to some medieval-cultural concept of respect, but actually to the biblical idea of divine

---

[626] Cited in Rutledge, *The Crucifixion*, p. 158.

righteousness or justice. As St. Anselm wrote in the same work: "There is nothing more just than supreme justice [righteousness], which maintains God's honor, [righteousness] in the arrangement of things, and which is nothing else but God himself" (1.13).[627] Moreover, Rutledge argues, it is a caricature of St. Anselm's thought on this subject to claim that he was only concerned with how Christ fulfills the requirements of Divine Justice. On the contrary, Anselm was concerned above all to show that God in Christ fulfilled the strictures of divine righteousness for us in order to manifest his merciful love; as St. Anselm wrote in a summary statement of what Christ had achieved: "He freed us from our sins, and from his own wrath, and from hell, and from the power of the devil, whom he came to vanquish for us, because we were unable to do it, and he purchased for us the kingdom of heaven; and by doing all these things, he manifested the greatness of his love toward us" (1.5).[628]

Anselm's theory has been subjected to criticism on other grounds as well. In particular, it seems to divorce the Son of God's saving work on the Cross from the rest of his incarnate life, so that it appears that the salvation of the world was accomplished by Christ's death alone. This would remove from the doctrine some of the insights we gleaned from Exemplarist theories of Atonement — a heavy price to pay. Besides, making Christ's entire work of redemption depend solely upon his death seems incoherent even on Anselm's own principles. We can rightly ask: what is it that makes Christ's undeserved death on the Cross, in loving obedience to his heavenly Father, a pleasing "satisfaction" to God, such that his death superabundantly compensates Divine Justice for all human sin? According to Anselm, the infinite value of Christ's death is supposed to rest on the fact that Jesus was an infinite, divine person in human flesh, not just a created, human person. By the same token, however, Christ's whole life of loving obedience to the Father also would have been infinitely pleasing to God, and not something merely owed to a benefactor (as would be the case with the loving obedience of a mere created human being in

---

[627] Ibid., p. 157. Words in brackets added by Rutledge.
[628] Ibid., p. 164.

relation to his Creator). Thus, it would appear more reasonable to say that Jesus Christ's whole-life offering, from cradle to grave, is what made a superabundant satisfaction for sin, and not his death alone. As we shall see, that is precisely the direction that St. Thomas Aquinas took the Sacrificial-Satisfaction Theory later in the Middle Ages.

The Sacrificial-Satisfaction Theory of St. Thomas Aquinas

By far the most in-depth Sacrificial-Satisfaction Theory was developed by St. Thomas Aquinas in the thirteenth century. It is not easy to summarize his perspective, because he seemed to start out as a fairly straightforward disciple of St. Anselm on this subject, and then gradually worked out his own distinctive version of the theory culminating in his *Summa Theologiae*.[629] Still, we can outline the main features of St. Thomas's mature perspective without great difficulty.[630]

Aquinas argues that in God's nature, Divine Mercy and Divine Justice coincide: They are one in the simplicity of God's essence. God is always and everywhere just and merciful, at one and the same time. When God acts mercifully, he does not act against justice, but, in a sense, goes beyond it. In other words, God's justice always furthers his work of mercy, and never detracts from it. Aquinas writes: "The work of divine justice always presupposes the work of mercy and is based upon it" (ST I.21.4).

Humanity was certainly in a dire predicament after the fall of Adam and Eve. However, according to St. Thomas God permitted the fall of man, with all its tragic effects on human history, because he knew he

---

[629] The classic scholarly study that traces the development of the thought of St. Thomas on Christ's saving work is Romanus Cessario, O.P., *The Godly Image: Christ and Salvation in Catholic Thought from Anselm to Aquinas* (New York: Fordham University Press, 2002).

[630] The paragraphs that follow consist of a slight revision of what I wrote in *Divine Mercy: A Guide from Genesis to Benedict XVI* (Stockbridge, MA: Marian Press, revised edition 2010), p. 120-128. This in turn was based primarily on an article by John Saward, "Love's Second Name: St. Thomas on Mercy" in *Canadian Catholic Review,* March, 1990.

would respond to it with the most amazing display of his merciful love, sending his Son Jesus to share our human nature, and to die for our sins on the Cross.

Aquinas holds that it is possible for sinners to restore a right relationship with God only if they make a proper "satisfaction" to God for sin. The problem is that making satisfaction to God for sin is precisely what humanity, by its own power, cannot do. We have no way to make up for our sins (for the past cannot be undone, and no one has anything "extra" in the present or the future to offer to God for his past sins, since a life of perfect obedience was owed by each one of us to God our Creator anyway). Besides, we owe to God an *infinite* compensation for sin, since by our sins we have betrayed and offended Infinite Love. Yet we have nothing infinite to offer to God to make up for our sins. Moreover, human nature, corrupted by sin, needs to be regenerated and renewed, but again, the regeneration of the soul is beyond human power.

Given that both a compensatory satisfaction for our sins, and the regeneration of our sinful souls are entirely beyond our capability, the human race desperately needs a Savior. Saint Thomas shows that only God himself can be our Savior, through Jesus Christ our Lord.

According to Aquinas, God supremely manifests his mercy by sending his divine Son into the world to share our human nature, and to make "atonement" or "satisfaction" for our sins, meriting for us also superabundant graces of regeneration and sanctification. In this way God as man did for humanity what we by ourselves could not do:

> For man to be liberated through the passion of Christ was in harmony both with his mercy and justice. With justice because by his passion Christ made satisfaction for the sin of the human race, and so man was liberated through the justice of Christ. But also with mercy, because, since man by himself could not make satisfaction for the sins of all human nature, God gave his Son to be the satisfier... and in so doing he

showed a more abundant mercy than if he had forgiven sins without requiring satisfaction (ST II.1.2).

Saint Thomas obviously sees the suffering, redemptive work of Christ as fitting to Divine Justice — that is, as making "satisfaction" (or compensation) for human sins. At the same time, it is the most stupendous act of merciful love for us, because God does all this for us himself, out of nothing but sheer mercy for us in our plight, since we are unable to help ourselves. In doing so, St. Thomas says, God manifests his merciful love far more than if he had just forgiven sins by "letting bygones be bygones."

In order to understand St. Thomas's theory of Atonement, we need to be clear by what he meant in saying that Jesus Christ makes "satisfaction" for our sins. Often, the theory of Aquinas (and that of his predecessor, St. Anselm) is confused with the theory put forward by the Protestant Reformers, for whom atonement meant a quasi-legal transaction in which Christ suffers the "retribution," "penalty," or "punishment" for sin *in the place of* sinners. In other words, God in Christ takes upon himself, in our place, what sinners deserve, and in this way he clears our debt to Divine Justice. For St. Thomas, "satisfaction" does indeed involve making up our debt to God's justice for our sins. But our moral debt for sin can be made up to God in a way that goes beyond mere penal retribution. Our debt can be cleared by another kind of reparative or compensatory act, which St. Thomas calls "satisfaction."

The word and the concept of "satisfaction" actually derive from ancient Roman law. According to St. Thomas, a person can be said to make satisfaction for an offense when he offers something that the offended party accepts with a delight matching or outweighing his displeasure at the original offense. The offender, we may say, "does enough to clear the debt." Take, for example, the case of someone who in a fit of anger throws a punch at another person and breaks his jaw. Strict retributive justice says that the offender ought to suffer to an extent comparable to the suffering that he has caused. Thus, someone should punch him in the jaw ("an eye for an eye"), or at least he ought to be put in jail and suffer a punishment of internment that fits the crime. However, "satisfaction" for the original transgression might be made to the offended party instead, if the offender offers appropriate acts of "reparation" or "compensation." For example, he could offer a sincere and public apology for his actions, offer to pay the injured man's medical bills (plus a compensatory payment for pain and suffering), and do other acts of help and public service to "make it up" to the victim, and to society as a whole, for his crime. All this would amount to "satisfaction" of the man's moral and social debt.

Saint Thomas states numerous times that what gives saving, satisfactory value in God's eyes to the life and death of his Incarnate Son is not just the sufferings that Christ endured for us, but also the loving obedience of the Son, in and through his sacred humanity. That is why Aquinas can argue that our Lord began to merit our salvation even from his cradle, because even his Holy Childhood was one continuous act of loving obedience to the Father. Moreover, St. Thomas quotes with approval St. Augustine's teaching that what made Christ's passion acceptable to the Father was the charity out of which he offered himself up for us (ST III. 48.3).

Furthermore, it is important to note that because he was the divine Son in human flesh, all of his human acts are "theandric" (that is, acts done by a divine person, in and through his human nature) and therefore of infinite value. It follows that Christ's perfect, loving obedience to the Father throughout his life and death is not only "sufficient" to "make up" for our sins — in fact, his life and death gains "superabundant" merit. It *more than* makes up for our sins.

Saint Thomas sums up his view of all this in his *Summa Theologiae* as follows:

> He atones appropriately for an offense who offers whatever the offended party equally loves, or loves more than he detested the offense. But Christ, by suffering out of love and obedience gave to God more than was required to compensate for the offences of the whole human race. First, by reason of

the tremendous charity from which he suffered; second, by reason of the dignity of his life, which he gave up in atonement, for this was the life of one who was both God and man; third, on account of the extent of the passion and the sorrows suffered ... and so Christ's passion was not merely sufficient but a superabundant atonement for the sins of the human race (III. 48.2).

We can see here that in the theology of St. Thomas, Divine Mercy not only fulfills the demands of Divine Justice, but goes *way beyond* those demands, meriting an infinite ocean of graces which our Savior wants to pour out upon a lost and broken world.

It should not be supposed that for the Catholic Tradition, St. Thomas answered every possible question about Christ's saving work on the Cross, or even that every nuance of his teaching on this subject is completely clear and coherent. For example, if all of Christ's acts and sufferings as incarnate are "theandric" and therefore of infinite value, and if all that is needed for our salvation is for the merits of his life and death to apply to us (through our incorporation into the Body of Christ), and the graces he won for us to be poured out upon us, transforming our hearts by the Holy Spirit to make us a new creation in Christ, then it would seem that the Cross was actually *superfluous* to his saving work, since he had already superabundantly merited our salvation even from his cradle. Knowledge of Christ's death on the Cross might help us subjectively to receive the benefits of his redeeming work, but the Cross does not seem to be essential for those benefits objectively to be won for us. Moreover, this whole Thomistic theory is based on an analogy between how reconciliation can happen between human beings (via "satisfaction"), and what is required for us to be fully reconciled to God. The question arises (and will be discussed later in this chapter) whether sin and reconciliation with God can be fully understood in such a "human" way.

Still, the basic outlines of the perspective of St. Thomas are unmistakable, and have been widely embraced in the Catholic world for many centuries: *Through offering to the Father in* *loving obedience his whole life on earth, and especially his passion and death on the Cross, our Savior compensated Divine Justice for our sins and merited not only our pardon, but also all the graces we need to be sanctified and saved.*

In the Anglican world, with the decline of the Anglo-Catholic movement in numbers and influence since the Second World War, there have not been many defenders of Sacrificial-Satisfaction theories. But two prominent figures stand out in this respect.

First, Lionel Spencer Thornton, a priest of the Community of the Resurrection (a religious order originally founded by Charles Gore), wrote a short and dense volume in 1937, just prior to the war, entitled *The Doctrine of the Atonement*. Drawing heavily upon the Fathers of the Church as well as on Scripture, Thornton cautiously outlined and endorsed elements of the traditional Satisfaction theories:

> Our lives belong to God. He claims all. Nothing must be held back. Human life is to be fulfilled in the devotion of uttermost self-giving and adoring love. Yet, like Ananias and Sapphira we keep back part of the price (Acts 5:1-11). We withhold the response of love, and so we insure the liability of debtors. Like the unmerciful servant, we cannot pay (Mt 18:21-35). We have no compensation to offer, no ransom-gift. No expiatory act of ours can avail in the slightest degree to restore us from the position of defaulting servants to that of children in the Father's house. But God "loved us and sent his Son to be the expiation of our sins." Him "God set forth to be a means of expiation by his blood." God Himself has provided the sacrifice (Gen 22:8). God alone can put away sin; but He wills to act through human response. In the old covenant there was developed a formal system by which man might symbolically co-operate in the divine forgiveness. Now in Christ the Father has set forth the innermost reality of expiation. We may define it as consisting in a costing [costly] act of compensation for sin,

offering to God the adequate gift, and so acting with cleansing power to remove the defilement of guilt.[631]

"He gave His life a ransom." He gave the unmeasured riches of His love in an act of compensation, whose cost is beyond computation. It is beyond computation in two ways: first, because we can never plumb the depths of the spiritual agony and desolation involved for Him; and secondly, because we can never measure the wealth of generous self-giving which was poured so freely into the doing of this saving act.

The expiation was the act of God in Christ. It was God's own vindication of His moral order in the very arena of its violation. God Himself in the person of His Son submitted to the spiritual laws of His own moral order. The incarnate Son, by subjecting Himself to the consequences of sin, reasserted the sovereign holiness of God against sin's violation. These unfathomed depths of the Atonement will always be mysteries transcending our understanding, although they may appear wholly reasonable to adoring faith so far as understanding is within our reach. Our insight into such mysteries must be fragmentary for two reasons; first, because we are finite creatures, who can attain only to a limited grasp of God's ways; and secondly, because we are sinners, who, by our own acts, have further restricted and dimmed such spiritual vision as has been granted to us.[632]

In addition to the two reasons that Thornton offers here, in all humility, for leaving the Satisfaction Theory in the end an unfathomable mystery, he might have mentioned a third reason: that since the 18th century this way of conceiving Christ's saving work has suffered powerful critique (or so it would seem) on rational grounds.

---

[631] Lionel Spencer Thornton, *The Doctrine of the Atonement* (London: The Unicorn Press, 1937), p. 122-123. In this passage Thornton writes of "expiation," but he evidently takes the meaning of the word to be closer to "propitiation."
[632] Ibid., p. 134-135.

As just one example, let us look at a book we have quoted and cited before: *Philosophical Approaches to Atonement, Incarnation, and the Trinity* (2016) by Christian Analytic philosopher C. Stephen Layman. In that work, Layman lays out numerous reasons why Sacrificial-Satisfaction theories do not seem to him to make much sense. We will restrict ourselves here to three of the principal ones he presents.

First, Layman asked why God "must kill someone" in order to be able to forgive us. After all, human beings often forgive one another, even for serious offenses, without requiring the equivalent of someone's death — especially if the offender is sincerely penitent and has apologized (Layman sees God's merciful love on display in this way in Christ's parable of the Prodigal Son). So, Layman asks:

> [W]hy should a human sacrifice please God? "God was displeased with human sin but God had Jesus killed as a sacrifice and that removed God's displeasure" — really? Such a claim is baffling, and hardly puts God in a good light.[633]

I will save a more complete response to these objections to the next two sections of this chapter. Suffice it to say for now that there are several elements of caricature in what Layman is attributing to the Sacrificial-Satisfaction Theory here. For starters, God did not exactly arrange for Jesus to be killed ("God had Jesus killed"), but God *permitted* his divine Son to be killed, knowing full well what sinful human beings would do when Infinite Love Incarnate was dwelling in their midst. Second, in the Thomist version of the Sacrificial-Satisfaction Theory, at least, *Christ's salvific sacrifice is not just his death, but his whole-life offering in obedient love, culminating in his death.* Most importantly, the Sacrificial-Satisfaction theories of Anselm, Aquinas and Thornton do not say that *"someone"* must live and die in loving obedience for the redeeming sacrifice to be accomplished: it says that *only the one who was God-and-man — in other words, only God Incarnate, because of the infinite, superabundant value of all his actions — could make such a sacrifice.*

---

[633] Layman, *Philosophical Approaches to Atonement, Incarnation, and the Trinity*, p. 25.

Layman takes up this subject again later in his book. He asks how it makes sense for God to accept as a sacrifice for sin one person's life as payment for another: "[I]f each human being owes God a life of perfect obedience, does it make sense for God to accept someone else's life (and death) as a payment instead?"[634] Layman likens this to a case of a student who owes a term paper to hand in to his professor. But when he fails to write one, he offers to the professor an extra-paper written by one of his classmates instead: would the professor be right to accept such an offering to make up for the student's un-written term paper? Or, to make the analogy closer to the Satisfaction Theory: would it be right for the professor to offer one of her own unpublished essays to be used by the student to offer in place of the missing term paper? Layman concludes:

> Similarly, given that you and I each owe God a life of perfect obedience, it's hard to see how Christ's life (and death) can compensate for either yours or mine. A moral debt (viz. owing God a well-lived life) is not like a financial debt which can be paid back (at least, in principle) with anything of equivalent value.[635]

But Layman is surely mistaken here. Moral and social debts *can* sometimes be paid back with an equivalent "satisfaction" (see our previous discussion of St. Thomas on satisfaction, and the example we gave of the man who punched another and broke his jaw, and of what he could do to "make up" for that offense).

Moreover, the analogy that Layman offers of the student and the term papers does not really mirror the Sacrificial-Satisfaction Theory, because in academia a student does not really "owe" his assigned essays, morally or financially, to the professor; rather, the term paper is simply an academic requirement for earning credit hours, and one of the practical means toward a good education. Substituting someone

---

[634] Ibid., p. 35.
[635] Ibid., p. 36.

else's written work for one's own, even with the professor's permission, obviously would violate the pedagogical purpose of the whole exercise. The professor sets the class assignments, collects them and marks them toward a good pedagogical end, but they are not in any sense "owed" to her. Being "in debt" to someone else is a moral or financial category, not a practical one. According to the Sacrificial-Satisfaction, however, we are in moral debt to God: we owe him compensation or satisfaction for the offence of our sins.

Finally, it is not always unreasonable for a creditor (morally or financially) to help a debtor to pay a debt, or otherwise make satisfaction for a debt owed to himself. Think of a parent who helps a child pay for a window that the child broke because the child could not foot the bill or fix the window all by himself. Morally and financially, the two clear the debt and repair the damage together, based on the love of the parent for the child, and not only on the sincere penitence of the child himself. Furthermore, we would think it odd (and poor parenting too!), if the parent merely accepted the penitential tears of the child as enough to clear the debt involved here. Sometimes, contrition and apology are just not enough.

It was considerations such as these that led (at that time Anglican) philosophical theologian Richard Swinburne to make a major attempt at re-stating and defending a coherent Sacrificial-Satisfaction theory. To his efforts we now turn our attention.

The Sacrificial-Satisfaction Theory of Richard Swinburne

In an essay first published in 1988, "The Christian Scheme of Salvation," **Richard Swinburne developed a Sacrificial-Satisfaction theory based on the premise that a righteous God cannot fully forgive us for our sins unless we have made an adequate atonement for them.**[636] **For God to do otherwise, for**

---

[636] For an excellent summary of Anselm's perspective on this point, see Mozley, *The Doctrine of the Atonement*, p. 127-128; 135-136.

him simply to overlook our past sins, requiring nothing of us, would trivialise our past wrong-doing, and imply that he does not take sin or personal relations very seriously.[637]

It would be a mistake to interpret Swinburne as insisting here on an abstract standard of justice "extrinsic" to our personal relationship with God. Rather, the strength of his theory is his insight that *real personal relationships include the need for just compensation to be offered when wrongs have been committed.* Only personal beings among God's creatures can practice this virtue of justice: it is only human beings who can say things like "that's not fair," or "I owe you an apology" or "he paid his debt to society"— expressive of what we all believe is an essential aspect of personal and social relationships. Presumably, our relationship with God has this dimension as well, who alone possesses the attribute of justice (i.e., the commitment to render to each person what is due to them) in an infinitely perfect way.

We must therefore make atonement for the past, and atonement usually means much more than just sorrow for our sins. A contrite heart is essential, but as in normal human relations, it is not enough to atone for grave acts of wrongdoing that have caused grievous harm. Authentic contrition must be expressed and completed in an apology to those we have wronged, in works of "reparation" (that is, by trying to repair as best we can any damage we have caused to others, to ourselves, and to the Kingdom of God, by our transgressions), and by the offering of "penance" (an extra gift to make up for sin).[638] Since

---

[637] Richard Swinburne, "The Christian Scheme of Salvation" in Michael Rea, ed., *Oxford Readings in Philosophical Theology 1*, p. 300-301.
[638] Swinburne defines "penance" as an "extra gift" or favor that constitutes our apology as "meant and serious" by making it "costly" (Ibid., p. 299). However, deep contrition, sincere apology and works of reparation can in themselves be quite costly, so we might do better to define penance in a slightly different way. I shall take "penance" to mean an extra gift or favor that makes up in an indirect way for what cannot be fully repaired. For example, if I knock a man down with my car, I should not only apologise and help to pay his medical bills; I should do some other extra favor, or make some other extra payment to help compensate

God is our Creator and Benefactor, however, we already owe him a worthwhile life. Thus, we not only lack any way of fully repairing the damage done to his Kingdom by our sins, we also have nothing "extra" to offer him as a "penance" that we do not owe to him already:

> If God has given us so much, we have a duty anyway to live a worthwhile life; and if we have failed to do so, it's going to be very difficult to find a bit extra to offer to God in compensation for past misuse. We are too close to the situation of the criminal who has spent his ill-gotten gains, and is unable to make reparation. We need help from outside …. Just as a good parent may put in the way of a child an opportunity for making amends (an opportunity which he would not otherwise have had) rather than just accept an apology, so a good God also may do just that.[639]

"Help from outside" comes from the merciful God himself. As Jesus Christ, the Divine Word made flesh, he makes his own perfect human life and death available to us to offer as the completion of our work of reparation and penance.[640] He himself can be our "extra gift." Swinburne explains:

> The living of a perfect human life by God himself forms a far more perfect offering for man to offer God than a perfect life lived by an ordinary human. For the ordinary human has an obligation to live a worthwhile life, and so [at least] some of

---

for the disruption to his life and lasting damage to his body or his life plans that my reckless driving has caused. These are aspects of the harm I have caused that I am unable to undo or repair directly. The law courts will often enforce such acts of penance by requiring that a payment to the victim should be made "for pain and suffering."

[639] Ibid., p. 306.

[640] I say "as the *completion* of our work of reparation and penance" here, because presumably there are many aspects of atonement that we can make (albeit only with the invisible aid of the Holy Spirit) which do not require any explicit relationship with Jesus Christ: for example, contrition and apologies to God and to others for our wrongdoing, and works to try to repair the offense and harm we have caused to others.

the perfection of his life would be owed anyway. An incarnate God does not owe it to any benefactor to live any particular kind of life, and so the whole perfection of that life would be available to others to use as their offering.[641]

In other words, an atoning penance must be an extra gift, over and above any service otherwise owed. The "extra" in Christ's obedience consists in the fact that his life is not a solely human offering to the Father, but actually the offering of the divine Son Incarnate. By identifying ourselves with his offering through the Holy Spirit and the Church, especially by participation in the Eucharist, we can utilize his total devotion to the Father, his loving and sacrificial life and death, as our own penitential offering. This completes our atonement, and enables God fully to forgive us on a moral basis.[642] In short, God himself, through the incarnate life, death and resurrection of his Son, has mercifully given us the means to offer up a complete reparation and penance for our sins, and thereby enabled us to receive the fullness of divine forgiveness.

Swinburne's theory of the Atonement has been widely discussed since its first presentation, and it has come under fire from several directions. We shall look at each of the major lines of critique in turn.

a) David Brown claimed that if our creation is God's free gift to us, then we do not actually owe him any compensation for our misuse or destruction of it:

> For if I receive something as a gift, while I am 'indebted' to that person, it does not mean that the donor has thereby put me under an obligation to do something for him in return .... Otherwise, the initial

---

[641] Ibid., p. 306-307.

[642] Again, by full "forgiveness" I mean that one neither exacts retribution on the offender (i.e., one pardons his offence) nor withholds friendship, but restores the relationship in full. In both respects, *divine* forgiveness is always expressed by the outpouring of the Holy Spirit and sanctifying grace into a repentant and receptive heart.

bequest, even when it is the gift of life itself, could not count as a pure gift.[643]

It would follow that we do not owe our Creator a full atonement before he can forgive us for our sins on a moral basis. Therefore, the life and death of the Incarnate Lord would not be needed to provide us with the means to complete our reparation and penance in the way that Swinburne suggests.

We might do better, however, to see the gift of life in a different light: as a gift entrusted to us for a special purpose. God has not just transferred the ownership of something from himself to us, with no more claim upon us, merely hoping that we do not squander the gift (e.g., as a father may give $20 spending money to his son). Rather, the Bible seems to teach that by creating us, God entrusted us with a special purpose, namely, the care of things that ultimately belong to him: ourselves, each other, and all living creatures. In the Garden of Eden, for example, the first human beings were not just there to enjoy themselves and do whatever they wanted. God gave Adam a definite responsibility: to "till the garden and keep it" (Gen 2:15). In the New Testament, Jesus speaks of a master who gives money to his servants to invest for him (Mt 25:14ff), of money owed to a master by an unmerciful servant (Mt 18:21-25) and of unfaithful tenants of the master's vineyard (Mt 22:33ff). The point is that God trusts us to be faithful stewards of all the gifts and responsibilities that he freely gave us, so that all the earth may share in his perfections and reflect his glory. Our creation may be seen as a pure gift in that God did not create us out of any need of his own (and of course, it was not merited by us or "owed" to us in any way either). He created us out of *pure love*: a selfless desire to share his glory and perfections with other beings. In other words, he made us in

---

[643] Brown, *The Divine Trinity*, p. 222. Brown's discussion of this point actually antedated the first publication of Swinburne's Sacrificial-Satisfaction Theory.

his own "image" so that we might learn to love and create as he does, in our own finite and human way, and he also intended to draw us to himself, so that we might reflect his love and share his joy. But the special dignity of this gift of existence in his image entailed a responsibility: to serve the good purposes for which we were made. *The idea of just compensation for waste and destruction is not out of place with regard to gifts originally given for a good purpose.*[644]

b) It may be objected that talk of "compensation," "penance" and the like makes the saving work of Jesus Christ a purely external, transactional affair. But this is far from the truth. Swinburne's Sacrificial-Satisfaction Theory merely supplements what we have already found to be true and helpful from Exemplarist theories and other Sacrificial theories, since it addresses aspects of our relationship with God that those other theories do not — and those theories hardly can be construed as merely "external' or "transactional." Swinburne's theory would just add one more dimension to the multi-dimensional mystery of Christ's redeeming work.

Besides, all that God requires of us in "atonement" or compensation for sin (sincere contrition, apology, reparation, and penance) he surely helps us to do by the Spirit of the risen Christ, working within us. Moreover, all that he demands and helps us to do is also "medicinal" in effect; **in other words,**

---

[644] An analogy may be found, for example, in a philanthropic benefactor who selflessly gives a man $100,000 to start a new school. If the man steals or wastes the gift, he betrays the benefactor's trust and good purpose, and owes the donor not only a sincere apology, but a return of the money, as much as possible (as reparation), and also an extra gift (or penance) to make up for the delay and disruption of the benefactor's purpose in entrusting the money to him in the first place. In fact, in St. Luke's version of the Lord's Prayer, the debts we owe to human creditors are likened to the moral debt for our sins that needs to be remitted by God: "and forgive us our sins, for we ourselves forgive everyone who is *indebted* to us" (Lk 11:4).

true contrition, the offering apologies, works to repair any damage done by our actions, and works of penance — *all of these acts of atonement, when accomplished by the grace of the Holy Spirit, help purge our hearts from attachments to evil, and sanctify our souls to adhere to his loving will. In this subjective sense, these acts accomplish the completion of our repentance, and repentance is what opens our hearts to divine forgiveness in the form of a renewal of the life of the Holy Spirit.* This is especially true if we have a Catholic understanding of the offering of the Eucharist as a penitential sacrifice, in which the penitential offering we make to God (when we offer sacramentally the death of Christ to the Father) includes at the same time his own gift of himself to us in the Body and Blood of his Son in Holy Communion. In short, by adopting Swinburne's theory, we certainly would not be committed to a purely external, transactional understanding of the Atonement.

c) One might fairly argue that in some of Christ's own parables, such as the parables of "The Prodigal Son" and "The Pharisee and the Publican," *the Father forgives sinners solely in response to their heart-felt contrition and apology: there is no sign that works of reparation and penance also are needed to complete our repentance,* that is, to open our hearts and clear the way for God's full pardon in the form of a restored friendship with him in the Holy Spirit (See Lk 15: 20-24, and 18:9-14).

On the other hand, it may be that since God can read the human heart, he is able to see whether sinners have attained such a depth of true contrition, or at least an authentic desire for it, that they would naturally desire to perform works of reparation and penance if they could, at the first reasonable opportunity. In other words, **authentic contrition surely carries within it a sincere yearning to make full atonement for one's sins.** *The divine "requirement" of works of reparation and penance, therefore, is not an arbitrary, additional obstacle that God has placed in our* *path and asked us to overcome so that he can fully forgive us on a just basis; rather, these works are essential to complete and in-depth repentance for sin.* **Acts of reparation and penance more fully distance our hearts from our sins, and thereby open our hearts to receive divine forgiveness in the form of a renewal of the life of the Holy Spirit, even as these same acts acknowledge the rights and dignity of those whom we have wronged.** For example, we can hardly imagine that after receiving his father's initial forgiveness and welcome-home banquet, the prodigal son would not intend to do some kind of special service, in at least partial reparation and penance for his misdeeds, such as making attempts to restore to his father at least some of the inheritance money that he had squandered. In the story of Zacchaeus, for example (Lk 19:1-10), the tax collector offered to repay *four times over* anyone whom he had cheated, and Jesus did not reject his offer on the grounds that his contrition and apology, and simple restitution were enough. Instead, Jesus replied "Today salvation has come to this house" (19:9).[645]

The point is: *truly in-depth repentance (i.e., true contrition and fully turning away from our sins) carries within it the sincere desire to make amends — in the form of apologies, works of reparation and penance — to the extent that we can.* The Sacrificial-Satisfaction Theory states that in union with Christ's sacrifice on the Cross we can do so without remainder, because, as the traditional Anglican Book of Common Prayer states, his passion and death are the "full, perfect, and sufficient sacrifice, oblation and satisfaction for the sins of the whole world." In our relationship with God,

---

[645] Notice that this is similar to what happens in the Catholic Sacrament of Reconciliation (sacramental confession): the priest pronounces absolution for sins in the name of Christ, but usually on the condition that the penitent promise (as an expression of true repentance, and to deepen and complete that repentance) to carry out works of reparation and penance, in order for full divine forgiveness to be received, and the temporal punishment due to sin fully to be remitted.

therefore (at least from a Catholic and Anglo-Catholic perspective), true repentance and faith in Christ includes the desire to perform works of apology (and confession), reparation and penance, as we have opportunity, and there is no more perfect "penance," or penitential offering that we can make to the Father than the "re-presentation" (*anamnesis*) of his Son's loving obedience unto death in the Holy Eucharist (I Cor 11:26). *If God sometimes seems to fully forgive sinners on the basis of their contrition and apology alone, it is the presence of true and in-depth repentance — including the sincere desire to express and complete it through acts of reparation and penance — and not some more shallow form of repentance, that forms the basis of his act.* Indeed, it may be on the basis of such a sincere desire that the Father sometimes fully remits even the mortal sins of sincerely contrite non-Christians, whose capacity to make an adequate reparation and penance is more restricted (in so far as they lack faith in Christ's saving work, and access to the sacraments).

d) An objection related to the previous one also frequently arises: *Why is it that God cannot do what human beings usually feel free to do: partially or fully forgive the wrongdoing of an offender even without requiring any works of reparation or penance?* As C. Stephen Layman puts it: "While it is true that a morally perfect God will take sin seriously, isn't it up to God to decide what that involves?"[646] Swinburne would certainly agree, up to a point: "What, however, is within the victim's power is to determine, within limits, just how much atonement is necessary before he is prepared to give the forgiveness which will eliminate [objective] guilt."[647] But, Swinburne continues, "if he chooses, the victim can insist on substantial reparation, and sometimes it is good that he do so, that he should insist on the guilty one, for his own sake, making a serious atonement; for that allows

---

[646] Layman, *Atonement, Incarnation and the Trinity*, p. 34.
[647] Swinburne, "The Christian Scheme of Salvation," p. 300-301.

him to take seriously the harm that is done."[648] Obviously, in our relationship with God this would be true especially with regard to grievous, "mortal" sins. As the party ultimately wronged by our sins, God has revealed through Scripture and Tradition the degree of atonement that he believes is best and appropriate for us to offer to restore our relationship with him: sincere contrition and confession, and works of reparation and penance, the latter consisting primarily in the sacramental offering up of his Son's perfect human life and death in compensation for our own misspent life. Nothing could be more fitting.[649]

While Swinburne's understanding of the works of atonement required of us seems defensible as far as it goes, it would seem that something is still missing from this picture. There is surely another reason why God does not do what humans sometimes do: require little or no reparation and penance as a condition of the offer of full forgiveness. It is not only that, given the gravity of some of our sins, God deemed it best for us to offer him a substantial reparation and penance for them. There is also *the metaphysically unique status of God* to consider, and *our unique relationship with him*, which has no direct human parallel. After all, God is our *Total Benefactor*, in that *every good thing we receive comes ultimately from him as our Creator and Sustainer*. Other human beings are at best secondary and partial causes of the many good things that he gives to us, and so to some extent, parents, friends, neighbors, and society as a whole, as mere partial benefactors, can require only partial atonement for acts of wrongdoing committed against them as a condition of pardon and the full restoration of relationships. For God, on the other hand, to offer unconditional forgiveness, or to require only minimal conditions for bestowing his full forgiveness would surely be unjust, for in sinning against him we are sinning against our *Total Benefactor* — and indeed,

---

[648] Ibid., p. 301.
[649] Ibid., p. 306.

betraying his infinite love for us. Thus, it would be a gross violation of his justice and holiness *not* to require from us a full and substantial atonement for our sins in order for the fullness of divine forgiveness to be poured out upon us. Nothing short of complete and in-depth repentance will suffice (and as we have seen, that includes a sincere desire to make amends in works of reparation and penance, as we have the opportunity to do so).

e) Some commentators have objected that on Swinburne's theory, Christ's sacrificial life and death is of very limited effect, since it only covers our sins when it is offered to God by believers as a compensatory, penitential gift in the sacramental rites of the Church, especially at the Holy Eucharist. This would seem to limit its sacrificial value solely to Christians — and indeed solely to Catholic and Eastern Orthodox Christians, the only ones who include in their sacramental theology the doctrine that at every Eucharist the sacrifice of Christ on the Cross is made present, and the only ones who plead on that basis for all the benefits of his sacrifice to be poured out upon them. Presumably, Protestant Christians, who do not accept such an understanding of the Eucharist as a re-presentation of Christ's sacrifice on Calvary, would be unable to access those benefits. Indeed, the way Swinburne phrases the matter seems to leave him wide open to this objection:

> Christ offered the sacrifice for all. But it can only atone for me if I use it — if I join my feeble repentance and halting words of apology to it, if I use it to pay my fine, to make my peace. There has to be a formal association with it in the process of my disassociating myself from my own sins and from involvement with those of others …. Christ founded a body to carry on his work. The Christian Church provides a formal ceremony of association in the pledges made by the candidates for admission in its ceremonies of baptism and

confirmation, and before participation in the Eucharist in which, as Paul puts it, we "proclaim the Lord's death until he comes" (I Cor 11:26).[650]

There are several ways to overcome this objection, however, including (1) that the Catholic and Orthodox Eucharist is a form of corporate prayer, and there is no reason why God could not accept other forms of prayer — such as the sincere supplications of repentant Protestant believers to receive all the benefits of Christ's saving passion — as the equivalent of the Eucharistic prayer in this respect (at least for those in honest doubt about the doctrine of the Eucharist as a re-making-present of the sacrificial death of the Lord). Moreover, (2) at every Catholic and Orthodox Eucharist, prayers are offered not only for the believers present, but for the whole Church and the whole world. Presumably, on the basis of Christ's one sacrifice on Calvary, made present and offered up at every Eucharist, many of the graces and benefits of his passion and death are thereby poured out on a much wider basis than just on the believers and communicants in attendance.

f) Now we come to what appears to be the strongest objection to Swinburne's theory — as we have seen, an objection sometimes also made against the Sacrificial-Satisfaction Theory of Aquinas. ***In short, these theories do not clearly show how Christ's death on the Cross was either necessary to, or decisive for his saving work.*** This objection was spelled out by Protestant theologian Steven L. Porter in an essay entitled "Swinburnian Atonement and the Doctrine of Penal Substitution":

---

[650] Ibid., p. 307. As a matter of fact, a more literal translation of the Greek of this New Testament passage is given by the King James version: we "show forth the Lord's death until he comes" — which seems even closer to Swinburne's position.

In fact, God could have required merely Christ's valuable life for this purpose without requiring the crucifixion. Surely all the good acts of Christ's life as well as the suffering and humiliation he endured in the incarnation constitute a substantive gift to offer as reparation and penance [NB: especially so if, as Aquinas maintained, all of the acts and sufferings of Jesus Christ, even from his cradle in Bethlehem onward, are "theandric" acts, and therefore of infinite value]. So, since the goods obtained by Christ offering reparation and penance on behalf of sinners could be accomplished without his suffering and death, it is implausible to think that a good God would require such an event for forgiveness. *For a voluntary sacrifice of life is not a morally valuable act unless there is some good purpose that can only or best be achieved by means of it.* Since the goods of reparation and penance can be achieved without Christ's death, it would appear that his voluntary death was either foolish or suicidal.

Swinburne does contend that Christ's life and death are a peculiarly appropriate means of reparation and penance in that they make up a perfect human life offered up for persons who led ruinous lives …. While this seems right, it is not clear why Christ's *death* is an important part of his perfect human life. Would Christ's life have been less perfect if he had ascended into heaven right after, say, the Garden of Gethsemane? … One might think that if Christ had avoided the Cross, then Christ would be seen as having dodged the inevitable result of the kind of life he led. But dodging bullets — even inevitable ones — seems a virtue, unless there is some good purpose to take the bullet. Since Christ's life alone accomplishes the goods of substantive reparation and penance, Swinburne's view of the atonement provides no good reason for Christ voluntarily to go to the cross.[651]

Of course, one might argue that Christ's crucifixion was valuable on other grounds, say, for example, on the grounds we discussed earlier in our survey of the Incarnational Exemplarist theory of Atonement: that our Lord thereby shares our lot by undergoing total human affliction with us, shows us the Way of Love in the midst of such suffering, and manifests the depth of his love for us by doing so. Still, this would not make the Cross of Christ a "satisfaction" of Divine Justice for our sins — sins already compensated for by the superabundant satisfaction that Christ offered for us by his whole-life of loving obedience to the Father. Thus, Porter's objection still stands: *on Swinburne's Atonement theory, the Cross is superfluous to the sacrifice that God-in-Christ must offer to make up for our sins, that is, to enable him to pardon our sins, and renew the gift of the Holy Spirit in our hearts, on a just basis.*

In short, it does not seem as if the Sacrificial theories of Aquinas and Swinburne — or indeed, any of the Sacrificial theories that we have considered so far — can provide us with an adequate answer to the second of the "unanswered questions" left over from our discussion of Exemplarist theories of Christ's saving work. That question remains: *In what way is the Cross God's decisive act to liberate us from the guilt and power of sin, and therefore the supreme revelation of his love, as the Christian Faith has always claimed?* For the New Testament is clear that *above all it is the death of Jesus on the Cross that accomplishes our salvation*: "But far be it from me to glory *except in the cross of our Lord Jesus Christ*" (Gal 6:14); "For I decided to know nothing among you *except Jesus Christ and him crucified*" (I Cor 2:2); "For I delivered to you as of

---

[651] Stephen Porter, "Swinburnian Atonement and the Doctrine of Penal Substitution" in Rea, ed., *Oxford Readings in Philosophical Theology, vol I*, p. 319-320; italics mine.

first importance what I also received: *that Christ died for our sins, according to the scriptures*" (I Cor 15:3); "God shows his love for us in that *while we were yet sinners Christ died for us*" (Rom 5:8); "And you, who were dead in your trespasses and the uncircumcision of your flesh, God made alive together with [Christ] having forgiven us all our trespasses, having cancelled the bond which stood against us with its legal demands: *this he set aside, nailing it to the cross*" (Col 2:13-14); "[S]ince all have sinned and fall short of the glory of God, they are justified by his grace as a gift, through the redemption which is in Christ Jesus, *whom God put forward as an expiation by his blood,* to be received in faith" (Rom 3:23-24); "and through him to reconcile to himself all things, *making peace by the blood of the cross*" (Col 1:20); "You know that you were ransomed from the futile ways inherited from your fathers, not with perishable things such as silver or gold, *but with the precious blood of Christ,* like that of a lamb without spot or blemish" (I Pet 1:18-19); "For the Son of Man also came not to be served but to serve, *and to give his life as a ransom for many*" (Mk 10:45).

It would not be hard to show that this same emphasis on the Cross as God's decisive act for our salvation can be found in the mainstream Christian Tradition as well. Just one example will suffice here: the Easter *Exultet* ("Rejoice now!") sung at the Easter Vigil service throughout the Christian world, probably from as early as the fifth century:

> It is truly right and good, always and everywhere, with our whole heart and mind and voice, to praise you the invisible, almighty and eternal God, and your only begotten Son, Jesus Christ our Lord; for he is the true Paschal Lamb, who *at the feast of the Passover paid for us the debt of Adam's sin, and by his blood delivered your faithful people.*[652]

---

[652] Cited in Rutledge, *The Crucifixion*, p. 227; italics mine.

The trouble with all of the Sacrificial theories that we have explored (except for the theory propounded by St. Anselm, which has its own set of problems) is that even though these theories *include* the crucifixion of Jesus as a fitting culmination of his whole life-offering to the Father, they do not really show that it was *Christ's decisive act that accomplished our salvation.* They do not show us how it "paid for us the debt of Adam's sin," as the Easter *Exultet* says, setting us free from our burden of objective "guilt" (i.e. our moral debt to Divine Justice and Holiness), and from the ongoing "power" of sin in our lives. Something is missing from the gospel of the Cross here.

Richard Cross and a Sacrificial-Merit Theory

Before we move on to consider other major categories of Atonement theory, we need to consider a unique one put forward by philosopher Richard Cross, which we can call a Sacrificial-Merit theory. Contra Swinburne, Cross is not convinced that any other form of compensation to God for human sin is needed than the making of sincere apologies:

> For the gifts [in creation] that God gives to human beings come at no expense to Himself, and their abuse causes God no harm other than the deprivation of service. So there is an important sense in which these divine gifts to us differ from standard cases of benefaction, which involve some kind of cost .... It seems to me that appropriate reparation in such cases is merely apology, where apology of course presupposes genuine repentance. Repentance is sufficient to remove a bad intention. As such, repentance does not pay back any loss to the wronged party .... [I]t seems to me that apology is just the sort of act that would satisfy the requirements of reparation .... [653]

[653] Richard Cross, "Atonement Without Satisfaction" in Rea, ed., *Oxford Readings in Philosophical Theology*, vol. I, p. 334-335.

It will be clear to the reader of the previous sections of this chapter that I would take issue with Cross on this point in a number of ways. First, our sins not only involve bad intentions and deprive God of our "service;" *they also take from him the ideal accomplishment of the very purposes for which we were made by our Total Benefactor.* As the chosen stewards of his creation, we were supposed to serve him and accomplish those good purposes. In addition, *our sins are actually a betrayal of his infinite love for us* (see section d above). Furthermore, if we follow O.C. Quick, et al, in positing a universal "sensational passibility" in God, consisting of some kind of divine sympathy for the plight of all his creatures, and if we also have a kenotic understanding of the Incarnation, in which God has taken into his divine nature a total identification with our human condition as Jesus of Nazareth, attaining thereby the closest possible compassion for us, then *it would certainly not be true to say that our sins do no other "harm" to God than "deprivation of service."* Moreover, from a biblical standpoint we would have to ask: *What was the point of the sacrificial system that God established for ancient Israel, if all that is needed in reparation to God for sin is the making of apologies? Arguably, one of the purposes of that sacrificial system was to enable the Israelites to express, deepen, and complete their repentance for sin by making (albeit in an imperfect manner) a compensatory offering to God.* Finally, as I argued earlier, we commonly believe that *a full and complete repentance for sin includes a desire to offer reparation and penance, where it is possible to do so.*

In any case, following the example of one train of thought that he finds in St. Anselm's *Cur Deus Homo*, Cross seeks to move away from the orbit of Sacrificial-Satisfaction theories altogether, and to develop instead "a different and in principle independent theory, according to which Christ's death *merits* certain rewards for human beings"— the central idea of his Merit Theory of Atonement.[654]

Unfortunately, Cross's theory is based on two rather shaky premises: (a) that sorrow for sin and apology are always all that is needed for God to forgive us on a moral basis (cf. my response to this, above); and (b) that even if the sinner sincerely apologizes, God is not morally

---

[654] Ibid., p. 341.

The Incarnation

bound to offer full forgiveness: "Forgiveness is not morally necessarily because … forgiveness is supererogatory — no one has a duty to forgive someone else who has wronged them," not even in response to repentance and reparation.[655] But this latter premise seems dubious as well. Imagine a man who has morally wronged another person in a serious way (e.g. by serious theft), and imagine that in sincere repentance for his wrongdoing, he has offered his victim the most complete atonement that he can: sincere contrition and public apology, promise of amendment, exhaustive efforts to repair any harm he has done by his sins (e.g. by returning the stolen goods), as well as works of penance that might compensate his victims for what cannot directly be repaired (e.g. compensating for the stolen money four times over, as Zacchaeus did). Granted that he has done all this, with the proper penitential dispositions, surely it would be wrong for his victims not to forgive him for the offense, at least for the most part[656] (unless, of course, it was a repeat offense, in which case one legitimately might doubt the full sincerity of the man's repentance — but since God can read the human heart, this would not be a problem in the malefactor's relationship with him. If the man had made a sincere confession, and accomplished the appropriate penance, then God would know whether or not all this expressed authentic sorrow for sin). In short, if one were *not* to offer a large measure of forgiveness to such a model penitent, we would commonly say that such a person "stubbornly refuses to forgive."

On the basis of these two (arguably faulty) premises, and given that Jesus is the divine Son Incarnate, Cross theorizes:

> On this scheme Christ's death is a supererogatively good act that merits a reward from God. The reward is to be whatever Christ asks for. (This reward is not rashly or irresponsibly ascribed by God if we suppose that Christ is necessarily good,

---

[655] Ibid., p. 329.
[656] I will leave to the next section of this chapter a discussion of whether or not there might be circumstances in which even all this would not be enough for *full* forgiveness to be offered on a sound and just basis.

and thus incapable of asking for anything bad.) Christ asks that God [the Father] forgive the sins of those who repent and apologize to God. God is then obliged to do so. So the redemptive result of Christ's sacrifice is God being obliged to forgive those who call upon him in penitence and sorrow.[657]

There are certainly some helpful features in the Merit Theory proposed by Cross here. Above all, it helps make sense of language we find in the New Testament about the risen and ascended Christ acting as our heavenly "advocate" and "intercessor" (Heb 7:25, 9:24; I Jn 1:21). In heaven, evidently, he is pleading before the Father that all the graces of the Holy Spirit that he merited by his supererogatory life and death might be poured out upon the world, especially on those who open their hearts to him in repentance and faith. This theory also helps to include in Christ's work of atonement the need for the graces of sanctification to be poured out upon sinners in abundance, to enable us to overcome the "power" of sin in our lives (i.e., our inner corruption and proclivity to sin). As St. Paul wrote, "Where sin increased, grace abounded all the more" (Rom 5:20). *The advantage of the Merit Theory, therefore, is that it shows us how sanctifying grace can be offered to us not only as an expression of Divine Love, but in a way that also accords with Divine Justice:* **for Jesus Christ, out of his merciful love for us, merited for us by his life and death the renewal of the Holy Spirit in our hearts, and all the sanctifying graces of the Holy Spirit that we need. Christ now pleads before the throne of heaven that all of these graces may be poured out upon us. Indeed this ought to be seen as a major aspect of Christ's saving work.** We shall return to this subject later in this chapter. Suffice it to say here that the New Testament certainly implies that Jesus has merited a great reward by his loving obedience to the Father in his life and death, and that he claims this reward now on our behalf: "Worthy is the Lamb who was slain, to receive power and wealth and wisdom and might and honor and glory and blessing …. Let us rejoice and exult and give him the glory, for the marriage of the Lamb has come, and his Bride has made herself ready; it was

---

[657] Ibid., p. 342.

granted to her to be clothed with fine linen, bright and pure" (Rev 5:12, 19:7).

Nevertheless the Merit Theory still has severe defects.

For one thing, the idea that the main goal of Christ's work of atonement was to insure that God would be morally "obliged" to forgive us (that is, in response to our sincere apologies for our sins), seems odd and unnecessary. God's own attribute of justice would naturally enable him to pardon us for our sins if a sufficient atonement had been made for them. Cross makes it seem as if God is actually reluctant to forgive us, and so we must "twist his arm," so to speak, and bind him by an extra and secure *obligation* to do so. The contrary is surely the case: the God of love is *eager* to offer us pardon and renewal, if the demands of his justice also can be met. His saving work through Jesus Christ, especially his sacrificial offering of himself on Calvary, is (among other things) his way of enabling himself to offer us pardon and renewal in accord with his perfect justice and holiness.

For another thing, *the Merit Theory still does not clearly explain how the crucifixion of Jesus was God's decisive act for our salvation, the act that supremely reveals his love for us.* As we have seen, Cross states that "Christ's death is a good act of supererogation that merits a reward from God." But *why* is it the only good act of supererogation that merits such a great reward? Surely, as God Incarnate, all of his acts of faithful love and obedience are "theandric," of infinite value, and therefore merit a great reward. Moreover, *what good does his violent death in itself actually do for us that needed to be accomplished for our salvation, and that could not be attained in any other way?* No doubt (as the Incarnational Exemplarist Theory would say) it was the culmination of his life of loving obedience to the Father, and by his death he also shares in the experience of total human affliction, in solidarity with suffering humanity. But as we have already seen, those accomplishments on the Cross, considered all by themselves, are insufficient for our salvation, and therefore insufficient to the Christian understanding of the mystery of the Cross. They do nothing to address *the moral debt we owe to God for our sins of the past, the burden of objective guilt for our sins which God cannot in justice remit apart from a full atonement being made for them.* The Cross of Jesus, as an example of love for us to follow, and as God's act of total solidarity with us (as in Incarnational Exemplarism) are certainly vital aspects of the mystery of our Redemption – and they certainly merit a reward, for which our Savior intercedes before the throne of heaven, and claims for us: the outpouring of the Holy Spirit and his saving, sanctifying grace upon penitent sinners. But all things considered, that is insufficient for the Cross to be lifted high by the Church as the decisive, divine act that accomplishes our salvation — if by "salvation" we mean what supremely liberates us not just from the *power* of sin, but also from our moral debt, our *objective guilt* for sin.

To close our consideration of Sacrificial and Merit theories of the Atonement, therefore, Anglican New Testament scholar Tom Wright leaves us with the fundamental question that still needs to be answered, when all Exemplarist, Sacrificial and Merit theories have been accounted for:

> Unless there was a *reason* for Jesus to die, and perhaps even a reason for him to die that particular and horrible kind of death, it is hard to see how this death could actually be an example of love. If Bill's dearest friend falls into a fast-flowing river and Bill leaps in to save him, risking his own life in the process, that would indeed provide an example of love (as well as heroic courage) for anyone who witnesses this event or hears about it. But if Fred, wishing to show his dearest friend how much he loves him, leaps into a fast-flowing river when his friend is standing safely beside him on the bank, that would demonstrate neither love nor courage, but meaningless folly.

> My point is this: unless Jesus' death *achieved* something — something that urgently needed to be done and couldn't be done in any other way — then it cannot serve as a moral example [or as the supreme demonstration of God's love for us, for that matter]. The "exemplary" meaning must always depend on something prior. As John puts it: "Love consists in this; not that we loved God, but that he loved us and sent his

son to be *the sacrifice that would atone for our sins*. Beloved, if that's how God loved us, we ought to love one another in the same way" (I Jn 4:10-11). John does not expect his readers to offer themselves as the sacrifice to atone for one another's sins. That has already been done. They are expected to *copy* the self-sacrificial love through which Jesus did something unique, something [on the Cross] that urgently needed doing. So our question presses: What was that "something"?[658]

The Legal or Penal Substitution Theory of Atonement

This bring us to consideration of what has been, since the Enlightenment, the most controversial understanding of Christ's saving work: the Legal or Penal Substitution Theory. **This theory basically states that God can only offer forgiveness to us in accord with the demands of his justice. Our sins against God are so heinous (because they betray and offend *infinite* love) that they demand the ultimate death penalty: the punishment of total and irrevocable alienation from God, the Author of Life, in other words, both bodily death and everlasting spiritual death.** *But God is so merciful that in the person of His Son, Jesus Christ, he offered up, in our place, his own death on the Cross to pay the penalty that we deserve. When we open our hearts to him in repentance and faith, the death-penalty that he paid can apply to us, we are "washed in the blood of the Lamb," pardoned for the guilt of our sins, and set free.* In his book *Consoling the Heart of Jesus*, Fr. Michael Gaitley, MIC, summed up this perspective on the Cross:

> By our sins we offended not just any man but the God-Man, an offense that deserves the penalty of death. Yet, instead of destroying us ungrateful creatures as we deserved, God in Christ Jesus chose to suffer the death penalty for us, so we

---

[658] Wright, *The Day the Revolution Began*, p. 47-48.

might be forgiven and have life with God. What unfathomable love and mercy![659]

We will analyze this theory of the Atonement in greater depth than the others surveyed in this chapter, not only because the Legal Theory is the most controversial of them all, but also because (as we shall see), along with the Incarnational Exemplarist Theory, it "fits" especially well with a kenotic understanding of the Incarnation.

1) Penal Substitution in Scripture and Ancient Tradition

To begin with, the historical origins of this understanding of redemption are hotly disputed. David Brown spoke for many when he wrote: "To my mind … it is hard to see in this position anything other than a creation of the Reformation with its own preoccupation with legal issues."[660] To be sure, this theory was first spelled out in depth and detail by a man with a legal background, John Calvin, as well as by the Lutheran theologian Philip Melanchthon. One of the surprising things about twentieth century Anglicanism, however, is that the theory received a scholarly defence by an Anglo-Catholic theologian, J.K. Mozley, not least because he believed that it had its origins in the writings of the ancient Fathers of the Church. Indeed, in recent years other important theologians claim to have made the same discovery as Mozley in this respect (e.g. the Reformed, and profoundly ecumenical Canadian theologian Hans Boersma, and the American Episcoplian Fleming Rutledge). From Boersma, for example, we learn:

> Saint Irenaeus [in the second century] expresses the connection between Christ's sacrifice and propitiation most clearly when he says that the Lord "did not make void, but fulfilled the law, by performing the offices of the high priest, propitiating God for men, and cleansing the lepers, healing the sick, and Himself suffering death, that exiled man might go free from condemnation, and might return without fear to his

---

[659] Michael Gaitley, MIC, *Consoling the Heart of Jesus* (Stockbridge, MA: Marian Press, 2010), p. 134.
[660] Brown, *Divine Humanity*, p. 185.

own inheritance. ..." Origen (c. 185-253) ... argues that Christ is the sacrificial victim through whose death on the cross "propitiation" is made. Similarly, St. Cyril of Alexandria (c. 375-444) argues that Christ "accepted the punishment of sinners." These judicial elements were reinforced in the West through the writings of St. Hilary of Poitiers (d. 367) and St. Augustine (354-430). "Christ though guiltless," comments Augustine, "took our punishment that He might cancel our guilt, and do away with our punishment." In the sixth century we find St. Gregory the Great (c. 540-604) explicitly discussing the question of God's justice in condemning the Mediator who "deserved not to be punished for Himself." Gregory answers the question with an eye to the outcome of Christ's death: "But if He had not Himself undertaken a death not due to Him, He would never have freed us from the one that was justly due to us. And so, whereas 'The Father is righteous,' in punishing a righteous man 'He ordereth all things righteously.'"[661]

In looking for the roots of a specifically "penal substitution" model, however, we need to be cautious, because when some of the ancient Fathers state that by his death Jesus Christ accomplished the "propitiation" for our sins (in other words, a sacrifice that turns aside the wrath of God), they could just as well be referring to an incipient Sacrificial-Satisfaction theory. In other words, similar language may be used, but the idea behind it may be that Christ *shared in the consequences of human sin, representing us and making a satisfaction-offering to God of loving obedience on our behalf,* rather than that Christ *bore the penal consequences of sin in our place.* Mozley, for example, found seeds of these theories as early as the second century. Regarding the *Epistle to Diognetus,* he writes that the author

> speaks of God as Himself taking our sins, which the reward of punishment and death awaited, and giving His Son as a ransom for us, 'the Holy for the wicked, the Innocent for the guilty.' 'For what else could cover our sins except his righteousness?

---

[661] Hans Boersma, *Violence, Hospitality, and the Cross* (Grand Rapids: Baker Academic, 2004), p. 162-163.

In whom was it possible for us sinners to be justified ... save in the Son of God alone? O sweet exchange and unexpected benefits! That the wickedness of many should be hidden in One who was righteous, and the righteousness of one justify many wicked.'

This is a "remarkable passage," Mozley concludes, "combining, as it does, ideas of man's sins deserving punishment, of God taking our sins in His love and giving His innocent Son as a ransom for us, and of the consequent covering of sin by righteousness represented as exchange."[662] In this case, the language of the *Epistle to Diognetus* could be seen to reflect a Penal Substitution theory, but it might fit even better with an incipient Sacrificial-Satisfaction theory. In looking for the Patristic roots of penal substitution, therefore, we do well to restrict ourselves to language of Christ suffering "in our place," coupled with some idea of a penalty being paid. Nevertheless, just in the few quotations from the Fathers given by Boersma, an implicit notion of penal substitution arguably might be on display in the words of St. Cyril of Alexandria, St. Augustine, and St. Gregory the Great.[663]

Moreover, in none of these authors is the idea of substitution taken to be exclusive of other dimensions of the mystery of redemption, such as Christ as our exemplar, or Christ setting us free from the power of the Devil. Taking all this into account, Fleming Rutledge found the concept of Christ dying "in our place" in several more of the ancient Fathers:

- Rutledge claims that in his great work *On the Incarnation*, St. Athanasius "put forward the idea of exchange ('in the stead of') as though it were obvious, using the phrase several times."[664] For example, Athanasius writes: "Taking a body like our own, because we all were liable to the corruption of death, He

---

[662] Mozley, *The Doctrine of the Atonement*, p. 97-98.
[663] Rutledge would agree with Boersma's reading of St. Cyril of Alexandria here (see Rutledge, *The Crucifixion*, p. 479), as would Mozley in *The Doctrine of the Atonement* (p.114), and Mozley would also agree with Boersma's reading of St. Augustine (Mozley, p. 122-123) and St. Gregory the Great (Mozley, p. 125).
[664] Rutledge, *The Crucifixion*, p. 477.

surrendered his body to death *instead of all*, and offered it to the Father …. Whence, as I said before, the Word, since it was not possible for Him to die, took to himself a body such as could die, that He might offer it as His own *in the stead of all.*"[665]

- According to St. Ambrose, "Jesus took flesh to abolish the curse of sinful flesh, and was made a curse *in our stead* so that the curse might be swallowed up in a blessing …. He took death too upon himself that the sentence might be carried out, so that He might satisfy the judgment that sinful flesh should be cursed even unto death."[666]

- According to St. Gregory Nazianzus, Christ saves us "because He releases us from the power of sin and offers Himself as a ransom *in our place* to cleanse the whole world."[667] And note here that by offering "a ransom in our place" Gregory cannot mean "a ransom paid *to the Devil* in our place," because he was a sharp critic of the "ransom to the Devil" theory.

- Rutledge also argues that St. John Chrysostom is the clearest of all: "Christ has saved us … by substituting Himself in our place. Though He was righteousness itself, God allowed Him to be condemned as a sinner and to die as one under a curse, transferring to Him not only the death which we owed, but our guilt as well."[668]

In Mozley we find several more purported references to penal substitution not mentioned either in Boersma or in Rutledge, in particular:

---

[665] Athanasius, *De Incarnatione* 8, cited in Rutledge, *The Crucifixion*, p. 477; her italics.

[666] Ambrose, *De fuga saeculi*, 44, cited in Rutledge, p. 479, her italics.

[667] Gregory Nazianzus, *Oratio in laudem Basilii*, 30.20, cited in Rutledge, p. 480; her italics.

[668] John Chrysostom, *Homiliae in epistulam ad Hebraeos, 15.2,* cited in Rutledge, p. 480. Mozley in *The Doctrine of the Atonement*, p. 113, also finds the idea of penal substitution in Chrysostom, noting that he even uses the (rather dubious!) illustration of a king who gives his son to die in the place of a bandit.

- In the fourth century, Eusebius "speaks of Christ as 'chastised for us and undergoing a penalty which He did not owe but we for our sins, and so gaining for us forgiveness of sins.'"[669]
- Mozley sums up the teachings of St. Hilary of Poitiers as follows: "The Passion was voluntarily accepted to satisfy a penal necessity; through Christ propitiation is made to God; in His death we see a guiltless sufferer paying the penalty for sins He had not committed. Hilary thinks of Christ as expiating by His death for sins for which others should have suffered; so far, at least, a penal significance is ascribed to the Cross ...."[670]
- Finally, Mozley cites the work of St. John Damascene in the eighth century, who summarized the thoughts on the doctrine of the Redemption of most of his saintly forbearers, including the notion that the death of Christ was, (in Mozley's words) "a sacrifice offered on our behalf and in our stead to the Father against whom we had sinned .... Exactly like Chrysostom, he compares Christ's action to an innocent man's readiness to step into the place of one condemned to die."[671]

---

[669] Mozley, *The Doctrine of the Atonement*, p. 108, citing Eusebius *Dem. Ev.* 10.1.
[670] Ibid., p. 120; see Mozley's footnotes for references to the passages in St. Hilary.
[671] Ibid., p. 116-117; see Mozley's footnotes for references to passages from St. Damascene. If Mozley is right, then the witness of St. John Chrysostom and St. John Damascene also shows that the penal substitution dimension of the doctrine of redemption, contrary to popular belief, is not foreign to the Christology of the East. We find another example in the writings of St. Tikhon of Zadonsk in Russia (1724-1783):

> But you, my Lord and Sovereign, have suffered in my place. The servant sinned, but my Lord suffered the punishment; the servant erred, but my Lord was scourged; the servant stole, and my Lord offered compensation; the servant was indebted, but my Sovereign paid the debt. And in what manner did He pay it? Not in gold and silver but with His disgrace, his wounds, His blood, His death on the cross. For me, wretched and accursed, He bore the infamy, He who is blessed throughout all eternity. (St. Tikhon of Zadonsk, "Confession and Thanksgiving to Christ, Son of God, The Savior of the World" in Fedotov, *A Treasury of Russian Spirituality*, p. 132)

While this new appreciation for the Patristic seeds of the Legal Theory is well worth noting, we do not have space to adjudicate these scholarly claims here. All of the passages cited from the Fathers (above) would need to be closely analyzed in the **context** of the documents from which they are taken, and in the context of each writers thought as a whole. Besides, **it is primarily the alleged strength of its *scriptural* basis that has continued to commend the Legal Theory to the heirs of the Reformation, and especially to those in the Evangelical tradition.**[672]

In the Old Testament, however, several key passages and concepts seem to point in the direction of penal substitution. For example, there is the all-important passage about the vicarious suffering of the Messiah for sinners,[673] the Suffering Servant of the Lord, in Isaiah 53: 4-6, 11-12:

> Surely he has borne our griefs and carried our sorrows; yet we esteemed him stricken, smitten by God and afflicted. But he was wounded for our transgressions, he was bruised for our iniquities; upon him was the chastisement that made us whole, and with his stripes we are healed. All we like sheep have gone astray; we have turned every one to his own way; and the Lord has laid on him the iniquity of us all … and he shall bear their iniquities. … [H]e poured out his soul to death, and was numbered among the transgressors; yet he bore the sin of many, and made intercession for the transgressors.

---

[672] Of course, this too is controversial. Roman Catholic theologian Gerald O'Collins, SJ, for example, offered an in-depth critique of the alleged biblical basis of the substitutionary doctrine of the Cross. See O'Collins, *Jesus Our Redeemer*, p. 138-160.

[673] I assume here that the Suffering Servant of the Lord refers both to an individual (the Messiah) and to the vocation of the people of Israel as a whole, a vocation that is supremely fulfilled by that individual; see Wright, *The Day the Revolution Began*, p. 125-126.

This passage is of special importance for an interpretation of the Cross because from ancient times it was used in the Church's liturgy for Good Friday. In fact, it was so central to the understanding of the Cross by the early Christians that in the first century St. Clement of Rome (in his first epistle, section 16) simply quotes it in full to explain what Jesus accomplished on Calvary. Given that it speaks of the Messiah as being "chastised" (that is, punished, in a sense even "smitten by God"), and as "bearing the iniquities" of all sinners, in order to make us whole, it is hard not to see penal substitution implied here. Moreover, this passage connects with several others in Scripture. For example, I Peter 2:24-25 alludes to it: "He himself bore our sins in his body on the tree, that we might die to sin and live to righteousness. By his wounds you have been healed. For you were straying like sheep …." Thus, if Isaiah 53 includes the element of penal substitution, then so does I Peter 2, at least implicitly. Jesus himself connects his coming arrest and persecution with the penal substitution theme of Isaiah 53 when he says to his disciples: "For I tell you that this Scripture must be fulfilled in me, '*And he was reckoned with transgressors*'; for what is written about me has its fulfilment" (Lk 22:37). In addition, when Jesus tells us that the Son of Man came "to give his life as a ransom for[674] *many*" (Mt 20:28; Mk 10:45), and that the New Covenant in his "blood" is "poured out for *many*" (Mt 26:28; Mk 14:24), he alludes to the same Suffering Servant passage in Isaiah, where the prophet says that "he bore the sin of many" (53:12).[675]

---

[674] It should be noted that the Greek preposition *huper,* usually translated here as "for" can also mean "instead of" or "in place of." See the discussion of this point in Millard Erickson, *Christian Theology* (Grand Rapids: Baker Academic, second edition, 1998), p. 830-832.

[675] According to New Testament scholar Joachim Jeremias, this concept of "the many," in its pre-Christian Jewish interpretation, referred to the godless among both the Jews and the Gentiles. The expression, therefore, was not meant to be exclusive (i.e., "many, but not all") but inclusive ("the totality, consisting of many"). On this see John Stott, *The Cross of Christ* (Downers Grove IL: InterVarsity Press, 1986), p. 146-147.

The Incarnation

This verse in Isaiah (53:12) also raises the question of what "sin-bearing" in the Old Testament might mean. Anglican Evangelical theologian John Stott summed up his study of the question:

> It is clear from Old Testament usage that to 'bear sin' means neither to sympathize with sinners, nor to identify with their pain, nor to express their penitence, nor to be persecuted on account of human sinfulness (as others have argued), nor even to suffer the consequences of sin in personal or social terms, but specifically to endure its penal consequences, to undergo its penalty. The expression comes most frequently in the book of Leviticus and Numbers. It is written of those who sin by breaking God's laws that they will 'bear their iniquity (or sin)' (AV and RSV). That is, 'they will be held responsible' or 'will suffer for their sins' (NIV). Sometimes the matter is put beyond question by the fact that the penalty is specified: the offender is to be 'cut off from his people' (i.e., excommunicated) and even, for example, in the case of blasphemy, put to death.[676]

In short, Isaiah 53 is central to a biblical understanding of the Cross, and it is almost impossible not to see an element of penal and substitutionary sin-bearing as part of the mystery of what the Messianic Suffering Servant of the Lord accomplished for us there.

In Isaiah 53:10 we are also told of the Suffering Servant: "it was the will of the Lord to bruise him; he has put him to grief: when he makes himself an offering for sin …." Here the Messiah is likened to the lambs offered as sin-offerings in the Temple. **Thus, if we take Isaiah 53 as a whole, the sacrificial death of the Messiah is essentially a sin-bearing sin-offering.**

In John 1:24, John the Baptist proclaims: "Behold the Lamb of God, who takes away the sin of the world!" But the Passover lamb was not

---

[676] Ibid., p. 143. In the footnote to this passage Stott cites as examples of penal sin-bearing Ex 28:43; Lv 5:17, 19:8, 22:9, 24:15 and Num 9:13, 14:34 and 18:22]

a sin-offering, and the language of "taking-away" sin in the Torah is used especially for one sin-offering above all: the one and only sin-bearing sin-offering in ancient Judaism.[677] It is widely accepted by Old Testament scholars that the animal sacrifices in the Jewish Temple generally did not function as sin-bearing penal-substitutes. The animals did not bear the punishment for sin in the place of the sinners who offered them; rather, they were offered as a satisfaction or penitential gift to the Lord to wipe the debt and stain of sin away, a compensatory gift expressing repentance. Yet there was one Jewish sin-offering that was different: a sin-offering that was also sin-bearing. This was the ritual on the Day of Atonement, the day when the High Priest was to take away the guilt of the community and make atonement for their sins by taking two male goats for a sin-offering (Lv 10:17, 16:5). One was to be sacrificed and its blood sprinkled in the usual way, while on the living goat's head the High Priest was to lay his hands and confess all the sins of Israel, transferring them to the goat (16:21-22). Then the

---

[677] While it is true that in most cases the sacrifices offered in the Temple in Jerusalem were not considered to be "penal substitutes" for the sinner, still, it would also be true to say that the *original* Passover Lamb, and the blood of that lamb that was spread on the door posts of the Israelites in Egypt, was indeed a kind of substitution. Timothy Keller brought out this point in his book *Jesus the King: Understanding the Life and Death of the Son of God* (New York: Penguin: 2011), p. 178-179, and 183:

> In every home that night there would either be a dead child or dead lamb. When justice came down, either it fell on your family or you took shelter under the substitute, under the blood of the lamb. If you did accept this shelter, then death passed over you and you were saved; that's why it was called Passover. You were saved only on the basis of faith in a substitutionary sacrifice. ...

> [W]hen Jesus says, "This is my body ... This is my blood ... poured out," he means: *I'm the One that Isaiah and John spoke about. I am the Lamb of God to which all other lambs pointed, the Lamb that takes away the sin of the world.*

> On the cross Jesus got what *we* deserved: The sin, guilt, and brokenness of the world fell upon him. He loved us so much he took divine justice on himself so that we could be passed over, forever.

goat was to be driven into the wilderness, "taking away" all Israel's sins along with it to die in a solitary place, far from the people (16:22). **Thus, the sacrifice of the goats on the annual Day of Atonement was arguably the one Jewish temple sacrifice in which sacrificial animals acted symbolically as a penal substitute, "taking away" both the guilt and power of the sins of the People of God, a sin-bearing sin-offering, just as the Suffering Servant of the Lord in Isaiah 53, the Messiah, was prophesied to be.**

The argument is frequently made that the scapegoat (etymologically the "goat that escapes") is not sacrificed. It is released into the desert to carry away the people's sins, but it does not have to be killed in punishment for them — the people are nowhere commanded to kill it. It is the other goat that is sacrificed. John Stott replies to this point:

> Some commentators make the mistake of driving a wedge between the two goats, the sacrificed goat and the scapegoat, overlooking the fact that the two are described as a 'sin offering' in the singular (Lev 16:5). ... Each embodied a different aspect of the same sacrifice, the one exhibiting the means the other the results of the atonement. In this case the public proclamation of the Day of Atonement was plain, namely that reconciliation was possible only through substitutionary sin-bearing. The author of the Letter to the Hebrews has no inhibitions about seeing Jesus as both 'a merciful and faithful high priest' (2:17) and as the two victims, the sacrificed goat whose blood was taken into the inner sanctuary (9:7, 12) and the scapegoat which carried away the people's sins (9:28).[678]

In the New Testament there are several key passages that seem to speak directly of substitutionary atonement. In Galatians 3:13-14, St. Paul tells us:

> Christ redeemed us from the curse of the law, having become a curse for us — for it is written, "Cursed be everyone that

---

[678] Ibid., p. 144.

hangs on a tree"— that in Christ Jesus the blessing of Abraham might come upon the Gentiles, that we might receive the promise of the Spirit through faith.

Saint Paul's main point here is that those who try to be set right with God by keeping the law will find themselves under a divine "curse," because all are cursed who do not follow every aspect of that divine law perfectly (Gal 3:10-11). Jesus Christ, however, sets us right with God (i.e., justifies us) by taking the curse upon himself of all those who fall short of complete obedience to the law, both Jews and Gentiles. Indeed, Paul is paraphrasing here a verse from Deuteronomy that occurs in the context of the harshest penalties meted out by divine law for evildoers: such as idolaters (Dt 13:15), murderers (19:21), and the stoning of a disobedient son (21:21). Fleming Rutledge concludes from this:

> The overwhelming effect of the Deuteronomic verse about the hanged man [on a tree] in this context [of Galatians 3] is that Christ is *taking the place* of all the stoned, massacred, enslaved, defiled and beheaded idolaters, rebels, apostates, and murderers (and all others) who have suffered under the Law. He is suffering the curse and defilement that would have fallen upon them — that is, upon *us*. Understanding the Galatians verse in any other way strains unconvincingly at the obvious meaning ....

> How can a crucified Messiah "who hangs on a tree," cursed by God, be an acceptable object of worship? [Saint Paul's] conclusion ... is that Christ became a curse *for us* (*huper hemon*) precisely in order to blow wide open every possible conditional version of the covenant. None of the categories of sinners cursed by the Law that are listed in Deuteronomy are beyond the reach of God's saving act. Paul's gospel is radically expansive, and clearly suggests that Christ substituted himself for us all, godly and ungodly, Jews and Gentiles alike (3:28),

under the curse of Sin. Other meanings can be found in Galatians 3:10-14, but substitution is clearly predominant.[679]

If this interpretation of Gal 3:13 is acceptable, then it also sheds light on two other cryptic passages in St. Paul that are notoriously difficult to interpret: "For our sake *he made him to be sin who knew no sin*, so that in him we might become the righteousness of God" (II Cor 5:21) and "For God has done what the law, weakened by the flesh, could not do: sending his own Son in the likeness of sinful flesh and for sin, *he condemned sin in the flesh*, in order that the just requirement of the law might be fulfilled in us, who walk not according to the flesh but according to the Spirit (Rom 8:3-4). In both cases, the thought seems to be that Christ the Innocent One ("who knew no sin") not only suffered the substitutionary "condemnation for sin" in his own person "in the flesh", but he did so with the goal of enabling us to fulfill "the righteousness of God," "the just requirement of the law," in other words, that we may "walk" from henceforth "in the Spirit."[680] The goal

---

[679] Rutledge, *The Crucifixion*, p. 473. It is true that in Galatians 3:13 St. Paul leaves out the words in Deuteronomy that those hanged on a tree are cursed "by God," but this does not alter the meaning of the passage. For St. Paul clearly wants to say that it is the standard of the divine Law, God's justice or righteousness, which declares us all accursed, Jew and Gentile alike (the same message as Romans 1-3), and it is God in Christ who bears that curse for us, in our place. O'Collins argues in *Jesus the Redeemer* (2007) that "On the cross Jesus was cursed by the law and by those who administered the law, but not by God" (p. 153). But this section of Galatians is not a denunciation of the Temple authorities who engineered Christ's execution: they are nowhere mentioned. Rather, it is a warning that anyone who tries to be set right with God merely by striving to keep his Law will fall short, and end up under a divine curse (Gal 3:10-11). If we are cursed by the Law, therefore, we are under the condemnation of God's justice, for it is *his Law* that we have disobeyed. And it is this curse, our condemnation before the scales of Divine Justice, that Christ took upon himself on the "tree" of the Cross.

[680] The connection with Gal 3:13, and the interpretation of II Cor 5:21 I am offering here — that they refer to Christ dealing with the objective guilt of sin on the Cross so that we can be empowered to live according to the Spirit — I am adapting from Anglican NT scholar Tom Wright in *The Day the Revolution Began*, p. 253.

of his substitutionary sacrifice, therefore, is to set us free to live by the Spirit of God.

Finally, in the Gospels we see Jesus offered a "cup" to drink by his heavenly Father in the Garden of Gethsemane. It is commonly assumed that this "cup" was simply the cup of his betrayal, and the excruciating sufferings he would have to undergo in his agony and passion. But a closer look at the biblical metaphor of the "cup" that the Lord sometimes gives people to drink shows that it is rooted in something deeper. In the Garden of Gethsemane, Jesus asked his heavenly Father that, if possible, the "cup" may be taken from him. No doubt this has several layers of meaning, but one layer surely refers to the "cup" of divine "wrath" for sin (that is, Divine Justice)[681] — a "cup" mentioned with this same connotation at least 10 times in Holy Scripture (see Job 21:20; Ezek 23:32-34; Is 51:17-22; Ps 75:8; Jer 25:15-29; Hab 2:16 and 49:12; also Rev 14:10, 16:1ff, and 18:6). **In short, Jesus knew very well what he was getting into by drinking that cup to the dregs on the Cross: he was offering himself as a sacrifice, as a sin-bearing sin-offering, for lost and broken humanity.**

Perhaps no one has summarized the biblical case for penal substitution better than Protestant New Testament scholar A.M. Hunter in his books *The Words and Works of Jesus* (1950) and *Interpreting Paul's Gospel* (1954):

> It is with this type of theory that the sayings of Jesus seem best to agree. There can be little doubt that Jesus viewed his death as a representative sacrifice for "the many." Not only is His thought saturated in Isa. 53 (which is a doctrine of representative suffering), but His words over the cup — indeed, the whole narrative of the Last Supper — almost demand to be interpreted as a sacrifice in whose virtue his

---

[681] In the New Testament divine "wrath" refers not to cruel vindictiveness or bad temper (!), but to God's personal and just attitude of total opposition toward sin and evil: see Rom 1:18, Col 3:6, and Eph 5:6.

followers can share. The idea of substitution which is prominent in Is 53 appears in the ransom saying. And it requires only a little reading between the lines to find in the "cup" saying, the story of the Agony, and the cry of dereliction, evidence that Christ's sufferings were what, for lack of a better word, we can only call "penal."[682]

Paul declares that the crucified Christ, on our behalf, took the whole reality of sin upon himself, like the scapegoat: "For our sake he made him to be sin who knew no sin, so that in him we might become the righteousness of God." Paul sees the Cross as an act of God's doing in which the Sinless One, for the sake of sinners, somehow experienced the horror of the divine reaction against sin so that there might be condemnation no more.

Galatians 3:13 moves in the same realm of ideas. "Christ redeemed us from the curse of the law, having become a curse for us." The curse is the divine condemnation of sin which leads to death. To this curse we lay exposed; but Christ on his cross identified himself with the doom impending on sinners that, through this act, the curse passes away and we go free.

Such passages show the holy love of God taking awful issue in the cross with the sin of man. Christ, by God's appointing, dies the sinner's death, and so removes sin. Is there a simpler way of saying this than that Christ bore our sins? We are not fond nowadays of calling Christ's suffering "penal" or of styling him our "substitute"; but can we avoid using some such words as these to express Paul's view of the atonement?[683]

---

[682] A. M. Hunter, *The Words and Works of Jesus* (London: SCM, 1950), p.100, as quoted in J.I. Packer and Mark Dever, *In My Place Condemned He Stood: Celebrating the Glory of the Atonement* (Wheaton, IL: Crossway Books, 2007), p. 99.

[683] A, M. Hunter, *Interpreting Paul's Gospel* (London: SCM, 1954), p. 31f, as quoted in Packer and Dever, *In My Place Condemned He Stood*, p. 100.

I have gone to great lengths here to make a case for the biblical and Patristic seeds of the notion of Christ's death as an act of penal substitution, not because the other major theories we have surveyed so far in this chapter lack a scriptural or Patristic basis, but because the roots of those theories are not disputed by most contemporary theologians, at least not to anything like the degree that the Legal Theory is questioned.

Still, establishing the seeds of this theory in the principal sources of revelation (Scripture, and for Catholics and Eastern Orthodox Christians at least, ancient Tradition), while it may enable the theory to receive a hearing, does not deal with the main objection usually advanced against it. Rather, *the principal complaint against it is that the theory of the Cross as an act of penal substitution violates both moral and theological logic.*

2) The Logic of the Legal Theory

For one thing, the Legal Theory involves an extremely low view of fallen human nature. Every adult we meet on the street must be seen as (in God's eyes) deserving the most terrible punishment — bodily death and everlasting spiritual death — if the theory is to make any sense.[684] This is hardly likely to appeal to the relatively humanistic Anglican temperament. Christian "humanism" rightly conceived, however, is not the same as optimism: rather, it is an abiding confidence in the capacity of the otherwise fallen and accursed human soul to attain sanctity, with the help of divine grace. Such was the humanism of St. Thomas More and Desiderius Erasmus, of Jeremy Taylor and St. Francis De Sales. "Optimism," on the other hand, consists in an overconfidence in the capacity of the fallen human soul to live virtuously *even apart from the help of grace.* Such was the naïve optimism of the Deists and the Enlightenment, of Thomas Jefferson and Voltaire. This latter attitude is condemned in Scripture: "Cursed is the man who trusts in man … whose heart turns away from the Lord ….The heart is deceitful above all things and desperately corrupt" (Jer

---

[684] On this see David Brown, *Continental Philosophy and Modern Theology*, p. 119.

16:5,9). Such "optimism" also underestimates the gravity of the offense of sin, which not only degrades the sinner and his victims, and compounds the misery of human life, but also "spits in the face" of our Creator, Redeemer, and Sanctifier — our Total Benefactor — and thereby betrays his *infinite love* for us.

The Penal Substitution Theory simply states that God himself has acted decisively on the Cross to remove this massive burden of human sin and guilt, which is the principal obstacle to the fulfilment of his loving plan for each one of us. He does so by sending his divine Son to die on the Cross, taking the penalty for our sins upon himself in our place. In this way he opens the way for us to true sanctification of the heart, and to the Kingdom of Heaven at our journey's end. Anglican Evangelical theologian J.I. Packer summarized the logic of the theory in his essay "What Did the Cross Achieve" (2007):

> The notion which the phrase "penal substitution" expresses is that Jesus Christ our Lord, moved by a love that was determined to do everything necessary to save us, endured and exhausted the destructive divine judgment for which we were otherwise inescapably destined, and so won us forgiveness, adoption, and glory ....
>
> [W]hat Christ bore on the cross was the God-forsakenness of penal judgment, which we shall never have to bear because he accepted it in our place. The appropriate formulation is that on the cross Jesus' representative relation to us, as the last Adam whose image we are to bear, took the form of substituting for us under judgment as the suffering servant of God on whom the Lord "laid the iniquity of us all" (Is 53:6).[685]

---

[685] J.I. Packer, "What Did the Cross Achieve?" in Packer and Dever, *In My Place Condemned He Stood*, p. 77 and 87. Some theologians and Scripture scholars claim that the true biblical perspective is that Christ acts as our "representative" in his life and death, or as a "vicarious representative," but they rarely make it clear what this means. Packer here admits that Christ as the New Adam "represents" all of humanity as the source and archetype of a new humanity, but this in itself still does not tells *how* he became the source of that new creation:

Unfortunately, there is no theory of the Atonement that has suffered more from caricatures than this one. Evangelical Anglican Norman Anderson, for example, decried the various forms in which the Penal Theory has been misunderstood:

> Not infrequently, it has been represented in terms of a stern and angry God being placated by the kind and loving Christ, or in terms of God visiting the sins of the guilty upon the only innocent man who was 'good enough to pay the price for sin.' Both perversions of the doctrine must be repudiated …. God in Christ identifies himself with our sin, and bore its penalty and consequences.[686]

Clearly, the doctrine sounds quite different if God himself, in the person of his Son Jesus Christ, is said to have borne the penalty we deserve. For our sake he accepted the penalty that his own Divine Justice demands, thereby enabling him freely to forgive the penitent sinner in accord with his attributes of mercy and justice. Anderson accepted that God would not allow one man to pay the penalty for another man's sins (e.g. Ez 18:1-4): "Only the one who made us, who put us in this world knowing what would happen, and who will be our judge at the great Assize, could do that."[687] In short, it is only because Jesus is our Creator and our Judge, God Incarnate, that he can die in our place, bearing our penalty for us.

The book *The Cross of Christ* (1986) by Anglican Evangelical John Stott is justly styled a classic for its in-depth and lucid defence of the theory of Penal Substitution. Like fellow Anglicans Packer and Anderson, Stott pointed to the Incarnation as the key to understanding the saving work of Jesus on the Cross:

---

in other words, it does not tell us what he did, especially on the Cross, to make that a reality. Thus, Packer rightly speaks in this passage about "representation" taking the form of "penal substitution."

[686] Anderson, *Jesus Christ: The Witness of History*, p. 103

[687] Ibid., p. 105.

It is the Judge who in this passion takes the place of those who ought to be judged, who in His passion allows Himself to be judged in their place. The passion of Jesus Christ is the judgement of God, in which the Judge Himself was judged ....

For in giving His Son He was giving Himself. This being so, it is the Judge Himself who in holy love assumed the role of innocent victim, for in and through the person of His Son He Himself bore the penalty which He Himself inflicted .... For in order to save us in such a way as to satisfy Himself, God through Christ substituted Himself for us .... The cross was simultaneously an act of punishment and amnesty, severity and grace, justice and mercy.

Seen thus, objections to substitutionary atonement evaporate. There is nothing even remotely immoral here, since the substitute for the law-breakers is none other than the divine Lawmaker Himself. There is no mechanical transaction either, since the self-sacrifice of love is the most personal of all actions. And what is achieved through the cross is no merely external exchange of legal status, since those who see God's love there, and are united in Christ by His Spirit, become radically transformed in outlook and character.[688]

---

[688] Stott, *The Cross of Christ*, p. 161 and 159. Stott's last paragraph here is an effective answer to Eleonore Stump's complaint that the doctrine of Substitutionary Atonement "leaves humans with just the same tendencies to will what is contrary to God's will, so that their wills are no more conformable to God's will, they are no more tending toward unity with God than they were before the Atonement." Stump, "Atonement According to Aquinas" in Rea, ed., *Oxford Readings in Philosophical Theology, I*, p. 269. According to I Pet 2:24, however, *the objective achievement of Christ's sin-bearing on the Cross actually prompts and enables our subjective transformation*: "He himself bore our sins in his body on the tree, that we might die to sin and live to righteousness. By his wounds you have been healed." Besides, Stump is assuming here that all defenders of the Legal Theory necessarily see it as the complete explanation of the saving work of Jesus Christ, rather than simply as one (albeit central) dimension of the mystery, among many others.

Stott also emphasized the *propriety* of substitution as the means of our salvation. At its root, human sin always involves the prideful attempt to "play God" — to do things our own way and rely on our own strength and cleverness, rather than trusting in the Lord. The Cross of Christ provides the perfect reparation for this offence:

> The concept of substitution may be said to lie at the heart of both sin and salvation. For the essence of sin is man substituting for God, while the essence of salvation is God substituting for man. Man asserts himself against God and puts himself where only God deserves to be; God sacrifices Himself for man and puts Himself where only man deserves to be. Man claims prerogatives that belong to God alone; God accepts penalties that belong to man alone. The biblical gospel of atonement is of God satisfying Himself by substituting Himself for us.[689]

Nevertheless, the Legal Theory remains under relentless assault in the academic community. As a result, even some Evangelical theologians tend to shy away from it. For example, in *The Enigma of the Cross* (1987), Anglican theologian Alister McGrath avoided the Penal Theory. He focused instead on the idea that by voluntary submission to humiliation on the Cross, God revealed to us the true nature of his divinity, and lent dignity to our suffering. God should not be seen as an impassible monarch; rather, he is our Servant King whose loving power is supremely exercised through his service and suffering for us.[690] This is evidently a version of the Incarnational Exemplarist Theory, a theory of the Atonement with which many theologians have felt more comfortable in the post-war era.

---

[689] Stott, *The Cross of Christ,* p. 160.
[690] Alister McGrath, *The Enigma of the Cross* (London: Hodder and Stoughton, 1987), p. 106, 117-124.

Why has penal substitution remained such a controversial topic? A closer look at the moral and theological logic involved will provide us with the key to its strengths and weaknesses.

a) Why does God need to exact a penalty of retribution before he can forgive penitent sinners?

First, we need to define what we mean by "retributive punishment." With Steven L. Porter, I shall take this to mean, on a human level, "The forcible withdrawal of certain rights and/or privileges from a wrongdoer in response to the intentional misuse of those rights and/or privileges by the wrongdoer."[691] **By analogy, therefore, *divine punishment for sin is the withdrawal of divine life from the unrepentant sinner: the loss of the life-giving Holy Spirit, resulting in temporal suffering and miseries of all kinds, and (in cases of unrepented mortal sin) eternal and irrevocable spiritual death.* But this punishment does not take the form of a divine act additional to the sin itself. Rather, by God's design, sin brings about its own punishment. In other words, divine retributive punishment for sin is an expression of God's *permissive will*: he permits us to misuse our free-will, if we so choose, and in accord with his justice allows the stubbornly impenitent to experience the inevitable consequences of their unrepented sins — *what sin by its very nature brings: the obstruction, or even eviction (so to speak) of the life-giving Holy Spirit from the soul, resulting in both increased temporal sufferings, and ultimately eternal loss. And it is just and right that God does this.* In other words, as an expression of his attribute of distributive justice by which he renders to each person what is their due, God has made the world and human life in such a way that ultimately, both in this life and the next, justice is done in the lives of those who refuse to repent for their wickedness, and who reject his mercy.**[692] Catholic

---

[691] Porter, "Swinburnian Atonement," p. 322.
[692] See *Catechism of the Catholic Church*, entry 1472. This is not to deny that God's retributive justice is also merciful. As we shall see later in this chapter, when he justly chastises sinners by his permissive will in this life, permitting them

theologian Roch Kereszty summed up for us this mystery of sin and punishment:

> The punishment I receive for my sin is not something extrinsic to sin itself. It is not like the application of a penal code whose penalties have only a legal connection with the sin committed. God respects our human dignity to shape freely our own being. If by sinning I freely distort my own reality and thereby my relationship to my neighbor and to God, God allows this freely chosen distortion to take effect. *The punishment of sin, then, is its necessary, "natural" consequence.* Thus, while sin is the freely chosen opposition to one's true self, to God, and to one's neighbor, the punishment is the suffering that results from this threefold estrangement. Yet as long as the sinful choice is not finalized in death, the suffering that comes from the estrangement remains a powerful incentive for sinners to seek a reversal of their state.[693]

Norman Anderson likened God's demand for the punishment of sinners to the theory behind civil penal codes. It is simply a matter of fairness or "justice":

> Both the reformative and deterrent purposes in punishment would lack any adequate moral basis were there not also a retributive element — the conviction that the criminal *deserves* such treatment, that his crime merits it, and that there is a

---

to suffer temporal consequences for their sins, it is also an expression of his remedial, "tough love" for them; and even when he justly allows unrepentant sinners to suffer eternal loss, it is also an expression of respect for the dignity of their free-will — the capacity he gave them as their Creator to choose their own destiny — and, as we shall see, even an expression of his merciful love for them.
[693] Kereszty, *Jesus Christ: Fundamentals of Christology*, p. 336. The only thing missing here from Kereszty's definition of divine punishment for sin is an acknowledgement that, while not *merely* the application of a penal code, nevertheless, it is just and right, on the scales of Divine Justice, that God permits this consequential suffering for the stubbornly impenitent.

necessary connection between the degree of his guilt and the severity of the punishment he must bear.[694]

Some might object here that Anderson held a distorted view of the intention of the law courts and the legal system. Arguably, the courts were not established to give people their "just desserts" with respect to divine law, but to protect compliance with civil law. A number of factors should be taken into account in sentencing: the need to quarantine criminals for the protection of society, the need to uphold essential community standards by expressing abhorrence, the need to deter other criminals from breaking the law, the need of the criminal to learn to take responsibility for his actions, to deter him from future law-breaking, and to effect some form of rehabilitation. All of these *utilitarian* factors might be taken into account in the process of sentencing a convicted criminal, without succumbing to the desire to punish criminals as an act of social retribution. In short, if we do not need to use retribution as a foundation of our legal system, why does God need to do so in his moral governance of the universe?

Similarly, some philosophers and theologians deny the need for *divine* retribution altogether. Fleming Rutledge, for example, draws our attention to the perspective of Nobel Prize winning Anglican Archbishop Desmond Tutu in South Africa, for whom "justice" was fundamentally restorative rather than retributive. This is why the famous Truth and Reconciliation Commission in South Africa limited itself solely to exposing the wrongs committed by the agents of the apartheid regime — through public disclosure, and the open confession of violations of human rights — rather than going after the perpetrators with retributory prison sentences or executions. While this may indeed have preserved a measure of social peace in South Africa, and opened the way for racial reconciliation to take place, there was still an element of retribution in what was done (at least in the form of the "shaming" of those whose evil deeds were made public). Furthermore, one could hardly expect God to agree that this limited measure of "owning up" to what they had done would be considered

---

[694] Anderson, *Jesus Christ: The Witness of History*, p. 102.

enough to atone for their grievous sins before the court of heaven. Rutledge, however, invites us to see Divine Justice in a different light:

> God's justice is not in competition with his mercy; *both* are manifestations of his redemptive purpose. If we can understand that God's righteousness (*dikaiosyne*, the same Greek word translated as "justice") is liberating and restorative, not crippling and retributive, then we can discuss sin with a more open mind and heart.[695]

But this is to miss some key biblical truths. In our relationship with God, his justice is indeed ultimately restorative *to those who repent*; but Scripture clearly shows that God's justice is rightly retributive, at least to those who stubbornly *refuse* to repent. Our Lord referred to this in Matthew 11:21, when he said: "Woe to you, Chorazin! Woe to you, Bethsaida! For if the mighty works done in you had been done in Tyre and Sidon, they would have repented long ago in sackcloth and ashes. But I tell you it shall be more tolerable on the Day of Judgment for Tyre and Sidon than for you." Again, in Matthew 16:27 he said, "For the Son of Man is to come with his angels in the glory of his Father, and he will repay every man for what he has done." This is also what St. Paul preached to the Athenians in Acts 17:30-31: "The times of ignorance God overlooked, but now he commands all men everywhere to repent, because he has fixed a day on which he will judge the world in righteousness." Saint Paul also taught in Romans 2:6-8: "For [God] will render to every man according to his works: to those who with patience in well-doing seek for glory and honor and immortality, he will give eternal life, but for those who are factious and do not obey the truth, but obey wickedness, there will be wrath and fury" (cf. Lk 13:3-5; Acts 3:19; Rev 16:8-11). According to Jesus and St. Paul,

---

[695] Rutledge, *The Crucifixion*, p. 168-169. Rutledge seems to contradict here what she had said earlier (and that we quoted earlier in this chapter) that "there are some things that cannot go unpunished" and in such cases it is important "that reparations be made, that sentences be served, that restitution be offered when there is a great offence" (Rutledge, p. 148).

therefore, Divine Justice is indeed retributive in the end for the stubbornly impenitent.

With regard to human justice systems, David Brown has pointed out that there is an element of proper "retribution in distribution" in the severity of punishments meted out, and the length of prison sentences assigned, akin to the common sense desire that "the punishment should fit the crime."[696] For example, consider the list of non-retributive, "utilitarian" reasons for punishing criminals that we previously discussed. Without also applying a standard of "retribution in distribution," one could argue that the most sure and certain way of achieving almost all of these utilitarian purposes at once would be to ascribe life-sentences for every crime. It is primarily because we know that such a severe sentences would be "unjust" for small crimes, that the perpetrators of such crimes do not "deserve" such treatment, that we refrain from utilitarian over-kill. Arguably, any proper theory of social punishment must therefore involve at least some retributive element.[697]

Porter also argues that there is more to retributive punishment than just "eye for an eye" calculations of proportionate response. The administration of a fair punishment actually upholds the dignity of everyone involved in the situation:

> While the potential utilitarian ends of retributive punishment are well known (deterrence, rehabilitation, and prevention),

---

[696] Brown, *Continental Philosophy and Modern Theology*, p. 119.

[697] Leonard Hodgson insisted that there is a difference between proper "punishment" and mere "revenge" in that the former is a social act in which a community "disowns and disassociate[s] itself from ... acts which contradict what it stands for" (*The Doctrine of the Atonement*, p. 57). As the rightful and sovereign King of the universe, in the process of re-establishing his rightful reign and kingdom on the earth, God may indeed have this kind of utilitarian, social right to punish unrepentant evildoers. Nevertheless, while this distinction between "punishment" and "revenge" may be true as far as it goes, as just another utilitarian consideration, it still leaves the question of whether or not the individual malefactor actually "deserves" the degree of punishment he/she receives.

there are also what might be called *intrinsic ends* that are secured in all cases of rightful, retributive punishment. For to demand that a wrongdoer suffer the loss that he deserves takes the harm done with moral seriousness; it treats the wrongdoer as a responsible moral agent; and it expresses the value of the victim as well as the value of the personal relationship involved. This in turn provides the wrongdoer the opportunity to take himself, his act, the victim, and the relationship involved with due moral seriousness by his abiding by and perceiving the justice of the enforced demands. In the case of serious wrongdoing or repeated offenses, the absence of punishment can trivialize all those elements.[698]

Based on these insights gleaned from Anderson, Brown, and Porter, therefore, we can make a strong case that retributive justice rightfully plays a part in human justice systems, and in the sentencing of convicted criminals, and by analogy this makes it likely that retributive justice plays a part in God's moral governance of the universe as well — as St. Paul, and Jesus himself clearly taught.

Still, our main question remains unanswered: even if Divine Justice legitimately can be retributive, in certain circumstances — because God can only forgive those who are authentically repentant for their misdeeds — why does there also need to be a punishment exacted before he can fully pardon the penitent? Why isn't repentance — especially repentance fully expressed and completed by what Swinburne would call acts of "atonement" (contrition, apology, works of reparation and penance) — why is that not enough to enable God fully to forgive us on a "moral" basis, in accord with his holiness and justice?

We need to remember that human relationships and justice systems are only *analogous* to Divine Justice, not its exact equivalent. Again, *God is our Total Benefactor, and our sins betray his infinite love for us. The context of our wrongdoing against God, therefore, is vastly different from the context of the*

[698] Porter, "Swinburnian Atonement," p. 322.

wrongs we do to other human beings or to society, even though these are often two dimensions of the same acts (take for example, theft from the poor, which is both a grave sin against God and a serious crime against humanity).[699] For God simply to forget about our mortal sins, even if we are sorry for them now and trying to make amends, hardly seems to be in full accord with his justice and holiness. To do so would still, to some degree, trivialize our offenses, and all the human suffering and disruption of divine purposes they have caused. Porter believes that the doctrine of penal substitution adequately addresses the gravity of sin, and provides the best the motive for true and deep repentance for it:

> In God demanding and Christ taking on the kind of punishment we deserve in our place, human sin is taken with utter seriousness, sinners are treated as responsible moral agents, and the high value of the Godhead and the divine/human relationship is expressed. Moreover, sinners are provided the opportunity *in the cross* to recognize the gravity of their offense, to realize their responsibility before God, to grasp the great value of the Godhead and the divine/human

---

[699] It is also important to remember that human justice systems are actually incapable of fairly adjudicating precisely what a perpetrator "deserves," since unlike God, we are not omniscient and do not have the gift of reading hearts. Some malefactors have been so wounded by others throughout their lives that the degree of moral culpability for their worst crimes is actually mitigated in God's eyes. As the saying goes: "hurt people hurt people." This is not to completely excuse all bad behavior, but to argue that human free-will is enmeshed in a web of social injustices and psychological wounds, secrets of the heart that only God can see. This is one reason why the courts should avoid as much as possible meting out irrevocable and extreme sentences, even if they seem to "fit the crime," such as the death penalty. Some penalties that appear to fit the crime may not actually fit the criminal. This is also one reason why St. Paul reminds us of the proverb: "Vengeance is mine, I will repay, says the Lord" (Rom 12:19). Only God is capable of knowing completely what someone's "just desserts" amount to in any situation. Human justice systems, therefore, must restrict themselves to the minimal degree of retribution that is needed for an equitable social order (in addition to utilitarian motives of deterrence, quarantine, and rehabilitation). For in the end, only God fully knows who deserves what.

relationship, and in all of this to become aware of the riches of God's mercy, grace, and love.[700]

Another reason why divine retribution is appropriate for serious human wrongdoing, even for the penitent, is *the inescapable human moral intuition that serious wrongdoing ought to be punished to some extent, even when the criminal is sorry for his misdeeds.* In other words, when we ourselves do wrong to others, our conscience convicts us and pronounces an inner sentence of "guilty" and "worthy of punishment." It was the Russian novelist Fyodor Dostoyevsky in his book *Crime and Punishment* who showed that this echo of the demands of divine justice lies so deep within the human heart that when we do something grievously wrong, even if we "get away with it" in the sense that we don't get "caught," we end up punishing ourselves anyway. Bit by bit we destroy ourselves, for we are eaten away deep within by guilt and self-hatred, no matter how much we may refuse to admit that truth to ourselves. This same truth is expressed in another way in the old saying: "The wicked flees when no one pursues" (Prov 28:1). Deep inside, we know our moral debts well enough — we know what we deserve.

The most grievous moral wrong that we can commit is when we betray the trust of someone who loves us — especially if the person we betray is innocent of all wrongdoing. Human sin is a betrayal of our heavenly Father's *infinite love* for us. His infinite love created us, gave us the gift of life, and invites us to share eternal life with him in Heaven. By our sins, we betray that infinite love, and that surely leaves us in a state of tremendous moral debt to God. We really owe him something that we can never repay — namely, a life of totally faithful service spent achieving the good purposes for which he made us. Having misspent our past, we have nothing extra to offer to God to make

---

[700] Ibid., p. 326; italics mine. Of course, it could be argued that a Sacrificial-Satisfaction theory can uphold these truths just as well, or better, than the Legal Theory can. The latter, however, can successfully locate much of this *on the Cross*, in accordance with Scripture and ancient Tradition. See our discussion of the main shortcomings of Sacrificial-Satisfaction theories in the previous sections of this chapter.

up for it, and by our mortal sins we owe an infinite penalty to his justice for having so seriously let him down. Even authentic repentance, completed by acts of restitution and penance, where possible, seems to fall short of making up that debt. In fact, Porter argues, even in human relationships, in cases of grievous moral crime malefactors acquire a further moral debt to their victims — what may be called a *"penal debt"* — that cannot be remitted by deep repentance alone:

> Let us say that I deliberately crash your car because I am jealous of you. Now … I am in moral debt to you and I ought to repent, apologize, and seek to make reparation and penance. I owe this to you, and just as it would be good of me to offer it to you, so it would be good of you to require such an atonement process as a condition of your forgiveness.

> But while it seems clear that I owe you this kind of response, it also seems clear that I deserve more than this. For even after engaging in the Swinburnian atonement process, it seems permissible for you to withdraw my car-borrowing privileges. I certainly don't deserve the privilege after what I have done, and in fact it appears that I deserve to lose that privilege — at least for a time. Due to my misuse of a certain privilege, you have a right to withdraw that privilege from me ….

> As another example, take the unfaithful husband who comes to his wife repentant, apologetic, and willing to make reparation and penance for his adultery. It seems permissible for the wife to accept these steps toward reconciliation but to nevertheless demand that he move out of the family home — at least for a time. The wife may say to her husband, "I will forgive you, but for now pack your things and get out of the house." If there was a debate about whether or not this was fair, I take it that we would side with the wife. For it appears that the husband deserves to be treated in such a manner —

he deserves to lose certain rights and privileges of family life due to his misuse of those rights and privileges.[701]

Let us add one more example: suppose a man rapes and murders your teen-age daughter. Suppose that before the trial, he is helped by a prison chaplain to realize the gravity of what he has done; he becomes authentically contrite, publicly apologizes in court, offers to do public service for the rest of his life to atone for his evil deed, and offers to foot the bill for the creation of a public memorial of the daughter you have lost. It is hard to see how he could do any more to "atone" for his sins (in Swinburne's sense of the word). But would you be wrong to insist that he also spend at least some time behind bars as a punishment for what he has done? — and wrong to insist that your *full* forgiveness of his moral crime would depend on that being accomplished? *It seems that in cases of serious wrongdoing in human affairs, in addition to what Swinburne would call accomplishing works of "atonement," there is also an additional, "penal debt" that ought to be paid, before the conditions for full forgiveness can be met. And if this is true on a human level, how much more so on the divine level?*

The truth is that having betrayed the *infinite love* of God, our *Total Benefactor*, by our mortal sins, we owe him an *infinite penalty*. The only thing that could even approach such a penalty would be our death: both the irrevocable punishment of bodily death and the everlasting punishment of spiritual death (in other words, the everlasting loss of divine friendship, and the deprivation from our hearts of his life-giving Holy Spirit). That is why the Bible says "the wages of sin is death" (Rom 6:23). The uncomfortable truth is: This is what we really deserve! **The Legal Theory, however, tells us that in Jesus Christ, God takes that penalty upon himself, in our place, as an expression both of his justice and of his merciful love for us, and in this way he clears our infinite "penal debt" on the Cross. As a result, our sincere faith and repentance, expressed and completed by works of "atonement" (in Swinburne's sense of the word: contrition, apology, acts of reparation, and penance) now amount to enough**

---

[701] Ibid., p. 321.

fully to re-unite us with our merciful Father, the sacrificial life and death of his Son, and the renewal of the life-giving Holy Spirit. By such repentance and faith, we are now fully able to receive the forgiveness that Christ won for us on the Cross.

b) How is justice being served if the innocent divine Son bears the penalty we deserve?

This question can be traced back to the eighteenth century philosopher Immanuel Kant, and has been repeated by many theologians ever since. For example, John Austin Baker argued that the whole idea behind the Penal Substitution Theory is unjust. Moral debts are not transferrable from one person to another; thus, God cannot take upon himself the punishment we deserve by being executed in our place:

> Justice can never be served by punishing the innocent .... If God then deliberately takes on himself the suffering which is my due for the evil I have done, he is not satisfying Justice; he is perverting it. His conduct may be considered admirable from a different point of view, but not from that of Justice.[702]

Here again, several lines of rebuttal are possible to the defender of the Legal Theory.

First of all, drawing upon the German theologian Pannenberg, Anglican writer (and later Archbishop of Canterbury) George Carey, in his book *The Gate of Glory* (1986), suggested that moral responsibility cannot be sorted neatly into individual compartments. We are woven into communities in which our lives and responsibilities intertwine:

> Pannenberg cites the case of the German people who had to bear the consequences of the war to varying degrees, especially in its division of East and West .... Hitler's monstrous crimes against humanity resulted in his own people's separation and hurt .... Pannenberg's point is that individuals or groups can,

---

[702] Baker, *The Foolishness of God*, p. 304.

indeed, bear guilt for others vicariously because such is the interpenetration of human life that abstraction of the individual from society is impossible.[703]

But this simply will not do. It is one thing to say that later generations of Germans had to live with the *effects* of Hitler's crimes. It would be another thing to say that they bear some objective guilt (i.e., some *moral responsibility*) for those crimes, and rightly can be punished for them. The point is that in human relationships, moral debt is simply not transferable, however difficult it may be for us to assign accurate amounts of blame to groups or individuals in complex situations. Presumably it is not difficult for our omniscient God. He sees clearly who is guilty of what.

The defender of penal substitution would do better to harken back to a distinction mentioned earlier in this chapter. **While our moral intuitions certainly tell us that one human person cannot fairly be punished in place of another,** *Jesus Christ is not a merely human person. Uniquely, he is a divine person: the divine Son of God in human form.* **And that makes all the difference.**

We also know that one human being cannot justly take upon himself the penalty for another human being. Transferring moral or legal penalties from one person to another does not suddenly become acceptable on the scales of justice because it is voluntarily undertaken. *But we do not know that it is unjust for the One who is our Creator and our Judge to take upon himself the burden and penalty for our sins.*

Interestingly, human beings can voluntarily pay fines on behalf of others — thus far, we seem comfortable with the idea of voluntary penal substitution. And people can even assume the role of "judge" (in a civil and temporal sense) over other human beings. This enables us to form the following analogy: Imagine a judge in a court of law who

---

[703] George Carey, *The Gate of Glory* (London: Hodder and Stoughton, 1986), p. 142.

pronounces a verdict of "guilty as charged," and justly sentences an accused man and his family to pay massive reparations for their crimes. Imagine also that those reparation payments are so huge that the family will have to pay off the debt for the rest of their lives. Then imagine the same judge, out of mercy and compassion for that family — and seeing their evident regret and contrition — coming down from the bench and offering to "foot the bill" to clear those payments, even at the cost of impoverishing himself. This judge has fulfilled the righteous demands of the law, and the cry for mercy and compassion, at one and the same time, in one and the same act of self-sacrifice. Here we have an analogy of what our Creator, Judge and Savior, Jesus Christ, has done for us.

Of course, on the Cross Jesus did not just *pay a fine for us*; he was *executed in our place.* This is another level of voluntary substitution altogether. The impossibility of finding an entirely adequate, merely human analogy in this case, however, should hardly surprise us — and is hardly a unique situation in theology. Consider the mystery of the Incarnation. The ancient Fathers looked for analogies for how one person could have both a divine and human nature at the same time in the fact that one human person can have both a soul and a body. And using narrative analogies, Kierkegaard compared the Incarnation to the story of a king whose love for a peasant girl moved him to become a peasant himself for a time in order to win her love. But all such analogies for the Incarnation break down at some point, because a mere human person cannot literally add a new nature (with all its limitations and experiences) to his old one. God is the only one who can assume a limited human nature without abandoning the infinite perfections of his divine nature. The uniqueness of divine action in the world — as the Infinite acting in the finite realm — can only be expressed in analogies with limited application, whether we are talking about the Incarnation, or the Atonement.

The analogy offered here for Christ's sacrifice on the Cross (the judge who pays a crippling debt in place of a convicted family of debtors) is nevertheless an appropriate one because it leans on the fact that even in our everyday human system of justice and law, we do not think it immoral for someone voluntarily to act as a "kind of" penal substitute by footing a bill owed by another. And we would certainly admire a compassionate judge for doing so, in the right circumstances.

With regard to the divine Son Incarnate, again, *he is in a unique relationship with all human beings. He alone is a divine person in human form; as such, not only is he our Final Judge, but also our Creator and Sustainer. It is precisely for these reasons that we may surmise that God (and God alone) can justly bear an extreme punishment — the temporal and eternal death penalty that his own justice demands for mortal sin — in the place of his creatures, and for their sake, whereas it would be wrong for a mere human being to bear such an extreme punishment in place of another.* All this does not make Divine Justice and Divine Goodness utterly incomprehensible and inscrutable to us. Like any proper analogy, this one (the judge who pays the costly fine for a family of debtors) comes close to the mystery and illuminates it, without fully capturing and exhausting it. **In fact, as we have already seen, divine revelation in Holy Scripture, arguably confirmed by one stream of the tradition of the ancient Fathers, assures us that God can indeed make such a sin-bearing, atoning self-sacrifice on behalf of his creatures.**

Catholic theologian Eleonore Stump offered a critical dissection of the Penal Substitution theory in this regard in her essay "Atonement According to Aquinas" (2009) — expressing at the same time her preference for the Atonement theory of St. Thomas. It is not clear from what she wrote, however, that she fully understood the position that she was criticizing:

> What [penal substitution] is really telling us is that any human being's sins are so great that it is a violation of justice not to punish that person with damnation. What God does in response, however, is to punish not the sinner but a perfectly innocent person instead (a person who, even on the doctrine

of the Trinity, is not identical with God the Father who does the punishing).[704]

Here we need to take a moment to dissect this dissection. First of all, a *Catholic* legal theorist, at least, would not say that *all* human sin merits eternal damnation: it is grave sin (in Catholic parlance, "mortal sin") that rightly deserves such a penalty: the everlasting loss of the life-giving Holy Spirit from our hearts, whom we have in a sense ejected from our hearts. Venial sin merits merely temporal punishment.[705] Secondly, it is no part of the theory to hold that on Calvary it is "God the Father who does the punishing": rather, God the Father simply accepted the suffering and death inflicted by sinful men on his Son as the equivalent of the death penalty due to sinners (i.e. he brought boundless good out of a foreseen and permitted evil). Third, even what I have just written in the previous sentence is an inadequate manner of speaking about the Trinitarian dimension of this mystery, because the moral debt that sinners owe to Divine Justice is not simply owed to the Father. Divine Justice is an attribute shared by all three persons of the Trinity, so that *the Cross satisfies the demands of the justice of the Son just as much as the justice of the Father.* Fleming Rutledge points to the striking phrase in II Corinthians 5:18 ("All this is from God, who through Christ reconciled us to himself"), a passage that she says nails down

---

[704] Eleonore Stump, "Atonement According to Aquinas" in Rea, ed., *Oxford Readings in Philosophical Theology*, vol. I, p. 268.

[705] The distinction between mortal and venial sin is foreign to most Protestant traditions; in the Catholic tradition it is seen as rooted in Scripture (Jn 19:11; I Jn 5:16-17). *Catechism of the Catholic Church,* entries 1855, 1861, and 1863 tell us:

> Mortal sin destroys charity in the heart of man by a grave violation of God's law; it turns man away from God, who is his ultimate beatitude, by preferring an inferior good to him. Venial sin allows charity to subsist, even though it offends and wounds it …. Mortal sin is a radical possibility of human freedom, as is love itself. It results in the loss of charity and of sanctifying grace, that is, the state of grace. If it is not redeemed by repentance and God's forgiveness, it causes exclusion from Christ's kingdom and the eternal death of hell, for our freedom has the power to make choices forever, with no turning back …. Venial sin … merits temporal punishment.

"the indispensable affirmation that the Father is acting, not *over against* the Son, but *through and in* the Son, whose will is the same as the Father's."[706]

Finally, Stump's appeal to the distinction between the persons of the Trinity here would only be a fair criticism of the Penal Substitution Theory if that theory necessarily involved a tritheistic doctrine of God. If the persons of the Trinity were three independent beings, three primary substances, it might indeed be immoral for one divine person to punish an innocent one in the place of all sinners, or even to accept the voluntary suffering of that innocent divine person as a penalty for human sin. But that is not the true mystery of the Trinity. Rather, in the case of God —and in a way we cannot fully comprehend — three "persons" (by which I mean three subjects or centers of self-consciousness, rational thought, and voluntary agency — see Part One, Chapter One, above), share the same act of being, that is, the same divine nature in act (see our discussion of the mystery of the Trinity in Part One, Chapter Five of this book). As Christ is one in being with His Father in this mysterious Trinitarian way, in some real sense the one paying the penalty is the same divine being as the one to whom the debt is owed, and the one to whom that debt is paid. And again, to be precise, that penalty is demanded by the justice and holiness of all three persons of the Trinity, not just by the Father.

By the same token, the substitutionary death of Christ was also an expression of the love of both the Father and the Son. It is not as if Jesus died to change the Father's attitude toward humanity from a one of retributive justice to one of merciful love. Evangelical theologian Millard Erickson explains:

> [I]t is helpful to recall the numerous references indicating that the Father sent the Son to atone for sin. Christ was sent by the Father's *love*. So it is not the case that the propitiation changed a wrathful God into a loving God. ... this is indicated quite clearly

---

[706] Rutledge, *The Crucifixion*, p. 100.

in I John 4:10: "This is love: not that we loved God, but that he loved us and sent his Son as an atoning sacrifice for our sins."[707]

c) How can it be said that Jesus bore in our place the temporal and eternal death-penalty we deserve if (1) all of us still have to die; and (2) if that penalty for Jesus did not consist in a state of guilt, despair and the loss of the Holy Spirit (that is, if it was not the true equivalent of the everlasting state of the damned); and anyway (3) if the penalty he endured was not an everlasting one, because his sufferings came to an end? Finally, (4) if Christ paid the penal debt for all sinners on the Cross, why do unrepentant sinners have to pay that penalty again?

Here again, we are dealing with objections to the theological and moral logic of the Legal Theory.[708] Let us take these objections in reverse-order.

First, what we know from divine revelation in Scripture and ancient Tradition is that the passion and death of Jesus Christ was in principle enough to redeem all of humanity, but it can only avail for those who access its benefits through repentance and faith. *The gift freely offered must be freely received.* His blood shed was sufficient for the salvation of all, but it remains only in potency for any particular individual, unless or until that soul consents to be united with Christ by the Holy Spirit, becoming a "new creation" (II Cor 5:17) and "one body" with him (I Cor 12: 12-13) through repentance and faith (a process which ordinarily includes, Catholics would say, Baptism and sacramental Confession, Confirmation and Holy Eucharist). In other words, one cannot be fully "washed clean in the blood of the Lamb" if one refuses to come to the covenanted fountains of grace, with the proper dispositions, so that this washing can be fully received. As St. Paul put it: "There is therefore now no condemnation *for those who are in Christ*

---

[707] Erickson, *Christian Theology*, p. 835.
[708] See Stump, "Atonement According to Aquinas," p. 268-269, where three of these objections can be found.

Jesus" (Rom 8:1), and again: "[S]ince all have sinned and fall short of the glory of God, they are justified by his grace as a gift, through the redemption which is in Christ Jesus, whom God put forward as an expiation by his blood, *to be received by faith*" (Rom 3:23-25; cf. Heb 10:19). That is why those stubbornly unrepentant of mortal sin to the end of their lives cannot be pardoned on the basis of the Cross of Christ. Thus, although this is a mystery of faith, we can at least see that *it is fitting that the saving death of Jesus Christ would only avail for those who open their hearts to union with him through (implicit or explicit) dispositions and acts of repentance and faith.* We separate ourselves from our attachment to our sins by repentance, and we welcome the grace that he offers to unite us to himself through faith. Moreover, given that God respects the free-will he gave to us as our Creator, he would never *compel us* to repent and accept in our hearts the renewal of the life of the Holy Spirit, from whom we have separated ourselves by our mortal sins.[709]

Second, the objection raised was that Jesus did not suffer on the Cross everlastingly: so how can he be said to have taken upon himself the everlasting penalty justly owed by the damned? Here we need to recall the mystery of the relationship of the Eternal God to the temporal order. On the one hand, on a kenotic understanding of the

---

[709] Oliver Crisp has recently proposed what he calls a "union" theory of the Atonement based on the idea that Christ and his elect ("Redeemed Humanity") somehow form one metaphysical entity that persists through time, analogous to the way Adam and his progeny do. "At the cross, Christ has transferred to himself the penal consequences for which they are guilty, as one part of the larger metaphysical whole" (*The Word Enfleshed*, p. 138). Crisp argues that this removes from the penal substitution theory any need for imputation, whereby God in Christ allows himself to be treated as if he were a sinner, and therefore is punished in our place. It is not at all clear, however, that imputation can be so easily side-stepped. After all, whatever this mysterious "metaphysical whole" may be, it does not erase the metaphysical distinction between persons in the Body of Christ, not even between Christ and the sinner. Even in the deepest mystical union with God, I am still a distinct creature, and he is still the transcendent Creator, Redeemer, and Sanctifier. Thus, it still must be true, even in this "union" version of the penal substitution theory, that Jesus of Nazareth, a person metaphysically distinct from myself, takes the punishment for my sins in my place as if he were guilty of the crimes that I had committed.

Incarnation, the sufferings of the human body and soul of the divine Son are included in the divine nature, preserved in the divine store of experience, *and since divine memories do not fade, his agony and passion remains, in that sense, everlastingly present to the divine Son.* Moreover, if one holds the view that God is beyond the temporal order altogether, then the sufferings of the Son of God on the Cross are in some way *eternally present and happening before him* (just as every one of his acts and experiences would be eternally present to him in his timeless state). These are issues to which we shall return in the final chapter of this book.

Third, **the objection was raised that on the Cross Jesus did not suffer the true equivalent of the penalty of damnation, since his suffering did not consist of a state of bitter despair, and the loss of the Holy Spirit.** *Here is perhaps the strongest objection to the Legal Theory.* **The defender of penal substitution ordinarily will appeal to Christ's descent into the experience of God-forsakenness on the Cross, and will want to say that** *at this moment Jesus plumbed the very depths of alienation from God. He shared in a kind of alienation and separation from God that is analogous to the lot of every lost soul.* The *Catechism of the Catholic Church* both hints at this — and at the same time seems to back away from it — in *Catechism* entry 603:

> Jesus did not experience reprobation as if he himself had sinned. But in the redeeming love that always united him to the Father, he assumed us in the state of our waywardness of sin, to the point where he could say in our name from the cross: "My God, My God, why have you forsaken me?" Having thus established himself in solidarity with us sinners, "God did not spare his own Son but gave him up for us all," so that we might be "reconciled to God by the death of his Son."

Notice that this *Catechism* entry states that Jesus "assumed us in the state of our waywardness of sin," and connects this fact with his cry of dereliction from the Cross as an act of "solidarity with sinners,"— but then the *Catechism* qualifies this with the opening words that this solidarity was not an experience of "reprobation." There is certainly a paradox here. On the one hand, Jesus did not experience a false burden of guilt for imagined wrongdoings — in other words, he was not suffering from a delusion that he had actually committed mortal sins. In that sense, the Catechism rightly says, "Jesus did not experience reprobation as if he himself had sinned." On the other hand, if he did not share on the Cross in an experience of subjective guilt and alienation from God akin to that of the lost, in what did his "solidarity" with the human state of the "waywardness of sin" consist?

One of the great Catholic writers of the twentieth century, the Ven. Archbishop Fulton Sheen, wrestled with this same paradox. In his famous *Life of Christ* (1958), Sheen attempted to "square the circle," so to speak, by saying that *the Son of God took upon himself the equivalent of our experience of guilt for sin and alienation from God due to sin, but not an experience of total despair:*

> Sinners can show a love for one another by taking the punishment which another deserves. But our Blessed Lord was not only taking the punishment but also taking the guilt as if it were His own ....

> In taking upon Himself the sins of the world [Jesus Christ] willed a kind of withdrawal of His Father's face and all Divine consolation.... This particular moment He willed to take upon Himself that principal effect of sin which was abandonment.

> *Man rejected God; so now He willed to feel that rejection. Man turned away from God; now He, Who was God united personally with a human nature, willed to feel in that human nature that awful wrench as if He Himself were guilty* .... In that cry [of dereliction on the Cross] were all the sentiments in human hearts expressive of a Divine nostalgia: the loneliness of the atheist, the skeptic, the pessimist, the sinners who hate themselves for hating virtue, and of all those who have no love above the

flesh; for to be without love is hell. It was, therefore, the moment when leaning on nails He stood at the brink of hell in the name of all sinners. As He entered upon the extreme penalty of sin, which is separation from God, it was fitting that His eyes be filled with darkness and His soul with loneliness. ...

Christ's cry was of abandonment which He felt standing in a sinner's place, but it was not of despair. The soul that despairs never cries to God .... The emptiness of humanity through sin, though He felt it as His own, was nevertheless spoken with a loud voice to indicate not despair, but rather hope that the sun would rise again and scatter the darkness.[710]

From Sheen's reflections here it follows that *the state of Christ at the moment of his cry of dereliction on the Cross was analogous to the spiritual state of souls eternally lost: it was the same state in so far as Christ shared in their crushing burden of subjective guilt for sin and feelings of total alienation from God* — even the *felt-experience of complete rejection and abandonment by God* — *but differed in so far as he did not succumb to despair.* To give in to the sin of despair would mean to allow oneself to be so overwhelmed by the feeling of alienation and abandonment by God that one actually ceased to believe or trust any longer in the existence or goodness of God. *Christ was plunged into the darkness of feelings analogous to despair, but sin is not a feeling; Jesus did not commit the sin of despair itself.*

---

[710] Fulton Sheen *The Life of Christ* (The Crown Publishing Group, 1977 abridged edition), from chapters 39 and 43; italics mine. Obviously, I would not want to endorse without qualification Sheen's opening sentence here that sinners ordinarily can take upon themselves the punishment other human beings deserve – at least not the *eternal* punishment they deserve for mortal sin, nor a temporal death-penalty or prison sentence for the crimes of another.

Catholic theologian Thomas Joseph White, OP, offered a substantial critique of this whole approach to the Cross in his book *The Incarnate Lord* (2015). White explains:

> True, Christ's passion is *like* an experience of damnation or despair in certain respects, because the agony he undergoes bears certain resemblances to the agony of the despairing. He can be said to suffer the pains of deprivation of the psychologically felt presence of God in a way that is *metaphorically* similar to that of the damned (through the absence of the *effects* of joy, consolation, etc.). Yet this similarity contains *nothing* that is *essentially* the same as the latter state, because Christ's suffering does not stem from an absence of or resistance to divine love. These latter faults, by contrast, contribute to the *essence* of despair and damnation ....
>
> The *essence* of Christ's agony, therefore, stems from something entirely different from such aversion to God (divine love) and therefore, strictly speaking, is not analogous to the state of the damned. In fact, at heart it is entirely dis-analogous.[711]

Of course, Sheen, White, and all orthodox Christian commentators would agree that Jesus was not actually in despair on the Cross (which would have been a mortal sin). His words about being "forsaken" actually are a direct quote from the first line of Psalm 22. It was common practice in ancient Israel to quote the first line of a psalm in order to refer to the entire text, and despite the words of total desolation at the start, the psalm ends on a note of trust in God and in the triumph of his saving will. Hence, it is probably wise to interpret the words "My God, My God, Why have You forsaken me?" (Mt 27:46; Mk 15:34) in conjunction with the sentence that Jesus spoke soon after that: "Father, into Thy hands I commend my spirit" (Lk 23:46). In other words, at that moment on the Cross, Jesus may have been expressing simultaneously both the feeling of sheer physical, emotional, and spiritual misery in the midst of all his afflictions, and

---

[711] White, *The Incarnate Lord*, p. 317-318.

yet, at the same time an underlying, almost blind surrender to divine providence.

Jesus went to the Cross believing that it was all in fulfilment of his Father's permissive will, in order to pay for us the ransom price for sin (e.g. Mt 20:28; Mk 10:45; Lk 22:42). When he descended into this darkest pit of human misery, however, afflicted at every level of his being at once, no doubt the purpose of his sufferings was only dimly grasped by him, if at all, on a conscious level. Total affliction has the capacity to shut off the human conscious and emotional faculties from any light, even from the most deeply held beliefs. Thus, Jesus' cry of dereliction may have meant, in effect: ***"My God, My God, why have you forsaken me? For I feel now that you are infinitely far away from me, that I am cut off from you by the most terrible guilt and burden of sin, that I am worthless and accursed, and that you have totally abandoned and rejected me in my misery and affliction when I most needed you ... you are my God, and yet in the midst of this horror your will is now utterly dark and impenetrable to me."***

White seems to have missed some of the significant similarities between this kind of experience and the penalty of eternal loss. Let us recall from the previous chapter what Simone Weil wrote about *the psychological and spiritual effects of the experience of total human affliction* into which Christ descended for us:

> There is not real affliction unless the event which has seized and uprooted a life attacks it, directly or indirectly, in all of its parts, social, psychological and physical .... Affliction constrained Christ to implore that he might be spared; to seek consolation from man; to believe that he was forsaken by the Father .... **Affliction hardens and discourages us because, like a red-hot iron,** *it stamps the soul to its very depths with the scorn, the disgust, and even the self-hatred and sense of guilt and defilement which crime logically should produce, but actually does not ... "Christ ... being made a curse for us."* It was not only the body of Christ

> hanging on the wood which was accursed, it was his soul
> also. In the same way, every innocent being in his
> affliction feels himself accursed.[712]

We should also bear in mind that for a soul that is very close to God, bonded to him by supernatural love, to lose all sense of his presence and love is an agony beyond compare. Such is the common testimony of those who have gone through the purifying mystical experience called "the dark night of the soul," an experience usually initiated by God's active withdrawal of all sense of his presence and love. If on the Cross Jesus Christ experienced total human affliction, then that experience must include this supernatural privation as well — the soul's dark night — and not just his physical and social afflictions, with all their psychological and spiritual effects (so vividly described by Weil).

To give us an idea of what the sufferings of Jesus on this, the deepest level of his soul might have been like, we can read St. Faustina Kowalska's description of her own journey through the dark night. She writes about it in her *Diary* under the title of "The Trial of Trials":

> At this point ... the soul is engulfed in a horrible night. It sees within itself only sin. It feels terrible. It sees itself completely abandoned by God. It feels itself to be the object of His hatred. It is but one step away from despair....
>
> The soul is drawn to God but feels repulsed. All other sufferings and tortures in the world are as nothing compared with this sensation into which it has been plunged; namely, that of being rejected by God. ... It falls deeper and deeper from darkness to darkness, and it seems to it that it has lost forever the God it used to love so dearly. This thought is torture beyond all description. ...

---

[712] Weil, *Waiting on God,* p. 64-65 and 80-81; italics mine.

If God wishes to keep the soul in such darkness, no one will be able to give it light. It experiences rejection by God in a vivid and terrifying manner. … This word *rejected*, becomes a fire which penetrates every nerve to the marrow of the bone. It pierces right through her entire being. The ordeal reaches its climax. The soul no longer looks for help anywhere. It shrinks into itself and loses sight of everything; it is as though it has accepted the torture of being abandoned. This is a moment for which I have no words. This is the agony of the soul. …

[T]he person's entire soul is in the hand of the Just God, the Thrice-Holy God, — rejected for all eternity! This is the culminating moment, and God alone can test a soul in this way, because He alone knows what the soul can endure.[713]

The objection will be made that Jesus could not experience such a dark night in his human soul, because his soul did not need to be purified of sin, self-reliance, and self-centeredness. On the other hand, his human soul was far more closely bonded to the supernatural love of his Father, by the Holy Spirit, than even the greatest of the saints. To lose all sense of his Father's presence and love surely would have been unimaginably excruciating for him. It would have added even deeper suffering to all that had been laid on his shoulders by the physical tortures and social rejection (with all its effects) that he endured. Of course, we cannot fully fathom what it must have been like on Calvary for the divine Son Incarnate to lose all sense of His Father's love and presence in his human soul, but St. Faustina's words give us at least some inkling of what such an experience may have involved.

Fleming Rutledge points to the close link in the New Testament between Galatians 3:10-14 and our Savior's cry of dereliction on the Cross. Christ, says St. Paul, "redeemed us from the curse of the law, having become a curse for us" (3:13). Rutledge sums up her exegesis of this passage:

---

[713] Saint Maria Faustina Kowalska, *Diary: Divine Mercy in My Soul* (Stockbridge, MA: Marian Press, 2009 edition), entries 98 and 101, p. 54-56.

The important thing for our discussion here is Paul's announcement (*kerygma*) that God, in the person of his sinless Son, put himself voluntarily and deliberately into the condition of the *greatest accursedness* — on our behalf and in our place. This mind-crunching paradox lies at the heart of the Christian message.[714]

Notice that what Weil described (above) — total human affliction — is not just an absence of spiritual "consolations" (as White had put it), but a psychological state of "self-hatred," subjective "guilt" and "defilement," a state "which crime logically should produce, but actually does not." St. Faustina calls the worst spiritual affliction for a holy soul, the dark night, an experience of "abandonment," "rejection by God," and "one step away from despair." And Rutledge, following St. Paul, called the state of Christ on the Cross one of "greatest accursedness." To put it in colloquial terms, Christ's total human affliction — bodily, social, emotional, and spiritual affliction all at once — is analogous to what we commonly refer to in English as *"living hell"* or *"hell on earth."* Perhaps the state of the soul of Jesus on the Cross was expressed most poignantly by G. Campbell Morgan in his book *The Crises of the Christ* (1945):

> Man sinned when he dethroned God and enthroned himself. He reaps the utter harvest of his sin when he has lost God altogether. That is the issue of all sin. It is the final penalty of sin, penalty not in the sense of a blow inflicted on the sinner by God, but in the sense of a result following upon sin, from which God Himself cannot save the sinner. Sin is alienation from God by choice. Hell is the utter realization of that chosen alienation. Sin therefore at last is the consciousness of the lack of God, and that God-forsaken condition is the penalty of sin that forsakes God. Now listen solemnly, and from that Cross hear the cry, "My God, My God, why hast Thou forsaken Me?"

---

[714] Rutledge, *The Crucifixion*, p. 100; italics mine.

> That is hell …. On that Cross He was made sin, and therein
> He passed to the uttermost limit of sin's outworking.[715]

It follows that White was mistaken when he characterized the likeness between the dereliction of Christ on the Cross and the state of the damned souls as merely "metaphorical," consisting only in the fact that in both cases, the persons involved no longer feel the joy and consolation of the divine presence. The similarities, however, go much deeper, *for in both cases the soul experiences the depths of subjective guilt (in the psychological-spiritual form of feelings of self-loathing, worthlessness, and defilement) and feelings of utter alienation from, and complete abandonment by God.*[716] The causes in each case may be very different (the total human affliction of a perfectly innocent soul versus un-repented mortal sin in a lost soul), but the psychological and spiritual effects are quite similar.

Of course, as previously discussed, these two states differ in that, unlike souls in the state of damnation, Christ never committed the sin of final despair, nor experienced its exact equivalent in emotional agony. On the other hand (as I argued in the previous chapter), **at least in one respect the alienation from God experienced by Jesus was *even worse* than any that sinners could feel, since it was borne by one who was completely pure and free from actual sin — plunging his soul into all the more unfathomable darkness, since all of his sufferings were so completely undeserved.** Here, too, in a strange way there is an analogy with the state of eternal reprobation.

---

[715] G. Campbell Morgan, *The Crises of the Christ* (London: Pickering and Inglis, 1945), p. 215.

[716] Of course, this does not mean the Father actually abandoned him on the Cross: that would be a metaphysical impossibility. The Father cannot actually separate himself from his Son, because the Blessed Trinity cannot be divided into separable parts. Rather, some theologians speculate (with Calvin, and Frank Weston) that in his human soul the Son on the Cross lost the Beatific Vision of his Father for a time; others say (with Aquinas) that the Son simply did not permit the comfort of that vision to sustain him on the Cross. In any case, if the Legal Theory of the Atonement is true, then it must have been possible for the divine Son Incarnate to "taste" in some way something closely analogous to the terrible penalty of eternal loss, and thereby bear that penalty away for all who turn to him in repentance and faith.

The souls of the damned passionately believe (falsely, in their case) that they too are innocent, and that their everlasting state is unjust: they take no responsibility for their crimes, and blame God and others for everything. That is surely why Jesus spoke of the damned as "weeping" — not with penitence, surely, but from self-pity — and "gnashing their teeth" (the latter a metaphor for ferocious hatred; e.g. Mt 8:12; Lk 13:28).[717] Christ on the Cross bore no hatred in his heart at all, but he did bear the burden of the deepest spiritual and psychological agony and darkness that totally innocent, unjust, and cruel suffering can cause.[718]

In volume two of this series we shall explore yet another aspect of Christ's experience of God-forsakenness: the claim of the Catholic tradition that in the Garden of Gethsemane, and during his agony and passion, Jesus suffered the most excruciating feelings of grief and loss. This unparalleled grief came from his supernatural foresight of all those who would reject and refuse his love, despite his sufferings on their behalf. In other words, *in the Garden and on the Cross Jesus suffered the most unutterable grief possible to perfect love: he foresaw how his agony and passion ultimately would be in vain for so many. If this is true, then even the causes of the God-forsakenness of Christ and of the damned bear a certain similarity: in the latter case, the bitterness of slavery to their own sin; in the former case, overwhelming grief at the final slavery to sin of much of humanity.*[719]

---

[717] In her mystical revelations, St. Faustina Kowalska had a vision of hell in which she heard the damned souls crying out with words of despair, hatred for God, curses and blasphemies; St. Maria Faustina Kowalska, *Diary: Divine Mercy in My Soul*, entry 741, p. 296-297.

[718] Saint Thomas Aquinas argued that the kind of suffering that strikes a person and overwhelms him with evil in response to his persistent efforts to do good is the worst human misery of all; see *ST* II-II. 30. 1.

[719] In *Did Jesus Know He Was God?*, p.99, Dreyfus explains this mystery as follows:

> It is this infinite dignity of the one who suffers which gives to his sufferings their unique and unsurpassable intensity: the physical

In the end, of course, there are mysteries here too deep for us to fathom.[720] What we *can* know about the sufferings of Christ on the Cross, however, certainly does not rule out the doctrine of penal substitution, and in some ways strongly suggest it. Perhaps Pope St. John Paul II said it best in one of his poems:

> But the depths of His words no one knows
> No one knows how far
> The farthest reason goes
> How limitless His suffering was —
> Solitude on the tree of the Cross.

---

sufferings of the passion, the sorrowful character of which comes not only from his wounded body but also and above all from his heart tortured by the fact that men have rejected his love; the sorrow caused by the sin of the world, for Jesus sees infinitely better than all of us both the hatred of God that it contains and the ravages that it produces in the hearts of men and the evils that it causes in the world.

[720] We need to say a word here about White's alternative interpretation of our Lord's cry of God-forsakenness on the Cross. He writes:

I have argued that the cry of Christ from the cross should be interpreted theologically as a prayer of desire related to his hope to introduce humanity into the eschatological gift of redemption. Hope implies an incomplete state in which both loving desire and painful deprivation can be simultaneously present. In examining the last words of Christ according to John and Mark, I have claimed that the cry from the cross is presented by each as a desire-in-agony (with more emphasis on agony in Mark, and more on desire in John). Therefore, both gospel writers affirm the existence of such a mixed state in the soul of Christ during his crucifixion. Furthermore, this cry has explicit eschatological overtones for both, since it is seen to usher in a new age of redemption that begins at Calvary. (White, *The Incarnate Lord*, p. 328)

Doubtless this passionate desire was one aspect of what was going on in the human soul of Jesus when he was dying on the Cross, but White's position here runs aground on one simple fact: if that was *all* or *primarily* what Jesus experienced on the Cross, then why would this prayer of (as yet unfulfilled) desire and eschatological hope cause him to say he felt "forsaken" by his Father?

There is one more objection in this group to which we still need to attempt an answer: the question of why we still have to die, if Jesus bore the death-penalty for sin in our place. To be sure, we no longer have to die spiritually and eternally, because the fruit of Christ's saving death for those who repent and believe, incorporated into the Body of Christ, the Church, through the sacraments, is the gift of the Holy Spirit and everlasting life with him in heaven. But the question remains: why do we even have to die in a temporal sense? Why do we have to endure the terrible separation of soul and body if Christ supposedly paid this price for us too?

We need to remember, however, that Christ came to save us not only from objective guilt and punishment, but also from the ongoing *power* of sin in our lives. Thus, for those who live in Christ, bodily death is not eliminated, but transformed into a principal means of our sanctification. From being merely part of the *penalty* for sin for the unrepentant, it becomes, in the Holy Spirit, an instrument of deliverance from sin's *power* over us.

Surely, to be sanctified in Christ — completely overcoming the power of sin in our hearts by the Holy Spirit — is to become fully mature in Christ, loving God with all our hearts and our neighbors as ourselves, as he did. But there is no greater love than this, Jesus said, than to lay down our lives for others (Jn 15:3). Martyrs for faith and charity do this in an instant: the shedding of their blood is at the same time the completion of their spiritual growth in Christ. But others shed their blood for God and neighbor drop by drop: through long and painful service and sacrifice, through ardent prayer in times of darkness, and through offering up their suffering and dying in union with Christ for the good of souls. Saint Athanasius wrote of this mystery too in *De Incarnatione,* section 21, when he reflected that Jesus put away death only insofar as it was penal, and symptomatic of humanity's sin.[721] It has been truly said that the Son of God came to earth not that we

---

[721] Mozley, *The Doctrine of the Atonement*, p. 106.

might not suffer at all, but that our sufferings should be like his, transforming us more and more into his likeness.[722]

Even though Christ paid the death-penalty for us, therefore, all of us still need to suffer bodily to the point of death.[723] As a result of Christ's passion and death, however, our dying has been transformed, and it no longer has dominion over us. It might be said that Christ suffered *bodily* death in our place to pay the penalty of what Catholics call the *temporal punishment* for our sin,[724] and he experienced the equivalent (by close analogy, at least) of *spiritual* death on the Cross to pay the *eternal punishment* due for our sin — so that for those united with him in the Holy Spirit, through repentance and faith, bodily dying can be transformed from a necessary temporal penalty into a refiner's fire, a furnace of his sanctifying love.

For the followers of Jesus Christ, united with him in a life-giving personal relationship (that is, in Catholic terminology, "in a state of grace"), dying bodily is no longer experienced primarily as a necessary and just punishment for sin. Rather, it is transformed into a process that can purge our hearts of all remaining pride and self-sufficiency, so that we are finally enabled to "let go," to open our hearts to the Holy Spirit, and entrust our lives fully to our Lord in penitence and faith. Our souls are thereby prepared for heaven, our hearts made open and able to receive the unimpeded inflow of the Holy Spirit. In this way also any remaining temporal punishment due for our sins (from what had been our half-hearted repentance for them) is finally remitted.

---

[722] On this mystery of the faith, see Robert Stackpole, *Jesus, Mercy Incarnate* (Stockbridge, MA: Marian Press, 2000), p. 32-38 and 55-87.

[723] Or almost all: in Scripture there seem to be some exceptions, such as Enoch and Elijah, and possibly Moses, according to the Jewish reading of the last chapter of Deuteronomy combined with the Transfiguration story in the New Testament. Some interpretations of the Catholic doctrine of the Assumption of Mary into heaven would also exempt her from the experience of bodily death.

[724] The concepts of temporal and eternal punishment for sin are explained in *Catechism* entries 1472 and 1473.

For the small number of Christ's disciples who have already attained, before the moment of death, a more perfect repentance for their sins and a *complete* union in faith and love with the Heart of Jesus, bodily death is no longer needed to aid such a spiritual purification process, or to clear away any remaining temporal punishment for sin. As a result, their sufferings and their dying can be fully offered up in love, in union with the merits of Christ's agony and passion. This is what Catholics would call a "co-redemptive" offering for the needs of the Church and the whole world. Catholics believe that this is why St. Paul can write that by his sufferings he "completes what is lacking in Christ's afflictions for the sake of his body, that is, the Church" (Col 1:24).[725]

And at least for one of us (or so Catholics believe), whose soul remained always without any stain of original and actual sin, and totally surrendered to God in faith, there was no necessity for her death at all. She received the greatest possible benefit of the merits of the saving life and death of Jesus Christ.[726]

> d) Does the Legal Theory necessarily involve a "strife of attributes" in the divine nature, with his merciful love in conflict with his justice, and the latter needing to be "bought off" before he can forgive us?

If we take a classical approach to the divine attributes, this objection will not have much force. According to St. Thomas Aquinas, all of God's attributes are really one in the absolute simplicity of the divine essence. That is one reason why, in the

---

[725] See the section of my book *Jesus, Mercy Incarnate*, p. 65-70, where the concept of co-redemption is explained. Suffice it to say here that the prefix "co" does not mean "equal to the Redeemer," but comes from the Latin "cum," which means "with the Redeemer," that is, in co-operation with him and on the basis of the graces he merited for us. Of course, our sufferings can be offered up, and to some extent become co-redemptive, even if we are not yet fully sanctified in Christ.

[726] On this see my book, *Mary, Who She is and Why She Matters* (Stockbridge: MA: Marian Press, 2016), p. 73-86.

Catholic spiritual tradition, the closer we come to God in faith and love, the more childlike we become. For in truth God is so utterly simple that only the childlike soul can begin to comprehend him; all his attributes are united in the one, simple, eternal act in which he is himself, manifests all infinite perfections, and does all that he does. This means that Divine Mercy and Divine Justice coincide in the simplicity of his nature. Thus, God is always and everywhere both just and merciful at one and the same time in all that he does. I touched upon this mystery in my book *Divine Mercy: A Guide from Genesis to Benedict XVI* (2009):

> Some of the greatest saints and theologians in the Catholic Tradition … have struggled to find a way to fuse together, in a single vision, the justice and mercy of God, without denying either one. How God's justice and mercy are one in the absolute simplicity of the infinite divine nature is, of course, a mystery that we can never completely fathom in this life. It is beyond the capacity of finite minds, and of our fallen nature, to comprehend ….
>
> And yet we can know right from the start that it must be so: [the Catholic philosophical tradition] shows us that God's nature is absolutely simple and indivisible, so that His justice must always be an expression of His mercy. [In fact] the simplicity and indivisibility of the divine nature was a truth solemnly defined at the First Vatican Council, Dogmatic Constitution on the Catholic Faith, Chapter One. Moreover, the Psalms clearly state that God's mercy is over all His works (see Ps 145:9).[727]

However, even if one cannot accept such a doctrine of divine simplicity, it is not clear that the Penal Substitution Theory of the Atonement necessarily involves interior conflict and contradiction in

---

[727] Robert Stackpole, *Divine Mercy: A Guide from Genesis to Benedict XVI*, p. 96. See further discussion of this issue in the "Conclusion" chapter of this present work.

God. To be sure, for human beings, it is very hard, if not impossible, always to meet the demands of both justice and merciful love at one and the same time. But on what grounds do we say that this is impossible for God? His own acts and revelations in salvation history show that he can do this:

> Even in this life, we can begin to see that God's justice — His occasional chastisements of us in this life, and His purgatorial punishments of us in the next — are also, at one and the same time, expressions of His mercy toward us. If He sometimes chastises us by permitting us to suffer, it is only to "wake us up" and summon us back to repentance and faith ("Those whom the Lord loves, He chastises" [Heb 12:6]), and purgatory is not only a place of temporal punishment for half-repented sin; it is also, at the same time, a "purging" that mercifully sanctifies and heals the soul (see *Catechism*, 1030).

> More difficult to fathom is how the final damnation of a soul is also, in another way, God's final act of mercy toward that soul …. In fact, as many of the saints teach, even hell itself is tempered by God's mercy (for example, St. Catherine of Siena and St. John Eudes). By allowing souls to reject Him and His love forever, God thereby respects human freedom — the ability He gave us to choose our own destiny …. Moreover, God knows that for souls who truly hate Him, to have to see Him face to face forever would make them even more miserable than their self-chosen exile. That is why Cardinal Newman wrote: "Heaven would be hell to the irreligious"— and Milton's Satan in *Paradise Lost* voices the sentiments of all the damned: "Better to reign in hell than serve in heaven." As C.S. Lewis put it: "The doors of hell are locked on the *inside*."…

> Most of all … the Cross of Jesus Christ is the supreme exposition of both the mercy and the justice of God.[728]

---

[728] Ibid, p. 96 and 272.

On the Cross, Jesus Christ reveals that *God is both holy and gracious love* (to borrow a phrase often used by P.T. Forsyth and J.K. Mozley). He is not holiness and justice *separable* from gracious and merciful love (as if he is sometimes holy and other times gracious, or as if he has a "just" side of his character that wars with his "merciful" side) — surely, it is safe to say that God has something analogous to an integrated personality! Anglican theologian J.K. Mozley insisted that this is precisely what the Cross reveals to us:

> The mystery of the Cross is the illuminating mystery. The word of the Cross is the power of God, telling of what God has done in taking upon Himself in His only Son a burden too great for sinful man to carry, revealing what sin is, and the judgment which falls upon it, and the atonement which is made for it, *revealing God as holy and gracious love*, as the Father of His people Who forgives their sins, not sparing the cost to Himself of a forgiveness which left no moral claim — the vindication of his holiness and the penalty of sin — unprovided for.[729]

e)   Does the Penal Substitution theory necessarily involve an individualistic, passive, and otherworldly doctrine of salvation that undermines Christian social concern, in other words, that contradicts real commitment to the pursuit of social justice and peace?

This objection is directed at extreme, fundamentalist leaders of the Evangelical movement who preach the Legal Theory of the Atonement combined with a largely extra-ecclesial, and individualistic doctrine of salvation, divorced from other dimensions of the mystery of Christ's saving work. The result tends to be a marginalization of Christian social concern (other than support for what leads to the wider dissemination of this form of the gospel, such as religious liberty). But the Penal Substitution Theory is not confined to this cultural and theological niche. As

---

[729] J.K. Mozley, *The Heart of the Gospel* (London: SPCK, 1925), p. 42; italics mine.

we shall see, it has taken Catholic and Anglo-Catholic as well as Protestant Evangelical forms. Moreover, the Evangelical movement can boast many figures down through history who have shown that their acceptance of some form of the doctrine of Substitutionary Atonement does not contradict an appreciation for the social implications of the gospel: for example, John Wesley, William Wilberforce, Lord Shaftesbury, and Karl Barth. Evangelical Christians led the way in the English-speaking world in the struggle for the abolition of slavery, for universal education, for an end to child labor and inhumane working conditions, and the founding of trade unions. In the nineteenth and twentieth centuries Evangelical missionaries not only spread the gospel of Christ's saving death to the ends of the earth, they often expressed the love of Christ in other ways as well by establishing schools, hospitals, and orphanages.

Some Evangelicals led the way in promoting racial harmony too. Most Americans have forgotten that Billy Graham's evangelistic Crusades were the first open, publicly integrated gatherings of blacks and whites in the southern United States since the Civil War. This was at Graham's insistence. In fact, in September, 1959, when he arrived at the location for a crusade in Little Rock, Arkansas and found that sections for "White only" and "Negro" had been cordoned off, he personally went into the stadium and tore down the barriers with his own hands.[730] Graham strongly believed that racial distinctions have no place at the foot of the Cross. In his best-selling book, *Peace with God*, he said of Christian social concern:

> Christians above all others, should be concerned with social problems and social injustices. Down through the centuries the church has contributed more than any other single agency in lifting social standards to new heights. Child labor has been outlawed. Slavery has been abolished in Britain, the U.S.A., and

---

[730] Lewis A. Drummond, *The Evangelist: The Worldwide Impact of Billy Graham* (Nashville: Word Publishing, 2001), p. 78.

some other parts of the world. The status of women has been lifted to heights unparalleled in history, and many other reforms have taken place primarily as a result of the influence of the teachings of Jesus Christ. The Christian is to take his place in society with moral courage to stand up for that which is right, just, and honorable.[731]

Fleming Rutledge issued a challenge to all those who suspect that a substitutionary understanding of the Atonement inevitably leads to social passivity and indifference:

> Can it really be shown that abandoning the substitution motif results in … more charity? If one believes that the very essence of God is shown forth in the Son's death on our behalf *and in our place*, then the logical outworking of this faith would be a style of living for others, even taking their place if necessary. How does the motif of substitution *not* teach that?[732]

It seems clear, therefore, that the doctrine of Penal Substitution is a defensible and even vital aspect of the Christian understanding of the saving work of Jesus Christ. It is not meant to stand alone, however, and I have argued that it completes and complements rather than replaces the insights we found in other theories, both Exemplarist and Sacrificial. Non-Incarnational Exemplarism reminds us that Jesus was fully and authentically human; his Spirit-inspired, self-giving love for His Father and for all people is the abiding, and supremely attractive example of ideal humanity that can move us to follow him as his disciples. For Incarnational Exemplarism, the divine Son of God Incarnate himself shows us this way of love — the way of his Kingdom — and shares with us in all the joys and sorrows of the human condition, even to the point of dying on the Cross in patient and forbearing love for us. According to the Pure Sacrificial Theory

---

[731] Billy Graham, *Peace with God* (Nashville: Thomas Nelson, second edition, 1991), p. 247.
[732] Rutledge, *The Crucifixion*, p. 502.

this same Son of God is the One who rose from the grave, and made the sanctifying power of his faithful love unto death, through the gift of the Holy Spirit, available to all the world, especially by our incorporation into Christ through prayer and the sacraments. And so that our repentance for sin may be deep and complete, and our sins forgiven in a way that is fully in harmony with both Divine Justice and Divine Love, (according to most Sacrificial-Satisfaction theories) Christ made his entire life of perfect, loving obedience to the Father available to us to offer up, especially in the Eucharist, as our penitential gift, to complete our repentance through works of atonement, and open our hearts to the gift of the Spirit; furthermore, (according to the Merit Theory) the ocean of graces that Jesus merited for us through his whole-life offering of faithful love, as the divine Son in human flesh, he now claims as his reward on our behalf, pleading for us at the right hand of the Father for the renewal in our hearts of the Holy Spirit, that the graces of the Holy Spirit may draw the whole world to salvation, and be poured out upon all who come to Christ in repentance and faith. Finally (according to the Legal Theory), because we also owed an unpayable penal debt to God, the God whose infinite love our sins betrayed, he came among us as Jesus Christ, and paid the penalty for those sins himself, in our place, to set us free from their guilt and power — in this way the Cross was God's decisive act, above all others, for our salvation, the act that supremely reveals his holy and gracious love for all humanity.

My contention would be, therefore, that elements from each of these theories can be fitted together in this way into a beautiful mosaic that begins (but only begins!) to unfold *the multi-dimensional mystery* of all that Jesus Christ has done to save us.

To close this section of the chapter, therefore, let us turn again to the (often neglected) work of early twentieth century Anglo-Catholic theologian J.K. Mozley, who strove to knit together the doctrine of Penal Substitution with other, more widely accepted aspects of the doctrine of Redemption.[733] For Mozley, the moral consciousness of humanity insists that "wrongdoing merits punishment,"[734] and so Christ's saving death must address this reality. God among us as Jesus Christ does indeed take upon himself, in our place, the punishment for sin that we deserve, but this vicarious suffering not only compensates Divine Justice: it also deeply moves us and transforms us by the knowledge of how deeply we are loved. We must lay hold of the value of Christ's passion and death as satisfaction-for-sin by a profound surrender of faith. In the end, this doctrine implies no strife-of-attributes in the divine nature, because everything is done in the service of God's merciful love for the human race:

> Is there anything immoral if God looks at men's inchoate moral achievements and forgives their moral shortcomings, that is, their sins, in the light of the moral completeness of Christ's life? If He reckons faith as righteousness, when in the act of faith man recognizes the moral obligations that press upon him for fulfilment, confesses his own failures, admits the justice of punishment as that which he has deserved, and at the same time points to the complete fulfilment of the law, the complete confession of God's holiness, and the voluntary endurance of penal suffering and death by Christ from within humanity? ...

---

[733] In fact, Mozley was not the only Anglo-Catholic theologian of his era to hold this position. We can find traces of it also in Frank Weston's *The One Christ* (1914 second edition), p. 308 and 301:

> [On the Cross] the manhood becomes inoperative, inactive, almost paralysed by the withdrawal of the Divine Vision. The medium of His self-expression seems to fail Him. Then by a supreme act of will Jesus sends up His cry of confidence, of penitence, of acceptance of penalty: and so crying, completes the atonement for sin. ... For "the Lord has laid on Him the iniquity of us all." He must bear the penalty of the very act that constitutes His murder!

[734] Mozley, *The Doctrine of the Atonement*, p. 207.

Much of the objection felt toward any doctrine of the Atonement which refuses to dispense with substitutionary and penal conceptions centres round the supposition that these connote either that God the Father was Himself anxious only to punish, while God the Son satiated that desire for vengeance by taking the punishment upon Himself, or that other ways to atonement being open God chose a way which entailed the infliction of suffering upon His incarnate Son .... But if it is once made clear that God's eternal counsels are the eternal movements of His love, and that the Incarnation, a doctrine inexpressibly dear to all who believe in it as being the temporal actualisation of those counsels and the record of that love, necessitates in the sinful world the endurance of a suffering and a death in which the penal element is inevitably included, then the objections lose their force.[735]

[T]here is something which we can by no means afford to give up in the old ideas of the satisfaction which [Christ] made to God, and of the penalty of sin which He took upon Himself. Get away from all feudal, commercial, and transactional, quantitative forms of thought, as most truly we need to do, and a deepened moral and spiritual insight will learn how to make use of the belief that God makes the cross of Christ at once the throne of judgment and the fountain of salvation.[736]

Classical and Ransom Theories of Atonement

The Classical theory essentially states that *God in Christ won a decisive victory over the demonic forces of evil that enslave humanity, especially by his death on the Cross for us, and his triumphant resurrection.* This theory is called "classical" primarily because some historians of theology have argued that this was the principal way of understanding the saving work of Jesus Christ in the

---

[735] Ibid.,, p.206-220.
[736] Mozley, *The Heart of the Gospel*, p. 31-32.

early Church, especially among the Fathers of the East. That the *metaphor* of victory over Satan and the forces of darkness (the "Christus Victor" theme) was prominent in early Christianity is doubtless true. The theme is certainly found in the New Testament as well (see Col 2:15; Heb 2:14-15, and I Jn 3:8). F.W. Dillistone saw the theme of a heroic act of redemption as one of the two basic forms of the Christian understanding of the Atonement. It is a narrative that occurs over and over again, both in Christian and pagan cultures: a savior-hero must struggle against evil, and although wounded by it, he ultimately triumphs over the forces of darkness on our behalf.[737]

Working out that metaphor and narrative in terms of a coherent *theory* of Atonement, however, has proven to be rather difficult. Several of the early Fathers attempted to do so, including Origen, St. Gregory of Nyssa, St. Augustine, and St. Leo the Great, resulting in what is commonly known as the "Ransom Theory."[738] Saint Gregory of Nyssa, for example, believed that the sins of humanity allowed the Devil to gain rights over us: we rightfully became his slaves. To set us free from that bondage, God the Father offered his Son Jesus as a ransom to the Devil, who then put Jesus to death. But God tricked the Devil into believing that Jesus was merely human, and raised Christ from death through his divine nature, liberating him from Satan's power.

The Ransom Theory allegedly suffers from a number of defects. First of all, it requires belief in Satan as a real, supernatural agent of evil, and for some contemporary theologians, including some Anglicans, this is seen as problematic.[739] Secondly, it is not clear why the Devil has any

---

[737] Dillistone, *The Christian Understanding of Atonement*, p. 413-414.

[738] On these Fathers of the Church see Mozley, *The Doctrine of the Atonement*, p. 102-103, 109, 122-123, and 124.

[739] See for example, Austin Farrer in chapter VII of *Love Almighty and Ills Unlimited: an Essay on Providence and Evil* (London: Collins, 1961). Trevor Williams sought to reinterpret the language about the Devil as "the symbol and symptom of human godlessness, the destructive power unleashed when human beings make what is less than God their God." See Trevor Williams, "The Atonement" in Robert Morgan, ed., *The Religion of the Incarnation: Anglican Essays in Commemoration of Lux Mundi* (Bristol: Bristol Classical Press, 1989) p.

"right" to hold us in bondage, or to demand a ransom for our freedom. As C. Stephen Layman puts it: "How could the devil have such a right? Isn't that like suggesting that a kidnapper has a *right* to demand payment?"[740] In addition, it is hard to believe that a Holy God would choose a dishonest scheme in order to gain our freedom.[741] Besides, it is not even clear how such a scheme could have worked. As Layman pointed out:

> Jesus raised some people from the dead. This being so, surely the Devil would be aware that God has the power to raise humans from the dead. Why, then, wouldn't it occur to the Devil that God might raise Jesus from the dead? Is the Devil, as presented in Scripture, as easily taken in as the Ransom Theory seems to suggest?[742]

Evangelical Anglicans, at least, have resisted the temptation to neglect the Ransom Theory altogether. Norman Anderson, for example, accepted the existence of the Devil. He then modified the Ransom Theory by saying "Satan had no rights over us, but he had acquired power over us."[743] By our sins we put ourselves under Satan's powerful influence. John Stott elaborated on this idea, outlining from the New Testament four ways by which Satan tempts and enslaves us: our condemnation under the moral law, our sinful proclivities, our fear of death, and the corrupt values of the world.[744] By these means Satan tempts us to

---

112. It is hard for Christians to sustain such scepticism, however, in the light of the fact that in the Gospels Jesus cast out demons, often spoke directly about the struggle against the forces of supernatural evil (e.g. Lk 10:17-20), and taught his disciples to pray "deliver us from the evil one" (Mt 6:13).

[740] Layman, *Philosophical Approaches to Atonement, Incarnation and Trinity*, p. 32.

[741] On the other hand, it could be argued that God did not hide the fact that Jesus was the divine Son Incarnate; Satan simply cannot penetrate the mysteries of Divine Love because he has eternally rejected the help of grace.

[742] Layman, *Philosophical Approaches to Atonement, Incarnation, and Trinity*, p. 33.

[743] Anderson, *Jesus Christ: The Witness of History*, p. 101

[744] Stott, *The Cross of Christ*, p. 241-243.

despair, and to further acts of sin. **Nevertheless, both Anderson and Stott admit that in order to understand** *how* **the Son of God sets us free from Satan's power, we need the help of other theories of Atonement.**

Two Anglican theologians in particular in the post-war era have made fresh attempts to explore how the Classical Theory might enrich our understanding of Christ's saving work.

In his *Principles of Christian Theology* (1977), John Macquarrie reinterpreted the theory to mean that Christ has triumphed over all the earthly idols that gain demonic power over human beings. Sin is at its root an act of idolatry, a centering of one's hope and allegiance on beings rather than on Being.[745] Nation, race, class, power, sex, wealth — all such idols have power to transfix and trap the human spirit. But Jesus refused to idolise any created being, and lived instead in faithful devotion to his heavenly Father. The culmination of his work came in his passion and death, when Jesus gave himself away completely on the Cross, for as Macquarrie wrote: "One's own self is the last idol, and to give oneself away unreservedly is indeed to have become like God, and to have vanquished the last demon.[746]

So, Christ has vanquished the idols that threatened him. But how does this help to vanquish the idols that threaten us? Macquarrie answered this question in three ways.

First, he extolled the life and death of Jesus as "the paradigm of human existence."[747] Christ's perfect example of self-giving love for God and for others opens us to new possibilities for living. Here the Exemplarist Theory plays a part in Macquarrie's thought.

---

[745] Macquarrie, *Principles of Christian Theology*, p. 319.
[746] Ibid., p. 319. Cf. Gustaf Aulen, *The Faith of the Christian Church* (Philadelphia: Fortress Press, 1960), p. 197.
[747] Ibid., p. 320.

Secondly, "the self-giving of Christ is continuous with the self-giving of God, and the whole work of Atonement is God's."[748] God himself has done this work through Christ, "bringing his constant self-giving love for his creation right into creation." Thus, the holy life of Jesus is from first to last the work of holy Being, and in the end "the cost is paid by God himself who holds the initiative throughout."[749] It is God himself who makes this self-sacrificial offering in Jesus. The Son gave himself away completely out of love for the Father and for humanity, even suffering the pangs of death for us. Here a specifically Incarnational Exemplarist theory played a part in Macquarrie's thought.

Finally, the Holy Spirit, unitive Being, is also active in the atoning Christ-event, working in the hearts of those who encounter Jesus Christ, and making possible their response of faith.[750]

In short, in Macquarrie's view, it is God the Word himself (holy self-expressive Being) who lives out for us in Jesus the Way of total self-giving, the Way of the Cross, so that with the aid of the indwelling Spirit (unitive Being) we might follow his lead and attain our true humanity, triumphant over the demonic idols that so powerfully tempt and enslave us. In this way Macquarrie shows how themes current in two of the schools of soteriology that we have explored (Incarnational Exemplarist, and Classical) might be woven into a single pattern around a central theme: Christ victorious over the demonic power of idolatry.

Unfortunately, Macquarrie did not really address in-depth the kinds of questions that have led so many theologians down through Christian history to go beyond Abelardian Incarnational Exemplarism, and the implications of the "Christus Victor" theme, into serious consideration of the Sacrificial-Satisfaction and Legal theories of Christ's saving

---

[748] Ibid.

[749] Ibid., p. 321; cf. Aulen, *The Faith of the Christian Church,* p. 197-198, and Dillistone, *The Christian Understanding of Atonement*, p. 414-415.

[750] Macquarrie, *Principles of Christian Theology*, p. 325.

work. For example, although the Cross plays a part in Macquarrie's thought as the culminating demonstration of how Jesus overcame the last and most powerful idol that enslaves us all — the idol of one's own self — it is not entirely clear how that demonstration overcomes either the *guilt* of our past sins, or the *power* of sin in our lives in the present. No doubt the Holy Spirit helps with the latter process, but it would seem that more is needed. If human sin requires an adequate "atonement" of some kind in order for God to forgive us in a way that is true to his own nature as the God who is just and holy, then merely demonstrating his love for us by setting a good example of love for us to follow in Jesus Christ does not really meet this need.

Also (going back to our critique of the sufficiency of the Incarnational Exemplarist Theory), if the process of our salvation is conceived exclusively as a Spirit-assisted response to new *knowledge,* that is, to Christ's *demonstration* of divine and human love, it is not clear what saving effect that work of Christ would have for those who never hear the gospel. Is the effectiveness of Christ's saving work through his incarnate life and death strictly limited to those who are lucky enough to hear about it and believe it? No doubt Macquarrie would respond that the Word of God (the same Word who was incarnate among us in Jesus), is universally present as self-expressive Being, addressing all human hearts with his grace. But as we have seen, the Christian message from the New Testament onward is that the Divine Word can only be a universal "saving" presence because of things that he objectively accomplished for us in his human life and death, even apart from human knowledge of those accomplishments. And this is precisely what Macquarrie's blend of Incarnational Exemplarist and Classical Atonement theories does not show.

More recently, Anglican New Testament scholar and theologian Bishop Tom Wright, in his book *The Day the Revolution Began* (2016), has explored how the implications of the classical motif in the doctrine of Redemption might be coupled with the exegetical and theological tradition of substitutionary atonement. Wright begins by noting the unanswered questions of the "Christus Victor" theme. In particular, he draws attention to the remarkable and paradoxical idea that on the cross Jesus won a victory — or at least God won a victory through Jesus — over the shadowy "powers" that had usurped his rule over the world. The idea was popular in some quarters during the first few Christian centuries. Many thinkers in the second half of the twentieth century and up to the present have advocated some version of this …. [But] who or what are these "powers"? Why would someone's death — anyone's death, the Messiah's death, the death of the Son of God himself — why would such an event defeat these "powers"? Why would that be a revelation of divine *love*? And — perhaps the most pressing question of all — if these "powers" have been defeated, why does evil still appear to carry on as before, to reign unchecked?[751]

As Macquarrie did, Wright then points to the importance of the power of idolatry over human life as a key theme in the Bible, and as the main bondage that must be broken if humanity is ever to attain the purposes for which the Lord first made us:

In the biblical model what stops us from being genuine humans (bearing the divine image, acting as the "royal priesthood") is not only sin, but the idolatry that underlies it. The idols have gained power, the power humans ought to be exercising in God's world; idolatrous humans have handed it over to them. What is required, for God's new world and for renewed humans within it, is for the power of these idols [e.g. wealth, sex, power, race, class, and nation etc.] to be broken. Since sin, the consequence of idolatry, is what keeps humans in thrall to the non-gods of the world, dealing with sin has a more profound effect than simply releasing humans to go to heaven. It releases humans from the grip of these idols, so they

---

[751] Wright, *The Day the Revolution Began*, p. 46.

can worship the living God and be renewed according to his image.[752]

Wright then develops an understanding of the Atonement that draws heavily upon both the idea of "substitution" (he prefers to call it "representative" rather than "penal" substitution) and the basic Classical Theory. He takes pains to show, however, that according to Scripture the goal of the substitutionary, saving work of Christ on the Cross is not just to bear the penalty for human sin so that those who accept him as Lord can find forgiveness and a free-ticket to heaven. Rather, Christ sets us free *from* the crippling burden of our guilt so that we can be free *for* a new life in the Spirit: a new creation in which the power of the idols to warp and destroy human life is finally broken.[753]

To begin with, according to Scripture the main problem is not the general one of human idolatry, Wright claims, but the more specific problem of the idolatry of the people of Israel, whose original vocation in Abraham was to bring the true worship and service of God to all the nations of the world (Gen 12:3; cf. Is 49:6). Israel must be renewed and its true vocation must be restored so that all the world can finally find salvation in God from sin, guilt, and idolatry:

> [J]esus, as Israel's Messiah, bears Israel's curse in order to undo the consequences of sin and 'exile' and so to break the power

---

[752] Ibid., p. 68.

[753] It would seem that Wright's theory would be strengthened if coupled with belief in the metaphysical reality of Satan and the demons (fallen angels). According to some of the early Christian writers, idols can gain such "power" over us precisely because they are *demonic* idols, that is, they are the instruments of the power of supernatural evil to hold us captive. Saint Paul, for example, writes that to offer sacrifices to idols is to offer them to demons (I Cor 10:20-21). The idea of Satan as a "supra-personal" force of evil in human hearts and human affairs played a significant role in Wright's earlier work (as in for example, *Evil and the Justice of God*. Downer's Grove, IL: InterVarsity Press, 2006, p. 81 and 109-112), but receded almost entirely into the background in *The Day the Revolution Began* (2016).

of the 'present evil age' once and for all. When sins are forgiven, the 'powers' are robbed of their power.[754]

Israel's sins had resulted in exile, exile had been prolonged, a new 'slavery' had been the result — so that the new Passover would need to be effected *through sins being forgiven*. And sins are forgiven, as we have seen in Paul's … letters through the representative and substitutionary death of Jesus …. Jesus *represents* his people as Israel's Messiah, and so he and he alone can appropriately be their substitute …. What I now want to suggest is that, within this larger picture, the evangelists have also explained *how* this forgiveness comes about. It comes about because the one will stand in for the many. It comes about because Jesus dies, innocently, bearing the punishment that he himself had marked out for his fellow Jews as a whole. It comes about because from the beginning Jesus was redefining the nature of the kingdom with regard to radical self-giving and self-denial, and it looks as though that was never simply an ethical demand, but at its heart a personal vocation. It comes about because throughout his public career Jesus was redefining power itself, and his violent death was the ultimate demonstration-in-practice of the redefinition.[755]

Here we can see Wright blending into a rich synthesis several scriptural themes, as well as the Atonement theories of Incarnational Exemplarism, Penal Substitution, and the basic Classical Theory of divine triumph over the demonic powers of idolatry.

Wright's treatment of the doctrine of Redemption through the Cross, however, still leaves the reader wondering about several things.

First, what does it mean to say that Jesus "represented" Israel as the Messiah, or even all of humanity as the New Adam? Granted that these concepts are biblical, but how does they translate into metaphysical

---

[754] Wright, *The Day the Revolution Began*, p. 241.
[755] Ibid., p. 279, 216, 210-211.

clarity? Let us attempt our own succinct definition here that fits with Wright's train of thought, since he does not give a clear definition of his own.[756] *It might be said that Jesus was Israel's representative because he was the archetype and the fulfilment in his own life of Israel's vocation: the true worship and service of God in the midst of a lost and broken world. On this basis, through his risen and glorified life among his disciples, he is now the archetype and source of the life of the New Israel, the Church, in her mission to extend the true worship and service of God to all peoples and to the ends of the earth.*

If that is what "representation" here really means (with echoes of the Pure Sacrificial Theory of Atonement that we discussed earlier in this chapter), then it is unfortunate that Wright decries — and sometimes even caricatures — the way Legal theorists of the Atonement have presented and analysed Christ's substitutionary sin-bearing. He sees them as ignoring the true doctrine of "representative substitution" in favor of abstract theories about Divine Justice and Divine Mercy. However, if Christ's death was to be the true sin-bearing sacrifice, the sacrifice that can bring all who believe to a new life in the Spirit that finally overcomes the power of idolatry and sin in their lives, then how

---

[756] Wright mentions briefly that representative substitution means "that the 'servant' [of Is 53], the quintessential Israelite, takes upon himself the fate of the nation, of the world, of the many" (p. 53). But often in his work it is not entirely clear whether this "taking upon himself our fate" means merely *sharing* in that fate with us, or doing so in some sense "in our place," *instead of* us. In *How God Became King: the Forgotten Story of the Gospels* (New York: Harper One, 2012), p. 243, Wright clearly states the latter: "As for the gospels themselves, there should be no doubt that ... Jesus, for them, is dying a penal death in place of the guilty, of guilty Israel, of guilty humankind." But then he writes of "Jesus's role precisely as Israel's representative Messiah, through which he is exactly fitted to be the substitute for Israel and thence for the world." Again, it is not clear what he means by "representation" here, or how that makes him "exactly fitted" to be the penal substitute for Israel and the world. While it was certainly *fitting* to his mission that Jesus the Messiah was the fulfilment of God's promise to Abraham that through Abraham's seed all the nations of the earth would be blessed (Gen 12:3), one would think that it was even more fitting — indeed, absolutely essential — to his saving work as the sin-bearing substitute for the whole world that Jesus was a divine person in human flesh and completely without sin. Wright does not deny the latter, but he puts all the emphasis on the former.

can theologians avoid translating that message into universally accessible metaphors and abstract categories that can communicate this gospel cross-culturally to all people everywhere? After all, the gospel message was not just meant for the Jews.[757] And isn't that translation process what we see happening, to some extent, in St. John's Gospel and letters? Wright himself never quite manages to do the same:

> [A]t the heart of [Paul's message in Romans 3:21-26] we find not an arbitrary and abstract "punishment" meted out upon an innocent victim, but the living God himself coming incognito … coming to take upon himself the *consequence* of Israel's idolatry, sin, and exile, which itself brought into focus the idolatry, sin, and exile of the whole human race ….[758]

> What God was doing through the Torah, in Israel, was to gather "Sin" together into one place, *so that it could then be condemned*. If anywhere in the whole New Testament teaches an explicit doctrine of "penal substitution" this is it — but it falls within the narrative not of a "works contract," not of an angry God determined to punish someone, not of "going to heaven," but of God's vocational covenant with Israel and through Israel, the vocation that focused on the Messiah himself and

---

[757] In *The Mission of the Messiah* (Steubenville, OH: Emmaus Road Publishing, 1998), p. 149-151, Catholic biblical scholar Tim Gray points to several allusions to the story of Adam and Eve in the Gospel According to St. Luke, passages in which the gospel writer evidently intends us to see that Jesus voluntarily bore not only the curses due to Israel for breaking their covenant with God, but also the curses due to all the sons of Adam for their betrayal of God's love from the Garden of Eden onward. For example, Luke traces the genealogy of Jesus right back to Adam; like Adam Jesus was tested in a garden; like Adam, who was cursed to labor 'by the sweat of his brow" (Gen 3:19), Jesus sweat drops of blood on the ground in his labor of agony in the Garden of Gethsemane (Lk 22:44); like Adam, who labored amongst the thorns (Gen3:18), Christ was crowned with thorns as he labored for our salvation; and finally, like Adam, Jesus bore the curse of death for sin (Gen 3:19), ultimately to restore "paradise" to the lost (Lk 23:43), making the tree of the Cross the new Tree of Life.

[758] Wright, *The Day the Revolution Began* p. 337.

then opened at last into a genuinely human existence ....
"There is no condemnation for those in the Messiah ...
because God ... condemned Sin right there in the flesh" [Rom
8:1-4]. The punishment has been meted out. But the
punishment is on Sin itself, the combined, accumulated,
personified force that has wreaked such havoc in the world and
in human lives.

Here is a point that must be noted most carefully. Paul does
not say that God punished Jesus. He declares that God
punished Sin *in the flesh of Jesus* .... The death of Jesus, seen in
this light, is certainly *penal.* It has to do with the punishment on
Sin — not, to say it again, on Jesus — but it is punishment
nonetheless.[759]

Here, again, Wright's metaphysics are elusive. Amid a stream of
caricatures of the Legal Theory ("an abstract punishment meted out
upon an innocent victim," "an angry God determined to punish
someone," etc. — notice how far these caricatures roam from the
thought of Legal theorists such as Norman Anderson and John Stott
that we explored earlier), Wright wants to replace the Legal Theory
with the idea that it was not Jesus who was punished, but "Sin" in his
flesh. But how does that work? Christ's flesh is an aspect of himself, it
is himself in person (especially if "in the flesh" here means not just "in
his body" but "in his human nature" as it sometimes does in Greek).
After all, if you nail Jesus' body to a cross, you don't just nail his "flesh"
to it, you nail "him." The point is: *the death of Christ was God the Son
himself, in his own person, in and through his own tortured body and tormented
soul, out of his merciful love for us and in accord with his own holiness and justice,
bearing the penalty for Israel's sins and for all human sins in our place.* Sadly,
Wright's failure to translate the biblical narrative of Christ's saving
work on the Cross into intelligible doctrine tends to obscure as much
as illuminate this gospel message.

---

[759] Ibid., 286-287.

And yet, his underlying point is well-taken: the gospel message is not just the offer of a "get-out-of-jail-free" card for eternal life because Christ paid the penalty for us on the Cross. Rather, it is a liberation *from* the guilt of sin so that we can be liberated *for* a new life in the Spirit, a life that can finally defeat the power of evil and idolatry over humanity once and for all.

The Kenotic Contribution to the Doctrine of Redemption

So far in this chapter, we have seen how the doctrine of the Incarnation forms a vital foundation for the mystery of the Atonement, no matter which of the four basic schools of Atonement theory (Exemplarist, Sacrificial, Legal, or Classical) one takes as a line of approach. We have done this primarily through a survey of post-World War II Anglican thought — a good vantage point on this issue, since in this era the Anglican Communion has wrestled with significant challenges to its historic, incarnational faith from within its own ranks. But again, Anglican thought on the doctrine of Redemption in this period, while it has its own emphases, is far from unique; to a considerable extent it mirrors and draws upon doctrinal developments elsewhere, as appropriate in an ecumenical age.

We can summarize our findings like this: *almost every dimension of the saving work of Jesus Christ is illumined and strengthened by the truth of the Incarnation.* Richard Swinburne's Sacrificial Theory, for example, like that of Aquinas, starts by assuming that our Lord wanted to come to our aid so that we could make a full atonement for our sins. In the context of this intention, the Incarnation is shown to be *essential* to Christ's redemptive work. Only if Jesus is the divine Son Incarnate can his life and death of faithful and obedient love have "theandric," supererogatory value, so that we can sacramentally offer up his whole-life self-sacrifice as an appropriate penance to God for our sins. The Merit Theory developed by Richard Cross also depends upon a robust doctrine of the Incarnation, for it is only because Jesus is God Incarnate that his human life and death can be of universal, meritorious value. The Incarnation is essential to the Theory of Penal Substitution too: only if Jesus is God Incarnate, our Creator and our Judge, can he pay the penalty for our sins in our place on the Cross.

In the Incarnational Exemplarist Theory and the Classical Theory, the Incarnation is held to be at least *fitting* to God's overall, saving purposes for humanity. As we have seen, if God our Creator desired to show us the Way of faithful love, the Way of the Kingdom that overcomes the demonic power of idolatry over our lives, and if he also wanted to move us to follow that Way, then he could accomplish both purposes at once. He could live out for us himself an exemplary human life, in human flesh. This would convincingly demonstrate his "sacrificial" and "merciful" (in the sense of patient and forbearing) love for us — especially if it cost him terrible suffering at the hands of sinners — and all this could certainly move us to open our hearts to his Spirit, and to love him in return.

By contrast, if (as the Non-Incarnational theologians would have it), Jesus was *not* God Incarnate, then he was a much less convincing demonstration of *God's* love and mercy. Jesus would be seen merely as an ambassador of God, called and inspired by him to show us the Way of faithful love, even unto death on the Cross, and the hope of eternal life. Thus, God would be standing on the sidelines, so to speak, like a good football coach. His contributions to the team would be commendable, and he might even have some kind of feeling for his players. But the real hero would be the captain on the field, showing how the game should be played, and risking life and limb in the process.

Clearly, the Incarnation needs to be affirmed if the Church is to have a gospel message of salvation through Jesus Christ to celebrate, and to proclaim to the world. Historically this has been a central belief of the Anglican tradition, as contemporary Anglican discussion largely confirms. *What is unfortunate, however, is how little the Anglican tradition has appreciated that its own incarnational heritage — especially its own distinctive form of the Kenotic understanding of the Incarnation — might enrich and illuminate these holy mysteries.*

506

As we have seen, a major problem with much of contemporary thought on the Atonement is its frequent failure to explain clearly why the crucifixion of Jesus was decisive to his saving work. In Macquarrie's Classical Theory, all the Non-Incarnational and Incarnational Exemplarist theories that we surveyed, the various Sacrificial theories of Quick, Mascall, White, Thornton, Aquinas and Swinburne, and the Merit Theory of Ricard Cross, the crucifixion is seen merely as the culmination and climax of his whole life of self-giving love. Only in the writings of those trying to incorporate the idea of substitutionary atonement into their Christology (e.g. Packer, Anderson, Stott, Mozley, Porter, Rutledge, and Wright) are we given reason to see the crucifixion itself also achieving something distinctive and decisive: Jesus Christ, out of his holiness and his merciful love for us, has taken upon himself the burden and penalty of our sins in our place. Whatever one may decide about the theological and moral logic of the Legal Theory, we can at least appreciate that it does justice to the traditionally cross-centered devotion of the Western Church. In the words of the refrain of the Catholic devotion "The Stations of the Cross": "We adore you O Christ and we bless you, because *by your holy cross* you have redeemed the world." We find the same focus at the heart of the Eucharist in almost every Western liturgy — for example, in the traditional Anglican Book of Common Prayer service of Holy Communion, in which the worshippers give glory to God, above all, because "thou of thy tender mercy didst give thine only Son Jesus Christ to suffer death upon the cross for our redemption; who made there, by his one oblation of himself once offered, a full, perfect and sufficient sacrifice, oblation, and satisfaction, for the sins of the whole world ...."

Historically, the passion and death of Jesus has indeed been seen as pivotal to his saving work. Now we shall make an important claim for Kenoticism in this regard. I shall argue that a kenotic interpretation of the Incarnation makes a vital contribution to our understanding of the Atonement: it provides further justification for the Cross-centered focus of Western Christianity by putting the Cross back at the centre of soteriology where it belongs. *For only a kenotic interpretation of the Cross can clearly establish for us that God the Son, as Jesus Christ, fully identified there with the depths of our broken, suffering, guilt-ridden and alienated human condition.*

The basic message of Kenoticism is that God has shared with us in his divine nature, through Jesus Christ, all the joys, sorrows, and pains that the human journey entails, from a limited human perspective on events. He created us knowing full well (or at least, knowing the strong probability!) that the human race would fall into sin, as well as experience affliction in a myriad of ways. According to Kenoticism, however, by coming among us and sharing our lot, the divine Son gave us the closest, divine-as-human companionship amid all our sufferings and struggles. His sharing on the Cross in the experience of "total human affliction" enabled him to enter into the most profound solidarity with our plight; now we can truly say that our Lord does not ask us to walk through any depth of suffering that he has not undergone himself.

In short, **Kenoticism (especially in the form of Moderate KM developed largely within the Anglican tradition) is the incarnational theory that enables us to affirm all this in the most coherent, intelligible and powerful way. It enables us to say that God, through Jesus Christ, has fully identified with human suffering, taking the sins and sorrows of the world upon his Heart (that is, right into the divine nature itself), in order that he might raise us to himself. If so, then the Kenotic approach to the Incarnation is the best foundation for those theories of the Atonement that depend upon a strong and clear affirmation of this truth for their coherence, and their power to move the human heart — in particular, as we have seen, this would be true of the Incarnational Exemplarist and Penal Substitution theories of Atonement. Only if the divine Son has truly shared our lot, right into the depths of total affliction and the subjective experience of God-forsakenness itself, can he truly light the way for us through the darkness, and bear for us— in his Heart and in our place — the burden of all the sins of humanity.** At the same time (as discussed in Part One of this book), in Moderate KM the one who suffered and died for us was, simultaneously and in a biblical sense, worthy of our worship and adoration: he was upholding all of creation with his universal wisdom and power — all the stars and galaxies — even while he was born among us on earth in Bethlehem, sharing all the limitations of our human condition, preaching and healing in Galilee, and giving his life for us on the Cross.

In fact, Kenoticism is not only the best foundation for underpinning these two important incarnational Atonement theories: it also adds important dimensions of its own to the doctrine of Redemption. We shall look here at four dimensions of the mystery of Redemption that can be enriched and illuminated by a kenotic perspective.

> 1) A kenotic understanding of the Cross can help us overcome our fear of affliction, a fear that can cripple our discipleship when the cost seems too great

Sin and affliction are not easily separated. Just as sin fills the world with needless suffering, so the threat of affliction can powerfully tempt us to sin. Consider how often people are tempted to despair, to lose confidence in God's loving providence, or to preserve themselves at any cost in the face of terrible suffering. The threat of persecution and torture, for example, has caused many to renounce their faith in God, or to compromise their commitment to the common good. In other words, fear of affliction and death have remarkable power to limit our trust in God, and our commitment to the path of self-giving love. This is the "cost of discipleship" that Christian martyr Dietrich Bonhoeffer wrote about so movingly in the face of the ideologies of radical hatred of our time (e.g., fascism and communism, and in our own day, radical Islamic terrorism). But it is not just the threat of socio-political persecution that can cripple our discipleship. Any major threat or occasion of total human affliction presents us with the choice between trust and anguish, and between hope and despair. For example, Cardinal Walter Kasper noted that during the outbreaks of the bubonic plague in the Middle Ages, infected people visited shrines with plague crosses where they could prayerfully identify with the suffering of the crucified Christ, and spiritually lift themselves up on the Cross with him.[760] Saint Augustine once wrote that that Jesus Christ entered into the fellowship of our afflictions precisely in order to disarm our dread of them, our fear that they necessarily have the power to separate us from him:

> It was by no necessity of his condition, but by the good will of his compassion, that our Lord Jesus took up these feelings of human weakness, as he also took the flesh of human weakness and the death of human flesh. He did it to transform into himself his Body, the Church, whereof he has deigned to be the Head, that if ever it happened to any of his holy and faithful ones to be saddened and sorrowful in the midst of human temptations, he should not on that account find himself estranged from the grace of his Savior, and should learn that such occurrences are not sins, but indications of human infirmity. Thus the body was to take the note of the Head.[761]

In short, fear of total affliction and death, and the very experience of affliction itself, has the power to lead us away from the call to love, and to tempt us to fall into despair in the face of suffering.

A kenotic interpretation of the Cross, however, addresses this situation directly. For Kenoticism tells us that in the face of grievous suffering, the Son of God not only reassures us (through his resurrection) that we may hope for eternal life. He also gives us the assurance, from his own personal journey through total human affliction, that we can never be totally bereft of him, even in the midst of terrible suffering.

Although she balked at interpreting the mystery of the Incarnation in a kenotic fashion, Anglican theologian Marilyn McCord Adams focused her Christology on the human experience of "horrors." She defined the horrors to which human beings are subject with brutal honesty:

---

[760] Kasper, *Mercy*, p. 152.
[761] Augustine, *Exposition on the Psalms*, 87,3, cited in Kasper, *Mercy*, p. 120.

Paradigm horrors include the rape of a woman and axing off of her arms, psychophysical torture whose ultimate goal is the disintegration of the personality, schizophrenia or severe clinical depression, cannibalizing one's own offspring, child abuse of the sort described by Ivan Karamazov, parental incest, participation in the Nazi death camps, the explosion of nuclear bombs over populated areas, being the accidental and/or unwitting agent in the disfigurement or death of those one loves best. Participation in horrors furnishes *reason* to doubt whether the participant's life can be worth living, because it engulfs the positive value of his or her life and penetrates into his/her meaning-making structures seemingly to defeat and degrade his/her value as a person.[762]

God's response to these horrors, Adams says, is not just to compensate its victims with everlasting felicity in the next life; rather, it is actually to begin to "defeat" these horrors here and now. By identifying with our human vulnerability and sufferings through his own incarnate life and death, the Son of God established a permanent basis for an intimate relationship with us, a relationship nurtured and sustained through the Eucharist, which in turn prepares us for eternal beatitude with him in heaven:

> God Incarnate shares not only our nature, but also our plight in a material world such as this, the Divine Word also becoming radically vulnerable to horrors.[763]

> Most obviously, the Gospels climax in Jesus' horror-participation as a victim, in His crucifixion. Not only was the method of killing degrading because crueler than that normally used to slaughter cattle; it was socially uprooting. Not only was Jesus betrayed, denied, and deserted by his closest followers: Deuteronomic law declared that death by hanging from a tree rendered its victim cursed, cut off from the people of God and from God (Deuteronomy 21:23; Galatians 3:13)! From a

---

[762] Adams, *Christ and Horrors*, p. 32-33.
[763] Ibid., p. 40

Jewish point of view, death by crucifixion clearly defeated Messianic pretensions and turned Jesus' earthly ministry into an evident failure.[764]

But if Christ came to save human persons from the ruinous power of horrendous evil, then crucifixion is precisely the sort of thing that would make His mission successful. If God takes God's stand with the cursed, the cursed are not cut off from God after all![765]

Divine solidarity with us in horror-participation weaves our own horror participation into the warp and woof of our own witting and unwitting intimate personal relationship with God …. By catching up our horror-participation into a relationship that is incommensurably good for us, Divine participation in horrors defeats their *prima facie* life-ruining powers.[766]

Although he also did not call himself a Kenoticist, it was the German Lutheran Jurgen Moltmann, perhaps more than any other contemporary theologian, who emphasized this aspect of the message of the Cross.[767] Moltmann claimed that we can walk with greater courage and faith in the knowledge that nothing can ever separate us from the crucified God. In the darkness of grief and pain, abandonment by friends and isolation from all companionship, amid shattered hopes and dreams — still, to be crucified with him is not to lose him. **We can always know two things: we can know that God deeply understands and sympathises with our plight, because as Jesus he once walked the same dark path; and we can claim an indestructible identity, even when everything else has been stripped away from us, as disciples crucified alongside him. God's close empathetic understanding, and an indestructible**

---

[764] Ibid., p. 69.

[765] Ibid., p. 41.

[766] Ibid., p. 40.

[767] In addition to his most famous work, *The Crucified God* (1972), these ideas can be found expressed in a more personal way in Moltmann's much shorter book, *Experiences of God* (Philadelphia: Fortress Press, 1980).

identity in union with him: these can never be taken from us if (as Kenoticism tries to establish metaphysically) God chose to experience the depths of total human affliction with us on the Cross.

If this is enough to liberate us *from* the crippling effects of our worst fears, then it liberates us also *for* faith and love, especially when the call to love others and trust in God becomes most costly.

We see all this on display in the life and writings of St. Thomas More, who never considered himself constituted with the bravery to be a martyr. But when for conscience sake he had to demur from the edicts of King Henry VIII, even under threat of being hung, drawn and quartered for treason, he wrote from prison of the comfort and courage he found in Jesus in his treatise, "The Sadness of Christ":

> [Since Christ] foresaw that there would be many people of such a delicate constitution that they would be convulsed with terror at the danger of being tortured, He chose to enhearten them by the example of His own sorrow, His own sadness, His own weariness and unequalled fear, lest they should be so disheartened as they compare their own fearful state of mind with the boldness of the bravest martyrs ....To such a person as this, Christ wanted His own deed to speak out (as it were) with his own living voice: "O faint of heart, take courage and do not despair. You are afraid, you are sad, you are stricken with weariness and dread of the torment with which you have been cruelly threatened. Trust me, I conquered the world, and yet I suffered immeasurably more from fear, I was sadder, more afflicted with weariness, more horrified at the prospect of such cruel suffering drawing eagerly nearer and nearer. Let the brave man have his high-spirited martyrs, let him rejoice in imitating a thousand of them. But you, my timorous and feeble little sheep, be content to have me as your shepherd, follow my leadership; if you do not trust yourself, place your trust in me. See, I am walking ahead of you on this fearful road .... [A]nd likewise remember that this light and momentary burden

513

of tribulation will prepare you for a weight of glory which is beyond all measure. For the sufferings of this time are not worthy to be compared with the glory that is to come which will be revealed in you. As you reflect on such things, take heart, and use the sign of my cross to drive away this dread sadness, fear, and weariness like vain spectres of darkness ...."

And so, among other reasons why our Savior deigned to take upon Himself those feelings of human weakness, this one I have spoken of is not unworthy of consideration — I mean that having made Himself weak for the sake of the weak, He might take care of other weak men by his own weakness. He had their welfare so much at heart that this whole process of His agony seems designed for nothing more clearly than to lay down a fighting technique for the faint-hearted soldier who needs to be swept along, as it were, into martyrdom.[768]

Thus, a kenotic understanding of God's incarnate passion opens up a way to face our deepest fears of affliction, the very fears that weaken our discipleship at the time of greatest testing. As the author of the book of Hebrews put it: through his death Jesus has overcome the power of Satan, who through fear of death held humanity in lifelong bondage (Heb 2:14-15).

---

[768] Saint Thomas More, "The Sadness of Christ" in *Selected Writings* (New York: Vintage Books, 2003), p. 17-19. Of course, in saying that Christ became weak for the sake of the weak, More did not mean that Jesus became weak in faith or courage. Rather, there were powerful and unique reasons why Christ was reduced to his own state of anguish and dread. In particular, the Catholic tradition would point to his grief in the Garden of Gethsemane from his supernaturally infused foresight of the multitudes whom he loved who would be eternally lost, despite of all his sufferings for them (a foresight rising to daylight consciousness by the Holy Spirit, perhaps from the universal, infused knowledge stored in his subconscious). The Catholic tradition also points to the natural shrinking of Christ's human nature from the approach of total affliction on the Cross, and his reluctance to drink of the "cup" of divine wrath that was offered to him by his Father, which meant bearing in his human soul an experience of God-forsakenness and alienation from God analogous to the eternal loss suffered by unrepentant sinners.

2) A kenotic understanding of the Cross can help us to overcome our residual fear of God

As we saw earlier in this chapter, most incarnational theologians claim that the Incarnation is the most direct and comprehensible way for God to reveal himself to human beings. God in flesh spoke to flesh. An infinitely personal God revealed himself through a finite personal life. The incarnate form of his self-revelation thereby gives clarity to our understanding of God that helps us to overcome our residual fear and dread of him: our fear of the unknown, our dread of the infinite divine mystery. Though much of that mystery remains, we are assured that nothing we shall ever discover about God can contradict the personal, self-giving, sacrificial love for us that he has clearly shown through his incarnate life and death as Jesus Christ. As St. John wrote: "In this the love of God was made manifest among us, that God sent his only-begotten Son into the world, so that we might live through him" (I Jn 4:9).

Kenoticism, however, strengthens and renders more intelligible this vital truth, for the *kenotic* form of God's incarnate self-revelation especially helps us to overcome our fear and dread of him.

The truth is that we are afraid of the almighty power of God. Omnipotence is frightening to those who have already been used or abused by the corruption of human power. Every wicked parent, teacher, boss, bureaucrat, and dictator leaves a mark on the soul, and further deepens the general store of human dread of authority. We are understandably suspicious of an *all-powerful* being. But God-in-*kenosis* disarms our fear of him. Austin Farrer once described this in a homily for Christmas:

> The universal misuse of human power has the sad effect that power, however lovingly used, is hated … we are made incapable of loving the government of God himself, or feeling the caress of an almighty kindness …. All his dear and infinite

kindness is lost behind the mask of power. Overwhelmed by omnipotence, we miss the heart of love ….

Yet Mary holds her finger out, and a divine hand closes on it. The maker of the world is born a begging child; he begs for milk, and he does not know that it is milk for which he begs. We will not lift our hands to pull the love of God down to us, but he lifts his hands to pull human compassion down upon his cradle. So the weakness of God proves stronger than men, and the folly of God proves wiser than men. Love is the strongest instrument of omnipotence, for accomplishing those tasks he cares most dearly to perform; and this is how he brings his love to bear on human pride[769]: by weakness not by strength, by need and not by bounty.[770]

As we have already seen in the important reflections of O.C. Quick on this point (see Part One, Chapter Three, above), *this is how God acts with power to achieve his highest purposes, the greatest aims of his Kingdom: he is neither coercive nor destructive, but draws us to himself by his compassionate love and patient suffering, that is, by the kenotic form of his love.* **If so, then we have little reason to fear his power.**

---

[769] Farrer might have been clearer at the end of this beautiful passage if he had said "fear" or "suspicion" here rather than "pride."

[770] Austin Farrer, *Said or Sung: an arrangement of homily and verse* (London: Faith Press, 1960), p. 34-35. Similar sentiments can be found in the meditations on the Nativity of Christ by St. Alphonsus Liguori (1696-1787):

> If our Redeemer had come to be feared and respected by men, he would have come as a full grown man, with royal dignity; but because he came to gain our love, he chose to come and to show himself as an infant, and the poorest of infants, born in a cold stable between two animals, laid in a manger upon straw, without clothing or fire to warm his shivering little limbs: "thus would he be born, who willed to be loved and not feared." ("Discourses for the Novena of Christmas, II" in *The Incarnation and Birth of Jesus Christ.* Brooklyn: Redemptorist Fathers, 1927, p. 37)

Perhaps this is also the hidden meaning of St. Mark's account of the passion of Jesus Christ. At the very end of that Gospel, in response to Christ's cry of dereliction on the Cross and the utter social shame and self-abasement of his death, a Roman centurion (symbol of the *coercive might* of the Roman Empire), was the first person in Mark's Gospel to confess faith in the crucified Lord, with the words: "Truly, this man was the Son of God" (Mk 15:39). As Lucien Richard puts it: "The crucifixion story in Mark dramatizes the mysterious paradox of authentic Christian existence: 'Power comes to its full strength in weakness' (2 Cor 12:9)."[771]

Indeed, this is the meaning of so many Christian devotional paradoxes. At Christmas, as Austin Farrer said: "The love of God is so strongly armed with weakness that it must prevail. Love is nowhere more truly omnipotent than in the manger."[772] And St. Paul says the same thing about the power and wisdom of Divine Love manifest on the Cross:

> For the word of the cross is folly to those who are perishing, but to us who are being saved it is the power of God …. For Jews demand signs and Greeks seek wisdom, but we preach Christ crucified, a stumbling block to Jews and folly to Gentiles, but to those who are called, both Jews and Greeks, Christ the power of God and the wisdom of God. For the foolishness of God is wiser than men, and the weakness of God is stronger than men. (I Cor 1:18-25)

Although he does not describe himself as a Kenotic theologian, a similar understanding of the power of God revealed on the Cross also has been a recurrent theme in the work of Anglican Bishop Tom Wright:

> At the heart of the gospel is a redefinition of power. That is one of the central ways in which early Christians interpreted the death of Jesus. The reason the cross carried such life-changing power, and carries it still, is because it embodied, expressed, and symbolized the true power of which all earthly

[771] Richard, *Christ: The Self-Emptying of God*, p. 72.
[772] Ibid., p. 38; cf. Quick, *Doctrines of the Creed*, p. 65-66.

power is either an imitation or a corrupt parody. It isn't the case that power as we know it in the "real" world is the "norm" and the Christian subversion of it is a kind of bizarre twist that might just work even though we don't see how. The gospel of Jesus summons us to believe that the power of self-giving love unveiled on the cross is the real thing, the power that made the world in the first place, and is now in the business of remaking it; and that the other forms of "power," the corrupt and self-serving ways in which the world is so often run, from global empires and multimillion businesses down to classrooms, families, and gangs, are the distortion.[773]

3) Kenoticism makes God's full offer of forgiveness for sin truly credible.

A kenotic position on the Incarnation enables us to say that God the Son has experienced, from within his authentically human perspective as Jesus of Nazareth, the terrible cost of human sin upon human life. He knows what it is to experience grief, betrayal, rejection, marginalization, racial and class hatred, persecution, and death by torture. He knows what it is to feel the injustice of the condemnation of the innocent. He even knows what it is to feel alienated, abandoned, and cut off from God, analogous to the subjective experience of guilt and judgement. As a result, with this experience of total affliction at the hands of sinners forever stored in his divine "memory," he now has a touchstone for the closest possible compassion for all those who

---

[773] Wright, *The Day the Revolution Began,* p. 398-399. Similarly, in *The Power of the Cross,* p. 277-314, **Graham Tomlin addresses the fears that drive so many post-modern thinkers today: e.g., that the Church (as well as other religious groups) propagates a metanarrative that masks a will to exercise power over others, and impose its religious doctrines on others. This fear is disarmed if the primary form of "power" that Christians are called to exercise through their metanarrative, centered on the Cross, is the power of voluntary servanthood and suffering love.**

suffer as victims and perpetrators of sin.[774] For he has had first-hand, human experience of the terrible cost of sin upon both victims and perpetrators alike.

Why does this make God's offer of forgiveness for sin more credible? Some theologians have argued that God may rightfully forgive any offenses in so far as they are offences committed against himself as Creator and Total Benefactor of the human race, but he can hardly claim the right to forgive our offences in so far as they are committed against our fellows, unless he truly understands and shares in the pain and agony which our sins have caused them.

The Russian author Dostoevsky addressed this problem in his novel *The Brothers Karamazov*. Through the character Ivan Karamazov, he put forward the argument that crimes against the innocent, such as young children, are beyond the reach of anyone else's forgiveness. The perpetrators of the terrible innocent suffering of children can never be forgiven by any save the victims themselves, for no one truly knows the misery their victims endured. Ivan argues:

> "When the mother embraces the fiend who threw her child to the dogs, and all cry aloud with tears 'Thou art just, O Lord!', then, of course, the crown of knowledge will be reached and all will be made clear. But what pulls me up here is that I cannot accept that harmony …. I don't want the mother to embrace the oppressor who threw her son to the dogs! She dare not forgive him. Let her forgive him herself, if she will, let her forgive the torturer for the immeasurable sufferings of her mother's heart. But the sufferings of her tortured child she has no right to forgive; she dare not forgive the torturer, even if the child were to forgive him! And if that is so, if they dare not forgive, what becomes of harmony? Is there in the whole

---

[774] For a discussion of Christ's experience of something analogous to subjective guilt, see Part Two, Chapter One above.

world a being who would have the right to forgive and could forgive?"[775]

Through the character Alyosha, Dostoevsky then points the way through this impasse, and shows how full forgiveness might be offered by all even to the torturers of the innocent:

> "Brother," said Alyosha suddenly, with flashing eyes, "you said just now, is there a being in the whole world who would have the right to forgive and could forgive? But there is a Being and He can forgive everything, all and for all, because He gave His innocent blood for all and for everything. You have forgotten Him … and it is to him they cry aloud, 'Thou art just, O Lord, for Thy ways are revealed.'"[776]

Dostoevsky found the right to offer full forgiveness only in the humiliated and tortured Christ. This is what Kenoticism enables us to affirm as well: Jesus the Son has borne our griefs and carried our sorrows. He has experienced total human affliction in his passion and death. He has thereby gained a reference point for the closest empathetic and sympathetic participation in the suffering of all living creatures. **Since the Son of God has shared as closely as possible the burden of human suffering, he can rightly offer forgiveness on behalf of its victims to those who cause it**.[777] Of course, in this respect he need only do so on behalf of those victims of our sins who cannot yet, or who forever refuse to forgive us (again, one thinks of innocent children whose words of forgiveness may never be heard until the next life, or those victims of our sins who will not forgive us and are lost forever, clinging to their hatred and vindictiveness). There is no need for Christ to forgive on behalf of those who are willing and able to forgive, in this life or the next. But if *all* wounds are to be healed

---

[775] Fyodor Dostoevsky, *The Brothers Karamazov*, vol. I, C. Garnett, trans. (London: J.M. Dent, 1927), p. 249-250.

[776] Ibid., p. 251.

[777] The close connection between Kenoticism and Dostoevsky's perspective is not surprising, given the strength of the Kenotic tradition in Russian Orthodox theology and spirituality from the mid-nineteenth to the mid-twentieth centuries; see Part One, Chapter Six, above.

for the blessed, forgiveness must one day be available to them on behalf of all those victims of their sins who will not or cannot offer it — and this only Jesus Christ, the crucified God, rightfully can do. F.W. Dillistone summed up the point like this:

> Through the encounter between Alyosha and Ivan Karamazov, [Dostoevsky] grapples with the question of the right to forgive sins and affirms that only the one who has borne in himself the suffering and torture which wicked acts entail can rightfully speak a word of forgiveness to the sinner. **'Only if it can be true that Christ really suffers in all suffering, and if upon Him all sin has actually fallen, can He have the right to forgive sin in the stead of those other sufferers who may not forgive us.'**[778]

4) Kenoticism shows us how God can awaken within us a deeper spirit of authentic penitence for our sins.

A kenotic doctrine of the Cross implies that God the Son bore — and continues to bear — the sins of the world upon his Heart; that is, he is deeply affected in his capacity for empathy and sympathy. He feels for our plight, sympathizing and grieving over the plight of the lost and the broken in the deepest way because he once shared their lot. By looking to his Cross, therefore we can now see clearly the sorrow we cause by our sins to the compassionate Heart of the divine Son. This can move us to a more perfect contrition for our sins, informed by love for the Heart of Jesus as well as by regret for the miseries we have caused to others.

Kenoticism thus opens a way through an Anglican theological "dead-end." At the beginning of the 20th century, Anglican theologian R.C. Moberly had argued in *Atonement and Personality* (1901) that God's forgiveness can only begin to be offered in response to awakening penitence. Yet men and women can never be perfectly contrite; even our acts of contrition are tainted by self-

---

[778] Dillistone, *The Christian Understanding of Atonement*, p. 297-299.

centeredness. The Son of God came to our aid, Moberly claimed, by assuming an "inclusive" human nature which, by indwelling and embracing all humanity, can be penitent on behalf of all. By identifying through the Holy Spirit with Jesus Christ, the perfect penitent, who deeply grieved for the sins of all of humanity in his agony and passion, we can enjoy a full measure of divine forgiveness, and grow in a spirit of authentic repentance.[779]

In his classic work of Christian apologetics, *Mere Christianity*, the Anglican writer C.S. Lewis popularized his own version of Moberly's perspective, in a chapter entitled "The Perfect Penitent":

> Now, what was the sort of 'hole" that man had gotten himself into? He had tried to set up on his own, to behave as if he belonged to himself. In other words, fallen man is not simply an imperfect creature who needs improvement: he is a rebel who must lay down his arms. Laying down your arms, surrendering, saying you are sorry, realising that you have been on the wrong track and getting ready to start life over again from the ground floor — that is the only way out of our 'hole.' This process of surrender — this movement full speed astern — is what Christians call repentance. Now repentance is no fun at all. It is something much harder than merely eating humble pie. It means unlearning all the self-conceit and self-will that we have been training ourselves into for thousands of years. It means killing part of yourself, undergoing a kind of death. In fact, it needs a good man to repent. And here comes the catch. Only a bad person needs to repent: only a good person can repent perfectly. The worse you are the more you need it and the less you can do it. The only person who could do it perfectly would be a perfect person — and he would not need it.

---

[779] See the helpful discussion of Moberly's rather elusive position in Dillistone, *The Christian Understanding of Atonement*, p. 256-259.

Remember, this repentance, this willing submission to humiliation and a kind of death, is not something God demands of you before He will take you back and which He could let you off if He chose: it is simply a description of what going back to Him is like. If you ask God to take you back without it, you are really asking Him to let you back without going back. It cannot happen. Very well, then, we must go through with it. But the same badness which makes us need it, makes us unable to do it. Can we do it if God helps us? Yes, but what do we mean when we talk of God helping us? ...

[U]nfortunately, we now need God's help in order to do something which God, in His own nature, never does at all — to surrender, to suffer, to submit, to die. Nothing in God's nature corresponds to this process at all. So that the one road for which we now need God's leadership most of all is a road God, in His own nature, has never walked. God can only share what He has: this thing, in His own nature, he has not.

But supposing God became man — suppose our human nature which can suffer and die was amalgamated with God's nature in one person — then that person could help us. He could surrender His will, and suffer and die, because He was man; He could do it perfectly because He was God. You and I can go through this process only if God does it in us; but we can only do it if He becomes man. Our attempts at this dying will succeed only if we men share in God's dying ... but we cannot share God's dying unless God dies; and He cannot die except by being a man.[780]

This expression of Moberly's theory was an improvement upon the original because Lewis side-stepped the most difficult notion that Moberly had introduced: that Christ must have had an "inclusive humanity," so that he that could somehow include all of

---

[780] C.S. Lewis, *Mere Christianity*, p. 56-58.

us in his own perfect penitence.[781] Lewis switched this around so that Christ does not need to include us in himself; rather, we need to include his perfection within ourselves. We do so by welcoming the presence of the risen and glorified Christ and his Spirit within our hearts, who unites us with the sanctifying power of the divine Son's perfectly penitent human nature. In this respect, Lewis's version of the Perfect Penitent theory can be seen as an aspect of the Pure Sacrificial Theory of Quick, Mascall, and especially of Vernon White that we previously discussed.

Unfortunately, Moberly's theory was saddled with two other incoherent elements. *It is just not clear how Jesus of Nazareth, innocent of sin, could really be "penitent," much*

---

[781] If, as mentioned earlier in this chapter, the Catholic tradition is true that Jesus had a supernatural foreknowledge in the depths (or subconscious) of his human soul of all those for whom he was giving his life on the Cross (cf. Gal 2:20), then there would be a sense in which Jesus did have an "inclusive" human nature. By this supernatural gift of knowledge, and by his love for all those whom he foresaw, he would have carried us each and all in his Heart on the Cross. We shall explore further this Catholic tradition, and its relationship with the doctrines of the Incarnation and the Cross, in volume two of this series. Suffice it so say here that even this concession would not render Moberly's Atonement Theory coherent. For even if Jesus did foresee in the depths of his soul, each and every sinner for whom he was dying on the Cross, and even if he grieved over their lost and broken condition, and over all of their sins, this still would not be the equivalent of "vicarious" penitence for those sins — a notion which is in any case far from clear. Presumably "vicarious" means (1) "I do something that enables you to do the same, without which you could not do it," or (2) "I do something in your place so you don't have to do it yourself." Regarding the first option: *how did Jesus "repent" for sins in a way that enables us to do it ourselves? — he was, after all, the sinless Lamb of God.* Real repentance involves disowning ones sins through authentic contrition, and a determination to amend one's life. Jesus never had to disown any sins, was never contrite for sins in that sense, and never had to commit himself to amend his life. His grief and sorrow over the sins of others was therefore only remotely analogous to human "penitence." The second sense of "vicarious" would be synonymous with substitutionary atonement, *and it is not clear how someone, even God Incarnate, can repent in place of another person*, given that repentance necessarily involves a subjective transformation of the attitudes and dispositions of the soul. Surely, no one can undergo such inner transformation in place of another.

less penitent on behalf of others. To be sure, his grief and sorrow over the sins of others was analogous to repentance, but only remotely so, for penitence essentially involves remorse for one's sins and the resolve not to commit them again. As Maurice Wiles once wrote: "The feeling of shame and sorrow at the sin of another to whom one is closely bound by nature and by love, which [Moberly] so eloquently describes, still falls short of constituting 'vicarious penitence' for that sin."[782]

Lewis stumbled here too, if only because he equated Christ's earthly self-surrender with a process of repentance. Our Lord's suffering and dying was a *kind of* loving surrender and death-to-self, to be sure, but not exactly the *repentant* kind. The sanctifying power of his love which Christ makes available to us, while it enables us to repent, therefore, does not seem to depend upon him leading the way as a perfect "penitent."

As a result of these difficulties, the Perfect Penitent theories of Moberly and Lewis have largely fallen out of favor both in Anglican and non-Anglican Christology since the Second World War. Nevertheless, it is clear that Moberly had hit upon something of vital importance. If God cares about the development and fulfilment of human personality, then he must want to help us *fully disown* our attachment to our evil deeds. This is an essential part of the process of our "at-one-ment" with him. Moreover, a true spirit of repentance seems to be a *sine qua non* for God to be able fully to forgive us on a moral basis, in accord with his holiness and justice. A truly contrite heart is also what enables us to *receive* his forgiveness, for we can hardly receive the grace and pardon of Divine Mercy, and a renewal of the life of the Holy Spirit in our hearts, if we cannot really admit that we are guilty of transgression.

To bring us to a state of true contrition and repentance must therefore be an essential aspect of Christ's saving work to rescue

---

[782] Maurice Wiles, *Faith and the Mystery of God* (London: SCM, 1982), p. 67.

us from the guilt and power of sin.[783] Saint Paul said as much in Romans 2:4: "Do you not know that God's kindness is meant to bring you to repentance?" Yet contemporary theology, both Anglican and otherwise, has often failed to explain how Christ accomplished this. No doubt, as Geoffrey Lampe emphasized, the attractive quality of graced, human love demonstrated in the life and martyrdom of Jesus can convict us of our sins. We know we fall far short of his shining example, and this can move us to repent. Furthermore, the depths of merciful and sacrificial love that God showed to all of humanity through Jesus Christ can also move us to the kind of contrition that flows from gratitude and love: the Incarnational Exemplarist, Sacrificial, Legal, and Classical theories of the Atonement that we surveyed demonstrate this clearly enough.

Kenoticism, however, strikes at the very roots of our stubborn attempts at self-justification. All too often we try to excuse our sins; we claim that our sins only harm the guilty, those who "deserve" their ill-treatment anyway. But if the Son of God has fully identified with the human condition, then he can closely empathise and sympathise with the afflictions of all people, even those guilty of harming others, and therefore his close compassion extends even to their plight. To unnecessarily harm anyone is to grieve the compassionate Heart of the Son of God himself.[784]

---

[783] In the Catholic tradition, "contrition" is said to be "imperfect" when it proceeds merely from a fear of the consequences of our sins (such as divine punishment or public shame) or from disgust with ourselves at our misdeeds; but contrition becomes "perfect" when it flows from love for God, that is, from sorrow at having betrayed the love of our Creator, wounding the Sacred Heart of His Son, our Redeemer, and blocking the work of the Holy Spirit in our own lives, and in the lives of others.

[784] Acts of "necessary harm" to the morally guilty would include the quarantine of criminals for the protection of society, and the killing in self-defence of relentless and violent aggressors. No doubt these tragedies grieve the compassionate Heart of the Son of God too, but not on account of any sin committed by those using the minimum force necessary to protect the relatively innocent from serious harm.

Whenever we set ourselves up as the ultimate judges over others, and seek to give them their full and "just desserts" according to our own lights, then we assume for ourselves a role which only God is capable of fulfilling: "'Vengeance is mine, I will repay,' says the Lord" (Rom 12:19). Paradoxically, in taking strict vengeance ourselves on those we see as guilty of causing harm, even if they *are* guilty, we crucify the innocent Son of God as well. His compassionate Heart is bonded even to the fate of the guilty; even to the last moment of their lives, from the depths of his Heart he longs to bring them to repentance, and to new life in the Holy Spirit. Thus, Rowan Williams once wrote of the Christian invitation "to recognize one's victim as one's hope."[785] True contrition and conversion are to be found only "as we return to our victims seeking reconciliation," even in circumstances where we must continue to believe in the rightness of our cause. The point is that even a just cause — even the manifest, objective guilt of our enemies — does not confer on us the right to victimise them, or to take "revenge" (that is, beyond the requirements of maintaining basic social order through a just and fair legal system). Williams therefore writes of seeing the face of Christ crucified even in the suicide of a terrorist. Christ's compassion extends even that deep and that far, even to the alienated condition of the terrorists, and even to their sufferings when they are tortured or victimised. In short, Christ's compassion is without any boundaries.

Kenoticism alone makes sense of this claim. For Kenoticism tells us that the divine Son once shared the lot of the crucified, the guilty and the alienated, and this experience, ever present in his unfading "memory" (that is, in his divine store of experience) remains the touchstone of his closest compassion for all human beings. It follows that whatever we have done to his brothers and sisters — even the very least of them, and even the guiltiest of them — we have done also to

---

[785] Rowan Williams, *Resurrection* (London: Darton, Longman and Todd, 1982), p. 67.

him (Mt 25:40: "Truly I say to you, as you did it to one of the least of these my brethren, you did it to me."). When we finally begin to appreciate that we crucify afresh the compassionate Heart of the Son of God by our sins (Acts 9:5; Heb 6:6), then, perhaps, our hearts might be moved to repent under the shadow of the Cross of the One who loved us.

In conclusion, we may say with some confidence that although Kenoticism does not bring us to a new or unique formulation of the doctrine of the Atonement, it does add several vital dimensions to the mystery of Christ's saving work which no mere Two-Nature model of the Incarnation can supply. For the Two-Nature model will always cushion the effects of the Cross. It will tell us that God in Christ "suffered impassibly," or suffered only from an omniscient perspective on events. If so, then we lose all the added benefits of the Kenotic view. First (section a, above), we lose God's close empathetic and sympathetic understanding of our worst sufferings, and therefore, in the midst of those sufferings, we lose his close, sympathetic companionship, and our indestructible identity in union with our crucified Lord; in short, we lose much that can help us overcome our fear of affliction, a fear that often cripples our discipleship. Second (section b), we lose the assurance that God's loving omnipotence on our behalf is supremely activated and expressed through his kenotic service and suffering for us, from the cradle to the Cross; in other words, we lose much that helps us overcome our suspicion and dread of Divine Omnipotence. Third (section c), we lose an aspect of the gospel of forgiveness, for only if God has shared as closely as possible in the effects of all our sins can he forgive us on behalf of any victims of our sins who cannot yet, or will never forgive us; thus, we lose an aspect of the pardon that sets us free. Finally (section d), we lose the idea that God the Son bears the sins of the world on his Heart, i.e., that he closely empathises and sympathises with the lost and the broken because he once shared their lot, especially on the Cross. In other words, we lose much that can move us to authentic penitence for our sins — sins which deeply affect others (even those guilty of committing grievous wrongs themselves), and therefore deeply affect the Heart of the Incarnate Lord as well, whose compassionate love embraces the good and the bad alike.

In all these ways, Kenoticism focuses our attention on the crucifixion of Jesus. The fact that God Incarnate literally tasted death for us in that event makes it his distinctive and decisive act in human history for our salvation. Acceptance of a kenotic model of the Incarnation, therefore, keeps the doctrine of Redemption centered on the Cross, where Christian devotion has always looked for saving grace.

Postscript: On Catholicism, Kenoticism and the Penal Substitution Theory

No doubt many Catholic readers of this book will be surprised that I have offered a defence of the Legal Theory as one of the vital dimensions of the mystery of Redemption. Ever since the era of Scholasticism in the Middle Ages, the Church in communion with Rome has tended to interpret Christ's saving work primarily in terms of the Sacrificial-Satisfaction theories of Anselm and Aquinas. Indeed, contemporary Catholics often see their view of redemption as in stark contrast to ideas of substitutionary atonement originating (allegedly) from the Protestant Reformation.

In this chapter I have already provided some grounds for believing that this latter claim is not true: the notion of substitutionary atonement has its seeds both in Scripture and (arguably, as a secondary theme) in the writings of the ancient Fathers. Moreover, as we have already seen, there are aspects of the Catholic liturgical and devotional tradition which at least fit best with, if not necessitate, a substitutionary interpretation (e.g., the Easter *Exultet*, which locates the Cross as the place where our moral debt to God is paid, or *the Stations of the Cross*, which also state that it is on the Cross that Christ redeemed the world). In so far as Sacrificial-Satisfaction theories of Atonement do not really show us, in a coherent way, how the Cross was truly the decisive act by which

The Incarnation

Jesus Christ accomplished our redemption, it is implicit, if only by default, that these Catholic liturgical and devotional traditions must refer to a substitutionary aspect of redemption instead: such is the intuitive grasp of the mysteries of the faith by the People of God in prayer and worship! Nor does the devotional and liturgical evidence end there. For example, one finds the theme of substitutionary atonement explicit in the Liturgy of the Hours, Morning Prayer Week III, for Wednesday, in the psalm-prayer for the third psalm:

> Lord Jesus, you have revealed your justice to all nations. We stood condemned and you came to be judged in our place. Send your saving power on us and when you come in glory bring your mercy to those for whom you were condemned.

In the Church's tradition of hymnody as well, there are occasional references to penal substitution, especially in the song for Good Friday often attributed to St. Bernard of Clairvaux, "O Sacred Head Sore Wounded":

> What thou, my Lord, hast suffered,
>   Was all for sinners' gain:
> Mine, mine, was the transgression,
>   But thine the deadly pain.
> Lo! here I fall, my Saviour:
>   'T is I deserve thy place;
> Look on me with thy favor,
>   Vouchsafe to me thy grace.[786]

In the writings of the saints we also find occasional references to substitutionary atonement. To some extent, this arose from the fact that the writings of Aquinas on Christ's saving work were

---

[786] Most scholars now believe this hymn was actually the work of Paul Gerhardt (1607-1676).

sometimes interpreted as including the notion.[787] Thus, as we have seen, a faithful Thomist like the Ven. Fulton Sheen believed that the "satisfaction" for sin that Jesus accomplished for us in his life and death included a penal substitutionary element. Saint Alphonsus Liguori (1696- 1787), who probably wrote more about this dimension of the mystery of Redemption than any other saint or Doctor of the Church, held much the same belief as Sheen. In his "Reflections and Affections on the Passion of Jesus Christ," for example, St. Alphonsus wrote:

> The Son of God, the Lord of the universe, seeing that man was condemned to eternal death in punishment of his sins, chose to take upon himself human flesh, and thus to pay by his death the penalty due to man. ... "But how is this?" continues St. Augustine. How is it possible, O Saviour of the world, that Thy love has arrived at such a height that when I had committed the crime, Thou shouldst have to pay the penalty? "Whither has Thy love reached? I have sinned; Thou art punished."[788]

> Our loving Redeemer, having come into the world for no other end but that of saving sinners, and beholding the sentence of

---

[787] This is a disputed point among Aquinas scholars even today. For example Gerald O'Collins in *Christology: a Biblical, Historical, and Systematic Study of Jesus* (Oxford: Oxford University Press, 1995), p. 207, claimed that Aquinas was the forerunner of the "monstrous" view of redemption of "a penal substitute propitiating the divine anger." At the opposite extreme, Rik Van Nieuwenhove in his essay "'Bearing the Marks of Christ's Passion': Aquinas' Soteriology," p. 290-291, claims that by "satisfaction" Aquinas did not have in mind any kind of juridical transaction at all; rather, the idea largely can be reduced to its medicinal, and subjectively transformative effects on the souls of the faithful. By their incorporation into Christ, his saving death attains satisfactory value for them, which means it turns the human will back toward the will of God. In this book, I have followed the *via media* position of John Saward, who does not see any element of true penal substitution in the soteriology of Aquinas, but also does not interpret "satisfaction" in Aquinas merely in personalist categories — at least not as the notion of "satisfaction" appears in the *Summa Theologiae*.

[788] Saint Alphonsus De Liguori, *The Passion and Death of Jesus Christ* (Brooklyn: Redemptorist Fathers, 1927), p. 25.

condemnation already recorded against us for our sins, what was it that he did? He, by his own death paid the penalty that was due to ourselves; and with his own blood cancelling the sentence of condemnation, in order that divine justice might no more seek from us the satisfaction due, he nailed it to the same cross whereon he died (Col 2:14).[789]

In his "Considerations on the Passion of Jesus Christ," St. Alphonsus wrote:

> In order that he might satisfy the divine justice for us, and at the same time inflame us with his holy love, [Christ] was willing to endure this burden of all our sins; that, dying upon a cross, he might obtain for us the grace of the life of the blessed. …

> Of this there were two express figures in the Old Testament; the first was the annual ceremony of the scape-goat, which the high-priest represented as bearing all the sins of the people, and therefore all, loading it with curses, drove it into the desert to be the object of the wrath of God. This goat was a figure of the Redeemer, who was willing to load himself with all the curses deserved by us for our sins; being made a curse for us, in order that he might obtain for us the divine blessing. Therefore the apostle wrote in another place, *He made him to be sin for us, who knew not sin, that we might be made the justice of God in Him.* …

> And Jesus accepted such a death. He died to pay the price for our sins; and therefore, as a sinner, he desired … in his Passion to be nailed upon the Cross to atone for our guilty wanderings: to atone for our avarice, by being stripped of his garments; for our pride, by the insults he endured; for our desires of power, by submitting himself to the executioner; for our evil thoughts, by his crown of thorns; for our intemperance, by the gall he tasted; and by the pangs of his body, for our sensual delights.

---

[789] Ibid., p. 130.

Therefore, we ought continually with tears of tenderness, to thank the Eternal Father for having given his innocent Son to death, to deliver us from eternal death. ...[790]

[T]hough he had not contracted the pollution of sin, nevertheless, he took upon himself the miseries contracted by human nature, as the punishment of sin; and he offered himself to the Eternal Father, to satisfy the divine justice for all the sins of men by his sufferings; he was offered because he himself willed it; and the Eternal Father, as Isaiah writes, *laid upon Him the iniquity of us all.* ...

We must understand that Jesus had taken upon himself all the sins of the world, although he was himself the most holy of all men, and even sanctity itself; since he had taken upon himself to satisfy for all our sins, he seemed the greatest of all sinners; and having thus made himself guilty for all, he offered himself to pay the price for all. Because we had deserved to be abandoned forever in hell to eternal despair, therefore he chose to be given up to death deprived of every relief, that thus he might deliver us from eternal death.[791]

Man sins, and the Son of God makes satisfaction for him. O Jesus! I have sinned, and hast Thou made satisfaction for me? Yes, I have deserved hell, and Thou, in order to deliver me from eternal death, hast been pleased to be condemned to death upon the cross! In a word, in order to pardon me Thou wouldst not pardon Thyself ....[792]

Most importantly, the *Catechism of the Catholic Church* in entry 443 combines the themes of satisfaction and substitution when it states about the Cross of Christ:

---

[790] Ibid., p. 230 and 232.
[791] Ibid., p.243 and 292.
[792] Saint Alphonsus De Liguori, *The Way of Salvation and Perfection* (Aeterna Press, Eugene Grimm, trans., 2016 edition), Part I, Meditation XCV, p. 97.

By His obedience unto Death, Jesus accomplished the substitution of the suffering servant who makes an offering for sin when 'He bore the sin of many, and who shall make many to be counted righteous, for He shall bear their iniquities.' Jesus atoned for our faults, and made satisfaction for our sins to the Father.

If this (all too brief) survey of the Catholic tradition regarding penal substitution is accurate, then it would be fair to say that Catholic theologians are not being disloyal to the voice of the Holy Spirit, speaking through Sacred Tradition, if they include a penal substitutionary aspect in their overall understanding of Christ's redeeming work. While very much a "minority report," it can still be offered as a legitimate part of an authentically Catholic perspective on this great mystery.

In fact, well before the Protestant Reformers began to emphasize the Legal Theory, Cardinal Nicholas of Cusa already understood this as a legitimate aspect of the doctrine of the Atonement. He preached:

> In its intensity of pain [His death] enfolded within itself the penalty of death of all those who were to be freed [from eternal death]. Thus, each individual who was rightly supposed to suffer death because of his transgression of, or disobedience to, the Law makes satisfaction in and through the death of Christ, even if [that individual] ought to have suffered the penalty of torment in Hell. Therefore, the intensity of the sorrow of Christ (who bore our sorrows and who took upon Himself the sentence of condemnation and who fastened the handwriting to the Cross, where He made satisfaction) was so great that no one could have suffered it except Him in whom there was most perfect love – which love was able to be present only in the Son of God. Hence, whatever punishment is either

written about or thought of is less than that satisfaction-making punishment that Christ suffered.[793]

Several contemporary Catholic theologians have continued this tradition. Hans Urs von Balthasar, for example, in his classic work *Mysterium Paschale* (1970), saw penal substitution as one aspect (albeit an elusive one to define) of the great story or "theo-drama" of our salvation:

> Since the sin of the world is 'laid' upon him, Jesus no longer distinguishes himself and his fate from those of sinners ... and thus in that way he experiences the anxiety and horror which by rights they should have known themselves. The possibility of such a real assumption of the sinful being of all sinners may be rendered intelligible ....[794]

> Christ must be God if he is so to place himself at the disposal of the event of love which flows from the Father and would reconcile the world with itself that in him the entire darkness of all that is counter to God can be judged and overcome ....[795]

> All of that presupposes for [St.] Paul the judgment of the Cross wherein God, as the man Christ, takes upon himself the totality of 'Adam's' guilt (Rom 5:15-21) in order that, as the 'bodily' incorporation of sin and enmity (II Cor 5:21; Eph 2:14), he might be 'handed over' (Rom 4:25) to be 'condemned through God' (Rom 8:3), and as the life of God, which died in God-forsakenness and was buried, to be divinely 'raised for our justification' (Rom 4:25). That is not myth, but the central

---

[793] From Nicholas of Cusa, Sermon 276 (Lent, 1457), which is discussed in-depth in Walter Andreas Euler, "Does Nicholas of Cusanus Have a Theology of the Cross?" in *Journal of Religion*, 2000, vol. 80, issue 3, p. 416-417, accessed online at http://www.academicroom.com /article/does-nicholas-cusanus -have-theology- cross . The full quote itself can be accessed online at jasper-hopkins.info/SermonsCCLXXVI-CCXCIII.pdf.
[794] Von Balthasar, *Mysterium Paschale,* p. 104-105.
[795] Ibid., p. 112.

biblical message and, where Christ's Cross is concerned, it must not be rendered innocuous as though the Crucified, in undisturbed union with God, had prayed the Psalms and died in the peace of God.[796]

The theme of penal substitution is also prominent — and more intelligible, perhaps — in the writings of Cardinal Walter Kasper. In his book *Mercy* (2013), Kasper expresses this as the very heart and center of Christ's saving work:

> God cannot simply ignore evil in history and treat it as something inconsequential and meaningless. That would be cheap grace and not authentic mercy, which takes human beings and their actions seriously. In his mercy God also wants to serve justice. Therefore, Jesus — taking our place [*stellvertretend*] — willingly takes the sins of all upon himself; yes, he even becomes sin (2 Cor 5:21) ….

> With the idea of substitutionary atonement, it is not — as a prevalent misunderstanding suggests — a matter of a vengeful God needing a victim so his wrath can be assuaged. On the contrary, by willing the death of his son on account of his mercy, God takes back his wrath and provides space for his mercy and thereby also for life. By taking our place in and through his son, he takes the life-destroying effects of sin upon himself in order to bestow upon us life anew. "So if anyone is in Christ, there is a new creation; everything old has passed away; see, everything has become new!" (2 Cor 5:17). It is not we who can reconcile God with us. He is the one who has reconciled himself with us (2 Cor 5:18).[797]

> He who was innocent has voluntarily discharged the requirement of justice in our place and for our benefit (Rom 8:3; Gal 3:13) …. According to human logic, [divine]

---

[796] Ibid., p. 122.
[797] Kasper, *Mercy*, p. 75

righteousness would have meant a death sentence for us as sinners. But now righteousness means acquittal for the sake of life. The law's demand is not thereby rescinded; rather, Jesus Christ has discharged the requirement of justice for us and in our place.[798]

One more contemporary example will suffice. In his book *The Gaze of Mercy* (2015), Fr. Raniero Cantalamessa, OFM Cap, for over three decades the preacher to the papal household in Rome, plumbed the depths of Christ's assumption of human guilt on the Cross:

> To say that Jesus took upon himself the penalty of sin does not mean that he took only the *punishment* on himself but that he also took upon himself something much worse, the *blame* for that very sin. He took sin on himself without having committed it …. We can understand, then, what depths are concealed behind the fact that Jesus was considered "answerable" to his Father for every sin in the world. Jesus experienced, to the highest degree, the most crushing, ingrained, and universal cause of suffering, the "sense of guilt." Even that, however, is now redeemed at its root.[799]

> In forgiving sinners, God is not renouncing justice, but vengeance, a desire for the death of the sinner. Instead, he takes upon himself the punishment due to sin. This is the mystery that was announced in the Old Testament and fulfilled historically in the expiatory death of Jesus.[800]

Sadly, the "legal" or "penal" dimension of Christ's saving work all too often has been caricatured by Catholic theologians. For

---

[798] Ibid., p. 78.
[799] Raniero Cantalamessa, OFM Cap., *The Gaze of Mercy* (Frederick, MD: The Word Among Us Press, 2015) p. 98-99.
[800] Ibid., p. 178.

example, in his book *Jesus our Redeemer* (2007), Gerald O'Collins, SJ, summarized his objections to the theory in these words:

> Some … interpret the biblical data to mean that Jesus as a substitute was personally burdened with the sins of humanity, judged, condemned, and deservedly punished in our place; through his death he thus satisfied the divine justice and propitiated an angry God. This theology of penal substitution directly attributes Christ's passion and death to God's 'vindictiveness' rather than to human violence and cruelty. … [W]hile sometimes speaking of the divine anger (e.g. Rom 1:18; 2:5, 8; 12:19; 13: 4-5), the NT never associates that anger with Christ's suffering and death. …
>
> Instead of needing to appease an angry deity who was 'out for blood,' Christ was sent by divine love (e.g. Rom 8:3, 32) to reconcile us with God and with one another.[801]

There are so many elements of caricature packed into a short space here that it is hard to untangle them all at once! Suffice it to say: (1) It is misleading to sum up the Penal Substitution Theory as Jesus "propitiating an angry God," since Jesus himself *is* God the Son Incarnate. He made a propitiatory offering of *himself* to clear our debt to *his own* Divine Justice, a divine attribute he shares with the Father and the Holy Spirit. (2) It is false to imply that our only choice lies between the notion that "an angry God who was out for blood" needed to be appeased, or on the other hand that Christ was sent to save us "by divine love." The whole point of the Legal Theory is that as an act of merciful love for us, the divine Son Incarnate, Jesus Christ, bore the just penalty for our sins in our place on the Cross; *this was an expression of perfect Divine Justice and perfect Divine Love at the same time*; (3) while it is true that the New Testament never explicitly connects Christ's passion and death with the propitiation of God's anger or wrath, we need to remember that the biblical words "anger" and "wrath" are

---

[801] O'Collins, *Jesus our Redeemer*, p. 177-178

metaphors for Divine Justice. As we have seen earlier in this chapter, the Bible does indeed connect divine retributive justice with the Cross both implicitly and explicitly, for example, in the Garden of Gethsemane when Christ asks that the "cup" be taken away from him; in Galatians 3:13-14, which speaks of Christ becoming a "curse" for us on the tree of the Cross; and also in Isaiah 53, which speaks of the Suffering Servant of the Lord as "bearing our sins" and being "chastised" for us, and proclaims that "the Lord has laid on him the iniquity of us all." Finally, (4) The Legal Theory certainly does not "attribute Christ's passion and death to God's 'vindictiveness' rather than to human violence and cruelty." As we previously discussed, God the Father did not kill his Son; he merely *permitted* his Son to die at the hands of sinful men, and brought the most wonderful good out of this permitted evil. Moreover, no defender of penal substitution speaks of divine "vindictiveness;" this pejorative term implies a desire for retributive justice *instead of, or apart from mercy and love* — a separation which is never true of God's nature or his acts.[802]

Even granted all this, most Catholic theologians today still would object to the Legal Theory of the Atonement on the grounds that it is just not needed: a Sacrificial-Satisfaction theory, such as the one passed down in the Catholic tradition from Aquinas, (allegedly) shows us how God can make atonement for our sins, and unite his justice and mercy in the work of our salvation, *without*

---

[802] O'Collins mentions several times in his discussion of the New Testament story of salvation "the representative death of the Messiah who atoned for human sin" (p. 106; see p. 102-106). But he can give no clear account of what this kind of language means, and in the end he appears to say that it refers not to the crucifixion itself, but to Christ's heavenly pleading for us on the basis of his death, in which Christ "freely represents human beings to God and before God, and on their side they agree to his redemptive representation" (I Jn 2:1) — leaving the actual efficacy of his death itself unexplained. In other words, he never answers the question: what is it about Christ's death that clears our moral debt — our objective guilt — for sin, and makes it a sound basis for such intercessory prayer before the throne of God?

involving the controversial notion of penal substitution. Typically, Catholic theologians will say something like this:

> While Protestants see Christ as suffering God's wrath so we don't have to, Catholics should see Christ as making to the Father a pleasing offering into which we ourselves can be incorporated through the sacraments and, with the help of God's grace, by uniting our will to that of Christ. Our Lord's perfect obedience, and his placing of God's Law of perfect love above all earthly things was a pleasing offering to God that made atonement for our sins. In other words, the divine Son made amends to the Father and restored justice by offering to God something more pleasing than our sins were displeasing: a whole human life, from cradle to grave, of faithful obedience and perfect love, even in the face of suffering and death.[803]

---

[803] A good example from recent Catholic Christology would be Roch Kereszty's "simple re-working" of St. Anselm's Satisfaction Theory. Kereszty writes:

> Sin is in fact an offence against God himself ... in some real sense of infinite gravity. If, consequently, God decides to treat sinful humankind as adults so that sinners must face the consequences of their actions and obtain forgiveness by making up for their "infinite offence," they cannot do this on their own. Only if God becomes a human being, if God takes upon himself the death of the sinner and turns the process of estrangement ending in death into the human expression of infinite divine love, only then can sinners "make satisfaction" for their sins, because only then can they unite themselves through faith with the life and death of the incarnate Son of God. To put it briefly, if God had not satisfied as a human being for the sins of humankind, human kind could not make its own this satisfaction. ...
>
> If our sins offended God in his fatherly love by refusing the grace of being a child of God, then it appears very appropriate that the only Son of God should become incarnate and as a human being offer to God that unique filial love which God the Holy Father deserves; only then can we, through faith, unite ourselves to the only Son and offer "through him, with him, and in him" the love and honor that the father deserves to receive from us. (*Jesus Christ: Fundamentals of Christology*, p. 341-342, cf. p. 413-415)

I want to suggest, however, that the Sacrificial-Satisfaction Theory of the Atonement just cannot "work" for Catholic theology in the way that this view implies.

First of all, the Satisfaction Theory, all by itself, cannot establish that Jesus in any sense accomplished an act of saving "substitution" on our behalf, which the Catholic *Catechism* tells us is part of the mystery of our redemption. Satisfaction theories claim that Jesus shares the human experience of suffering and death, which is the inevitable and natural consequence of original and actual sin upon human life (and in that sense, he shares in our "punishment" for sin) — but *sharing in an experience of something with others, even in order to accomplish something on their behalf,* is certainly not the same thing as *substituting oneself for others*: substitution means suffering something for others in their place, so that they don't have to suffer it themselves. In what sense was Jesus acting as our saving "substitute" if not by bearing in our place the punishment for sin that we deserve?[804]

One might argue that Jesus bore the depths of human affliction for us without benefit of the companionship of a divine person incarnate. He "trod the winepress alone" (Is 63:3), so to speak, so that we do not have to do so ourselves — as we briefly discussed in Part Two, Chapter One of this book. But if that is all that saving "substitution" means, then we are left with the same unanswered question that we discussed earlier in this chapter about the moral intelligibility of a God who, in seeking to save us, does not also seek to meet the demands of his holiness and retributive justice in the face of the moral debt of human sin. I have made the case at

---

[804] In *The Light of Christ* (Washington, DC: Catholic University of America Press, 2017), Thomas Joseph White, OP, tries to sidestep the Legal Theory by claiming that "Jesus' substitutionary atonement for our sins is above all something positive, not something negative. He substitutes his love, his justice, and obedience where the human race has lacked love, justice, and obedience" (p.170). But to "substitute" presumably means to do something for another in their place, so that they do not have to do it themselves. It does not just mean to do something for the benefit of another that they cannot yet do themselves.

length that this move leaves an important aspect of God's redeeming work unfulfilled, as that work is portrayed in Scripture and, arguably, in the ancient Tradition of the Fathers.

Second, as we have already seen in our discussion of the theories of Aquinas and Swinburne, the Satisfaction Theory seems to make Christ's actual death on the Cross, in one major respect at least, not decisive for the forgiveness of sins and for our salvation. Here, again, is why: Their theory states that Jesus loved his Father and all of humanity with all of his Heart, perfectly fulfilling the law of love, and that he was even willing to be killed rather than compromise this love in any way. The Father was well pleased with this whole-life offering of his divine Son in human flesh. It thereby merited the removal of our moral debt to God for our sins, applying fully to those who are incorporated into Christ's life by faith, repentance, and the sacraments. No doubt all of this has elements of truth in it as far as it goes. But why, then, would Christ's actual death on the Cross be necessary? Given that he was the divine Son Incarnate, and that all his human acts are "theandric" and therefore of infinite value, Christ's mere willingness to die, if it came to that, would have been enough to make his self-offering of love complete. Some of the saints have held that even the shedding of one drop of Christ's Blood would have been enough all by itself to save the world. This is the Satisfaction Theory of Aquinas and Swinburne taken to its logical conclusion.[805] But if that is so, then surely Christ saved the world in the Garden of Gethsemane when he surrendered himself in love to the Father and sweat drops of blood! How, then, could the teaching of the 16th century Council of Trent of be true that it was "by His most holy Passion *on the wood of the Cross*" that Christ "merited justification for us" and "made satisfaction for us unto God the Father"?[806] And how could the teachings of Pope St. John

---

[805] For example, St. Thomas Aquinas writes in ST III. 46. 5. 3: "The very least one of Christ's sufferings was sufficient of itself to redeem the human race from all sins."

[806] Council of Trent, session VI, chapter seven.

Paul II be true that Jesus offered a just "compensation" for our sins *on the Cross*?[807] Jesus said to the disciples on the road to Emmaus: "Was it not necessary that the Messiah should suffer these things and enter into his glory?" (Lk 24:26) For some reason, he could only say of his saving work "It is finished" at the moment of his death, and not before (see Jn 19:30).[808]

Typically, Catholic theologians will respond to all this that even though our Lord's crucifixion may not have been strictly necessary to save us, to pay our debt to his justice, still, it showed the magnitude of God's love for us in that he was willing to undergo such a death and make such a sacrifice. But again (as we discussed earlier in this chapter), authentic "love" can only be fully expressed in action for the benefit of another. *If Christ's crucifixion was not really needed in order to save us from objective guilt, that is, to make the atoning sacrifice for our sins and to obtain the forgiveness of our sins, then how would it express the magnitude of his "love" for us?* **No doubt it establishes and expresses his deepest solidarity with the afflictions of humanity — which is certainly a great act of love for us — but not in a way that directly and objectively redeems us from our sins: and *it is the Cross as the locus of redemption from sin (as we have seen) that is the clear witness of both Scripture and Catholic Tradition.***

In short, I would argue that what made the Son's offering of himself on the Cross pleasing to the Father was that by dying on the Cross, he thereby carried to completion the loving plan of the Blessed Trinity of bearing in our place the penalty we deserve for our sins — a sacrifice really necessary to win our pardon. It was a

---

[807] Pope John Paul II encyclical letter *Dives in Misericordia* (Rich in Mercy, 1980), no. 7.

[808] The same word, "finished" (Greek: *tetelestai*) was commonly used in the Greco-Roman world to write on a bill that had been paid. Thus, the word could mean "finished" in the sense of "over and done with: the amount owing has been paid off." On this see Wright, *How God Became King*, p. 8.

plan that the Son willingly accepted when he was sent into the world in the first place (see Mk 10:45; Jn 3:16).

The Sacrificial-Satisfaction Theory, it would seem, just does not work in the way that Catholics have often claimed, and much that it seeks to express can be found in a different way: in a combination of the Penal Substitution and the Merit theories of Christ's saving work.

Suppose that human "sin" against God differs radically from the moral debts we accrue from the wrongs we do to one another. The main difference would be that our sins cannot be fully "atoned for" in the very "human" way that Aquinas and Swinburne describe. In other words, suppose we cannot make sufficient "satisfaction" for sin, not even with the help of Christ, since there is nothing that we could weigh in the balance in our favor against the betrayal of the infinite love of our Total Benefactor that all our sins imply. In short, suppose it just is the case that temporal punishment is due for venial sin, and both temporal and eternal punishment for mortal sin, and no amount of repentance, on its own (that is, no amount of contrition, apology, works of reparation and penance, not even devoutly offering up Christ's perfect life and death at the Eucharist), could completely cancel that debt. After all, even our works of atonement and our sacramental worship are almost always tainted by half-hearted repentance and weak faith (Rom 7:14-25; I Jn 1:8-9). And even when they are not, the full demands of justice, the "penal debt" that we owe, remains to be paid.[809]

What we know from Scripture and Tradition is that "the wages of sin is death" (Rom 6:23), both as an inevitable consequence and as a just punishment. Thus, to betray God's infinite love (as every mortal sin does) on the scales of his justice surely deserves a relatively infinite penalty: the penalty of bodily suffering and death (the temporal punishment due for all sin) and everlasting spiritual

---

[809] See our discussion of the reflections of Steven L. Porter on the Legal Theory of the Atonement earlier in this chapter.

death (the eternal punishment due for mortal sin) — that is, complete alienation from God. And by God's just ordinances from the beginning, these are also the inevitable effects (the "natural consequences," so to speak) of unrepented mortal sin on human life: the loss of the life-giving Holy Spirit, resulting in the decay and ultimate loss of both physical and spiritual life — in other words, the state of "death" from sin that St. Paul describes in his letters (e.g. Rom 5:12-21). But Jesus Christ substitutes himself for us on the Cross by experiencing there in his body and soul — and thereby paying for us — the equivalent (by close analogy) of that temporal and eternal penalty, so that those who are in faithful and loving union with him do not have to pay that penalty themselves: "There is therefore now no condemnation for those who are in Christ Jesus" (Rom 8:1; cf. Gal 5:6). Our Savior's act of loving "penal substitution" takes care of our moral debt to God. When we are united to him by repentance and faith, informed by love (and *to the degree* that we are thus united with him), it clears our account and wins our pardon.[810]

Nevertheless, a cancelling of debts and a full pardon for the past, on its own, still does not obtain for us all the graces that we need

---

[810] See note 783, above. Catholics would say: to the degree that we are united with Jesus by repentance and faith informed by love, to just that degree his substitutionary penalty can apply to us. If our repentance is still imperfect, then his sin-bearing sin-offering covers the eternal punishment for our sins, but not yet all the temporal punishment that remains due. In this way, the offering of grace-assisted "satisfaction" to God in the form of Swinburne's works of "atonement" is still an aid to our salvation, because, as we explored earlier in this chapter, deep and authentic repentance for sin always seeks to express and complete itself in true contrition and apology (or confession), and works of reparation and penance. Without doing so — or at least, without the desire to do so, though our opportunities to carry out that desire may be obstructed by circumstances beyond our control — our repentance is not complete, and therefore we cannot fully partake of the benefits of the saving death of Jesus Christ. We can neither be fully pardoned on the basis of the penalty he paid to Divine Justice on the Cross for us, nor can our hearts be fully open to the renewal of the life of the Holy Spirit that Jesus Christ merited for us, and that he longs fully to bestow upon us as the expression of his forgiveness.

to be fully sanctified and prepared for everlasting life. In other words, what adequately deals with the *past* (on the scales of justice) does not necessarily take care of all the needs of the *present* and the *future*.

Here is where elements of the Merit Theory of Christ's saving work address our need. *Jesus not only died for us: he also lived for us. From cradle to grave, he offered his whole life as one continuous act of love for his heavenly Father, and for us.* Since this was an offering of a divine person in human flesh, it was a "theandric" self-sacrifice well-pleasing to the Father, and its meritorious value before the scales of Divine Justice was therefore infinite and super-abundant *for its purpose* (which was not to compensate Divine Justice for our sins, but to merit for us sanctifying grace). As a result, when we are spiritually united with him through authentic repentance and faith, informed by love (and to the *degree* that we are thus united to him), we can receive the renewal in our hearts of the life of the Holy Spirit, and all the graces we need for the sanctification of our whole life-journey, in preparation for eternal life.[811] Indeed, by His whole-life offering, Christ has merited all the graces needed for the sanctification of the entire world and the coming of the new heavens and the new earth portrayed in the Book of Revelation (chapter 21), the Kingdom of God that abides forever.

In short, Jesus made up for our misspent past when he bore the penalty that we deserve on the Cross. He also merited for us, by his whole life and death of loving obedience to the Father, all the sanctifying graces that can heal us and set us free from sin's power in our lives. That's not just some cold, impersonal, judicial transaction. It's a wonderful gift of his mercy that sets us free from both the guilt and power of sin!

---

[811] St. Irenaeus of Lyons summarized this aspect of the Atonement when he wrote: "The Son of God ... was incarnate and made man, and then summed up in himself the long line of the human race, procuring for us a comprehensive salvation, that we might recover in Christ Jesus what in Adam we had lost, namely, the state of being in the image and likeness of God." St. Irenaeus of Lyons, *Adversus Haereses*, 3.18.1, cited in O'Collins, *Jesus our Redeemer*, p. 85.

All we need to do to receive that gift is to open our hearts to Jesus Christ more and more by repentance and faith.[812]

An understanding of Christ's saving work such as this includes all that is true and helpful from the Sacrificial-Satisfaction Theory, without the added problem of making Christ's death on the Cross, in a major respect, superfluous to our redemption. Catholics could still say that in offering up the life and death of Jesus Christ to the Father at every Eucharist, we are pleading for the (penal) benefits of his Cross to be applied to our souls, and for all the sanctifying graces he merited by his life and death to be poured out upon us, and upon the whole world.[813] And Catholics would thereby embrace an understanding of the Cross that puts us one step closer to our Protestant Evangelical brothers and sisters in Christ, without sacrificing anything essential to the Catholic heritage. Indeed, from our insistence upon the role of the Merit and

---

[812] In *Divine Humanity*, David Brown expressed concern that the preaching of Christ's saving death as an act of penal substitution, while it clearly brings relief from guilt for some believers, might inadvertently be a stumbling block to others, especially those who suffer from false guilt, those "traumatized by an exaggerated sense of guilt and for whom the only release seems to be escape from the Church rather than a deeper entering into its life" (p. 149). He does not make clear, however, precisely how the message of Christ's substitutionary death exacerbates such a psychological condition. If one believes that Jesus Christ died to pay the penalty for all of one's sins, then that should bring with it a sense of being deeply loved by him in spite of one's sins, and release from the burden of every kind of guilt that weighs upon the heart, that is, relief both from actual guilt and from false guilt. Of course, it may not actually *heal* false guilt, which may return to trouble the heart – and for that the sufferer might need to have recourse to pastoral counselling, and in some cases to prayer for inner healing and the healing of memories.

[813] In fact, the 16th century ecumenical Council of Trent alluded to the penal substitution model with regard to the Eucharist when it spoke of the "propitiatory" nature of the Sacrifice of the Mass offered "for the sins, punishments, satisfactions, and other necessities of the faithful" (Council of Trent, Session 22, chapter 2). O'Collins laments: "By aligning 'satisfaction' with 'punishments,' and speaking of God being 'appeased,' the Council of Trent accepted penal elements …. Satisfaction was now officially depicted as involving punishment." See *Jesus our Redeemer*, p. 138-139.

Satisfaction theories, we would be calling them one step closer to us as well.

To recap: it is clear that the Legal or Penal Substitution Theory of the Atonement fits best with a kenotic understanding of the Incarnation. Much like the Incarnational Exemplarist Theory, the Legal Theory has clarity and power only if the divine Son of God truly identified with the human condition, bore our griefs and sorrows, and descended into the depths of our guilt and alienation from God due to sin. Our contention throughout this book has been that a kenotic theory of the Incarnation — and especially the Moderate Kenotic Model developed primarily in the Anglican tradition — can make that claim of divine identification with human suffering with greater clarity and coherence than any other incarnational theory.

The Exemplarist Theory of the Atonement tells us that in the midst of his identification with our plight, the divine Son Incarnate showed us the Way of faithful love, and revealed the depths of God's love for us as well, for he willed to show us that Way at terrible cost to himself. The Legal Theory of the Atonement tells us that by bearing in his Heart and in our place the ultimate penalty for human sin, he thereby cancelled our moral debt to Divine Justice, setting free all those who truly repent and believe. In short, *Kenoticism strengthens and illumines both of these Atonement theories that lie at the very heart of the gospel — in addition to the four dimensions that a kenotic perspective on the Incarnation adds to the Christian doctrine of Redemption.* And all that is "good news" indeed.

Chapter Three
Kenoticism and the Social Implications of the Gospel

The saving work of Jesus Christ cannot be reduced just to the redemption and sanctification of individual souls in preparation for the life to come. As we saw in the previous chapter, especially in our discussion of the writings of Anglican New Testament scholar Tom Wright, there are also vital *social* ramifications of the gospel which are not just "optional-extras."

According to Leonard Hodgson, "the Christian must learn that being saved, he is saved *to serve*."[814] Christ saves us not just by taking away the *objective guilt* of our sins on the Cross, and not only by beginning to overcome the *power* of sin in our lives, by the gift of the Holy Spirit that he pours into our hearts. All of this is of central importance, but it is not the fullness of the gospel. For the "good news" is also that we are called to a whole "new creation" in Christ: a transformative grace that overflows the lives of individuals, sanctifies the entire human community, and ultimately heals the whole created order (Rom 8:19-21). Hodgson emphasized this wider divine purpose in his book *The Doctrine of the Atonement* (1951):

> To be a full grown, adult Christian is to be one through whom the love and power of God are flowing out into the world around for the overcoming and casting out of all that is ugly and base and evil, for the discovery, encouragement, and building up of all that is true and good. But, as we have seen, men are not by nature fit for this work. Our cowardice, our selfishness, our lusts and our ambitions get in the way. We have to born again and become penitent and forgiven selves before we can give ourselves to our Lord for Him to use. ...
>
> We need to think of the church as the body through which our risen and ascended Lord is seeking to rescue His world from all the evil with which it is infected, the body in which artists

---

[814] Hodgson, *The Doctrine of the Atonement*, p. 94, italics mine.

may be cleansed and inspired for the service of beauty, scholars for the pursuit of truth, politicians and industrialists, merchants and labourers, doctors and lawyers and countless others for the better ordering of our common life. ...

Sinners converted, cleansed and forgiven are commissioned and empowered, through the arts and the sciences and in every department of life, to bring all the natural world into captivity to the obedience of Christ.[815]

To put it another way: *sin has a powerful social dimension*. All too often, human sins become enshrined in socio-economic systems that oppress and degrade human beings. Social injustice itself is a product of sin, and so its destruction must be an important aspect of the salvation brought to the world through Jesus Christ, and the Kingdom he came to establish "on earth as it is in heaven" (Mt 6:10). In short, if the gospel message is that Christ came to save humanity from the "guilt" and "power" of sin, then all that he has done, and will do in human history to break the rod of the oppressors and set captives free (Is 9:4), overcoming the power of sin in which human society is held in bondage, must be an integral part of that gospel.

Throughout much of the twentieth century, Anglican prophetic witness against social injustice was largely the work of outspoken bishops (for example, Gore, Temple, Bell, and Sheppard in England, and Desmond Tutu in South Africa), and the movements they spawned (such as the COPEC conference in 1924, or the Malvern conference of 1941). However, with the work of the Church of England's Board for Social Responsibility, and the publication of the notable *Faith in the City* report in the 1980s, Anglicans entered upon a new era.[816] The Anglican Communion in England, and elsewhere, was now more ready to use its official research and communication powers, and its moral leverage within the nations it serves, to stand as a body against what it perceives to be structural injustice. In some areas

---

[815] Ibid., p. 92, 95, and 118.
[816] The role of the Board for Social Responsibility was subsequently assumed by the Church of England's Mission and Public Affairs Division.

of the world, such as Uganda, this resulted in many Anglicans bravely resisting tyrannical forms of government, even at the cost of their lives.

Unfortunately, the theological roots of this prophetic social witness remain shallow. In an article in *The Church Observer* in 1985, Rev. Jeremy Sheehy complained about the "very, very thin" discussion of theological foundations in the famous *Faith in the City* report. The report pointed toward the gospel preached *by* Jesus, Sheehy noted, but not enough to the gospel *about* Jesus. The Incarnation, the Cross, and the Resurrection of Jesus, as well as the doctrine of the Holy Trinity, were almost completely neglected as foundations for Christian social teaching.[817] Surely, the social witness of the Church must be based on the *fullness* of the gospel and the Catholic faith, if it is to avoid secular ideological subversion from either the left or the right.[818]

Throughout the twentieth century, Anglo-Catholics in particular assumed that the doctrine of the Incarnation is an essential foundation for Christian social thought. They commonly claimed that Christian concern for social justice, and for the economic plight of the poor in particular, depends in some important respect upon an acceptance and understanding of the orthodox faith: that Jesus Christ is the divine Son of God, the second person of the Trinity, living a fully human life among us. Hence, Fr. Sheehy wrote: "Our belief that the physical and social and economic conditions in which people live are of religious value rests on our conviction that God himself has lived a human life and has himself become flesh."[819]

Was Sheehy, and the Anglo-Catholic movement in general, correct about this? **Are there social imperatives implied in the doctrine of the Incarnation, and if so, what are they? Moreover, which social**

---

[817] Jeremy Sheehy, "Looking for the Theology," in *The Church Observer*, autumn, 1986, p. 7-8. Sheehy's criticisms seem well founded; cf. *Faith in the City: The Report of the Archbishop of Canterbury's Commission on Urban Priority Areas* (London: Church House, 1985), p. 47-55.
[818] See E.R. Norman, *Christianity and the World Order* (Oxford: Oxford University Press, 1978), who argued that the educated leadership of the Church had adopted the Western bourgeois liberalism espoused by the secular intelligentsia.
[819] Sheehy, "Looking for the Theology," p. 9.

teachings actually depend upon the truth of the Incarnation, and in particular a kenotic understanding of the Incarnation? In short, what difference does Kenoticism make to the Social Gospel?

Several possible answers to these questions have been proposed in twentieth and twenty-first century Anglican discussion, and this was itself something of a microcosm of the debate going on in the wider Christian world in this era. We shall look at these answers in turn, beginning with the most radical viewpoint.

The Incarnation has Oppressive Social Implications

Anglican theologian Don Cupitt argued that the Incarnation is an example of "theological anthropomorphism." He warned that the idea that deity and humanity can be united in a single person suggests a possible connection between things human and divine which Jesus would have rejected.[820] Jesus emphasized a radical distinction between the human and divine in his parables, an overthrowing of established values which left people free to decide the authentic meaning of their own existence for themselves.[821] Thus, there is no absolute divine person or divine teaching in human history. God is utterly mysterious and transcendent. **Since Cupitt saw belief in the Incarnation as akin to an act of idolatry, it is not surprising that he abhorred its implications for the Social Gospel. Among contemporary Anglican theologians, he led the way in arguing that the Incarnation has significant connections with absolutist, intolerant, and persecuting elements in Christian tradition.**[822]

Cupitt presented a view of Western history in which the doctrine of the Incarnation plays a leading and sinister role. For example, he tells us that in the age of Constantine, Gentile Christians added the Nicene

---

[820] By way of contrast, see what I wrote in Part One, Chapter Four on Christ's implicit claims in the synoptic gospels to a divine identity.

[821] Don Cupitt, *The Debate About Christ*, p. 138, and "The Christ of Christendom," p. 138.

[822] Ibid: *The Debate About Christ*, p. 51, and "The Christ of Christendom," p. 141.

doctrine of the Incarnation to the primitive faith, and thereby sanctified a more or less permanent world-order through a more or less permanent institutional church.[823]

In other words, Christianity blessed the ancient status quo by fashioning Christ in the image of an exalted Roman Emperor (see, for example, the Byzantine *Pantocrator* icons); Jesus was held to be the universal God-man, the Celestial Emperor blessing the earthly Christian empire of Constantine. In Christ, universal manhood was said to be united with divinity; therefore, all humanity was blessed in Christ, including the prevailing social order.

At best, however, this is a collection of half-truths.

On the one hand, the Byzantine emperors sometimes justified their authority over both church and state by appealing to the fact that Christ himself was a single person, both divine and human. As Christ united these two natures in harmony in his indivisible person, it was argued, so the Christian Emperor alone can unite the divine Church and human civil order in true harmony under his indivisible authority. This was the social doctrine known as "caesaropapism."

On the other hand, in the age of Constantine the triumph of Christianity actually brought about a significant transformation of the old Greco-Roman social order. For example, the evils of slavery were mitigated: slave families were kept together, baptized and married in the Church, and sometimes even ransomed by the Church. In the era of the Fathers it was generally considered a good work before the Lord to free a slave.

Christians also elevated the social status of women in the Greco-Roman world. Timothy Keller sums up the evidence for us:

> It was extremely common in the Greco-Roman world to throw out new female infants to die from exposure, because of the low status of women in society. The church forbade its

---

[823] Ibid., *The Debate About Christ*, p. 7 and 69.

members to do so. Greco-Roman society saw no value in an unmarried woman, and therefore it was illegal for a widow to go more than two years without remarrying. But Christianity was the first religion to not force widows to marry. They were supported financially and honored within the community so that they were not under great pressure to remarry if they didn't want to. Pagan widows lost all control of their [first] husband's estate when they remarried, but the church allowed widows to maintain their husband's estate. Finally, Christians did not believe in cohabitation. If a Christian man wanted to live with a woman he had to marry her, and this gave women far greater security. Also, the pagan double standard of allowing married men to have extramarital sex and mistresses was forbidden. In all these ways Christian women enjoyed far greater security and equality than did women in the surrounding culture.[824]

Indeed, educated women played a key role in Christendom throughout late Antiquity and the early Middle Ages: for example, in Byzantium women served both as doctors and as lawyers. In the West, women in the new religious orders ran the schools that often educated the nobility and the future bishops of the Church.

Some of the most savage aspects of Greco-Roman culture were abolished in the era of Constantine: for example, Christians put an end to the practice of infanticide, and to bloody gladiatorial contests. The laboring classes found relief when Sunday became a day of rest from work for all, and church charities for the poor received imperial financial support. Saint Basil started what may have been the first public hospitals; later, Benedictine houses of prayer, study, and hospitality, both to travellers and to the poor, spread across the landscape. Bishop St. Ambrose of Milan forced the Christian Emperor Theodosius to do public penance for an act of mass murder — so even the Emperor was held to be accountable to the laws of God. In short, from the fourth through the ninth centuries, incarnational Christianity

---

[824] Timothy Keller, *The Reason for God* (New York: Penguin, 2009), p. 261.

did not simply baptise and bless the old pagan imperial culture; rather, it significantly reformed and transformed it.[825]

In any case, the burden of Cuptitt's argument is that "A high incarnational Christianity says the things feudalism wants to hear; that man was created for serfdom, and that there is an historical absolute to which he must wholly submit himself."[826] It is hard to see, however, why the doctrine of the Incarnation must be more "absolute" or oppressive than any other truth claim. Every assertion about God and his relationship to the world, insofar as it is held to be true, involves the claim that people should freely accept it precisely because it is true (e.g. the name "Islam" literally means "submit"). Nor is it obvious why the Incarnation necessarily implies that man was created for oppression, exploitation and "serfdom." Brian Hebblethwaite, for example, argued just the opposite. **The Incarnation shows us that God is not an indifferent cosmic monarch or heartless despot. Rather, Hebblethwaite claimed, the doctrine tells us that God has come among us *as* one of us, and for love of us made himself our servant as Jesus of Nazareth (Mk 10:45; Phil 2:7). Rulers and subjects alike are to be inspired by this as the pattern for loving service of others:**

> **[I]t is quite clear from the New Testament and from Christian piety down through the ages that what has given Christianity its characteristic moral and religious force is the conviction that its Lord has humbled himself and taken the form of a servant ... the Incarnation has been taken as the pattern of Christian ministry, as a matter of involvement and service in every area of human life.[827]**

---

[825] See Henry Chadwick, *The Early Christian Church* (Harmondsworth: Penguin, 1967), p. 60, 128, 167-168, and Morton Kelsey, *Healing and Christianity* (Minneapolis: Augsburg, 1995), p. 103-143.

[826] Don Cupitt, "The Finality of Christ," in *Theology*, December, 1975, p. 626.

[827] Hebblethwaite, *The Incarnation*, p. 30, and 43-44.

We shall return to this important point later in this chapter. Suffice it to say here that Cupitt's claims lack both historical balance and logical clarity.

In a somewhat similar way, American Episcopalian theologian Carter Heyward lamented the alleged patriarchal implications of traditional, incarnational Christianity. For example, in her essay "Can Anglicans be Feminist Liberation Theologians and Still be Anglican?" (1988) she felt able to answer this question in the affirmative, because once the obstacle of the Incarnation is extracted from the Christian faith, she claimed, the whole conceptual framework becomes more supportive of the cause of human liberation:

> From a feminist liberation perspective, we are able to understand our relationship to Jesus as that of participation: we are *with* Jesus; as such we are *in 'Christ': the active cooperation of the human with the divine.* The 'maleness of the historical Jesus' need not be a stumbling block for women, for we do not worship this man as God. We act *with* him. In Christ we stand with Jesus as we stand with one another; we love Jesus as we love one another. In this way Christians love and honour God, just as many, countless many who are not Christians, love and honour God. ...
>
> *We who are Christians are empowered by the memory and presence of Jesus.* The one whom we call 'Christ' mirrors our own vocation, to love our neighbors as ourselves and, in so doing, to offer to God the one spiritual sacrifice required of us — to take the risks involved in standing with humankind on behalf of a better world. We look to Jesus as a brother, an advocate, a friend, a liberator, because he stood *with* us on the earth. Only insofar as we take seriously the human brother can we discern, in what he did, the divine spirit moving with and in and through him. In looking to Jesus, we see that we are put on the spot to make decisions not unlike his, and to take the consequences. Jesus' story does not let Christians off the hook of our own moral responsibility; his story is ours not because

he lived and died in our stead, but rather because his story mirrors our own lives and pilgrimages.[828]

This is evidently another form of Non-Incarnational Christology, combined with an Exemplarist theory of Christ's saving work: Jesus is our companion and model as the one who lived alongside us in history, cooperated with the divine Spirit in his own time, and who still accompanies us now in the struggle for human liberation. From Heyward's perspective, key aspects of all this would collapse if it included devotion to Jesus as the divine Son of God Incarnate, for then women would be required to worship and obey a male human being as their Lord and Savior.

Heyward fails to comment, however, on the Catholic and biblical Tradition that God's own Son, seeking out his lost sheep as a male human being and giving his life on the Cross for his "Bride" the Church (Mt 25:1-13; Mk 2:19-20; Eph 5:21-33) is more a *spousal* than a *patriarchal* mystery. In other words, if Jesus Christ is the Bridegroom of a new, redeemed humanity, the one who reaches out in gracious love to his people, then the Church as his Bride is essentially feminine in relation to him, in responsive love. This means that women are the members of the human race who can best embody the way to sanctity, and the new humanity in Christ. In Catholicism, therefore, the highest of all creatures is the Blessed Virgin Mary, the Mother of God, and the fundamental Christian charism that is lived out by all the saints, as von Balthasar famously wrote, is the baptismal "Marian charism" of all Christians: to receive and return the love of God with our whole being, as she did.[829] Thus, it is not at all clear that the doctrine of the Incarnation stands as a threat to the dignity of women.

---

[828] Carter Heyward, "Can Anglicans be Feminist Liberation Theologians and Still be Anglicans?" in Peter Eaton, ed. *The Trial of Faith* (West Sussex: Churchman Publishing, 1988), p. 39 and 34-35.
[829] On this see the apostolic letter of Pope St. John Paul II, *Mulieris Dignitatem* (On the Dignity of Women, 1988).

The Incarnation

It has been argued by some feminists, however, that the Christian obsession with self-sacrificial love exemplified by Christ in his Incarnation and on the Cross has promoted a culture of passive acceptance by women of the patriarchal oppression that they suffer. Women are encouraged to identify themselves with Jesus on the Cross as helpless victims, rather than encouraged to struggle for liberation from male social dominance and violence.

Once again, however, we are in the realm of half-truths here. While there certainly have been times and places in the Christian world in which the cult of the suffering Christ has been used to promote mere passive endurance of injustice, still, such historical failures should not be confused with logical entailment. In other words, the Incarnation and the Cross do not necessarily imply such an outcome. As we have already seen (in Part Two, Chapter One of this book), authentic love does not always take the form of suffering and self-sacrifice. The highest form of love, by definition, means seeking the good of others *if need be* at the expense of our own temporal good: this is no endorsement of merely passive endurance of suffering at the hands of others, bearing a cross of *needless* suffering and victimization that does no one any good. Similarly, in the Incarnation and the Cross, the divine Son came to share in our sufferings and die for our sins *because we needed him to do this, with us and for us.* It was not a glorification of innocent suffering in itself. Moreover, the doctrine of the Incarnation tells us that the Son of God shared in all the characteristic blessings and joys of human life as well, hallowing them as a fitting vehicle of his divine life; he did not just share in our struggles and afflictions (again, see Part Two, Chapter One, above). There is no legitimate basis here for a "cult of suffering."

In fact, it is precisely the woman (or man, for that matter) who knows that she has been the object of the infinite love of God Incarnate who then can embrace the sacrifices of love to which she may be called from a position of self-worth and inner strength, rather than from a position of broken self-esteem and servility. David Brown points to the nature of authentic sacrificial love when he writes:

The encouragement of passivity in women on the basis of Christ's example in death was of course wrong. But sacrificial service of others should in any case never have been presented as always necessarily a passive, joyless activity. Instead, it will characteristically bring its own positive fulfilment in the joy of seeing others flourish. Indeed, so far from deriding mothers' pride in their children as a lost opportunity for self-fulfilment, the natural opportunities afforded for self-fulfilment through the fulfilment of others (in numerous other ways also) need to be taken with much more seriousness.[830]

The Incarnation is Not of Vital Importance to Social Christianity

Some Anglicans over the past century and a half have believed that the Incarnation is superfluous; it does not add anything to our stock of essential Christian social principles that we cannot glean just as well from other areas of Christian doctrine, such as the doctrines of God, Humanity, and Creation.

One Anglican representative of this perspective, for example, was Maurice Wiles. In his book *The Remaking of Christian Doctrine* (1974), he neatly summarized his whole theological outlook. We can use this summary as a springboard for reflection on the social implications of Non-Incarnational Christianity (for Wiles actually wrote little on these implications himself):

> The pattern of belief I have been trying to develop is belief in God upon whom the world depends for its very existence, a God who cares about human suffering, who has a purpose for the world which men can come in part at least to know, and who elicits from men a mature response of faith and love in which sin can begin to be overcome, and the goals of human life to be realised. Moreover, the central figure within history who focuses for us the recognition and realisation of these things is Jesus Christ. In Christian history all this has

---

[830] Brown, *Divine Humanity*, p. 259.

undoubtedly been held together and vividly expressed by the doctrine of the unique incarnation of God in Jesus Christ. I have been arguing that that particular doctrine is not required for the whole pattern of belief to be true, or indeed for our having good grounds for believing it to be true.[831]

Nothing vital in Christianity depends upon believing in the Incarnation. All that we need to believe is in a caring God who bestows upon us the gift of existence. This appears to be Wiles' position. And its implications are easy to see. God is the free, all-loving, infinitely wise Creator who made us in his own "image" (Gen 1:26-27); in other words, he created us with a degree of free-will, and the potential to use our freedom to create, love, and reason after his own likeness. Moreover, he set us amid his wider creation, entrusting us with the care of ourselves, each other, and with the stewardship of the whole earth (Gen 1:28, 2:15). Thus, *each person has both inherent dignity and purpose as a child of God.*

The social implications of such an approach are also easy to see. Human beings are not to be treated as mere pawns on an economic and political chessboard. *We belong to God, first of all, as his created children.* Thus, we each have an inherent worth and purpose in his eyes that does not depend upon membership in a particular gender, race, class, nation, or religion, or upon our usefulness to society or to the State. It follows that God demands that his human creatures, made in his image, should never be oppressed, exploited, or terrorised, and that each person's inherent, created potential for freedom,[832] for creative work, for love, and for the search for truth and fulfilment, should be given an opportunity to flourish.

Unfortunately, human beings habitually fall short of realising their potentials, and all too often abuse others in their social relationships,

---

[831] Wiles, *The Remaking of Christian Doctrine*, p. 117-118.
[832] "Freedom" is used in this context simply as self-determination under the guidance of reason, and an absence of social coercion in so far as that is compatible with the common good.

thereby betraying their Creator's trust. In other words, we are all habitual sinners, still on the way to being fully cured, and so none of us in society can be trusted with absolute power over his fellows. Nevertheless, our Creator's purpose is that we live in community, in a fellowship of mutual support and respect. Only in this way can we fully develop our potentials, and become all that he made us to be. *It follows that whenever human beings suffer under tyranny on the one hand, or grinding poverty and deprivation on the other, human society is violating the will of God. Our righteous God then demands social change.* We see this clearly expressed by the prophets and the Psalms in the Old Testament:

> Is this not the fast that I choose: to loose the bonds of wickedness, to undo the thongs of the yoke, to let the oppressed go free, and to break every yoke? Is it not to share your bread with the hungry, and bring the homeless
> poor into your house; when you see the naked to cover him, and not to hide yourself from your own flesh? Then shall your light break forth like the dawn, and your healing shall spring up speedily; your righteousness shall go before you, the glory of the Lord shall be your rear guard. Then you shall call, and the Lord will answer; you shall cry, and he will say, Here I am. (Is 58: 6-9)

> "Hear this word , you cows of Bashan, who are in the mountain of Samaria, who oppress the poor, who crush the needy, who say to their husbands 'Bring, that we may drink!' The Lord God has sworn by his holiness that, behold, the days are coming upon you, when they shall take you away with hooks, even the last of you with fish-hooks. And you shall go out through the breeches, every one straight before her; and you shall be cast forth into Harmon," says the Lord. ... But let justice roll down like waters, and righteousness like an ever-flowing stream. (Amos 4:1-3, 5:24)

> Give the king thy justice, O God,
> and thy righteousness to the royal son!
> May he judge thy people with righteousness,

and thy poor with justice! …

May he defend the cause of the poor of the people,
give deliverance to the needy and crush the oppressor! …

May all kings fall down before him,
and all nations serve him!
For he delivers the needy when he calls,
the poor and him who has no helper.
He has pity on the weak and the needy,
and saves the lives of the needy.
From oppression and violence he redeems their life;
and precious is their blood in his sight. (Ps 72: 1-2, 4, 11-14)

On the basis of the created dignity of every human being, therefore,
— and also on our tendency to misuse the freedom that God gave us
— Christians today must speak out for *democracy* (that is, the dignity of
having a voice in choosing one's own government, and non-violent
means to check abuses of state power: in other words, the capacity to
remove corrupt or unjust rulers through the ballot box). Christians
must also promote *human rights* (that is, protection of innocent human
life from violence, and within reasonable limits, the dignity of freedom
of expression, association, religious worship and practice, and
emigration). Also, Christians must support *economic rights* for all (the
dignity of having access to the basic and necessary means for survival
and the development and use of one's God-given gifts and talents: this
includes food, clothing, shelter, health-care, and educational and
employment opportunities; inevitably this will involve some form of
public and private social welfare "safety net").

I have endeavored to show just how far one might go towards
developing Christian social principles based solely on the doctrines of
God, Humanity (i.e., biblical anthropology), and Creation, *without any
reference to the Incarnation at all*. In a similar way, Jurgen Moltmann
derived "fundamental human rights" and the need for
"democratisation" from the biblical teaching that all human beings are

made in the image of God, and therefore each person has inalienable dignity.[833]

In fact, even Anglican incarnational theologians often have neglected the social implications of the doctrine. For example, the Incarnation received only a single mention in Charles Gore's work *Christ and Society* (1927). Gore based Christian social teaching primarily upon the message of Jesus about the Kingdom of God.[834] Most of the contributors to the book *Essays Catholic and Radical* (1983) followed the same path. Social Christianity allegedly centres upon the message of the dawning of the Kingdom[835] -- a perspective which we shall explore later in this chapter.

Nor are Anglican theologians the only ones who have struggled to locate any distinctive social relevance for the Incarnation. American Roman Catholic Michael Novak, for example, found political implications in the Incarnation, but on closer inspection, these simply turn out to be reaffirmations of what is found in other traditional doctrines, such as the doctrine that human beings are made in the divine image, and yet have fallen from grace into sin. The Incarnation, Novak says, merely calls us to acknowledge the limitations, weaknesses and evils which plague our utopian dreams.[836]

---

[833] Jurgen Moltmann, *On Human Dignity* (London: SCM, 1984), p. 22-24. Another good example of this whole approach to the Social Gospel can be found in the sermons and addresses of Martin Luther King Jr., especially in the address "How Should a Christian View Communism?" in *Strength to Love* (Glasgow: Fount, 1963), p. 96-105. For an Anglican equivalent, see Trevor Williams, *Form and Vitality*, p. 314-315.

[834] Charles Gore, *Christ and Society* (London: George Allen and Unwin, 1927), p. 37-62.

[835] Kenneth Leech and Rowan Williams, eds., *Essays Catholic and Radical* (London: Bowerdean, 1983), p. 91 and 171. In a similar way, see the report of the Church of England's Board for Social Responsibility, *Not Just for the Poor* (London: Church House, 1986), p. 15-31, which derives social principles from Christian doctrine about Creation, the Kingdom, and the death and resurrection of Jesus.

[836] Michael Novak, *The Spirit of Democratic Capitalism* (New York: Touchstone, 1982), p. 341, and 349-351.

Similarly, in Archbishop of Canterbury William Temple's influential book *Christianity and Social Order* (1942), the Incarnation played only a small, supporting role. Temple derived the "primary" Christian social principles from belief in God as our loving Creator, and the created free-will of human beings.[837] God intended people to use their freedom to respond positively to his love, and to build up a fellowship of love among themselves. But humanity misuses its freedom and falls into self-centeredness instead. Chronic self-centeredness becomes a taint affecting all persons, and complete deliverance can only be achieved by "winning the whole heart's devotion, the total devotion of my will — and this only the Divine Love disclosed by Christ in his life and death can do."[838]

On this basis, Temple argued that respect for persons is the central Christian principle. We should remember that Temple wrote these words in the midst of the Second World War, when most of the globe was under threat from Fascist and Communist totalitarianism:

> The primary principle of Christian ethics and politics must be respect for every person simply as a person. If each man and woman is a child of God, whom God loves and for whom Christ died, then there is in each a worth absolutely independent of all usefulness to society. The person is primary, not society: the State exists for the citizen, not the citizen for the State. The first aim of social progress must be to give the fullest possible scope for the exercise of all powers and qualities which are distinctly personal …."[839]

It is remarkable how small a part the Incarnation played in Temple's social theology here, especially given that he had written at length about the Incarnation earlier in his life in books such as *Christus Veritas*

---

[837] William Temple, *Christianity and the Social Order* (London: SPCK, 1976 edition), p. 62-63.
[838] Ibid., p. 60.
[839] Ibid., p. 67.

(1924), where he emphasized its central importance. In *Christianity and the Social Order*, the Incarnation is said to highlight and dramatize God's love for humanity, and thereby help draw us out of our habitual and destructive self-centeredness. Otherwise, however, it appears that the doctrine has little else to say. In fact, one could argue that Temple's "primary" Christian social principles can be preserved without it. If every person is created by a loving God and made in his image, with the potential to respond positively to his love, then it would still be true that there is in each person a worth "absolutely independent of all usefulness to society." The fostering of each individual's highest personal qualities could still be seen as the best way for society to cooperate with God's benevolent purposes for us, and therefore remain "the first aim of social progress."

The Incarnation was also relegated to the periphery in the work of the Anglican theologian V.A. Demant. In his book *Theology of Society* (1947), Demant placed his hope for the recovery of human solidarity in a common realisation that human beings are creatures of a loving God: "The only effort demanded of him is to admit his creaturehood, to renounce the torturous activity to make his own world."[840] Solidarity involves living a common life that is already given by the common structure of our being. The highest expression of this human solidarity is found in the Church, in the worship of God: "the worshipful creature is at once at unity with the whole hierarchy of being, for he is at unity with the Creator."[841] Demant then adds, almost as an afterthought:

> As Christ in his blessed Incarnation pierced through all forms of created order and became, not society, not a culture, not an idea, but man — and not only man, but *this* man, born of *this* woman, a concrete individual in all his social relations — nay more, in the Blessed Sacrament enthrones himself even in the material — so union with Christ, which is of the nature of the

---

[840] V.A. Demant, *Theology of Society* (London: Faber and Faber, 1947), p. 24.
[841] Ibid., p. 26.

Church as priest of earthly society, redeems society at each level of its being.[842]

Here Jesus Christ is seen as the representative of the true, worshipful humanity, incorporating material, social, and spiritual levels of being in his total devotion to God. But it is not clear why he needs to be God Incarnate to be the exemplary representative of humanity (would not a solely human Jesus, filled to overflowing with the Holy Spirit, serve just as well?), nor is it clear how Demant's teaching here adds anything to our stock of Christian social principles except the call to spread the gospel of Christ to the ends of the earth, incorporating more and more people into union with Christ, our Creator and Redeemer, through the Eucharist.

Demant derived basic Christian social principles from Christian anthropology: human beings are limited by their finitude, prone to sin, and yet created in the spiritual image of God. According to Demant, political philosophy which forgets human limitations and sin tends toward over-optimism and utopian rationalism, while one that forgets the spiritual side of humanity ends in cynicism and moral relativity.[843] True as all this may be, the doctrine of the Incarnation seems to play no part in this framework at all.

Thus, we are still left with our central question: does the Incarnation add anything vital to our Christian social principles — anything over and above what the doctrines of God, Humanity, Creation, and the Kingdom can teach us?

The Incarnation has Vital Social Implications

Early in the twentieth century, many Anglo-Catholics claimed that the Incarnation does indeed have important social implications. Some essential Christian social principles were said to rest upon it, and to stand or fall with it. Unfortunately, the reasons given to justify this viewpoint were often rather poor.

---

[842] Ibid.

[843] Ibid., p. 213-214.

Indeed, lack of clarity pervaded early twentieth century Anglican theology in this area.

Maurice Reckitt, for example, saw the Incarnation as central to the Christian social movement. In his book *Faith and Society* (1932), for example, he wrote:

> The whole effort of the Church and of the Christian in the social sphere is founded upon faith that in the Incarnation God has identified Himself with the fate of His creation. ... Its social consequences are profound. For the Incarnation testifies to both the potential perfection of earthly things, and even, by its extension in the Sacraments, specifically of man-made things (e.g. bread and wine); and also to the inestimable spiritual significance of the individual. God did not save man *from* his earthly surroundings, but amidst these surroundings. Again, the created being whom Christ came down to redeem must clearly be of precious significance to God to demand such a stupendous condescension.[844]

The main problem with Reckitt's analysis here was that most of the social principles he derived from the doctrine of the Incarnation might be justified in other ways, from other Christian doctrines. For example, take the doctrines of Creation and the Kingdom. If we believe that human beings receive their existence as the free gift of a loving God who made each one of us in his own image, with the inherent potential to receive and return his love, and if we also believe that Jesus was the most inspired of God's prophets, and that he taught us that God is working in human history to bring about his Kingdom on earth, a kingdom that includes forgiveness of sins, compassionate service of the poor, and the removal of economic and social injustice, then we would still have adequate grounds for believing that God cares about the fate of human beings, that he

---

[844] Maurice Reckitt, *Faith and Society* (London: Longmans and Green, 1932), p. 31-32.

intends earthly things and human society to be "perfected" in the coming Kingdom of God on earth, and that each person is of "inestimable spiritual significance" to him. We would also have adequate grounds for believing that God does not "save man *from* his earthly surroundings, but amidst these surroundings," for we could say that God inspires social prophets such as Jesus to call us to the ways of the Kingdom, and that God sends forth his Spirit into human hearts to enable us to respond to that call. In short, we could properly believe all this without any reference to the doctrine of the Incarnation at all.

Of course, the Incarnation does add something to this framework, for it shows us the very depths and extent of God's love for us. Like Temple, Reckitt believed that we must be of "precious significance to God" for God himself to come among us in the flesh as one of us, and even to suffer death upon the Cross for us in order to save us. The Incarnation and the Cross thereby give us *added* reasons to see each person as precious in God's sight, and we are called by Christ to share this good news to the very ends of the earth (Mt 28:20). But as we have seen in our discussion of non-incarnational social theology, and even in our discussion of Temple's thought, we *already* have adequate grounds for working for a just society in which each person is respected and valued as a child of God without having to refer to the Incarnation. The doctrines of God, Humanity, Creation, and the Kingdom would seem to be enough on their own.

An Anglican contemporary of Reckitt, W.G. Peck, put great emphasis on the Incarnation in his principle work *The Divine Society* (1925). **Peck saw the Incarnation as the guarantee of the divine authority of the social teachings of Jesus:**

> Jesus asks of men a new attitude to life, which must display itself in every sphere, and this he asks not as a teacher of morals and philosophy, but as God suffering for them. ... Thus, the

dogma of the Incarnation becomes the final sanction of all the principles laid down in our Lord's teaching.[845]

Peck found this authoritative social teaching primarily in Jesus' preaching about the Kingdom of God. Christ's Jewish hearers expected the coming of the Kingdom to involve the end of social and economic injustice:

> Seeing therefore that Jesus accepted for his teaching a conceptual mold which was so clearly connected with anticipations of social and economic change, we may suppose that if He had considered those anticipations to be entirely irrelevant, He would have spared no pains to make this abundantly clear. But He offered no criticism of these anticipations in themselves. Where He parted company with the popular enthusiasm of His day was as to the manner in which they were to be realised.[846]

Implied in Christ's authoritative teaching about the Kingdom, therefore, is the promise that God is working in human history to overturn oppressive and dehumanising social structures: "[Jesus] opened the book and found the place where it was written, 'The Spirit of the Lord is upon me, because he has anointed me to preach good news to the poor, he has sent me to proclaim release to the captives and recovering of sight to the blind, to set at liberty those who are oppressed, to proclaim the acceptable year of the Lord.'… and he began to say to them, 'Today this scripture has been fulfilled in your hearing'" (Lk 4:16-21; cf. 2:46-55).

Other teachings of Jesus were seen by Peck to have social implications as well. For example, Jesus taught that God is our Creator; the whole of human existence is a free gift of God's love, and thus there can be no absolute human ownership. A man does

---

[845] W.G. Peck, *The Divine Society: Christian Dogma and Social Redemption* (London: SCM: 1925), p. 179; cf. Gore, *Christ and Society*, p. 22.
[846] Ibid. (Peck), p. 164.

not even own his own life, and he should see himself as a mere *steward* of God's creation: "All is given, and it is the Giver's purpose which must be considered and served in all things: and that is why Jesus is constantly speaking of the Will of His Father."[847] Moreover, Jesus taught us that the purpose of our existence lies first not in material things, but in total devotion to the Kingdom of God (Mt 6:33). The pursuit and enjoyment of personal riches is therefore not a refuge from anxiety, rather, it is a distraction from life's true purpose and fulfilment. Hence, the rich man will have a hard time entering the Kingdom of God (Mk 10:23). Finally, Jesus taught that true discipleship can only be found in a life of dedicated service to others (Mk 10:42-45). Peck concluded:

> His attitude appears to be an utter condemnation of the accepted standards of our present society. ... Jesus conceived a complete revolution of human standards, a revolution which was to be based upon a supernatural reality.[848]

In a similar way, in a memorable passage of his book *The Incarnation of the Son of God* (1892), Bishop Charles Gore spelled out in detail the profound challenge that the teachings of Jesus Christ make to many of the accepted standards of socio-economic behavior in the Western world:

> Jesus Christ is the same yesterday, today, and for ever. The claim which He made on the contemporaries of His life on earth, is the claim which He makes on his disciples today. Many will come to Him at the last day — so we cannot but paraphrase His own words — with manifold pleas and excuses derived from the maxims of what is called the Christian world: 'Lord, we never denied the Christian creed: nay, we had a zeal for orthodoxy, for churchmanship, for Bible distribution, but of course in our business we did as everyone else did; we sold

---

[847] Ibid., p. 173.
[848] Ibid., p. 178-179.

in the dearest and bought in the cheapest market: we did not, of course we did not, entertain any other consideration when we were investing our money, except whether the investments were safe; we never imagined that we could love our neighbors as ourselves in the competition of business, or that we could carry into commercial transactions the sort of strict righteousness that we knew to be obligatory in private life. Lord, in all these matters we went by commonly accepted standards: we never much thought about Christianity as a brotherhood.' Then will He protest unto them: 'Did I not say to thee, in that written word wherein thou didst profess to have eternal life: "A man's life consisteth not in the abundance of things that he possesseth"? Did not I warn thee, "How hardly shall they that have riches enter into the kingdom of God"? Did I not bid thee seek first the kingdom of God and His righteousness? Did I not tell thee that except a man, in spirit or will at least, forsook all that he had, unless he took up his cross and followed Me, he could not be My disciple? Not everyone that saith unto Me, Lord, Lord, shall enter the kingdom of heaven, but he that doeth, that hath done, the will of My Father.'[849]

Whatever one decides about the central *content* of the authoritative social teachings of Jesus — and Gore and Peck may indeed have located the essential core of them — we still need to ask if they cannot be claimed to be normative on grounds other than the Incarnation. For example, Christ's teachings might be said to be sufficiently vindicated by the echo they find in the human conscience, and by the fact that God raised Jesus from the dead, putting a divine seal of approval on his life and mission. These would be adequate grounds for the supremacy of his social teachings over those of other sages and philosophers, even without leaving the orbit of non-incarnational Christianity.

---

[849] Gore, *The Incarnation of the Son of God*, p. 214.

The Incarnation

On the other hand, if Jesus is indeed the divine Son Incarnate, then we can go further and claim that the principles of his teaching are utterly indefectible as they stand, and unsurpassable in the future as well. They do not need to be completed or corrected by some later sage or prophet (e.g., by Mohammed, or Joseph Smith, or Guru Nanak), because *no one can reveal the essential truths about God and humanity more clearly or more fully than God in person, in human flesh.*[850] *In short, Peck was surely correct when he claimed that the Incarnation is "the final sanction of all the principles laid down in our Lord's teaching."*[851]

In what may be the most in-depth discussion of the social implications of the Incarnation ever written by an Anglican, Peck went on to argue in *The Divine Society* that the doctrine necessarily leads to "four postulates of direct economic significance." We shall look briefly at each of these in turn.

---

[850] See our discussion in Part Two, Chapter Two of this book of the entire trustworthiness or "infallibility" of Jesus, at least on matters of significance to his mission, such as "faith and morals."

[851] Peck, *The Divine Society*, p. 179. This perspective is shared by many in the Evangelical tradition as well. Anglican Evangelical Oliver O'Donovan, for example, has written of "the foundation of Christian ethics in the incarnation":

> Since the Word became flesh and dwelt among us, transcendent divine authority has presented itself as worldly moral authority. It comes to us not as a *mysterium tremendum* which simply destroys all worldly order, but as creation restored and renewed, to which God is immediately present in the person of the Son of Man. The teaching and life of Jesus must be *morally* authoritative if we are not to be thrown back upon the gnostic gospel of a visitor from heaven who summons us out of the world. ... The meaning of Jesus' life and teaching must be a worldly meaning, a reality of human existence which can command our lives in the world and reorder them in the restored creation. (*Resurrection and the Moral Order: An Outline for Evangelical Ethics*. Leicester: Apollos, second edition, 1994, p. 143)

1) *The corporate unity of humanity*

Peck found social significance in the fact that "Jesus does not come to the [human] race as to a series of isolated individuals. He came to one place for a few years, and thus to all mankind; and He wrought an act for a corporate body which is Man."[852] Peck's expressions are a bit confusing here, but it would seem that by the "corporate unity of mankind" he meant the interdependence of human lives in society and in history. It is not clear, however, how he then derived opposition to market competition from the mere fact of such interdependence, or from the principle of the primacy of "the common good."[853] Historically, arguments in favor of relatively free-market capitalism are usually based on the idea that fair and competitive free markets best *promote* the common good, for example, by preserving liberty, encouraging wealth-creation via entrepreneurship, and efficiently producing and making widely available affordable, quality consumer goods. These claims by apologists for capitalism may be disputed, of course, with reference to the empirical facts about capitalist economies and how they have performed in practice, but theoretically, at least, the case for capitalism is based on the principle that the fair and free exchange of goods and services is best for the rising prosperity of almost everyone.

2) *The equality of all human beings*

Peck believed that "All alike owe their existence and their redemption to God. … Thus, upon the deepest levels of life they are all perfectly equal in having no grounds of personal merit."[854] From this Peck sought justification for relatively equal levels of income: "The economic implication is that though functions may differ, the intrinsic worth of *man's functioning* is in all cases equal where it is the best service that a man can bring, and consequently wide disparity of material

---

[852] Ibid., p. 181.
[853] Ibid., p. 181-182.
[854] Ibid., p. 182.

rewards represent no spiritual reality."[855] The problem with this analysis, however, is that there are disparities (even "wide" ones), not only between different amounts of effort which different persons put into their jobs, but also between the different amounts of education and training needed to equip them to do those tasks, and often quite dramatic differences in the degree of responsibility for the life and prosperity of others that those social roles entail. A just and fair social order will surely reward people accordingly.[856] In any case, it is not clear that Peck can derive the principle of "the equality of all men" from the Incarnation alone. In fact, his wording suggests that it is the doctrines of Creation and Redemption, and not the Incarnation as such, which implies that, in important respects, all people are of equal value in the eyes of God.

3) *Material things find their significance only as they are employed for moral-spiritual ends*

We find a similar problem with Peck's logic here, for it would seem that this social principle could just as well be founded on what Jesus *taught* ("Seek first [God's] Kingdom and his righteousness," Mt 6:33) and from the way Jesus *lived* (especially the secondary role that material possessions played in his life of total devotion to the will of his Father, and the service of human need), rather than from the Incarnation. Also, the doctrine of the Incarnation all by itself does not necessarily imply that material things *only* have significance when used for moral-spiritual ends. Admittedly, it implies that material things *can be* used for such ends; this was the famous argument that St. John of Damascus employed in the eighth century to justify the use of icons in prayer and worship. Since the Word reached out to save humanity by assuming flesh, we may communicate heavenly and spiritual realities through painted icons.[857] Nevertheless, it is the *content* of Christ's teaching and

---

[855] Ibid., p. 183.

[856] One might also add that in a market economy, entrepreneurs and investors will need to be offered sufficient financial incentives to risk their capital to establish new businesses, and create new jobs and products.

[857] Anglican-Orthodox Joint Doctrinal Commission, *Dublin Agreed Statement*, p. 39-40.

example, and not the fact that Jesus is God Incarnate, that can lead us most directly to the principle that material things find their significance *only* as they are employed for moral-spiritual ends.

Peck goes on to claim that the capitalist system, with its selfish, materialistic profit motive, violates this incarnational principle. Capitalism "has only one God and that is Mammon," Peck wrote, "material wealth grasped, possessed, and worshipped for its own sake, and as the ultimate standard of well-being."[858] But this hardly seems a fair critique of all forms of capitalism. Peck would have done better to blame secular materialism and consumerism more than capitalism per se. Clearly, there are some Christian businessmen and women who do not shamelessly "grasp" wealth, but seek to maximise profits in honest ways, that do not exploit their employees or the natural environment. They seek profit not "for its own sake," or "as the ultimate standard of well-being," but in order to create quality consumer goods, provide for their families, pay their fair share of taxes, and come to the aid of the Church and the poor. In short, the profit-motive is not necessarily based upon "greed," or the worship of wealth for its own sake. To Christian capitalists, profits morally attained may be seen as the means both to socially beneficial productivity and philanthropy. In fact, the founding father of capitalism, Adam Smith, argued in his work *The Theory of Moral Sentiments* (1759) that society could not function properly without an infusion of moral virtue, and sentiments that hold self-interest in check.[859]

4) *The Incarnation inspires in men a motive of gratitude and a desire for service*

Here the doctrine of the Incarnation was seen to have social implications because it is included in the doctrine of Redemption.[860]

[858] Peck, *The Divine Society*, p. 186 and 238-239.
[859] R. Ekelund, R. and R. Hebert, *A History of Economic Theory and Method* (USA: Waveland Press, fifth edition, 2007) p. 105. See also Malcolm Brown, "The Case for Anglican Social Theology Today" in Malcolm Brown, ed., *Anglican Social Theology* (London: Church House Publishing, 2014), p. 15 and 33.
[860] Peck, *The Divine Society*, p. 188.

The Incarnation

God's incarnate, redeeming love inspires in us both gratitude and service: we love because he first loved us (I Jn 4:10). But we have already met this line of argument in the thought of William Temple and Maurice Reckitt. The fact is that belief in a God who is both loving Creator and providential Guide of history — as in the Jewish faith — has also been taken as grounds for gratitude and service. Faith in the Incarnation and the Cross can certainly *deepen* one's spirit of thankfulness and social service, without being the *sole* ground, or a *sine qua non* for such dispositions.

In short, it is not clear that either Peck or Reckitt found vital social implications in the Incarnation which could not be derived from other basic Christian doctrines. To be sure, God's love for all persons, supremely expressed through his Incarnation and his Cross, can inspire us to a deeper thankfulness to God, and a greater willingness to love our neighbors. It can thereby *motivate* social service in a dramatic way (as some of the great Christian social reformers down through history have shown). Christians are also called to share the gospel of Divine Love to the ends of the earth (Mt 28:18-20). Moreover, Peck has reminded us that the Incarnation gives us a firm guarantee of the unsurpassable authority of the social teachings of Jesus. But all things considered, we have not yet found anything implicit in the Incarnation which might add significant *content* to Christian social teaching.

As we move on to consider some post-World War II Anglican writers, we find much the same difficulty. Given that the Anglican tradition is distinctive in the central place it accords to the doctrine of the Incarnation,[861] one would have thought that Anglican theologians would lead the way in unfolding the social implications of the doctrine. But such is not the case. In fact, among Anglican writers both before and after the Second World War, we find no satisfactory answer to the central question of this

---

[861] On this point see the Introduction to this book: "The Anglican Heritage and the Incarnation."

chapter: does the doctrine of the Incarnation have vital socio-economic implications — social principles which rest upon it, and stand or fall, with it — and if so, what are they? In fact, we find a scarcity of writing on this subject altogether. For example, one commentator pointed out that the *Myth of God Incarnate* debate of the 1970s and 1980s included almost no discussion at all of its implications for political theology.[862]

Even in that era, however, there were a few exceptions. For example, in *Principles of Christian Theology* (1977), John Macquarrie stated that Jesus Christ is the Incarnate Word, the particular being in whom divine, Expressive Being has most fully expressed himself. Macquarrie found this significant for Christian ethics:

> The awareness of the divine presence becomes the determinative factor in any distinctly Christian understanding of ethics. Differently stated, this means an extension of the sacramental principle to the whole of life. ... [T]he faith that holy Being presents itself and manifests itself in the neighbor and even in material things lends a new depth to the world and profoundly influences behavior in it.[863]

Once again, however, we may rightfully ask why we need to believe in the Incarnation in order to hold that there is a divine presence and self-manifestation throughout creation, in our neighbors, and in material things. Surely, an adequate doctrine of Creation, and of God's omnipresence and immanence would be enough.

Anglo-Catholic theologian Kenneth Leech claimed, both in *The Social God* (1981) and *True God* (1985), that the Incarnation is absolutely central to the Social Gospel. He called the Church to rediscover

---

[862] Rex Ambler and David Haslam, eds., *Agenda for Prophets: Towards a Political Theology for Britain* (London: Bowerdean, 1980), p. 9-10. Obviously, the writings of Don Cupitt, discussed earlier in this chapter, would be an exception.
[863] Macquarrie, *Principles of Christian Theology*, p. 510.

"theological materialism," the truth that grace and healing come to us through the flesh because the Word became flesh: "The assertion of the sacredness of the flesh and of matter is of prime importance in the recovery of Christian social theology."[864] Christianity is not about an otherworldly or pietistic salvation. It is about *this* world, Leech insisted; it is about the sacraments, and fleshly issues such as abortion, racism, and sexuality, where God's presence can be encountered and human lives made whole. **But Leech failed to consider that the doctrine of Creation might give us adequate support for belief in the sacredness of matter and of the flesh. The Bible tells us that God looked upon his entire creation and pronounced it "very good" (Gen 1:31). His beauty, wisdom, and power are seen reflected in the things that he made (Wis 13:1-9; Rom 1:18-21), and his Spirit fills the universe (Wis 1:7). The Psalms are replete with wonder at the creation (e.g. Ps 19:1-6), and praise for the immanent yet transcendent Creator (Ps 148). In short, non-incarnational Christians, Jews, deists and theists of many kinds seem to be quite able to believe in the sacredness of matter and of all human life without embracing incarnational Christianity. The Incarnation may reinforce that belief, but it is well established in other ways, by other biblical doctrines.**

John Austin Baker seemed to fall into a similar error. In *The Foolishness of God* (1970), he argued that the Incarnation gives dignity to the human race as never before:

> When above all we learn that God himself has become our partner and our brother, sharing our condition, this gives imperishable glory to every created thing. Never again can we despise or hate the earth trodden by the feet of God, the food and drink by which he lived, the family bonds which he shared, the human form which was found sufficient to express even his innermost being. Man is not merely Man, but in the old phrase, *capax Dei*, someone in whom God can be himself.[865]

---

[864] Kenneth Leech, *The Social God* (London: Sheldon Press, 1981), p. 35-38.
[865] Baker, *The Foolishness of God*, p. 313.

In direct response to Baker, Maurice Wiles rightly asked why the full dignity of creaturehood is not adequately safeguarded and expressed by the doctrine of Creation.[866] **We do not have to believe in the Incarnation in order to have sufficient grounds for loving the earth, our food and drink, our family bonds, or our human form. We can love these things because they are creations of a good and all-wise God who often blesses us through matter. The Incarnation does indeed *reaffirm* the value of human flesh. We are given *added* reason to cherish human life, for God did not think it beneath his dignity to dwell among us as one of us. But the inherent worth of every human life is already established by the fact that God made us in his image, body and soul, with the potential to know and love him in return.**

In *Travels in Oudamovia* (1976), Baker claimed that the Incarnation is the foundation of human brotherhood:

> [B]ecause the Son of God has become man, all men and women are brothers and sisters of the Son of God. ... This relationship to the eternal Son is a fact about all human beings. ... It is something that has been done for them unilaterally by the Son's becoming man, long before they were born.[867]

As true as this certainly is, we still need to ask whether the doctrine of the Incarnation is really necessary to establish our kinship with God. For presumably, we are each created in the image of God, loved into being and held in being by the loving Father of us all. This gives us a common kinship as "children," in a sense, of our common heavenly Father (Acts 17:27-29). In fact, many Old Testament scholars see the creation accounts in the book of Genesis as conveying the message that God established an initial covenant with human beings and with all of creation: he chose

---

[866] Wiles, *The Remaking of Christian Doctrine*, p. 119.
[867] John Austin Baker, *Travels in Oudamovia* (Leighton Buzzard: Faith Press, 1976), p. 27.

to form a kinship-bond, so to speak, with all of his creatures right from the start (e.g. see Lk 3:38).[868] To be sure, the Incarnation of the Son reaffirms and strengthens this kinship-bond, making us not only children of God, but now brothers and sisters of God Incarnate. But the Incarnation is not the sole ground of human kinship with God.

Kenneth Leech offered another possible social implication of the Incarnation. In a way highly reminiscent of the thought of the nineteenth century Anglican theologian F.D. Maurice, he argued that the doctrine of the Incarnation implies that "all theology is social":

> [I]f manhood has been taken into God, then the human race is a solidarity, men are oned with God and with each other. ... If Christ has raised manhood into God, it follows that there is a true sharing in the common life of the Godhead.[869]

However, it would seem, that all this depends upon an ancient notion of the Incarnation derived from Christian Neo-Platonism: that the divine Son united himself with a timeless, universal form called "manhood" or "humanity" in which all human beings participate. On this view, simply by becoming incarnate in the womb of Mary, the divine Son somehow began to transform the inclusive "humanity" of us all, bringing the divine life into contact with this universal form in which we all share. This book is not the place for a philosophical discussion of the notion of "universals;" suffice it to say that almost all contemporary philosophers — including those working within the Anglo-American orbit of Analytic philosophy (as most post-World War II Anglican theologians have), would be very reluctant to accept such an understanding of universals today, or of the Incarnation based on that philosophical foundation.[870]

---

[868] For example, see Scott Hahn, *The Father Who Keeps His Promises: God's Covenant Love in Scripture* (Cincinnati: St. Anthony Messenger Press, 1998), p. 51.

[869] Leech, *The Social Gospel*, p. 27 and 38. Cf. Mascall, *Whatever Happened to the Human Mind*, p. 48-51.

[870] Historically, it was the Scholasticism of the high Middle Ages which buried Platonic realism and replaced it with more Aristotelian forms – and later, many

In his book *The Anglican Vision* (1997) James Griffiss expounded the implications of the doctrine of the Incarnation from the perspective of the "liberal Catholic" tradition. The nineteenth century Catholic renewal in the Anglican Communion, Griffiss claimed, recovered Richard Hooker's insight that the sacraments of Baptism and the Eucharist unite us with the Incarnate Christ, through whom we participate in the life of the Triune God.[871] In fact, the Church itself may be thought of as an extension of the Incarnation: it is a sacramental sign and instrument of Christ's mission to transform all of society and incorporate all of humanity into the Kingdom of God.[872] In a way similar to Leech, Griffiss echoes the Platonic view of F.D. Maurice that the Incarnation breaks down the barriers between sacred and secular by including all of human life in the person of Christ and in the worship and Kingdom of God, and therefore: "an incarnational faith calls for the transformation of the 'secular' or 'political' world in Christ, a transformation for which all Christians must take responsibility."[873]

Even if all this is true as far as it goes, once again we are left asking if the Incarnation is the only aspect of Christian belief that calls for this kind of social responsibility and social transformation in Christ. The Evangelical tradition, for example, with far less emphasis on the Church and the sacraments as an extension of the Incarnation, nevertheless, can boast a long and honorable heritage of seeking greater social justice.[874] Moreover, as we have seen, even non-incarnational Christianity — basing itself on the doctrines of God, Creation, Humanity, and the Kingdom — can provide a solid foundation for social democracy, for human and economic rights, and

---

early modern philosophers tended to undermine philosophical realism altogether in favor of various forms of nominalism.

[871] Griffiss, *The Anglican Vision*, p. 111.

[872] Ibid., p. 44 and 52-53.

[873] Ibid., p. 52.

[874] For example, see Part Two, Chapter Two above, where we discussed the social ramifications of the Legal Theory of the Atonement in the Evangelical world.

for social transformation inspired by these ideals without any need for the doctrine of the Incarnation at all.

In *The Challenge of Change: The Anglican Communion in the Post-Modern Era* (1998), American Episcopalian Michael Harris sought to redefine the Incarnation, in part to establish its social relevance. According to Harris, the Incarnation as traditionally conceived — in other words, seeing Jesus as the divine Son dwelling among us as a fully human being — tends to obscure the vocation to which all Christians are called:

> I believe the prevailing understanding of the uniqueness of Jesus as the Christ has made it increasingly difficult to understand our mission in relation to his or to think of ourselves as participants in the Incarnation. ... So I want to look at the notion that the Incarnation needs to be freed from the notions that it is a unique event, and that the Incarnate One is *white, male,* or *western.*[875]

Harris claims that the Incarnation is better understood as the human experience of divine compassion, a compassion present throughout all of creation, to which Jesus responded positively, and with which he cooperated to an eminent degree. In fact, we are all called to be "incarnations" of divine compassion, just as he was:

> When Jesus, as human, responds to the grace of God by faith, it is with a completely open heart, with work that "does not count the cost." He is the full linking of the human and the divine. ...
>
> Belief in Jesus as the Incarnation of the Word or Wisdom of God is the result of what we understand he was about, in

---

[875] Mark Harris, *The Challenge of Change: The Anglican Communion in the Post-Modern Era* (New York: Church Publishing, 1998), p. 126 and 125. Presumably, Harris was aware that Jesus of Nazareth was neither "white" nor "western," but Semitic and Middle-Eastern?

particular of his life, as the compassion of God made real in the world. The uniqueness of Jesus as God's own Son is not a logical requirement of such a doctrine, as if God's compassion could only be made real through the particular person of Jesus. Rather, the uniqueness is in the matching of Jesus' compassion and our allegiance to him in that compassion. When Jesus says, "As the Father has sent me, so I send you" (Jn 20:21), we are called to follow him in the way of compassionate action. Indeed, the reference to Jesus being "the first fruits" (I Cor 15:23) is an indication that God's indwelling compassion is incarnated in other persons who follow him.[876]

That there is a metaphorical sense in which all Christians are meant to "incarnate" the same divine compassion that was manifest in the life of Jesus is doubtless something with which all Christians could agree. But reducing the doctrine of the Incarnation itself to such a metaphor is hardly the best, or the only way to provide a foundation for compassion-in-action.

First of all, as I argued in Part One of this book, "incarnation" is not a word belonging privately to theologians, but a solemnly defined doctrine of the community of faith. Theological dialogue becomes confused and cacophonous when private definitions of words replace the terms of ecclesial discourse. The Incarnation is the doctrine that Jesus Christ was one person in two natures, fully human and fully divine. Harris does not believe in that doctrine in any of the forms which might be said abide within the parameters of that definition (forms which we explored in depth in Part One of this book) — therefore, he has not found social relevance *in the Incarnation*: he has simply ditched the truth of the Incarnation altogether, while retaining the term.

Second, his view is almost indistinguishable from the Action Christology of Anglican writers such as Norman Pittenger that we also unpacked in Part One — and in whom we found the same semantic

---

[876] Ibid., p. 113, and 104-105.

confusion between "incarnation," divine "immanence," and "inspiration."

Third, it is not clear what Harris means by his claim that belief in a unique incarnation of God in Jesus Christ is not needed to assert the universal compassion of God: "as if God's compassion could only be *made real* through the particular person of Jesus." What does "made real" here mean? In the first chapter of Part Two of this book, I argued at length that we do indeed need to assert that God has shared our lot from the perspective of a limited human consciousness as Jesus of Nazareth, if we are to make an intelligible claim that he has a close empathy and sympathy with the struggles and sorrows of every human being.

Much wiser in this regard has been Anglican Archbishop Desmond Tutu of South Africa. Tutu has impeccable credentials for aligning with divine compassion-in-action through his many decades of non-violent struggle against racism and apartheid in his native land, for which he was awarded the Nobel Peace Prize. Like Kenneth Leech, Tutu has also written of the need for an appreciation of "theological materialism," but he is careful to base it upon the teachings and deeds of Jesus as well as upon the Incarnation:

> As a Jew, Jesus would have been confused by our popular dichotomies, because the spiritual and the material, the holy and the profane, for him belonged together. When God sought to intervene decisively in human affairs, he did not send an angel, as he might well have done; no, he sent his only-begotten son, who became true man as he was already truly God in the shattering miracle of the Incarnation, the permanent union of divinity and humanity, of pure spirit with matter, a union which dualism would have ruled out of court as quite impossible.
>
> Jesus came to save not just souls but human beings, real persons of flesh and blood; consequently it was as integral a part of his mission to have ministered to the bodily needs of those who came to hear him as it was to have preached the

good news. When the hungry came, he did not send them off with a cheery wave and talk about pie in the sky when they died; he fed them.[877] He healed the sick, he cleansed lepers; he opened the eyes of the blind and the ears of the deaf; he forgave sins; he preached the good news to the poor and he raised the dead to life again. All these activities he considered of seminal importance to his mission to inaugurate the kingdom of his Father, and they were all of a piece as demonstrations that the power of that kingdom had broken into the world. They were all clues to Jesus' identity for those with eyes to see (Mt 11:1-6). ...

The incarnation means that we must take all human life seriously, body, mind and spirit. We must confess our belief not in the immortality of the soul, but in the resurrection of the body; and we claim that God communicates his divine life in and through ordinary, mundane, material things such as bread, water, wine and oil.[878]

What Tutu shows us is that the doctrine of the Incarnation, and the teachings and deeds of Jesus all converge and point to the same truth: It is God's desire to bring "integral salvation" to his people: healing and wholeness in body, mind, and spirit, in society and in human relationships.[879] This is a fitting synthesis of much of what we have gleaned from the Anglican heritage of social theology in this chapter — but it still leaves us wondering: is the doctrine of the Incarnation really essential to this

---

[877] To be more accurate, however, Jesus did both: as soon as he finished his Sermon on the Mount, for example, including his teachings that the poor, the hungry and those who mourn will be blessed in the Kingdom of Heaven and will see God, he then immediately began to heal the sick and raise the dead (see Mt 6-9 and Lk 7-8).

[878] Desmond Tutu, "The Theologian and the Gospel of Freedom" in Eaton, ed., *The Trial of Faith*, p. 62-63.

[879] "The salvation offered in its fullness to men in Jesus Christ . . . is salvation for all people and of the whole person: it is universal and integral salvation." (*Compendium of the Social Doctrine of the [Catholic] Church*, no. 38).

framework? Couldn't a merely human Jesus, inspired and empowered by the Spirit of God, have taught and done the same things, and conveyed the same message about God's plan for integral human salvation?

We have nearly reached the end of our survey, and our central question remains unanswered. Does anything in the social implications of Christian doctrine really depend upon the truth of the Incarnation? *Must we abandon the claim that the Incarnation adds something distinctive and essential to our set of Christian social principles?*

Have We Been Asking the Wrong Question? Tom Wright and the Social Implications of the Cross and the Kingdom

Given that our search for essential and "distinctive" social principles founded primarily upon the Incarnation has so far been largely fruitless, we do well to ask at this point whether we have been (as the saying goes) "barking up the wrong tree." Perhaps we have fallen into what Tillich called "the Anglican heresy" after all, by assuming a centrality for the Incarnation among all the doctrines of the faith that it does not possess, and then expecting to find "distinctive" elements of Christian social teaching that stand or fall with it.

Anglican Bishop and Scripture scholar Tom Wright, however, encourages us not to take the Incarnation out of context of the gospel as a whole. The Incarnation, he claims, is certainly vital to the saving work of Jesus Christ on the Cross, and the inauguration of the Kingdom of God he came to bring "on earth as it is in heaven." Thus, it is a *sine qua non* of the heart of the gospel, presupposed in the good news of the Cross and the Kingdom. But the mystery of the Incarnation was never meant to stand on its own, with its own distinctive set of soteriological or social implications:

> We in the West, perhaps, ever since Chalcedon, or even Nicea, have read as the main text what the gospels treated as a presupposition. In all four gospels, Jesus is the embodiment

("incarnation") of Israel's God. But this is not the gospels' main theme. Not even, I think, John's. The main theme is that, in and through Jesus the Messiah, Israel's God reclaims his sovereign rule over Israel and the world. …

What we call "incarnation" thus lies at the heart of, and gives depth and meaning to, the kingdom-and-cross combination that, in turn, lies at the heart of the four gospels. … The "divinity" of Jesus is not to be separated from his kingdom work, his cross-accomplishing kingdom work. It does not, as a dogma, "come away clean."[880]

Much of the heart of Wright's own work has been to remind the Church of what he takes to be the central message the gospel: God has become King in and as Jesus Christ, who defeated the forces of evil and sin on the Cross, and now reigns as the rightful Lord of all:

What I miss, right across the Western tradition, at least the way it has come through to the twentieth and twenty-first centuries, is the devastating and challenging message I find in the four gospels: *God really has become king — in and through Jesus!* A door has been opened that nobody can shut. Jesus is now the world's rightful Lord, and all other lords are to fall at his feet.[881]

---

[880] Wright, *How God Became King*, p. 240 and 189-190. Some Scripture scholars would dispute Wright's understanding here of the main theme of St. John's Gospel. For example, *The Ignatius Catholic Study Bible* tells us that "the most pervasive theme in John, which in many ways is the master key that unlocks the Gospel as a whole, is the revelation of God as a family. Nearly every chapter is marked by familial language that explains the inner life of God as well as our relation to God through the grace of divine generation. The 'divine family' of God revealed as Father, Son, and Spirit is the towering mystery of the Fourth Gospel" (p. 158). Moreover, John's Gospel begins and ends with a solemn confession of the mystery of the Incarnation (Jn 1:14; 20:28, 31) as the mystery that supremely manifests the love of God for humanity (Jn 3:16; cf. I Jn 4:9), and as the gateway to the great mystery of God's eternal, intra-Trinitarian love (see 13:1-3, the preamble to the Trinitarian mystery unfolded in chapters 13-17).
[881] Ibid. (Wright), p. 37.

What matters is that we are constantly brought back in touch with the center of the faith: that Jesus "gave himself for our sins, to rescue us from the present evil age, according to the will of God our Father" (Gal 1:4). Each element of that is vital; each informs and undergirds the others. The loving purpose of God, working through the sin-forgiving death of Jesus, frees us from the power of the "present evil age," so that we may be part of God's new age, his new creation, launched already when Jesus rose from the dead, awaiting its final completion when he returns, *but active now through the work of the rescued rescuers*, the redeemed human beings called to bring redeeming love into the world — the justified justice-bringers, the reconciled reconcilers, the Passover People. ...

The gospel was — and is — the powerful announcement that the world has a new lord and the summons to give him believing allegiance. The reason the gospel carries this power is that it's true: on the cross Jesus really did defeat the powers that held people captive. For the early Christians, the revolution *had happened* on the first Good Friday. The "rulers and authorities" really had been dealt their death blow. This didn't mean, "So we can escape this world and go to heaven," but "Jesus is now Lord of this world, and we must live under his lordship and announce his kingdom." The revolution had begun. It had to continue. Jesus's followers were not simply its beneficiaries. They were to be its agents.[882]

The reign of God on earth through Jesus Christ, however, will only spread by means of the Cross: that is, by the suffering love of his Spirit-empowered disciples, following in the footsteps of their Master. **In short, for Wright the *kenosis* of the Son of God is not so much an abstract theory of the Incarnation as it is an understanding of the Cross as the only way that God's Kingdom ultimately can triumph in this world:**

---

[882] Wright, *The Day the Revolution Began*, p. 364-365 and 391-392.

[T]he victory of the cross will be implemented through the means of the cross. ...

[T]hose who are eager for "bringing the kingdom," for social and cultural renewal in our day, can easily forget that the revolution that began on the cross only works through the cross. And those who are eager to "save souls for heaven" are likely to regard suffering simply as something through which most of us some of the time and some of us most of the time will have to pass, rather than as something *by means of which* the rescuing love of God is poured out into the world. The latter is closer to the mark. ... [S]uffering or dying for the faith is not simply a necessary evil, the inevitable concomitant of following a way that the world sees as dangerously subversive. Suffering and dying is *the way by which the world is changed*. This is how the revolution continues. ...

Did we really imagine that, while Jesus would win his victory by suffering, self-giving love, we would implement that same victory by arrogant, self-aggrandizing force of arms? (Perhaps we did. After all, James and John, so close to Jesus as anyone, made exactly this mistake in Luke 9:54 and again in Mark 10:35-40). ... Once you understand the kind of revolution Jesus was accomplishing, you understand why it would go on being necessary for it to be implemented step by step, not all at one single sweep, and why those steps have to be, every one of them, steps of the same generous love that took Jesus to the cross.[883]

Wright sees this call to Christian discipleship and mission inevitably leading to confrontation with the social idols that warp and destroy human life (the inordinate lust for sex, wealth, and power — what he sums up as the reign of the false gods "Aphrodite, "Mammon," and "Mars"). Social injustice is to be

---

[883] Ibid., p. 366, 368, and 374.

challenged through non-violent love in action, for the sake of true social justice and peace, by a faith-filled and Spirit-filled people who confess only Jesus as the Lord of all:

> Mission, as seen from the New Testament perspective, is neither about "saving souls for heaven" nor about "building the kingdom on earth." It is the Spirit-driven, cross-shaped work of Jesus's followers as they worship the true God and, confronting idols with the news of Jesus's victory, work *for* the signs of his kingdom in human lives and institutions.[884]

The Incarnation, therefore, is but the necessary presupposition and backdrop of all this: unless Jesus was God Incarnate, he could not have died for the sins of all, nor could he rightfully claim our allegiance as Lord of all — which means Lord of every aspect of our lives, including the socio-economic and political aspects. Indeed, the Evangelical tradition has emphasized that the proclamation of the Lordship of the risen and ascended Jesus Christ is a challenge to all other "lords" and "idols" that vie for our allegiance: charismatic government leaders, political parties or ideologies, ethnic, tribal, racial or national loyalties, institutional religious structures or even international unification schemes. Anything other than Christ that claims our highest loyalty is a sinful rejection of his rightful claim to reign as king.[885] And it is only in a world in which he reigns as king that conflict and social injustice can finally be ended. Thus, *the doctrine of the Incarnation plays a supporting role for the real center of the gospel, which is the revolutionary message of the Cross and the Kingdom.*

And yet, such are the unfathomable riches of the mysteries of the Christian faith that we can view each one of them from more than one angle, without necessarily contradicting ourselves. The various

---

[884] Ibid., p. 407.

[885] This perspective seems to lie near the heart of the work of Anglican Evangelical theologian Oliver O'Donovan as well; see, for example, his discussion of the famous Barmen declaration of German Christians (in response to the claims for allegiance made by Nazi ideology and Adolf Hitler) in *Resurrection and the Moral Order*, p. 90-97.

dimensions of the mysteries of Christ complement one another, and we can unfold the divinely revealed truth about him in various ways, leading to an ever greater fullness of understanding.

That is why, without contradicting anything that Bishop Wright has taught us, it could be said that just as the Incarnation is the presupposition and back-drop for the good news of the Cross and the Kingdom, so, at the same time, the Cross and the Kingdom are a *sine qua non* of the truth of the Incarnation. For the mystery of the Incarnation is that Jesus was (and is) "God self-limited in manhood" (Weston), "Emmanuel ... God with us" (Mt 1:23), the Divine Word who "became flesh and dwelt among us" (Jn 1:14; literally in Greek: "tabernacled" or "pitched his tent" among us). This means that the divine Son of God has really shared *all* the conditions of humanity — and truly to identify with our human condition and share our lot must include his descent into the very *depths* of our human state: right down to the utter weakness and helplessness of the manger in Bethlehem, and the experience of total human affliction on Calvary. Moreover, along the way the life journey of God Incarnate had to include proclaiming and living out the ways of God's Kingdom, for to "Seek first [God's] Kingdom and his righteousness" (Mt 6:33) is included in what it means to be *fully human* in the midst of God's world.

It is only because the Son of God was willing to do *all that*, with us and for us, that we can say he *truly* shared our lot, assuming the *fullness* of what it means to be human. After all, the Incarnation is not merely about a moment: not just the moment of the Annunciation or the manifestation of his coming among us at the first Christmas. Nor is it merely the truth that Jesus was, in the abstract, one person in two natures, fully human and fully divine. It is that truth played out and actualized *in chronological time and in an authentically human life-journey*. The proclamation and living out of the ways of the Kingdom — and the persecution and suffering this inevitably entails in a fallen world — *all this is included in the mystery of the Incarnation, the fulfilment of what it means for God to take flesh and dwell among us as one of us*. This is what it necessarily means for God to become *fully human* in self-giving love, as he intended humanity to be. Moreover, it is only because the divine Son, out of his infinite love for us, was willing to assume the fullness of our human condition that he is now worthy to be praised, honored and adored as the rightful King of humanity, and the rightful Lord of all.

Saint Paul expresses this with matchless beauty when he writes to the Philippians about the divine Son "emptying himself" (*ekenosen*: "pouring himself out"), taking the form of a servant: humbling himself, first of all by being "born in the likeness of men," and ultimately by sharing our "human form" unto death, "even death on a cross" (Phil 2:7-8). "Therefore" (i.e., "For that very reason") God has "highly exalted him," raising him to new and glorified life in his human nature, and calling all people everywhere to bow the knee and confess that "Jesus Christ is Lord, to the glory of God the Father" (2:9-10). **In other words,** ***God's incarnation as an expression of his infinite love for us, even unto death on a cross, is what makes Jesus truly our Lord and Savior, and rightful King of the coming reign of God.***

The book of Hebrews tells us much the same thing. In a passage that we emphasized in Part Two, Chapter One of this book, the author of Hebrews says that the divine Son, out of his great love for us "for a little while was made lower than the angels," which even included "tasting death for every one" (Heb 2:9). Read in context, these phrases refer primarily to the sufferings of temptation that Christ shared with us, but implicitly they have a much wider resonance:

> For it was fitting that he, for whom and by whom all things exist, in bringing many sons to glory, should make the pioneer of their salvation perfect through suffering. For he who sanctifies and those who are sanctified have all one origin. *That is why he is not ashamed to call them brethren.* … Since, therefore, the children share in flesh and blood, *he himself likewise partook of the same nature,* that through death he might destroy him who has the power of death, that is the devil, and deliver those who through fear of death were subject to lifelong bondage. … *Therefore he had to be made like his brethren in every respect, so that he might become a merciful and faithful high priest in the service of God,* to make expiation for the sins of the people. For because he

himself has suffered and been tempted, he is able to help those who are tempted. …

For we have not a high priest who is unable to sympathize with our weaknesses, but one who in every respect has been tempted as we are, yet without sinning. Let us then with confidence draw near to the throne of grace, that we may receive mercy and find grace to help in time of need. (Heb 2:9-18; 4:15-16; italics mine)

In fact, one could say that the completion of the Incarnation even includes the incorporation into Christ of all the faithful in his Body the Church, and ultimately into the final Kingdom of God at the end of time. For Christ's "body" is not only his earthly flesh and blood, now risen and glorified, but the mystical extension of his body in his Church (e.g. I Cor 12:27). In this present age, therefore, we are to do "the work of ministry, building up the body of Christ" (Eph 4:12), so that ultimately "we are to grow up in every way into him who is the head, into Christ" (4:15) — and even now God the Father "has put all things under his feet and has made him head over all things for the Church, which is his body, the fullness of him who fills all in all" (Eph 1:23). **Thus, even the mission of the Church to proclaim and live the Cross and the Kingdom is, in the end, all about seeking the *pleroma* of Christ in his Body, the fullness and completion of the mystery of the Incarnation when Christ finally will reign as Lord of all.**

Seen from one angle, therefore, the gospel is all about the Incarnation: the Crib, the Cross, and the proclamation of the Kingdom are all moments and subsets of this great mystery.

If all this is true, then perhaps we are not remiss in seeking to find "distinctive" and "essential" social implications of the Incarnation. The whole vast mystery of the Incarnation, after all, may have ramifications which go beyond the ramifications of each of its parts. We should be especially encouraged to look for them by the fact that the great incarnational *kenosis* passage in Philippians 2 (discussed above) occurs in the context of St. Paul's exhortations to the Christians

593

in Philippi to practice "humility," "love," "affection," and "sympathy" toward one another (Phil 2:1-4). "Have this mind among yourselves, which was in Christ Jesus," St. Paul wrote (2:5). In other words, he who was originally "in the form of God" has shown us the Way: we are to love one another as he has loved us (Jn 13:34), according to the very pattern he gave us in the Incarnation.

The Social Implications of Kenoticism

Let's remind ourselves of the terrain we covered in the previous chapters of this book. According to the Kenotic stream of interpretation, the doctrine of the Incarnation means that God came among us in the form of a servant; through an act of self-limitation, the divine Son shared with us all the conditions of human life from the perspective of a human range of consciousness, even unto death, to reveal to us the truth about God and to bring us salvation. This human experience was taken into his divine nature, and now forms the touchstone for his deepest compassion for the joys, struggles and sorrows of all humanity.

As the Gospel tradition has it, he was born in a cattle stall, and as a child became a political refugee in Egypt. He later lived and worked in the rural village of Nazareth as a carpenter, then followed a divine call to travel as a penniless preacher, teacher, and healer in Galilee, with nowhere to lay his head. Finally, abandoned by his friends and unjustly accused, he was nailed to a cross. **In short, God the Son, "self-limited in manhood," has known what it is to be poor, to walk the way of struggle for truth and love, and even to suffer injustice and total human affliction as one of us.**

Understood in this "kenotic" way, all of these fully human experiences have been assumed into the divine nature of the Son of God, and this carries with it four vital implications for Christian social theology.

1) *A kenotic interpretation of the Incarnation means that we can affect, in the most profound way, the Heart of God the Son*

By causing suffering to our neighbors through cruelty or neglect, *we actually cause suffering to the "Heart" of the Son of God himself,* in the mystery of his divine person and divine nature, and especially in his capacity for compassion for us. If Kenoticism is true, we cannot escape this conclusion. When the Son was risen and ascended to new life by the Father, he took with him into the heavenly realm, in and through his human nature, a deepened capacity to empathise and sympathise with those who are tempted and afflicted, for he himself had journeyed through the human experience of temptation and affliction (Heb 2:18, 4:15). This human experience, now present in his unfading human memory as the risen Savior, and also preserved in the unfading store of experience in his divine nature, is the touchstone of the closest possible compassion for his creatures. **His own compassionate Heart, both human and divine, therefore, is inextricably bound to the fate of the hearts, minds, and bodies of the people he came to save.** This is why St. Paul heard him say on the road to Damascus, "I am Jesus, whom you are persecuting" (Acts 9:5): by arresting and imprisoning the early Christians, Paul had been persecuting Jesus himself. This is also the underlying truth in Christ's parable about the Judgment Day — establishing this parable as *literally*, and not just metaphorically true — when Jesus said that he will turn to the righteous of all the nations and say: "[F]or I was hungry and you gave me food, I was thirsty and you gave me drink, I was a stranger and you welcomed me, I was naked and you clothed me, I was sick and you visited me, I was in prison and you came to me. ... *Truly, I say to you, as you did it to one of the least of these my brethren, you did it to me*" (Mt 25: 35-40).

For all of its occasional lapses into sentimentalism, here is a vital element of truth in Catholic devotion to the Sacred Heart of Jesus. For whenever we are cruel or indifferent to our neighbors in need, and whenever we wantonly neglect our own bodily and spiritual needs, we grieve the Son of God's own heart of love, both human and divine. As

The Incarnation

Pope Pius XI wrote in his encyclical *Miserentissumus Redemptor* (Most Merciful Redeemer, 1928):

> The sins of men and their crimes committed in every age were the cause why Christ was delivered to death, and now also they would of themselves bring death to Christ, joined with the same grief and sorrows, since each several sin in its own way is held to renew the passion of Our Lord: "Crucifying again to themselves the Son of God, and making him a mockery" (Heb 6:6). ... and so, even now, in a wondrous yet true manner, we can and ought to console that Most Sacred Heart, which is constantly wounded by the sins of thankless men.[886]

To be sure, the truth of these biblical and papal statements must be carefully expressed, lest in speaking of the Heart of Jesus as continually vulnerable to compassion and grief, we contradict the truth of his resurrection and his glorified life in heaven. We shall need to return to the metaphysics of all this in the second volume in this series. Moreover, the cult of the Sacred Heart has traditionally focused on consoling Christ primarily through prayer, and devotion to his Heart in the Blessed Sacrament.[887] **But the neighbors whom we daily bless or oppress, curse or care for, are Jesus Christ's very brothers and sisters, tied to him by the closest possible bonds of compassion. To love them is to love him as well, in the mystery of his Heart.**

Bishop Frank Weston famously expressed this same truth in the conclusion of his speech at the 1923 Anglo-Catholic Congress in London:

> When you come out from before your tabernacles, you must walk with Christ, mystically present in you, through the streets of this country, and find the same Christ in the people of your cities and

---

[886] Pope Pius XI, *Miserentissimus Redemptor*, in *Papal Encyclicals: 1901-1939* (Raleigh: McGrath, 1981), article 13, p. 325.
[887] Timothy O'Donnell, *Heart of the Redeemer* (San Francisco: Ignatius Press, 1989), p. 171-182 and 277-278.

in your villages. You cannot claim to worship Jesus in the tabernacle if you do not pity Jesus in the slum. ... It is folly, it is madness, to suppose that you can worship Jesus in the sacrament and Jesus on the throne of glory when you are sweating Him in the bodies and souls of his children. ... You have your Mass, you have your altars, you have begun to have your tabernacles. Now go out into the highways and hedges, and look for Jesus in the ragged and the naked, in the oppressed and the sweated, in those who have lost hope and in those who are struggling to make good. Look for Jesus in them: and when you find Him, gird yourselves with His towel of fellowship, and wash His feet in the person of His brethren.[888]

2) *A kenotic understanding of the Incarnation thereby establishes compassionate love as the central Christian social principle*

As we have seen, even without belief in a kenotic Incarnation of God in Christ, one could legitimately hold that Jesus of Nazareth taught and lived with compassion, following the will of his Father by the Holy Spirit, and that this justifies compassionate love as a central Christian social principle. **A kenotic model of the Incarnation, however, ties together love for God and humanity, Christ's Two Great Commandments (Mt 22:34-40), in the closest possible way, giving us the most powerful motive for prioritizing and practicing compassion.** *If the exercise of compassionate love for our neighbours is the principal way given to us by which we can love the Lord in return, for all his love for us, then it should stand at the very center of Christian social theology.* Anglican theologian Stuart Headlam (d. 1924) summed it up well long ago: "You are literally, as he himself said, feeding, clothing, housing Jesus Christ when you are feeding, clothing, housing any human beings; bad food,

---

[888] Cited in Mark D. Chapman, "Christ and the Gethsemane of Mind: Frank Weston Then and Now," in *Anglican Theological Review*, Spring, 2003, p. 284. Chapman also cites a prayer by Weston expressing somewhat similar sentiments: "Eternal Love, God, my Father, truly I did not see Thee in others when I hurt them in soul and body; I did not see Thee in the hungry, the ragged, the sick, the unhappy; I did not even see Thee in myself when doing sin" (p. 290).

ugly clothes, dirty houses, not only injure the body, but injure the soul; nay more, they do great injury unto God himself."[889]

By way of contrast, consider the central principles of capitalism. In *Essays Catholic and Radical* (1983), Michael Langford argued that the foundation of Adam Smith's whole capitalist philosophy (as Smith himself confessed) was set out in his *Theory of Moral Sentiments*. Smith claimed that there is a "natural" tendency for human beings to sympathise with and emulate the rich, and to recoil from poverty, and on this principle he based the whole capitalist economic order.[890]

From an authentically Christian perspective, however, we can say that it was by identifying with our human poverty, and finding there a touchstone for deepest compassion for our afflictions, that the divine Son has acted to reverse this "natural" tendency (a tendency which is not "natural" at all, of course, but a symptom of original sin and its corrosive effects on human attitudes and relationships). Prior to the Incarnation and passion of the Son, to abuse or ignore the poor and helpless was to abuse or ignore the needs of the children of God, violating God's good purposes for human life, and betraying God's trust as our Creator. But now, as a result of his incarnate life and passion, to abuse or neglect those in need is also deeply to affect the very heart of God the Son himself. Now we can draw nearer to God than ever before by serving the poor, the afflicted, and the lost. **For the risen Jesus Christ must surely have a compassionate "bias to the poor,"[891] a special bond with them and concern for their plight, not because they are necessarily "better" than other**

[889] Attributed to Headlam by Kenneth Leech in *True God*, p. 247, although the specific work by Headlam referenced there is inaccurate.
[890] Michael Langford, "Hard Times: Catholic Theology and the Critique of Capitalism," in Leech and Williams, *Essays Catholic and Radical*, p. 270.
[891] Anglican Bishop David Sheppard of Liverpool used this phrase in his book of the same title, *Bias to the Poor* (London: Hodder and Stoughton, 1983), but did not give it adequate theological foundation. Roman Catholic social teaching phrases it as a "preferential love for the poor" (*Catechism of the Catholic Church*, entry 2448).

people, but simply because they suffer the most, as he once suffered.

It might be objected that Christ's compassion is merely personal, focusing on the personal needs of each individual, rather than having anything to do with unjust social structures. It is not possible, however, to make such a sharp distinction. Human beings do not exist as isolated individuals, but within a whole socio-economic context that deeply affects their lives. *To have authentic compassion for any human being, therefore, means to be concerned for the totality of their well-being, including the extent to which the social and economic structures in which they live warp, disfigure and hamper the fulfilment of their human nature, and their growth in the likeness of God.*

Here we need to be clear, however, that in defining compassionate love as "the central Christian social principle," we are *not* saying that it is the single foundation upon which everything in the Church's social teaching can be based, and from which everything else can be deduced.[892] As we have already seen, the doctrines of God, Creation,

---

[892] In recent years, some theologians have thrust the doctrine of the Trinity into this foundational position, without realizing its limitations in this regard. In *Christ the Key* (2010), Katheryn Tanner did her best to set the record straight. She argued that the *vast differences* between human and divine persons, and between human societies and the divine Trinitarian society, make any simple equation between human relationships and the Trinity difficult to conceive:

> Direct translation of the trinity into a social program is problematic because, unlike the peaceful and perfectly loving mutuality of the trinity, human society is full of suffering, conflict, and sin. Turned into a recommendation for social relations, the trinity seems unrealistic, hopelessly naïve, and, for that reason, perhaps, even politically dangerous. To a world of violent, corrupt, and selfish people, the trinity seems to offer only the feeble plaint: "Why can't we all just get along?"…

> The trinity tells us what human relations should be like ideally. The understanding of humans as creatures and sinners tells us what sort of

The Incarnation

Humanity, the Cross, and the Kingdom each have their own role to play in this mosaic (for example, in establishing inalienable human dignity, and a basis for human rights).

Compassionate love, flowing from the divine Son's love for us in the Incarnation, is "central" in much the same way that a transept in a cathedral is central: everything passes through it and connects with it, but the cathedral as a whole is much greater than just its transept. **Thus, loving others with compassionate love, as we have been loved by the incarnate Son, and with the intention of loving him back, gathers up the social truths established by other Christian doctrines and motivates them for action. So, for example, we are moved in a special way to seek for human rights for all, and for the relief of the poor from hunger and disease, by the desire to love and serve the one who loved us in our need — the compassionate Heart of Jesus — whose Heart has a special bond of compassion for the plight of all who suffer (Mt 25: 31-46). In other words, the human intellect can establish the social implications of many Christian doctrines, but what moves the heart in an affective and powerful way to pursue them is a pure desire to love the Heart of Jesus, the Son of God, present in the struggles and sufferings of all people, and whose compassionate love extends to all.**

3) *A kenotic understanding of the Incarnation establishes the pattern for attaining true compassion*

Compassion divorced from truth quickly descends into mere sentimentalism or ideological blindness. As a result, all too often efforts at social reform or social revolution end up doing as much harm as good (one thinks, for example, of the results of the French Revolution in the 1790s, and the Russian Revolution of 1917). We are called by the Incarnation, however, to strive to attain a well-informed compassion that transcends social and cultural barriers, even as the

---

approximation of the ideal we are in fact capable of. (*Christ the Key*, p. 221, and 228-229)

Son of God became incarnate in a kenotic way in our world, and thereby gained the closest possible compassion for our human condition.

Alone, the doctrine of Creation gives us a benevolent, though somewhat aloof Creator. Some versions of Two-Nature Christology (as we saw in Part One of this book) claim that God in Christ shared our human condition to some extent, but always tempered by his omniscient perspective on events. **According to Kenoticism, however, God has come to know what it is to be human "from the inside," i.e., from a fully human perspective on events. As Jesus of Nazareth, he has suffered as we suffer, and struggled as we struggle.[893] We are thereby called to love our afflicted brothers and sisters in a similar way,** *as best we can attaining true compassion, trying to understand the plight of the spiritually and materially poor from their perspective.* Evangelical Anglican theologian John Stott spelled out what this means in his book *Issues Facing Christians Today* (1999):

> If this Christian mission is to be modelled on Christ's mission, it will surely involve for us, as it did for him, an entering into other people's worlds. In evangelism, it will mean entering into their thought world, and the world of their tragedy and lostness, in order to share Christ with them where they are. In social activity it will mean a willingness to renounce the comfort and security of our own cultural background in order to give ourselves in service to people of another culture, whose

---

[893] Given that the Kenotic Model of the Incarnation that I have defended in this book entails that Jesus was necessarily infallible and sinless in his human soul, some might object that this model undermines my claim that "As Jesus of Nazareth, he [the divine Son] has suffered as we suffer, and struggled as we struggle." Throughout this book, however, I have endeavored to show that, according to the metaphysics of Moderate KM, while Christ's divine identity entails that he was *always victorious* in his struggles to grow in conscious apprehension of truth and the practice of virtue, *it does not entail that he had no struggles in these aspects of his human life at all* (see above: Part One, Chapters Four and Five, and Part Two, Chapter Two).

needs we may never before have known or experienced. Incarnational mission, whether evangelistic or social or both, necessitates a costly identification with people in their actual situations.[894]

This is evidently the New Testament pattern of Christian mission as well. In *The Power of the Cross*, Graham Tomlin has shown how St. Paul reached out to the Corinthians in a kenotic fashion in order to share the gospel with them in the most fruitful way:

> Paul decided to work with his hands in order to be in a position to reach the poorer levels of society in Corinth, rather than just the rich. Paul's evangelistic reasons for this course of action [in I Corinthians 9] ... has a double edge. It means partly the benefits of being able to reach a greater number and variety of people, but it also included the idea that he might "share in its blessings." This tactic is in part an evangelistic strategy, but not purely so: it is also "soteriologically significant." There is an inner dynamic in the gospel that if Paul is to share in its benefits, he will need to take the same self-lowering path taken by the Christ who was crucified. ...
>
> The true response to the God who saves through a crucified Messiah is a life of voluntary servanthood, self-lowering love, distinctly different from the attitude shown by his opponents, and even his supporters in Corinth.[895]

An example of this kenotic love-in-action can be seen in the life and witness of St. Roque Gonzalez (1578-1628). Devoting himself to serving the needs of the oppressed Indian tribes under Spanish rule in South America, St. Roque rooted his apostolate, first of all, in identification with the people he came to help. He learned to speak their language, and to share their cultural life (to the extent compatible

---

[894] John Stott, *Issues Facing Christians Today* (Basingstoke: Marshalls, 1984), p. 21.
[895] Tomlin, *The Power of the Cross*, p. 95 and 98.

with his Catholic faith): eating their food, living in their houses, and witnessing first-hand the tragic injustices that they suffered. By the end of his life he had established Jesuit missions and largely self-governing refuges (called "reductions") for tens of thousands of native Indians throughout Paraguay, southern Brazil, northeastern Argentina, and Uruguay. The effort was lauded even by the anti-Catholic French *philosophe* Voltaire:

> [T]he Paraguayan missions ... had arrived at what is perhaps the highest degree of civilization to which it is possible to lead a young people .... In those missions, law was respected, morals were pure, a happy brotherliness bound men together, the useful arts and even some of the graceful sciences flourished, and there was abundance everywhere.[896]

In concrete terms today, this means that the Incarnation calls middle and upper class Christians, where possible, to spend time among the poor and oppressed, to become more aware of their true needs, to listen to their perspectives — and in some cases to their demands as well. As St. Teresa of Calcutta once said: "Today it is very fashionable to talk *about* the poor. Unfortunately it is very unfashionable to talk *with* them."[897]

Authentic, incarnational presence and listening inevitably will mean that in addition to supporting public and private charities for those already poor and dispossessed (and beyond the ideology of benevolent paternalism that has predominated in Christian social thought in the past), *Christians must open their eyes and ears to the need for the reform of society, so that it no longer produces an underclass of deprivation and powerlessness in the first place.*[898] Fair and

---

[896] Alban Butler, *Butler's Lives of Saints: New Full Edition; November,* David Hugh Farmer, ed. (Collegeville, MN: The Liturgical Press, 1997), p. 126.
[897] Cited in Brandon Vogt, *Saints and Social Justice: A Guide to Changing the World* (Huntingdon, IN: Our Sunday Visitor, 20140, p. 26.
[898] On Anglican theology and benevolent paternalism, see Rowan Williams, "Liberation Theology and the Anglican Tradition," in R. Williams and D. Nicholls, *Politics and Theological Identity* (London: The Jubilee Group, 1984), p. 28-29.

sufficient access for all to health care and educational opportunities will therefore become a Christian priority in the social sphere.[899] These services provide the social foundation for individuals to make the best of themselves, and to develop their God-given gifts and talents in ways that enable them to flourish and to serve the common good. In addition, to remove the state of relative powerlessness of the working classes, new forms of social ownership should be explored, including profit-sharing arrangements, employee share ownership, and worker representation on company Boards.[900] In other words, there ought to be a wide scope for exploration of new forms of ownership and production toward what Chiara Lubich has called "an economy of communion,"[901] that is, of participation and cooperation among free and dignified persons — rather than an economy dominated by stifling bureaucratic government control on the one hand, or cutthroat private competition and greed on the other. **In short, the Incarnation, understood in a kenotic way, calls us to do what we can to empathise and sympathise more deeply with the sufferings,**

---

[899] I have not used the common phrase "equality of opportunity" here, for good reason. First, it is impossible to attain as a social ideal: to some extent there will always be privileged pathways of some kind or other to social advancement and rewards. For example, the mere fact that most children grow up in their own families means that they will not have entirely equal opportunities in life: some families will foster their academic and social achievement, while other families will hinder their development. Second, the attempt to hammer the ideal of full equality of opportunity into reality in socialist countries has inevitably led to centralized, uniform, government provision of health and education services for all — a state of affairs that is usually corrosive of academic freedom, political liberty, pluralism, efficiency of delivery of the services offered, and consumer choice. It could be that government subsidized vouchers for health care and education, for example, would open fairer access to such services for the lower classes (and better delivery of services for all) than the more centralized, bureaucratically controlled, "one-size-fits-all" solutions usually favored by those on a quest for complete equality of opportunity.

[900] On this see Pope St. John Paul II, encyclical letter *Laborem Exercens* (Through Work, 1981), no. 14.

[901] See Luigino Bruni, "Chiara's Economy of Communion: When a charism changes even the economy" in *Nuova Umanità* n.177, vol.XXX, 2008, accessed online at http://www.edc-online.org/en/publications/papers/english-papers. htm .

needs, and perspectives of the poor, the powerless, and the oppressed, just as God himself has done with us.

It is important to add here, however, that middle and upper class Christians should not automatically assume that concerns about "ownership" or civil and economic "rights" are always the primary concern of the aggrieved and the downtrodden. Just as important, if not more so in some circumstances, is the desire of most people not to be treated as the mere *objects* of government programs or corporate investment (one thinks, for example, of the social failure of the vast government housing projects erected in the 1960s and 1970s in many western nations, and the sudden incursion — and often just as sudden exodus — of large factories in what had been settled and functioning towns and neighborhoods). The need is for a more *participatory* approach in which people have a say in the future of their own cherished local communities.

In this respect, Anglican social theology and Catholic social teaching have converged in the twentieth and twenty-first centuries. There is a common recognition of the vital importance of intermediate associations (mid-way, so to speak, between the individual and the state), communities in which people often find their worth and identity: this includes the "natural" communities into which one is born, such as the family, and non-governmental ethnic or national identity groups, and also local "voluntary" associations such as parishes, schools, charitable groups, clubs, drop-in centers (including local pubs), small businesses, local trade unions and professional associations. It is within these intermediate-level social associations that people often find a place where they are known by name and welcomed; where they can take part in relationships of mutual dependence and personal care both given and received; where they find ways to make their own personal contribution to the common good, and feel as if they count for something. All of this can serve to promote their human dignity and their growth in virtue. Central governments and mega-corporations need to insure that their social programs and private investment initiatives respect, support, and cooperate with the positive role played by intermediate groups, and must not seek to undermine or replace them.

All this should serve to remind us that the Incarnation alone cannot be the sole foundation of the social implications of Christianity. Here the doctrine of the Trinity also has its place. For the revealed truth is that human beings are created in the image of a God who is a Trinity of divine and equal persons in an eternal communion of mutual love and self-giving; this is why we find our own true fulfilment by participating in human communities of mutual love and respect. This Trinitarian pattern of communion can play a key role in the foundation of any society that seeks to embody the principles of the Kingdom of God that Jesus preached. Moreover, this pattern serves as a prophetic challenge to all social groups and structures — even to intermediate associations (however "natural" or indispensable they otherwise may be) — lest they allow themselves to be infected by the contagion of the sins of their members, and end up breaking down rather than building up human dignity and the common good.[902]

Some have complained that Kenoticism by implication promotes the maintenance of oppressive social hierarchies (such as patriarchy and aristocracy); it merely "softens" this oppression through encouraging social condescension by the wealthy and powerful, after the pattern of the condescension of the divine Son in assuming our human condition, limiting himself to come among us and come to our aid. In his book *Divine Humanity* (2011), David Brown found an element of truth in this

---

[902] Rowan Williams rightly sounded a cautionary note, therefore, in the Church's endorsement of "natural" social groupings such as the family or the nation: "The question the Church is authorised to ask of any human association is whether it is making it more or less difficult for people to grow into a maturity in which they are free to give to one another and nourish one another .... So it will not do simply to think of the Church uncovering the rationale of natural human associations. The Church, I suggest, judges and interacts with all of these, and in some circumstances gives thanks for them just as in others it questions or resists them." Rowan Williams, *On Christian Theology* (Malden, MA: Blackwell Publishing, 2000), p. 236-237.

critique. In the past, Kenoticism all too often seemed to promote socio-economic structures of benevolent paternalism:

> What one misses in all these [Kenotic] writers is any real sense of the need to get alongside the person one seeks to benefit: instead of just handing out largesse, actually empowering the weak. Perhaps it was simply the overwhelming nature of the great contrast between God and ourselves that led them astray. ...[903]

> I suggest that the reason theology has been slow to pursue such lines is because of residual attachment to notions of hierarchy of being, deep seated as these are within Christian thinking. Not only is God still thought of as at the head of a great chain of being but also we continue to think of ourselves in consequence as superior to the rest of creation. ...[904]

> The reason why we do and should value God so highly is because of what he has done for us, not because he is simply in some sense higher up on the scale than we are. ... So to me even more problematic than the class and sexual assumptions in the various kenotic analogies is the unquestioned presupposition that in kenosis God was entering a *lower* form of existence rather than just a *different* kind of being. Of course, it was lower in the sense that there was less power, knowledge, and so on, but that does not carry with it any necessary implication of a lesser degree of value or potential fulfilment in this quite different form of existence. ...[905]

> Kenosis is the best language for what occurred in the incarnation not because God stepped down from a great height in order to become human (though true), but because the logic of creativity and love to which Christianity is already

---

[903] Brown, *Divine Humanity*, p. 190.
[904] Ibid., p. 191-192.
[905] Ibid., p. 192.

committed combine to imply a coming alongside the other in any such endeavor.[906]

Perhaps Brown overstated his case here, for *both* God's "stepping down" and his "coming alongside us" seem essential to understanding his love for us in the Incarnation, and its social implications.

First, there is clear biblical warrant for speaking of a scale or hierarchy of being, which includes a hierarchy of *worth*. For example, Psalm 8 speak of the majesty and glory of God above the heavens, and then of humanity as made just a "little less than God," crowned with its own glory and honor, and given dominion over all the other creatures of the world. The three steps of the scale of being (God, humanity, and other living creatures) are on full display here. Jesus tells us several times that God cares for all his creatures, but also calls us to "Look at the birds of the air; are you not of *more value* than they?" (Mt 6:26; Lk 12:24), and he thereby invites us to trust in God's care for us, because we are "*worth more* than many sparrows" to him — creatures he also cares for with his all-seeing providence (Mt 10:29-31; Lk 12:6-7).

Second, the Bible teaches that God should be of supreme value to us not only because of what he has done for us, but *also* because of his inestimable worth or "greatness." Psalm 145, for example, begins with three verses of sheer adoration of the greatness of God (as in verse 3: "Great is the Lord, and greatly to be praised, and his greatness is unsearchable") before proceeding to give thanks to the Lord for all his "wondrous works." Psalm 148 praises God for all his work of creation, and then closes with adoration of his greatness: "Let them praise the name of the Lord, for his name alone is exalted; his glory is above earth and heaven (148:13)." Psalm 150 sums it up in one verse "Praise him for his mighty deeds; praise him according to his excellent greatness" (150:2).

Third, the wonder of the Incarnation is precisely the amazing love of this infinitely great God that led him to "send his only Son into the

---

[906] Ibid., p. 200.

world" (I Jn 4:9) to restore to us the life of grace and the Holy Spirit which we had lost by our sins. And he did so not only by entering our "different" kind of being, but also by descending into the depths of our limited, broken, "lower" form of being, doomed to die: he "emptied himself, taking the form of a servant, being born in the likeness of men. And being found in human form he humbled himself and became obedient unto death, even death on a cross" (Phil 2:7-8). For our sake, he who was "rich" made himself "poor," so that by his poverty we might become rich (II Cor 8:9).

In short, a strong biblical argument could be made that God is worthy of adoration as inestimably greater in every perfection of being than we are (just as we are of greater value to him than all his other creatures, whom he also cares for); and his love for us expressed in the Incarnation was indeed the kenotic condescension of one who in some sense left the riches of the divine life of heaven for the relative lowliness and poverty of a human existence, and died for us on the Cross. The Incarnation is therefore an act of *authentically loving divine condescension*.[907]

---

[907] In her review of David Brown's *Divine Humanity*, Kathryn Tanner worried that by denying the element of divine condescension in the Incarnation, Brown was drifting away from clarity about *kenosis* itself: "Are we still talking about kenosis if that no longer involves any relinquishment of the higher position for the sake of the lower — no condescension, that is, within a hierarchical framing of the relation between God and creatures? ... [A]lterations of the usual metaphorical associations of kenosis leave me wondering whether the term has been broadened beyond recognition." Kathryn Tanner, "David Brown's *Divine Humanity*," in *Scottish Journal of Theology,* 68 (I), 2015, p. 109. But in the end, despite his misgivings about the hierarchy of being, Brown did not deny that *in some sense* "God stepped down from a great height in order to become human" (*Divine Humanity*, p. 200); what he denied was the social importance of that fact compared with the fact that the Incarnation also involved a "coming alongside" humanity in its suffering and struggles. My contention is that *both* aspects are essential to our understanding of the great love that he showed us, and the pattern for attaining true compassion that the Son of God gave to us in the Incarnation (Jn 1:14).

At the same time, if we accept a kenotic understanding of the Incarnation, then it need not provide social warrant for mere condescension by the upper and ruling classes toward the poor and the powerless; for as we have already seen, **Kenoticism also implies that** *the only way to attain authentic love and compassion for those in need is really to step down and come alongside them: to abandon one's comfortable distance from their plight, and come to share in it alongside them as much as possible, learning to understand the world of their need from their perspective.* **For God, "stepping down to us" in the Incarnation also involved "coming alongside us." This is precisely what made it such an astounding manifestation of his love for us, and establishes the pattern whereby (when our own afflictions are less severe) we should step down and come alongside others who, for the time being, are in greater need.**

All this about Christ "coming alongside us" is not to say that Kenoticism necessarily compels us to accept what came to be known as "Liberation Theology," in other words, seeing Jesus as our Marxist "comrade." To highlight the differences between the Kenotic and the Liberation approach, we can examine a passage on the Incarnation from the Roman Catholic Liberation theologian Gustavo Gutierrez. Gutierrez tells us that Christ's *kenosis* was an act of love and liberation, an act of solidarity and struggle:

> Thus, true Christian poverty has redemptive value. If the ultimate cause of man's exploitation and alienation is selfishness, the deepest reason for voluntary poverty is the love of neighbor. Christian poverty has meaning only as a commitment of solidarity with the poor, with those who suffer misery and injustice. The commitment is to witness to the evil which has resulted from sin and is a breach of communion. It is not a question of idealizing poverty but rather of taking it on as it is — an evil — to protest against it and to struggle to abolish it. As Ricoeur says, you cannot really be with the poor unless you are struggling against poverty. ... Christian poverty,

as an expression of love, is solidarity *with the poor,* and is a protest *against poverty.*[908]

For Gutierrez, therefore, Christ became incarnate among the poor and oppressed of Israel in order to protest against social evils, to struggle in solidarity with those suffering social injustice, and to proclaim the abolition of those social evils as God's plan for the Kingdom.

Liberation Theology, so conceived, suffered widespread critique in the final decades of the twentieth century. To begin with, it offered a much too narrow notion of Christian voluntary poverty. A Christian may indeed choose to embrace poverty in solidarity with the poor and oppressed, to live alongside them and share in their struggle for social justice — but Christian voluntary poverty is hardly limited to that form. Arguably, St. Francis of Assisi and the early Franciscan movement embraced voluntary poverty in order to protest against *the spiritual bondage caused by wealth and riches,* more than the social evils of poverty. At the same time, of course, by living among the poor as poor themselves, the early Franciscans gained a special, kenotic compassion for the most poor and outcast members of medieval society, especially lepers. Others have embraced a life of gospel simplicity in order to be maximally free and available to serve the immediate needs of the poorest of the poor (one thinks of St. Teresa of Calcutta and her Sisters of Charity), without prioritizing in their own charism a commitment to social action for the change of unjust social structures. This is not because Mother Teresa and her Sisters were *opposed* to social action or social change; they simply did not presume to know what form that action and change should take, and in any case, usually did not see it as their particular charism and calling directly to pursue it.

Moreover, the concern of Gutierrez and other theologians for human "liberation" was often held to be far too narrow. The divine Son did not take flesh among the poor and oppressed *solely* as an act of protest against poverty and injustice. ***Jesus Christ was concerned above all***

---

[908] Gustavo Gutierrez, *A Theology of Liberation* (Maryknoll, NY: Orbis Books, 1973), p. 300.

with the integral salvation of God's people in the Kingdom of God, a kingdom that would include God's benevolent reign over every aspect of human life: over the human mind with faith and truth, over the human will with love, over the human heart and affections with hope, over the human spirit in authentic prayer and true worship, over the human body with health and wholeness, and over human communities with justice and peace.

A specifically "Moderate" Kenotic Christology may take the Liberation theologians to task on another point. *Incarnational "solidarity with the poor" should not mean uncritical acceptance of the political demands of the poor and the powerless. For the divine Son Incarnate did not blindly accept all the perspectives of his oppressed people.* Though he took flesh as an oppressed Jew under the Romans, he spurned the moral and religious legalism characteristic of the scribes and the Pharisees, the revolutionary utopianism of the proto-Zealots of his time, and the narrow ethnic and religious nationalism so endemic among his countrymen. The divine Son was born among the poor of Israel, lived as one of them, addressed his ministry primarily to them, and believed that they above all would be able to welcome the message of the Kingdom (Lk 2:24, 5:18, 6:20-26, 9:58). But his vision of all social classes and sub-groups was unclouded by class hatred and racial or religious prejudice. Moreover, his realistic appraisal of fallen human nature would not allow him to throw in his lot with the utopian revolutionaries (Mt 7:3-5; Mk 7:20-23, 26:52; Lk 11:13, 18:9-14, Jn 6:15, 18:36). **In short, Kenoticism enables us to believe that Jesus the Son identified with the poor, walking with them and for them through all their joys and sorrows, struggles and afflictions, and yet looked with a sinless and critical eye on the illusions and prejudices of his own class and people. As Christians who seek to follow Jesus Christ in solidarity with the poor, we too must cleanse our consciences and our social vision of all social hatred and prejudice, by the power of his Holy Spirit.**

At first glance, one would think that the "Radical" Kenotic models of the Incarnation could offer a better analogy for this pattern for attaining true compassion than "Moderate" Kenotic models. After all, in Radical KM, the divine Son enters our human condition and assumes all its limitations by abandoning some or all of his divine prerogatives, so that he no longer has access (or full access) to his own omnipotence, omniscience, or omnipresence. It is by the power of the Holy Spirit alone that the Son of God himself, in the human nature that he assumed, overcomes the illusions and prejudices of the communities that nurtured and educated him. He literally achieved what we must try to achieve by the power of the Holy Spirit, on whom we too must rely.

On the other hand, Radical KM *exaggerates* the *kenosis* that is needed for attaining true compassion, plunging the divine Son totally, without remainder, into the condition of others. Moderate KM actually tracks closer to the pattern for attaining true social compassion that the divine Son gave to us in the Incarnation. Real compassion does not involve the complete mental abandonment of one's own, original worldview and social perspectives in order to enter into the perspectives of others. Rather, it is an addition without necessarily being a total subtraction, an addition ultimately leading to the formation a new synthesis. It calls for sharing in the condition of others to whatever extent may be possible, leading to closer empathy and sympathy for them, with the help of the Holy Spirit, *while at the same time putting that new range of experience into dialogue with elements of truth that one brought into the situation in the first place.* In other words, one doesn't gain true compassion by turning oneself into an *amnesiac* in order to experience and understand the situation of others. By continually putting the new perspectives gained into dialogue with one's original store of experience and knowledge, one thereby attains a true and wiser synthesis: a synthesis that is unlikely to be strictly bound by artificial barriers such as gender, race, class, or nationality. Our social perspectives are therefore *enriched* by doing what is needed to identify with others empathetically and sympathetically, not simply *replaced.* In this respect, Charles Gore's analogy for the Incarnation based on the human act of "redemptive sympathy" strikes a realistic chord:

> He must not abandon his own higher standing-ground if he is to benefit the object of his compassion; but remaining essentially what he was he must also find himself in the place

of the lower; he must come to look at things as he looks at them; he must learn them again from his point of view. This is ... how Origen would have us understand the mystery of the divine condescension. It is the grown one learning to speak as a child: it is the Divine putting Himself at the point of the view of the human.[909]

In the second volume of this study we will need to take a closer look at the metaphysics of the knowledge and consciousness of Christ. We have already seen some of the keys toward understanding this mystery in Part One, Chapter Four of this book, especially in our discussion of the contributions of Richard Swinburne and Thomas Morris to the logic of Moderate KM. There we spoke of the divine Son extending his divine mind or range of consciousness into an additional, limited, human range of consciousness and action, to which his properly divine mind has an "asymmetric accessing relationship." In this way the divine mind contains the contents of his human mind, but is not contained by the human mind of Jesus, and there is a "flow" of experience and knowledge between the two minds, analogous to the flow between the subconscious and conscious life of a single human person. Suffice it to say here that the proper pattern for attaining true social compassion is quite similar to this: it involves an extension of one's own mental life and range of experience into an *additional* range of knowledge and experience — the result of "identifying with the poor and oppressed" as much as possible — including and incorporating the contents of that additional experience and new knowledge into one's original store of experience and overall worldview.

In a similar way, Rowan Williams pointed out "how important it is to distinguish God's identification with the victim from some kind of divine approval of the victim's cause."[910] **God Incarnate, Jesus Christ, has the deepest possible compassion for oppressed groups, but this compassion does not amount to a blanket**

---

[909] Gore, *Dissertations*, p. 218-219.
[910] Williams, *Resurrection*, p. 78.

endorsement of their methods of redress (e.g. acts of revolutionary violence or terrorism), nor an automatic declaration of their innocence and social wisdom. Jesus alone is the fount of all wisdom and innocence;[911] as the Incarnate Son he is "full of grace and truth" (Jn 1:14), and therefore he has compassion for the struggles and afflictions of *all* individuals and *all* groups of people, even for those outside one's own oppressed group. The Cross, therefore, must not be turned into a narrow ideological weapon, as if Christ identifies only with the plight of *my* group, and not with the plight of another.[912]

4) *The Kenotic doctrine of the Incarnation calls us to ministries of caring in the form of in-person involvement and service*

An authentically "Kenotic" Christology tells us that we are to care for the afflicted as the divine Son has cared for us all (Phil 2:5-11): each in our own way, as circumstances permit, emptying ourselves, as St. Paul wrote, taking the form of servants — caring in-person with incarnate concern, that is, caring love embodied and in-the-flesh. We are called to do what Jesus asked us to do when at the Last Supper he "laid aside his garments, and girded himself with a towel. Then he poured water into a basin, and began to wash the disciples' feet .... [H]e said to them ...'If I, your Teacher and Lord, have washed your feet, you also ought to wash one another's feet. For I have given you an example, that you also should do as I have done to you" (Jn 13:4-5, 12-15).

Indeed, the example that Christ set for us throughout his earthly life echoes this Kenotic doctrine of the Incarnation. At the Last Supper, he said to his disciples: "For which is greater, one who sits at table or

---

[911] In Catholic theology, Mary too is innocent of sin, by divine grace, and grows into all wisdom, but only because her heart completely adheres to the Heart of Jesus at every step of her life journey, for he is the divine source of her wisdom and purity. Mary is then a sign of hope for the human race: that in Christ we too can become all that we were meant to be.
[912] Ibid., p. 78-80.

one who serves? Is it not the one who sits at table? But I am among you as one who serves" (Lk 22:27). And when he was instructing his disciples on the need for them to practice servant-leadership, he pointed to his own example as the Messiah who practiced voluntary servanthood and loving self-sacrifice, even unto death: "For the Son of Man also came not to be served but to serve, and to give his life as a ransom for many" (Mk 10:45).

In concrete, socio-economic terms, this means that supporting impersonal, bureaucratic programs for the needy will never be enough. Some Christians are apt to believe that their duty to care for the afflicted ends with their voting support for the welfare state, or their financial contributions to charity. But ministries of personal caring — of self-limiting, self-forgetful acts of love even to the point of personal self-sacrifice — are also vitally important: for example, visiting the housebound elderly or looking after elderly relatives, serving in soup kitchens for the poor, assisting at shelters for battered women and for women with crisis pregnancies, adopting a child or accepting a foster child into one's home, visiting the sick and those in prison, befriending immigrant families in one's neighborhood, and sharing the gospel with friends and colleagues. God the Son has shown us the way himself, when he came to our world to aid us in-person, in the flesh, taking the form of a servant — even, in the end, at terrible cost to himself. He did not just send us angelic or human emissaries. And we are called to do the same.

This divine pattern of love, even to the extent of personal sacrifice, is best preserved by a kenotic approach to the Incarnation. For in Two-Nature Christology, God's experience of loving identification with the human condition is held to be shielded, so to speak, by his absolute divine impassibility (Mascall), or at least greatly tempered by his omniscient perspective on events (e.g. in Brown's version of TNC). Thus, his saving work does not involve a true self-limitation to the point of full "identification" with human life, from the perspective of a fully human consciousness (on this see Part Two, Chapter One, above). In Kenoticism of any form, on the other hand, God the Son is seen as entering into the very depths of total human affliction in order to save us. For our sake he journeyed through the abyss of human suffering and injustice. God thereby shows that his love for us is so deep he is willing to bear any personal cost for our salvation.

Kenoticism on War and Peace, and Care for the Environment

All of this has led some writers to speculate that the kenotic pattern of God's love manifest in the Incarnation points Christians toward a totally self-sacrificial, pacifist stance on issues of war and peace. George F.R. Ellis put it this way in his essay "Kenosis as a Unifying Theme for Life and Cosmology":

> [T]he strong kenotic position of pacifism is the only truly profound way to deal with real evil, and its supposed lack of success is quite misleading: the true situation being that it is almost never tried, and if it were, things would often be radically different; the problem is that we do not have the courage and strength to try it, for it is an extremely costly road to go. If we regard other persons involved as always human *and always open to generosity invoked by sacrificial behavior*, we will be taking the high road and imitating the true nature of God, thus opening the way to true transformation. In contrast, the use of force is a way of responding to like with like; it does not have the power to transform the situation.[913]

It is the italicized portion of this quote, however, that should give us pause. "Radical" and "Pure" Kenoticism, as we discussed earlier in this book, may seem to call Christians to the total abandonment of all

---

[913] George F.R. Ellis, "Kenosis as a Unifying Theme for Life and Cosmology" in Polkinghorne, ed., *The Work of Love*, p. 125; italics mine. It should be noted that Ellis sees an absolute pacifist approach taken by society as a whole as impossible, because those committed to a non-coercive and non-violent stance, if they are to be consistent with their own principles, cannot compel the rest of society to restrict itself to kenotic forms of action. Thus, absolute kenotic love on issues of war and peace can only be practiced voluntarily by some, not imposed by law upon all.

comfort and earthly security for the sake of peace. This would seem the best "fit" with a model of the Incarnation that emphasizes that the divine Son actually abandoned some or all of his divine attributes in order to save us from evil. But as we have already seen (in Part Two, Chapter One of this book), God's love is not always kenotic in nature. To achieve some of his good purposes in history, he sometimes uses power as a determinative principle, rather than the power of self-limitation and self-sacrifice (e.g. he uses determinative power in bringing creatures into being *ex nihilo*, in raising Christ from the dead, and in the final resurrection and triumph over the unrepentant forces of evil at the end of time). To be sure, to achieve the *greatest* purposes of his love — the salvation of the lost — God utilizes the special power of his kenotic self-sacrifice in the Incarnation and on the Cross.[914] But he is not so naïve as to believe that all people are "always open to generosity invoked by sacrificial behavior;" he knows the depths of evil in human hearts (Jer 17:9; Lk 11:13); he knows that even the matchless, generous love manifested in the kenotic earthly life and death of his divine Son was not sufficient to convert the souls of many — either during the lifetime of Christ, or in any age thereafter — especially among the socially powerful. And it is precisely the powerful, addicted to the further expansion of their power, who are the ones principally responsible for acts of unjust and relentless aggression against peoples and nations.

The recourse to arms by Christians, therefore, has usually been seen as justified as last resort, to prevent the continuation or spread of violence and grievous injustice against the relatively innocent.[915] It should not be intended as an instrument of social transformation or salvation: it is merely "damage control" that aims to restore the tranquility of a reasonable social order so that the real kenotic work of salvation through Jesus Christ, and the mission of his Church, can be undertaken in peace. In fact, Ellis mentions a "just war theory with an

---

[914] Saint Thomas Aquinas, for example, wrote that the salvation of souls is a greater work of God than the creation of the whole world, because it has an eternal effect: *ST* I-II, 113, 9.
[915] On this see *Catechism of the Catholic Church*, entries 2307-2317.

explicit kenotic slant" that sounds more realistic. He envisages "policing and warlike action undertaken with minimal use of force, and that at all times offers the other a way out, and takes their humanity and needs into account."[916] In such situations, non-kenotic determinative power is used, but combined with kenotic limitations on military action, and supplemented by overtures of peace and reconciliation.

Some writers have found in Kenoticism an implicit call for the renunciation of humankind's powerful dominance over the biosphere. The need is said to be urgent for an abandonment of human striving for economic growth in favor of a radical simplification of lifestyle that is both environmentally "friendly" and sustainable. Here again, a Radical Kenotic understanding of the Incarnation would seem at first to fit best with this near total act of self-limitation and self-sacrifice: in this case, the abandonment of market models of economic growth in favor of a sustainable economic stagnation that sharply limits human impact on the natural world. While not going quite that far, Holmes Rolston, III sees some kind of environmental *kenosis* as necessary in the present global crisis of materialism and greed:

> The secular world looks for the management of nature, for reducing all nature to human resource, and plans a technology and an industry to accomplish that in the next millennium. But in that aspiration, humans only escalate their inherited desires for self-actualizing, tempted now into self-aggrandizement on scales never before possible. ... The Christian opportunity today is to limit such human aggrandizement on behalf of the five million other species who also reside on Earth. Such kenosis is a Christian calling for the next millennium.[917]

Rolston has offered us a false dichotomy here. There is surely a middle way between, on the one hand, the "secular management" of nature

---

[916] Ibid., p. 123.
[917] Holmes Rolston, III, "Kenosis and Nature" in Polkinghorne, ed., *The Work of Love*, p. 64-65.

that turns it into a mere instrument of economic growth (i.e., treating nature as a mere object of human determinative power and exploitation, with all the environmental damage to the planet, and resource depletion over time that this involves), and, on the other hand, a vision of human use and interaction with nature based solely on the notion of kenotic self-limitation.

From a biblical perspective, the governing principle of humanity's relationship with the biosphere is *stewardship*, not *kenosis*. Humanity was called from the very beginning to have "dominion" over the rest of creation (Gen 1:28), but this was to be a *responsible* dominion: we were to "till" the Garden of Eden and to "keep it" (Gen 2:15). The first term implies the reasonable use and development of natural resources to meet human needs — a non-kenotic form of relationship with nature — while the latter terms implies "protection," "keeping it safe," as something that ultimately belongs to God our Creator and not to us — which inevitably involves kenotic self-restraint by humanity in its exploitation of natural resources. It follows that kenotic "self-limitation" of the human management and use of the natural world is necessary to the extent that it is needed to achieve the goal of responsible stewardship.

In both cases that we have just surveyed, therefore, — the issue of war and peace, and the issue of environmental care — Kenoticism envisaged primarily according to Radical or Pure Kenotic models tends to distort the social implications of the Incarnation. The Moderate Kenotic Model of the Incarnation, on the other hand, offers a better analogy for the social ramifications of the doctrine. For with Moderate KM, the true *kenosis* of the divine Son in entering into all the conditions and limitations of human life as Jesus of Nazareth is coupled with his (uninterrupted) wise and providential care over the whole cosmos. In other words, with Moderate KM both kenotic and non-kenotic forms of Divine Love are operative *simultaneously*, just as they properly are in humanity's dealings with relentless aggressors on the international scene, and in human interaction with the environment.

Many have been inspired by the Kenotic pattern of God's love for us manifest in the Incarnation (whether or not they were actually adherents of any full-blown kenotic theory): Evangelical missionaries sacrificing their lives for the spread of the gospel in foreign lands; Catholic clergy and religious orders taking up residence in the heart of inner cities and slums to serve the poor; lay Christians reaching out to those living on the margins of society in their local communities, or becoming personally active in movements for the promotion of social justice; parents working long hours year after year in arduous jobs in order to provide for their families as best they can, or sacrificing some of their career goals to serve the needs of their children at home. As Brian Hebblethwaite wrote: "The Incarnation has been taken as *the pattern of Christian ministry*, as a matter of involvement and service in every area of human life."[918] For the Incarnation tells us that the Word of God has humbled himself, taking the form of our servant. He has even laid down his life for us. And Jesus said: "Love one another, even as I have loved you" (Jn 13:34).

---

[918] Hebblethwaite, *The Incarnation*, p. 43-44.

Conclusion
Kenoticism and the Mystery of God

As the introductory chapter of this book makes clear, at the heart of what is distinctive about Anglican identity lies the mystery of the Incarnation, and within that heritage, over the past 130 years, lies a particular stream of interpretation of this doctrine waiting to be rediscovered by Anglicans themselves, and by the wider Christian community. As a result, this book has offered a comprehensive defence of the Kenotic Theory of the Incarnation, rooted primarily in the way that theory has developed within the Anglican tradition since the early twentieth century. This "moderate" version of Kenoticism has been shown to be not only coherent in itself, but also remarkably powerful in its impact on the wider pattern of Christian belief. Above all, we focused on its implications for God's identification with human suffering, for the doctrine of the Saving Work of Jesus Christ, and for the social witness of Christianity. In short, I have argued that this incarnational heritage is a special gift that Anglican Christianity can make to the enrichment of the faith of all Christian traditions, as appropriate in an ecumenical age.

At every step of this study, we have seen the importance of the doctrine of the Incarnation (as defined above all at the Council of Chalcedon) to the whole pattern of the Christian Faith. We have also seen that some of the most difficult questions that remain about Kenotic Christology arise in the area of our understanding of the divine nature. On the surface, at least, even the more moderate versions of Kenoticism that developed primarily within the Anglican world require a significant revision of the Patristic, Scholastic, and Reformation consensus concerning the essential simplicity, immutability, and impassibility of God.

Some final, and crucial questions, therefore, need to be faced if Anglican Moderate Kenoticism really can make a profound and lasting contribution to ecumenical Christology. I criticized several versions of Kenotic Christology in this book ("Radical" and "Pure Kenoticism" in particular), for leading us into significant distortions of the biblical and mainstream Christian understanding of the divine nature — heading us into tritheism and voluntarism in particular. But, as we have seen, even "Moderate Kenoticism" hardly fits with some features of the traditional Christian understanding of God. Moderate KM requires us to hold that the divine Son has taken into the divine nature itself, and preserved there human experiences of limitation and suffering from the perspective of his fully human consciousness on events as Jesus of Nazareth. Can a God who has subjected himself to limitation, change and suffering in this way really be the God of the Bible, the Church, and the mainstream Christian Faith? If not, then my claim that the Anglican heritage of Kenoticism can make a special contribution to ecumenical Christology is certainly a spurious one.

Analytic vs. Classical Conceptions of God

One way forward for those seeking to fashion an understanding of God that fits well with a kenotic model of the Incarnation (especially with the Moderate Kenotic Model that we explored and defended throughout this book), would be to swim within the stream of Analytic theism. This is a philosophical school that many contemporary Kenoticists find congenial. As we saw in Part One, the philosophical theologies of O.C. Quick, Brian Hebblethwaite, Thomas Morris and Richard Swinburne all hold, with the mainstream Christian tradition, that God is "an all-powerful, all-knowing, perfectly good, eternal and transcendent being who has created our entire universe and preserves it in existence from moment to moment."[919] Divine attributes such as self-existence, goodness, omniscience, and omnipotence are held to be essential to the divine nature, but God is neither completely immutable nor completely impassible: he can have new experiences, take new initiatives, make himself vulnerable to suffering (without being overwhelmed by it), and respond in time to human prayers. Indeed, according to many Analytic theists, God does not dwell in a realm of timeless eternity (with all times present to him at once), but within linear time (or within a parallel time sequence to our linear time); thus he is not able to foresee

---

[919] Morris, *Our Idea of God*, p. 17.

all the free actions of his human creatures, but responds to them step by step with his gracious and powerful love in order to achieve his loving purposes for his world.

We have already explored some aspects of this philosophical perspective in Part One of this book, and we have seen that it enables us to hold that, at least in some respects, God is immutable and impassible. As the Old Testament says, he abides "from everlasting to everlasting" (Ps 90:2); his essential divine attributes (such as those listed above) cannot be lost or rendered inaccessible to him, although he can will to restrain their full use. He does not know all the future actions of free beings, but he knows how he will respond to every possible situation that may arise, and every possible prayer so that his loving purposes for his creation can be fulfilled; thus, he knows his own inexhaustible resources for bringing good out of evil. As a result, he can assure us (through biblical prophecy) of his final triumph over evil in this world, and at least the general outlines of what that triumph will look like. Arguably, the kind of God that this stream of Analytic theism offers us is also very close to the biblical understanding of God — and very close to the picture of the divine nature in-*kenosis* that Sergius Bulgakov outlined for us. Moreover, as we saw in the work of Quick, Hebblethwaite, Swinburne and Morris, we can attain a fairly intelligible and coherent picture of how a God like this could become incarnate in his world in a kenotic way, and what that incarnate state might look like.

This is certainly one possible philosophical framework for a Moderate Kenotic Christology: that is, for the kind of Christology for which I argued earlier in this book, and found so richly expressed in the Anglican heritage. Indeed, throughout Part One and the first chapter of Part Two, I assumed, explained and even defended this general Kenotic and Analytic theist perspective, and implied that this is a fairly intelligible and coherent, and therefore legitimate path for mainstream Christian theologians to tread.

The question, however, is not whether this path in philosophical theology is an *acceptable* one, but whether it is *the best* path to take.

In fact, powerful arguments can still be made that in some stronger sense God is immutable, and dwells in a state of timeless eternity. First of all, if he is the transcendent cause of the initial cosmic "Big Bang," and at that first moment of creation time and space itself came into existence, then the cause of these realities must in some sense transcend space and time. Second, if some form of the philosophical argument from the contingency of creatures to the existence of a Creator holds water, then it gives us a God who is Being itself, Pure Act, infinitely Perfect Being, and it is very hard to see how infinitely Perfect Being could undergo any kind of change, since he has no unrealized potentials which might be actualized.[920] Indeed, some philosophers argue that any changes in his nature could only involve a loss of divine perfection, a diminution of the fullness of Being.[921] Third, a stronger biblical case can be made for divine timeless

---

[920] For a brief, contemporary re-statement of a theistic argument from contingency, see my book *Letters to a College Student* (Chilliwack, BC: The Chartwell Press, 2015), p. 101-116.

[921] This argument is not convincing. David Brown stated in *The Divine Trinity* (p. 257) that only a change in "moral perfection" or goodness would threaten the fullness of divine perfection. That seems to assume, however, that the only significant value is moral in nature, whereas changes in beauty or knowledge (truth) would seem to be equally significant. In other words, if changes in the divine nature do not amount to diminishment of any of God's three transcendentals (goodness, beauty or truth), or the power to enact these transcendentals in the greatest possible way, then, arguably, they qualify as "value-neutral" changes with regard to divine perfection. I would argue that the *kenosis* undertaken by the divine Son, assuming our human condition out of love for us by adding an experiential knowledge of human life and death to the store of his omniscient, factual knowledge, was an amazing expression of Divine Goodness, as well as something infinitely beautiful that only God can do. Perhaps Walter Kasper said it best: "The cross is the utmost that is possible to God in his self-surrendering love; it is 'That than which nothing greater can be thought;' it is the unsurpassable self-definition of God." See Walter Kasper, *The God of Jesus Christ* (New York: Crossroad, 1976), p. 194. Thomas Morris argues persuasively that there can indeed be value-neutral changes in God:

eternity than many seem to realize. In his *Systematic Theology* (1994), Evangelical theologian Wayne Grudem makes a persuasive argument that Holy Scripture actually implies this view of Divine Eternity (see especially his exegesis of Is 46: 9-10 and 2 Pet 3:8): God stands above time and sees all earthly times and places, and all the free actions of his human creatures in one simple glance; past, present and future all remain before his gaze.[922] This connects also with the matter of biblical prophecy. While not all biblical prophecy is predictive prophecy, and much of it that is predictive is either cryptic or general in nature, still, it would be hard to understand how God could foresee (and enable his prophetic spokespersons to foretell) certain specific events, such as the birth of the Messiah in Bethlehem, or the threefold denial of Christ by Peter, or the future mission of St. Paul the apostle, without having a timeless gaze on the future.[923]

Many of the arguments commonly used against the notions of divine immutability and timeless eternity seem to be exceptionally weak. For example, it is said that God cannot dwell in a realm of timeless eternity because that would mean he has an Olympian, immovable indifference to the plight of his people on earth: a God who cannot be moved with

---

As I write this sentence I change from forming one letter to forming the next, but I see no reason to think that such changes necessitate an increase or decrease in my intrinsic value or metaphysical stature at all. And if there are value-neutral changes, it will not follow from the fact that God cannot change for the better or for the worse that God cannot change at all. So his perfection does not clearly motivate a doctrine of absolute immutability after all. (*Our Idea of God*, p. 127)

[922] Wayne Grudem, *Systematic Theology* (Grand Rapids: Zondervan, 1994), p. 168-173.
[923] Unless, of course, we are going to say that God uses determinative power to make everything happen exactly the way he wants to at every moment (and thus he can accurately foretell the future, because he has decided in advance exactly what he wants to happen in the future) — in which case there is no real angelic or human free-will. In such a scenario, God could indeed foresee the future from within linear time, because none of his creatures have any free-will to make things happen in any way different from the way God wants them to happen. This scenario, however, fits better with some streams of Islamic thought than anything resembling Classical Christianity.

compassion for our plight, it is said, cannot really care about us. But this is surely a *non sequitur*. If God is all-good, and goodness is always diffusive of itself, then God would not need to be "moved" by our plight in order to come to our aid: as Perfect Being and Pure Act, he would ever and always be "moving" and acting to help and save us. He would be actualizing all the divine perfections at once, including Divine Love; he would be "immutable" in the sense of unchangeably active in love: Pure Act, not Pure Stasis.

Furthermore, it is argued that we cannot have a real, personal relationship with God if he cannot "respond" to our prayers, and if our prayers can make no difference to the way things are or will be (which are fixed in his gaze from all eternity).[924] But this too does not follow. It assumes that divine timeless knowledge is founded on a divine universal determination of all events — but such determinism is not necessarily implied in the notion of timeless eternity. As Boethius and others have argued, timeless eternity does not mean that God "fixes" all events *by* his gaze. It simply means that in one simple act of vision God can see what his human creatures are doing with their free-will at every moment of linear time: past, present, and future. In other words, the doctrine of divine timeless eternity holds that some of what God knows is contingent on our free choices, even though his mode of knowing these choices is not temporal.[925] Moreover, just because we cannot *imagine* how God can hear a prayer at time X and respond to a prayer at time Y in one and the same a-temporal, eternal act, this does not mean he is unable to do so. "Timeless" knowledge, after all, is not exactly the same as "simultaneous" knowledge: the latter is merely an analogy for the former, and what it would really be like to have a time-less gaze on all events is not something we can fully comprehend with the human mind.[926] But since when is our

---

[924] For a clear expression of this argument, see Robert W. Jenson, "Ipse Pater Non Est Impassibilis" in Keating and White, eds., *Divine Impassibility and the Mystery of Human Suffering*, p. 125-126.

[925] On this see Morris, *Our Idea of God,* p. 97-98.

[926] Simultaneous knowledge is a single act of knowledge or awareness of more than one event occurring at the same moment in linear time, whereas timeless

understanding of God confined to what we can fully comprehend or completely imagine? For Christians who confess the mystery of God as Holy Trinity, the answer to that question should be obvious.

These are vast issues, of course, and they cannot be settled here in three paragraphs! Suffice it to say that there is more to be said for the Classical tradition that God is Perfect Being — simple, immutable and impassable, with a timeless and all-encompassing knowledge of all times and events — than some theologians today realize. Indeed for Roman Catholic and Eastern Orthodox Christians, these truths are not only defensible, but, arguably, authoritatively taught by the Church.

To begin with, the doctrine of absolute divine immutability and impassibility was the teaching of the overwhelming majority of the ancient Fathers and medieval Scholastics. In his classic study of the history of the notion of divine impassibility, J.K. Mozley summed up his findings like this:

> The material brought together up to this point shows the existence of a steady and continuous, if not quite unbroken, tradition in Christian theology as to the freedom of the divine nature from all suffering and from any potentiality of suffering. ... [A]s against Patripassianism, Monophysitism and Theopaschitism, the Church as a whole pursued a course and made distinctions which were intended to safeguard against any ascription of passibility to the divine nature, and to rule out any form of doctrine which seemed logically to involve such an error.[927]

Saint John Damascene in the eighth century summed up the view of most of the Fathers when he wrote in his book *On the Orthodox Faith*:

knowledge would be a single act of knowledge or awareness of more than one event occurring at different moments of linear time.
[927] J.K. Mozley, *The Impassibility of God: a Survey of Christian Thought* (London: Cambridge University Press, 1926), p. 127.

"[W]e say that God suffered in the flesh, but never that his divinity suffered in the flesh, or that God suffered through the flesh" (III, 26).[928]

Given the importance of the witness of the ancient Fathers to the Eastern Orthodox tradition, it is not surprising that even a full-blooded Eastern Kenoticist like Sergius Bulgakov would feel compelled to cling to a di-polar understanding of the divine nature. For Bulgakov, as we have seen, the "immanent Trinity" remains unchangeable and unchanged by the kenotic life of the "economic Trinity;" that is, the immanent Trinity remains completely unaffected by God's outreach toward his creatures. Better a split-level God than to abandon the near consensus of the Fathers and the saints on divine impassibility altogether!

For Roman Catholics, divine simplicity and immutability are taught definitively by the magisterium of the Church. The nature of God was solemnly defined (to the extent that it can be defined) at the First Vatican Council in the very first chapter of its *Dogmatic Constitution on the Catholic Faith*:

> The Holy, Catholic, Apostolic, Roman Church believes and confesses that there is one true and living God, Creator and Lord of heaven and earth, almighty, immense, incomprehensible, infinite in intelligence, in will and an all perfection, who as being one, sole, absolutely simple and immutable spiritual substance is to be declared as really and essentially distinct from the world, of supreme beatitude in and from Himself, and ineffably exalted above all things beside Himself which exist or are conceivable.
>
> This one, only, true God, of His own goodness and almighty power, not for the increase of His own happiness, nor to acquire but to manifest His perfection by the blessings which He bestows on creatures, with absolute freedom of counsel,

---

[928] Cited in Emery, "The Immutability of the God of Love," p. 33.

> created out of nothing, from the beginning of time, both the spiritual and corporeal creature, to wit, the angelic and the mundane ... all things are naked and open to His eyes, even those which are yet to be by the free action of creatures.[929]

This magisterial Tradition also solidly affirms that the divine nature remained impassible despite the temporal sufferings of the Word made flesh. As previously discussed (in Part One, Chapter Five), The Council of Chalcedon (451 AD) rejected the heretical Monophysite confusion between the two natures of Christ, for "they fantastically suppose ... that the Only-begotten is passible;" and the same Council expressly "expels from the assembly of the priests those who dare to say that the divinity of the Only-begotten is passible."[930] The Third Council of Constantinople (The Sixth Ecumenical Council of the Church, in 680-681) reiterated the same teaching when they rejected the Monothelete heresy (that Christ has one divine will, and not also a human will), in part "so as not to attribute passions to the divinity."[931]

All of this would seem to stand directly against the claims that we made in the "Introduction" to this book: that the Anglican stream of Kenoticism gives us the best pathway toward a deeper understanding of the great mystery of the Incarnation, and that this model of the Incarnation can be a special gift from the Anglican tradition to the

---

[929] First Vatican Council, "Dogmatic Constitution on the Catholic Faith," Chapter One, in *Dogmatic Canons and Decrees* (Rockford, IL: TAN Books, 1977), p. 218-220. Similarly, the Fourth Lateran Council in 1215 spoke of the "immutability' and "simplicity" of the divine essence shared by all the persons of the Trinity.

[930] The Council of Chalcedon, "Definition of the Faith," in Norman P. Tanner, ed., *Decrees of the Ecumenical Councils*, vol. I (Washington, DC: Georgetown University Press, 1990), p.85-86, cited in Emery, "The Immutability of the God of Love," p.30-31. As previously discussed, we need to remember that according to the Catholic Tradition, disciplinary and pastoral applications of papal and conciliar doctrinal definitions do not fully share in the infallible guidance of the Holy Spirit granted to the definitions themselves.

[931] Council of Constantinople III, "Address to the Emperor Constantine IV," in *Sacrorum conciliorum nova et amplissima collection,* vol. II, Johannes Domenicus Mansi, ed. (Paris-Leipzig: H. Welter, 1901), col. 664, cited in Emery, "The Immutability of the God of Love," p. 32.

wider Christian world. How can this be so, if neither the Eastern Orthodox nor the Roman Catholic communities of faith can embrace it? For it seems to violate the ancient, medieval and magisterial traditions they hold dear concerning the simplicity, immutability, and impassibility of God.[932] Far from being an ecumenical gift to these major portions of Christendom, for them it would seem to be a "non-starter"!

It would appear that if we wish to preserve a truly incarnational faith, we are left with only two live options. On the one hand, we may approach the mystery of the divine nature from the perspective of Analytic theism, a perspective easy to harmonize with the Moderate Kenotic Model of the Incarnation that we found so fruitful for the wider pattern of Christian belief. On the other hand, we could approach the mystery of the divine nature from a perspective more in tune with Patristic and Scholastic philosophical theism, a perspective easy to harmonize with Two-Nature Christology. These forms of incarnational Christology would seem to be mutually exclusive, with ecumenical enrichment between them simply impossible.

To close this study, however, I want to suggest that this may be a false dichotomy: that there may be a way that one could, in fact, hold to an understanding of God as (in a sense) timeless, infinitely Perfect Being, and yet embrace a Moderate Kenotic Model of the Incarnation, without self-contradiction. A bridge that spans this divide — in this respect, also, an ecumenical divide between the Anglican heritage of Kenotic Christology on the one hand, and the Catholic and Eastern Orthodox traditions on the other — may be possible to construct after all.

---

[932] In Catholic theology the doctrine of God's timeless, "eternal now" perspective on all events (see *Catechism of the Catholic Church*, entry 600) also has important connections with the doctrine of the Eucharistic Sacrifice — the Mass as a true *anamnesis* (re-making-present) of the sacrifice of Christ on the Cross — as well as with the doctrine of the Immaculate Conception of the Blessed Virgin Mary, in which Jesus on the Cross merits the graces poured out upon the soul of his mother Mary at the moment of her conception.

Toward A New Kenotic Understanding of the Nature of God and His Acts of Creation and Incarnation

To help us chart this new way forward, we can turn to Anglican philosophical theologian Keith Ward's careful summary of the Classical Christian understanding of the mystery of God — this review will help us explore what is essential to retain from that tradition, and what is not. Ward writes:

> The traditional concept of God in Christianity is that God is eternal, in the sense of being timeless — that is, without temporal relation to anything in time, and without internal relations of a temporal nature. It follows from this that God is strictly immutable. Whatever happens in the created cosmos makes no difference to God[933], and does not change God in any way. The cosmos is created by a non-temporal act, and God created every moment of time, from first to last, in one and the same act of intentional causation.
>
> This in turn entails that the incarnation of the second hypostasis of the Triune Being of God is effected by God in the very same non-temporal act by which God also creates and consummates the created order. The incarnation causes no change in God, but lies in a particular relation of the created nature of Jesus to the creator. It is not literally true that "the Word became flesh" (Jn 1:14), since the eternal Word cannot become anything. It must always remain timelessly and changelessly what it is. The situation is rather that the human nature of Jesus has a unique relation to the eternal Word, a

---

[933] Obviously, Ward would be incorrect if by "makes no difference to God" here is meant "God is indifferent; he does not care about what happens in his world." Classical theology certainly held that God is good and cares for his creation; he seeks the good of his creatures. But "makes no difference to God" could simply mean "does not have any effect on him, does not cause any changes to his being."

relation of enosis,[934] unity, by which it expresses in time the nature of the Word and manifests in a uniquely direct way the salvific intentions of the Triune God. The human nature is said to be "assumed" by the divine person of the Word, but exactly what the assumption consists in remains a mystery of faith. While it can be imagined as a possibility, the human mind cannot gain a clear comprehension of it.

Important points for the traditional account are that the incarnation causes no change in the nature of God, and that it is not a new idea which occurred to God subsequently to his creating the universe. It is part of the one creative divine act, and thus may rightly be said to have been willed from the beginning of creation.[935]

As we proceed, we must bear in mind that for Classical Christianity, the divine works of creation, incarnation, and redemption are all simply aspects of, and included in, the one, simple, infinite, immutable, eternal act in which God is all that he is, manifests all his divine perfections, and does all that he does.

Without completely contradicting this Classical perspective on Divine Eternity, suppose we lean on Ward again, this time extracting some insights from his work *Christ and the Cosmos*, in order to build up a preliminary understanding of God and his relationship with creation. In Chapter Four of his book, he argues that God is in some respects "necessary" and in other respects "free." He sets out the argument in 10 formal steps, the latter five are directly related to our concerns here:

---

[934] Ward states in a footnote that *enosis* is an English word that occurs in the Oxford English Dictionary, based on the Greek *henosis*.
[935] Ward, "Cosmos as Kenosis" in Polkinghorne, ed., *The Work of Love*, p. 152-153.

6. God exists by necessity (usually held by classical theists).

7. The universe is contingent, at least in part: it could have been different and might not have existed — God did not have to create this universe in particular, or maybe any universe.

8. Therefore God as Creator of this universe must act contingently ….

9. And God as omniscient knower of this universe must include contingent epistemic states.

10. *Therefore God is not simple:* God, while being necessary, does some things contingently and so is necessary in some respects and contingent in other respects.[936]

Ward goes on to explain:

> It seems a perfectly coherent supposition that a God who has to exist and has the general nature God has (say, of being the most powerful being possible and having the greatest possible knowledge and being the best possible being) might yet act in contingent ways. …

> The idea might be that in God there is a necessary knowledge of all possibles, a necessary 'feeling' or sensitivity to their value or disvalue, and a necessary ability to create (to make some states actual). … [P]ossible universes exist in the divine mind that has the capacity freely to choose to actualise a specific set of values out of all those possibilities. The set of values and the mind which cognises them are necessary, whereas the actual choice to create is free and thus contingent.[937]

Ward believes that his view of God entails that God "is temporal in some respects," because "free creation entails choosing between alternative states, and choosing entails change from potency to actuality, and change entails a form of temporality." But suppose we take on-board Ward's view of the divine nature, yet *not* his conclusion

---

[936] Ward, *Christ and the Cosmos*, p. 19; italics mine.
[937] Ibid., p. 19-20, and 27.

that this God must necessarily change in a time sequence from potency to act when he chooses to create the world, and comes to know the changing states of his world. **Suppose we stubbornly insist that even a God who freely brings into existence a contingent world and knows contingent states, can do so in one, simple, timeless, eternal act.**

Several things would seem to fit well this perspective.

(1) It would be fitting that God eternally express his *perfect goodness* by creating a world, and by becoming incarnate within it, for goodness is always diffusive of itself

Classical Christianity has always wrestled with the question of why a God who eternally actualizes and expresses all his perfections within himself would choose to create a world distinct from himself. In his book *God in a Single Vision*, David Brown suggests that we should not think of God deciding to create a world as if he ever seriously considered the option of *not* doing so. Rather, in accord with many of the ancient Fathers and earlier medieval Scholastics (e.g. Aquinas, Bonaventure and Duns Scotus), the key to this mystery lies in the insight that goodness is always diffusive of itself. Brown reflects on this mystery when he writes:

> [I]t is of the nature of goodness to share, and so, if God is good, he must also share his being with others. Note that this is not at all the same as saying that God needs to share …. Rather, what is envisaged is pure gift, pure grace, if you like. God does not create the world because he needs something from the world, or even because he needs to give something to the world, but rather the world comes into existence because on this analysis of goodness there can be no perfect goodness that is not defined by generosity, by giving without receiving a return. Now of course to make sense of this notion one must assume that what is given is itself a good, but that is precisely the claim that the earlier tradition makes, by asserting that existence of itself is good. God as perfect Being and perfect Goodness imparts to the world some of that existence, some

of that goodness, and nothing is lost from him thereby because he is infinite Being, infinite Goodness. ...

[This] avoids the anthropomorphic idea of God needing to make a decision about whether or not to create the world. The world exists simply in virtue of the fact that he is what he is, namely perfect goodness. ... [T]hough it thus makes the emergence of something other than God inevitable, it does not rob God of all choice: some world was inevitable, but not necessarily this particular world. An element of choice thus remains.[938]

If "inevitable" here sounds a bit too much like "necessary" (and the Christian tradition has always been hesitant to say that God created the world out of a necessity of some kind, for creation has always been seen as a free and gracious gift of God), we can at least say that it was entirely "fitting" to his nature as pure "goodness" that he bestow existence, and a share in his perfections on beings other than himself,[939] and it is very hard for us to imagine him choosing to do

---

[938] Brown, *God in a Single Vision*, p. 14.

[939] "Fitting" I understand to be the mean between logical, metaphysical or moral "necessity" on the one hand, and mere "absence of contradiction" on the other. A truth claim about God may be said to be "fitting" if it is consonant and in harmony with the other things we know about the nature of God, such that we almost could have guessed the truth of it from what we already know to be true about him. Richard Swinburne has argued that making such speculations about what it is "fitting" for a good God to do is a legitimate way to proceed in philosophical theology:

[G]od's perfect goodness makes it probable that he will do certain things rather than other things. For we have some understanding of what a good person will do. ...

We derive this understanding of what it is to be a good person by reflecting on what a good ordinary human person will do. But a divine person, of course, although personal, is different from ordinary human persons. And so we must reflect what difference it would make to how a good person would act if there were no limits to his power,

otherwise. Perhaps it was *possible* for God not to create — but how he would then live out the diffusion of his perfect goodness is impossible for us to conceive.[940]

Furthermore, given the kind of God he is (perfect in goodness), it is entirely fitting that he would fashion at least some of the creatures in his world quite closely in his own "image," that is, able in a finite way to create, love, and reason as a reflection of his own infinite creativity, love, and reason. Such creatures could thereby come to know and love him, and come to know and love each other. All of this necessarily entails bestowing upon them the gift of *personhood*: the inherent capacity for self-consciousness, rational thought, and voluntary agency

---

knowledge, etc., and if he were the source of existence from moment to moment of all other things. (*Was Jesus God?*, p. 24)

[940] Thomas Morris makes a helpful distinction between what is "natural" and what is strictly "necessary," arguing in effect that it is "natural" (and therefore, we may say, "fitting") for God to diffuse his goodness by creating a world, but not strictly "necessary" for him to do so:

It is natural for a man and woman who love each other and who are good people, to want to bring into existence a child, or children, with whom to share that love and toward whom to express that goodness. But it is not necessary for marital love and moral goodness to be expressed in this way. A person is not necessarily any less loving or good for choosing to remain celibate. A person physically or biologically prevented from having children of his or her own is not necessarily thereby condemned to an incomplete state of personal goodness. Bringing new life into existence is a natural expression of love and goodness. But it is not essential. ...

[I]t surely would seem greater for God to have the most extensive range of freedom we can imagine, consistent with his never acting in such a way as to violate his character or nature. And in addition, with the conception of God as free never to have created any contingent beings, we have secured the basis for another important insistence of Christian theologians: that the very existence of the universe at all should be experienced and accepted by us as a free gift of God. (*Our Idea of God*, p. 148-150)

(without which authentic creativity, love and reason would be impossible; after all, robots and puppets on a string cannot do such things!) — and that also means that by an act of *kenosis* God would need to limit his power and control over those free creatures to allow them truly to exercise their voluntary agency.[941]

Given all this, it could be said that for God to become incarnate in his world also would be entirely fitting. It would be perfectly in harmony with his goodness — indeed, a true and supreme expression of his goodness — if he chose to draw as near as possible to the creatures that he made in his image, to share their lot, and to show them the way to live out their finite form of being in accord with the divine *shalom* (God's proper reign and Kingdom in this world). By doing so he would reveal his Divine Goodness to them in the most intelligible way, addressing his creatures on their own level: in human words and human deeds.

Given that God also knew that these creatures would, in the course of time, misuse their free-will and thereby usher disorder, evil, and suffering into his creation, it would also be fitting to his perfect goodness for him to mount a rescue operation for those same creatures that he loves so much, even if it cost him dearly in some way to do so.

Of course, in all this Christians have the benefit of hindsight: we have plenty of reason to believe that there actually is an all-powerful, all-wise, and all-good God, and that he actually has done all of these good things! But looking back, we can see in hindsight that they were all perfectly fitting to infinite goodness, diffusive of itself. And again: these are all just various aspects of the one changeless eternal act in which God is all that he is, chooses all that he chooses to do, and does it.

---

[941] Recall our discussion of O.C. Quick's concept of divine "external passibility" in Part Two, Chapter One, above.

(2) It would be fitting that God eternally express his perfect goodness through *perfect creativity*, creating a world as an expression of his perfect goodness, including a kenotic self-limitation on his determinative power to enable at least some of his creatures to exercise authentic free-will

Surely, divinely perfect creativity can be understood as an aspect of divinely perfect goodness. And Divine Creativity certainly includes the capacity to diffuse perfect goodness by expressing the infinite divine perfections in and through a created medium with finite creaturely limitations. To do so God utilizes his attributes of omnipotence and omniscience in a special way, a way that he would not otherwise have done had he not chosen to create a world. His creation, therefore, reflects in a finite way his infinitely perfect power, wisdom, and goodness.[942] As Scripture says: "The heavens are telling the glory of God; and the firmament proclaims his handiwork" (Ps 19:1).

In addition, it is surely a higher expression of creativity to bring creatures into being who are close "images" of the divine than not to do so. As we have already seen, this *necessarily* involves a kenotic self-limitation on his determinative power and control of events, so that these creatures can exercise authentic voluntary agency. Indeed, it is hard to see how God could actualize his capacity for perfect creativity, as an expression and diffusion of perfect goodness, without creating a world with at least these basic features.

(3) It would be fitting that God eternally express his perfect goodness in the form of *perfect love*, which means seeking the good of others, especially by becoming incarnate among them in their world, and even, if need be, by doing so through kenotic self-limitation, and self-sacrifice

---

[942] See St. Bonaventure's extended meditation on this mystery in his *Breviloquium* in *The Works of Bonaventure: Cardinal, Doctor and Saint* (Patterson, NJ: St. Anthony Guild Press, Jose de Vinck, trans., 1963), p. 69-106.

The Incarnation

What could perfect goodness mean without perfect love? Apart from the revelation of God in Christ, we might not know what perfect love really looks like in its fullness, but basic rational reflection on this world, and on human life within it, surely leads us to recognize that perfect goodness includes love, at least in the sense of a general "benevolence" that seeks and wills the good of all.[943] And what act could be more loving and benevolent toward his human creatures than for God to take flesh among them, sharing their life, showing them the Way of the Kingdom, and revealing his goodness to them in an accessible and intelligible human form? Indeed, it would be an even more perfect expression of Divine Love to accomplish all this through a kenotic incarnation. *For one clearly possesses a more perfect form of goodness if one is able to limit oneself, and even suffer for the good of others, if need be, than not to be able to do so.*[944] In Part Two of this book we made the case that *a kenotic Incarnation, especially in the form we called Moderate KM, would meet the needs of humanity in significant ways*: for example, in God's identification, close empathy and sympathy with the human condition, in accomplishing important dimensions of his saving work, and in giving to the Social Gospel its center and full expression. Indeed, if at least the Incarnational Exemplarist, Sacrificial-Merit and Legal theories of Atonement represent essential aspects of Christ's saving work (as we claimed in Part Two, Chapter Two of this book), then one could argue that it would not only be *fitting* for God to choose to become incarnate in a kenotic way, but also *necessary* to the effective accomplishment of his rescue operation for lost humanity.

---

[943] In the Appendix to his book *The Abolition of Man* C.S. Lewis marshals the evidence for a cross-cultural "Law of General Beneficence" manifest in the literature of all the ancient civilizations of the world; see *The Complete C.S. Lewis Signature Classics* (New York: Harper Collins, 2002), p. 731-733.

[944] Just think of the implications if we deny this: it would mean that the loving self-sacrifice of a St. Damien the Leper, or a St. Maximillian Kolbe, or a St. Gianna Molla was more heroic, more selflessly brave and generous, than the love of the divine Son incarnate on the Cross, who (according to classical Two-Nature Christology) "suffered impassibly," such that his divine nature remained unaffected by his own human life and death.

In short, what I have tried to show in these reflections is that it is entirely fitting to perfect Divine Goodness, in seeking to diffuse his goodness, to do so by creating a world, including a kenotic dimension to that creative activity to permit the operation of human and angelic free-will (indeed, we can hardly imagine him doing otherwise); and it is also entirely fitting to his goodness for him to choose to become incarnate within his world, especially by an act of kenosis, identifying with and sharing in human sufferings out of love for us. Moreover, these acts of creation, incarnation, and redemption could be just so many aspects of the one, infinite, eternal act in which God is what he is, manifests all of his perfections, and wills to do all that he does.

The objection will be raised that I am just trying to introduce into the divine nature experiences of change and suffering through a kenotic incarnation — experiences that God by definition cannot have because he is by nature Perfect Being: completely simple and immutable in his perfection, and therefore completely impassible.

There is an important sense, however, in which the theology of divinely perfect goodness that we are sketching here does *not* introduce any real change into the divine nature. Change is presumably a move from potency to act: from having a potentiality to actualizing that potentiality. Thus, a person may need a holiday on the Mediterranean, and if he gets a good Christmas bonus in his paycheque, he may be able to actualize that potential, and change from being a cold, wet and tired out employee in London to one refreshed and invigorated by the sun and the sea. But suppose he was actually born, raised, and lived his whole life by the Mediterranean Sea. Indeed, that he *always* worked there. It would still be true to say that he is actualizing his potential for receiving the refreshment and invigoration of the sun and the sea, but he is doing so perpetually, changelessly, if you will. He does so while in one sense not having to undergo any change at all, but just by being who he is and changelessly choosing to live where he lives.

The Incarnation

Perhaps something similar is true of God. He surely has the eternal capacity in his divine nature to create a world, and to become incarnate by *kenosis* within it, as a fitting expression *ad extra* of his perfect goodness, creativity and love. But to do so he does not need to undergo actual change *in a time sequence*, that is, to go from temporal potency to temporal act, from being a non-creator and non-incarnate to actually becoming so *in linear time*. In other words, he can actualize the potentials of his nature for creative and redemptive action *timelessly*, in the one, changeless, eternal act in which he is all that he is, and wills to do all that he does, and does it.

This also means that God eternally (and changelessly, so to speak) chooses to assume the experience of relating to a world of creatures distinct from himself, and chooses to assume also the human experiences of growth and change, suffering and sorrow in and through his kenotic life as Jesus of Nazareth. In other words, in choosing to create a world and to become incarnate within it as an expression and diffusion of his perfect goodness, *he wills to experience his divine reality as that of a God who has chosen to relate to creatures in these ways, rather than experiencing his divine reality as a God who did not will to create a world or become incarnate among his creatures.*[945] **In that sense, perhaps, Bulgakov was right: God freely wills to give up his complete immutability and impassibility, his *absolute immunity* from the experience of all change and all suffering, by his single, eternal act of creating and redeeming a world. He has thereby added to his divine experience what it is like to be a creator, and what it is like to come among as one of us, "self-limited in manhood" (as Weston would say). But this is an eternal, timeless addition to his divine experience, an eternal, unchanging actualization of these potentialities — and in that sense it is a form of**

---

[945] Of course, we do not have any clear conception of what it means for God to "experience his divine reality" in various ways, save by some distant analogy with our own, human way of experiencing things. But it does not seem presumptuous to say that in some sense God does uniquely experience what it is like to be God, and that there is likely to be some difference between eternally experiencing what it is to be an *actual* creator and redeemer, as opposed to eternally experiencing what it is like only to be a *potential* creator and redeemer.

"immutability," for it is all part of the one, infinite, eternal act in which God is himself, does what he chooses to do, and perfectly diffuses his goodness.

We need to remember also that God's immutable, changeless perfection is a profound mystery, not something we can *fully* comprehend, and certainly not *a priori*. Even so strong an immutabilist and impassibilist as Fr. Gilles Emery, OP, admitted that "The divine mode of immutability, as concerns its very reality, escapes us, because it is the immutability of the pure actuality of God, indicative of his plenitude of being, love, and life."[946] Why should we be prevented, then, from "fleshing-out" the meaning of divine changelessness by pondering that "plenitude" of his being as divinely perfect goodness, diffusive of itself, and what seems most fitting to the perfect, eternal diffusion of that goodness? Also, why should we hesitate to let ourselves be informed also by divine revelation, which enables us to see how God has actually enacted and manifested that plenitude of being and goodness in what he has actually done?

One of the benefits of this way of seeing things is that it helps to solve a conundrum that we faced in Part Two, Chapter One of this book. There we argued that God could only have a close empathy and sympathy for the human condition if he actually "identified" with our condition at some point, that is, by experiencing human life and human suffering from a limited, human perspective on events. In other words, to attain real compassion for our plight,[947] God would have to have more than just a complete *factual* knowledge of human life: he would need to add to that knowledge in his divine nature an *experiential* knowledge of all the limitations and conditions of what it means to be

---

[946] Emery, "The Immutability of the God of Love," p. 63.

[947] By attaining through Christ a deep "compassion" for our plight, of course, I do not mean to imply that God would not have "cared" what happens to us before that point in time. In Part Two Chapter One we defined "compassion" merely as the affective accompaniment of true empathy, and we argued that even apart from or prior to attaining deep compassion for our plight, God would still have known (factually) about our predicament, and would still have "cared" in the sense of seeking our good.

fully human. We argued that if God thru Christ actually experienced human life in that way, then this would become the touchstone and reference point of his close compassion for the plight of all people — and it would even apply "retroactively." In other words, we said that when his human sufferings were completed in ca. 33 AD, God the Son would not only have gained a deep compassion for all present and future sufferers, but he would even be able from that point onward to sympathize more deeply with the sufferings of all those who had lived before his incarnation.

All of this discussion presupposed, of course, that God operates within some kind of time sequence similar or parallel to our own. Moreover, all of this still does not make sense of the biblical witness that even before the incarnation of his Son, God already had some kind of sympathy and compassion for the human condition (Is 63:9; Hos 11:8). We were unable to shed any further light on this mystery.

Suppose that we now join Kenoticists such as H.R. Mackintosh and Frank Weston in affirming that God exists instead in a realm of timeless eternity, with all events in linear time present before his gaze, and all his actions in time merely so many aspects of the one, infinite, eternal act in which he is all that he is and does all that he does. Then it would be the case that God had the kenotic sufferings of his human form as Jesus of Nazareth *eternally* present before him, from all eternity included and preserved in the store of experience in his divine nature, and this would be the timeless, eternal touchstone and reference point for his close sympathy and compassion for all his creatures, at all times and places, past, present and future. Thus, it would be literally true to say that God heard with compassion the cries of suffering of his people Israel when they were enslaved in Egypt (Ex 1:7-8), and that this experience of deep empathy and sympathy for their plight was grounded in his own experience of suffering and oppression as Jesus of Nazareth, eternally present to his divine nature. In short, we would now have some way of beginning to understand the mystery that God ever and always has had the closest possible compassion for the plight of humanity.

One could also argue that this perspective is not entirely opposed to the witness of the early Fathers of the Church. In his study of the history of the notion of divine impassibility, J.K. Mozley found that some early orthodox Christian writers — and at least one saint — accepted that some forms of suffering could be ascribed to the divine nature. For example, Lactantius taught that all of God's affective reactions to his creatures are always under the direction and control of his reason and his love, and that to deny him emotions such as graciousness, pity, and righteous anger (in response to sin) is to evacuate the divine life of all reality.[948] The most in-depth meditation on this matter, however, comes from St. Gregory Thaumaturgus (213-270 AD). According to St. Gregory, it does not count as "suffering" in God if he takes upon himself an experience of suffering for the sake of defeating evil, and in order to heal the sufferings of his creatures. In so far as God is always triumphant over evil and suffering, the suffering he assumes in the process is really a manifestation of his immortality and goodness — and in that sense he remains "impassible." Saint Gregory wrote:

> In God, those are not to be accounted sufferings which of His own will were borne by Him for the common good of the human race, with no resistance from His most blessed and impassible nature. For in His suffering He shows His impassibility. For he who suffers suffers, when the violence of suffering brings pressure to bear on him who suffers contrary to his will. But of Him who, while His nature remains impassible, is of His own will immersed in sufferings that He may overcome them, we do not say that He becomes subject to suffering, even though, of His own will, He has shared in sufferings.[949]

Mozley then summarizes the thought of St. Gregory on this issue:

---

[948] Mozley, *The Impassibility of God*, p. 50-52.
[949] Ibid., cited on p. 66.

What he is particularly concerned to say is that *passio* may be predicated of God when the experiences which God takes upon Himself are directed by God's will to a good end, and display not any weakness on the part of God, but His power and triumph. Gregory may not have found the exact point at which it is necessary to limit any ascription of *passio* to God; nevertheless, he has opened out and set foot upon an important line of advance to a true understanding of the problem. Further, Gregory makes what is, in effect, the valuable suggestion that we must not sacrifice the idea of God's moral action and of the love from which His energy proceeds to a supposed necessity for maintaining a metaphysical conception of the quiescence of the divine life.[950]

The question that the faithful Roman Catholic or Eastern Orthodox Kenotic theologian asks is whether a perspective similar to that of Lactantius and St. Gregory Thaumaturgus on divine impassibility can be held today without incurring a charge of heterodoxy.

Although he appears to be a thoroughgoing impassibilist, Paul Gavrilyuk has argued that the early Fathers did not cling to belief in absolute divine impassibility as a matter of philosophical speculation. Rather, it was primarily "an indicator of the divine transcendence" and "a marker of God's undiminished activity."[951] Gavrilyuk writes:

> Used adverbially, as in the expression of the Lenten Triodion "and impassibly thou has submitted to thy passion," divine impassibility qualifies the manner in which God endures suffering. To read such statements in a Nestorian manner as saying that the divine subject is not affected by suffering in any

---

[950] Ibid., p. 71. Along the way, Mozley also argues that both Origen and St. Augustine expressly contradicted themselves on this matter: see pages 60-62 and 108-109.
[951] Paul Gavrilyuk, "God's Impassible Suffering in the Flesh," in Keating and White, eds., *Divine Impassibility and the Mystery of Human Suffering*, p. 143.

way at all is to misinterpret them. When the Fathers spoke of God suffering impassibly, they wanted to express that God was not conquered by suffering, and that God's participation in suffering transformed the experience of suffering. In the incarnation God made human suffering his own … in order to transform suffering and redeem human nature.[952]

Expressed in that way, all of this can be affirmed in the context of the "New Kenotic Theology" that I am proposing here. **We surely want to respect this intuition, common to all the Fathers (as Gavrilyuk has described it):** *God could never have been conquered or overwhelmed by any human suffering he assumed for our sake, and in freely choosing to participate in human suffering, he also has a boundless capacity to bring good out of it.* **In these senses, at least, God is truly "impassible."**

In fact, our whole kenotic approach here also may be closer to the mind and intentions of St. Thomas Aquinas than might appear at first glance. In the process of explaining his own Two-Nature Model of the Incarnation in his book *The Divine Trinity* — a model in which he posited a flow of experience between the two natures of the Incarnate Son[953] — David Brown found a measure of common ground with St. Thomas in the latter's understanding that the union of the two natures in the single person of the Son of God is a "real" relation not in God, but only from our point of view:

> [In *Summa Theologiae* III.2.7, Aquinas] should not be interpreted as denying that the union is really in God in one sense of union, i.e. with it viewed as timeless, eternal divine intention that a human nature be united with him at a specific point in time, and since taken into God's timelessness, presumably also

---

[952] Ibid. The key here, of course, would be unpacking what Gavrilyuk might mean by saying "the divine subject" can be "affected by suffering" and in the Incarnation that he "made human suffering his own." I argued in Part One of this book, above, that this kind of language is not really intelligible if it is coupled with a classical Two-Nature model of the Incarnation.

[953] See our discussion of this model in Part One, Chapter One, above.

timelessly present to him, though with a datable beginning. It is just that ... 'union' in the passage is being used exclusively in an active sense of uniting and in that active sense there was nothing new happening to God that was not already timelessly present to him. Perhaps the point can be made clearer by drawing a parallel with answers to prayer on a timeless view of God. For, just as then intervening in the world to answer our prayers would constitute no real change in God, such intervention being part of God's purposes from all eternity, so on this view neither do the changing events of Christ's life. All the God-man's attributes *qua* God remained unaltered: it was only his attributes *qua* his relationship with the world that appeared to change, and such 'changes' as these, like answers to our prayers, must be viewed as being eternally present to the timeless, changeless mind of God.[954]

We could fairly say that at least this aspect of the incarnational doctrine of St. Thomas is not far removed from the New Kenotic theological perspective on offer here. **For in one sense, God the Son does not undergo "change" by becoming incarnate in a kenotic way, because all of his human experiences of change and suffering through his Incarnation — timelessly willed, experienced and accepted by him — are thereby eternally and "immutably" present to his divine nature.**

What about the definitive Catholic magisterial teaching on the "absolutely simple and immutable" nature of God? Perhaps we have something similar here to what theologians in other contexts have called a "remainder concept." For example, in the Catholic theological tradition we find a discussion of "pure (human) nature": that is, created human nature considered apart from any modifications and elevations of it by divine, supernatural grace, and any modifications and corruptions of it caused by original and actual sin. Of course, this "pure human nature" is in one sense merely a theoretical construct: no human being has ever existed in that state. Adam and Eve were enriched by grace from the first moment of their creation, and their descendants enter the world already wounded and corrupted by original sin. Thus, pure human nature is what some theologians have called a "remainder concept": what remains of the concept of a "human being" when all supernatural grace and all corruption of sin have been removed from the picture. A merely theoretical concept it surely is, but not without its uses, for it enables us to see more clearly what is essential to the created structure of human nature, and what the definition of human nature in itself really is.

Perhaps the same could be held with regard to the definition of "God" provided by the First Vatican Council. Let us repeat here the first crucial paragraph of that definition:

> The Holy, Catholic, Apostolic, Roman Church believes and confesses that there is one true and living God, Creator and Lord of heaven and earth, almighty, immense, incomprehensible, infinite in intelligence, in will and an all perfection, who as being one, sole, absolutely simple and immutable spiritual substance is to be declared as really and essentially distinct from the world, of supreme beatitude in and from Himself, and ineffably exalted above all things beside Himself which exist or are conceivable.[955]

This statement by the Council could be held to apply (in Bulgakov's terms) to the reality of God "in himself and for himself": what the divine nature essentially and eternally is apart from any divine choice to create a world and to become incarnate within it. In that sense, it would be a mere "remainder concept," for the truth is, of course, that God did choose to create and to become incarnate, from all eternity. But this "remainder concept" would define for us the fullness of what God is in and for himself, and the infinite resources from which he acts *ad extra*. That would include the infinite capacity of his divine

---

[955] First Vatican Council, "Dogmatic Constitution on the Catholic Faith," p. 218-219.

nature to absorb the experiences of human suffering and affliction that he freely assumed in his incarnate life as Jesus of Nazareth, without being overwhelmed by those experiences, and the unfathomable depth of his ability to bring good out of permitted evils.

To see this conciliar definition at Vatican I as expressing a "remainder concept" would still preserve the main intention of the definition itself, which was to protect the Church from all pantheistic and Hegelian notions of the divine nature, all of which clearly failed to distinguish the reality of God from that of his creation. The Council was faced with the fashionable philosophical movements of the nineteenth century that collapsed the transcendence of God into his immanence, or into some kind of necessary, organic relationship between God and his world. And that is clearly not our intention here in proposing this New Kenotic Theology of the nature of God, and of his creative and redeeming activity.

This understanding of the conciliar definition also could open up a new notion of divine "simplicity." A God who from all eternity voluntarily undergoes human experiences of temporality and suffering, and includes and preserves these in his divine store of experience in his divine nature, is clearly not an "absolutely simple" substance in quite the way that Classical Christian orthodoxy held him to be. But the New Kenotic Theology does not thereby have to abandon the notion of divine simplicity altogether. *For simplicity need not be equated merely with undifferentiated singularity.* When we encounter beauty in this life, for example, we sometimes speak of the "simple beauty" of a whole, manifest when a whole has perfect, mathematical harmony and proportion among its parts, rather than an absence of all internal distinctions whatsoever. Think, for example, of the simple beauty of the major triad in music. In a similar way, the Trinitarian God is "simply beautiful." He is not reducible to an undifferentiated substance (a notion which puts extreme strain on both the doctrines of the Trinity and the Incarnation, as we have seen throughout this book). The Catholic mystic Saint Maria Faustina Kowalska summed up the ineffable mystery and simple beauty of the Trinity when she wrote:

> On one occasion I was reflecting on the Holy Trinity, on the essence of God. I absolutely wanted to know and fathom who God is. … In an instant my spirit was caught up into what seemed to be the next world. I saw an inaccessible light, *and in this light what appeared like three sources of light* which I could not understand.[956]

Perhaps this is also the reason why children (as well as those abiding in a state of spiritual childhood) are attracted by natural manifestations of God's simplicity. The expressions of his simple beauty in the world that he made fill them with joy and wonder, from the unfolding of a flower to the rays of a star or a snowflake. Regarding the latter, Caryll Houselander once wrote:

> Each one is a minute mandala, a circle of vibrant light radiating from a cross. Multitudinous though they are, there are no two alike — tiny ferns and stars and wildflowers of frost, each having its own exquisite design that is invisible to the naked eye. … It is the pattern in creation of the Creator, in whom is the being of all that is.[957]

It would not be true to say, therefore, that all of God's properties and attributes are in reality reducible to the one simple property of being Divine, or undifferentiated Being. God is indeed the greatest possible being, infinitely Perfect Being, but he cannot possess absolute "property simplicity" because on any orthodox notion of the divine nature, he must have both "necessary" (i.e., essential) properties, and certain "contingent" properties flowing from their exercise or self-restraint. Thomas Morris explains:

> We believe that he is necessarily powerful, but that it is only contingently true of him that he used that power to create our

---

[956] Kowalska, *Diary*, entry 30, p. 17; italics mine.
[957] Caryll Houselander, *The Little Way of the Infant Jesus* (Manchester, NH: Sophia Institute Press, 1995 edition), p. 39 and 38.

world. He could have created another universe instead, or, perhaps, he could have refrained from creating any physical realm at all. We also believe that it is only contingently, not necessarily, true of God that he called Abraham out of Ur, spoke through Moses, and sent the prophets he chose. Moreover, I happen to be wearing a striped shirt today. I could have worn a plain shirt instead. It is a contingent fact that I am garbed in stripes. And God knows this fact. He thus has a belief, or is in a specific state of knowledge, which is contingent. He has the property of being in this cognitive state contingently, since its status must mirror the contingent status of the fact known. God is necessarily a knower. God contingently has the knowledge that I have on a striped shirt. Thus, there is both necessity and contingency with respect to God. And there seems to be no other way to capture this truth than to say that God has both necessary (essential) and contingent properties. But if that is so, then he cannot "have" just one and only one property, a single property with which he is identical. Nor can he be said to literally have no properties. The thesis of property simplicity therefore must be false.[958]

While Kenoticism necessarily has to abandon the traditional notion of "property simplicity" in God, it can uphold at least three other significant forms of divine simplicity: (1) "spatial simplicity," because God is not a physical object, and so he does not have spatially located parts; and (2) "temporal simplicity," because the eternal fullness of divine existence is not divisible into temporal segments, as our lives in linear time are.[959] Moreover, all of his essential properties and attributes are perfectly harmonious and integrated, and immutably and inseparably bound together. Thomas McCall refers to divine simplicity in this sense as (3) "generic simplicity," and defines it for us as follows:

---

[958] Morris, *Our Idea of God*, p. 117.
[959] Ibid., p. 114.

God is simple in the sense that within God (i) there is no composition whereby God is made up of parts or pieces that are ontologically prior to or more basic than God; (ii) there is no metaphysical complexity that would bring contradiction or moral complexity of any kind; (iii) there are genuine distinctions within the divine nature; and (iv) all essential divine attributes are mutually entailing and coextensive.[960]

In other words, the divine nature includes an array of essential, inseparable and compossible divine attributes. Again, Thomas Morris explains what all this can mean:

[I]n the case of God's possession of his defining, distinctively divine [essential] attributes, there is no question of coming-to-be and ceasing-to-be. He possesses these properties in all possible circumstances. There is no fragility or tenuousness to his character. His divinity is neither accidental nor temporary. His properties cannot "come apart." The instability and contingency which accompany complexity in our [human] case offer no threat to his exalted status whatsoever. Thus, there is no need to endorse property simplicity to provide for the recognition of God's greatest possible metaphysical stature. The purported benefits of simplicity can be had otherwise. ...

---

[960] McCall, "Trinity Doctrine Made Plain and Simple," in Crisp and Sanders, eds. *Advancing Trinitarian Theology*, p. 55. McCall further explains point (i) by stating: "Since it is not so much as possible that any of the divine persons exist without the others or apart from the divine essence, they are not, strictly speaking, *parts of God*" (p. 55). This seems very close to what McCall defines as the "Formal Simplicity" doctrine of Bl. John Duns Scotus, which states that the only distinctions within the divine essence are what Duns Scotus called "formal" distinctions: distinctions which are neither "real" distinctions (that is, between independent and separable things) or merely "conceptual" distinctions (that is merely notional, or matters of formal logic). See McCall, p. 52-53. This may be an additional dimension of divine simplicity, which still leaves us short of having to embrace the doctrine of absolute divine simplicity of St. Thomas Aquinas.

[The traditional doctrine of divine simplicity] is an attempt to express a true mystery concerning the real, metaphysical unity of God. It is sensible to think that there is a special kind of integrity to the being of God. The thesis of property simplicity, as it stands, just fails to capture it. So by rejecting the [traditional] doctrine of divine simplicity ... I don't mean to be turning my back on any legitimate inklings of divine uniqueness which may ultimately stand behind it. I just mean to indicate that insofar as those inklings can be captured in language, the thesis of property simplicity, and its associated general doctrine, is just not what we need for that expression.[961]

In short, along with the First Vatican Council, the New Kenotic Theology can say that God is as "absolutely simple" as it is possible to be — but the traditional understanding of divine simplicity has not expressed that mystery well enough. Let us say, rather, that God in his eternal simplicity essentially consists of three divine persons — St. Faustina's three sources of one light — in perfect Trinitarian communion. That one light is radiant with distinct divine attributes or properties, but these elements exist in perfect, timeless, and eternal harmony, manifesting in that harmony an infinitely "simple beauty" beyond our comprehension.

Of course, in one sense it is a misnomer to speak of a "New Kenotic Theology," when all I am really doing is calling us back into the orbit of the Anglican stream of Moderate Kenoticism, as found above all, and in various ways, in the writings of Gore, Weston, Quick, Hebblethwaite, Swinburne, and Brown (with a bit of help from the Protestant philosopher Thomas Morris, and the Russian Orthodox theologian Sergius Bulgakov). So there is really not much "brand new" here at all: just a plea for Anglicans not to forget their rich heritage of reflections on the kenotic dimensions of Divine Love, and for Christians from other churches and traditions to receive these reflections in a way that can enrich their own appreciation of this great

---

[961] Ibid., p. 117-118.

mystery. This is the mystery in which God himself, in the person of his Son, came among us as one of us, to share our lot and to save us. Any theological tradition that can help us receive with deeper understanding and greater joy that mystery of Divine Love is well worth recovering.

Appendix A

Sed Contra:
A Response to Keith Ward's *Christ and the Cosmos: a Reformulation of Trinitarian Doctrine*

As luck (or divine providence) would have it, just as I was putting the finishing touches on the first draft of this manuscript, one of the leading philosophical theologians in the English-speaking world, Keith Ward, published a treatise that clearly advocated positions precisely the opposite of the ones I defend in my book. Rather than rewrite major portions of my manuscript in response to his, however, I thought it best to devote an entirely separate "appendix" solely to his work.

In this book Ward provides important clarifications and developments of positions he had stated earlier in his career. In addition, to my mind his book is also the best defence of a Unitary Model of the Trinity, and an Action Model of the Incarnation to be found anywhere in Anglican thought over the past 130 years. As such, it should be required reading for students and scholars of these issues in the 21st century. On the other hand, as I shall presently explain, I do not find that he makes a very persuasive case. It still seems to me that a Social-Organic Model of the Trinity, and a Moderate Kenotic Model of the Incarnation fit with Holy Scripture, mainstream Christian Tradition, and the canons of rational coherence and intelligibility better than the alternatives that Ward offers to us.

Unity-in-Trinity or Trinity-in-Unity?

One of the most helpful aspects of Ward's book is the clarity with which he maps out his position. **With regard to the mystery of the Holy Trinity, he proposes that** *God is one center or subject of consciousness and will, manifest in the world in three distinct forms of divine activity*:

> [T]here is one stream of consciousness operating in three significantly different ways of relating to creation. There is one

wholly integrated divine consciousness and will with three necessary, inseparable, and complementary modes of activity.
…

The mode of being that sustains the whole universe in existence is different from the mode of being that identifies itself with and acts in and through one (human) part of the universe [Jesus], and it is different again from the mode of being that cooperates inwardly with all created intelligent agents to shape them into one all-inclusive communion of being. Yet these are all distinctive activities of the one supreme mind and will of God, expressed in different ways. God is one cosmic Subject, expressed in three distinct but indivisible and inseparable modes of being.[1]

Thus, for Ward we find in God

three different modes of subsistence — creative, self-communicative, and unitive — of one unitary will and knowledge. The same God acts in three ways and therefore manifests the same agency in three different forms, instantiations, and loci of action. And that is not a social doctrine of the Trinity at all.[2]

The attentive reader will notice that all this is very close to the Trinitarian perspective offered by John Macquarrie in his magnum opus, *Principles of Christian Theology* (1977). Indeed, toward the end of Ward's book, he praises the Trinitarian theology of Macquarrie, and explains it in a way that shows its close proximity to his own point of view:

What Macquarrie calls the primordial, expressive, and unitive forms of divine action are co-present and cooperative in every divine act. … Macquarrie names these three forms [of divine

---

[1] Keith Ward, *Christ and the Cosmos: A Reformulation of Trinitarian Doctrine* (New York: Cambridge University press, 2015), p. 242 and 90.
[2] Ibid., p. 216.

activity] as the primordial (source of all possibilities), the expressive (expressing or manifesting itself in and through particular beings and 'above all in the finite being of Jesus'), and the unitive (uniting finite beings with Being itself). In every divine act, God is active as the primordial source of possibilities, the creative power that gives form to actual beings, and the unitive power which works to include them in the final goal of Being.[3]

Ward makes several major points in favor of this Unitary Model of the Trinity.

First, he insists that in St. John's Gospel the divine "Word" who "became flesh" in Jesus Christ is not described as a "person." For example, he notes:

> [T]he Greek word *Logos* can be translated in many ways — as 'Word,' 'Speech,' 'Thought,' 'Intellect,' 'Wisdom,' or even 'Reason.' It is a strangely impersonal term, and it does not seem to refer to a self-subsistent being, or one who exists as a person, in the sense of having a distinct and unique consciousness and agency. It suggests, rather, the act or quality of a personal being. For it is persons who have wisdom or intellect or speech, as a quality of their being.[4]

This is a curious argument, however, because for St. John the Divine Word is not just a mode of divine activity that generates ideals, possibilities, and intentions. The pre-incarnate Word is referred to as a "he" in almost all English translations of John 1:2-4: "*He* was in the beginning with God; all things were made through *him*, and without *him* was not anything made that was made. In *him* was life, and the life was the light of men" (RSV-CE). A literal translation of these verses would actually involve a repetition of "that one" or "that Logos," not "he." What makes almost all translators think that they are justified in

---

[3] Ibid., p. 260 and 258.
[4] Ibid., p. 53; italics mine.

using "he" throughout verses 2-4, however, is the context of the passage as a whole. For example, in verse 1 St. John says that in the beginning "the Word was *with* God," in Greek: *pros ton theon*. The word *pros* does not connote merely proximity to the Father, but also an intimacy of fellowship.[5] In verses 4-5, the Logos is identified as the "light of men" to whom John the Baptist "bore witness" (and John bore witness to a person, Jesus Christ, not just to a divine attribute or mode of activity, cf. verse 15); also, in verse 14 we are told that the Logos became *sarx*, "flesh" (in other words a fully human reality), and "we have beheld his glory, as of the only Son from the Father" — so the "Word" is the same as the Son, sent from the Father. There is also the implicit identification of the Logos with Jesus Christ at verses 17-18.[6] *On balance, then, there appears to be an implicit "personalization" of the Logos throughout this whole passage (verses 1-18) — and that was certainly the way most of the early Fathers of the Church understood John's "Logos."*[7] In order to remain consistent with his own Trinitarian model, however, Ward actually has to refer to the Divine Word or Son in a way that the consensus of New Testament translators never does — with an impersonal pronoun, as an "it":

---

[5] Erickson, *Christian Theology*, p. 357.

[6] I am grateful to the Rev. Dr. David Brown for some of these biblical insights. Note also the other "bookend" of St. John's Gospel: chapter 20, where St. Thomas addresses Jesus as "My Lord and My God" (20:28), and also Christ's great confession of his own divine identity using the name that God gave to himself in Exodus: "I am" in Jn 8:58.

[7] Among many examples, we may cite the following. St. Justin Martyr writes in *Apologia* II, xiii: "[F]or we worship and love, next to God, the Logos which is from the unbegotten and ineffable God; since it was on our behalf that he has been made man, that, becoming partaker of our sufferings, he may also bring us healing." St. Irenaeus of Lyons writes in *Adversus Haereses* V.i.1: "[T]he all-powerful Word of God, who never fails in justice, acted justly even in dealing with the Spirit of Rebellion. For it was by persuasion, not by force, that he redeemed his own property." And again, in IV.Xii.4: "From the beginning he was accustomed, as the Word of God, to descend and ascend for the salvation of those who were in distress." And again, in IV. XX. 6: "[T]he Word was made the minister of the Father's grace to man, for man's benefit. For man he wrought his redemptive work."

I would say that 'the Son' (also called 'the Word') is an aspect of the divine as it conceives and relates to a specific cosmos. *It* is not the whole of the divinity, but *it* is one of the forms of the divinity as humans are able to conceive it. Infinite Being turns in thought towards a cosmos, taking form as Wisdom. It creates the cosmos 'through' that Wisdom — not another person, but a personalized aspect of the divine.[8] ...

In fact, [in St. John's gospel] the impersonal nature of 'the Word' is remarkable. A 'word' is spoken by a person but is not itself a person. The one who speaks is the Father. This suggest that the Word is God's communicative and expressive thought. This thought has an eternal existence; the thought of the world exists before the world exists. A thought does not speak — *it* is the speech of the Father; we may say '*it* does what *it* hears.' The thought 'becomes flesh,' as the thought takes form as a human subject. Though *it* is the thought of God, *it* becomes expressed in the mind of a human being.[9]

What Ward has done, here, however, is simply collapse one side of the paradox in the first chapter of St. John's Gospel into the other side. Yes, the Divine Word is the expressed thought of God — but paradoxically, what makes the Divine Word different from a human word or thought is that this Word is also a fully divine person (Jn 1:1): The Word who became the subject of fully human "flesh" (1:14), he is the Divine Word or Son who came and dwelt among us as Jesus Christ (1:14, 17-18).

---

[8] Ibid., p. 69; italics mine. It is not clear what Ward means here by a "personalized" aspect of the divine: perhaps he means an aspect of Infinite Being that has been "personified" by Christians, so they can discuss it. In that sense, for Ward the divine Word or Son is not a divine person, but a form of divine activity given a "personal" literary form.

[9] Ibid., p. 55; italics mine. The next to last sentence quoted here lacks clarity on its own. As Ward explains elsewhere, the Word does not take flesh *as* a human subject, but in and through a created human subject.

Ward makes similar oversights in his reading of the first chapter of Colossians. Christ, he says, is there described as "divine wisdom itself, which was embodied on earth in a human person. And that wisdom is destined to include all things in *itself*, liberated from evil and transformed by the Spirit."[10] But in almost all English translations St. Paul refers to the pre-incarnate Wisdom (or Image) in verses 15-17 as a "he," not "it": "for in *him* all things were created ... all things were created through *him* and for *him*. *He* is before all things, and in *him* all things hold together." One major reason for the use of all the personal pronouns here is that the whole meditation on Christ in verses 15-20 evidently describes "the Son" mentioned in verses 13-14. Moreover, the title "the first-born" in verse 15 surely refers to a person (the first-born Son), who is clearly the same one whom St. Paul claims is the divine Image through whom and for whom all things exist (verse 16). In short, Ward's impersonal interpretation of St. Paul's use of the Wisdom tradition in this passage runs afoul of the wider context, and again the consensus of almost all biblical translators.

The Book of Hebrews too speaks in personal terms of the pre-Incarnate "Son" as the one "through whom God [the Father] also created the world. *He* reflects the glory of God and bears the very stamp of his nature, upholding the universe by *his* word of power" (Heb 1:2-3). In other words, the subject being referred to as performing all these divine functions (such as upholding the whole universe) in verses 2-3 is the "Son" mentioned near the start of verse 2 (again, see Colossians 1, where the "Son" of verse 13 and the "first-born" of verse 15 is the same one who performs the cosmic role of holding together the entire universe in verse 17). Surely these cannot all be mere literary personifications of an aspect of divine activity better described, but never referred to in the New Testament, as an "it"! And again, there is plenty of evidence that the early Church Fathers spoke of the Divine Word or Son in fully personal terms.

In fact, the Classical, orthodox tradition of Christology can do justice to the dimension of the Divine Logos that Ward wants to highlight —

---

[10] Ibid., p. 71; italics mine.

the Word as divine communicative thought, expression, and idealization — without depersonalizing the Word. Indeed, the two sides of the paradox are not contradictory, for as Aquinas taught, the Father can be said eternally to generate a true Image and Logos of his own nature by an act of his divine intellect, and yet the fruit of that intellectual act also can be said to be a divine person or Son. The Divine Word is no less a divine person for being generated *per modum intellectus*. It is a mystery we cannot fully fathom, to be sure, but divine revelation in Scripture and Tradition indicates that it is so, and we have no grounds for saying that this is logically impossible. In Hebrews the paradox is clearly evident: "but in these last days [God] has *spoken* to us by a *Son*" (Heb 1:2).

Ward contends that the Holy Spirit also is not presented to us in the New Testament as a personal subject in his own right:

> The Spirit lives 'in' the disciples (John 14,17), whereas persons do not normally live in one another. The Spirit is sent either by the Father or by Jesus and has the specific job of guiding the disciples into truth, but he does not seem to have a will of his own: 'He will not speak on his own, but will speak whatever he hears' (John 16,13). The Spirit is certainly active and causally effective. But is this a distinct person, with a will and experience of his own? ... [T]he Spirit does not seem to be a participant member of a group of three individuals who together decide upon what is to happen in the world. ...

> [T]he Spirit does not speak of *itself.* Sent by Jesus (John 20,22), or by the Father at the request of Jesus, it is in that sense that *it* is the 'Spirit of truth' (14,16) .... Spirit does not here seem to be an independent personal reality who has conversations with the Father and the Son in some internal Trinitarian society.[11]

---

[11] Ibid., p. 41-42 and 63; italics mine.

Notice that once again, to be consistent with his Trinitarian model, Ward has to do something that New Testament translators (other than the Jehovah's Witnesses) never do: refer to the Holy Spirit with an impersonal rather than a personal pronoun. **In the New Testament, however, the emphasis on the personal reality of the Holy Spirit is so pronounced that in John 16:13-15, Jesus refers to the Spirit as "he" nine times in three verses.** In his *An Expository Dictionary of New Testament Words*, W.E. Vine writes: "The Personality of the Spirit is emphasized at the expense of strict grammatical procedure in John 14:26; 15:26; 16:8, 13, 14, where the emphatic pronoun *ekeinos*, 'He,' is used of Him in the masculine, whereas the noun *pneuma* [Spirit] is neuter in Greek, while the corresponding word in Aramaic, the language in which our Lord probably spoke, is feminine (rucha, cp. Heb. ruach)."[12] **Doubtless, St. John inserted the masculine pronoun for the Spirit in this passage (16:13-15) because it refers back to Christ's use of the Greek *parakletos* in verses 7-11 (usually translated as "Counselor" or "Advocate"). The "Spirit of truth," then, is seen as in apposition to *parakletos*, which justifies continued use of the masculine personal pronoun in verses 13-15:**[13]

> Nevertheless I tell you the truth: it is to your advantage that I go away, for if I do not go away, the Counselor will not come to you. And when he comes, he will convince the world of sin and of righteousness and of judgment....
>
> I have yet many things to say to you, but you cannot bear them now. When the Spirit of truth comes, he will guide you into all the truth; for he will not speak on his own authority, but whatever he hears he will speak, and he will declare to you the things that are to come. He will glorify me, for he will take

---

[12] W.E. Vine, *An Expository Dictionary of New Testament Words* (1940), accessed online at https://www.blueletterbible.org/search/Dictionary/viewTopic.cfm?topic=VT000 2735.
[13] Again, many thanks to the Rev. Dr. David Brown for the substance of some of these biblical insights.

what is mine and declare it to you. All that the Father has is mine; therefore I said that he will take what is mine and declare it to you. (Jn 16: 7-8 and 13-15)

Ward is certainly right to point out that the Spirit is spoken of as "sent" by the other two divine persons, and never as a "sender." But this does not necessarily imply that he is not a person. After all, in the New Testament the Son is said to be "sent" into the world by the Father and to "send" the Spirit, while the Father "sends" the Son and the Spirit into the world for their mission, but is not himself "sent" by anyone. In classical western orthodoxy, at least since St. Augustine, this threefold distinction in roles, that is, this distinction in their mode of activity in the world, was held to be an expression of the distinct, eternal mode of origin of each divine person. The Father is the "origin without origin," the Son is originated and originates, the Spirit is originated but does not originate. The way they act in the economy of salvation, therefore, reflects their hypostatic distinction of origin. It does not reflect any lack of "personhood" in any of the three.

There is also plenty of evidence in Luke-Acts and in the epistles of St. Paul that the apostolic Church both experienced and spoke of the Holy Spirit in fully personal terms (that is, as a divine center of consciousness and will). At least implicitly, the Holy Spirit is said to be omnipotent (Lk 1:35), omniscient (Rom 8:27), omnipresent (Acts 2:17) and eternal (Heb 9:14) — all attributes of divinity (cf. Mt 28:19). Fully divine, the Spirit is also "personal." He conceives purposes (Acts 8:29: "And the Spirit said to Philip, 'Go up and join this chariot;'" cf. Acts 13:2); he guides the understanding and decisions of the apostles (Acts 15:28: "For it has seemed good to the Holy Spirit and to us to lay upon you no greater burden than these necessary things …."), and he "intercedes" for us in prayer ("[T]he Spirit himself intercedes for us with sighs too deep for words," Rom 8:26). The Spirit can be "grieved" by the sins of humanity (Eph 4:30), and he can even be lied to (Acts 5:3: "Ananias, why has Satan filled your heart to lie to the Holy Spirit?"). Moreover, contrary to what Ward claims, the Holy Spirit appears to be a distinct personal reality who does indeed "have conversations with the Father and the Son in some internal Trinitarian society."[14] According to St. Paul, the Spirit within us in prayer bears witness by enabling us to cry with him "Abba, Father" (Rom 8:15-16 and 26-27). As previously discussed (in Part One, Chapter Five), the implication here is that when our prayer falters, it is taken up by the Spirit into his own dialogue with the Father.

Ward is right to point out that the New Testament often refers to the Spirit in ways that seem to make him other than a "person." For example, he is called a "power"; he is said to be "sent" by the Father and the Son; he lives within human hearts and can be "poured out" upon us from on high. But all of this only stands to reason: the Holy Spirit is an infinite *divine* person, not a finite human person, and infinite persons surely can do many things that shatter the boundaries of human personhood. As we have already seen: if he is said to be "sent" by the Father and the Son, this does not make him a mere divine "mode of activity," in the universe. It simply means that his personal mode of living out and expressing the divine nature reflects his unique and eternal relationship of origin. In addition, while our mode of speaking of the presence and activity of the Spirit in the world must of necessity be analogical, an infinite person surely can be said to "dwell within us" in "power" in a way that a human person cannot, for he can be present and act in the depths of the human heart, strengthen the will and illumine the mind in a far more direct and effective way than any human person could ever do.

The divine, personal identity of the Holy Spirit was something that only attained greater clarity in the mind of the Church over time (and was only officially defined at the Second Ecumenical Council, Constantinople I, in 381 AD). Some confusion over the Holy Spirit arose from the ambiguity of the notion of the "Spirit of the Lord" in the Old Testament, and the very close relationship in the New Testament between the presence and activity of the ascended Christ, and the role of the Holy Spirit in the life of the Church and the heart

---

[14] Ibid., p. 63.

of the believer.[15] Still, my contention would be that the fully divine and distinct personal identity of the Holy Spirit was implicit in the apostolic witness in the New Testament from the beginning, and this teaching makes better sense of the apostolic faith in this regard than any rival interpretation, including Ward's.

One of Ward's principal objections to all social models of the Trinity (that is, to any model that seems to say that there are three personal subjects, three distinct centres of consciousness and will in God), is that the New Testament shows them to be hierarchically ordered:

> The three centres of consciousness do not seem to be equal persons. It is the Father who commands, who sends, and who ultimately controls. The Son's role is to ask, to hear, and to obey the Father's will, not to initiate any independently chosen sources of action. And the Spirit seems to be almost entirely passive, carrying out what he is sent to do but not apparently taking any part in a divine conversation about what is to happen. ... If these are three individuals, there seems to be a clear hierarchical line of authority between them, which makes

---

[15] Lionel Spencer Thornton argued in *The Incarnate Lord* (London: Longmans, Green and Co., 1928), p. 323, that according to the New Testament "Both Christ and the Spirit dwell in the Christian soul, but not in the same way." Christ is the "indwelling content of the Christian life" that is being "formed" in us, so that we conform "to the likeness of Christ's character." The Holy Spirit is the one at work within us who conforms us to Christ."St. Paul nowhere says that the Spirit is formed in us, or that we are to be conformed to the image of the Spirit." Similarly, as Gerald O'Collins, SJ, points out:

> It is the indwelling Spirit that helps us pray *Abba*, and witnesses to Christ (Rom 8:15-16; Gal 4:6; I Cor 12:3), and not an indwelling Christ who makes us pray like that and witnesses to the Spirit. ... Finally, unlike the Spirit, it is the crucified and resurrected Christ who at the end will subject all things to the Father (I Cor 15: 24-28). (Gerald O'Collins, SJ, *The Tripersonal God: Understanding and Interpreting the Trinity* (New York: Paulist Press, 2014, p. 63-64).

any thought that they are three fully individual persons who are equal with one another dubious.[16]

This also seems a curious argument, on two counts.

First, it hardly seems fair to object to Social Trinitarianism on the grounds that there is no evidence in the New Testament of three "fully individual" persons who "initiate independently chosen sources of action" — as if Social Trinitarianism only works if there is clear evidence of tritheism in the Scriptures! Social Trinitarians do not hold that any of the three persons initiate *independent* actions; rather, they always act in harmony, in accord with the purposes and decisions fully shared by all three. In other words, Social Trinitarians seek to remain true to the mystery and paradox of the Trinity; they simply insist that one side of that paradox — the side that says that there are three "persons," three centres of consciousness and will in God who relate to each other in self-giving, mutual love and total cooperation — must not be erased by being collapsed into mere modes of activity of just one divine person.

In addition, Ward's argument here is a curious one because even in human experience we know that human persons can be entirely equal in worth and dignity, as children of God made in his image, and yet carry out social roles differing greatly in authority and responsibility, and in the exercise of distinct natural skills and spiritual gifts. For example, in the Church there are bishops, priests, deacons, religious, and laity; in the economy there are shareholders, employers, and employees; in the political realm there are rulers and subjects, those who mostly govern and others who are mostly governed. None of these distinctions in social roles necessarily implies a sub-human status for anyone (although the way these roles are carried out by sinful human beings can sometimes "dehumanize" others). By analogy, in the mystery of the Holy Trinity the fact that the Father is the ultimate and eternal source of the other two divine persons, and therefore instantiates and expresses the divine nature in a different way from the

---

[16] Ibid., p. 36.

Son and the Spirit does not necessarily contradict the equality of nature of the three divine persons.

To be sure, in the run-up to the First Ecumenical Council at Nicea it took some time for the early mainstream Christian theologians fully to appreciate and clarify the divine equality of all three persons of the Trinity — especially regarding the Holy Spirit, as we have seen. Also, a degree of "subordination" of the Son to the Father can be found in the writings of some of the earliest Christian writers, such as St. Justin Martyr and Origen. Doubtless, one of the difficulties here was that the existence of the divine Son was revealed to the world through a lowly human vessel — an instantiation of human nature — an earthly vehicle that both revealed and at the same time veiled the full reality of the divine personhood of the Son. The mainstream Church, however, remained faithful to the apostolic witness in the New Testament in this regard, culminating in the Nicene Creed.

Ward contends that conceiving the Trinity on his more unitary than social model does not mean that in the gospels, when Jesus is praying to the Father, God is actually praying to himself. For (as we shall see) according to Ward, Jesus is not personally divine. Here Ward is responding to William Hasker, who had claimed that if the Son is not clearly distinguished from the Father as a distinct divine person, then when Jesus was praying to the Father, a mere uni-personal God would have been praying to himself. Indeed, on the Cross, Jesus would have cried out that he had forsaken himself![17] But Hasker's argument only succeeds if we presuppose that Jesus had a divine identity — a presupposition which, again, as we shall see, Ward disputes. Conversely, Ward says, from the mere fact that Jesus prayed to the Father we cannot deduce that there are at least two persons in relationship within God:

> Starting from the Patristic formulation that the [Divine] Word is the subject of Jesus' experiences, it is easy to move to the conclusion that it is the Word who prays to the Father and that

---

[17] Ibid., p. 35.

this establishes a relationship of two personal individuals within the being of God itself. But this does not quite seem to be what the New Testament writings imply. ... It is Jesus who prays to the Father, not the Father who prays to the Son. Praying, after all, is not conversation; it is or includes, requests addressed to a being of infinitely greater power. So while the fact that Jesus prays to the Father distinguishes Jesus from the Father, it does not seem to refer to a distinction between two persons of the same sort.[18]

Ward then offers us an alternative way of understanding Christ's prayer that (allegedly) does not require us to say that there are at least two divine persons, and that "turns the tables," so to speak, on Hasker's argument:

When Jesus prays to the Father, it is the human person, limited in power and knowledge, one finite being among others, wholly dependent upon the creator for his existence and nature, who voices his desire and intentions, and attests his total dependence upon the transcendent creator of all. It is not God as the eternal Word who prays to God as Father — which *would* be a case of the divine speaking to itself.[19]

Here again, we are beset with curious arguments. After all, prayer is traditionally defined, in part, as a "conversation" with God, as St. Theresa of Avila once wrote in her autobiography: "Mental prayer is, as I see it, simply a friendly intercourse and frequent solitary conversation with Him who, as we know, loves us." Jesus not only speaks to the Father in prayer: the Father also speaks to him (Lk 3:22; Jn. 12:28). The fact that Jesus has a relationship of prayer with the Father counts as evidence that there are at least two "persons," two centers of consciousness and will, in-relationship with each other. Moreover, if Jesus is God the eternal Word in person, then his prayer life would *not* be "a case of the divine speaking to itself," but evidence

---

[18] Ibid., p. 40.
[19] Ibid., p. 78; italics mine.

of one divine person, the divine Son or second person of the Trinity conversing with another divine person, the Father, in an through the human form that the divine Son had assumed as his own. In short, if Jesus is a divine person, then there is evidently more than one "self" in God, and one of those "selves" is engaged in the human pole of prayer. This does not leave us with three gods, however; for as we saw in Part One, Chapter Five, the One God may be conceived as a self-sustaining, organic and relational union of three divine personal subjects. In other words, when Jesus prays he is not praying to his creator; rather, the only-begotten, eternal Son, dwelling under all the conditions and limitations of human life, is praying to his eternal Father, who is another "person" within the eternal communion of love in the life of the Blessed Trinity.

Missing in Ward's whole approach here is not only faithfulness to the full range of the Trinitarian ramifications of the New Testament, but also faithfulness to the guidance of the mainstream Tradition of the Church in the unfolding of these mysteries. After all, the Church is "the Body of Christ" on earth (Rom 12:4-5; I Cor 12:12-13, 27) and "the pillar and bulwark of the truth" (I Tim 3:15). Regardless of one's ecclesiology or denominational allegiance, it should be common ground among Christians that at least the *consensus fidelium*, especially the consensus of most of the faithful prior to the tragic divisions between Christians in the second millennium, and especially in the highest, official expressions of the Church (such as the ecumenical creeds), would be considered as a trustworthy guide in the Holy Spirit to what can be said with confidence about the mysteries of God, Christ, and salvation. Historically, and at least officially, this has certainly been the assumption of Ward's own Anglican Communion. If Ward is right, however, then the mainstream, creedal Tradition of Christianity has been substantially and tragically mistaken on this central mystery of the faith.[20] For in its highest expression, the Nicene-

---

[20] Oliver Crisp sums up the issue well when he writes: "I suggest that God would not permit the church to come to a substantially mistaken account of the person

Constantinopolitan Creed, the pre-incarnate Word or Son is clearly held to be a "person," a "who" not an "it": "through *whom* all things were made: *Who* for us men and for our salvation came down from heaven." In fact, he is a fully *divine* person: "God of God, Light, of Light; Very God of Very God; Begotten, not made; Being of one substance with the Father …." Moreover, the Holy Spirit is confessed to be a divine person too, "*who* proceedeth from the Father and the Son, *who* with the Father and Son together is worshipped and glorified, *who* spake by the prophets." If neither the fullness of the (at least implicit) New Testament witness, nor the guiding voice of the ancient, mainstream creedal Tradition of the Church in interpreting and unfolding that witness can be trusted on these matters, then on what grounds can Ward fairly claim that his Unitary Model of the Trinity properly reflects God's self-revelation given to the world through Jesus Christ and his apostles? That Tradition does not strictly necessitate a social doctrine of the Trinity — for a unitary, subsistent relations doctrine also has roots in the mainstream Tradition, in a tributary rooted in scripture, and running from Augustine to Aquinas — but (as I argued in Part One, Chapter Five of my book), Holy Scripture and mainstream Christian Tradition at least *permit* Social Trinitarianism within their parameters, even as they clearly *exclude* the form of the doctrine of the Trinity offered to us by Ward.

Of course, Ward might fairly argue that here I am just the proverbial "pot calling the kettle black"! For it could be said that the Social Trinitarian doctrine that I have proposed, as well as all kenotic theories of the Incarnation — even the Moderate Kenotic Model I defended in my book — also lie outside the boundaries of classical Christian orthodoxy. After all, these theories involve a significant revision of the traditional understanding of God's absolute divine simplicity, immutability, and impassibility. True enough. But there are at least three mitigating circumstances here. (1) The absolute simplicity,

---

of Christ and to encode this in a canonical decision in an ecumenical council, for what we think about the person of Christ touches the heart of Christian doctrine and therefore the heart of the gospel. It is an impoverished doctrine of providence that claims otherwise." (Crisp, *The Word Enfleshed*, p. 76).

immutability, and impassibility of the divine nature, while accepted by almost all of the ancient Fathers and medieval Scholastics, by divine providence never received formal, dogmatic definition by any ecumenical creed or papal decree (prior to Vatican I, at least). This surely leaves a bit of "wiggle room" for fresh developments of philosophical and theological thinking in these areas, as long as such developments remain respectful of the fundamental concerns that led to the formation of that informal, historical consensus on these matters in the first place. I have endeavored to "proceed with caution" in just that way (as I hope the final chapter of my book fairly shows). (2) Besides, as I have also tried to show, the version of Social Trinitarianism and Kenotic Christology proposed in this book does not, in fact, contradict the guidance and parameters of the core definitions of the faith issued by the ancient ecumenical councils and decrees — nor do these doctrines contradict at least the underlying intentions of the councils and decrees of the Catholic Church in communion with Rome of the second millennium. (3) Finally, given that no major theologian ever put forward for discussion any truly "kenotic" theory of the Incarnation prior to the 19th century, then it is only fair that the theory should be given a hearing in its best forms. After all, legitimate developments of doctrine sometimes happen in the life of the Church in just this way. A new idea is put forward in some half-baked, or rash and imprudent form, and at first it is sharply rejected, even by great saints and doctors, but then after many generations of more careful analysis and consideration, the "wheat" is extracted from the "weeds," so to speak, and aspects of the original proposal are actually found to unfold implications of the apostolic deposit of faith, and the ancient Tradition of the Church that were not fully appreciated before. For Roman Catholics, the historical development of the doctrine of the Immaculate Conception of the Blessed Virgin Mary is surely a case in point.

Ward's theory of the Trinity, however, sails too close to the shores of ancient Modalistic Monarchianism and Sabellianism, and more modern forms of Unitarianism to make any plausible claim to be a legitimate development of doctrine rooted in scripture and the ancient councils and creeds.

Indeed, the cost of skirting the scriptural and creedal Tradition of the ancient Church on the Trinitarian mystery of God manifests itself in some of the conclusions that Ward inevitably reaches.

(1) **Ward is forced to admit that *on his Unitary Model, God must be dependent upon a relationship with his creation for the fulfilment of his potential for the actualization and exercise of the divine attribute of "love."*** Ward explains that on his view:

> That does not mean that God must necessarily and always have created others to love. It means only that the expression of God's nature makes it natural that God will (not necessarily without beginning or intermission or end!) at some point create other persons in order to realise the divine nature as loving in relation to them.[21]

For Ward, this also means that God does not need to have internal "persons" in loving relationship with each other to be a relational God with the attribute of perfect love. An isolated, loving, divine person, he reasons, is not a contradiction in terms:

> [I]n the unique case of God, the one and only creator of everything other than itself, isolation might be bliss, since God would presumably enjoy unlimited bliss in the contemplation of infinite perfection (and that would not be selfish, since there are no other realities in existence). What would be wrong with that, or what would be ontologically impossible with that?[22]

---

[21] Ibid., p. 180.

[22] Ibid., p. 122-123. Given that the Holy Scriptures, and our Lord, teach us to refer to God as "he," the frequent use of the impersonal pronoun "it" for God in this book is also open to objection — but we do not have the space to tackle this

The trouble is that a solitary, uni-personal God would not possess the "infinite perfection" needed to be the object of such blissful self- contemplation, precisely because he would not possess in his own nature the infinite perfection of love (love infinitely given, infinitely received, and infinitely returned). On Ward's Unitary Model of the Trinity, therefore, God would be required to create a world of persons to love and to love him back in order to fulfill his potential for exercising the attribute love. One wonders how that kind of metaphysic fits with St. John's definition that "God is love" (I Jn 4:8), and how it fits with the biblical understanding of the sovereignty and aseity of God, "as if he needed anything" (Acts 17:25). Besides, no finite creatures could ever fully meet God's needs in this respect, for a finite person cannot infinitely receive divine love, nor infinitely return it. *It follows that unless there is a real distinction of persons within God who can relate to each other in infinitely perfect loving communion, then God could never attain or enjoy the perfection of love.*

Ward's position here has other dire ramifications as well. Roch Kereszty, O.Cist., summed these up in *Jesus Christ: Fundamentals of Christology*:

> In such a system humankind becomes a necessary partner for God, without whom God would not be wholly God because he would not be loving. This conclusion, which implies a temporal process of growth in God, would change the very heart of the biblical message, which insists that creation, and even more so the incarnation are pure gifts of God's unselfish love. God has created the world and humankind not for personal gain but for our good. He became incarnate and died for us not to perfect himself

---

issue here. See Robert Stackpole, "Why Does St. Faustina Call Jesus 'My Mother'?" at https://www.thedivinemercy.org/library/article.php?NID=2468.

but to save us and   assure us a share in his own fullness.[23]

Ward argues, however, that self-giving love among infinitely perfect and   co-equal divine persons does not make much sense:

> There is, to put it bluntly, no point in a divine person giving itself to another divine person, since they both already possess everything that is worthwhile. …[24]

> The terminology of 'giving and receiving love' belongs to societies of needy and dependent beings who would be grateful for any help or encouragement they can get. A society of such beings would be good, but it would hardly be an example of absolute perfection. …[25]

> What sort of love could exist between three perfect persons of the social Trinity? Love in the ordinary human sense involves caring for others in distress, helping them achieve their unique goods, creating and valuing such goods, developing together as different personalities, helping but leaving free, and cooperating when required. Difference is important to love, involving a sharing of different perspectives and interests. All this depends on persons not being omnipotent and omniscient and wholly good, but sometimes being in need of help, needing to learn other's viewpoints, and learning patience, tolerance, empathy and understanding.

> What would love among three omnipotent, omniscient, perfectly good beings be like? They might

---

[23] Kereszty, *Jesus Christ; Fundamentals of Christology*, p. 348.
[24] Ibid., p. 200.
[25] Ibid. p. 178.

know each other completely and admire each other tremendously. But … they need no help, need to learn nothing, do not need to put up with one another's foibles. What is the point of sharing when there is nothing new to learn, nothing one cannot already do, no possibility of development in self-sacrifice? … Can you really value someone who is exactly the same as you?[26]

Here Ward seems to have fallen into a misunderstanding of the nature of love that I addressed earlier in my book (albeit in a different form). Even on the merely human level, it does not seem to be the case that "giving and receiving love" always takes the form of merciful, compassionate love, that is, the kind of love that seeks to meet the essential needs or overcome the sufferings of others. Not all authentic human love is of that sort. For example, it can be a truly loving act to praise the Lord in worship, to engage in the conjugal act with one's spouse, to play a game with one's children, or simply to share any common and wholesome joy, such as listening to good music or watching a beautiful sunset together. *Similarly, divine persons can completely give themselves in love to each other through sharing eternal joys, cooperating harmoniously in divine purposes, and expressing (in some mysterious way, no doubt) gratitude and appreciation for who and what they eternally are: unique, personal instantiations of the divine nature.*

Ward asks: but how are they unique? Can you really love someone who is exactly the same as you? These questions might be a significant challenge to the Subsistent Relations Model of the Trinity of St. Augustine and St. Thomas Aquinas, but they hardly apply to the Social-Organic Model of the Trinity that I have defended here, and in Part One, Chapter Five of my book. Rooted in aspects of the thought of Leonard Hodgson, Brian Hebblethwaite, Richard Swinburne, David Brown, Cornelius Plantinga, Jr., Keith Yandell, and C. Stephen

---

[26] Ibid., p. 179.

Layman, this is the doctrine that the divine persons are unique, first of all, in their relations of origin, and therefore that *each divine person possesses, expresses, and experiences the divine nature in his own unique and characteristic fashion — paternal, filial, or pneumatic — in a way reflective of his unique mode of origin.* To begin with, they each have their own eternal act of self- consciousness, and the (not fully communicable) experience of being a particular divine person. For example, only the Father is aware of himself as Father, and fully experiences what it is to be the Father. Also, each divine person performs distinct acts in the world, albeit in harmony with the other divine persons, and experiences those acts in his own unique way. For example, only the Son became incarnate, and experienced the fullness of what it was like to be the divine Son incarnate, but he did so by the power and assistance of the Holy Spirit.

This does not mean that there are three gods. What it does mean is that God is (to speak analogically) a social and organic communion of divine persons — "social" in that there are three persons, three distinct subjects of consciousness and will in God, united by bonds of mutual love and cooperation, and "organic" in that they are ontologically and eternally dependent upon each other in their relations of origin. Only together in these ways does each of the three persons fully actualize all his divine attributes, and eternally sustain and enact the Tripersonal divine reality. I am compelled to repeat in summary form here what I argued in my own book in Part One, Chapter Five, because Ward's arguments seem to have less force against that Trinitarian model than the other Social Trinitarian models that he critiques.

(2) **Ward's Unitary Model ultimately forces him to conclude that *there is no mutual love among the persons of the Holy Trinity*:**

Does it follow that there is no mutual love between Father and Son? It does. There cannot be mutual love between two aspects of divine experience and action. Love only truly exists where there is an 'other' to receive and return love. Of course, the human Jesus is just such an other, so there is mutual love between [the] Father and the human aspect of the incarnate Son. This emphasizes the point that the eternal Word is not a separate Subject from the Father. But Jesus is precisely a separate Subject, though one who has been subsumed from the first moment of his human life into the divine life. Thus there is mutual love between the infinite God and the human who is assumed into the divine life but not obliterated by that life.[27]

On the contrary: the New Testament explicitly states (and sometimes implies) that there is the deepest possible love between the eternal Son and his eternal Father. For example: "The Father loves the Son and has given all things into his hand" (Jn 3:35) — the context here is a discussion of the mystery that the Son "comes from above" and was "sent" by the Father into the world "to bear witness to what he has seen and heard" (3:32, that is, seen and heard in his eternal, pre-incarnate life with the Father). Thus, the Father eternally loved the Son by giving him the eternal truth to which he would bear witness when he was sent into the world, so that the whole world would ultimately belong to his Son. Again: "For the Father loves the Son, and shows him all that he himself is doing (5:20) … for whatever he does, the Son does likewise" (5:19). Christ's high priestly prayer is perhaps the best example:

Father, the hour has come; glorify your Son, that the son may glorify you [A]nd now, Father, glorify me in your own presence *with the glory which I had with you before the world was made.* Father, I desire that they also, whom

---

[27] Ibid., p. 242.

you have given me, may be with me where I am, *to behold my glory which you have given me in your love for me before the foundation of the world.* O righteous Father, the world has not known you, but I have known you; and these know that you have sent me. I made known to them your name, and I will make it known, *that the love with which you have loved me may be in them,* and I in them. (Jn 17: 1, 5, 24-26; italics mine)

"Most importantly," Ward writes, if we adopt his Unitary Model of the Trinity "we can unhesitatingly affirm the words of Jesus, "Hear O Israel, the Lord your God is one Lord" (Mk 12:29)."[28] Ward evidently intended this to be the "clinching" biblical argument for his position (hence his introductory phrase "Most importantly ...."). A closer look at this passage, however, reveals just the opposite. Jesus is here quoting the Israelites' daily prayer called the *Shema,* taken from Deuteronomy 6:4-5. But the Hebrew original of this verse, with which Jesus must have been familiar, speaks of God as "one" not by using the Hebrew word for numerical singularity (*yachid*), but by using the word for a composite or group unity (*echad*), the very same word used to describe Adam and Eve as "one flesh" (Gen 2:24), and to describe the one, united "whole assembly" of Israelites returning from exile (Ezra 2:64).[29] Of course, I am not claiming here that the author of

---

[28] Ibid., p. 256.

[29] See Erickson, *Christian Theology*, p. 354-355. The early Fathers of the Church recognized other passages as well in the Hebrew Scriptures that foreshadowed the Divine Trinity, especially instances where the Lord God spoke of himself in a plural form (e.g. Gen 1:26-28 and Is 6:1-8). Such foreshadowing is often dismissed on the grounds that it merely represents God as the King of Heaven using the "royal we" to refer to himself and the whole angelic court. But this argument is anachronistic: the "royal we" was largely the invention of Medieval Christendom, and not customary in ancient Israel or the ancient Near-East; see Erickson, p. 353-354. Along with Deuteronomy 6:4-5, these biblical passages also speak to the objection sometimes raised against Social Trinitarianism that it leaves matters unclear whether we should worship and address God as a group (them) or as an individual (he). However, Scripture sometimes seems to do both (see also Mt 28:19 and I Cor 8:6) which signals that the infinite and heavenly

Deuteronomy consciously and explicitly thought of God as a plurality of persons. But the author was guided by the Holy Spirit to choose this word and this way of expressing Jewish monotheism, rather than another, more obvious way. **In other words, here in the daily prayer of all Israel, and at the start of our Lord's Two Great Commandments, we have an implicit statement that the mystery of the unity of God is more than a numerical unity: it is a mystery of persons-in-relation.**

Action Christology and the Incarnation

Keith Ward's book also offers a straightforward explanation and defence of what I called in Part One, Chapter One an "Action" Model of the Incarnation. This model involves the use of traditional titles for Jesus Christ such as "Lord" and "Word" in ways that simply do not match the classical, conciliar parameters of what "incarnation" might mean. Ward's book is more helpful than many in this respect, however, because at least he clearly defines his reinterpretation of the classical terminology:

---

mystery of the Tri-personal God transcends any sharp, earthly distinction between "me" and "us." As C.S. Lewis once wrote:

> On the human level one person is one being, and any two persons are two separate beings — just as, in two dimensions (say, on a flat sheet of paper) one square is one figure, and any two squares are two separate figures. On the Divine level you still find personalities, but up there you find them combined in new ways which we, who do not live on that level, cannot imagine. In God's dimension, so to speak, you find a being who is three Persons while remaining one Being, just as a cube is six squares while remaining one cube. Of course we cannot fully conceive a Being like that: just as, if we were so made that we perceived only two dimensions in space we could never properly imagine a cube. But we can get assort of faint notion of it. And when we do, we are then, for the first time in our lives, getting some positive idea, however faint, of something super-personal—something more than a person. (*Mere Christianity*, p. 162)

The Incarnation

The actions of God are so intertwined with the actions of Jesus that it is possible to speak of God and Jesus together as *kyrios* [Lord].[30]

Jesus could express and incarnate the eternal wisdom of God in human form, and in that sense he would be God the Word.[31]

[W]e may say that there is only one personal 'subject' in Jesus; but it is not the [Divine] Word, which is not a distinct subject of consciousness and will at all. There is only the human subject in Jesus, but that subject perfectly expresses the divine Ideal or self-communicative expression of God. ... The Word, on this model, is an eternal possibility made actual, first, as an eternal Ideal in the mind of God, and then (incarnated) in a finite subject.[32]

As David Brown has shown, however, this kind of unity of divinity and humanity in Jesus would be merely a *contingent* unity that could be broken by Jesus at any time (that is, if the human free will of the created person, Jesus, is to be respected). Thus, it would seem that Ward is offering us just an up-dated version of Nestorianism — a close cooperation and synergy between two persons: the divine person of God the Father through the influence of his Word, and a created, human person. As Ward puts it: "Jesus is a real human creative subject of action, whose unity with God is synergistic or one of total cooperation (that is essential, in my view, to believing that Jesus is fully human)."[33]

To be sure, no orthodox Christian would dispute that the divine Son of God, in his human nature anointed by the Holy Spirit, fully cooperated synergistically with the will of his heavenly Father. Historically, however, that perfect synergy was said to be the result and

---

[30] Ibid., p. 49.
[31] Ibid., p. 41.
[32] Ibid., p. 57.
[33] Ibid., p. 80.

expression of the Incarnation; it did not constitute or define the Incarnation itself. Rather, the Incarnation was defined by the ancient ecumenical councils as the mystery that Jesus is one divine person in two natures, fully human and fully divine (see the full discussion of this point in Part One, Chapter One, above).

Of course, this raises the whole question of what properly is meant in Christology by the word "person." Following C. Stephen Layman, I have argued that in general a person is a subject or bearer of properties of a "personal" kind (especially the capacity for self-consciousness, rational thought, and voluntary agency, as well as the capacity for loving inter-personal relationship).

Ward's book is most helpful when he dissects the view of some theologians that persons are *nothing but* "relations." There is little doubt that persons are essentially relational beings. A "person," divine or human, can only completely fulfill his or her nature through relationships of sharing and cooperation with other personal beings — and sometimes in relationships of dependence upon others. But this does not mean that persons are relationships, and nothing more. Ward explains:

> There is no doubt that cultivation of distinctively human capacities requires membership in society. … [But] it would be a mistake to dissolve persons simply into their relations or to say that persons are 'nothing but' the sum of their social relationships, as Karl Marx put it. … [I]n each person there is a core of individuality evidenced by more than just the ways in which they relate to others. Each person has a unique chain of experiences, a unique responsibility for acting, and a continually developing set of feelings and attitudes that may remain unknown even to his or her closest companions.
>
> I could not play the violin part of a Beethoven symphony unless I was related to others who helped me develop my talents, added their parts to the symphony, and shared my musical experiences. But what the symphony means to me and

The Incarnation

how it is experienced by me remains a privileged secret of my inner life. So we might well say that human persons are relational — they are properly social animals — but they retain an inner core of unique individuality which is more than the relations which have helped make them what they are. They are certainly not just relations.[34]

The doctrine of the Incarnation, as I understand and articulated it in my book, refers to the fact that Jesus is a *fully human* person (that is, a person with a fully human nature), but uniquely, not a *merely human* person; he is the divine Son of God dwelling among us *as* a fully human person (that is, he is the second person of the Trinity, who has made himself the subject of a definably human form of existence, with all the characteristic human attributes, such as possessing a human body and a human soul).[35] **In other words, the divine Son is the divine person who, without ceasing to be essentially divine, and without ceasing to uphold the whole universe with his wisdom and power, limited himself, restraining the exercise of some of his divine attributes at a particular time and place in human history in order to dwell with us under all the conditions of human life. It follows that *the divine Son is the one subject or bearer of all the fully human attributes, acts, and experiences of Jesus of Nazareth.* To put it in classical language, the human reality of Jesus is "enhypostasized" in the person of the Divine**

---

[34] Ibid., p. 172 and 173-174.

[35] Aaron Riches in *Ecce Homo*, p. 117 helps us understand in what sense Jesus is a divine-as-human person:

> If the human Christ is not a human hypostasis (or person) as Cyril, Leontius of Jerusalem, and [John] Damascene commonly hold, the human Christ is still "personally" human, in the sense that he incarnates "the characteristic and distinctive properties of the divine filiation of the Logos." In this way we see that the doctrine of the "enhypostatos," far from compromising the integrity of the humanity of Jesus, rather "throws into maximum relief the condescension of the divine action: it is the divine Son who lives a fully human life, subject to the contingency and vulnerability of fleshly existence."

Word. This is the traditional doctrine of the Incarnation in a moderately "kenotic" key.

For Keith Ward, however, to be truly human Jesus must be a *solely* human person: "Human beings in general are persons who have their own centres of creatively free action — that is an important part of the definition of a 'person,'" and again, "Jesus is a real, creative subject of action, whose unity with God is synergistic or one of total cooperation (that is essential, in my view, to believing that Jesus is fully human)."[36]

But this is a non-sequitur. As I argued in Part One, Chapter Five, if Jesus is a *divine* center of consciousness and will — a *divine* personal subject, dwelling among us under fully human conditions and limitations — then he has not necessarily violated or overwhelmed any human aspect of Jesus. For one thing, there is not a created being named "Jesus" who exists apart from or prior to the act of the incarnation of the divine Son *as* Jesus. Rather, Jesus is a divine person who has placed himself under human conditions and limitations, including suffering temptation and acting freely from within that fully human state and context. He is not God united with a created man that has been "hollowed out" of his human personhood, so to speak, or that is in any way "missing" human personhood or human freedom, as Ward fears.[37] On the contrary, he is God living among us *as* a man: the divine Son as the uncreated personal subject of all the fully human attributes, acts, and experiences of Jesus of Nazareth.[38]

---

[36] Ibid., p. 74 and 80.

[37] Ibid., p. 39.

[38] Stated in this way, the doctrine that the one personal subject in Jesus Christ is the divine Son, the second person of the Trinity, is *de fide* for Roman Catholics. Besides being implied in the Nicene Creed and at the Ecumenical Councils of Ephesus (431 AD) and Chalcedon (451 AD), as well as taught explicitly by the Second Ecumenical Council at Constantinople (553 AD), it has been clearly reiterated by the Catholic magisterium on several occasions: for example, by Pope Pius XII in 1951 in *Sempiternus Rex*, 32 ("It is indeed the truth that from the earliest times and in the most ancient writings, sermons and liturgical prayers, the Church openly and without qualification professes that our Lord Jesus Christ, the only Begotten Son of the Eternal Father, was born on earth, suffered, [and] was nailed to the cross."), and by Pope St. John Paul II in 1990 in *Redemptoris*

The Incarnation

Ward's hesitations on this vital point of Christian doctrine are certainly understandable. Down through history, many formally "orthodox" theologians on the person of Christ have portrayed his divine identity in ways that made it hard to see him as fully human, subject to real human limitations. While all agreed he had a human body, he was often said to be omniscient in his human mind, and able to command infinite divine power by means of his human will. Early Kenotic theologians such as Gore and Weston wrote many chapters detailing the sad story of how, at least up until the 19th century, and with very few exceptions, many of the greatest saints and theologians believed that in his human soul the pre-Paschal Son of God could not *really* be ignorant of the day and hour of the end of the world (despite Mk 13:32), and could not *really* have grown in wisdom as a youth (despite Lk 2:52) — all such ignorance must have been a veiled or consciously feigned ignorance, for didactic purposes.[39] Moreover, when Jesus performed great miracles, such as multiplying loaves and fishes and calming the storm at sea, he permitted his divine nature, normally held in reserve, to go beyond what his human will could accomplish through the limitations of human nature alone — an interpretation of the Gospels that goes right back to the *Tome* of Pope St. Leo the Great. **In the writings of many mainstream theologians of the Church, therefore, the *kenosis* of the divine Son stopped short of abiding by the authentic limits of the human condition; in other words, the one who supposedly "for us men and for our salvation came down from heaven" did not actually come *all the way down*. There was**

---

missio, 6 ("To introduce any sort of separation between the Word and Jesus Christ is contrary to the Christian Faith. St. John clearly states that the Word who 'was in the beginning with God,' is the very one who 'became flesh' [Jn 1:2, 14]. Jesus is the incarnate Word — a single, indivisible person."), and finally, in the *Catechism of the Catholic Church* entry 468: "[E]verything in Christ's human nature is to be attributed to his divine person as its proper subject, not only his miracles but also his sufferings and even his death ...."

[39] For a contemporary defence of this position, see William Most, *The Consciousness of Christ* (Front Royal, VA: Christendom Press, 1980).

too little appreciation of the fact that the divine Son, dwelling among us under all the conditions and limitations of manhood, would have had to rely on the Holy Spirit for whatever measure of supernatural knowledge and supernatural power he needed to carry out his earthly mission (Acts 10:38). "Full of grace and truth" in his human soul he surely was (Jn 1:14), and therefore full of all virtue as well, but all this flowed from his unique, supreme, and total surrender, as a divine person incarnate, to the power and guidance of the Holy Spirit and to the will of his Father who sent him. It did not come from a hidden "power-pack" in his divine nature that he could access in his incarnate state whenever he wished.[40]

Nevertheless, *the reduction of Jesus to a solely human person, as Ward does in his Christology, is just not needed to preserve Christ's full humanity* (as the greatest of the British Kenotic theologians, such as Gore, Weston, Mackintosh, and Hebblethwaite, in various ways endeavored to show).

Moreover, *Ward's reductionism has the effect of making it impossible to claim that God in Christ has truly shared our lot.* For on Ward's Action Model, *there would be no true unity of experience between Jesus and the Divine Word.*

On the one hand, Ward says that "the Word, as omniscient, would have intimate knowledge of all human experiences anyway," a view I critiqued in Part Two, Chapter One of my book.[41] But Ward explains further:

> The eternal Word is expressed in [Jesus] in the fullest way that is possible in a human life, and he contributes to the Word the

---

[40] As previously mentioned in Part Two, Chapter Two, limits of space prevent us from exploring the ongoing debate in Catholic theology over the traditional teaching of St. Thomas Aquinas that due to the hypostatic union, Jesus possessed the beatific vision and beatific knowledge in his human soul during his sojourn on earth. I shall address this issue in depth in volume two of this series.
[41] Ibid., p. 38.

experiences of human relationship and suffering that could only exist by the real participation of the divine in time. ... So the unity of the human subject and divine Word consists in the fact that the human experience is included and accepted into (owned and acknowledged by) the divine experience, and the divine character and intentions are expressed without distortion in the free, creative actions of the human agent. For Christians, this is uniquely, fully, and indissolubly the case only in Jesus.[42]

Another curious argument, surely: for we need to know how God can just take "ownership" of the experiences of another person (in this case, on Ward's model, the experiences of a created human person, Jesus of Nazareth), experiencing them as if they were his own. Presumably, a "person" by definition has a unique, self-conscious experience of being a particular person; this experience is his own, and not fully communicable to others. In other words, another person may know all about my experience in an objective, factual way, and may even have a very close empathy and sympathy for my experiences, but an essential aspect of being "me," a distinct person, would be my unique ownership and privileged access to the full experience of being "me."[43]

Even if God can fully assume the experience of a created human being as his own (recall that David Brown attempted to show that this is possible through his "method-acting" analogy for the Incarnation), still, several important questions remain. First, how would we then distinguish God's unity of experience with Jesus from his unity of experience with every other human being, given that Ward has claimed that God already has "intimate knowledge of all human experiences anyway"? Second, even if we can make such a distinction, then **why would God not unite himself in the same fully intimate way with everyone, just as he did with Jesus? If such a union, initiated by**

---

[42] Ibid., p. 39-40.
[43] Ward elsewhere seems to agree that this is an essential feature of personhood; see Ward, p. 173-174.

God, of total inspiration and shared experience does not violate Christ's created human nature, it would not violate the authentic humanity of any other created person. **God could have prevented a great deal of human misery and suffering in human history if only he had been more generous with his Action-Christology-style unions with human beings!**

Ward contends that God chooses to assume as his own only the *non-sinful* thoughts and feelings of created human persons, but not their sinful thoughts and feelings:

> In the case of all human beings, God has complete knowledge of all they feel and think. But the feelings and thoughts of most human beings often conflict with the will of God, and so God must preserve a certain distance from them. God knows what the feelings are, and in a sense this means that God feels them.[44] But God does not identify with them, and no one can say that these are God's own feelings or feelings in accord with God's own nature.

> In the case of a grace-perfected life, however, there would be no alienating distance between God's nature and this human nature. ...[45]

Most Christians think that God's knowledge of the human experiences of Jesus will not be distanced in the same way as it is from other human experiences, influenced as they are by sin. Since Jesus is sinless and filled with the divine Spirit, God will be able to 'own' Jesus' experiences, to accept them as the experiences of a human fully united to the divine. Thus, Jesus' experience on the cross, for instance, will in a special way be

---

[44] Ward would need to clarify here in what sense God "feels" the sinful feelings of human beings. Just knowing about them — and even having a measure of empathy and compassion for those who experience them — is not the same as feeling them oneself as one's own, as Ward himself states. It is awkward, therefore, to say that "God feels them."

[45] Ibid., p. 76.

both known and acknowledged by God as experiences of the divine in human form. They will express in a definitive way how God shares in the suffering of creatures, and they will define how God shares in the suffering of creatures, and they will define the way in which such suffering can be transformed when human lives become truly united to God.[46]

In the end, however, on his own principles Ward would have to admit that even this kind of divine, experiential union with the sinless Jesus — and even such a union, to a lesser degree, with the non-sinful thoughts and feelings of other human beings — would not establish that God has ever really experienced human joys, sorrows, and sufferings from a fully human, finite perspective on events:

> So God's knowledge of the interior lives of other persons will not simply be a duplicate of those personal experiences as they are experienced by other persons. It will be a 'reflected' knowledge of a unique kind, embracing a total empathy, a 'feeling-with' another, but accompanied by the knowledge that it is the experience of another that is known. In the case of God's infinite knowledge of finite human experiences, part of that otherness will be that human knowledge is sense-based, fallible, limited, and [though not in the case of Jesus] infected by the prejudices and estrangement of human lives from God. Since God suffers no such defects and limitations, it will be quite clear that divine knowledge of human mental contents, however empathetic, will differ in quality from human knowledge itself.[47]

Thus, a major "distance" would remain between all non-sinful thoughts and feelings of created human beings, including those of Jesus, and God's "acceptance" and assumption of those thoughts and feelings onto the level of his transcendent and omniscient perspective

---

[46] Ibid., p. 226.
[47] Ibid., p. 225-226

on events. After all, the human experience of Jesus too was "sense-based, fallible, and limited" as Ward puts it. The translation of Christ's human and finite experiences onto the level of God's infinite and omniscient perspective, therefore, would surely radically alter those experiences as shared by God, who has an utterly immaterial, universal, and infinite mind. Unless, of course, those human experiences of Jesus were also included and preserved in the divine nature through a divine incarnational *kenosis* — but Ward is not offering us any version of Kenotic Christology here.

Besides, as I argued in Part Two, Chapter One, **it is not at all clear how God can *closely* empathise and sympathise with the human condition if he has never limited himself to share in all the conditions of humanity. He would have no touchstone, no in-person, fully human experience as a reference point for his compassion for our plight. The burden of my account was to show that only a Kenotic Model of the Incarnation can establish in a coherent and intelligible way that as Jesus Christ, God has fully identified with human joys and sorrows, struggles and sufferings, experiencing them from the perspective of a human consciousness, with fully human limitations.**

With regard to Action Christology, despite Ward's valiant defence, it seems clear that David Brown's verdict on it long ago remains accurate:

> A unity of will in a common purpose [between God and Jesus], no matter how complete, would not justify us in speaking of a single person rather than two persons. In the first place, it would remain a contingent unity (one person could will differently from the other, and so break the unity at any moment) and, secondly, there remain vast areas of personhood which still would not be united, there continuing to be no unity of common experience, despite the common purpose.[48]

---

[48] Brown, *The Divine Trinity*, p. 230.

Conclusion: The Wider Problem

It is not just the inadequacy of Ward's models of the Trinity and the Incarnation that should cause us concern, however; it is also the ramifications of his perspective for the wider pattern of Christian belief. Much of my own book was written to address these concerns, along with concerns about similar perspectives expressed by many other contemporary theologians, both from within and from outside the Anglican world. There is no need to repeat myself here. It will suffice to quote the reactions of one of the great Kenotic theologians of the 20th century, P.T. Forsyth, as he confronted similar, heterodox, "idealist" Christologies in his own day, and tried to show how deeply damaging they are to the logical coherence and saving power of the Christian Faith.

According to Forsyth (echoing the thought of St. Athanasius and St. Cyril),[49] only God in person can perform the saving work that rescues humanity from sin; only God in person can clearly and definitively reveal his love for us; and only God in person can decisively establish his Kingdom in this world. In fact, Christ's love for us would be no more than that of many other great martyrs for righteousness and truth, and he would merit neither our worship nor our allegiance as "Lord," *unless he was sent from above* — a divine person who chose to come and dwell among us and share our lot, and who lived and died as one of us for our salvation:

> Christ is much more than the personal realization of the [divine] idea of Humanity and the guarantee of its universal attainment. ... For only God can reveal God. And the King of God's Kingdom must be God. ... Is not the creation of God's Kingdom a task beyond the power of any instrument, any creature? Is it not God's own work? Whoever did it must be God himself. God must directly perform and sustain the great

---

[49] Forsyth, *The Person and Place of Jesus Christ*, p.84.

act that set up such communion. God must do it in person. ...
[O]ur Redeemer must save us by his difference from us,
however the salvation get home by his parity with us. ... His
obedience as man was but the detail of the supreme obedience
which made him man. His love transcends all human measure
only if, out of love, he renounced the glory of heavenly being
for all he here became. ... Unlike us, he *chose* the oblivion of
birth and the humiliation of life. His life here, like his death
which pointed it, was the result of his free will. It was all one
death for him. It was all one obedience. And it was free. He
was rich and for our sakes he became poor. What he gave up
was the fullness, power and immunity of heavenly life. ... The
self-determination to be man went the whole divine length to
the self-humiliation of the cross. ... It is what he did in
becoming man, even more than what he did as man, that
makes the glory of his achievement so divine that nothing
short of absolute worship from a whole redeemed humanity
can meet it.[50]

---

[50] Ibid., p. 323, 324, 326-327, 342, and 271-273.

Appendix B

Catholicism and Social Trinitarianism

In his survey of recent metaphysical and theological approaches to the doctrine of the Trinity, Thomas H. McCall states the sobering truth for Catholic theologians who might wish to embrace some form of Social Trinitarianism: "[T]he ST theorist should admit ... that ST is not consistent with Lateran IV," and clearly inconsistent with other "official, 'high-water mark' pronouncements of Latin Trinitarianism."[1] McCall admits that this is probably the case with *all* forms of Social Trinitarian theory. Indeed, any comparison of what I wrote about the Trinity in Part One, Chapter Five of this book with the *Catechism of the Catholic Church*, entries 253-255, shows that my own attempt to develop an orthodox ST theology cannot possibly be harmonized with official Catholic statements such as entry 253, "each of [the divine persons] is God *whole and entire* .... In the words of the Fourth Lateran Council (1215): '*each person is that supreme reality*, viz., the divine substance, essence or nature;'" and also entry 255, "because it does not divide the divine unity, the real distinction of each of the persons resides *solely* in the relationship which relates them to one another." I have added italics to the entries above just to show that the *Catechism*, like the Fourth Lateran Council,[2] clearly endorses the absolute simplicity of the

---

[1] McCall, *Which Trinity? Whose Monotheism?*, p.103.

[2] The relevant sections of the decrees of Lateran IV state the following:

> There is one highest, incomprehensible and ineffable reality, which is truly Father, Son, and Holy Spirit; the three persons together, and each person distinctly; therefore there is in God only Trinity, not a quaternity, because each of the persons is that reality, viz., that divine substance, essence or nature which alone is the beginning of all things, apart from which nothing else can be found. This reality is neither generating nor generated, nor proceeding, but it is the Father who generates, the Son who is generated, and the Holy Spirit who proceeds, so that there be distinctions between persons but unity in nature.
>
> Hence, though the Father is one person (alius), the Son another person, and the Holy Spirit another person, yet there is not another reality

divine substance and the identity of each divine person with that one divine substance, whole and entire, as well as the teaching of St. Augustine, St. Thomas Aquinas and the Council of Toledo that the persons of the Trinity are "subsistent relations"— teachings that I criticized at various points in this book.[3] Does this mean that Social Trinitarianism is necessarily *heretical*, from an authentically Catholic point of view?

I hope and pray it does not. I have also given some reasons in this book (in Part One, Chapter Five) why I think there still may be some latitude here for further doctrinal development in the Catholic Tradition in a Social Trinitarian direction. In particular, I stated:

1) The Ecumenical Councils of Lateran IV in 1215, Lyons in 1274, and Florence in 1439-1442, although they offered in-depth teaching on the mystery of the Holy Trinity, never saw fit to condemn the Social Trinitarian teachings of Richard of St. Victor (d. 1173), although his book *De Trinitate* was perhaps the most prominent work on the subject between St. Augustine and St. Thomas Aquinas.

2) I find it almost impossible to believe that the Roman Catholic Church will require the Orthodox churches of the East to accept the full-blown Latin doctrine of the Trinity of Lateran IV, Lyons, and Florence as a condition for re-establishing full communion between the two sister churches of Christendom.

(aliud), but what the Father is, this very same reality is also the Son, this the Holy Spirit, so that in orthodox Catholic faith we believe them to be one substance. ... Thus, the Father and the Son and the Holy Spirit who proceeds from both are the same reality. (J. Neuner, SJ, and J. Dupuis, SJ, *The Christian Faith: Doctrinal Documents of the Catholic Church*. New York: Alba House, fifth revised and enlarged edition, 1990, p. 117)

[3] Several times in Part One, Chapter Five, and in Appendix A, I referred to all three of these teachings together, for convenience, as "The Subsistent Relations Doctrine." To be precise, however, they are three distinct truth claims, although almost always found together, and only one of these is the proposition that the divine persons subsist as mere "relations."

3) I also find considerable merit in the idea proposed long ago by Bertrand De Margerie, SJ that although all the ecumenical councils accepted by Rome are true ecumenical councils, nevertheless, they also manifested diverse and unequal realisations of ecumenicity. Some councils included the full participation or representation (in various ways) of the entire, universal episcopate while other ecumenical councils did not. Thus, near-maximum ecumenicity was operative at Nicea and Chalcedon, at Florence and at Vatican II — but far less so at Lateran IV. It is the teachings of those councils that were less ecumenical that may be the best candidates for re-reception, and reformulation in and through the ecumenical dialogue process between East and West.[4]

4) Finally, I add here a fourth consideration: that the doctrine that the divine persons subsist as mere "relations" expressed in *Catechism* entry 255 is based primarily on the teachings of the Council of Toledo (675 AD), which was a regional, not an ecumenical council of the Church — in fact, a council whose teachings have never been formally and expressly approved by any general council or pope. In other words, Toledo is not a definitive expression of the Church's universal magisterium, and its teachings are not therefore an expression of the Church's infallible teaching authority.[5]

Of course, for Catholics this is not a judgement that can be made by an individual theologian, either for himself or for others. In the end, it is a judgement that only the authentic Catholic magisterium can make, under the guidance of the Holy Spirit.

---

[4] Discussion in English of De Margerie's perspective can be found in Aidan Nichols, O.P., *Rome and the Eastern Churches* (San Francisco: Ignatius Press, 2010), p. 370-375.

[5] It is also important to note that that the mere appearance of the teachings of Toledo in the *Catechism* does not automatically raise them to the level of "infallible." As Cardinal Joseph Ratzinger explained (who was head of the commission that prepared the *Catechism*): "The individual doctrines which the *Catechism* presents receive no other weight than that which they already possess" (Joseph Ratzinger and Christoph Schonborn, *Introduction to the Catechism of the Catholic Church*. San Francisco: Ignatius Press, 1994, p. 27).

Quite apart from the issue of the relative weight of those medieval councils and *Catechism* entries in defining doctrine, however, we should recognize at the outset that Catholics who wish to be Social Trinitarians, and those more committed to the full Latin and Thomistic doctrine of the Trinity, have important, foundational commitments in common. In his book *The Trinity* (2011), Gilles Emery, OP, summarizes for us the Patristic consensus on this doctrine that certainly must be (at a minimum) common ground for any attempts at reformulation or doctrinal development in this area:

> The mature doctrine of the Fathers of the Church (starting from around the year A.D. 350) can be described by the three following characteristics: first, a clear vision of the distinction between person and nature, entailing the principle that all that is attributed to the divine nature is found in an equal and simple way in each divine person; second, a formulation of the generation of the Son that clearly signifies that this generation occurs within the incomprehensible divine being; third, a clear expression of the inseparable action of the divine persons. The technical vocabulary, however varied, serves to express these fundamental themes that constitute the foundation of a Trinitarian theological culture. These themes should not be filed away as mere relics of the past. Rather, they form the matrix of Christian reflection on the mystery of the triune God.[6]

Authentically Catholic Social Trinitarians should heartily agree. We would part company with Emery, however, when (as in the next few pages of the very same book) he unpacks what he takes to be the optimal meaning of these fundamental Patristic commitments in terms of the Thomistic philosophy of the absolute simplicity and absolute immutability of God. I offered some reasons for amending this philosophical vision in the "Conclusion" section of my book — and how all this pertains to the Trinity will be discussed below.

---

[6] Emery, *The Trinity*, p. 90.

Meanwhile, Catholic Social Trinitarians need not be wary of the teachings of all three medieval councils that tackled the doctrine of the Trinity. It is time to unpack the bold claim I made in passing in a footnote: that nothing of what I have written about the Trinity in this book contradicts the teachings of the (maximally ecumenical) Council of Florence of the 15th century. Surely, the Council of Florence echoed the teachings of Lateran IV and Lyons that preceded it! Indeed, one could fairly argue that Florence intended to endorse the teaching of Augustine, Aquinas, and the Council of Toledo that the divine persons subsist as "relations." Thus, in its decree for the Jacobites (1442), the Council of Florence stated: *"These three persons are one God and not three gods, for the three are one substance, one essence, one nature, one Godhead, one infinity, one eternity, and everything (in them) is one where there is no opposition of relationship."*[7] There was no express intention at Florence to alter or water-down the teachings of the previous councils on the Trinity in any way, and this conciliar statement certainly can be read as consistent with those previous councils. But, whether deliberately or not, the way the mystery of the Trinity was phrased at Florence leaves out much of what was said at Lateran IV, and is thereby (providentially?) less restrictive on the mystery of the Trinity than that earlier council. Florence admits of other, possible interpretations, leaving the door open to a Social Trinitarian expression.

To begin with, it is possible to have a relationship of "relative opposition" between two personal subjects that does not require that the persons are merely "relations." For example, a human relationship may be founded on a completed or ongoing action of some kind (e.g. parent and child, or mover and moved). In these cases, the oppositional relation, that is, the relationship of contrast between the persons, is accidental and external to the personal subjects involved.

According to the Thomists, given *the absolute simplicity of the divine essence,* there can be no real distinction between substance and accident in God (or, for that matter, between his essence and his existence, his essence and his attributes, form and matter, or act and potency). Whatever is in God, is God. Thus, the relationships of opposition in God (that is,

---

[7] Neuner and Dupuis, *The Christian Faith: Doctrinal Documents*, p. 119.

the ones revealed to us by God in Holy Scripture, traditionally called Fatherhood, Sonship, and passive Spiration) cannot be accidents: they must be identical to the divine essence itself. In other words, they must "subsist" as "relations," with no real distinction between each one and the divine essence itself, "the supreme reality … whole and entire." At the same time, however, each subsistent relation (allegedly) is distinct from the other two by reason of their relations of opposition.

I see two major problems here.

First, the Thomists' conclusion that there is a "real" distinction between the persons in God equivocates on the meaning of the word "real," using the word at times in a rarefied sense. On their theory, since God's essence is *absolutely* simple, everything in God must be identical to the divine essence whole and entire. Thus, it should follow that there can be no ontologically "real" distinctions in God whatsoever — only distinctions from our human perspective, to our way of thinking. Whatever relationships of opposition may be said to exist in God, therefore, cannot be predicated of him in an ontologically "real" and "really distinct" way, only in a logical or notional way. If there are relations of Fatherhood in God, Sonship in God, and passive Spiration in God, then each relation must be absolutely, numerically, and generically identical with the one divine essence — and therefore absolutely, numerically, and generically identical to each other. Thus, the names of the three divine persons are just three names for exactly the same reality: there are no ontologically "real" distinctions between the divine persons in God. The doctrine of the Trinity vanishes.

Aquinas tries to escape this conclusion by positing that that the category of "relation" is unique among accidents. All other kinds of accidents (such as accidents of quantity and quality) refer solely to the subject in which they inhere, and which they modify. A "relation," however, by definition refers not so much to the subject in which it inheres but to something other than the subject. It is pure referentiality, a reference of one thing to another, a tendency from the subject toward something else.

The trouble is that Aquinas has already attributed to the divine essence a property (absolute simplicity) which completely forbids any true ontological "otherness" in God, any ontologically real "something and something else" within God that might exist in a real relation. There are no distinct parts, aspects or personal modes of the divine being that could form such a relationship. Again, we may see in God logical or notional relations of opposition, from our point of view — but not in "reality," for in the divine essence itself, all is one.

Second, the philosophical gymnastics that the Thomists undertake in order to avoid this conclusion only succeed in making the doctrine ever more opaque.

Consider this passage from a book by Roman Catholic philosophical theologian Anselm K. Min, *Paths to the Triune God*, in defense of the Thomistic tradition in this regard:

> In creatures relations are accidents, but in God they are the divine essence itself. Hence, in God essence is not *really* distinct from relation and person, although the persons are *really* distinguished from one another. The person signifies relation as subsisting in the divine nature, but relation does not differ *really* [re] from essence, except in our way of thinking [ratione], while as referred to an opposite relation, relation has a *real* distinction by reason of that opposition. There is a *real* identity — with only a logical distinction — between person and essence in God, but a *real* distinction among the three persons themselves. The relations and persons are *really* distinguished from one another insofar as they are relationally opposed to one another, but not insofar as they are identical with the essence. Thus, there are one essence and three persons, one God, Father, Son and Holy Spirit.[8]

Min's explanation of the Subsistent Relations Doctrine, again, seems to equivocate on the meaning of the word "real." If the three divine

---

[8] Anselm K. Min, *Paths to the Triune God; An Encounter between Aquinas and Recent Theologies* (Notre Dame, IN: University of Notre Dame Press, 2005), p. 210-211; italics mine.

person-relations "do not differ *really* [re] from [the divine] essence except in our way of thinking [ratione]," as Min says, then surely that means that they do not differ in reality from each other. When Min then goes on to say "the relations [persons] are *really* distinguished from one another insofar as they are relationally opposed to one another," he seems to be using the word "really" here in a different sense than the first time. The divine persons-as-relations may be logically and notionally distinguished from each other, and in that sense "really" distinct, but they are not in any way *ontologically* distinct from each other, for each one is simply the same thing as the one divine essence, whole and entire. Thus, *in reality* there are not three distinct persons in God.

In another place Min writes: "[The Three divine persons] are identical with the divine essence and remain 'one God,' but are distinct from the divine essence in their real and pure referentiality, which also makes each really distinct from the others."[9] But on Thomistic grounds, there can be nothing in God that is not God, certainly nothing in God that is really, ontologically "distinct" from the divine essence — so, if the persons in their "pure referentiality" *are* "distinct from the divine essence," then those persons in their pure referentiality are not really *in God* — and once again, that means there are no really (ontologically) distinct divine persons in God.

The standard Thomist response to this critique of the coherence of their doctrine of the Trinity is that those who make it are defining the divine persons *anthropomorphically* rather than *analogically*. In other words, neglecting the divine transcendence, we are treating the divine persons as if they were precisely the same thing as human persons; we are defining divine persons as centers of consciousness and will just as human persons are defined today in modern philosophy. It is no wonder, then, that we find a logical contradiction in the idea that each distinct divine person is the one God, whole and entire, for how could three distinct centers of consciousnesses be, at one and the same time, one center of consciousness? As a matter of fact, however, some Social Trinitarian theorists are doing their best to avoid this univocity trap

---

9 Ibid., p. 304.

(see my discussion, below). In any case, as Thomas McCall rightly points out, the appeal to an analogical use of religious language still does not overcome the main problem with the Thomists' doctrine:

> [E]ven if we deny that the notion of "person" is univocal and allow for the traditional kinds of qualified differences between human persons and divine persons, we are nevertheless left with the [coherence] argument. Nothing about this argument ... depends on a univocal account of personhood, nor does it assume that the divine persons are "modern individuals." For *whatever* they are, if the Father is identical to the divine essence, which is also identical with the Son, then the Father and the Son are identical.[10]

If it is permissible to amend the doctrine of *absolute* divine simplicity (see my discussion of this point in the "Conclusion" chapter of this book), then it would be possible to have "relationships of opposition" in God (as the Council of Florence requires) which are neither accidental to the divine persons themselves, nor "subsistent relations." Indeed the mystery of the eternal relation of origin of each divine person could be said to be essential to the existence and the distinct identity of each one, and all three relations of origin would be essential to the existence and essence of the Tripersonal God as a whole.

Here we can draw upon a distinction made by Cornelius Plantinga, Jr. between the "generic" divine essence (that is, all the essential divine attributes, such as eternity, omnipotence, omniscience, and goodness; each divine person possesses these attributes in common) and the "personal" essence of each divine person (that is, their unique, eternal relations of origin, and the characteristics and properties unique to each divine person as a result of their relations of origin, such as their unique self-consciousness, and their distinct modes of action in, and experiences of the world — e.g. being incarnate). In addition, there is another essence that Plantinga did not discuss: the

---

[10] McCall, "Trinity Doctrine, Plain and Simple," in Crisp and Sanders, eds., *Advancing Trinitarian Theology*, p. 58.

unique *"Tripersonal essence"* of God as a whole — for God presumably is an individual substance that simply is, in one act of being, the divine "generic essence" in act, from the organic and social union of all three fully (generically) "divine" persons, each with their own "personal essence." God is one, Tripersonal, fully divine being (not "a being," actually, but Infinitely Perfect Being — see again the "Conclusion" chapter of this book).

In other words, a Social Trinitarian too can claim that the relations among the persons of the Trinity are not mere "accidents" in God or in any divine person; they are essential to the Tripersonal divine nature, in that the divine nature can only really exist in this Tri-personal way, with Father, Son and Holy Spirit as three centers of consciousness and will, essentially and inseparably united by eternal, relational bonds of origination and cooperation in one act of being. As the Social Trinitarian is not bound by the extreme Thomist doctrine of absolute divine simplicity, he/she has less to fret about — in this regard, at least.

Thus, we can confess with the Council of Florence that in God "everything is one" (that is, there is one, divine "generic essence" possessed in common by each divine person, and by the Tripersonal God as a whole; and there is only one divine substance — again, the Tripersonal act of being that is God), considered in the abstract and separately from all "relationships of opposition" within God (that is, the eternal relationships of origin and cooperation among the divine persons). It is especially the relationships of origin in God flowing from the Father that eternally produce three distinct, generically divine persons, with their unique personal essences.[11]

---

[11] Given that the loving and wise *cooperation* among the three divine persons necessarily follows from the fact that the very being and divine reality of each divine person flows from his unique relation of origin, it is primarily the eternal relations of origin that grounds both the unity of the Trinity, and results in the distinct identity ("personal essence") of each divine person. The "social" cooperation of the divine persons with each other is therefore a maintenance and expression of that underlying, "organic" unity of origination.

Three more questions immediately arise with regard to this social Trinitarian option.

1. Does this doctrine of the Trinity "divide the substance" of God, sharing it out among the three persons, so to speak, a concept of the Trinity that was forbidden by the Ecumenical Councils of Lateran IV and Lyons?

If by "substance" here we mean the Aristotelian "secondary substance" (i.e., "kind-substance," in this case, the generic divine essence, the divine attributes), then our Social Trinitarian model does not at all "divide the substance." Each one of the divine persons, participating "organically" (by origination) and "socially" (by cooperation) in the life of the Trinity, possesses and exercises *all* the generic divine attributes (e.g., eternity, aseity, omnipotence, omniscience, goodness and love); each one is, in that sense fully divine, and so is the Trinity as a whole — for the Tripersonal God too possesses all the generic divine attributes (albeit in a unique, threefold way). But our model does "divide the substance," in a sense, if by that we mean the Aristotelian "primary substance," in this case God's one act of being, which can only exist in a Tripersonal way, with none of the persons the equivalent of God's act of being "whole and entire."

Nevertheless, it remains appropriate to refer to each of the divine persons as "God", in so far as that is shorthand for "God the Father," "God the Son," or "God the Holy Spirit," **for the presence and action of each one in the world is a pure outreach and expression of the Tripersonal God as a whole, that is, of the common mind and intentions, common will and shared exercise of love and power of the Trinitarian Communion that God is.** Thus, Mary is truly called "The Mother of God" (meaning, of course, the Mother of God the Son), and God (meaning God the Son) truly suffered and died on the Cross.

2. What about the passage in the Athanasian Creed implicitly endorsed by the Council of Florence (when Florence recommended that creed to the Armenians, with whom the Catholic Church was seeking reunion): "Likewise the Father is

God, the Son is God and the Holy Spirit is God. Yet they are not three gods, but one God."

There are several things that a Social Trinitarian might want to say about this passage.

The first is: **why not read each "is" in these sentences as an "is" of predication rather than an "is" of identity? In other words, the Athanasian creed could be saying here: "The Father is divine (that is, he has all the divine attributes; he possesses the divine "generic essence"), the Son is divine, and the Holy Spirit is divine, but they are not three separate or separable divine beings; rather, they make up only one act of being which also has all the divine attributes, the Tripersonal God."**

This would fit precisely with the **Social-Organic Model of the Trinity proposed in this book. For, again, my contention is that the Tripersonal God is a single act of being with all the same generic divine attributes as each divine person (of course, God possesses these attributes in a unique, triplicate, tripersonal way, through the relations of origin and cooperation among the three). Moreover, only the One God includes within his Tripersonal act of being the unique "personal essence" of each divine person; in other words, the Tripersonal God includes all three distinct, personal ways of "being divine," with their unique characteristics (the paternal way of being a divine person, the filial way, and the pneumatic way).**

Consider again the social-organic analogy of conjoined triplets. Each person of a conjoined triplicate is, generically, *fully human* (i.e., each has a fully human soul united with a fully human brain and a genetically human body), and the triplicate as a whole also is *fully human* (albeit in a unique, threefold way). But each triplet is not the living, conjoined triplicate "whole and entire." Only the triplicate as a whole includes *all three ways of being a triplet* (the left way, the center way, and the right way) *in one single, living act of being.*

Consider also the quite different social-organic analogy of the Church. The Church is in one sense one substance, the risen and glorified Son of God, who, in a mysterious way incorporates into himself, through baptism, each and every unique Christian person, with all of his/her natural and spiritual gifts, interdependent roles of service, and unique experiences. Together they make up his one mystical Body (Rom 12:3-8; I Cor 12: 4-30). Each member of that Body is fully human, but so, in a unique way, is the mystical reality of Christ as a whole. Only the "social" (lovingly cooperative) and "organic" (completely interdependent) communion of persons as a whole, growing into full unity in the Spirit in truth and love, ultimately attains in each member the fullness of the stature of Christ (in human sanctity, at any rate; Eph 4:12-16). And each member thereby participates in making the glorified humanity of Christ himself whole and complete (Eph 1:23). Only the Body of Christ as whole, therefore, ultimately includes in one living reality all the ways in all its members of manifesting the life and light of Christ.

These analogies with the Trinity are imperfect, of course, as all analogies for supernatural, transcendent realities must be, but they help us at least to begin to unfold the mystery.

The Athanasian Creed was written long before Aquinas filled out all the details of the full Latin doctrine of the Trinity, so we must not project all of those details back into the thinking of those who composed this creed. Moreover, I am certainly not saying those authors were really Social-Organic Trinitarians after all, and would recognize what I have written (above) as exactly what they intended to say! What I do suggest is that their meaning was not entirely clear, as they were groping to grasp this mystery (as we all must do, even though we today have the benefit of access to many more centuries of reflection on the mystery of the Trinity than they did). Their words are ambiguous as they stand, and patient of a Social Trinitarian interpretation.

Richard Swinburne has argued that the only alternative to a Social Trinitarian reading of this passage of the Athanasian Creed would be a thoroughly *uncharitable* one: that is, we would have to interpret the words in a *self-contradictory* sense, as if they were saying that God is three divine individuals and yet only one divine individual, and that the Father, Son, and Holy Spirit are each of them the same individual thing

(God), and yet they have distinct properties (mentioned elsewhere in the creed, such as the properties of begetting and being begotten) — which is also self-contradictory, Swinburne says, for if three things are the same identical thing, then they must have identical properties. Of course, Swinburne's argument here only holds if the full Latin doctrine of Lateran IV that he does not want to attribute to the Athanasian Creed is almost completely unintelligible, and even if intelligible, is logically incoherent (as I argued in Part One, Chapter Five of this book).[12]

3. What precisely is the metaphysical status of a divine "person" in the Social Organic Model of the Trinity proposed here?

First of all, it is important to say that much more work needs to be done to "flesh out" the metaphysics of Social Trinitarianism. There are far wiser heads than mine engaged in this work — and have been over the past few decades.[13]

Still, this is one of the most difficult questions of all for the Social Organic Model — indeed for the mystery of the Trinity itself. **For if divine persons are *not* three independent, separate or separable entities, three divine primary substances (which would be tritheism, pure and simple) and if they are also *not* "subsistent relations" in an absolutely simple divine essence (which collapses into mere logical and notional distinctions between the divine persons, not ontologically real distinctions)** *then what are they?* **In truth, it is easier to say what a divine person is not than what a divine person is!** Keith Ward has argued that they are three distinct modes of divine activity of one divine center of consciousness and will (see Appendix A of this book; this ultimately results in a form of Unitarianism). Karl Barth sees them as three modes of the act of

---

[12] Swinburne, *The Coherence of Theism*, p. 186, discussed in McCall, *Which Trinity? Whose Monotheism?*, p. 16.
[13] At this time of writing, the most in-depth treatment of Social Trinitarianism may be found in the work of Christian Analytic philosopher William Hasker in *Metaphysics and the Tri-personal God* (Oxford: Oxford University Press, 2017 edition), although Hasker would not describe his version of ST as a "social-organic" model.

Revelation of a unipersonal God, and Brian Leftow sees them as three distinct Lockean "streams of consciousness" of one divine subject (which, in all three cases, leaves no room for the perfection of real, loving, personal relationship in God).

McCall has suggested a re-examination of the theory of Bl. John Duns Scotus regarding the "formal distinction" between the divine persons. McCall explains:

> For Scotus two entities are formally distinct if the distinction is genuine (that is, within the thing itself, and not merely rational or mental) but not between two different essences, or between separable parts or pieces of the same thing. ... So two entities can be formally distinct ... if they are both really inseparable and genuinely distinct on account of distinctions found in themselves. ... [Scotus] holds that the divine persons are "fully real, subsistent entities" who are, in the words of Richard Cross, "necessarily interdependent." Thus the persons are genuinely distinct, and modalism is avoided. But the divine persons are also really — even logically — inseparable, thus polytheism is avoided as well.[14]

All of this might fit very well with a Social-Organic Model of the Tripersonal God, but it awaits a monograph by someone to explore the possible connections in-depth.

I would also hope to see someone, someday draw out the connections between a responsible Catholic Social Trinitarianism and the philosophical work of W. Norris Clarke, SJ. All theologians wear philosophical lenses, whether they recognize them or not, and mine have certainly been colored in recent years by those of Clarke (not surprising, given the affinity between Clarke's perspectives and those of Pope St. John Paul II, the patron saint of the "Institute of Divine Mercy" which bears his name, and which I have served for the better

---

14 McCall, "Trinity Doctrine Plain and Simple," in Crisp and Sanders, eds., *Advancing Trinitarian Theology*, p. 52-53.

part of 22 years). For Clarke, all being is relational, "substance-in-relation," from the lowest creature to the Blessed Trinity itself.[15]

---

[15] For those who are unfamiliar with Clarke's Trinitarian ontology, Matthew Levering offers a helpful summary in *Scripture and Metaphysics: Aquinas and the Renewal of Trinitarian Theology* (Oxford: Blackwell, 2004), p. 202-205. The following extracts may be helpful:

> In a programmatic essay, "To Be is to Be Substance-in-Relation," W. Norris Clarke approaches the topic of Trinitarian ontology from the standpoint of Thomistic metaphysics. Clarke contrasts the standard Aristotelian account of "being" with the insight that "being" must be "substance-in-relation."... In the realm of creatures, all beings are, no matter how apparently autonomous, constituted by relation. In itself, the creature is constituted by its relation to God, its Creator. Therefore, in the realm of creatures, ontology or metaphysics — the study of being qua being — must recognize that created being is relational by definition. As Clarke states with regard to creatures, "To be a substance and to be related are distinct but complementary and inseparable aspects of every real being. The structure of every being is indissolubly dyadic: it exists both as *in-itself* and as *toward others*."...

> Clarke criticizes Aquinas for remaining overly cautious in this aspect of his metaphysics. Clarke notes, Bonaventure was bolder. Following the school of the Victorines, Bonaventure argues that since being (as good) is self-communicative, the highest good must be self-communicative in the absolutely highest degree. ...

> For Clarke, philosophy can achieve the insight that divine being must be relational, but it cannot determine the precise *mode* in which the divine nature communicates itself. ...

> Christian revelation goes beyond, and super-eminently confirms, the insights of philosophy by identifying the mode of the Trinity. In his presentation of the Trinity, Clarke suggests that the self-communicative impulse of the divine being is fulfilled super-eminently in the divine Persons flowing forth from the divine nature or being. According to Christian revelation, Clarke notes, "the inner being of God is by the very necessity of its nature *self-communicating love*, which flowers out into the internal processions of the three Persons within the unity of the divine nature" ... a flowering expected by philosophy, but whose exact mode could not have been determined. ... Being, at its most intense, is relational being: perfect Trinity. The intrinsic meaning of "being" is

My own inclination is to say that it is precisely here — in the mystery of divine personhood — that the mystery of the Trinity lies most beyond our comprehension. We can say in a general sense that a "person" is the subject or bearer of properties of a personal kind, such as the capacity for self-consciousness, rational thought, voluntary agency, and loving relationships with other persons. **By *analogy*, then, each divine person also could be said to be a subject of which similar personal properties can be predicated — but those personal properties or attributes are *infinite and eternally in act* (e.g., infinite knowledge, infinite love). The divine persons are three centers of consciousness and will indeed, but not three centers of *human* consciousness and will!**

Moreover, when we call a divine person a "subject" we do not mean (as we do when referring to a human person), a primary substance, a distinct, separate and independent entity, a really existing thing in *that* sense, but something uncreated: *an uncreated subject that is eternally generating, and/or being generated by, another divine person (or persons)*. A divine "person" (or "subject") is therefore not a primary substance in itself, but an uncreated subject who participates in the one divine

---

"relational being" — at its divine source, is the infinite relational Being that Christians call the Trinity.

Clarke goes on to endorse the Thomistic doctrine of the divine persons as "subsistent relations," seeing in this doctrine an echo of what he wants to say philosophically about Being itself as relational. Obviously, Social Trinitarians prefer a more robust doctrine of personal relations in God, and might see a social-organic model of the Trinity as reflecting Clarke's insights here even better than the Thomistic model. Moreover, we should be wary of seeing all three divine the persons as generated by or flowering-forth from the divine nature or infinite Being per se: the Catholic tradition surely requires that the persons flow from the nature and infinite Being *of the Father*. Saint Bonaventure, in fact, insists, in his *Commentary on the Sentences* (*I Sent.*, d.27, p. 1, a. un., q. 2, discussed in *Bonaventure*, p. 24-27) that the Trinity flows from the self-diffusive goodness, "fountain-fullness" or "fecundity" of the Father. In other words, Perfect Being itself is relational because the divine Father is necessarily relational, eternally begetting his Son, and with and through His Son, the eternal Spirit.

primary substance (the act of being of the Tripersonal God as a whole), both "organically" (by origination) and "socially" (by cooperation).

In short, our Trinitarian ontology runs straight into the mystery here of divine "begetting" and "procession" (see our discussion of this mystery in Part One, Chapter Five). As we cannot fully comprehend what these eternal, divine relations of origin are — since divine begetting and procession (or spiration) are ultimately unfathomable to us — how can we fully comprehend what divine persons are, who are the eternal fruit and product of those relations of origin?

The Trinity, then, remains veiled in mystery. All we can know is that each divine person possesses all the essential divine attributes (the divine "generic essence") and that each divine person is distinct from the other two as a result of his unique relation of origin (resulting also in distinctive characteristics and properties, the unique "personal essence" of each one) — and each divine person cannot possess either "essence" apart from the fact that he is eternally united to the others "organically" (by eternal origination) and "socially" (by loving and wise cooperation) in the one act of being of the Tripersonal God.

Selected Bibliography

Adams, Marilyn McCord, *Christ and Horrors: The Coherence of Christology.* Cambridge: Cambridge University Press, 2006.

Althaus, Paul, "Kenosis" in K. Galling, ed., *Die Religion in Geschichte und Geganwart,* vol. III. Tubingen, 1959.

Ambler, Rex, and Haslam, David, eds., *Agenda for Prophets: Towards a Political Theology for Britain.* London: Bowerdean, 1980.

Anderson, Norman, *Jesus Christ: the Witness of History.* Leicester: InterVarsity Press, 1985.

_____, *The Mystery of the Incarnation.* London: Ecclesia, 1978.

The Archbishop of Canterbury's Commission on Urban Priority Areas, *Faith in the City.* London: Church House, 1985.

Aulen, Gustaf, *The Faith of the Christian Church.* Philadelphia: Fortress Press, 1960.

Baillie, Donald, *God Was In Christ.* London: Faber and Faber, 1948.

Baker, John Austin, *The Foolishness of God.* London: Darton, Longman and Todd, 1970.

_____, *Travels in Oudamovia.* Leighton Buzzard: Faith Press, 1976.

Balthasar, Hans Urs von, *Mysterium Paschale: The Mystery of Easter.* San Francisco: Ignatius Press, 1990.

Barth, Karl, *Church Dogmatics,* vol. 11; G. Bromiley and T.F. Torrance, trans. Edinburgh: T and T Clark, 1936-1977.

_____, *Dogmatics in Outline,* G.T. Thomson, trans. London: SCM, 1949.

Bayne, Tim, "The Inclusion Model of the Incarnation: Problems and Prospects" in *Religious Studies,* no. 37, vol. 2, 2001, p.125-141.

Bettenson, Henry, *The Early Christian Fathers*. Oxford: Oxford University Press, 1956.

_____, *The Later Christian Fathers*. Oxford: Oxford University Press, 1970.

Boersma, Hans, *Violence, Hospitality and the Cross*. Grand Rapids: Baker Academic, 2004.

Bonaventure, St., *Bonaventure: The Soul's Journey into God, The Tree of Life, The Life of St. Francis* (New York: Paulist Press, Classics of Western Spirituality Series, 1978),

Brown, David, *Continental Philosophy and Modern Theology*. Oxford: Blackwell, 1987.

_____, *Divine Humanity*. Waco, TX: Baylor University Press, 2011.

_____, *The Divine Trinity*. La Salle, IL: Open Court Publishing, 1985.

_____, *God in a Single Vision: Integrating Philosophy and Theology*.

Abingdon, Oxon: Routledge, 2016.

Brown, Macolm, ed., *Anglican Social Theology*. London: Church House, 2014.

Brown, Paul D., and Stackpole, Robert, *More Than Myth? Seeking the Full Truth about Genesis, Creation and Evolution*. Chilliwack, BC: The Chartwell Press, 2014.

Brunner, Emil, *The Christian Doctrine of Creation and Redemption: Dogmatics*, vol. II; Olive Wyon, trans. London: Lutterworth, 1952.

Bulgakov, Sergius, *The Lamb of God*; Boris Jakim, trans. Grand Rapids: Eerdmans, 2008.

Burgess, Paul, "Three are the Perfection of Charity: the *De Trinitate* of Richard of St. Victor" at http://www.paulburgess.org/richard.html.

Cantalamessa, Raniero, OFM. Cap., *The Gaze of Mercy*. Frederick, MD: The Word Among Us Press, 2015.

Carey, George, *The Gate of Glory*. London: Hodder and Stoughton, 1986.

Catechism of the Catholic Church. New York: Image Books, 1995.

Cessario, Romanus, OP, *The Godly Image: Christ and Salvation in Catholic Thought from Anselm to Aquinas*. New York: Fordham University Press, 2002.

Chadwick, Henry, *The Early Church*. Harmondsworth: Penguin, 1967.

Confer, William, and Ables, Billie, *Multiple Personality*. New York: Human Sciences Press, 1983.

Creel, Richard, *Divine Impassibility*. Cambridge: Cambridge University Press, 1986.

Crisp, Oliver D., and Sanders, Fred, *Advancing Trinitarian Theology: Explorations in Constructive Dogmatics*. Grand Rapids: Zondervan, 2014.

Crisp, Oliver D., *The Word Enfleshed: Exploring the Person and Work of Christ*. Grand Rapids: Baker Academic, 2016

Cupitt, Don, *The Debate About Christ*. London: SCM, 1979.

_____, "The Finality of Christ" in *Theology*, December, 1975.

Currie, David, *What Jesus Really Said About the End of the World*. San Diego: Catholic Answers Press, 2012.

Davis, Stephen T., Kendall, Daniel, SJ, and O'Collins, Gerald, SJ, *The Trinity: an Interdisciplinary Symposium on the Trinity*. Oxford: Oxford University Press, 1999.

Dawe, Donald, *The Form of a Servant: an historical analysis of the Kenotic motif*. Philadelphia: Westminster Press, 1963.

De Margerie, Bertrand, SJ, "L'analogie dans l'oecumenicite des Conciles. Notion clef pour l'avenir de l'oecumenisme" in Revue Thomiste LXXXIV. 3 (1984), p. 425-426.

Demant, V.A., *Theology of Society*. London: Faber and Faber, 1947.

Dillistone, F.W., *The Christian Understanding of Atonement*. London: SCM, 1968.

The Doctrine Commission of the Church of England, *Believing in the Church*. London: SPCK: 1981.

_____, *The Mystery of Salvation*. London: Church House, 1995.

_____, *We Believe in God*. London: Church House, 1987.

Doctrine in the Church of England: The Report of the Commission on Christian Doctrine Appointed by the Archbishops of Canterbury and York in 1922. London: SPCK: 1938.

Dostoevsky, Fyodor, *The Brothers Karamazov*, vol. 1, Constance Garnett, trans. London: J.M. Dent and Sons, 1927.

Dreyfus, Francois, OP, *Did Jesus Know He Was God?* Chicago: Franciscan Herald Press, 1984.

Drummond, Lewis A., *The Evangelist: The Worldwide Impact of Billy Graham*. Nashville: Word Publishing, 2001.

Dubay, Thomas, SM, *The Fire Within*. San Francisco: Ignatius Press, 1989.

Eaton, Peter, ed., *The Trial of Faith*. West Sussex: Churchman Publishing, 1988.

Emery, Gilles, *The Trinity: an Introduction to the Catholic Doctrine of the Triune God*. Washington, DC: The Catholic University of America Press, 2011.

Erickson, Millard, *Christian Theology*. Grand Rapids: Baker Academic, second edition, 1998.

Evans, C. Stephen, ed., *Exploring Kenotic Christology*. Vancouver, BC: Regent College Press, 2006.

Farrer, Austin, *A Celebration of Faith*. London: Hodder and Stoughton, 1970.

_____, *Faith and Speculation*. Edinburgh: T and T Clark, 1967.

_____, *Interpretation and Belief*. London: SPCK, 1976.

_____, *Lord, I Believe: Suggestions for Turning the Creed into Prayer*. London: The Faith Press, 1955.

_____, *Love Almighty and Ills Unlimited: an Essay on Providence and Evil*. London: Collins, 1961.

_____, *Said or Sung: an arrangement of homily and verse*. London: The Faith Press, 1960.

_____, *Saving Belief*. London: Hodder and Stoughton, 1964.

Fedotov, George P., *A Treasury of Russian Spirituality*. Buchervertriebsanstalt, 1988.

Forsyth, P.T., *The Person and Place of Jesus Christ*. Grand Rapids: Eerdmans, third edition, 1909.

Freddoso, Alfred J., "Human Nature, Potency, and the Incarnation" in *Faith and Philosophy*, 3 (1986).

Gavrilyuk, Paul, "The kenotic theology of Sergius Bulgakov" in *Scottish Journal of Theology*, vol. 58, issue 3, August, 2005.

Gore, Charles, *Christ and Society*. London: George Allen and Unwin, 1927.

_____, *Dissertations on Subjects Connected with the Incarnation*. London: John Murray, 1907.

_____, *The Incarnation of the Son of God*. London: John Murray, 1891.

_____, *The Reconstruction of Belief*. London: John Murray, 1926.

Gorodetzky, Nadejda, *The Humiliated Christ in Modern Russian Thought*. London: SPCK, 1938.

Goulder, Michael, ed., *Incarnation and Myth*. London: SCM: 1979.

Graham, Billy, *Peace with God*. Nashville: Thomas Nelson, second edition, 1991.

Gray, Tim, *Mission of the Messiah*. Steubenville, OH: Emmaus Road, 1998.

Green, Michael, ed., *The Truth of God Incarnate*. London: Hodder and Stoughton, 1977.

Griffis, James E., *The Anglican Vision*. Lanham, MD: Cowley Publications, 1997.

Grudem, Wayne, *Systematic Theology*. Grand Rapids: Zondervan, 1994.

Gunton, Colin, *Yesterday and Today: A Study of Continuities in Christology*. Lo33ndon: Darton, Longman and Todd, 1983.

Gutierrez, Gustavo, *A Theology of Liberation*. Maryknoll, NY: Orbis Books, 1973.

Hahn, Scott, *The Father Who Keeps His Promises: God's Covenant Love in Scripture*. Cincinnati: St. Anthony Messenger Press, 1998.

_____, *First Comes Love: Finding Your Family in the Church and the Trinity*. New York: Image Books, 2002.

Hall, Francis J., *The Kenotic Theory*. London: Longmans, Green and Co., 1898.

Hanson, A.T., *Grace and Truth: a study of the doctrine of the Incarnation*. London, SPCK, 1975.

_____, *Reasonable Belief*. Oxford: Oxford University Press, 1980.

Harris, Mark, *The Challenge of Change: The Anglican Communion in the Post-Modern Era*. New York: Church Publishing, 1998.

Harvey, A.E., *God Incarnate: Story and Belief.* London: SPCK: 1981.

Hebblethwaite, Brian, *The Incarnation: Collected Essays in Christology.* Cambridge: Cambridge University Press, 1987.

_____, *In Defence of Christianity.* Oxford: Oxford University Press, 2005.

_____, *The Philosophical Theology of Austin Farrer.* Leuven: Peeters, 2007.

_____, *Philosophical Theology and Christian Doctrine.* Oxford: Blackwell, 2005.

Hick, John, ed., *The Myth of God Incarnate.* London: SCM, 1977.

Hodges, H.A., *The Pattern of Atonement.* London: SCM, 1955.

Hodgson, Leonard, *The Doctrine of the Atonement.* New York: Charles Scribner's Sons, 1951.

_____, *The Doctrine of the Trinity.* London: Nisbet and Co., 1943.

Holloway, Richard, ed., *The Anglican Tradition.* Wilton, CT: Morehouse-Barlow, 1984.

Holmes, Urban T., *What is Anglicanism?* Wilton, CT: Morehouse-Barlow, 1982.

Hooker, Richard, *The Works of Richard Hooker*, vol. II, arranged by John Keble. Oxford: Oxford University, 1836.

Hunter, A.M., *Interpreting St. Paul's Gospel.* London: SCM: 1954.

_____, *The Words and Works of Jesus.* London: SCM, 1950.

Hurtado, Larry, *Lord Jesus Christ: Devotion to Jesus in Earliest Christianity.* Grand Rapids: Eerdman's, 2003.

The Ignatius Catholic Study Bible: RSV, Second Catholic Edition. San Francisco: Ignatius Press, 2010.

International Theological Commission (Roman Catholic), "Select Questions on Christology" section 7, at www.vatican.va/roman_curia/congregations/cfaith/cti_documents/rc_cti_1979_cristologia_en.html.

Jenkins, David, *The Glory of Man*. London: SCM: 1967.

John Paul II, Pope, Apostolic Letter *Mulieris Dignitatem* (On the Dignity of Women), 1988.

_____, *Crossing the Threshold of Hope*. New York: Alfred A. Knopf, 1994.

_____, Encyclical Letter, *Dives in Misericordia* (Rich in Mercy), 1980.

_____, Encyclical Letter, *Laborem Exercens* (Through Work), 1981.

Jungel, Eberhard, *God as the Mystery of the World*. Edinburgh: T and T Clark, 1983.

Kasper, Walter, *The God of Jesus Christ*. New York: Crossroad, 1976 and 1984 editions.

_____, *Mercy: The Essence of the Gospel and the Key to the Christian Life*. New York: Paulist Press, 2014.

Keating, James F., and White, Thomas Joseph, OP, *Divine Impassibility and the Mystery of Human Suffering*. Grand Rapids: Eerdmans, 2009.

Keller, Timothy, *Jesus the King: Understanding the Life and Death of the Son of God*. New York: Penguin, 2011.

_____, *The Reason For God*. New York: Penguin, 2009.

Kereszty, Roch A., O.Cist, *Fundamentals of Christology*. Staten Island, NY: Alba House, third edition, 2002.

King Jr., Martin Luther, *Strength to Love*. Glasgow: Fount, 1963.

Kowalska, Saint Maria Faustina, *Diary: Divine Mercy in My Soul.* Stockbridge: Marian Press, third edition, 2011.

Lampe, Geoffrey, *Explorations in Theology: 8.* London: SCM, 1981.

_____, *God as Spirit.* Oxford: Clarendon Press, 1977.

Langford, Thomas, *In Search of Foundations: English Theology 1900-1920.* Nashville: Abingdon Press, 1969.

Laporte, Joseph, "What Does it Mean to Have Free Will?" at https://www.bigquestionsonline.com/2017/10/11/what-does-mean-have-free-will/.

Law, David R., "Case Studies in Lutheran and Anglican Kenoticism: The Christologies of Gottfried Thomasius and Frank Weston." English version available from the author. Published only in French as "Le kenotisme lutherien et anglican: les christologies de Gottfried Thomasius et Frank Weston," in *Etudes Theologiques et Religieuses*, vol. 89, no. 3 (2014), p. 313-340.

_____, *Kierkegaard's Kenotic Christology.* Oxford: Oxford University Press, 2013.

_____, "Luther's Legacy and the Origins of Kenotic Christology" in *Bulletin of John Ryland's Library,* 93, 2, 2017.

Layman, C. Stephen, *Philosophical Approaches to Atonement, Incarnation, and the Trinity.* New York: Palgrave Macmillan, 2016.

Leech, Kenneth, *The Social God.* London: Sheldon Press, 1981.

_____, *True God.* London: Sheldon Press, 1985.

_____, and Williams, Rowan, eds., *Essays Catholic and Radical.* London: Bowerdean, 1983.

Levering, Matthew, *Scripture and Metaphysics: Aquinas and the Renewal of Trinitarian Theology.* Oxford: Blackwell, 2004.

Lewis, C.S., *The Complete C.S. Lewis Signature Classics.* New York: Harper Collins, 2002.

_____, *Mere Christianity*. New York: Harper Collins, 2001 edition.

_____, *The World's Last Night and Other Essays*. New York: Harcourt, Brace and World, 1960.

Liddon, H.P., *The Divinity of Our Lord and Saviour Jesus Christ*. London: Pickering and Inglis, 1864.

Liguori, St. Alphonsus De, *The Passion and Death of Jesus Christ*. Brooklyn: Redemptorist Fathers, Eugene Grimm, trans., 1927.

_____, *The Way of Salvation and Perfection*. Aeterna Press, Eugene Grimm, trans., 2016 edition.

Loofs, Friedrich, "Kenosis," in *Encyclopedia of Religion and Ethics*, vol. 7. Edinburgh: T and T Clark, 1908.

Lucas, J.R., *Freedom and Grace*. London: SPCK: 1976.

Mackinnon, Donald, *The Problem of Metaphysics*. Cambridge: Cambridge University Press, 1974.

_____, *Themes in Theology: The Threefold Chord*. Edinburgh: T and T Clark, 1987.

Mackintosh, H.R., *The Doctrine of the Person of Jesus Christ*. Edinburgh: T and T Clark, second edition, 1913.

Macquarrie, John, *Christian Hope*. Oxford: Mowbrays, 1981.

_____, *The Humility of God*. Philadelphia: Westminster Press, 1978.

_____, "Kenoticism Reconsidered" in *Theology*, March, 1974.

_____, *Principles of Christian Theology*. New York: Scribners, second edition, 1977.

Magee, Peter, *God's Mercy Revealed: Healing for a Broken World*. Cincinnati: Servant Books, 2005.

Marmadoro, Anna, and Hill, Jonathan, eds., *The Metaphysics of the Incarnation*. Oxford: Oxford University Press, 2011.

Martensen, Hans Lassen, *Christian Dogmatics*. Edinburgh: T and T Clark, William Urwick, trans., 1880.

Mascall, Eric, *Christ, the Christian and the Church*. London: Longmans and Green, 1946.

_____, *Corpus Christi*. London: Longmans, 1965.

_____, *Whatever Happened to the Human Mind*. London: SPCK: 1980.

Matthews, W.R., *The Problem of Christ in the Twentieth Century*. Oxford: Oxford University Press, 1950.

McAdoo, H.R., *Anglican Heritage: Theology and Spirituality*. Norwich: The Canterbury Press, 1991.

McCabe, Herbert, "The Involvement of God" in *New Blackfriars*, November, 1985.

McCall, Thomas H., *Which Trinity? Whose Monotheism? : Philosophical and Systematic Theologians on the Metaphysics of Trinitarian Theology*. Grand Rapids: Eerdmans, 2010.

McCool, Gerald A., ed., *A Rahner Reader*. London: Darton, Longman and Todd, 1975.

McGrath, Alister, *The Enigma of the Cross*. London: Hodder and Stoughton, 1987.

_____, *The Making of Modern German Christology*. Oxford: Blackwells, 1986.

Milbank, John, *Being Reconciled: Ontology and Pardon*. London: Routledge: 2003.

Min, Anselm K., *Paths to the Triune God*. Notre Dame, IN: University of Notre Dame Press, 2005.

More, Saint Thomas, *The Sadness of Christ* in *Selected Writings*. New York: Vintage Books, 2003.

Moltmann, Jurgen, *The Crucified God*. New York: Harper Collins, 1974.

_____, *Experiences of God*. Philadelphia: Fortress Press, 1980.

_____, *On Human Dignity*. London: SCM: 1984.

Morgan, G. Campbell, *The Crises of the Christ*. London: Pickering and Inglis, 1945.

Morgan, Robert, ed., *The Religion of the Incarnation: Anglican Essays in Commemoration of Lux Mundi*. Bristol: Bristol Classical Press, 1989.

Morris, Thomas V., *The Logic of God Incarnate*. Ithaca: Cornell University Press, 1986.

_____, *Our Idea of God*. Downer's Grove, IL: InterVarsity Press, 1991.

Mozley, J.K., *The Doctrine of the Atonement*. London: Duckworth, 1915.

_____, *The Heart of the Gospel*. London: SPCK, 1925.

_____, *The Impassibility of God: A Survey of Christian Thought*. London: Cambridge University Press, 1926.

Murphy, Francesca Aran, *The Oxford Handbook of Christology*. Oxford: Oxford University Press, 2015.

The Nature of Christian Belief. A Statement and Exposition by the House of Bishops of the General Synod of the Church of England. London: Church House, 1986.

Neuner, J., SJ, and Dupuis, J., SJ, *The Christian Faith: Doctrinal Documents of the Catholic Church*. New York: Alba House, fifth revised and enlarged edition, 1990.

Nichols, Aidan, OP, *Rome and the Eastern Churches*. San Francisco: Ignatius Press, second edition, 2010.

Nieuwenhove, Rick Van, and Wawrykow, Joseph, eds., *The Theology of Thomas Aquinas*. Notre Dame, IN: University of Notre Dame Press, 2010.

Norman, E.R., *Christianity and World Order*. Oxford: Oxford University Press, 1978.

Novak, Michael, *The Spirit of Democratic Capitalism*. New York: Touchstone, 1982.

O'Collins, Gerald, SJ, *Christology: a Biblical, Historical, and Systematic Study of Jesus*. Oxford: Oxford University Press, 1995.

_____, *Jesus Our Redeemer*. Oxford: Oxford University Press, 2007.

_____, *The Tripersonal God: Understanding and Interpreting the Trinity*. New York: Paulist Press, second edition revised, 2014.

O'Donnell, Timothy, *The Heart of the Redeemer*. San Francisco: Ignatius Press, 1989.

O'Donovan, Oliver, *Resurrection and the Moral Order: An Outline for Evangelical Ethics*. Grand Rapids: Eerdmans, second edition, 1994.

Packer, J.I., and Dever, Michael, *In my Place Condemned He Stood*. Wheaton, IL: Crossway, 2007.

Packer, J.I., *Knowing God*. Downer's Grove, IL: InterVarsity Press, 1995.

Papinikolauo, Aristotle, "Person, *Kenosis*, and Abuse: Hans Urs Von Balthasar and Feminist Theologies in Conversation" in *Modern Theology*, 19:1, January, 2003.

Paul VI, Pope, "The Credo of the People of God" (1968) at http://w2.vatican.va/content/paul-vi/en/motu-proprio/documents/hf_motu-proprio_19680630credo.html.

Pitre, Brant, *The Case for Jesus*. New York: Image Books, 2016.

Pittenger, Norman, *The Christian Church as Social Process*. Philadelphia: Westminster Press, 1971.

_____, "Christology in Process Theology" in *Theology*, March, 1977.

_____, *Christology Reconsidered*. London: SCM: 1970.

_____, *The Lure of Divine Love*. New York: Pilgrim Press, 1971.

Quick, O.C., *Doctrines of the Creed*. London: Nisbet, 1938.

_____, *The Gospel of the New World*. London: Nisbet, 1944.

Ramsey, A. Michael, *An Era in Anglican Theology: From Gore to Temple*. London: Longmans, 1960.

_____, *The Anglican Spirit*. New York: Seabury, 2004 edition.

_____, *God, Christ and the World*. London: SCM, 1969.

_____, *Introducing the Christian Faith*. London: SCM, 1969.

Rawlinson, A.E.J., ed., *Essays on the Trinity and the Incarnation*. London: Longmans, 1928.

Rea, Michael, ed., *Oxford Readings in Philosophical Theology 1: Trinity, Incarnation, Atonement*. Oxford: Oxford University Press, 2009.

Reckitt, Maurice, *Faith and Society*. London: Longmans and Green, 1932.

Richard, Lucien J., *Christ: The Self-Emptying of God*. New York: Paulist Press, 1997.

Riches, Aaron, *Ecce Homo: On the Divine Unity of Christ*. Grand Rapids: Eerdmans, 2016

Robinson, John A. T., *The Human Face of God*. London: SCM, 1973.

Rutledge, Fleming, *The Crucifixion: Understanding the Death of Jesus Christ*. Grand Rapids: Eerdmans, 2015.

Saward, John, "Love's Second Name: St. Thomas on Mercy" in *Canadian Catholic Review*, March, 1990.

Sellers, R.V., *The Council of Chalcedon*. London: SPCK: 1953.

Sheehy, Jeremy, *"Looking for the Theology"* in *The Church Observer*, Autumn, 1986.

Sheppard, David, *Bias to the Poor*. London: Hodder and Stoughton, 1983.

Sproul, R.C., *What Is Reformed Theology?* Grand Rapids: Baker, 1997.

Stackpole, Robert, *Divine Mercy: A Guide from Genesis to Benedict XVI*. Stockbridge, MA: Marian Press, revised edition, 2010.

_____, *Jesus, Mercy Incarnate*. Stockbridge, MA: Marian Press, 2000.

_____, *Letters to a College Student: On the Light of Reason and the Search for Truth*. Chilliwack, BC: The Chartwell Press, 2015.

_____, *Mary, Who She Is and Why She Matters*. Stockbridge, MA: Marian Press, 2016.

_____, "Promise and Perils in Contemporary Jesus Research" in *Journal of the Canadian Chapter of the Fellowship of Catholic Scholars*, Winter-Spring, 2012.

Staley, Vernon, *The Catholic Religion*. Wilton, CT: Morehouse-Barlow, centenary edition, 1983.

Stott, John, *The Cross of Christ*. Downer's Grove, IL: InterVarsity Press, 1986.

_____, *Issues Facing Christians Today*. Basingstoke: Marshalls, 1984.

Swinburne, Richard, *The Christian God*. New York: Oxford University Press, 1994.

_____, *The Coherence of Theism*. Oxford: Clarendon Press, 1977.

_____, *Was Jesus God?* Oxford: Oxford University Press, 2008.

Sykes, Stephen, *The Identity of Christianity.* London: SPCK, 1984.

_____, *The Integrity of Anglicanism.* Oxford: Mowbrays, 1978.

_____, Booty, John, and Knight, Jonathan, eds., *The Study of Anglicanism.* London: SPCK/Fortress Press, revised edition, 1998.

_____, and Clayton, J.P., eds., *Christ, Faith, and History.* Cambridge: Cambridge University Press, 1972.

Tanner, Kathryn, *Christ the Key.* Cambridge: Cambridge University Press, 2010.

_____, *Jesus, Humanity, and the Trinity.* Minneapolis: Fortress Press, 2001.

_____, "David Brown's *Divine Humanity*" in *Scottish Journal of Theology*, 68 (1), 2015.

Tanner, Norman P., *Decrees of the Ecumenical Councils*, vol. 1. Washington, DC: Georgetown University Press, 1990.

Taylor, Vincent, *The Person of Christ.* London: Macmillan, 1958.

Temple, William, *Christianity and the Social Order.* London: SPCK, 1976 edition.

_____, *Christus Veritas.* London: Macmillan, 1924.

Thornton, Lionel Spencer, *The Doctrine of the Atonement.* London: The Unicorn Press, 1937.

_____, *The Incarnate Lord.* London: Longmans, Green and Co., 1928.

Tomlin, Graham, *Looking Through the Cross.* London: Bloomsbury, 2013.

_____, *The Power of the Cross: Theology and the Death of Christ in Paul, Luther, and Pascal.* Carlisle: Paternoster Press, 1999.

Turner, H.E.W., *Jesus the Christ*. Oxford: Mowbrays, 1976.

Vanstone, W.H., *Love's Endeavour, Love's Expense*. London: Darton, Longman and Todd, second edition, 2015.

Vidler, Alex, ed., *Soundings*. Cambridge: Cambridge University Press, 1966.

Vogel, Arthur A., *Theology in Anglicanism*. Wilton, CT: Morehouse-Barlow, 1984.

Ward, Keith, *Christ and the Cosmos: A Reformulation of Trinitarian Doctrine*. New York: Cambridge University Press, 2015.

_____, *Holding Fast to God*. London: SPCK, 1982.

_____, "Incarnation or Inspiration: A False Dichotomy?" in *Theology*, July, 1977.

_____, *The Living God*. London: SPCK: 1984.

Ware, Timothy, *The Orthodox Church: An Introduction to Eastern Christianity*. Milton Keynes: Penguin, third edition, 2015.

Weil, Simone, *Waiting on God*. London: Fount, 1977 edition.

Weinandy, Thomas, OFM Cap, *Does God Change?* Still River, MA: St. Bede Publications, 1985.

_____, "Does God Suffer?" in *First Things*, November, 2001.

_____, *Jesus: Essays in Christology*. Ave Maria, FL: Sapientia Press, 2014.

Welch, Claude, ed., *God and Incarnation in mid-19th Century Lutheran Theology*. New York: Oxford University Press, 1965.

Welsby, Paul A., *A History of the Church in England: 1945-1980*. Oxford: Oxford University Press, 1984.

Wenham, John, *Christ and the Bible*. Guildford, Surrey: Eagle, 1993.

Weston, Frank, *The One Christ*. London: Longmans, Green and Co., second edition, 1914.

White, Thomas Joseph, OP, *The Incarnate Lord: A Thomistic Study in Christology.* Washington, DC: Catholic University of America Press, 2015.

_____, *The Light of Christ.* Washington, DC: Catholic University of America Press, 2017.

White, Vernon, *Incarnation and Atonement.* Cambridge: Cambridge University Press, 1991.

Wiles, Maurice, *Faith and the Mystery of God.* London: SCM, 1977.

_____, *The Making of Christian Doctrine.* Cambridge: Cambridge University Press, 1967.

_____, *The Remaking of Christian Doctrine.* London: SCM, 1974.

_____, *Working Papers in Doctrine.* London: SCM, 1976.

Williams, Daniel Day, *The Spirit and the Forms of Love.* New York: Harper and Row, 1968.

Williams, H.A, "Incarnation: Model and Symbol" in *Theology*, January, 1976.

Williams, Rowan, *God With Us: the meaning of the cross and resurrection. Then and now.* London: SPCK, 2017.

_____, *On Christian Theology.* Malden, MA: Blackwell, 2000.

_____, and Nicholls, D., *Politics and Theological Identity.* London: The Jubilee Group, 1984.

_____, *Resurrection.* London: Darton, Longman and Todd, 1982.

Williams, Trevor, *Form and Vitality: in the World and God.* Oxford: Clarendon Press, 1985.

Wright, N.T. (Tom), *Evil and the Justice of God.* Downer's Grove, IL: InterVarsity Press, 2006.

_____, *How God Became King: The Forgotten Story of the Gospels.* New York: Harper One, 2012.

_____, *Simply Jesus.* New York: Harper One, 2011.

_____, *The Day the Revolution Began.* London: SPCK, 2016.

Zycinski, Jozef, *God and Evolution: Fundamental Questions of Christian Evolutionism.* Washington, DC: Catholic University of America, 2006.

Index of Names

Index of Names

Index of Names

Index of Names

Index of Names

Index of Names

CPSIA information can be obtained
at www.ICGtesting.com
Printed in the USA
BVHW041820050121
597053BV00019B/444